Bernard Brodie and the Foundations of American Nuclear Strategy

Bernard Brodie and the Foundations of American Nuclear Strategy

Barry H. Steiner

University Press of Kansas

Modern War Studies

Theodore A. Wilson
General Editor

Raymond A. Callahan
J. Garry Clifford
Jacob W. Kipp
Jay Luvaas
Series Editors

© 1991 by the University Press of Kansas

Published by the University Press of Kansas (Lawrence, Kansas 66045), which was organized by the Kansas Board of Regents and is operated and funded by Emporia State University, Fort Hays State University, Kansas State University, Pittsburg State University, the University of Kansas, and Wichita State University

Library of Congress Cataloging-in-Publication Data

Steiner, Barry H. (Barry Howard), 1942–
    Bernard Brodie and the foundations of American nuclear strategy /
Barry H. Steiner.
        p.   cm. — (Modern war studies)
    Includes bibliographical references (p.   ) and index.
    ISBN 0-7006-0441-3 (alk. paper)
        1. United States—Military policy. 2. Nuclear warfare.
    3. Brodie, Bernard, 1910–   . I. Title. II. Series.
    UA23.S687   1991
    355.02'17—dc20   90-22618
                                                                                          CIP

British Library Cataloguing in Publication Data is available.

Printed in the United States of America
10 9 8 7 6 5 4 3 2 1

The paper used in this publication meets the minimum requirements of the American National Standard for Permanence of Paper for Printed Library Materials Z39.48-1984.

To the memory of
Bernard and Fawn Brodie

Contents

Foreword

We are delighted to welcome the publication of this book. Barry Steiner's study of Bernard Brodie and the impact of Brodie's work, which he has been working on for over ten years, has been supported since its inception by the UCLA Center for International and Strategic Affairs during both of our terms as the first two directors of CISA. We welcomed and encouraged Steiner's thoughtful and detailed evaluation of Brodie's contributions because, even though Brodie's work was seminal in the development of strategic thinking in the postwar period, it has not been adequately analyzed for its influence and continued relevance. Steiner's book provides such an evaluation and analysis, thereby enabling us both to see where we have come in the study of strategy and to treat a whole set of issues that have not been adequately dealt with in previous studies.

Steiner confirms our prior belief that Brodie was truly a founder of the modern study of strategy—namely, strategy in the nuclear and missile age. The issues that Brodie analyzed and the strategic choices that flowed from his analyses were at the forefront of the debate over nuclear strategy. Brodie had the remarkable ability to pose questions and treat issues years before anyone else, and his conclusions, based on logic, history, and psychology, typically became the established paradigms in the analysis of nuclear strategy. He developed our basic ideas on deterrence, on the role of nuclear weapons, on escalation, on limited war, and on many other aspects of modern strategy.

A frequently told story about Brodie is that when he opened his newspaper one morning in August 1945 to read that the United States had dropped an atomic bomb on Hiroshima he turned to his wife, Fawn, and said, "Everything I have done up till now is obsolete." He was, of course, ahead of anyone else in realizing this, and he immediately turned to the strategic implications of the new weapon. This new work led to his contributing to and editing the highly influential book *The Absolute Weapon*, published in 1946.

Brodie played an important role in the establishment of the Center for International and Strategic Affairs at UCLA in 1975. He was a member of the UCLA Department of Political Science from 1966 until his death in 1978, and he influenced and inspired colleagues in the department and elsewhere, university administrators, and external sponsors, stimulating work on strategy at UCLA. Brodie also worked with us in editing the volume of case studies of lessons learned from various postwar conflicts, crises, and debates over strategy, *National Security and International Stability* (Oelgeschlager, Gunn, and Hain, 1983), a volume that, in addition, included papers presented at the memorial conference, War and Politics held at UCLA one year after Brodie's death. We established the Bernard Brodie Distinguished Lecture on War and Politics, sponsored by CISA and presented annually at UCLA since 1980, for outstanding analysts of politics, strategy, and warfare to present their thoughts and research within the scholarly and humanist tradition exemplified by Bernard Brodie. The titles of both the memorial conference and the annual lecture were based on the title of Brodie's last book, *War and Politics* (Macmillan, 1973).

Our work at the Center for International and Strategic Affairs has continued in the tradition established by Bernard Brodie in the analysis of nuclear strategy. For example, books on nuclear strategy that appear in the CISA series Studies in International and Strategic Affairs include Roman Kolkowicz, editor, *The Logic of Nuclear Terror* (Allen & Unwin, 1987), and Roman Kolkowicz, editor, *Dilemmas of Nuclear Deterrence* (Frank Cass, 1987). Books on arms control, another area of Brodie's concern, that appear in the CISA series include Roman Kolkowicz and Neil Joeck, editors, *Arms Control and International Security* (Westview Press, 1984), and William C. Potter, editor, *Verification and Arms Control* (Lexington Books, 1985). Yet another area of Brodie's concern, East-West relations, is also treated in this series, including Michael D. Intriligator and Hans-Adolf Jacobsen, editors, *East-West Conflict: Elite Perceptions and Political Options* (Westview Press, 1988).

We would like to conclude with a personal reminiscence. Bernard was not just a leading strategic analyst. He was, in fact, a remarkable man of sense, grace, and culture. We had many meetings with him as we worked with him in developing the book that was eventually published after his death. We would usually meet at Bernard and Fawn's beautiful home in the Pacific Palisades, with a dramatic view of Santa Monica Bay and the Pacific Ocean, which he used to liken to the view of the Bay of Naples. In their home he was surrounded by beauty, including not only the view but also the orchids that he grew and the music and art that filled their home. Brodie was, of course, known internationally for his work on strategy, but he was also a highly refined person with broad interests and knowledge.

University of California, Los Angeles
May 1990

> *Michael D. Intriligator, Director, 1982–*
> *Roman Kolkowicz, Founding Director, 1975–1982*
> *Center for International and Strategic Affairs*

Preface

Since the Second World War, military strategy and policy have been far more studied, examined, and debated in public than ever before. To this situation Bernard Brodie contributed enormously. He pioneered "grand strategy"—the broad adaptation of military instruments to statecraft—with unexcelled logic and refinement. In so doing, he not only invigorated debate by reexamining conventional strategic beliefs, but as a professor in an open university educated others as he struggled for originality, coherence, policy relevance, and analytic balance. As a result, he prompted many to concentrate on the issues he addressed.

This work records and probes Brodie's intellectual contribution, amplifying official strategy and policy only as he referred to them. Generally uneasy about and critical of prevailing policy, Brodie forcefully argued for ideas not yet officially accepted, with a wide-ranging treatment that was generally less instructive about policy details than about general concepts. Further, Brodie was preoccupied as much with assumptions behind policy preferences and policy analysis as with the substance of policy. Much of his accomplishment as a strategist was to express and clarify assumptions underlying existing policies and policy viewpoints, making them part of the strategic debate. This study highlights Brodie's assumptions and their implications, comparing them with those of others with whom he disagreed. The purpose is not to produce categorical conclusions but rather to permit the reader to make an independent judgment and to prompt further inquiry where important questions remain.

Political scientists do not usually carry on the work of historians, but at least two defenses for doing so can be offered. First, historians and political scientists have long enjoyed overlapping research interests in the study of national security affairs. Brodie, a political scientist by training, frequently found historical references to back his interpretation of contemporary strategic problems. Second, closer familiarity with the historical record can affect the terms of more recent debate. In the field of security studies, the excitement and uncertainty associated with the earliest efforts to understand nuclear weaponry appear to have waned as analysis has become more mature and analysts more confident of their views. In some respects, as in the question of whether plans for counterforce attack with nuclear weapons have any validity, debate has become increasingly scholastic and sterile. Further, because of the passing of the pioneering generation of nuclear strategists, memory of the intellectual ferment attending early influential postwar strategic analyses is also in danger of being lost. This book argues for using intellectual history to search out antecedents for ideas and issues recently discussed and to sharply distinguish old elements from new ones in the debate.

It is a pleasure to list the many institutions and individuals who have assisted this project and to whom I am greatly indebted. The Center for International and Strategic Affairs of the University of California, Los Angeles, supported this study from its inception in 1979 and provided three grants (two in its first year) to spur it to completion. A separate grant from the Ford Foundation in the spring of 1982 facilitated the writing of chapters 7 and 8. A research fellowship during the academic year 1982/83 from the Center for International Studies of the University of Southern California, under the auspices of the National Resource Centers Program of the U.S. Department of Education, which coincided with a sabbatical grant from California State University, Long Beach (CSULB), permitted the writing of an early draft of chapter 2. Much preliminary work on the project was done during academic year 1979/80 while I served as a Research Fellow in the Center for Science and International Affairs of the Kennedy School of Government at Harvard University.

Many people offered assistance in obtaining documents pertinent to this study. Malcolm Palmatier, Claude Culp, and Richard Solomon of the RAND Corporation helped to clear for public use a large number of informal working papers prepared by Brodie while at RAND. These papers were assembled in 1980 as "Fourteen Informal Writings from the Unpublished Work of Bernard Brodie, 1952–1965," and many were subsequently included in a six-volume facsimile series edited by Marc Trachtenberg, *The Development of American Strategic Thought, 1945–1969* (New York: Garland, 1988).

The following people undertook repeated searches of documentary collections to assist this project: Malcolm Palmatier at the RAND Corporation; Ed Coffee, Edward J. Reese, Charles A. Shaughnessy, and John Taylor at the Modern Military Branch of the National Archives, Washington, D.C.; Cary Conn at the Suitland Reference Branch of the National Archives, Suitland, Maryland; Lynn Gamma and Judy G. Endicott at the Air Force Historical Research Center, Maxwell Air Force Base, Montgomery, Alabama; Susan Cooksey at the headquarters of the Air Force Intelligence Service, Fort Belvoir, Virginia; Nancy Bressler at the Seely Mudd Manuscript Library, Princeton University; and Anne Caiger at the Special Collections Library, University Reserach Library, University of California, Los Angeles. Searches in the Special Collections Library at UCLA were considerably expedited by an inventory, completed by Steven L. Isoardi in March 1979 and on file at that library, of Bernard Brodie's writings, virtually all of which are included in the Bernard Brodie Collection housed there.

Other searches of documentary collections were made by Ruth Griffin, Air University Library, Maxwell Air Force Base, Lt. Col. Elliott Converse III (USAF), William Heimdahl, and Walt Moody, Office of Air Force History, Bolling Air Force Base, Washington, D.C.; David Wigdor, Manuscript Division, Library of Congress; Lt. Comdr. Scott Wilson (USN), Naval Personnel Command, Washington, D.C.; Dennis Bilger, Truman Library, Independence, Missouri; David Haight and Tim Leyerzaps, Eisenhower Library, Abilene, Kansas; Richard J. Sommers, U.S. Army Military History Institute, Carlisle Barracks, Pennsylvania; Roger Anders, History Division, Department of Energy, Germantown, Maryland; Dwight Miller, Hoover Presidential Library, West Branch, Iowa; R. Michael McReynolds and Ann Ronan, Judicial and Fiscal Branch, National Archives; Frank Burch, Science and Technology Policy Branch, National Archives; William Montgomery, Office of Science and Technology Policy, Washington, D.C.; David Stowe and Elmer Staats, Washington, D.C.; Roy Webb, Special Collections Division, University of Utah Libraries; Evelyn Cherpak, Naval Historical Collection, Naval War College, Newport, Rhode Island; Patricia Stark, Yale University Archives; and the staff of the Washington National Records Center (Accession and Disposal Branch), Suitland, Maryland.

Individuals who provided pertinent materials from their personal collections were Fawn Brodie, William T. Golden, Malcolm Hoag, James E. King, Roman Kolkowicz, Charles E. Lindblom, and Joseph E. Loftus.

The following individuals graciously consented to be interviewed for this project: Gerald Aronson, Bruce Brodie, Fawn Brodie, Cyril E. Black, Berend D. Bruins, Samuel T. Cohen, James Digby, Mrs. Ladislas Farago, James David Fisher, Alexander George, Alfred Goldberg (psychiatrist practicing in Los Angeles), Alfred Goldberg (historian of the Office of the Secretary of Defense, Washington, D.C.), Joan Goldhamer, William T. Golden, Mrs. Ralph Greenson, Jack Hershleifer, Michael Howard, William W. Kaufmann, James E. King, Nathan Leites, Joseph E. Loftus, Andrew Marshall, Maj. Gen. Lauris Norstad (USAF, Ret.) Peter Paret, Brig. Gen. Noel Parrish (USAF, Ret.), Ernest Plesset, Thomas C. Schelling, Warner R. Schilling, Hans Speier, T. G. Walkowicz, Albert Wohlstetter, and Roberta Wohlstetter. Others who responded in writing to my questions included Cyril E. Black, William T. R. Fox, Joseph M. Goldsen, Lawrence J. Henderson, Malcolm Hoag, Charles J. Hitch, Klaus Knorr, Henry Rowen, and Herbert York.

A number of people read and commented upon earlier drafts of this study. They include Claude Culp, Ross N. Berkes, Alexander George, James E. King, Klaus Knorr, Joseph E. Loftus, Michael Mandelbaum, Malcolm Palmatier, and George Quester. Peter Paret commented upon chapter 9, and William C. Potter upon chapter 2.

Fawn Brodie and Joseph E. Loftus offered valuable encouragement in the early stages of this study, and Loftus was thereafter particularly generous with suggestions, comments, and criticism.

Most of the final manuscript was typed with great efficiency by Donna Yankovich. Others who assisted in the typing were Mary Ann Spano, Candy Yamagawa, Joyce Komai, Cathy Strickley, Steve Tyman, and Carol Weil. The Office of the Dean,

School of Social and Behavioral Sciences at CSULB, underwrote costs of some typing of the manuscript and nearly all of its photocopying.

The staff of the University Press of Kansas gently but effectively pushed for the completion of this project and did a superb job of editing the manuscript and preparing the index.

An earlier version of chapter 2 was published in the *Journal of Strategic Studies* 7 (December 1984).

My wife, JoAnn, who attended classes taught by Brodie, demonstrated her usual superb editing skills with good cheer.

1 · Introduction and Overview

For forty years, until his death in 1978, Bernard Brodie's career as a strategist coincided with, and spurred on, the dispersion of strategic thinking away from the professionals on active military duty who had long monopolized it. This dispersion has been reflected in the activities of such interwar British intellectuals as Maj. Gen. J. F. C. Fuller, Capt. B. H. Liddell Hart, and Vice Adm. Sir Herbert Richmond, retired officers disturbed, according to the historian Robin Higham, by

> their feeling that Britain had not won the First World War. It had not been for them an exhilarating military experience. It had lacked the glamour of the Boer War or the Indian frontier with their mobile operations. It had degenerated into an amateur affair fought by civilians, in which politicians and not generals were in control. The military intellectuals wanted to know why. And they believed that they had found out. It was an industrial war that required managers, and so the pundits became planners and management consultants. They saw their job as producing victories. But not just military successes, not simply a clearing of the bottlenecks, but rather a re-establishment of a profitable equilibrium, which we call peace. And like good consultants, their aim was largely to avoid a breakdown in the first place.[1]

Then as later the dispersion of strategic thinking was produced by the growing legitimation of the subject of military strategy, by the rising demand within the military establishment for reflection about it, and by the unprecedented change in the conduct of war. But following the Second World War, when Brodie became especially prominent in rationalizing and guiding American ideas about strategy—that is, about the shaping of war-making forces to national objectives—the extent of the dispersion has been unparalleled.[2]

When Brodie enlisted in the Naval Reserve with the rank of lieutenant in December 1942 at the age of thirty-two, he became a navy planner and management consultant, but unlike his British counterparts, who all held military rank from their service in the First World War, he had a civilian background. Brodie had published two books on naval strategy and made his initial reputation after the war had begun, whereas his British colleagues had made their reputations in peacetime. His first book, published as *Sea Power in the Machine Age* (Princeton University Press, 1941), grew out of his Ph.D. dissertation—originally entitled "Major Naval Inventions and Their Consequences in International Politics, 1814–1918." Completed at the University of Chicago in 1941 under the guidance of the distinguished economist Jacob Viner, it was perhaps the first American study of strategy and tactics at the doctoral level.[3] The dissertation was revised and extended for publication at the Institute for Advanced Study in Princeton during 1940 and 1941, where Brodie joined a seminar on American foreign policy and national security questions, a small and virtually unique project recently established by Edward Mead Earle that included nearly all American academicians then engaged in the study of strategy.[4] Brodie's second book, *A Layman's Guide to Naval Strategy* (Princeton University Press, 1942), completed in his first year as a member of the teaching staff of the Political Science Department at Dartmouth College, synthesized recent naval combat developments in Europe and the Pacific and was widely circulated within the Naval Fleet.[5]

A final difference between Brodie and earlier British thinkers was that he was engaged by the navy to rationalize American conduct in the war and not to affect its conduct in any important way, unlike Liddell Hart, who helped introduce tank warfare during the First World War. Brodie was assigned first to the Bureau of Ordnance (BuOrd) where he edited the bureau's *Bulletin of Information* (a quarterly confidential document distributed to Fleet officers), wrote speeches for its chief, Adm. William P. Blandy, and commented for Blandy on other writings on naval subjects.[6] Following his preparation of the BuOrd contribution to the first of the reports submitted by Fleet Admiral Ernest J. King, chief of naval operations (CNO), to the secretary of the navy, Brodie moved in November 1943 to the Office of the Chief of Naval Operations, specifically to the Office of Naval Intelligence (ONI), taking responsibility for editing the entire King report.[7] These experiences were less than fully satisfying to Brodie; in a letter to Earle that month he indicated that "ghosting for King is something of a promotion over ghosting for Blandy, but my voice is getting more and more sepulchral all the time, and I expect soon to be able to walk through closed doors without opening them."[8]

Still, given temporary duty status in ONI in January 1944 and working in its Special Warfare section (ONI section 16-W), which was almost entirely providing for the needs of the Office of War Information (OWI), Brodie had access to the navy's best intelligence about adversary strength and dispositions, employing it when contributing to confidential "combat narratives" of the war at sea.[9] His later celebrated criticism of axiomatic thinking by military professionals appears to have originated in his observation that neglect of combat intelligence produced missed strategic opportunities. An example he was to refer to many times was Admiral Halsey's decision to keep his fleet concentrated in the Battle of Leyte Gulf in October 1944. At the time of that battle, Brodie wrote in 1973,

> we had the information telling us exactly what carriers and other warships remained in the Japanese navy. This information, which had proved highly reliable, told us *at the time* that the four carriers sighted with Admiral Ozawa's force were all the Japanese had

left, and that except for the *Zuikaku*, the last survivor of the Pearl Harbor attack, they were small vessels converted from light cruisers and merchant vessels and of trivial military value. We also knew that the pilots left in the Japanese fleet were nothing like those our ships had encountered earlier in the war. . . . Halsey and his staff had the same intelligence, and our war experience over the previous year and a half should have confirmed its accuracy, yet they totally disregarded it. The two axioms that held their minds fast were (a) "the enemy's main force is where his carriers are"—true earlier in the war but now ludicrously wrong and (b) "don't divide the fleet in the presence of the enemy"—an idea designed to assure superiority or minimize inferiority of one's own force against the enemy's, but totally inapplicable in this instance because of the vast superiority we enjoyed.[10]

The Halsey example is also significant in that, as Brodie indicated, "it happens to be a case in which my judgment about it took form concurrently with the event";[11] all such instances, including his negative reactions to the failure of air force officials in 1951 to respond to his criticism of target selection priorities, the American failure to advance north of the 38th parallel in Korea in 1951, and the resolution of the Cuban missile crisis in 1962, impressed him strongly and categorically enough to permanently direct the course of his future thinking.

By the end of the war, having also participated in the planning of the April 1945 inaugural United Nations conference in San Francisco[12] and served as a special assistant to the secretary of the navy while still on active naval duty,[13] Brodie had become, well before his fortieth birthday, among the top strategic thinkers in the U.S. Navy and in the country. He terminated his active naval duty in September 1945, having already joined the teaching faculty of the Yale Department of International Relations. As anxious to be of service to policymakers in the postwar period as before it, Brodie was to become still better known as a nuclear strategist, being one of the very few American strategic thinkers to establish a major reputation both before and after the development of atomic weapons in 1945.

This work deals, however, almost entirely with Brodie's writing after that date. By November 1945, he had set forth his initial arguments about the military implications of atomic weapons (published in expanded form in Bernard Brodie, editor, *The Absolute Weapon* [Harcourt, Brace, 1946]) that remain more than forty years later a landmark in contemporary thinking about nuclear weaponry. His ideas continued to evolve in subsequent years at Yale; as a consultant to the RAND Corporation while on the Yale faculty; as special assistant to the air force chief of staff for periods in 1950 and 1951; as a senior member of the Social Science Staff of the RAND Corporation beginning in 1951, in which much of his writing grew out of contract work with the U.S. Air Force; and finally as a member of the Political Science Department and founder of the Center for International and Strategic Affairs (CISA) at the University of California, Los Angeles, from 1966 until his retirement in 1977 (see appendix). But his characteristic contemporary focus and breadth of appreciation of his subject had been established in his earliest writing on nuclear weaponry.

The Nuclear Divide

The critical approach Brodie adopted in the postwar period toward military professionals and conventional wisdom contrasted sharply with his earlier acceptance, before the advent of atomic weaponry, of prevailing strategic concepts. "The manner in which I have treated naval strategy in this book," he wrote in the preface to *A Layman's Guide,*

> might be classified as "orthodox." That approach may not prove popular in a day when we are being told on every hand that we must repudiate all the ideas of the past and develop a whole new strategy overnight. But what is required is an attitude of fine discrimination and adjustment, not nihilism. . . . Only those to whom the study of war is novel permit themselves to be swept away by novel elements in the present war.[14]

To be sure, even then Brodie chided those who subscribed uncritically to such axioms as the principle of not dividing the fleet, contending in regard to the American problem of fighting in two oceans that "even the soundest strategic principles must be considered as flexible and in any case they must be governed by necessity."[15] But instead of questioning the appropriateness of principles or the biases lurking in their reiteration, Brodie condemned inadequate attention to the straightforward meaning of broad strategic concepts. "Unfortunately," he wrote in that same study,

> the very preoccupation of commanders with specific and inevitably complex problems sometimes tends to make them impatient with the age old verities. Long-tested doctrines which are utterly simple are rejected in part because of their very simplicity, and in part too because of the dogma of innovation so prevalent in our age. . . . We live in an age when the basic theories of naval warfare are being rejected out of hand by responsible officials on the wholly unwarranted assumption that they do not fit modern conditions.[16]

Defending received strategic wisdom, Brodie's naval analyses took a broader focus and were more detailed than his work after 1945. With respect to focus, his *Layman's Guide* explored a wide range of topics relevant to defeating an enemy through naval power, such as command of the sea, defense of shipping, naval bases, air power, the tactics of naval engagement, and naval personnel, dwelling on the error of isolating any one of them. "Even if one insists on regarding as a separate branch of military power the forces which move through the air rather than upon land or water," he wrote, with reference to air-power advocates,

> it is a rather limited outlook which concentrates upon the spectacle of the airplane over its target to the exclusion of the long chain of circumstances which are responsible for putting it there. The air forces which so vitally aided the Japanese armies in their quick conquests of Malaya, the East Indies, and Burma operated from airdromes which in almost every instance had been seized by Japanese armies landed from ships. Many of the aircraft involved, especially the fighter planes, and all their fuel, cargoes, and maintenance crews and supplies were brought to the scene of operations in ships. Their local air superiorities, in other words, were derived from sea power.[17]

By contrast, his point of departure for analyzing atomic weapons was the much greater destructive potential afforded by those weapons compared with their predecessors, especially in bombing attacks against urban areas, which in turn raised the issue of whether the latest bombing efficiency would be associated with mutual suicide in two-sided atomic warfare. By 1952, when he first dealt with fusion weapons and their still more revolutionary destructive potential against cities, Brodie strongly advocated sparing cities, even if doing so rendered nuclear bombing operations less efficient.

Brodie's definition of his subject and his use of information also changed in 1945. His *Layman's Guide,* defining strategy as the "general handling of the tools of war to realize their purpose," masterfully attended to analytic detail, developing fine discrimination and adjustment in operational naval needs.[18] On the other hand, his understanding of strategy after 1945 went beyond the military mode of gaining victory under a specific set of circumstances, to "anticipate the trials of war, and by anticipation . . . seek where possible to increase one's advantage without unduly jeopardizing the maintenance of peace or the pursuit of other values."[19]

In addition, as in his critiques of conventional wisdom, his observations about nuclear weapons were usually pitched at a general level. He asserted in 1945 that atomic bombs were adequate to achieve military victory through strategic bombing and that they should be used in a retaliatory mode. In 1951, on the question of how to "maximize the *overall strategic* results of our strategic bombing campaign through manipulating the rate of expenditure of an A-bomb stockpile . . . absolutely limited in size," he argued that "we must consider all . . . aspects in a mutually connected fashion, but we should not betray ourselves into devising a specific schedule of delivery. The latter enterprise we can leave to the Air Force."[20] It was enough for him in the latter instance "to simply jar the prevalent complacency on the doctrine of shoot-from-the-hip-and-empty-the-magazine."

These discrepancies were due in part to Brodie's judgment of American military needs. In 1942, following the Japanese attack at Pearl Harbor, he was fully in accord with the American wartime priority of sustaining the Soviet Union and especially Great Britain until the United States could take the offensive against Germany,[21] rejecting the alternative of giving primacy to the defeat of Japan. He furthermore accepted the need for balanced military forces to implement the strategy. But in the contemporary period, the potential of a shorter war and less complex operational conditions to gain military victory seemed to some, including Brodie, to be afforded by strategic bombing with atomic weapons. Highlighting this possibility, and with faith in the destructive power of the newer weapons, presumed an in-being atomic force capable of carrying out war on very short notice as well as the highest reliance upon atomic bombs regardless of the state of political tensions.

Each of these presumptions, which Brodie held in 1945, several years in advance of American planners and policymakers, was associated with what Michael Howard termed a "strategic approach" to world politics. "From 1948 onwards," Howard argued, the United States . . . adopted the "strategic approach" to international relations which the Soviet Union had probably never abandoned. It visualized the world in terms of possible armed conflict and so conducted its policy as to maximize its military effectiveness in the event of such a conflict; much as the Powers of Europe had done between 1870 and 1914. It wooed and armed allies, attempted to intimidate neutrals and set itself the task of building up and maintaining a nuclear strike capability which would enable it to retaliate massively, at times and places of its own choosing, to Soviet aggression anywhere in the world.[22]

Brodie's newer orientations were ideal for employing this strategic approach: His definition of his subject widened to take account of the possibility of using weapons of war as a means to keep the peace, his focus narrowed to concentrate on the newer weapons assigned such burdensome duty, and his thinking beyond conventional strategic categories positioned him apart from those complacent about prior wartime experience. But his newer strategic approach was not well positioned to deal with operational detail about nuclear war scenarios. Exhorting planners and officials to shift to nuclear strategy, his own initial operational assumptions for doing so were optimistic. However, during his very sensitive work for Vandenberg, Brodie became aware of the war-making assumptions employed by American planners and consequently grew much more skeptical about victory in atomic warfare.

Another reason for the discrepancies was that Brodie knew he lacked much information about atomic capabilities and plans, because he did not have the highest security clearance. He would have been subject, therefore, to gross errors in his estimates of military requirements, a problem he did not have to confront in his earlier analyses of naval power. The contribution this made to Brodie's characteristically broad style of postwar analysis was in turn reinforced by his interest in breaking out of older strategic outlooks. When strategic concepts and attitudes were stable, as in the prewar period, the information appropriate for developing them tended to be well identified; conversely, when concepts and attitudes were being transformed, as in the period immediately following the attacks against Hiroshima and Nagasaki, the information reflective of newer ideas would ordinarily be less easy to establish.

It is also clear, on the other hand, that Brodie retained his broad style of analysis even as highlighting nuclear weapons became conventional among strategic thinkers. That he did so must be ascribed to the satisfaction that it presumably gave him, satisfaction not unrelated to the great assurance and intellectual authority he displayed in practicing it.[23] In the contemporary period, as evidently in the past, the most esteemed strategic thinking seems to have been carried on by those relatively few individuals "who could," as Higham wrote, "draw the broad lessons and conclusions, and who could master the mysteries of the military profession and explain them clearly to the public."[24]

The Emancipation of Strategic Analysis

One of Brodie's major postwar accomplishments was to legitimate the study of military strategy for civilians lacking a military background, based primarily on the wholly changed position of the major powers. "[What] is needed in the approach to strategic problems," he argued in a widely noted article in 1949, "is *genuine analytical method.* Formerly the need for it was not great, but, apart from the rapidly increasing complexity of the problem, the magnitude of disaster which might result from military error today bears no relation to situations of the past."[25] Earlier than anyone and thereafter more persistently and relentlessly, Brodie insisted upon differentiating (1) weapons of mass destruction from their predecessors; (2) recent combat experience from newer strategic doctrine; and (3) axioms from careful analysis. The importance of the analytical method, to which a broad array of disciplines could contribute, presupposed the limitations of combat experience as a source of strategic insight, especially in light of the novelty of atomic bombs. "Military planners," Brodie wrote in 1949,

> are obliged to make far-reaching decisions on issues concerning which there is little or no directly applicable experience. We certainly have no experience today with the mass use of atomic bombs. There is a good deal of experience which is in some manner relevant, but it must be sought out and applied with subtlety and discrimination and with constant concern for the qualifications enjoined by the elements of dissimilarity.[26]

Contemporary axiomatic strategy was mostly confined, not surprisingly, to doctrines of the offensive use of military forces, particularly the earliest possible use in war of atomic weapons. Such doctrines could ensure horrendous casualties without necessarily forcing an end to hostilities. But perhaps because they were so strongly believed, those doctrines were historically often not clearly related to combat experience, Brodie found. "Why had not the most obvious lessons of combat experience been absorbed by commanders who were to send great new armies into battle?" Brodie asked in 1973.

> Because for the most part experience not personal to themselves was not really alive to these commanders, who were not students of history, even of military history, but who had absorbed an intensive indoctrination laced through with religious fervor on the merits of the offensive. What was worse, in World War I the unprecedented separation of high command from front lines made it possible for the commander to be ignorant even of the experience of his own forces.[27]

The novelty of air bombardment in the First World War combined with the subsequent widespread interest in finding alternatives to indecisive ground combat to give to air-power advocates the status of ultimate intellectual authority.[28] "The fact that the military have to practice only intermittently the function for which they exist," wrote Brodie in 1973, referring to this situation, "means that a doctrine that is congenial can be adopted and cherished and given a dominating place in strategic planning without ever being put even to those tests that are feasible in peacetime."[29]

Brodie believed the military establishment could not be relied upon to provide the necessary checks against axiomatic thinking, at least not in a form available to the general public. "In the effort to explore the ramifications or specific application of those questions which 'are generally self-answering when explicitly and correctly stated,'" Brodie noted in 1949,

> the economics profession has produced a tremendous body of literature of impressive quality. The far older profession of arms, content with mere reiteration of its wholly elementary postulates, which change not with the changing years, has yet to round out a five-foot bookshelf of significant works of strategy. The purpose of soldiers is obviously not to produce books, but one must assume that any real ferment of thought could not have so completely avoided breaking into print.[30]

Dwelling upon analytic method to head off these difficulties, Brodie believed that strategy was associated with "problems involving economy of means, i.e., the most efficient utilization of potential and available resources to the end of enhancing our security," and that economists competent to weigh use of limited resources should be competent to study strategic questions as well. He went on to say that decisions about the appropriate characteristics of a military force needed to be informed by "multiple-contingency analysis [sensitive] . . . to the well-known concept of *marginal utility*. . . . [A] balanced force could be defined as one in which the marginal utilities, tactically and strategically considered, of the last increments to each of the existing components were approximately equalized. . . . In short, what we are discussing is the difference between thought and dogma."[31]

The distinction between thought and dogma was not unappreciated in the past. In 1973 Brodie lauded the nineteenth-century German strategic thinker Carl von Clausewitz for his "modernity," because his book *On War* "helps warn the general not to be too rigid in his conceptions, especially those that in our own times he is likely to have received in the form of simple axioms in his staff college or war college courses."[32] The British strategist B. H. Liddell Hart understood the same distinction when in his study of the American Civil War campaigns of Gen. William T. Sherman he consulted the seventy volumes of the *Official Records of the Union and Confederate Armies* to gain what he called "an ample education in historical wariness."[33] Objective strategic analysis may not have been as rare historically as Brodie implied: Liddell Hart argued in the interwar period that "conditions of the next war had often been foretold by students of war who were really objective in examining the previous war, and the deadlock of 1917/18 was foreshadowed as early as the American Civil War, being the natural result of the improvement in firearms."[34]

Still, the most incisive students of strategy prior to 1945, including Clausewitz and Liddell Hart, were motivated to study the subject by their combat experience.[35] Further, those (again including Clausewitz and Liddell Hart) willing and able to advocate more refined approaches to strategy invariably lacked a group of commonly motivated individuals to assist and support them. The potential of the analytic method would be very much enhanced if it could be institutionalized in research on strategic issues. This was likely to happen only when a need was perceived—as it is today—for individuals of different backgrounds to collaborate in tackling complex strategic problems. "It has not been altogether a new problem for the military," Brodie wrote in 1973,

> especially in the Navy, to have to think ahead technologically, but certainly the dimensions of the problem since World War II bear no comparison to those existing previously. One has to rely on specialists, on teams of technicians who will maintain an alert understanding of the evolving state of the art in each of several quite distinct technological fields like electronics, rocket propulsion, decoys or "penetration aids," and so on.[36]

And as long as military commanders interpreted combat experience by easy generalization, it could truly be said, as it was in Britain during the interwar period, that "the military mind is a limited mind owing to the nature of the calling" and that "military affairs were definitely second-rate."[37]

Brodie stimulated the introduction of the analytic method at policy-oriented research institutions such as the RAND Corporation, which he joined as a senior staff member in 1951 and where many contributions to military doctrine, force selection, and budgetary decisions were attributable to the practice of this method. During the 1960s, many members of the RAND staff and other strategic analysts were recruited by the military establishment, and their power became enormous. "All the leading civilian strategists who were willing to be consulted," Colin Gray wrote, "were drafted, at least on an *ad hoc* basis, into the official defense community. Their intellectual dominance in the early 1960s was nearly absolute."[38] The subject of strategic studies became widely legitimated by the reputations of those who analyzed it, by the growing published literature about strategic problems, and by the large number of individuals, most academically inclined, who were attracted to it.[39]

A highly qualified elite studying strategic problems offered new potential for criticizing and exposing entrenched ideas in the military establishment. Brodie, to be sure, had been one of the earliest and most incessant critics of the military establishment among the distinguished postwar military thinkers. At first he gently prodded the military services to consider atomic weapons as distinctive strategic weaponry;[40] then, beginning with his short but highly eventful service for air force chief of staff Gen. Hoyt Vandenberg in 1950 and 1951, he gave vent to outrage and scorn. This tone, which he adopted long before the emergence to ascendancy of the civilian analysts in the military establishment, suggests that Brodie was for the most part not optimistic about keeping military professionals accountable for their ideas. Having advised the chief of staff about the selection of strategic targets in the Soviet Union to accompany the emergency war plan, he noted much later that he had been shocked by "what I observed as sheer frivolousness and stupidity with respect to the treatment of the No. 1 strategic problem confronting the U.S. at the time. [The experience] also made me skeptical of the net utility of the intense secrecy which served as a shield for the perpetration of such blunders."[41]

Challenging Conventional Wisdom

Advocating objective analysis to counter what he considered the unprecedented dangers of military professionals' intellectual conformity, Brodie also strongly supported objectivity to moderate exaggerated claims for any viewpoint, even the commitment to objectivity itself. "Inherited axioms had almost no effect upon my thinking," he wrote in his 1959 study *Strategy in the Missile Age*. "I say 'almost' because it is possible they had an inverse influence, due to my deep-seated impulse to shy at axioms."[42] In some instances, he opposed uncritical application of historical experience. For example, in 1949 he criticized the idea, based on official evaluations of the results of strategic bombing during the Second World War, that morale was an unsuitable target for nuclear weapons.[43] In 1952, while proposing the use of thermonuclear weapons against enemy troop concentrations in Europe upon the outbreak of war, he rejected views reinforced during the Korean War that nuclear weapons were unsuited to battlefield targets[44] and that the nuclear stockpile should be conserved for attacks against the Soviet Union.

Elsewhere, notably when discussing limited contemporary warfare in Europe, Brodie took issue with arguments that were not historically validated but that he nevertheless believed were held too unreflectively. For example, he challenged the view that limited war ought to be based upon the use of nuclear weapons, asserting that "the conclusion that nuclear weapons *must* be used in limited wars has been reached by too many people, too quickly, on the basis of far too little analysis of the problem."[45] Later, in the early 1960s, he returned to advocate a limited war strategy predicated on nuclear use, on the ground that preponderant opinion had swung too uncritically to the other side.

Ironically, Brodie in the 1960s came to criticize those who enthusiastically applied economic methods to the analysis of strategic problems, as he had previously urged, at precisely the time of their intellectual dominance. He noted that such analysts — for example, those at RAND who did fruitful work comparing the cost-effectiveness of two or more weapons systems — neglected the study of history, the sole source of insights for strategists prior to 1945, and he stressed the importance of judgment and intuition in strategic affairs, particularly in connection with "the question of ends," which, he wrote, "is usually a much more important question than that of optimum means, and the systems analyst is not only without special equipment for handling the latter but may even be negatively equipped, that is, he may have a trained incapacity for giving due weight to political or social imponderables."[46] These examples illustrate Brodie's tendency to favor those ideas that, as H. Stuart Hughes put it, "have still to win their way"[47] and to be suspicious of those that seemed entrenched and secure.

At still other times, Brodie made largely cautionary challenges of concepts accepted as slogans but lacking clear referents. For example, in his 1949 critique of classical principles of strategy such as "economy of effort," he maintained that these principles "not only contain within themselves no hints on how they may be implemented in practice, but their very expression is usually in terms which are either ambiguous or question-begging in their implications—a trait which has grown more marked since Jomini's day under the effort to preserve for them the characteristic of being unchanging."[48] He took the same approach to deal confidentially with more sensitive concepts governing air force doctrine. For example, he noted in 1951 that air force officials sought to launch the American Strategic Air Command (SAC) against the Soviet Union upon the outset of a Soviet-American war in order to forestall a U.S. "collapse" to Soviet strategic bombing before American attacks had progressed very far. "We can scarcely learn how to produce collapse," Brodie wrote, "unless we know what collapse is. No doubt there are different kinds of situations which can legitimately be called collapse, but it is these very differences which oblige us to spell out what we mean by the word in any given context. The requirement that this and comparable words be spelled out would expose within the Air Force, and possibly elsewhere, the prevalence of some pretty bizarre fantasies."[49]

In these cases, Brodie did not articulate a categorical or highly structured view of his own. Rather, he confined his arguments to the more general level of military doctrine, making it difficult to discern the policy significance of the divergence of views. For example, when arguing for the use of atomic bombs against Soviet morale in a Soviet-American war, he denied "in practice . . . any essential conflict" between striking at Soviet morale and striking at the most expeditious Soviet economic targets;[50] when arguing against using thermonuclear weapons against battlefield targets in Europe, he seemed to have in mind threats of massive retaliation against the Soviet Union as a substitute; and when he argued for a nuclear demonstration strategy in Europe in the early 1960s, he conceded the need for *some* strengthening of the conventional forces of the North Atlantic Treaty Organization (NATO) in Europe. Brodie invariably aimed at a subtle difference of emphasis, depending upon his judgment of the arguments of others. He revealed his dependence upon other strategic thinkers to help him refine his preoccupations by arguing with others and broadening his field of acquaintances.

For example, his tour of service for Vandenberg sensitized him for the first time to the enormous destruction that the preferences of target planners in Washington and at SAC headquarters in Omaha—who were in sharp dispute, as will be noted—would have brought about in the first thirty days of a Soviet-American war, and he consequently shifted his primary concern from the destructive potential of nuclear weapons to the problem of inflicting excessive damage. His shifts in view, here as elsewhere, were largely intuitive, though he appreciated that objective analysis, which forced advocates to wrestle with detail and with divergent contingencies, could check the tendency to take ideas too far. "The reasoning processes by which the conclusions are reached in any modern systems analysis," he wrote in 1973,

are not only more detailed than anyone's intuitive judgment is likely to be but also more open and explicit and therefore more accessible to correction at any particular point where the reasoning may have gone astray. A briefing will be presented with many charts, graphs, and figures to series of audiences who will have every opportunity to challenge various assumptions or findings as they are presented. Those briefed are not put in the position of being required simply to accept or reject the conclusions.[51]

But Brodie, who was later to stress that systems analysis was most appropriate for dealing with peacetime decisions that are narrow in scope, generally was not guided by the analyses of others when shifting his views. Moreover, in spite of his early exhortation for strategic study based on the analytic method, Brodie was distinguished less for that than he was for spotting weaknesses in the arguments of others. He relied instead upon his own instincts, not hesitating as we have seen to criticize overplaying the importance of the analytic method.

Not surprisingly, Brodie's criticism of conventional wisdom and of military professionals as strategists undermined the influence he openly sought on strategic doctrine and decision making. Especially in his project for the director of air force intelligence, General Samford, which culminated in *Strategy in the Missile Age,* Brodie sought to have a major role in the development of a military doctrine appropriate for the contemporary period, but his shifts in view and great strengths as a critic showed him to be a better challenger of consensus than a forger of it. On the other hand, as H. Stuart Hughes noted, historically some of the most reflective writing has been completed by people who suffered great professional disappointments.[52] Brodie, who seems to have been frustrated at not achieving by the 1960s the power and reputation gained by other strategic thinkers, reflected that frustration in increasingly polemical writing in his later years. However, had he been as successful as he aspired in advising policymakers, he might not have been as inclined or as well equipped (given the sensitivity of the issues with which he would have dealt at the official level) to write for the general public.[53]

Deterring General War

Brodie remains best known for signaling, in his 1946 essays in *The Absolute Weapon,* the new importance nuclear weapons brought to the objective of preventing war. "Thus far the chief purpose of our military establishment has been to win wars," he wrote. "From now on its chief purpose must be to avert them. It can have no other useful purpose."[54] Supporting this statement was Brodie's own fear of the enormous consequence of nuclear war on the scale anticipated, especially when nuclear bombs were directed most devastatingly against cities. "The atomic bomb," he wrote in the same essay, "will be introduced . . . only on a massive scale. No belligerent would be stupid enough, in opening itself to reprisals in kind, to use only a few bombs. The initial stages of the attack will certainly involve hundreds of the bombs, more likely thousands of them."[55] Rejecting in this instance the association of all-out war and national suicide, Brodie took the narrowly military approach that war necessitated military victory to protect national survival. But he accepted the conventional wisdom of the military profession, confirmed in the two world wars, that "all war is total war." As did air-power advocates in the interwar period, for whom the deterrent objective was supported by the view that enemy morale would collapse at the outset of war,[56] Brodie coupled deterring war with the most dire threats against enemy life and treasure—that is, the threat of general war. When he argued, in other words, that the only "useful purpose" of military establishments was to prevent war, he did so on the basis of an unrefined all-or-nothing view of deterrence.

Continuing to focus on preventing general war, Brodie later allowed for wider choices in superpower hostilities. In an unpublished 1949 paper, written for the RAND Corporation, he dwelled upon the strategic value of threatening rather than destroying enemy cities in a nuclear war. "It is by no means clear," he wrote, "that the kind of morale consequences [from strategic bombing] I have been discussing could best be produced by a one-blow war. The expectation of worse to come seems to be an essential ingredient of critical morale disturbances leading to surrender situations."[57] Building upon RAND research on the warning of target populations during the Second World War,[58] Brodie viewed the threat value of the then relatively small American atomic bomb stockpile as the most promising means of forcing victory over the Soviet Union. In this paper and also confidentially to General Vandenberg in 1951, Brodie proposed limiting the first wave of attacks to only one-quarter of Soviet urban-area targets available to American bombers, keeping the remainder for coercive use. "The Soviet Union," he wrote categorically in September 1951, "looks like a perfect setup for the attack which exploits psychological weapons, and the atomic bomb looks like the perfect weapon for psychological exploitation. Why not bring these two things together?"[59]

Brodie now envisioned using in war the fear of nuclear holocaust he had previously conceived as a deterrent to war. Departing in this respect from the view that "all war is total war," he limited this contribution in three ways. First, still lacking any concept of limited war, he envisioned restraint only in the utilitarian sense of providing assurance that a small nuclear force would be adequate to gain victory. Second, he had in mind only the scenario of one-sided nuclear war, with the Soviets unable to deliver nuclear weapons against the United States. And third, he favored nuclear attacks not to bring about Soviet-American negotiation on surrender terms but to counter the presumed unwillingness of the Stalinist government to negotiate for any reason. Brodie believed that coercive bombing would help topple the Soviet regime by stirring mass disaffection toward it.

Not until 1952, in his earliest writing on fusion bombs, did Brodie break fully with the view that "all war is total war" and elevate the concept of deterrence *in* war to the center of his strategic analysis. Presuming that cities would be attacked in any Soviet-American strategic war and that the American people would be unable to persevere,[60] he could not find any rational military purpose for strategic nuclear attacks and was determined to prevent them at any cost. Consequently, he vigorously emphasized the futility of a two-sided Soviet-American strategic air war and of ensuring, through the threat of retaliating with nuclear weapons, that these weapons would not be directed against targets inside the United States or the Soviet Union even if superpower hostilities occurred elsewhere, such as in Europe. Anticipating the nonuse of nuclear weapons on the pattern of the Korean War, Brodie departed from the Korean experience by advocating American threats of massive retaliation to force the Soviets to stop fighting in Europe.

For the rest of the 1950s, he was pessimistic that a war in Europe would remain limited. Contending that "war . . . does have an inherent and almost necessary tendency to be orgiastic,"[61] he worried about the same military dynamics that prompted him in 1946 to anticipate all-out nuclear war. "When we are talking about a war in which weapons of the magnitude described are actually being dropped in large numbers in Europe," he wrote confidentially in 1955, "we are talking about a war in which rationality as an inhibiting factor has already been left far behind."[62]

The most important reason for his pessimism about controlling war in Europe and hence the strength of deterrence in Soviet-American hostilities was the mutual vulnerability to attack of American and Soviet long-range strike forces. As he put it in 1959, "In a world in which there was very little incentive on either side, or at least on the Soviet side, for surprise strategic attack . . . we should have much less reason to fear the quick spiraling upward of the level of violence."[63] Brodie later insisted, in fact, that subsequent development and deployment in large numbers of protected intercontinental ballistic missiles (ICBMs) and submarine-launched ballistic missiles (SLBMs) had critically lessened not only the possibility of surprise attack but also the danger of employing nuclear weapons in a European war. "It was not until sophisticated persons began to discern the possibility, through restraint in fighting, of avoiding the worst imaginable kind of holocaust, which is to say unlimited war," he wrote in his 1966 study *Escalation and the Nuclear Option,* "that the abhorrence that most civilized people feel towards nuclear weapons tended to be focused on the tactical use of such weapons in limited war. The intense desire to avoid any use of nuclear weapons quite naturally provoked the allegation that use of them in limited war would be critical in tripping off uncontrolled escalation."[64]

In writing about nuclear weapons as deterrents, Brodie connected nuclear war limitations with the threat value of those weapons and especially with the efficacy of making threats that could lead to general war.[65] If inhibitions upon general war were low enough that the threat to take actions to increase the danger of strategic attacks would probably not be efficacious, it would be difficult or impossible, he believed, to ensure that limitations in a European war would last. However, large inhibitions in the making of general war increased the chances that steps raising the danger of general war would inhibit intensification of limited war. But though he pioneered in analyzing deterrence in war, his portrayal of that problem as a derivative of the likelihood of general war meant that his concept of limited war tended to be weak. To be sure, Brodie's later complacence about the risks of any Soviet-American confrontation, and specifically his 1963 justification of "going for broke on deterrence,"[66] narrowed the problem of limited war in sharp contrast to his earlier playing up of that problem beginning in 1952. In both cases his judgment about limited war depended on whether, as he put it, a "strategic nuclear umbrella" could have a "deterrent effect on all war, not merely the strategic exchange."[67]

Nuclear Weapons and National Interests

Dissatisfied with analyzing the military implications of security questions — especially with reference to newer weaponry — Brodie sought to guide military imperatives by the choice of political interests and objectives. First, political considerations could be used to criticize wanton and politically counterproductive destruction in war. For example, in a memorandum Brodie wrote for Vandenberg in which he criticized the selection of the electric power system in the Soviet Union as a primary comprehensive target for the American strategic bombing campaign, Brodie pointed out that several electric power targets were located in or close to major Soviet cities and that attacking them would lead to needless destruction. Such a bombing campaign, he observed, disregarded an American congressional resolution expressing friendship for the Soviet people and distinguishing them from Soviet leaders.[68]

The same point underpinned his categorical rejection of strategic air war with fusion weapons, the first discussion of which, in April 1952, made reference to his conversion to the ideas of the nineteenth-century German strategic thinker Carl von Clausewitz. "Six months ago," he declared,

> I could and in fact did deny in print that the famous, often-quoted statement of Clausewitz's, "War is a continuation of policy by other means," could have any meaning for modern times. I felt that modern war, modern total war, is much too big, much to [*sic*] violent to fit into any concept of a continuation of diplomacy. I felt that war by its very outbreak must create its own objective — in modern times, survival — in comparison with which all other objectives must hide their diminished heads.
>
> I have since come to believe that Clausewitz was in fact saying something very profound. What he was saying, it now seems to me, is that war is violence — to be sure, gigantic violence — but it is planned violence and therefore controlled. And since the objective should be rational, the procedure for accomplishing that objective should also be rational, which is to say that the procedure and the objective must be in some measure appropriate to each other.[69]

Despairing that the United States would be able to continue war after being subjected to major attacks with fusion bombs, Brodie concluded that "the political objectives of war cannot be consonant with national suicide — and there is really no use talking about large-scale *reciprocal* use of fission and thermonuclear weapons against cities as being anything other than national suicide for both sides."[70] Consequently, Brodie advocated that "we ought at least to begin considering the feasibility and utility of exercising some restraint upon our own capabilities when hostilities begin and obliging the enemy to use a similar restraint."[71]

Brodie also denounced inflicting unnecessary and excessive destruction when he complained in his most mature work, *War and Politics,* about the tendency of military professionals to value victory above all else in war and more particularly about the depreciation of political aims by Western governments in the two world wars. He wrote, with respect to the First World War, that "hope of gain mattered far less than the feeling that one's own side must and will win, at whatever price and however long it might take. We are, in short, confronted not with simple greed but with some deep psychological need expressed on the national rather than the personal level. The obsession from first to last was with winning."[72] Although Brodie had anticipated and even endorsed this obsession in his essays in *The Absolute Weapon,* he became critical of it after his evaluation of fusion weapons.

Second, the use of political standards to determine whether to go to war or to risk hostilities supported Brodie's anticipation of sober and enlightened governmental behavior during crises. He argued that what Harold Lasswell termed the "critical level of exacerbation" in international affairs—that is, the point at which a sense of damaged national self-interest or propriety brought about belligerence—had risen since 1914 and was rising still more because of the growing destructiveness of weapons arsenals.[73] For example, Brodie did not believe that the nuclear superpowers of today would allow a diplomatic démarche such as the Ems Telegram, which had brought on the Franco-Prussian War in 1870 because of perceived injury to French "national honor," to precipitate hostilities.[74]

The idea that nuclear powers were fully aware of the military implications of weapons of mass destruction and consequently were less prone to be provoked to hostilities—a view fully consistent with Brodie's own known fears of general nuclear war—was perhaps his most important argument for the stability of a nuclear-armed world. "The only thing that will keep diplomacy from breaking down ultimately," he wrote in 1949, "is the conviction *on all sides* that war is far too horrible even to be contemplated. And the great dilemma is that that conviction can be sustained only by our making every possible effort to prepare for war and thus to engage in it if need be."[75] Three years later, after his analyses of fusion weapons had deepened his preoccupation with calamitous two-sided nuclear war, Brodie linked the potential devastation with reduced risk of war. "Believe me," he declared in 1952, "we are entering into an era in which no government, not even a Hitler government if it existed, would undertake this business of war lightly. I myself, concerning the Soviet Union, have never felt the hot breath of imminent war on my back."[76]

In the late 1950s, when the problem of a surprise attack concerned many strategic analysts, Brodie persisted in his optimism. "I do not at all think [the risks of Soviet attack] are substantial," he wrote to Quincy Wright in 1959, "but I think they are not altogether nil either. Certain respected and very well-informed specialists in the field rate them higher than I do."[77] He was also not alarmed during the Cuban missile crisis: "When the crisis broke, I personally lost no sleep over it. I felt utterly confident that this crisis would not deteriorate into war. This confidence separated me from some of my friends, and I am sure it annoyed them. I felt this confidence simply because I had information which convinced me that we were enormously superior in every important branch of arms to the Russians, and that *they knew it.*"[78]

These writings were silent on the quality of diplomacy employed to defuse crises, focusing instead on inhibitions that would presumably permit diplomats greater time and leeway to defuse tensions than in the past. Brodie did not elaborate, moreover, on the source of the inhibitions. If the latter were produced by American strategic force superiority over the Soviets,[79] it could be argued that such superiority had persisted from 1945 through the 1960s. On the other hand, Brodie had implied in his earlier writings that the inhibitions were produced largely by rational considerations independent of force differentials. Finally, as indicated in his references to "orgiastic" warfare in Europe, he did not seem to think that the level at which states were emboldened to initiate hostilities was associated with limitations *in* war.

A third way Brodie used a political standard was to point up omissions of cost-effectiveness analysis, as when he focused on political objectives in dispute and on the need to make available power relevant to them—steps he believed those who performed cost-effectiveness studies generally did not take.[80] The failure of cost-effectiveness studies to analyze vital political considerations was the basis of his criticism of Albert Wohlstetter's classic 1959 essay on the "delicate balance of terror," in which Brodie argued that Wohlstetter, using conclusions of a cost-effectiveness study on the basing of bomber aircraft, took "no account whatever of the inhibitory political and psychological imponderables that might and in fact *must* affect the conditions implied by that word *delicate*."[81]

Brodie himself, in the late 1950s, evaluated Soviet intentions in light of Soviet strength. In *Strategy in the Missile Age,* for example, Brodie, despite citing the high threshold of exacerbating disputes, dwelled upon the advantages of striking first with nuclear weapons[82] and upon the imperative to Soviet leaders to destroy the West if they were able to do so—as he put it, the "very high incentive [to the Soviets] for destroying us"[83]—which he gleaned from Nathan Leites's portrayal of the Soviet operational code.[84] Soviet incentives to destroy the United States supported Albert Wohlstetter's assertion that the balance of terror was delicate.[85]

Only later, following the Cuban missile crisis, did Brodie firmly conclude that "it has in fact become abundantly clear since the Wohlstetter article was published, and indeed since the dawn of the nuclear age, that the balance of terror is decidedly *not* delicate."[86] His belief also that Soviet leaders were quite cautious, as in the missile crisis, became a major underpinning of his companion confidence in the strength of deterrence of general war. In this connection, Brodie cited (as he had not in *Strategy in the Missile Age*) Leites's assertion that Soviet leaders were politically cautious and willing to accept tactical retreat to protect vital interests.[87] And he wrote in *Escalation and the Nuclear Option* that "our defense efforts, large as they are, are considerably below what they could be if we became really alarmed about our chances of keeping the peace. Surely then, our composure argues a persuasion that the opponent does not mean to have a war with us, at least not soon."[88]

Fourth, Brodie employed the political standard to discuss both the perils of failure to resist Soviet coercion and the opportunities of doing so. The possibility that fear of war would be a danger was opposed by the idea that fear of war would enhance international stability. Noting that fear of nuclear hostilities could be a handicap, Brodie in 1952 pointed to American plans for using foreign bases in Europe to implement a strategic bombing campaign and observed that "the fact is that in a crisis our allies would be utterly unable to face up to the threat of atomic weapons being used strategically against them."[89] Later, in 1959, he wrote in the same vein that "if the American people should ever really become panicked at some development in Russian capabilities, experience suggests that their response is likely to take the form of demanding greater withdrawal from risk rather than the reverse."[90]

In practice, however, Brodie argued, the president could disregard such attitudes "for long enough to accomplish a commitment to war. . . . It is the President's conviction, will, and decision which chiefly determine the issue of war or peace."[91] Following the Cuban missile crisis, Brodie insisted upon "the elementary but important lesson that while a strong military posture can support a strong policy or diplomacy, it cannot substitute for it. The same posture that enabled us to force an ignominious retreat on the Russians could obviously have enabled us to keep Soviet missiles and bombers out in the first place."[92]

Finally, in the aftermath of the Cuban crisis, Brodie challenged the assumption — which he found implicit in the proposals of those counseling the buildup of conventional forces in Europe during the 1960s — that the Soviets were superior to the Western powers in political nerve. "The United States," he argued, "is unquestionably much better at resisting aggression than in initiating it, but the Russians act as though they have grounds for treating us with respect. One strong reason for resisting the movement to put nuclear weapons out of bounds in limited war is to avoid changing the very favorable image that our opponents already have of us."[93]

Evaluating Strategic Targets

Documents that Brodie characterized as "the most important and best thought out . . . I ever wrote"[94] and that even now remain little known were two top-secret papers written for the air force chief of staff, General Vandenberg, in 1950 and 1951 on the selection of strategic targets.[95] Coinciding with American fighting in Korea, the assignment was made still more urgent by U.S. intelligence predicting a major Soviet-American war in December 1950, when Brodie began his second tour of duty for Vandenberg. "The Joint Chiefs in Washington," Brodie later recalled, "were utterly convinced that the Russians were using Korea as a feint to cause us to deploy our forces there while they prepared to launch a 'general' (total) war against the United States through a major attack in Europe. In early December 1950, they were actually persuaded . . . that a Soviet initiation of a general war was only two or three weeks away."[96] He went on to note that his position allowed him to witness Vandenberg's then "intense anxiety."[97]

Thus the broad target systems and specific targets in the Soviet Union (SAC's attacks against these constituted the only significant American military response available at that time for war against the Soviets) were not hypothetical but of overriding priority when Brodie was summoned to air force headquarters; Brodie's access to Vandenberg put him in position to affect the form and substance of the strategic bombing campaign. Also important as Brodie weighed his views was that the choice of strategic targets—or, more precisely, of the contents of the so-called target destruction annex to the 1951 emergency war plan—was disputed by the Air Targets Division (ATD), established by and responsible to the Joint Chiefs of Staff (JCS) and staffed by all the military services but dominated by air force general officers and civilians on one hand and SAC on the other.

Brodie was asked specifically to critique an ATD study that in late 1950 and early 1951 served as the target destruction annex in the absence of any other plan but had yet to be approved by the JCS.[98] The study was based upon two constraints: (1) JCS selection guidelines, which required that targets in the Soviet war economy (or "Delta") portion of the annex be chosen from among electric power, petroleum, and atomic energy target systems;[99] and (2) JCS and air staff "hypotheses" or planning factors which, dictated by the assumption that SAC would not be prepared at the outset of war for air operations beyond ninety days, required, among other things, that "the initial, three-month, atomic phase of the strategic air offensive will be selected as an integrated program and will not depend for major effects upon subsequent phases of the strategic air offensive."[100] The system of Soviet electric power stations, which took up the largest share of targets contained in this ATD study, seemed to the ATD staff to be the most promising system of targets that could be destroyed within ninety days and not depend on operations after that date for its full effects to be felt. But SAC officials, for their part, challenged this decision on the ground that a substantial portion of Soviet electric power plants included in the annex were isolated from other targets and otherwise difficult to detect and that the accuracy sought for these bombing attacks, another constraint upon the choice of targets, would probably not be attained against that system.

In a detailed and thorough critique of the ATD study, Brodie proposed the complete elimination of electric power targets from the annex. Questioning, as had SAC officials, whether assumed bombing accuracies would be fulfilled in practice against this target system, he cited how a Nagasaki steam power plant had escaped blast damage from atomic attack in spite of the fact that it was much closer to the surface point immediately under the center of bomb burst than were the mean miss distances established early in 1951 by the air staff to govern selection of nuclear targets.[101] (In January 1951, the air staff dropped electric power plants from the target destruction annex to the 1952 emergency war plan, because they were regarded as generally unfeasible with the mean miss distance constraint then established by the staff.[102]) He went on to argue, as did SAC, not only against the electric power system in particular but also against comprehensive strikes in depth against any single type of target, preferring instead to maximize the destructive potential of a relatively small atomic stockpile.

Some of Brodie's most original observations about the annex discounted what others saw as the lessons of the Second World War. For example, he disputed a conclusion of the U.S. Strategic Bombing Survey staff that atomic bomb attack was the most efficient way to disable electric power plants, noting that the physical vulnerability of hydroelectric plants to atomic bombs was smaller than had been presumed. And he questioned the contention of former Nazi armament minister Albert Speer, which had later guided high-ranking ATD officials in their selection of targets, that knocking out 60 percent of Soviet electric power capacity would have led to the collapse of the Soviet war economy. The postwar choice of electric power as a target system, Brodie stated, "looks like an effort to redeem the supposed lost opportunity of World War II."[103]

In the first of what were to be many distinctive critiques of war plan hypotheses over the years, Brodie criticized the ATD and SAC for advocating comprehensive attack, insisting that war plans be based on logically anticipated results rather than on operational considerations or the volume of economic assets destroyed.[104] He questioned, for example, "on what basis we are able to declare that while delivering 100 atomic bombs will be neither decisive nor lasting in its results, delivering some 300 during the same period will certainly be both."[105] Proposing bombing on a very different standard, he rejected "that we must shoot from the hip" in comprehensive attack and advocated instead "playing by ear" by attacking in stages and capitalizing on the threat of more attacks to come.[106] This meant destroying perhaps seventy-five of the most important Soviet industrial concentrations in the first bombing phase and keeping the remaining three-quarters of the atomic stockpile in reserve.

The effect that Brodie's tour of duty with Vandenberg had on him was much greater than its direct policy effects. As a result of his work for Vandenberg, a struggle ensued between him and the air force director of intelligence, Maj. Gen. C. Pearré Cabell, to control the appointment of a high-level committee, endorsed by Cabell and recommended by Brodie, that would undertake a more detailed target study for the chief of staff. Brodie lost this struggle and soon afterward his position at air force headquarters. Inasmuch as Brodie aspired to long-term responsibility to advise upon the selection of bombing targets, this development was undoubtedly a bitter defeat for him, as was the substance of the report of the follow-up committee, chaired by Henry C. Alexander, which largely affirmed ATD priorities, including comprehensive attack and the priority to be given to the Soviet electric power target system.

Brodie's work for Vandenberg did not have wholly negative results, however. Norstad, who had been transferred to NATO while Brodie was at air force headquarters, was now commander in chief of American air forces in Europe and commander in chief of Allied air forces in Central Europe. He continued to consult with Brodie and summoned him to NATO headquarters to do another study soon after Brodie completed his tour of duty for Vandenberg.[107] (The substance of this study is not known with certainty but may have pertained to targets for that portion of the American nuclear bomb stockpile under Norstad's jurisdiction.) Still more important, perhaps, though not for nuclear weapons policy, was the attention Brodie received from another air force general officer, Lt. Gen. John A. Samford, who had been impressed by the reports Brodie had prepared for Vandenberg. In 1952 Samford, Cabell's successor as director of air force intelligence, arranged with the RAND Corporation in Santa Monica for Brodie to complete on virtually a full-time basis a major study articulating contemporary air force doctrine. This study was published in 1959 as *Strategy in the Missile Age.* Ironically, the air force, which had derailed Brodie's quest for a permanent high-level position, ended up commissioning the study that brought him postwar popularity and enhanced his reputation.

Retrospective Evaluations

Brodie's rapid anticipation of the broad outlines of nuclear strategy and contemporary superpower relations has been widely recognized in recent years, beginning with the military historian Michael Howard, who pointed in 1969 to passages from *The Absolute Weapon* as having "outlined the concept of a stable balance of nuclear forces."[108] Echoing Howard's observation four years later, in *War and Politics,* Brodie noted that "much of the debate on atomic-age strategy" focused upon ideas expressed in five sentences written by him in that same study:

> Thus, the first and most vital step in any American security program for the age of atomic bombs is to take measures to guarantee to ourselves in case of attack the possibility of retaliation in kind. The writer in making that statement is not for the moment concerned about who will *win* the next war in which atomic bombs are used. Thus far the chief purpose of our military establishment . . . has been to win wars. From now on its chief purpose must be to avert them. It can have almost no other useful purpose.[109]

The explicit attention given to these words following Brodie's death in 1978 underscored their significance. Michael Mandelbaum, for example, characterized Brodie as one of "two prophets" (the other, Henry Stimson) who "foresaw the lines of strategy and diplomacy that would enable the world to live with nuclear weapons."[110] He went on to say that "Brodie foresaw the principal features of the nuclear age before they had come fully into being. A state could guard itself against nuclear attack if it had the ability to retaliate in kind." For Mandelbaum, this was the "central insight of Brodie's essays" and was perhaps the "foremost strategic proposition of the nuclear age."[111] Mandelbaum argued that the realization of the potential of nuclear weapons as deterrents came with the advent of fusion bombs — "the sheer physical power of nuclear weapons gave these armaments a deterrent force."[112] Authoritative perception of nuclear weapons as deterrents, Mandelbaum continued, had occurred by 1962 when the American secretary of defense, Robert S. McNamara, rationalized the stability of the Soviet-American nuclear standoff. The latter development made clear, according to Mandelbaum, that "the overriding purposes of the American stockpile of nuclear armaments was [*sic*] deterrence."[113]

Those who played up the prescience of Brodie's early writings played down the novelty of subsequent contributions to the strategic debate, though, as in the work of Robert Jervis, the focus was less on the institutionalization of Brodie's ideas than on their legitimacy. "Very little new has been said since 1946," Robert Jervis wrote in 1985.

In that year Bernard Brodie published his essays as *The Absolute Weapon* and William Borden published *There Will Be No Time*. Brodie's work is well known, and much of the thinking underlying MAD [mutual assured destruction] can be found there. Borden's book is all but forgotten. I came to know it only through references in James King's unpublished history of strategic thought. Although later strategists also ignored this book, many have ended up repeating it. Most of the arguments of our current doctrine — the "countervailing strategy" — are there, including present and projected technology. Forty years of thought have not taken us very far.[114]

Much closer intellectually to Brodie than to Borden, Jervis strongly criticized the "countervailing strategy" proposed by Secretary of Defense Harold Brown in the late 1970s. According to this strategy, deterrence of war was best achieved by retaining the ability to retaliate in kind, especially against an attacker's remaining military capability, following a nuclear offensive.

As did Brodie in his later writings, Jervis fastened upon continuities among enormous changes in contemporary weapons technology, played down the force of those changes, and used earlier writings as a tool of debate. "It is widely believed," Jervis wrote in 1984,

> that the rapid pace of technological progress since 1945 requires equally rapid change in basic ideas. For example, in the bibliography of *Nuclear Weapons and Foreign Policy*, Henry Kissinger refers to Brodie *et al., The Absolute Weapon* as "dated." Since these essays were an early and terribly prescient analysis of the effects of nuclear weapons, Kissinger's evaluation of them is symptomatic. Indeed most of his writings fail to grasp the essentials of the nuclear revolution. The technological changes which had occurred between the time of Brodie's essays and Kissinger's book a decade later were significant. But they did not alter the crucial points. The most important developments were the invention of the hydrogen bomb, the growth of the nuclear stockpile, and the progress of the Soviet program; but they only brought the revolution to full fruition.[115]

Public debate over strategy has intensified recently as the McNamara concept of mutually assured destruction and the Brodie idea of deterrence underpinning it have been sharply challenged. In a 1981 lecture, Howard declared that for almost thirty-five years, our whole military posture was based on Brodie's prescient definition of deterrence that the fear of any nuclear war would deter large-scale violence. Thus, he opined, the "policy of the United States, its allies, and perhaps also its adversaries was to create a strategic framework that made . . . certain that a nuclear attack would provoke a nuclear response [and] likely that an attack with conventional weapons would do so as well." Howard continued that although few then argued that nuclear wars on any scale were winnable given the unacceptable degree of damage they would inflict, this consensus was beginning to disintegrate when Brodie died. Accordingly, it was now widely doubted that nuclear defenses, however structured, would prevent "a Soviet Union that accepts nuclear war as an instrument of policy and has built up a formidable nuclear arsenal from thinking the unthinkable, from not only initiating but fighting through a nuclear conflict in the expectation of victory."[116]

Brodie's prescience as a strategic thinker cannot be disputed, but those asserting it are thus far evidently unable to agree in detail about its extent. Moreover, the focus on the prescience of Brodie's earliest writing on nuclear strategy is too narrow for understanding the full scope of his originality over a quarter-century of contemporary writing. Given Brodie's prolific output, it is doubtful whether he can be adequately appraised with reference to a few sentences that lacked the characteristic refinement that he brought to much of his later work. In these studies, he struggled for depth, breadth, coherence, refinement, and authority; he was impatient with unsupported assertions; he investigated the same military and political questions over and over again; and he was haunted, particularly in the 1950s, by the fear that newer developments would make his ideas obsolete, much as the advent of fusion weapons in 1952 had in his mind undermined what he had written in *The Absolute Weapon*.[117]

Brodie's thesis in *The Absolute Weapon* (however much it was later acclaimed) was also subject to the difficulty of taking rapid account of wholly new weaponry. We have seen that he persisted in that study in conceiving of victory in war on the pattern of prior wars. By contrast, the competing idea advanced in that study of deterring war by preparations to retaliate in kind was much less established at that time and therefore quite tentative, because it lacked any historical referent. Yet the inevitable tentativeness of that idea conflicted with the assurance commonly associated with prophecy, and from this perspective Brodie would not have had empirically convincing reason to anticipate that the balance of nuclear forces could or would become stable. Systematic examination of the evolution of Brodie's strategic thinking undertaken in this book suggests instead that Brodie's early statement about accumulating retaliatory forces in kind was supported chiefly by his antiwar values and fears of nuclear holocaust, which remained constant and strong throughout the contemporary period.

This book is informed by the antecedents in Brodie's earlier work of ideas advanced more recently by others and also Brodie's much less appreciated intellectual dependence upon others. It strives for a detachment that permits critical evaluation of the merits of Brodie's writings.[118] And it endeavors to keep distinct the major ingredients in Brodie's analyses, including his critical bent, his empirical supports, and his values and fears, in order to yield a more refined interpretation of his overall contribution.

The Conception of This Study

Brodie's numerous published and unpublished writings are used in this study to develop his most original and distinctive ideas, many summarized in this chapter, allowing him wherever possible to speak for himself. They are also employed to document Brodie's analytical strengths, among the most frequently displayed being his forcefulness and elegance in communicating his ideas; his critical interpretations of the writings of others, which played a key role in the development of his own views and significantly defined strategic issues for many informed people; his continuing efforts to plumb the meaning of essential concepts important for policy debate; and his wariness about the unforeseen consequences of nuclear weapons employment. Less often displayed, and therefore much less appreciated, was his ability to do detailed analysis under more limited assumptions. Brodie did not enjoy constraining his strategic thinking, preferring instead to give his views the widest range. However, it is his more detailed work, limited in its empirical referents, that may have the most lasting significance.

Highlighting Brodie's strengths, this study makes explicit the assumptions and circumstances that validate his ideas. Often Brodie specified his assumptions, as when he distinguished one-sided possession of nuclear weaponry from nuclear duopoly and the implications of small-sized nuclear arsenals from arsenals plentiful enough to cover all targets or when he critiqued the target list appended to the emergency war plan. At other times, especially when he highlighted arguments applicable to a wide range of circumstances and did not illustrate them, he did not define his assumptions carefully, an omission attributable to his general distaste for detail; to the wide-ranging manner in which he developed his ideas, which often required him to sacrifice systematic treatment; to the rapidity with which he completed many of his pioneering analyses, which often required him to forego extended treatment of original and provocative arguments; to his relative complacence, especially by the early 1960s, about the dangers of a Soviet-American nuclear war; and to his belief that detailed thinking on such subjects as plotting nuclear targets and spacing nuclear strikes ought to be done by Pentagon military planners rather than by outside consultants.

The concern with referents in this study reveals that when Brodie sacrificed detail, his analyses often became unclear and tended toward abstraction, perhaps his most serious analytical weakness. This development was understandably associated with Brodie's pioneering efforts on atomic and fusion weapons, when uncertainties about his subject matter and the novelty of the material would have forced him to simplify concepts and arguments; but it was also visible elsewhere in his work. For example, he categorically summarized and pushed some detailed work written by others in a much more refined, guarded fashion, as in his strong endorsement of classified RAND work on the warning of enemy civilian populations during the Second World War. Alternately, his fears discouraged more detailed analysis, as when he seemed to expect the worst in a major nuclear war and was therefore disinclined to study it. Elsewhere, his central argument drove his analysis, and he gave inadequate attention to circumstances and developments limiting the force of what he argued for, as in his general unwillingness to discuss the implications of defenses to nuclear attack. Again, he left out apparently essential details from his analyses, as, for example, when he failed to define what he meant in the early 1960s and afterward by "effective" use of battlefield nuclear weapons. Finally, he introduced highly arbitrary central assumptions, as when he presumed in his earliest postwar writings, in accordance with the experience of the two world wars, that any nuclear war between the major powers would bring about total war.

Focusing on the connection between Brodie's writings and his attitudes about the strategic questions he addressed, this study is limited to a careful reading of the substance of his work and does not ordinarily make inferences about Brodie's state of mind that lack strong support in the written record. Such an approach, which gives primacy to Brodie's intellectual orientation, seems warranted in this case by Brodie's tendency to use his writing as a tool of thought, refining and elaborating upon his ideas as he wrote; by his prolific output, which makes it possible to track shifts and nuances in his thinking to a degree not possible for other major thinkers; and by his evident concern to be original.

This is not to suggest that nonintellectual motives behind Brodie's writings have no importance. First, Brodie may have withheld important information for security reasons, as on the question of effective use of battlefield nuclear weapons.[119] Or, known to be especially discreet in security matters,[120] he may have avoided entering into details on a subject that interested him because of security sensitivities; the more than twenty years' delay between the time Brodie wrote his reports for Vandenberg and his initial reference in his private correspondence to the substance of those reports is explained partly by this discretion. Although discretion in the use of information is not a primary focus of this study, it appears to deserve more attention than I give it here, not only for Brodie's outlook but also for that of the policymakers and administrators with whom he dealt.[121]

Second, some of Brodie's personal motivations behind his writings have already been established in these pages — for example, his desire to be of service in policy matters and his immense intellectual self-assurance. Others suggested by the evidence include his desire for approbation, his great sensitivity to criticism of his own writing (in contrast to his willingness to provide it to others), his great attachment to reputation enhancement and material satisfaction, and his great frustration at not being called upon to exercise policymaking or policy-advising responsibility at high levels of government. Less established but also suggested by materials introduced in this book were Brodie's tendency to suppress ambivalence in his writing through his forceful mode of presenting his ideas and his tendency to use his writing to confront others with whom he sharply disagreed as a substitute for interpersonal discussions, in which he seems to have been more inhibited.[122]

Brodie's desire to cultivate a reputation, as well as be of service to policymakers, is probably a major reason for his prolific output. His high regard for his own great intellectual strengths may have been associated with his difficulty in facing his intellectual shortcomings, as reflected in his tendency to place the most favorable gloss on earlier events that had impeded his career.[123] This frustration also helps explain his very critical remarks about the military establishment, first informally and later in his final study, *War and Politics.* The apparent parallels between Brodie's understanding of his later frustrations and those he ascribed to Clausewitz in his psychoanalytic explanation of Clausewitz's career are described in chapter 9 of this book.

A third nonintellectual influence upon Brodie's writing was his relations with his colleagues.[124] Very incomplete and inconclusive evidence is weighed in chapter

10 of this study pointing to Brodie's suppression of written criticism of his RAND colleagues during the 1950s and of his strong interest in displaying such criticism during the 1960s, a shift explainable by Brodie's later belief that his reputation as a RAND analyst was stagnating relative to that of others. If true, this shift in orientation raises important questions (not answered in this book) about Brodie's broader and more personal relations with his RAND colleagues, one being the degree to which the RAND environment fulfilled Brodie's aspirations for intellectual influence over other strategic anaylsts, an aspiration that had evidently influenced his decision to join RAND. "One may have a lesser audience, measured in numbers of readers," he wrote to Harvey DeWeerd in October 1952, a little more than a year after joining the RAND staff on a full-time basis, "when writing from RAND rather than from a university; but one is likely to be a great deal more influential."[125]

A second question is the quality of interaction between Brodie and his colleagues, to which Brodie also referred in his letter to DeWeerd. "There are certain indefinable amenities which are known in a university environment which are somehow lacking [at RAND in Santa Monica]," he wrote. "We have friends here whom we like, but so far we have not made quite the kind of intimate friendships that we made at Yale. That is possibly due to the fact that we are now six or seven years older and possibly less outgoing ourselves. But there is not the same broad array of interests among one's colleagues that is found on a good university faculty."[126]

The available written record does not include later reactions by Brodie to life at RAND,[127] though he was later to call attention to the limited interaction across RAND departmental lines, a condition that would have affected him disproportionately inasmuch as most RAND social scientists moved to Santa Monica only some years after Brodie elected to do so. Further, his need for approbation would have required that others at RAND defer to him, yet Brodie's major project at RAND during the 1950s, published as *Strategy in the Missile Age,* was largely one of synthesis and conceptualization, following rather than leading other RAND analysis and apparently not receiving at RAND the great attention it inspired among informed people outside the organization. These impressions are suggested but not confirmed by evidence presented here; detailed inquiry into this phase of Brodie's career would, it seems, be fruitful.

Finally, on its own level, that of intellectual history, this study uses Brodie's contribution and his disputes with others to help document how a generation of individuals reconstructed its ideas about strategy after 1945 and to revive issues inadequately studied in the past. However, I tried to focus on analysis rather than on chronicling or recollecting; at this level, the book has important limitations. First, although I sought detachment, avoiding arbitrary policy positions, and spelled out all the evaluative elements, my evaluations remain tentative rather than categorical. Second, in my choice of topics and themes, I was necessarily selective rather than comprehensive.[128] The force of my conclusions, if they are apparent, must come in the repeated examples with which they are manifested, the examples being as important for integrating the whole as the themes they amplify.

2 · Using the Absolute Weapon

Shortly after the bombing of Hiroshima and Nagasaki, Bernard Brodie began to give major consideration to the military and political implications of the atomic bomb, then a wholly uncharted area. The bomb had been used to hasten Japanese surrender in the war just concluded, but its capacity to realize this objective had not been carefully thought through. Moreover, it had been examined militarily and politically in isolation, without reference to wider American strategy toward the Axis powers or to the larger military requirements believed necessary to subdue them. Developing, as Brodie sought to do, a strategy in which the atomic bomb would be the centerpiece had to proceed without prior debate or consensus.

The circumstances under which the bomb had been developed during the Second World War make it understandable why so little sustained attention had been given to its military and political aspects. The bomb's development had been a most closely guarded secret, about which few if any strategists were informed. Further, nearly all those individuals aware of the bomb's development were preoccupied with the urgent technological problems of quickly assembling a usable version of the weapon and had little time or reason to assess its long-term implications. Finally, the small number of people aware of the bomb and concerned with its military implications faced the problem that the weapon was of uncertain value and availability prior to the bomb's initial test in July 1945. Hence it was difficult to assess.

These conditions had been transformed by the war's end. First, much information about the bomb and its development had been made public. Second, once others besides atomic scientists were no longer concerned with the urgency of bringing a workable bomb into existence, they began to express their views about the implications of the weapon. Third, the test and initial use of the bomb demonstrated its awesome effects and fueled much optimism about its future potential. When Brodie began to write about nuclear weapons, however, there was little scholarly consensus on the weapon's impact or, for that matter, much scholarship on the subject.

Atomic Bombs as Deterrents

Brodie's first major contribution to atomic strategy was to stress the need to deploy nuclear weapons to prevent war. "The first and most vital step in any American security program for the age of atomic bombs," he wrote in *The Absolute Weapon*, "is to take measures to guarantee to ourselves in case of attack the possibility of retaliation in kind. The writer in making that statement is not for the moment concerned about who will *win* the next war in which atomic bombs are used. Thus far the chief purpose of our military establishment has been to win wars. From now on its chief purpose must be to avert them. It can have no other useful purpose."[1] He would later have much to say about "who will win the next war." At this early point, however, his interest in preventing war emerged from his anticipation that cities would be targets for nuclear weapons, that they would remain vulnerable to such attack, and that it would be difficult to continue to wage war once the major cities of one's own country had been destroyed. "Consider what it means," he told a National War College audience in September 1946, "to fight a war in which your cities may be knocked out within the first few hours, all your major cities. Remember your industries are gathered in your cities, and it seems to me strategic thinking has to start from those premises. What kind of a situation does that create?"[2]

For Brodie, once cities were quickly knocked out, war promised to be much briefer and more intense than in the past[3] and, in addition, would almost certainly be aimed at the enemy's "ability to absorb punishment [which] seems to vanish in the face of atomic attack."[4] Supporting this last statement, Brodie observed, was that in nuclear attack, "a far greater proportion of human lives would be lost even in relation to greater physical damage done"[5] than in an attack by conventional force — a point verifiable by comparing the results of nuclear explosions at Hiroshima and Nagasaki with the results of incendiary attacks against other cities in the Second World War.[6]

Since it was possible that the atomic bomb would be used intensively against cities, some strategists saw it as a very promising deterrent: If atomic warfare were to consist solely of urban offensives, rational attackers would certainly reconsider the planned assault if they anticipated proportional retaliation.[7] When Brodie emphasized that "*in no case is the fear of the consequences of atomic bomb attack likely to be low,*"[8] he evidently believed that cities would become "vast catastrophe areas" during atomic war.[9]

Yet Brodie also understood that the bomb's deterrent value could not be based entirely on the assumed limitation of atomic warfare to attacks against cities. In fact, he soon moved beyond this attack concept after concluding that "preservation of striking power" might be critical in order to reduce incentives to attack and that such striking power had to be separated from vulnerable cities.[10] If atomic forces were vulnerable to attack and therefore attractive as targets, they would be much less useful as deterrents and might well encourage attack if air war were viewed, as Brodie later put it, as "a race against annihilation, in which the only way to escape that end is to be swifter than the enemy in dealing out destruction."[11] The need to pause before initiating a nuclear attack was diametrically opposed to the conception of air war as a "race against annihilation."

Perhaps because atomic forces were not yet even considered for use in retaliation at the time his contributions to *The Absolute Weapon* were published, Brodie did not theorize much about the prospects of attacks against atomic forces. For example, he did not explain why cities would still inevitably be major targets for atomic attack if separating strike-back forces from cities and protecting them were so important. Brodie's preoccupation with atomic bombs as weapons of punishment may have steered him away from the nonpunitive purposes of bomb use, such as against the enemy's bomb stockpile as well as his strike-back force. An adequate assessment of atomic bombs as deterrents to attack could not be made until the latter issue was taken into account.[12]

But deterrence of attack could fail, not only because of shortcomings in a defender's preparations but also because of an aggressor's miscalculations. Such mistakes could trigger atomic war on a scale unforeseen at the start of hostilities. Mistakes could include attacks without any unifying strategic conception against both strike-back forces and cities, as occurred during the Second World War. "Again and again," the historian Ernest L. Woodward declared in 1945, "overconfidence has been followed by defeat, and yet the mistakes are repeated. Once more, who will dare to say that this type of error will not recur? It is not inconceivable that by sudden and unannounced aggression a nation may think that it can make retaliation impossible."[13]

Woodward believed that other reasons, apart from overconfidence, explained why nations had attacked in the past without pausing in fear of retaliation. Even if it were true, he observed, "that a user of the atomic bomb will suffer as much damage as he inflicts, . . . we must remember that human beings do not act on calculations of this kind. Hitler was prepared to sacrifice a whole generation for an imagined German future. Lenin was prepared to make a similar sacrifice of the Russian people. It is to our lasting credit that we ourselves did not flinch from an ordeal of this kind in 1940."[14]

A closer examination, however, indicates that in none of Woodward's examples did a national leader demonstrate unlimited boldness: The German and British governments were prepared to sacrifice assets only to a limited extent when the Second World War started in 1939,[15] and Lenin took his country out of the First World War. Still, the German and British cases seemed to show that deterrence of attack could fail in stages as belligerents became progressively bolder.[16] But Brodie conceptualized instead that if deterrence failed, it would fail all at once and catastrophically. "The atomic bomb," he wrote in *The Absolute Weapon*, "will be introduced . . . only on a gigantic scale. No belligerent would be stupid enough, in opening itself to reprisals in kind, to use only a few bombs. The initial stages of the attack will certainly involve hundreds of the bombs, more likely thousands of them."[17]

Although illustrative of a war in which the destructive and strategic effects of nuclear weapons would dominate (a point Brodie vigorously endorsed), this outlook did not wholly encourage attempts at deterring attack. Presumably, policy-makers would pause when confronted with the choice of an all-out nuclear war or no war at all, unless they were far more reckless than other major war-making countries in the twentieth century. Except for the Japanese attack against Pearl Harbor in 1941, massive deterrence failures also had no parallel in the immediate past, and they seemed ever more remote in view of the carnage suffered in the world war just concluded.

But the world wars of the twentieth century seemingly demonstrated to Brodie that war could become uncontrollable too easily, whatever the belligerents' prior political objectives. Unlike Woodward, he did not attribute this lack of control to miscalculations but rather to limitations dictated by national survival. "If there is anything characteristic of modern total war among great powers," he told a 1950 Air War College audience, spelling out what he termed the "heart of the matter" in "our planning of strategy,"

> it is that the nation engaged in it has precious little margin of choice for deciding the physical circumstances which it wishes to prevail at the moment of victory. If it wishes above all else to preserve its own physical plant from impending disaster, it can surrender, in which case it loses control of what it preserves. But if it is determined upon victory, then it is markedly confined by the requisites of that victory. The stages and risks involved in modern war are so great, the objective of victory so necessary and at the same time so vastly difficult to attain, that any strategic plan must be gauged first and foremost on the basis of its effectiveness in achieving that objective. War is not now, if it ever really was, a continuation of diplomacy by other means — to use Clausewitz's time worn and, in my opinion, outworn expression.
>
> By its mere outbreak war demolishes the diplomatic objectives of the preceding peace and creates its own. The chief of these is simply survival, against which all others must hide their diminished heads.[18]

If modern war took away political controls and military choices in this fashion, war presumably should be avoided altogether. On the other hand, nuclear war did not need to recall the most destructive war-making of the past. Conceiving of a war perhaps more destructive than any conceived before, Brodie looked for analogies to the employment of very-high-yield weapons. He could find some only by assuming that nuclear powers would be unwilling or unable to learn from the worst aspects of war-making in the past. (If belligerents were somehow able to integrate nuclear use with political interests, they would have to reject total war. Thus when Brodie came to categorically reject total war, he focused on the need for military leaders to work under some guiding political concept.) It also appears that he was summarizing the lessons of prior wars in very general and largely abstract terms. In so doing, he failed to recognize that even in those wars, diplomacy significantly guided war-making.[19]

Stressing narrow military concerns rather than the politico-military considerations for which he was to become well known, Brodie was in accord with many earlier strategists, such as the air-power advocate Giulio Douhet, who envisioned warfare as giving first priority to efficient and effective application of military force.[20] It was not surprising that when first considering a new weapon that he regarded as revolutionary, Brodie concentrated heavily on the obvious military differences between it and its predecessors.[21] But his assumptions about nuclear war-making were hardly flattering to the individuals involved in war decisions.

Atomic Bombs and Decisive Warfare

By 1946 Brodie had concluded that a strategic bombing program using atomic weapons could for the first time in history achieve military victory.[22] Elaborating on this point in much of his early work, Brodie stated that the only requirement for decisive atomic bombing was a sufficient supply of atomic bombs.[23] In other words, the decision whether "we ought to stop talking about wars as they used to be fought" and instead think of the revolutionary implications of nuclear weapons for strategy depended solely on the anticipated size of the nuclear force.[24] "[With] the experience of World War II," he wrote in 1948,

> none but extremists could argue that strategic bombing was sufficient unto itself for winning a war against a great nation. Moreover, despite the increasing range of bomber aircraft, there were a variety of technical reasons, quite impressive in the aggregate, to support the conclusion that a comprehensive program of strategic bombing over what might be called intercontinental distances would not become practicable "in the foreseeable future." That conclusion assumed, of course, an evolutionary improvement in known types of bombs and incendiaries, roughly approximating in magnitude the developments of the preceding score of years. At any rate, it was as nearly certain as any military predictions can be that a conflict between the two major centers of power would be a prolonged one — comparable in duration to the two world wars — and not promising the same finality of decision achieved in each of these instances.
>
> The atomic bomb has changed all that. Unless the number of atomic bombs which it is possible for any nation to make in, say, 10 years' time is far smaller than the most restrained estimates would indicate, there can no longer be any question of the "decisiveness" of a strategic bombing campaign waged primarily with atomic bombs. . . . Finally, it is difficult to see how the decisive phases of a war fought with substantial numbers of atomic bombs could be anything but short.[25]

In arguing that sizable numbers of nuclear weapons would determine winners and losers in the next war, Brodie moved beyond the axiom that no weapon could be strategically significant until integrated into existing or new military plans and into a nation's armed forces.[26] Apparently he understood the application of nuclear weapons in terms of his general concept that the decisiveness of a particular weapon would depend on the scale of its use.[27] In this instance, furthermore, his conception of large-scale nuclear-weapons use may well have put to rest for him any question about the will to resist attack—a question that had so bedeviled theorists of decisive warfare in the past. As Brodie later put it with reference to the two world wars, "Military theories, which tend always to assume that the opponent's strength is brittle, collapsed in the face of the enemy's refusal to collapse. Each side revealed under test a previously unimagined capacity to endure losses in life and treasure."[28] Although nuclear weapons foreshadowed a new mode of warfare, Brodie's conclusion about the decisiveness of atomic bombing had not yet been spelled out. The conclusion would be based largely upon faith until the elaboration had been done.[29]

In doing this work in 1946, Brodie could hardly have foreseen many of the intervening developments that would bear critically on the decisiveness of atomic bombing. With respect to nuclear capabilities, there was a question whether an attacking air force's bombs and planes would be adequate to destroy all or nearly all the designated targets, particularly as the latter sharply increased in number. Much of the growth in targets would result from the adversary's development of a large, well-equipped air force capable of carrying atomic bombs. Neutralizing that force was vital to reducing the damage to assets in one's own country. However, the capability to destroy an enemy air force was not easily achieved—it depended, for example, on whether the latter received warning of an attack, on the degree to which it was protected against an attack, and on whether it had already embarked upon an attack of its own. Therefore it was foreseeable that enemy air power might escape major destruction.

Brodie initially refrained from discussing targeting details, content to assume that "in the hypothetical war of the future the atomic bomb will be available to both sides in numbers which are large relative to the number of appropriate targets."[30] This was critical to his assertion that atomic bombing would be decisive, for it suggested that atomic bombs would have no difficulty covering the full enemy target list. But it slighted the difficulties and uncertainties of covering a large list of targets, including some highly elusive ones.

Mainly because of these difficulties and uncertainties, Brodie's assumption also underplayed the degree to which nuclear targeting would become a critical priority for strategic planners in its own right. For many years after Hiroshima, American plans for strategic air war with the Soviet Union were to focus on mating bomb capabilities to appropriate targets. To be sure, this focus did not result merely from targeting problems. For example, American planners lacked political guidance from their leaders that would have enabled them to relate war plans to national objectives. Still, war plans such as the Single Integrated Operations Plan (SIOP), approved in 1960 as the first instrument for continuous coordinated target planning under unified service guidance, were limited to ensuring that the targets would be covered, as previously envisioned by Brodie. Referring to this plan, David Rosenberg stated that "little effort was made to develop an objectives plan based on what targets would have to be destroyed to achieve U.S. war aims. Instead the SIOP was a *capabilities plan*, aimed at utilizing all available forces to achieve maximum destruction. As a result, although it eliminated duplication in targeting, it did not reduce the size of the target list."[31]

The making of capabilities plans for master target lists helps clarify why preparations to implement decisive atomic bombing resulted in war-making plans on the largest scale. Planners were not asked to couple nuclear hostilities with prior political objectives. As a result, plans for strategic nuclear war with the Soviet Union reflected the same disjunction between war aims and war plans apparent in Brodie's early writings. They also favored the interests of war planners over those of strategists. More complex targeting requirements, for example, contributed to the increasingly rigid war-making procedures[32] instituted by planners. This was done as a precaution against rapidly changing war conditions, particularly given the need to respond quickly to a Soviet attack. This rigidity strongly supported the view that only one plan for the use of nuclear weapons was appropriate and that it would necessitate war-making on the largest scale.[33]

Since planners viewed war on the largest scale as necessary to provide the largest assurance—everything else being equal—that the enemy air force would be destroyed and that strategic superiority would be established, Brodie probably had planners' interests foremost in mind when he first conceived of nuclear war on this scale. To support his contention that large-scale warfare was feasible, he also must have believed that American military superiority over the Soviets would remain and that it might even increase after the Soviets acquired atomic weapons.[34] Such superiority, in his view, would make decisive atomic bombing and continued American dependence upon nuclear weapons feasible for the foreseeable future.

By 1949, however, Brodie began to modify his earlier views, arguing that superiority might be imposed without attacks on a large scale. "The fact that the enemy possesses *some* atomic bombs," he declared,

> may, on the one hand, put a greater urgency upon our using those we have in order to anticipate his attack and to weaken the potential strength of that attack; or it may, on the other hand, cause us to hold our bombs as a threat to induce him to withhold his. The latter procedure would, of course, nullify the offensive significance of our superiority unless our plan was to withhold our bombs only until the enemy was no longer in a position to use his effectively.[35]

As this last point indicated, imposing superiority required more than merely possessing larger numbers of atomic bombs and planes than the enemy; it also presupposed a greater willingness to take risks and some understanding of the enemy's likely intentions in risky situations.

Finally, Brodie asserted that in the absence of superior bomb numbers and the accompanying willingness to take risks, preventing war altogether was all the more essential. "The burdens of diplomacy for avoiding war," Brodie wrote in 1949, referring to all-out hostilities between equally strong nuclear powers, "are unimaginable, but the task is incomparably important. But the only thing that will keep diplomacy from breaking down ultimately is the conviction *on all sides* that war is far too horrible even to be contemplated. And the great dilemma is that that conviction can be sustained only by our making every possible effort to prepare for war and thus to engage in it if need be."[36]

In other ways as well, opportunities for decisive atomic bombing depended on more than capability levels. For example, the variety of bombs, the accuracy with which bombs could be delivered to their targets, and intelligence about targets would likely improve independent of large growth in stockpiles of bombs, but so too might dispersal and hardening of many key enemy targets. Second, bombing opportunities depended on the extent to which nuclear-armed belligerents maximized their advantage. For example, if, as Brodie wrote in 1946, the fear of nuclear retaliation compelled an attacker to evacuate its cities prior to launching an offensive, the advantage of surprise—a plausible prerequisite for military victory—would be lost.[37]

Finally, even with efficient destruction of all or most targets with nuclear weapons, the enemy might not surrender. Much would depend on whether imposing increased casualties would hasten the war's end. Intuitively, maximizing casualties in atomic strikes ought to discourage or make impossible the enemy's further belligerence, but such strikes could so quickly that the imposition of still greater casualties could become a matter of strategic indifference. If mounting casualties did have a strategic effect in past wars, it was presumably only because the enemy could reevaluate its strategic goals as its casualties grew. If a nuclear attack denied the enemy this opportunity, the threat of future attacks might not make any strategic difference.[38]

Changing Bomb Production Estimates

Conceptualizing atomic plenty and, more specifically, what Brodie termed the "drastic . . . changes in character, equipment, and outlook which the traditional armed forces must undergo if they are to act as real deterrents to aggression in an age of atomic bombs"[39] would be purely abstract without some basis for anticipating that bombs and bombers would indeed be sufficient to cover strategic targets. Moreover, Brodie was not likely to extol a plentiful bomb supply unless he believed it was realistically obtainable. However, he apparently lacked the appropriate security clearances and was not privy to the best estimates of actual and potential atomic bomb production. He therefore depended on less precise second-order information, adequate only for very broad observations about atomic plenty.

Instead of using bomb production estimates to inform his early analyses, Brodie usually employed estimates of the *capacity* of the United States to produce atomic bombs. Illustratively, as in *The Absolute Weapon*, he wrote that

> even a relatively slow rate of production can result over a period of time in a substantial accumulation of bombs. But how slow need the rate of production be? The process of

production itself is inevitably a slow one, and even with a huge plant it would require perhaps several months of operation to produce enough fissionable material for the first bomb. But the rate of output thereafter would depend entirely on the extent of the facilities devoted to production, which in turn could be geared to the amount of ores being made available for processing. The eminent Danish scientist, Niels Bohr, who was associated with the atomic bomb project, was reported as having stated publicly in October, 1945, that the United States was producing three kilograms (6.6 pounds) of U-235 daily. The amount of plutonium being concurrently produced might well be considerably larger. Dr. Harold C. Urey, also a leading figure in the bomb development, considers it not unreasonable to assume that with sufficient effort 10,000 bombs could be produced, and other distinguished scientists have not hesitated to put the figure considerably higher.[40]

The "sufficient effort" needed to obtain ten thousand bombs entailed a heavier commitment to bomb production than was being invested at the time. But even given that commitment, Brodie acknowledged, the bomb would "remain, for the next fifteen or twenty years at least, scarce enough to dictate to its would-be users a fairly rigorous selection of targets and means of delivery."[41] In 1946 this seemingly postponed the condition of a plentiful bomb supply to a future beyond the range of effective strategic planning, because most planners could not anticipate what the value of ten thousand nuclear bombs would be fifteen or twenty years later. With such a distant payoff date, planners would probably not invest heavily in a nuclear program.

On the other hand, there was no clear reason why ten thousand bombs was the best benchmark for a plentiful bomb supply, or why the capacity to produce this number was a necessary prerequisite for the shift to nuclear strategy. Late in 1948 Brodie acknowledged the excessiveness of earlier estimates of atomic bomb production. "Information which would enable private citizens to make intelligent estimates concerning rate of bomb production has not been made public," Brodie wrote, "but there appear to be hints in various quarters that the maximum feasible rate of bomb production is substantially less than was being generally assumed two years ago."[42] At about the same time, he reassessed the number of bombs sufficient to permit decisive bombing — suggesting that a "large number [of bombs meant] one measured in three figures."[43] Elaborating on this relatively low new number, Brodie declared that "if our present rate of production were two bombs per month and were to continue unchanged, our accumulation of atomic bombs (or rather the materials for assembling them) would be entering the 'large numbers' category about four or five years hence."[44]

Whether approximately one hundred bombs were sufficient for decisive bombing depended on the prospective targets. In fact, it appears that diminished prospects for atomic bomb availability required Brodie to consider more carefully the relation between bombs and targets. Consequently, he asserted that the decisive bombing capabilities could be determined only in connection with the targets and that there was no single required stockpile level that could be specified for this purpose. "We know that one bomb will not win a war against a major power," Brodie wrote in October 1948,

> since it took two to produce the surrender of an already defeated Japan. The same may reasonably be held to be true of five or ten. But there appears to be little idea anywhere what number would be "significant" and even less conception of how many it takes to make the weapon "decisive." Much will of course depend on how the bombs are used, but then the significance of the whole issue is that the number available and estimates concerning the capabilities of that number will in large part govern the way in which they are used.[45]

At the extreme, very low bomb production might make it impossible for planners to anticipate how decisive atomic bombing might be. "I might say in passing," Brodie remarked in a January 1949 lecture,

> that at least one of my military friends, who is in a position to know the current rate of [atomic bomb] production, has argued with me that numbers are not as important as I seem to think in terms of the effect it has [*sic*] upon strategic planning. I cannot see that that can be so, unless the range of numbers with which they are dealing is very small indeed. I would grant that it doesn't make much difference whether you are talking about ten or twenty bombs for use in war, but I would argue that it makes a great deal of difference whether you are talking about twenty or two hundred, or about certainly between twenty and two thousand.[46]

Still, the potential rewards from two hundred bombs in ten years' time might seem distant to a war planner focused on more immediate problems. Responsible American military authorities may have had little notion, as Brodie suggested, of "what number [of bombs] would be 'significant' and even less conception of how many it takes to make the weapon 'decisive,' "[47] because stockpile estimates gave them no incentive to depend to any greater extent on nuclear weapons.[48]

If planners lacked incentives to think in terms of new concepts, Brodie certainly did not. Admittedly, his analysis at this point was very pragmatic, because he was using a totally different set of assumptions about nuclear bomb capabilities than he had employed in *The Absolute Weapon*. Further, he firmly believed in the military effectiveness of strategic bombing, even if it was not yet confirmed by experience.[49] But he contributed greatly to thinking about nuclear weapons under the most discouraging set of circumstances for planners — circumstances in which the immediate payoff from nuclear weapon use might seem very low or nonexistent[50] and in which such weapons might be treated in much the same way as were large nonnuclear bombs. If such a condition raised the problem of conserving the relatively small nuclear stockpile, the attempt to attribute disproportionate effects to nuclear weapons becomes very understandable. In particular, such a condition was favorable to the use of atomic bombs for coercive rather than purely destructive purposes. "It can readily be seen," Brodie wrote in 1949,

> that the magnitude of terror created [in such bombing] might well make a rather small number [of bombs] decisive, and then again it might not, depending largely on the pre-

paration of the target population, psychological and otherwise, and on their degree of awareness or ignorance of what is going on (in this case ignorance might be an asset). In any
case, there is a large problem area here demanding a great deal of intensive investigation.
The essential question to be answered is: "How many bombs will do what?" And the
"what" must be reckoned in over-all strategic results rather than merely in acres destroyed.[51]

The preoccupation with "over-all results" followed logically from the assumed
availability of only a relatively small number of atomic bombs and entailed a major
change from Brodie's earlier preoccupation with volume of destruction. Given the
very large capabilities stipulated in *The Absolute Weapon*, saturation bombing of
cities would be quite feasible, even if as many as eight atomic bombs were required
to destroy a single large city.[52] By contrast, a force too small for saturation bombing
would force nuclear weapons advocates to refocus their attention on nonmaterial
results of nuclear bombing.

Overcoming Enemy Defenses

The most difficult test for Brodie's assertion that atomic bombing would be decisive
was in the area of bombing operations against "a strong and well-alerted enemy."[53]
No consensus existed that bombing would pass this test. Those, especially navy personnel, who asserted that bombing would fail, highlighted technological trends
early in the postwar period that were, as Brodie conceded,

> decidedly in favor of the defense against the offense in ordinary strategic bombing. Means
> of detection and interception of subsonic bombing aircraft are making great strides.
> Guided or homing missiles of the rocket type, fitted with proximity fuses, promise to
> give new potentialities to anti-aircraft fire. Jet propulsion, permitting speeds far above
> those available to propeller-driven craft, is much more suited to short-range fighter planes
> than to large long-range bombers, due to the tremendous and rapid fuel consumption
> involved in the jet principle.[54]

According to another informed analysis, Allied bombing operations against Germany during the Second World War had shown that "unescorted deep penetration
raids in conditions of good visibility and in daylight are always likely to be costly
affairs for the unescorted raiding bombers of the future."[55] In the postwar period,
U.S. attacks would probably come at night to avoid Soviet fighter defenses. Since
most targets were in the Soviet interior and many of these heavily defended, and
since fighter planes of sufficient range were lacking to accompany American bombers
to their targets, it was expected that U.S. planes would suffer considerable attrition
in bombing runs.[56] Furthermore, night bombing would make the sighting of targets
more difficult. These considerations make understandable Brodie's 1952 assertion that
"attrition rates to the bombing forces, operational losses, navigational and gross aiming errors, may mean that well under 50% of the bomb sorties reach the so-called
bomb proper release point."[57]

Such an assessment reinforced the need for a large bomb stockpile and delivery capability, to allow for considerable wastage of bombs and planes in the bombing campaign. However, the expense of modern strategic bombing forces, especially bombers, ruled out the enormous number of planes employed in the Second World War[58] and made more urgent the question of acceptable losses in bombing operations. "In World War II," Asher Lee wrote,

> it was reckoned that if any air defense system could inflict average losses in excess of 5 per cent of the attacking bomber force, the air campaign would be slowed up. And in the face of a repeated loss of 10 per cent, a bomber force could not be kept up to effective strength. This was due to the difficulties of crew and aircraft replacements. But nowadays a figure of 5 to 10 per cent is too low a target for an air defense system to aim at. With mass destruction weapons, tremendous damage and casualties can be inflicted in all too short a time. If air defense is going to neutralize nuclear and hydrogen weapons before they achieve decisive results, then it must inflict even more than 25 per cent casualties on the raiders in certain operations.[59]

Obtaining the requisite defensive capabilities depended, in part, on the proportion of resources allocated to defensive and offensive objectives. As Lee put it, "The pattern of attack and defense is always changing in aviation and much depends on what local resources can be spared to do the job in hand."[60] A nation concentrating on air defense capabilities could force a potential attacker to launch a huge and perhaps prohibitive bombing offensive in order to prevail; then, if an attacking nation lacked an adequate bomber force, it might have to delay its bombing campaign until it could gain air superiority over the enemy.[61] Such a condition had handicapped American bombing units operating in Germany early in the Second World War and impressed participating airmen such as Curtis LeMay, who was later appointed commanding general of the American Strategic Air Command.[62]

Whether air defenses could significantly impede strategic bombing also depended on the choice of bombing targets. Lee's own acceptance of greater bombing attrition in the nuclear age than in the past had been linked to using atomic bombs to inflict "tremendous damage and casualties"—apparently with cities as targets, where damage and casualties would be greatest and more intense than in the past. Brodie made the same point even more categorically. Provided enough bombs could play a decisive role, he argued, planners could sacrifice bombers for their vital cargo and virtually abandon protection of scarce and vulnerable bombers in bombing operations. "It is easy to demonstrate," he wrote in August 1947,

> that if available in sufficient numbers, *atomic bombs need not require nearly as "reliable" a means of delivery as ordinary bombs.* . . . [I]f atomic bombs were plentiful enough to make the B-29s or their counterparts the critical items in computing loss tolerance rather than the bombs themselves—and if we could discount entirely effects on crew psychology—it would be acceptable to lose ten planes for every one which got through to the target with an atomic bomb, which gives us a loss tolerance of over 90 percent.[63]

These remarks, reflecting Brodie's unequivocal commitment to atomic bombing, seem to suggest that the strategic offensive would be more than adequate to overcome the enemy's actual and potential defensive refinements.[64] They can also be understood, however, in terms of Brodie's assumption that cities would be used as targets for decisive atomic bombing. "From the point of view of logistics and of mobilization of war potential," Brodie wrote in 1949,

> the important thing about the atomic bomb is not that one bomb can destroy a city but that *one plane* can destroy a city. But if it is so scarce that it can be used "only when the user has air superiority," that is, only when the situation has been well prepared in advance and when the plane carrying the atomic bomb is attended on its mission by a large number of other planes, then one must conclude that it will make strategic bombing more effective without essentially changing the gigantic character of the effort from that which had to go into the strategic bombing campaigns of World War II.[65]

Even though one atomic bomb could not destroy an entire large city, it was apparent, from a planning perspective, that the smaller the number of atomic bombs reaching their target (following the inevitable wastage during the air campaign), the more compelling the argument to target cities.

If, early in the nuclear age, only a small number of bombs could be expected to reach their targets, analysts could only conclude, as Herman Kahn stated, that "The bombs were too precious to be used on anything but important cities or the most valuable production targets."[66] Brodie's description in 1946 of a city as "a made-to-order target"[67] for atomic bombs would then have been especially apt, since both planners and strategists would have wished to gain maximum strategic advantage from the atomic bomb's large lethal radius. "Since," Brodie wrote in 1949,

> the atomic bomb in its minimim efficient size is necessarily of "city buster" destructiveness, there are relatively few targets on which its full destructive power can be utilized. Even Nagasaki, because of its configuration, suffered much less damage than Hiroshima, despite the fact that the Nagasaki bomb was more powerful. When we say that a plane carrying an atomic bomb can do the same amount of damage as 200 or 300 planes carrying conventional bombs, we are speaking of an exceptionally favorable target. We must therefore consider the effectiveness of a bomb partly at least in terms of the target. It happens, of course, that the most appropriate of indicated targets—that is, the large city—is an extraordinarily important one. It may be used on other targets if it is plentiful enough, but on most other targets its relative advantage over TNT bombs will not be nearly so great. On the other hand, we must ask ourselves whether it would ever have to be used on "other targets" after the main cities of a nation were destroyed.[68]

Again, as early in the nuclear age, when "the number of *critical* targets is quite limited,"[69] and when these targets consisted almost entirely of cities, an atomic attack would have been most revolutionary in its effects. Brodie probably had such an attack in mind when he wrote in 1946 that a limited bomb supply would impose a rigorous selection of targets,[70] for then strikes against industrial concentrations and administrative centers inside or adjacent to cities would be at a premium. Conceivably, even a small nuclear force could be decisive against such targets.[71] However, logistics would have discouraged excessive preoccupation with such a scenario, however revolutionary, since the chances that atomic bombing would be decisive would be significantly reduced if planners either rejected any wastage in atomic bombs or accepted heavy bomb wastage. Paradoxically, atomic bombs would seem to be most efficient in the course of such an early hypothetical air campaign only if enemy air defenses were totally disregarded — which, from a planning standpoint, was an unreachable ideal.

The opposite extreme, involving sufficiently large numbers of atomic bombs and bombers in relation to strategic targets, even allowing for wastage, was, as we have seen, Brodie's early long-term ideal. Only if the supply of bombs and bombers were very large in relation to targets could heavy attrition of bombers be accepted in the belief that a substantial number would still reach their designated bombing points.[72] But much depended here on the role of cities in relation to other targets on the list. If most targets consisted of cities, even extreme bomber losses might be acceptable; if many or most of the targets were not cities or if atomic bombs were deliberately withheld from cities as targets, the acceptability of extreme bomber losses would be undermined.

The latter two possibilities might well increase in importance as the supply of atomic bombs and bombers grew. For one thing, newer targets for the American air campaign such as the Soviet long-range air force, which would dictate growing American nuclear bomb supplies, would likely be perceived as more immediate and vital than cities since they affected Soviet ability to damage the United States. For another, the objective of sparing cities from atomic destruction to prevent orgiastic and suicidal warfare would be dictated to policymakers and planners as nuclear arsenals grew in size and especially once Soviet-American nuclear warfare began.

Conforming less to Brodie's ideal vision of nuclear warfare but more interesting were cases in which those directing air operations would have to determine whether the gains from atomic attacks would likely overshadow the losses from bomber attrition. The experience of the Second World War indicates that military leaders would proceed with bombing in these marginal cases. During that war, champions of strategic bombing in the Allied countries often launched bombing operations without fighter escorts that resulted in heavy losses of attacking planes.[73] Brodie's interest in exploiting nuclear weapons in all possible situations led him to weigh the anticipated effectiveness of nuclear bombs against their targets more heavily than the logistics required for their proper delivery over such targets. "It is possible," Brodie wrote in 1949, "that military leaders are underestimating the strategic effects to be gained from a bolder use of even a small number of atomic bombs. The stipulation that so far as possible each one must be delivered to its intended target has implications which conceivably might diminish rather than enhance the military effectiveness of the bombs available."[74]

This statement suggests that Brodie was more concerned that nuclear weapons be used *earlier* (upon the outbreak of war) than that a large number of bombs be used or bomb damage maximized. This accords with his later preoccupation with overall war-making results and contrasts with his earlier interest in the volume of destruction from nuclear weapons. Nevertheless, it seems to discount the possibility that wastage in air attacks would mean the difference between success or failure in the bombing campaign. Concentrated and very bold use of a small atomic force could become subject to heavy wastage of bombs and bombers. This wastage might mean that a small force would not be sufficient to compel Soviet surrender. By contrast, a piecemeal bombing campaign, which could be especially effective against enemy morale, would have the important additional benefit of lessening wastage. However, if Soviet leaders successfully used the wastage of American air power as a propaganda point to boost their people's morale, they would undermine the objective behind the piecemeal campaign.

Target Selection

When Brodie shifted his focus toward overall bombing results and away from the scale of bombing destruction, he differed from those still primarily committed to ensuring that sufficient bombs and bombers arrived as planned over their operational targets. This difference was not over selecting cities as targets, since Brodie, like the strategic planners primarily interested in maximum target destruction, clearly favored targeting cities, given scarce bombing capabilities. Rather, the dispute was between those favoring targeting flexibility in an air campaign versus those intent upon overcoming enemy defenses, which would preclude such flexibility because of the heavy wastage entailed.

Since the United States did not have enough atomic bombs in the 1940s to destroy all critical Soviet targets in case of a Soviet-American war, the feasibility of target flexibility depended on how a relatively small nuclear force would be utilized. This in turn depended on the goals of a strategic bombing analyst. Target planners who defined bombing objectives in terms of destroyed targets would use atomic bombs and bombers to maximize destruction of Soviet targets, especially those in and around large Soviet cities, ensuring formidable attack even with effective Soviet air defenses. Particularly if coupled with major warfare on land, air strikes against Soviet munitions factories and against existing forces waiting to be deployed to the front would likely affect Soviet ability to fight. By contrast, if the objective was to force the Soviets to sue quickly for peace, the bombing's primary function would be to instill as much fear as possible in the Soviet leadership and population rather than to destroy targets. Fear of additional bombing, instilled by relatively small-scale and sporadic bombing strikes, could then have a strategic effect equal to or greater than a much larger bombing campaign.

If scarce bombing capabilities required making the most of a relatively meager bombing force, there was plenty of opportunity for ingenuity, given nonelusive targets. (Elusive targets such as long-range bomber forces, not yet systematically considered by American planners, presented far more difficult problems.) As mentioned above, atomic bombs were quite adaptable as military instruments. But the full potential for adapting them could not be utilized unless target selection became a critical aspect of military priorities and was defined more broadly than in the past. In 1949 Brodie contended that "the strategy of strategic bombing is very largely a matter of target selection, where the economist (possibly also the psychologist) has at least as much to offer as the military specialist."[75] Arguing that strategy needed to be understood not just in narrowly military terms, he suggested that "problems involving economy of means, i.e., the most efficient utilization of potential and available resources to the end of enhancing our security," were critical for war and peace.[76]

Target selection, which Brodie subsequently defined as including "what targets you choose and how you go about planning to hit them and in what order,"[77] needed to be coupled with detailed war-making scenarios, in which guidelines would direct employment of scarce bombing capabilities in the most effective manner. In turn, this required defining atomic bombing objectives more precisely than Brodie had previously done and relating them to war-making circumstances. That relationship would additionally require planners to consider a large array of war-making conditions and the limited and limiting operational capabilities associated with them. "Although the Soviet Union has very conveniently narrowed" the question of who the probable adversary would be and where the probable theater of war would be located for American forces, Brodie wrote in 1949, "the sets of circumstances which might govern a conflict with that country still cover an extraordinarily broad range. It is all the more necessary, therefore, that we develop a conceptual framework adequate not only as a base of departure for specific strategic plans but also as a means of weighing one plan against another."[78]

The subject of target selection raised the question of whether bombing campaigns ought to be directed at the enemy's material capabilities or at its will to fight. Since cities would be the object of attack in either case, attention was directed to the appropriate timing of attacks for the two types of campaign. Studies of the huge logistical requirements of carrying atomic bombs to their targets could provide insights into the "economy of means" in target selection and could pinpoint weaknesses in Brodie's ideas. For example, even if "the scale of tolerable losses in [bombing attacks] is much greater for forces delivering A-bombs than for those conveying ordinary T.N.T., so long as a substantial number of the A-bombs are getting through,"[79] losses acceptable in restrained, prolonged bombing might well be different from those in concentrated attacks. Brodie did not do detailed work on the air defense problem, but his rationale for discounting its importance seemed to be critically weakened where substantial numbers of atomic bombs were not needed to penetrate to targets in the air campaign. If Soviet surrender could be ensured despite economizing on attacks, discounting or even ignoring Soviet air defenses might be justifiable. However, a close connection between more economical attacks and desired overall results still had to be demonstrated.

Brodie was most comfortable with more abstract strategy, in which the broadest significance of operational questions and logic was appreciated. On this level, wider questions were raised about bombing operations strongly justified on narrower grounds. For example, atomic attacks could inflict far more damage than justified by military objectives, particularly if the target concepts of many planners prevailed. "There is no guarantee," Brodie concluded in 1950,

> that a strategic bombing campaign would not quickly degenerate into pure terroristic destruction. The atomic bomb in its various forms may well weaken our incentive to choose targets shrewdly and carefully, at least so far as use of those bombs is concerned. But such an event would argue a military failure as well as a moral one, and it is against the possibility of such failure on the part of our military that public attention should be directed.[80]

Bombing that was most likely to "degenerate into pure terroristic destruction" would presumably be directed solely against enemy cities. Brodie's earliest writings present the logic of such a campaign. However, a great many enemy targets were likely to be located within cities, so it was unclear how a bombing campaign could abstain from striking cities altogether. Many who agreed that it was proper to use atomic bombs against Soviet cities nevertheless disagreed about concentrating or prolonging the bombing campaign. Adopting the first view in his earliest writings when he was discussing atomic attacks for maximizing damage inflicted on an enemy, Brodie later strongly adhered to the second position when advocating employing atomic bombs to coerce rather than to destroy.

Conclusions

Brodie's major contribution in his early postwar writings was to demonstrate the paramount strategic importance of nuclear weapons in the years to follow. His method of ferreting out the ideas of others (including military officers and nuclear scientists) about atomic weapons, placing them in broad context, and subjecting them to extended logical critique was very original, especially in his contribution to *The Absolute Weapon*, and would have been sufficient to merit enduring appreciation.[81] This early work also seems remarkably prescient about access to plentiful supplies of fissionable materials, mobilizing standing forces to deter attack, using long-range strike forces as atomic carriers, and accumulating sufficient numbers of nuclear weapons to cause unparalleled damage to countries employing them aggressively.

Thus in method and in substance, Brodie's writings were far ahead of their time in 1946. Considering the inertia in planning and the attendant risk of retaining obsolescent ideas, his theories came none too soon: Much time and effort would be required to integrate military outlook and planning with large supplies of nuclear weapons. In the long term, Brodie's essays in *The Absolute Weapon* were only the first step in refining ideas and procedures for calculating strategic or planning payoffs from the new weapons. Ordinarily, the lengthy peacetime gap between developing a new weapon and thinking about its military and political implications might be acceptable. However, if Brodie were correct that nuclear weapons—especially when available in large numbers—transformed the security of states, such a delay would have been irresponsible. Even if military planners added long-term concerns to their short-term ones in the first postwar years, they still would have been distracted by the immediate problems of war planning not solvable by the atomic bomb, which was then available only in very limited numbers.

Inasmuch as Brodie directed his vision of plentiful nuclear capabilities toward a more distant future, he not surprisingly found it difficult to detail the conditions of nuclear plenty. He paid little attention to detail when presenting his case for depending on nuclear weapons, partly perhaps because his data (such as bomb production estimates) usually lacked precision, but also because he apparently feared being mistaken if he narrowed his analyses by too great an extent.[82] He therefore had to adjust them to allow for intervening developments that he had not initially anticipated, such as the very low rate of bomb production early in the nuclear age that critically affected projected plentiful nuclear bomb supplies.

Brodie was always concerned about short-term uses for the atomic bomb, but his downgrading of American bomb-production potential centered his analyses on short-term preoccupations. One of his more important substantive contributions, the idea of coercive nuclear weapons use with a relatively small nuclear force—an idea that was not likely to be noticed by more traditionally inclined and short-sighted individuals—seems to have been stimulated at least in part by this shift. It testified to the pragmatic quality of his analyses and to his ability to accommodate such shifts.

Brodie's initial long-term focus resulted in analyses that were more incisive in discussing the more permanent features of nuclear weapons, such as their tremendous potential to destroy cities, than in treating intangible, temporal issues, such as the security interests of nuclear powers.[83] Highlighting how nuclear weapons were spectacular tools of destruction or threat making, Brodie's analyses never really examined whether nuclear powers would employ the weapons in these ways. Thus although Brodie was successful in showing how nuclear weapons changed the security position of all nations, he was less so in showing how they could enhance that position. His assertion that nuclear weapons and their delivery systems would be ideal tools of destruction could only be true for specified security interests.

Certainly, as Brodie made clear, there were scenarios in which nuclear weapons contributed to the security interests of the countries that possessed them. However, there were other scenarios in which nuclear weapons would prove far less useful. Comprehensive analysis needed to address both cases as well as the problems discounted by Brodie's simplified working assumptions (for example, overcoming enemy defenses in a bombing campaign).

Indeed, the breadth of Brodie's own perspective was at odds with the narrowly defined scope of his scenarios highlighting the usefulness of nuclear weapons. Of interest here is Brodie's exclusion in his earliest analyses of issues such as diplomacy or the refinements in weapon yields that affected the mating of bombs and targets on which his deductions about decisive atomic warfare were based. Even a few years after *The Absolute Weapon*, when his analytical focus shifted from the volume of destruction to overall bombing results, he showed virtually no concern—in sharp contrast to his later work—that war-making should serve diplomatic objectives. Perhaps it was because Brodie imagined nuclear war as so short and so potentially catastrophic that he failed to connect atomic bombing with diplomatic negotiation in his writings.

Brodie's contributions to *The Absolute Weapon* (circulated in its final form in February 1946)[84] were limited in scope and originality because they had been completed in a short period—soon after the atomic bombs had exploded over Japan. For example, virtually all of his ideas about air power in *The Absolute Weapon*, including the use of air-delivered bombs against cities, use of the air arm as a decisive mode of warfare, and the most efficient military utilization of a relatively small air force, can be traced, as Brodie later acknowledged, to earlier writings of the Italian air power theorist Douhet.[85] Further, Brodie's early narrow focus upon the connection between atomic bombs and their targets, something which he later (beginning in the 1950s) discounted,[86] seems to have been influenced not only by Douhet but also by Brodie's awareness of the scale of bombing during the Second World War and by his initial acceptance of the traditional idea (reflected in much prior strategic thinking) that military operations should be evaluated primarily on their effectiveness in damaging the enemy.

In spite of Brodie's attempts to project strategic concepts that took the atomic bomb into account, his early analyses also looked to the past. As Kenneth Whiting pointed out, any timely study of a major new weapon can err by overestimating characteristics of the weapons system and also by too complacently reconciling the new weapon with traditional war-making.[87] In some respects, such as his neglect of the air-defense problem, Brodie might have overestimated the atomic bomb's contribution to decisive warfare; in other respects, such as his early commitment to military victory even at the price of enormous destruction, he might have been too complacent about the costs. In both cases, however, he had not come to grips with the military and political inadequacies of a growing nuclear force.

3 · Using History: Morale as a Bombing Target

One of Bernard Brodie's important contributions to nuclear strategy, virtually un-known to the general public during his lifetime, was to argue for using atomic weap-ons upon the outbreak of war to undermine enemy morale. This argument, which matched the interest of air force planners in making decisive use of American nuclear capabilities in a Soviet-American war, was addressed to the short-term reality of the American nuclear monopoly and the small American atomic bomb stockpile. Brodie carried on this work, on a subject neglected early in the contemporary period,[1] first in a project on psychological warfare at Yale University commissioned by the RAND Corporation in 1949,[2] then when he served as special consultant to the air force chief of staff, Gen. Hoyt S. Vandenberg, in 1950 and 1951, and finally during his first months as a full-time senior staff member of the Social Science Division at RAND in 1951.

Brodie built this work upon a 1949 RAND social science analysis of what attacks against German and Japanese populations during the Second World War implied for postwar bombing with nuclear weapons. The RAND analysts made a case for mating nuclear weapons attacks with psychological objectives and for practicing bombing restraint by using nuclear weapons for demonstration value—that is, to shock the enemy, warn it ahead of time about future attacks, and coerce it to sur-render short of comprehensive attack.[3] Brodie also drew upon reports of the effects of bombing on German and Japanese morale completed by the United States Strate-gic Bombing Survey (USSBS). Without investigating in detail the earlier bombing experience, as did the RAND and USSBS staffs, he frequently demonstrated the revolu-tionary features of contemporary nuclear weapons by showing how those weapons would have made a decisive difference had they been applied to that experience. In this general approach, he wrote in 1949, "the analyst who wishes to derive general lessons applicable to the future, who is anxious to find the solution which will mini-mize the appalling human cost of war . . . will be obliged to go beyond history—*i.e.*, beyond experience—to explore the feebly lit realm of 'what might have been.'"[4]

Vindicating both nuclear bombing and its restraint, Brodie interpreted history to bolster his rejection, in reports for General Vandenberg, of the prevailing "shoot from the hip" philosophy in air force targeting circles and his recommendation instead of a philosophy of "playing by ear."[5] By advocating nuclear weapons use for psychological effect, Brodie also helped to head off discongruity between the air staff's preference for comprehensive nuclear attack on one hand and civilian policymakers' horror of the enormous destruction in such an attack on the other. Unless the latter disassociated nuclear bombing from the worst destruction, the American nuclear arsenal might become strategically worthless because of policymakers' unwillingness to employ it and at a time when, as a result of a major retreat by UN forces in Korea brought about by the Chinese army, American policymakers were considering air war against mainland China. "We have thus far given the Chinese every possible assurance that they could intervene with impunity," Brodie wrote in December 1950 while a consultant for Vandenberg. "[We] should begin publicizing right now the fact that strategic bombing does not necessarily mean mass slaughter. All the gasping of horror which occurs every time the use of the atomic bomb is mentioned is extremely harmful to us politically and diplomatically."[6]

The Critique of British Area Bombing

Bombing attacks by the British Royal Air Force (RAF) against German morale during the Second World War had been heavily justified by the view that breaking the enemy's will would terminate war production demanded by large-scale European ground operations. As Brodie subsequently observed, "Land operations have the great function of causing the enemy to consume what one's air attacks are depriving him of. When production and inventory fall to zero and demand continues unchecked, collapse follows; but the demand is a necessary ingredient in the process."[7] Referring for example to the economic utility of attacks against enemy housing and population centers, Brodie had in mind the German position at the very end of the war in Europe. "The effects of morale upon German production," he wrote in 1953,

> look very different if one concentrates on the last two months of the war rather than on the entire two years of heavy bombing. In the end the overwhelming conviction that there was simply no use in going on did indeed control events. The efforts to restore damaged facilities finally collapsed for complete want of incentive. One might expect that with atomic attack such a state of affairs might occur at relatively a much earlier date.[8]

Brodie's appraisal of morale attacks (or area attacks, as they came to be known), inflicted upon Germany throughout the war and not merely in the last two years of hostilities, was likewise based upon the effect of bombing upon economic production, but in this instance he unequivocally condemned the attacks as "an inordinate waste of bombs and of bombing effort."[9] German morale had suffered, he noted, but that effect had been dissipated, "spread out over all industrial enterprises, including nonessential ones, and in the end was trivial compared to the results of knocking out vital industrial complexes."[10] Borrowing heavily from the USSBS report on the effect of bombing upon German morale, Brodie attributed this failure to the successful maintenance of Nazi authority under the bombing pressure. Nazi leaders, he observed, sharply distinguished between the attitudes and the behavior of German workers, rigorously controlling worker behavior without seriously penalizing war-weariness and defeatism. "It was extremely difficult," Brodie wrote in 1949,

> to observe and measure changes in German morale and practically impossible to measure the effects of depressed morale upon the overall German war effort. What on the contrary became overwhelmingly obvious was that a people who had apparently lost all expectation of victory and who seemed desperately anxious to see the end of the war on almost any terms could still, through a political control system relying heavily on coercion, be kept in a routine though apathetic continuance of war production. That that discovery has been of tremendous importance in the evaluation of the morale factor cannot be gainsaid.[11]

Whether the German morale collapse to which he attached such importance might have been hastened by the RAF bombing Brodie did not indicate, but it is clear that area bombing was by no means the only preoccupation of the RAF during the last two years of the war. "From April till September [1944]," according to Sir Arthur Harris, commander of the RAF Bomber Command,

> all strategic bomber forces, both R.A.F. and American, were placed under the direction of the Supreme Allied Commander, General Eisenhower, when these were engaged on operations connected either with the reduction of the German air force or with the invasion of Europe. . . . Thus the strategic bombing of Germany had lasted for almost exactly a year, and for no longer. This is a point which I cannot emphasise too strongly. The average man considering the effects of the bombing of German industrial towns is apt to think of it as a campaign which went on for three years during which a force of 1,000 bombers regularly hammered away at all the enemy's main industrial centres. Actually only 45 per cent of Bomber Command's effort during the whole of the war was directed against German cities and this 45 per cent includes a number of exceptionally heavy raids carried out towards the end of the war which were tactical rather than strategic in their aim and were designed to have a short term effect on the land campaign by blocking the communications of the German army. In April of 1944 I certainly had no illusion that the strategic bombers had done their work; it never occurred to me that we could reduce the largest and most efficient industrial power in Europe to impotence by a year's bombing with an average striking force of six or seven hundred bombers which were never certain to find the target if it lay east or south of the Ruhr. On the contrary, I expected that the damage we had done to German industry—and for the size of the force it was most impressive—would be repaired in five or six months if we gave the enemy any respite from strategic bombing. . . . That respite we were now proposing to give him.[12]

Thus even RAF bombing had changing emphases, but Brodie's failure to trace these changes made him unable to establish whether the strategic failure of the RAF

campaign was primarily psychological (in that the German people were not sufficiently divided from their government) or primarily economic (in that area bombing
did not significantly reduce German war production). By the latter stages of the
war, with the growth of the RAF, the limitations of area bombing were likely to
have been more psychological than economic; at that time, for example, the Nazi
regime's success in retarding the collapse of morale would have become more important insofar as, according to the USSBS report, "the apathy resulting from the heaviest bombing made people more susceptible to the controls of the regime."[13] But
early in the RAF bombing, when the small size of the RAF limited the scale of
area attack and when considerable slack remained in the German economy, area
bombing floundered mainly for economic reasons.

For example, according to the official history of the RAF Bomber Command,
the attack against German communications

> was . . . closely linked with that on the morale of the civil population. . . . [E]mphasis
> was laid [in the summer of 1941] on the fact that "the best railway targets . . . lie in
> the main, adjacent to workers' dwellings and congested industrial areas." It is clear that
> it was this aspect of the communications target system which caused it to be accepted
> as the primary objective. It was added that morale might become the primary objective
> when the bomber force had been expanded and when German morale showed signs of
> weakening from other causes.[14]

These limited attacks failed because British planners grossly underestimated the resiliency of the German economy. According to the official history, "The impression
remained, not only in [1941] but in subsequent years, that Germany was so severely
strained that an additional burden might well produce a complete breakdown in the
national economy. This misconception was particularly important in considering the
possible effects of area bombing."[15]

Later, much larger area attacks, designed primarily for psychological effect, failed
to have major economic consequences for the same reason. For example, as the result
of four successive days of bombing against Hamburg in July and August 1943, during which about forty-five thousand Germans were killed, about 1.2 million people
evacuated the city, stimulated by fear of more attacks to come and by city leaders'
appeals for nonessential inhabitants to leave. These evacuations were later termed
"visible evidence that Area Bombing operations had stopped the normal life of a
major city."[16] Yet as John Kenneth Galbraith, who served on the USSBS staff, later
put it in reference to the firebombing of the center of Hamburg, a large industrial
city: "Waiters, bank clerks, shopkeepers and entertainers forcibly unemployed by the
bombers flocked to the war plants to find work and also to get the ration cards
that the Nazis thoughtfully distributed to workers there. The bombers had eased
the labor shortage."[17]

USSBS analysts generally agreed that "as in most other cases in the history of
wars — the collapse [of Germany] occurred before the time when the lack of means
would have rendered further resistance physically impossible."[18] Still, German eco-

nomic collapse came about more from material shortages than from any lack of will, unlike the German collapse during the last months of the First World War, which fit Brodie's description of "the effects of morale on German production" in 1945.[19]

First, whatever the will of the German regime and people, the closing in of the Allied armies would have badly damaged the German war economy in 1945 by denying to Germany critically valuable industrial centers such as the Ruhr. In this sense, major land operations helped undermine enemy production as effectively as did the bombing of key German economic targets. But the German will to resist continued despite the retreat on the ground. Second, the German labor force, which should logically have reflected any morale collapse toward the end of the war, did not weigh heavily in the final result. According to the USSBS summary report on the German war economy, "throughout the period following July [1944]" — that is, after the successful Allied bombing of German oil refineries from May to July 1944 — "despite maintenance of the labor force, production declined and after January 1945 the entire economic situation disintegrated into final collapse. In the final desperate period emphasis was placed on expansion of manpower and its concentration in war production and direct defense. But plant installations were hit too badly and transportation was too greatly hampered for labor to prove the limiting factor for production as a whole."[20] Following the collapse of the German oil industry, fuel limitations critically impeded utilization of continuing war production. The attitude of the German people counted for little in the end.[21]

The more effective the attacks were against German industrial targets, the less effective the area attacks were. This condition would no longer apply in a nuclear bombing campaign interdicting enemy war production in two simultaneous ways — directly, by destroying key war production sites, and indirectly, by undermining morale through area effects of the same atomic attacks. Brodie, who stressed just such a combination of effects in his analyses of nuclear bombing potential,[22] used his analysis of the RAF bombing to argue for capitalizing upon it.

Area Bombing and Direct Morale Effects

Brodie believed, as did British and American bomber commanders during the Second World War, that strategic bombing could be decisive even in the absence of land warfare, a point he argued not with reference to enemy war production but in connection with undermining the enemy's will to wage war. "We need not dwell," he wrote in 1949,

> on the extreme case of the attacker throwing all his A-bombs within a period of two or three days; even if he spreads his deliveries through a year of more, the experience of the target population will be vastly different from that of the Germans in World War II. Experiences comparable to those suffered by the inhabitants of Cologne, Essen, and Hamburg — and vicariously by other Germans — only in the fourth year of World War II will mark the beginning of the attack. Depending on the A-bomb resources of the

attacker, the weight of attacks through any given time span will be far greater than would be possible with HE [heavy explosives]. . . . [Earlier,] the buildup of attack was quite slow. . . . The Germans were thus permitted to make all sorts of adjustments such as are likely to be made only under the stimulus of disaster but which require time to effect. What we would have to investigate before we could make any really valid generalizations about cities as a target system would be somewhat as follows: what would have happened to the German national structure—political and social as well as industrial—if the thirty or forty largest German cities had been visited with the same magnitude of destruction that was inflicted on Hamburg at about the same time that that city was subjected to its greatest attacks. Essen and Cologne might be even better examples since the attacks on them came somewhat earlier in the war. In Japan the cases of Tokyo and Hiroshima would be relevant. Without prejudicing the results of such investigation, it appears fair to say that the consequences for each of the countries mentioned would have been of quite a different order of magnitude from what actually occurred.[23]

This logic underpinned Brodie's emphatic contention that *"there is clearly no basis at all for assuming that conclusions about German urban bombing in World War II would apply to war in the atomic age."*[24]

Identifying the German political and social structure as a target objective, Brodie evidently had in mind the later stages of the war, when RAF strength was increased. Harris similarly wrote after the war that such a larger force might have brought the Germans to their knees much sooner, without an Allied land invasion of Europe. "I am certain," Harris contended,

that if we had had an adequate bomber force to attack Germany a year earlier, that is, in 1943, or if we had not had the pre-invasion bombing and the bombing of the V-weapon sites to divert us in 1944, we should never have had to mount an invasion on anything like the scale that proved necessary. . . . [I]n the last three months of 1944 Bomber Command had dropped as great a weight of bombs as in the whole of 1943; there was no reason at all why we should not have been as ready for the offensive in 1943 as in 1944 except that we did not get the men, aircraft, and equipment when we asked for them, and we were always being diverted from the main offensive by the demands of other services. As the Americans also suffered continuously from similar diversions without these diversions the results would have been the inevitable and total collapse of Germany and there would have been no need for the invasion.[25]

On the other hand, Brodie pinpointed the shallowness of Harris's strategic concepts, as when he wrote that Harris expected "substantial results from area bombing . . . because, despite his utter disdain for what we now call 'psychological warfare,' he shared Douhet's faith in the critical vulnerability of civilian morale."[26] Indeed, Harris and his associates seem to have given little attention in practice to German morale. "The morale of the enemy under bombing," Harris wrote after the war,

could be taken as an imponderable factor. Just possibly a break in morale might lead to the collapse of the enemy, and more probably bad morale would add to the loss of production resulting directly from air raid damage, but it was not necessary to take these possibilities into account; bombing, there was every reason to suppose, would cripple the enemy's war industries if it was carried out for long enough and with sufficient weight.[27]

Equating the German will to resist with surviving German war potential, the destruction of which the British air staff intended, the staff found "a definite correlation . . . between acreage of concentrated devastation and loss of man hours" and of "the cumulative effect on industry of its extensive destruction in a large number of towns,"[28] an outlook that connected the largest available bombing force to the most effective undermining of German morale. Brodie, unlike Harris, strongly supported the study of enemy morale and of affecting it in a bombing campaign. Such study during the Second World War would have discouraged the launching of bombing attacks against German cities without reference to anti-Nazi activity or to industrial importance. According to Gabriel Almond, a member of the USSBS staff, "The bombing of workers' quarters through raids on industrial areas, and area raids[,] created difficult problems of explanation for the oppositional leadership everywhere."[29] Study of German morale would presumably have attempted to discern whether RAF bombing contributed to enemy opposition, whereas in the actual case, intelligence that the bombing did not do so was evidently ignored.[30]

Whether British study of German morale or more general strategic preoccupations could have overriden the dictates of efficient target destruction was unclear. Brodie observed, for example, that concentrated area bombing during the Second World War resulted inevitably from operational limitations such as large bombing inaccuracies. "The limitations [of radar-assisted night bombing] could be accepted, and a campaign carried out despite them," he pointed out, "only if the attacker expected substantial results from area bombing."[31] The large inaccuracies of RAF bombers early in the war, and the small size of the bombs initially used, limited damage from bombing attacks to specific targets and consequently contributed to the decision to target the centers of German cities. Decisions about bombing tactics such as "stick-bombing" (the dropping of two bombs in each bombing run) grew out of the earliest operational limitations. According to Sir Solly Zuckerman,

> Stick-bombing in general assumed small bombs, since aircraft could not carry vast loads. Small bombs meant relatively small foci of damage, and small foci of damage limited the choice of target systems to built-over-areas whose destruction could not have had much effect upon war industry. The more one attacks a bad system, the more you have to justify your actions so that the bad system becomes a good system. We were definitely caught up in this vicious circle.[32]

Moreover, because of the enormous logistical requirements of launching massive area attacks with the heavy explosives and incendiaries then available, which made it very difficult to follow up one area bombing success with other comparable operations, the goal of making bombing decisive in itself could hardly be more than an ideal.[33] For one thing, the conditions by which even major attacks, such as those launched in what Brodie termed "the entire two years of heavy bombing," could produce the necessary terror and panic were quite limited. As Martin Middlebrook wrote of the 1943 Hamburg raids,

> In not one of the four nights [when raids were carried out] was there any really concentrated bombing in that area of Hamburg chosen for attack on that night. But, because Hamburg was such a large city, other areas of it had received the bombs instead. The Battle of Hamburg had been a success because of Hamburg's situation near the German coast and on a very wide river which helped the Pathfinders to use their radar sets more profitably, because Sir Arthur Harris was prepared to persevere until a sufficient tonnage of bombs had been dropped and because he applied the strict principle of Area Bombing — that is, that the most densely built-up areas of a large city should be attacked and destroyed by fire. Subsidiary factors were the exceptionally dry weather, which helped to produce the firestorm, and the use of Window [a technique to foil enemy defenses by using pieces of aluminum foil] which helped the bomber force to arrive at the city and fly over it in a relatively unharassed manner. It was very rare for the R.A.F. to find such a favourable set of conditions for night bombing.[34]

Finally, RAF officials guided their selection of targets by anticipated or actual attrition to RAF planes from German defenses. For example, the Lübeck attack of March 1942, the first test of saturation incendiary bombing tactics, subsequently rated by the RAF Bomber Command as "a first class success" with "large areas of total destruction amounting to probably 45–50% of the whole city,"[35] also brought about unacceptable attrition to the attacking force.[36] Harris wrote later that "the principle of concentration in time and space would have been forced upon us in any case by the growing strength of the German defence."[37]

Sensitive to tactical considerations when he explained Harris's target selection, Brodie elsewhere seemed to reject out of hand Harris's choice of targets, as when he declared in March 1950 that "area bombing," by which he clearly referred to the characteristic pattern of RAF attack, "far from being the only way to carry on a strategic bombing campaign, . . . is the worst way."[38] Such an approach he specifically rejected for atomic warfare. "We cannot accept," he wrote in August 1950, "the conclusion that because atomic bombs are a convenient way of destroying cities, it is sound strategy to use them for that purpose. Even narrow military considerations might dictate other targets, and strategy cannot be guided exclusively by narrow military considerations."[39]

Although cautioning against allowing bombing tactics to dictate strategy, this statement presumed that those wielding an atomic capability would not be as constrained in their targeting decisions as Harris had been earlier. On the other hand, though highly informed by a bombing experience in which tactics were sharply constraining, the statement did not acknowledge that efficient target destruction would still be required *to some extent* at present. Atomic bombing would need to satisfy pressures for "substantial results" similar to those under which Harris labored, and those pressures would encourage, as in the Second World War, equating satisfactory area bombing results with great tangible destruction. "While particular tactics may call for particular weapons," Solly Zuckerman wrote, "it is usually the weapon which dictates the tactics; and inevitably strategy then becomes conditioned by what is practically possible." Zuckerman pointed out in a 1957 lecture that "weapons systems which might be pre-eminent in range and destructive power might impose inefficient strategies both from the point of view of cost and of results — in the same way as good strategy may be nullified by inefficient weapons, using the word 'weapon' in its broadest sense, and using the term 'inefficient' as implying inadequate for the purpose in view."[40]

Whether atomic bombs ought to be mated to morale objectives was distinct from whether area bombing was most appropriate to pursue those objectives. Had Harris's campaign wielded atomic weapons, it might have affected German conduct as well as morale, overcoming the impact of the Gestapo upon the German public;[41] the largest of the area attacks against Germany did assist that objective in the short term. For example, the German armament minister, Albert Speer, later recalled informing Hitler after the Hamburg attacks "that a continuation of these attacks might bring about a rapid end to the war."[42] Speer seems to have felt the same way after a 1945 Allied attack against Dresden killed an estimated one hundred thirty-five thousand Germans, the largest number of any specific bombing offensive in the war. This attack aimed at and provoked large-scale civilian evacuations to hamper the retreat of German forces on the eastern front. According to Speer, "in every attack in which the R.A.F. *suddenly* increased the weight of its attacks, as for example . . . in the attacks on Dresden, the effect not only upon the population of the town attacked but also upon the whole of the rest of the Reich was terrifying, even if only temporarily so."[43]

Brodie also attributed the British area bombing failure to RAF inability to produce more such attacks. However, by condemning Harris's area bombing method, Brodie undermined his comparison of the failure of RAF bombing with current nuclear bombing potential. In practice, Brodie argued for targeting industrial concentrations on the outskirts of cities,[44] a difference from the RAF approach that was insignificant for targeting efficiency but critical for bombing results. In any case, Brodie's own acceptance of very large urban casualties may have narrowed his perspective about strategic outcomes, much as Harris's outlook about such outcomes had been narrowed earlier by the demand for heavy enemy casualties to compensate for bombing inaccuracy and bombing attrition. In spite of his commitment to a deeper appreciation of enemy morale than that shown by Harris, Brodie remained as constrained by efficient target destruction as Harris was. This suggested some of the difficulty, even with atomic weapons development, of making strategy rather than tactics the primary focus of a strategic bombing campaign.

Bombing Scale and Its Effect on Morale

Brodie's interest in using strategic bombing independently of land warfare to bring about enemy surrender was understandable given his view that contemporary American ability to wage sustained land warfare had yet to be demonstrated.[45] It was also inevitable given his belief that an atomic war would be far shorter than the Second World War. Even when Brodie presumed that a Soviet-American war would last up to a year, for example, he did not clearly link atomic bombing with major invasion by the land armies of Central Europe or the Soviet Union in that period of time. And in the extreme condition in which, as he put it in 1959, "efforts to restore damaged facilities finally collapsed for complete want of incentive . . . [in nuclear war] within days or hours of the onset of the attack,"[46] such coordination was surely ruled out entirely, even for western armies already mobilized for major land warfare. However, as wars were shortened and land combat made less significant, what Brodie referred to as the demand aspect of morale collapse, the deprivation to the enemy by air strikes of what land battles were consuming, came into question.

In practice, early contemporary advocates of heavy area attacks had little concern for this problem, being uninterested in how nuclear strikes against area targets inside the Soviet Union would affect Soviet ability to fight on the battlefield. For example, one emergency war plan (in effect by the end of 1948) favored by American SAC officials aimed at destroying seventy Soviet cities with one hundred thirty-three atomic bombs in a massive attack.[47] It proposed to capitalize upon "the destructive and psychological power of atomic weapons," to contain advancing Russian forces at the Rhine, and generally to force Soviet capitulation through American atomic bombing. An atomic attack against seventy Soviet cities, according to a JCS review group writing in 1949, "could produce as many as 2,700,000 mortalities, and 4,000,000 additional casualties, depending upon the effectiveness of Soviet passive defense measures. A large number of homes would be destroyed and the problems of living for the remainder of the 28,000,000 people in the 70 target cities would be vastly complicated."[48] Such a plan surely assumed the same "faith in the critical vulnerability of civilian morale" that Brodie ascribed to Harris and Douhet and, more particularly, the same association between heavy bombing and enemy collapse.

Brodie accepted Harris's point that strategic bombing independent of land warfare would ordinarily be more destructive than bombing coordinated with it. "Exclusive reliance upon strategic air power," Brodie, reflecting this outlook in the postwar period, wrote in 1949, "would mean among other things, a completely different system of target selection, and *a far greater magnitude of destruction* than would be necessary to achieve *decisive air results* if the air offensive were coordinated with land operations. There is only one factor which might change this conclusion, and that is the morale effect of atomic bombs used on a large scale. As yet this factor is an almost complete unknown."[49] The scale of attack that Harris would have liked to deliver in the Second World War and the scale of nuclear attack that SAC preferred to deliver against the Soviet Union presumably illustrated the greater magnitude of attack designed to be decisive independent of land warfare. This view was probably strengthened by the presumption that only the heaviest attacks would overcome resistance by an enemy government similar to that of Nazi Germany.

This presumption was challenged in Brodie's exceptional case. In that case, atomic attack aimed at enemy morale would be decisive with smaller expenditure of force if nuclear bombing did not exhaust area targets, if the opponent were compelled to surrender even when possessing considerable remaining war potential, and if bombing success did not depend merely upon the scale of bombing destruction. That case provided a major rationale, therefore, for giving independent thought to Soviet morale as a bombing target.

But the reality Brodie described in his writings in 1949 was a neglect of morale as a target, "a quite pronounced tendency in various RAND [Corporation] discussions and documents to eliminate morale effects of bombing as a factor worth considering in evaluating the military worth of various A-bomb target systems or modes of laying on attacks."[50] He explained this neglect with reference to the failure of earlier area bombing against Germany. "The fact," Brodie wrote in 1951,

> that these [targeting] questions are considered almost exclusively in terms of economic results is only another example of the heavy economic bias which has prevailed in this area of thought since World War II. This bias was confirmed by the fact that *under the conditions and methods of World War II,* morale attacks on cities were or appeared to be a complete bust. The question now is whether we should not be ready to revise our thinking in view of the radically new conditions created by atomic and other weapons, of the availability of new methods of attack, and of the great difference in political climate between Nazi Germany and the Soviet Union.[51]

An early example of this "economic bias" may have been the conclusion of the USSBS staff in 1945 that since morale effects in the bombing of Germany had not been successful, bombing attacks under way against Japan should avoid aiming at morale effects and concentrate instead on the Japanese transportation network.[52] Subsequently, even when target analysts, including many economists, were well aware of the destructiveness of atomic attacks, they may not have felt competent to challenge the USSBS conclusion, propounded in ignorance of the atomic bomb, that heavier RAF attacks would not have had an appreciable effect against German morale.

The USSBS report on German morale, noting that "the maximum morale effect of dropping a given weight of bombs [on Germany] would be attained by widely scattered bombing rather than by concentrating available tonnage on a few areas," asserted that "morale changes resulting from a given weight of bombs are produced principally by the amount of personal involvement incident to the bombing" and questioned whether the heaviest bombing possible was the most appropriate instrument to induce such changes.[53] "The amount of serious personal involvement," the report stated,

> does not increase in proportion to the weight of the bombs dropped. The percentage of people suffering such consequences increases with tonnage, but the change is very small where bombing is severe. Only 5 percent more people were involved where 30,000

tons of bombs had been used than with 6,000 tons. This pattern of diminishing increase in personal involvement as bomb weight mounts parallels closely the pattern of change in morale with increasing bomb tonnage.[54]

Finally, target analysts may have accepted that larger explosive power was required against enemy morale than against specific war industries, believing the latter to be more suitable for the relatively small American nuclear stockpile of the late 1940s and early 1950s.

Contemporary acceptance that heavier bombing brought diminishing returns for attacks against enemy morale and that aiming at enemy morale required a large bomb stockpile neglected the terrorizing effect of nuclear attacks comparable to but on a much larger scale than the earlier bombing of Hamburg and Dresden. Planners neglected this effect, for example, when at first they equated targeting people with the killing impact of nuclear weapons.[55] Brodie for his part insisted that personal involvement of the adversary population in atomic bombing would be significantly greater than in the RAF bombing of Germany. "The fact remains," he noted in 1953,

> that the great majority of Germans escaped the more serious kinds of heartbreak or horror. Under atomic weapons the proportion of persons exposed to risk through residence in town or cities would perhaps not be substantially greater, but among those exposed the incidence of casualties and of lost homes would be far greater and the disorganizing effects upon the country-side (or "hinterlands") would be immeasureably [*sic*] more immediate and direct.[56]

Accepting very large casualties in nuclear war, Brodie sought the strongest reasons for terrorizing the enemy population. For example, he observed in 1949, "high rates of casualties among urban populations will . . . tend to have disproportionate effects upon the control group,"[57] because of the concentration of enemy leadership cadres in large cities. "The facts remain that under all forms of government," he wrote in 1953,

> an orderly surrender requires the initiative of political leaders who are either already in authority or close enough to it to acquire it without popular revolution, and that in any [case] popular revolutions do not thrive under conditions of wholesale destruction from the air. The kind of extreme destruction which can be envisaged with nuclear weapons is more likely to dissolve all government than to cause the replacement of an incorrigible regime by an amenable one. That indeed may be an objective worth pursuing, provided the attacker knows what he is doing.[58]

If the objective was to cause political chaos in the enemy country, bringing about heavy casualties in the shortest possible time might be appropriate. "The fact that a given amount of damage can be effected in a far shorter period of time with atomic bombs than with conventional bombs," Brodie declared in January 1949,

> has enormous implications in terms of the ability of the target state to repair damage and to adjust its defenses to the attack. For example, by the middle of 1944 Germany was still going strong, and it could hardly be said that the strategic bombing to which

she had been subject during the previous five years had yet accomplished anything like "decisive" results. For one thing, it had not been strictly cumulative. But if the same amount of destruction—or even half the amount—had been telescoped into, say, one week, it is hard to imagine how that nation could have been anything other than completely prostrate.[59]

Heavy attacks of this kind, all of which seemed to exclude warning the enemy population beforehand,[60] would plausibly undermine the authority of the enemy control group. The same objective might alternatively be promoted by bombing that stimulated enemy evacuations of cities, separating the population from a regime intent upon discrediting an atomic attacker and also interested—as was the Nazi regime—in keeping war industries in or close to cities manned by a labor force. Large-scale evacuations—obtainable, as the Hiroshima attack showed, by atomic strikes against cities[61]—might also be obtained by nuclear demonstrations and warnings of future attacks. In the latter case, focused upon by RAND Corporation social scientists, warnings might actually substitute for more comprehensive attacks. Once atomic bombs were used, Paul Kecskemeti concluded, "the outcome of the [atomic] demonstration will prescribe the future course of events. The people themselves will base their action on actual evidence rather than mere fears and predispositions, and such behavior will be far less modifiable by official manipulation than behavior in the absence of tangible experience."[62]

As we will see, Brodie came to acknowledge that personal involvement in bombing attacks included forced evacuation and that promoting such evacuation formed part of the terror effects of nuclear bombing.[63] However, evidently because he probably was not aware of emergency war plan targets prior to his work for General Vandenberg in 1950 and 1951 or sensitive until that time to the horrendous costs in lives and property produced by plans of that kind, Brodie appears at first to have given greater emphasis to allowing explicitly for morale as a target, even in large-scale nuclear warfare, than to bombing restraint.

Focusing on Enemy Surrender

Those linking bombing scale and morale effects envisioned, in the extreme case of comprehensive attack against enemy cities, prompt enemy surrender. By 1949, however, even though advocating area bombing with atomic weapons, Brodie acknowledged that heavy bombing—however decisive—might not suffice to force enemy surrender. "We should never be justified," he wrote in that year, "in basing our overall strategy on the assumption that devastating [strategic attack plan] attacks would produce a morale collapse leading immediately to surrender, but neither should we be justified in neglecting to prepare for the quick exploitation of such collapse and of resulting surrender movements."[64]

Supporting the idea that the Soviet Union would not immediately collapse, Brodie hypothesized the resoluteness of the Soviet regime, like its Nazi predecessor, in the face of attack. In 1949 he associated last-ditch resistance with popular identification with the top leaders,[65] and in 1951 he labeled the Soviet government a "last ditch fight regime." "Hitler knew damn well," Brodie declared,

> that the skin of himself and his people were involved and yet he continued to exercise control over Germany . . . after the Russian armies were already in Berlin and were making the rest of the city a complete shambles. And where he was even dictating his own successor after he had determined upon suicide. Now that's the kind of last ditch fight regime which we really have to think about when we're talking about the Soviet Union.[66]

Air force general officers and target planners, by contrast, took the link between comprehensive attack and rapid Soviet surrender as virtually axiomatic. Referring in 1951 at RAND to "the 'paralyzing' or 'devastating' blow idea," Brodie wrote that it "implicitly places very heavy reliance on psychological effects, but assumes — wrongly, in our opinion — that these effects are maximized by concentrating on one big crack of doom. There is little doubt that the more ardent supporters of this idea really expect the enemy to fold up immediately upon receiving this 'Sunday Punch' of A-bombs, though they will not readily own to such expectations."[67] Expectation of rapid Soviet surrender was not matched by systematic targeting of Soviet morale. For example, Brodie discovered during his work for General Vandenberg that the target objectives in the emergency war plan of 1951 included disrupting vital elements of the Soviet war-making capacity; retarding Soviet advances into Western Europe; and blunting Soviet capabilities to deliver an atomic attack against the United States and its allies. All three, it seemed to him, "must be strictly economic."[68]

The willingness of air force officials and planners to consider only tangible bombing effects while presuming that heavy bombing would take the Soviet Union out of the war recalled the error made by RAF commanders in bombing operations against Germany. It suggested, moreover, that expectation of rapid Soviet surrender may have inhibited differentiating psychological effects from general target destruction and, if so, that it was necessary to relax anticipation of immediate Soviet surrender before Soviet morale could be explicitly considered as an atomic bombing target. By contrast, once delayed surrender was allowed for, target selection became more complex, for then even the most favorable assumptions about *decisive* results — such as Brodie's view that war would be decisive in a matter of days[69] — would require distinguishing the psychological and economic consequences of bombing *at the outset* and outlining the opportunity costs of bombing primarily for psychological effect.

There was a tension, however, between Brodie's interest in explicitly considering morale in targeting decisions on one hand and his applying of nuclear weapons to the Second World War on the other. The former concern, for example, was supported by his 1951 criticism, written after his service for Vandenberg, that "almost all references to psychological results of a bombing campaign reflect the quite unexamined assumption that such results are increased only through killing more people."[70] It also suggested to Brodie that there could be inconsistencies in the psychological and economic results of bombing insofar as "the results we achieve on the political front may be the opposite to those we desire and may tend to offset to some extent the favorable economic results."[71] According to this perspective, striking at psychological and economic targets "are after all only means to an end, that end being the early and favorable conclusion of the war, and on a basis that will make the peace at least livable."[72]

On the other hand, comparing nuclear weapons potential with the experience of the Second World War flattered those weapons by dwelling upon the economic and psychological results of nuclear attacks as though they were fully consistent and therefore additive. To some extent, as Brodie noted, their effects *were* consistent. "*It cannot be too much stressed*," he wrote in 1951, "*that there is no essential conflict between economic objectives and psychological ones.* Bombs must in any case destroy structures, and whether the structures chosen reflect primarily a PW [psychological warfare] objective or an economic one is a matter of degree rather than kind."[73]

For this reason, Brodie observed, "choice of targets may be much less important than methods of attack."[74] Yet much of his writing defended area attack with atomic weapons by dwelling on simultaneously producing multiple bombing effects, better designed to gain decisive results than to force the enemy out of the war. If the objective was decisive bombing results, or if decisive results were equated with enemy surrender, the magnitude of the atomic potential directed against enemy cities might render comparative analysis of target systems unnecessary.

For these reasons, Brodie could establish the case for explicit concern about morale effects only by relaxing his interest in efficient nuclear target destruction — that is, in the destructive potential of nuclear weapons against a combination of targets. Efficient target destruction would surely be decisive against an enemy that lacked means of retaliation, such as the Soviet Union. But comparative analysis of bombing targets, including trade-offs in economic and psychological objectives, became important only as the focus of analysis shifted away from *decisive* attack and toward the requirements of producing enemy *surrender*. Giving explicit consideration to enemy morale as a bombing target was strongly justified, paradoxically, by scaling down expectations about nuclear bombing effects — such as those Brodie and many air force planners initially held — against *any* kind of targets.

The Value of the Threat of More Attacks to Come

Challenging those who failed to consider explicitly morale objectives in nuclear war, Brodie also questioned those who associated the largest psychological effects with the heaviest bombing attacks. "We appear," he wrote in 1949,

> to be giving an unduly low estimate of the pure shock and confusion effects of devastating attacks highly concentrated in time, but it is by no means clear that the kind of morale consequences I have been discussing could best be produced by a one-blow war. The expectation of worse to come seems to be an essential ingredient of critical morale disturbances leading to surrender situations.[75]

Specifically, Brodie suggested in 1949 that it might "be desirable to destroy the top ten enemy cities within a short space of time without necessarily concluding that it would be desirable to take also the next thirty within the same or a similar time."[76] And in 1951, when he proposed confidentially to the air force chief of staff "the elimination of say the 75 most important industrial complexes" in the Soviet Union upon the outbreak of a Soviet-American war,[77] Brodie would again have withheld perhaps three-quarters of the existing atomic bomb stockpile, which totaled about three hundred, from first phase attacks.[78]

At his most optimistic about using atomic attacks to force the enemy out of the war, Brodie stressed the killing effect of those attacks. By contrast, his most elaborate advocacy of the threat of more attacks to come — particularly beginning in 1951 — not surprisingly stressed the reactions of the *survivors* of nuclear attacks. He concluded in this latter connection, for example, that although the added destruction meted out in a comprehensive bombing campaign would considerably worsen the survivors' lives, it might not decisively impair the authority of the enemy control group; that is, it would leave the enemy political system largely intact. "The kind of mass attack envisioned for the opening period of the [nuclear] war," he wrote in 1951,

> will leave an urban population completely unnerved, distraught, and for the most part benumbed. It will be preoccupied with personal loss and with bare problems of existence. If comparable World War II experience is any guide, such a population is politically apathetic. Any attack of the intensity and duration now envisioned would undoubtedly be a terrible period for the Russian people. But we have no valid grounds for supposing that the governmental structure, with all its coercive apparatus, will be critically impaired.[79]

At the same time, evidently on the basis of this logic, Brodie no longer justified urban bombing by its effect in undermining the enemy control group. "Indiscriminate bombing of populations," he argued in 1951, would "very likely have a disproportionate affect [sic] upon the ruled as against the rulers."[80]

Contending that massive atomic attack might not, after all, critically impair the Soviet political system, Brodie may have been sensitive to Germany's experience under air bombardment during the Second World War. For example, H. Phillips Davison of the RAND social science staff wrote in August 1949 that "bombing was a terrible experience for the average German. It is fairly well established that after very heavy air attack he usually became apathetic, preoccupied almost exclusively with physical survival. Until that point was reached, however, bombing caused violent emotions — anger, hate, fear, indignation."[81] From his study of wartime Nazi security police and security services internal documents, Davison — of whose writing on this subject Brodie was aware — also cautioned that

> the power which engages in large-scale bombing of civilian populations *cannot* reasonably expect that the resentment aroused by this bombing will be directed against the home government. This may be the case only if the home government is weak or shows little aptitude for manipulating the affects of the bombed population. The Nazi government

was in a relatively unfavorable propaganda position when its cities were attacked by Allied bombers: It had claimed that no enemy bombers could reach its cities; it had been the first to engage in large-scale bombing of civilian populations; . . . . Nevertheless, the German control system was sufficient to direct the bulk of resentment, caused by bombing against the enemy, until a point when the shooting war had in any event been lost.[82]

The value of the threat of more attacks to come was sharply underscored by Davison's analysis of German reactions to Allied bombing. "Any large increase in the weight or extent of bombing," Davison noted, "caused increases in apprehension . . . , even though it may previously have seemed that the outer limit of anxiety had been reached."[83] By contrast, he suggested, "continuous use of a single pattern of bombing, whether heavy or light, day or night, will result in adaptation on the part of the population." He concluded that, "above all, adaptation to air attack is hindered by the belief that the worst is yet to come. As long as people suspect that they have not yet felt the full weight of the enemy's bombing potential they will continue to be apprehensive. . . . Conversely, those people who believed that they had already experienced the worst were reported as having shown little apprehension."[84]

Brodie appears to have wholeheartedly accepted this argument, which fit Speer's reactions to the bombing of Hamburg and Dresden, mentioned earlier. "The German people," Brodie wrote in 1953,

> underwent serious bombing for a period of some two years, during which the reach and spread of the bombers and the weight of bombs dropped steadily increased. It is abundantly clear that the bomb explosion causes fear and strain chiefly as a probable foretaste of what lies ahead. The one that has already burst is interpreted by all concerned as having done all the harm it can. It was a commonplace in Germany that people who had undergone the heaviest bombing often wrote their evacuated relatives to return home on the grounds that since there was nothing left to destroy the enemy would probably let them alone in the future. It is therefore conceivable that a massive atomic attack carried through over a relatively short period of time might have, despite the much greater damage and casualties inflicted, a less coercive effect than the *prolonged and mounting* agony which the Germans suffered in World War II. The fateful question is always: "What will tomorrow bring?"[85]

If Davison and Brodie were correct, the threat of more to come would have affected German morale without being consciously manipulated by the RAF; we have seen that target destruction rather than coercive warfare guided RAF bombing against Germany. But the presumed failure of area attacks against Germany raised questions about the importance of "the prolonged and mounting agony" brought about by bombing in that case. Brodie himself had earlier applied atomic bombs hypothetically to the RAF bombing of Germany because he was presumably dissatisfied with the "coercive effect" that "prolonged and mounting agony" had caused the Germans.

The American bombing of Japan did not, according to USSBS findings, contradict Davison's assessment about German adaptation to continuous bombing. "Urban people," the USSBS report on Japanese morale concluded, "who experienced more continuous bombing and therefore represent a better test on the question of adaptation, clearly indicate that they became better adapted as their bombing experience increased, while rural people, who had less direct and less frequent experience, became more afraid."[86] The bombing of Japan was more empirically suggestive, however, of the potential for manipulating the threat of more attacks to come than was the German case, for following the Potsdam Conference in July 1945 (and continuing to the end of the war some weeks later), specially worded warning leaflets were dropped over Japanese cities to be attacked, urging civilians to evacuate those areas ahead of time. The leaflets were subsequently characterized by the USSBS survey of Japanese morale as "one of the most spectacular efforts of the war" and were said to have "helped separate some citizens from their leaders, and generally capitalized effectively upon military and home front situations which were known to the people, and from which only a moral needed to be drawn."[87] In three operations between 27 July and 5 August 1945, thirty-one Japanese cities were warned of forthcoming attacks, of which fourteen were attacked by the end of the war.[88]

Large-scale Japanese evacuation of cities in advance of attack began to be significant in May 1945, before American policy had encouraged it, underscoring how major evacuations would have occurred in any event from what Brodie termed "the fury of our attack."[89] Without distinguishing between Japanese evacuations before and after initiation of the warning leaflets, Brodie regarded the leaflets as something of a model for a present-day air campaign to undermine enemy morale. "There is a more tangible objective to pursue in the attack on population than merely 'low morale,'" Brodie wrote in 1953,

> and one which is more profitable to the attacker as well as more humane than the production of corpses — the compulsion of huge evacuations. Some eight and one-half million Japanese left their homes during the American air campaign to become refugees in other towns or in the surrounding countryside. The magnitude of this figure must be considered not in proportion to the whole population but rather in relation to the populations of the larger industrial cities which fed the exodus. Although comparable evacuations took place in Germany, the flight of urban dwellers from Japanese cities was more concentrated in time and hence more disorganized and included very much larger proportions of workers previously engaged in war industries. This tide of panicked humanity not only spread throughout Japan the full account of the horrors occurring in the cities but also created for the government burdens with which it was conspicuously unable to cope.[90]

In short, when Brodie conceptualized morale depression by 1953 as varying "directly with [the] degree of personal involvement, such as the death or severe injury of someone near and dear or the destruction of all one's worldly goods or forced evacuation,"[91] he probably had the Japanese bombing experience particularly in mind. But the bombing of Japan represented even more systematic target destruction than the bombing of Germany. Gen. Curtis LeMay, then commander of the Twenty-First Bomber Command, which implemented the area attacks against the Japanese, set

out to systematically assault all Japanese cities, large and small; LeMay, in fact, originated the warning leaflets, evidently to protect his bombing campaign (which began
in March 1945) from American political opposition.[92] In contrast to Davison's conclusions about the German bombing, results of the Japanese campaign showed that
even regular and systematic bombing could be manipulated with threats of more
attacks to come.

Much of the American benefit from the warning leaflets in Japan came from
Japanese perceptions that the United States was using warnings to save lives — perceptions evidently stimulated by a portion of the American leaflets that sought humanitarian credit for the United States[93] — paradoxically, in a most intense bombing campaign not governed by humanitarian considerations. In the contemporary period,
nuclear bombing could easily be more intensive than warranted by humanitarian objectives, but even if it were not, major attacks would likely be necessary to gain
the evacuations from which political credit would be derived. "Dispersal is primarily
a function of the scale and intensity of bombing," wrote Victor Hunt, of the RAND
social science staff, following analysis of the Japanese case.

> Many other factors such as the government's approval of or opposition to evacuation,
> the state of morale, and the availability of transportation and a place to go, will also
> affect a target population's willingness to evacuate. But widespread and intensive bomb-
> ing with extensive physical damage and a high casualty rate is the essential element in
> bringing about dispersal.[94]

The Japanese Case: Bombing Effectiveness

Brodie found the American air offensive against Japan to be more productive than
the RAF area bombing of Germany. It was, in his words,

> remarkably different from that against Germany in character as well as result. It was
> much more concentrated in time, and had the benefit of the more advanced technology
> then available. Japan was more urbanized than Germany, its cities were more vulnerable
> to fire, and its active defenses at the time of the campaign were of a low order of effec-
> tiveness, being almost confined to antiaircraft guns. Thus, more was accomplished with
> fewer bombs.[95]

The effectiveness of the bombing, which began in November 1944 but became
highly effective only when implemented at night beginning in March 1945, Brodie
attributed not only to American operational capabilities but also to Japan's position
in the war. "In Japan, unlike Germany," he wrote in *Strategy in the Missile Age*,

> the urban-area bombing seems to have contributed more to achieving the desired results
> than did the precision bombing of specific industries. This was due not alone to the
> fact that there was less opportunity for recuperation among Japanese cities than there
> had been in Germany, but more importantly to the fact that in Japan economic objectives
> counted for less than psychological ones. . . . Japan had already lost the battle of produc-

tion . . . [and] was already defeated. It was necessary only to make her government develop a clear consensus on that fact, and then openly concede it.[96]

The atomic attacks against Japan—designed by American officials, according to Herbert Feis, "to make a profound psychological impression on as many of the Japanese as possible"[97]—Brodie also understood as having been psychologically effective. "Insofar as the explosions at Hiroshima and Nagasaki hastened the end of World War II," he wrote in 1951, "as they undoubtedly did by some unknown margin, it was not the two expended but the threat of more to come which tipped the balance. The damage done by those two explosions was, in terms of remaining overall enemy capabilities, literally nothing; the demonstration value was everything."[98]

American bombing of Japanese cities was dramatically enhanced by LeMay's decision, described as "one of the classic air decisions of the war," to lower the bombing altitude from about twenty-five thousand feet to about seven thousand feet.[99] As the result of this decision, according to a USSBS report,

> bomb loads more than doubled; using radar bombing methods, the weather ceased to be a serious factor; the number of aircraft dropping on the primary target soared from 58 to 92 percent; enemy fighter opposition was negligible; decreased bombing altitude meant less operating strain which added up to more sorties per aircraft; crew morale rose with each attack; . . . . Of equal importance, Japan's urban industrial concentrations had been proved highly vulnerable to destruction by incendiary attack.[100]

Because of the great incendiary effects against Japanese urban areas from low-level night bombing—referred to by LeMay as the "castastrophe bonus" from urban-area bombing[101]—aircraft factories and other economic targets were generally neutralized even if not directly hit. For example, LeMay subsequently recalled that in the devastating firebombing of Tokyo on the evening of 9 March 1945, an aircraft plant that had been targeted was destroyed by fire in the surrounding area even though the bombers had missed the plant itself.[102]

LeMay's success also illustrated the limitation of efficient target destruction as strategy. First, unlike Germany, Japan was unable to convey war production to Pacific island battlefields because it was effectively blockaded by the American navy; as Theodore Ropp pointed out, Japan was actually defeated twice—once by bombing and once by blockade.[103] Second, the threat of more attacks to come against Japan, supported to a considerable extent by the devastating air campaign implemented by LeMay, paradoxically may also have been undermined by the virtual exhaustion of area targets in that same campaign. The bombing of nearly all Japanese cities, large and small, by the end of the war reflected the sacrifice of coercive use of force to actual target destruction in that campaign.

Brodie, we have seen, criticized the heavy area bombing against Germany because it seemed to interfere with threatening more attacks to come, but he failed so far as is known to criticize the American bombing of Japan on this ground. This was perhaps because he relied strongly upon the Japanese case to dramatize the potential of threatening more attacks to come. Yet the heavy bombing accompanying the threat of more attacks to come against Japan came about from interest in targeting efficiency rather than in coercive strategy: The early American tactic of high-altitude day bombing against the two Japanese target systems LeMay had been ordered to destroy—namely, aircraft factories and urban-industrial concentrations—had not yielded satisfactory results. Although the combination of heavy bombing and the threat of more attacks to come was fortuitous in the Japanese case, it was also necessarily delicate, for even spectacular results from the threat of future attacks, such as those achieved against Japan, could be negated over the long run by progressive and efficient target destruction.[104]

Because of its destructive potential, nuclear weaponry was much more suited to the catastrophe bonus objective than older high-explosive and incendiary bombs, and it followed that efficient target destruction in atomic bombing could conflict much more with threatening more attacks to come than did the Japanese bombing. What the catastrophe bonus meant was spelled out by Dan B. Dyer, a staff member of the Air Targets Division at air force headquarters. "Today," noted Dyer in 1951,

> with your present atomic weapons the [S]trategic [A]ir [C]ommand can operate only against areas, areas which contain various types and various combinations of industry, capital equipment, government control, housing and population. The atomic attacks of SAC's war plan, however, are not area attacks with the connotation which is usually associated with the type of bombardment laid on by the RAF during all except the latter part of World War II. The SAC attacks when they come will be precision attacks with an area weapon.[105]

For example, the Soviet control structure was a target system to whose destruction SAC officials gave high priority; the importance of that target was used to justify targeting the center of Soviet cities, which would also destroy population, housing, and industrial complexes.[106]

Brodie categorically opposed maximizing the catastrophe bonus in nuclear attacks. "We have no justification," he wrote in 1951, "for regarding whatever large scale slaughter results from our bombing as a 'bonus'. It may be a negative bonus, harmful to our strategic and political goals. If we do not know that it is a bad thing to kill Russians indiscriminately, that is not the same as saying that we know it to be a good thing."[107] In place of the bonus concept, he would have modified attack points so that material destruction, not casualties, was magnified. "If we find ourselves," he wrote in 1951,

> obliged for a variety of reasons to bomb targets situated within cities—as seems almost inevitable—it may becomes [*sic*] a matter of great urgency so to space our attacks and to attend them with such warning that the Russian population will not inexorably conclude that we are solely bent upon their destruction, denying them all opportunity of reprieve or escape. Also, it might be a very important factor in helping us to decide such problems as whether the centers of cities or industrial concentrations within cities should be the RGZs [required ground zeroes] selected.[108]

Brodie's critique of the catastrophe bonus was undoubtedly a more specific assertion of his general view that strategy rather than tactics ought properly to guide a strategic bombing campaign. "The operational factor," he wrote in 1951,

> is after all not the only one that matters. It gives us the limits of the possible. Within those limits, the operational factor becomes one input among several—a vitally important one to be sure, but nevertheless subject to other considerations. If we have to pay a somewhat higher price for one kind of campaign rather than another, we should not only seek to determine the price disparity between the two but we should also leave the planner free to gauge the payoff in each case against the cost. The ultimate payoff is the only thing that counts, the forces involved being a means to that end (and an expendable one at that).[109]

In practice, however, his view that industrial concentrations rather than the center of cities ought to be attacked was not easily distinguished from SAC's own concept of precision bombing with an area weapon; it was much more at odds with the RAF bombing campaign against Germany, which, without aiming at specific precision targets, attacked the center of German cities to maximize casualties.

Although pursuit of precision attacks was the major targeting difference between the area bombing of Japan, which Brodie commended, and the area bombing of Germany, which he rejected, Brodie himself seemed to question the significance of precision attacks in the Japanese case. "What was wanted," he wrote in reference to the bombing of Japan, "was not a discriminating pruning out of this or that kind of military production, but simply the maximum of direct military pressure upon the population and the government."[110] Moreover, in spite of LeMay's low-altitude bombing innovation, which undoubtedly added to the accuracy of attacks against large targets such as industrial complexes, the decision to bomb at night signified, as did the earlier RAF bombing of Germany, a decision to attack indiscriminately.[111] Atomic bombing would be even more conducive to indiscriminate warfare.

Those charged with carrying out postwar strategic bombing against the Soviet Union (such as LeMay, who became SAC commander in 1948) believed that weaknesses in American bombing capabilities would narrow American targeting choices in such a campaign, much as they had against Japan. LeMay's choice of area bombing tactics against Japan had been as much dictated by operational difficulties as Harris's against Germany. "Basically," wrote Maj. Gen. Haywood S. Hansell, Jr., of the American bombing of Japan,

> there is every reason to believe that General LeMay would have welcomed an effective tactic to destroy selected targets rather than urban areas. But his equipment was limited and his crews were untrained in this technique. He concluded that [his available] radar bombing equipment was inadequate for precision bombing. This was almost certainly true in the absence of good quality radar maps and selected offset aiming points that would provide good radar returns. He chose to adopt and adapt the RAF night bombing technique which, late in the European war, had produced surprisingly accurate bombing results.[112]

Having aimed successfully at the catastrophe bonus against Japan because of insufficient bombing accuracy, LeMay subsequently wished to capitalize upon it in nuclear bombing operations against the Soviet Union. Citing the persisting inaccuracy of bombing attacks in the contemporary period against poorly documented and/or small targets as his reason for doing so,[113] LeMay evidently discounted the improved RAF and American bombing accuracy attained late in the Second World War as well as improvements in accuracy to be expected in the contemporary period.

For his part, Brodie accepted the efficient use of atomic bombs, as demonstrated by his preference for targets inside cities, but his position was supported by the logic of strategic objectives rather than by the need to maximize a given weight of destructive potential. The latter he assumed would have to be satisfied in any event, as when he expressed the view that to obtain a more prolonged nuclear bombing offensive, "we have to prove first of all to ourselves and to others that such spacing of attacks as will result from deliberate prolonging of the campaign need not unduly hazard or excessively reduce our overall delivery capabilities."[114] Those most interested in bombing efficiency would surely find significant Brodie's point that "it would probably require far fewer bombs per thousand head to create fugitives than to create an equal number of corpses."[115]

Whether advocates of applying the catastrophe bonus in comprehensive attack could ever regard a more prolonged nuclear bombing campaign playing up the threat of more attacks to come as acceptably efficient might be doubted. For example, prolonging bombing attacks also created the likelihood—mentioned by Brodie—that bomber commanders would lose more of their attack force to enemy defenses alerted by advance warning of bombings. Brodie noted in 1951 that "the most successful penetration is presumably the first one; subsequent attacks become increasingly costly and thus less effective."[116] For this reason also, threatening future attacks might need to be reevaluated if Soviet surrender were not forthcoming by a given time. On the other hand, persuasive reasons could be adduced for defining overall delivery requirements over a longer period and not just over the short term, particularly if rapid dissipation of American atomic capabilities brought what Brodie termed "the worst possibility"—namely, "that of the Soviet Union having the last bomb."[117]

The Japanese Case: The Will to Resist

For Brodie, the relative effectiveness of the American bombing of Japan depended to a significant degree on preventing the diehard resistance exhibited in Nazi Germany from taking place in Japan. This objective was fulfilled, he noted, when the Japanese emperor intervened in the last days of the war to "crystaliz[e] an effective (and, incidentally, legal) opposition against the war party."[118] Brodie strongly implied that devastating and virtually exhaustive area bombing had been necessary to force the Japanese monarch to take action. The Japanese people's veneration of their emperor permitted not only his intervention into military affairs but also, presumably, Japan's surrender to the United States on the condition that the emperor be retained.

Brodie's argument that the bombing was effective rested, therefore, on the very tardy negotiation that took place between the major antagonists in the Pacific war. By contrast, during much of the U.S. bombing of Japan, American officials appear to have misjudged Japanese determination to resist. Specifically, according to Paul Kecskemeti, the U.S. government

> acted as if the problem were that of defeating Japan, when in fact the problem was to avoid an unnecessary last battle *after* Japan was defeated. The same misconception prevented the United States from assessing the real significance of Japanese last-ditch resistance. Since the American leaders could not keep the concepts of "defeat" and "surrender" apart, they saw in Japanese resistance at Iwo and Okinawa proof that the Japanese did not recognize that they were defeated and needed convincing.[119]

The American demand, until the very last days of the war, for the unconditional surrender of Japan was partly linked to the presumption that Japanese leaders were not prepared to acknowledge defeat; those implementing the bombing of Japan argued that relaxing this demand while major land combat was under way might be interpreted by the Japanese as weakness.[120] However, this demand, also directed at Germany, may have postponed Japanese capitulation because of the Japanese government's desire to retain the emperor in the postwar period. In short, the Japanese case suggests that as officials sought to maximize the morale effects of bombing, they risked being too insensitive to the attitudes of the enemy control group.

The persistent Allied demand in the Second World War for unconditional surrender of the Axis powers helps to elucidate Hans Speier's observation that "the offensive against the morale of the enemy was waged primarily by bombs, both in Germany and Japan,"[121] for in that war, the demand for unconditional surrender supported virtually unlimited bombing. Brodie, particularly when advocating the strategy of threatening future attacks, by contrast strongly wished to couple contemporary bombing with psychological warfare. "One would think," he wrote in 1951,

> that the aim of producing important psychological and political results would demand above all the capacity to continue exerting pressure in some way comparable to that exploited in an initial blow. . . .
> Under present conceptions, it is not too much to say that we shoot our bolt and then wait for something to happen, being then quite unable to affect what will happen. We permit ourselves little or no opportunity for coordinating bombing attacks with political warfare. We permit ourselves no means of tying our attacks, especially on cities, to specific war acts of the Russian government and armed forces in a manner calculated to impress the Russians, first, that the sole responsibility lies with their government and, secondly, *that they have an alternative to being destroyed.*[122]

Dismissing the importance of negotiations to end the war with Japan, Brodie seems to have ruled out any accommodation with the Soviet leadership. "In a full-scale war with the Soviet Union," Brodie observed in 1951, "it would be almost axiomatic that there could be no surrender by the enemy, or readiness to negotiate on our terms, without a revolution in his government—that is, without collapse in the control of the present regime such as would permit some other group to take over."[123] He asserted that the chances of Soviet accommodation were reduced by the absence of organized dissent inside the Soviet Communist party, much as in the Nazi regime. The latter had

> succeeded in eradicating or incarcerating any organized political opposition, so that no means existed for giving direction to and translating into action the feelings of disaffection which undoubtedly developed. There could be no *peace party* in Germany (outside the Army, where the dissident group was liquidated after the abortive putsch of July 1944) because there could be no *party* outside the control of the Nazi leadership. This absence of an organized opposition, which is even more conspicuous in the case of the Soviet Union than it was in Nazi Germany, is perhaps the most important single feature of totalitarian countries which must give pause to those who would count heavily on defeating them by psychological means.[124]

However, if American officials dismissed from the outset any possible accommodation with the Soviet regime and substituted the demand for unconditional surrender, they might become too insensitive to Soviet leadership attitudes, as their predecessors had been earlier with the Japanese. For example, Nathan Leites, in research commissioned by the RAND Corporation, had concluded by 1950 that Soviet leaders would compromise on matters of less than fundamental importance and indeed sought considerable tactical flexibility in negotiating with the West.[125] The potential afforded to the West by such a tendency might well be forfeited if Western leaders demanded that the Soviets surrender unconditionally and if, as seemed likely, Soviet leaders refused.

The demand for unconditional surrender might also inhibit psychological warfare aimed at the Soviet population, much as it had interfered with Allied psychological warfare in Germany earlier. "To subvert the Germans by strategic sykewar," Daniel Lerner wrote,

> the Allies would have had to offer them alternatives more attractive than the hope of winning the war. A policy based mainly on persuasion, rather than coercion, would have had to offer more than a "better 'ole." It would have had to include offers of a "better life" for Germans than the prospects offered by a German victory. Such offers would have been incompatible with the policy of Unconditional Surrender.[126]

Inasmuch as Brodie does not seem to have doubted that the one-sided balance of nuclear force in this early period would lead to inevitable Soviet defeat in a war with the United States, his failure to move beyond the imposition of defeat to increase the incentives for the Soviet Union to surrender is difficult to understand.[127] Had a Soviet-American war broken out early in the contemporary period, a quick end to hostilities would have depended partly on the ability of the American and Soviet governments to sharply distinguish military defeat from political surrender.

The radically different origin of the Communist regime in the Soviet Union from the Nazi government in Germany enhanced the chances that Soviet leaders would understand the difference between defeat and surrender. Hitler flourished because of the widespread German grievance about being unjustly denied the opportunity to gain military victory in the First World War, whereas the Soviet Communists were not initially committed to wartime heroics.[128]

Strategic Bombing and Psychological Warfare

Emphasizing the difficulties of using strategic bombing to force the Soviet regime to surrender, Brodie accepted, as we have seen, the similarities between the present-day Soviet regime and the totalitarian government of Nazi Germany: They both sought to eliminate internal dissent toward their policies and they both displayed the potential for last-ditch military resistance. Conversely, Brodie diverged from the German model when conceptualizing that bombing could assist in undermining an enemy regime, permitting, for example, "civil disturbances generated by personal anxiety to develop into mass assaults or pressures upon the regime."[129] Popular governments such as Hitler's would presumably not be vulnerable to such a strategy because, as Brodie put it in 1949,

> in a tightly controlled totalitarian system, the control group may be able to suppress overt manifestations until its own morale—and thus initiative—is corroded, from which time total collapse may proceed very swiftly. In the Germany of World War II, this process was greatly retarded by the extraordinary degree of personal identification of the control group with the Fuehrer.[130]

Brodie sharply distinguished the Soviet system from the Nazi regime in this respect. "Several very close observers of the Soviet scene (George Kennan, for example)," he wrote in 1949, "are convinced that there is far less identification of the Soviet populace with the control group and its ideology than was true in Germany. Whether this be true or not would appear to be a very important field of investigation for the planners of [the strategic attack plan] as well as [psychological warfare]."[131]

By 1951 Brodie had considerably strengthened his view on this matter, declaring that "all the evidence we do have from subrosa sources, from published materials, from memoirs, etc., indicate overwhelmingly that . . . the Russian people by and large do not love the regimist [sic] government."[132] Terming as "conceivably . . . our greatest single asset" in a Soviet-American war "the distaste of the Russian people for the regime which covers them,"[133] he suggested that coercive use of nuclear force would compel the Soviet Union to surrender whatever the attitude of its leaders. "We should remember," he wrote in September 1951,

> that the spectacle which Germany provided in World War II of fighting to the very end of her capacity is the rare exception in modern times—an exception for which we have no reason to be proud. The surrender of Italy and Japan in the same war, and of

Germany and especially of Russia in the previous war, show that the will to resist may collapse long before the physical capacity to do so—provided that that will is properly conditioned by the conqueror and that the seeds of disaffection already exist in the target population. The Soviet Union looks like a perfect setup for the attack which exploits psychological weapons, and the atomic bomb looks like the perfect weapon for psychological exploitation. Why not bring these two things together?[134]

Specifically, Brodie suggested that a bombing campaign begin with nuclear strikes against small cities, saving lives in comparison with the more destructive options, yet also attacking where least expected and maintaining the threat to attack large cities in which dissidents would be presumed to be more active.

Whether *comprehensive* bombing could capitalize upon an enemy regime's unpopularity might indeed be doubted, particularly if bombing magnified casualties. Kennan may have had such a campaign in mind when he wrote in 1960 that

> outright war is itself too unambivalent, too undiscriminating a device to be an appropriate means for effecting a mere change of regime in another country. You cannot logically inflict on another people the horrors of nuclear destruction in the name of what you believe to be its salvation, and expect it to share your enthusiasm for the exercise. Even if you were sure that the overwhelming majority of another people wished in theory to be freed by external intervention from a given situation of political subservience (and in the case of Russia I am not at all satisfied that this would be the case today), it would still be senseless to attempt to free it from the limited internal embarrassment of an unpopular regime (which still permits it, after all, the privilege of life in the physical sense) by subjecting it to the far more fearful destruction and hardships of modern war.[135]

Even if not designed to magnify casualties, comprehensive attack might be incompatible with separating the enemy population from its rulers, a standard technique of psychological warfare.[136] For example, Brodie, who in 1951 knew that the emergency war plan target list no longer emphasized the catastrophe bonus but instead so-called vertical targeting of specific Soviet economic installations, reported to General Vandenberg that "our strategic bombing plan is in violent conflict with the sense of Secretary Acheson's warm approval of the McMahon [Congressional Concurrent] Resolution expressing friendship for the Russian people and with the whole tenor of our Voice of America Program."[137]

Others argued to the contrary that psychological warfare could be important even if nuclear bombing aimed for the catastrophe bonus. The Harmon Committee, which evaluated just that type of bombing program, concluded that it would create "a psychological crisis . . . within the U.S.S.R. which could be turned to advantage by the Allies through early and effective exploitation by armed forces and psychological warfare. Failing prompt and effective exploitation, the opportunity would be lost and subsequent Soviet psychological reactions would adversely affect the accomplishment of Allied objectives."[138]

This conclusion appears to have depended heavily on the views of Charles Thayer, then director of the Voice of America. Thayer argued that the payoff in morale effects of atomic attacks required prior psychological preparation, and he advocated psychological warfare at the outset of war to urge evacuation of cities and then the destruction of Soviet cities "at once and completely in order to get the maximum effect." Evidently abandoning the threat of more attacks to come, he envisioned, according to a summary of the Harmon Committee's deliberations, that

> there would be two phases of PW [psychological warfare]. We should start in now by telling them of the dangerous effects of the Atom bomb. This could be done by a series of radio broadcasts on atomic energy. In the second phase, the radio would be very effective for the first 72 hours after the declaration of war and before the first attack, as well as leaflets, telling the people to get out of the cities because we are coming to bomb them. Not more than one week should elapse between the last phase of PW and the first actual attack.[139]

The issue here was whether psychological warfare was to limit political damage from a bombing program decided upon other grounds, as in the war against Germany and Japan earlier and as LeMay now urged for war against the Soviet Union, or whether it should instead govern the scale and pace of bombing attacks, as Brodie urged in the event of Soviet-American hostilities. During the Second World War, the RAF area bombing of German cities may have caused difficulties for Allied propaganda against Germany; according to one contemporary account, the Allies "have not been able to make up their minds whether the destruction of Germany as a military power or simply the liberation of Germany from the Nazi yoke is their real aim."[140] Comprehensive bombing against Soviet cities would raise the same difficulty for psychological warfare efforts. As in the bombings of Germany and Japan, the bombing of Soviet cities required that propaganda acknowledge the distinctive qualities of the Soviet people working against their government under horrific conditions in spite of bombing that ignored those qualities.

But a coercive bombing campaign needed to tread delicately between projecting strength and restraint. Paul Kecskemeti concluded from his study of German evacuations in the Second World War that

> the population's will to continue the war depends on its perception of both the enemy's strength and the destructiveness of his attitude. The power conducting an air offensive is clearly interested both in appearing overwhelmingly strong and in not being intent on destroying the target country and its population. There is, however, a certain inconsistency between these two objectives.[141]

Projecting overwhelming strength on one hand was presumably enhanced by attacks engendering fear and doubts about the attacker's restraint; projecting restraint on the other hand could interfere with the threat value of prior attacks. For Brodie, who proposed heavy attacks in the initial phase of the campaign, the projection of strength would come first and the projection of restraint would depend on a significant pause in bombing. Others, such as Herbert Goldhamer, thought it desirable that "the threat should increase over time in certainty and temporal proximity"[142]— in which case bombing restraint would be projected first, with the attacker's strength becoming apparent to the enemy population only gradually.

The smoothing by psychological warfare of tensions between projecting major military strength and demonstrating restraint could be undone by more traditional characteristics of an air campaign, especially if the campaign were prolonged. "I am struck," Thomas C. Schelling wrote in 1962,

> with how customary it is to propose that advance warning be given to cities that are to be destroyed, so that the people can evacuate. That is going to extremes. It involves not only pursuing a strategy of limited nuclear destruction, but doing so consciously, avowedly, publicly, dramatically, with announcements, with an almost incredible deliberateness, patience, and self-confidence, and on a time schedule that is not only nerve-wracking in suspense but imprudent in its relinquishment of initiative. It seems to reflect a peculiar American penchant for warning rather than doing, for postponing decision, for anesthetizing the victim before striking the blow, for risking wealth rather than people, and for doing grand things that do not hurt rather than small things that do. It seems to me much more likely that any realization of such a strategy would be less clearly differentiated, more in the guise of "military tactics," more impetuous, more mixed and confused in its purposes and effects.[143]

Other problems, some discussed in connection with the RAF bombing, pertained to the association of bombing attacks with the progress of Soviet political dissidence. If attacks were first aimed at small Soviet cities, dissidents remaining in the large cities would have to anticipate nuclear attacks and those who departed in fear of attacks against those cities would be neutralized as a political force.

Finally, during the Stalinist period, the success of any terror bombing was conditioned upon overcoming the counterterror of the Soviet regime. George Kennan noted in this connection that the estrangement of a totalitarian regime from its population could not be regarded as complete. "The very experience of holding and exercising supreme power in a country," Kennan wrote in 1960,

> saddles any ruler, whatever his original ideological motives, with most of the traditional concerns of government in that country. . . . However despotic he may be, and however far his original ideas may have departed from the interests of the people over whom he rules, his position of power gives him, as Gibbon once pointed out, a certain identity of interest with those who are ruled.[144]

The resiliency of a terrorist regime was best shown, perhaps, by the depth of popular resistance to the Nazi invasion of the Soviet Union in the Second World War. To be sure, German propaganda in that case had poorly capitalized upon Soviet political weaknesses, but Soviet police tactics appear to have been very effective in enforcing resistance to the Nazi invasion.[145] More generally, the Soviet police state, in its more and less overt manifestations, seems to have produced a legacy impressed strongly enough into the popular Soviet psychology to make the effort to replace one terror by another highly difficult.[146]

Conclusions

Fully aware of the capability of strategic bombing to undermine morale in the Second World War and frequently referring to it in his writings, Brodie was nevertheless not interested primarily in historical evaluation.[147] Rather, he used history to support his independent analyses of present-day strategic problems. Antecedents that legitimated his contemporary positions he incorporated into his analyses of Soviet-American war. For example, Brodie used the warnings of American attacks delivered to the Japanese, the demonstrated ability of heavy attacks to cause large-scale evacuations, and the last-ditch resistance of totalitarian dictators such as Hitler to strengthen his case for restraint in the scale and pace of nuclear bombing attacks. And antecedents that did not seem to fit Brodie's contemporary preferences, such as the RAF area bombing of Germany, Brodie dealt with most notably by using the hypothetical past (for example, when he validated morale as a nuclear bombing target) or by underscoring how atomic warfare could fail (for example, in his assertion that a poorly directed A-bomb attack could actually be less effective than the RAF bombing).

In some ways, Brodie's use of history was faulty. For example, when he presumed that bombing should contribute to rapidly decisive results and also overcome a stubborn last-ditch control group such as the Nazis, he used history to flatter large destructive strategic bombing. Yet he neglected that the bombing directed against Japan, in which the bombers were able to attack with impunity and thereby cause enormous destruction, was made possible by army and navy successes that ensured the air bases for the logistical side of the assault.[148] Those same successes, it is now clear, would have brought defeat to Japan in the absence of the bombing. Moreover, if the bombing were not essential to ensuring decisive results, it also was probably not the major contributor to the Japanese surrender. The diplomacy salvaging a role for the Japanese emperor was by all indications more important.

To be sure, scenarios could be conceived in the present period in which nuclear-equipped air forces would rapidly decide the result of a Soviet-American war. I have noted Brodie's exclusive early postwar concern with such scenarios, abstracting from the other military arms and from American diplomacy in the same manner that he did in his treatment of strategic bombing in the Second World War. Yet as he broadened his analyses to distinguish between *decisive results* and *surrender* in a nuclear war, this abstraction, already subject to question, became still less defensible. For example, one of Brodie's strongest arguments for *coercive* warfare was that the consequences of the initial bombing would be uncertain. As he put it in 1951, "The possibility that the war may last five years instead of five weeks is one of the major weaknesses of the Sunday Punch idea."[149] But it was hard to believe that other military arms and diplomacy would not be given major roles as hostilities lengthened.

A full strategic analysis of the bombing of Japan needed to take into account its indispensable role in making possible the effective use of warning leaflets. Yet even here, difficulties not cited by Brodie interfered with drawing clear-cut lessons for a Soviet-American war. First, the demonstration of bombing impunity entailed using the catastrophe bonus targeting concept, which Brodie is known to have opposed for nuclear warfare; once nuclear weapons were employed, the enormous *additional* destruction of human life brought about through the catastrophe bonus was totally antithetical to the concept of saving lives by warning of future attacks. Second, the strategic value of the warning leaflets in the Japanese case was lessened by the comprehensive aspect of the Japanese bombing and (if Davison was correct) by the absence of large increases in the extent of the bombing.

And third, irrepressibly optimistic about mating nuclear weapons to psychological objectives, Brodie failed to take account in his analyses of cautions by the RAND staff about mass reactions to strategic bombing. For example, Kecskemeti concluded from his study of wartime Germany that

> the target population's will to continue the war would be weakened if an air offensive—supplemented by a suitable warning policy—established both the attacker's superior strength and his active concern for saving lives. However, the assumption does not seem to be warranted that this weakening of the will-to-war would go as far as to result in the overthrow of the war leadership and the assumption of control by a peace party ready to accept terms.[150]

As to why these errors occurred, the answer lies in Brodie's interest in exerting an immediate impact on policy debates and in his willingness to do what he believed needed to be done to gain it, particularly in rebutting the conventional wisdom. Indispensable for this purpose were references to history, because the current debate about options focused significantly on lessons deduced from history. Indispensable also were rapidly mobilized, persuasive arguments directed toward the novel aspects of the contemporary period, in which the choice of war plans carried larger stakes than ever—justifying for many the making of deductions about history in advance of adequate historical assessment. The full character of these stakes was impressed upon Brodie when he saw the emergency war plan hypotheses, which dictated, as he put it much later, that "all bombs in the stockpile . . . be expended as quickly as possible (on whatever deviation from the target list LeMay felt he could get away with)."[151]

The contrasting approach of detailed historical study not only would have been too insensitive to the unique aspects of Soviet-American relations; it also would have been too isolating for immediate participation in and too independent of the shifting contemporary policy debate. We have seen, regarding the latter point, how Brodie switched analytical emphases as the debate around him changed. Widening his contacts between 1949 and 1951 and moving away from an undifferentiated concern with decisive nuclear warfare to a preoccupation with coercive bombing to induce enemy surrender, Brodie adjusted his use of history accordingly.[152]

A loose, imaginative approach to history might suffice to gain consideration of a neglected bombing option. However, to *vindicate* that option against others, careful historical assessment needed to be applied to the operational and strategic concerns of earlier bombing experiences. We saw in the last chapter that Brodie was not interested in the detailed operational aspects of a nuclear bombing program. He continued to insist that desirable decisive outcomes would be produced by nuclear bombing despite the operational problems such bombing entailed, making it unnecessary to give the details. We also saw in the last chapter, however, that Brodie, in his choice of cities as nuclear targets, was very sensitive to the operational requirements of nuclear bombing, not only by flattering the destructive characteristics of the early postwar nuclear weapons but also by allowing heavy wastage in planes to suit strategic objectives.

Brodie's use of history was not inconsistent with these outlooks. It strengthened his ability to discuss cities as nuclear targets without having to determine the practical requirements or details of implementing a strategic bombing plan.[153] And it showed how his choice of cities as targets depended partly on the operational advantages of striking at large targets. In this last regard, he was ironically in the same position as Harris, whose earlier RAF bombing campaign against Germany Brodie had sharply criticized on strategic grounds. The difference between them was that Harris, who did not have a clear idea of what enemy morale signified, detailed his operational constraints, whereas Brodie, who understood much better than Harris the meaning of enemy morale, assumed that operational constraints were so secondary that a strategist need not spell them out.

4 · Using History: Economic Targets

Supplementing Brodie's work on morale as a bombing target in the late 1940s and early 1950s was his analysis of economic targets and objectives for nuclear weapons, which took up a major part of his time as special assistant to General Vandenberg. This analysis was preceded by an evaluation of Allied bombing strikes against Axis economic targets during the Second World War, work that came to the attention of Gen. Lauris Norstad, Vandenberg's deputy chief of staff, who then arranged for Brodie to meet with Vandenberg in August 1950.[1] Later that year, at Vandenberg's request, Brodie was asked to evaluate what was apparently the first study recommending to the JCS detailed nuclear bombing targets to accompany an emergency war plan.[2] The study, proposed for attachment to the emergency war plan for fiscal year 1951, was authored in 1950 by the Air Targets Division, a unit designated by the Joint Chiefs to make detailed recommendations about targets. The study and the plan it accompanied were the basis for Brodie's assertion that target objectives "must be strictly economic."[3]

Brodie considered his critique of this study to have been among his best work.[4] In it, as in his counterpart work on morale, Brodie sought to promote decisive use of atomic weapons in hypothetical war, to assist the immediate needs of the air force in this direction, and to meet the very large but fading opportunity provided by the American monopoly of nuclear weapons. He strove, as he did in his study of morale, for the breadth that characterized all his major strategic studies and adapted his ideas to those of individuals he met in the course of his work. He drew as well upon the bombing experience of the Second World War,[5] employing the hypothetical past to erase doubts about the decisiveness of the bombing of economic targets in that war. Unlike his study of morale, however, his ideas about mating atomic bombs to economic targets were developed almost entirely with the aid of highly classified documents that contained information not available to the general informed public. Another difference was that although Brodie used history to point up the potential of atomic attacks upon Soviet morale, he also used it to highlight the dangers of overoptimism about atomic attacks against Soviet economic targets.

Inasmuch as Brodie as special assistant held Vandenberg's mandate and confidence, he was well positioned in his critique of target plans to exercise a far-reaching influence upon war planning. Brodie by all indications was very conscious of his influence potential and wished to maximize it. Unfortunately and tragically, the very incisiveness and frankness of his critique of economic targets and of those authorized to manage JCS staff work on targets helped to undermine his tenure as a high-level adviser and to ensure that his influence upon planning fell far short of his aspirations.

Bombing to Facilitate the Normandy Invasion

The American bombing of Germany and Japan during the Second World War aimed at undermining war production irrespective of the state of Axis morale. Primarily a daytime campaign, it was similar to area bombing in that it was designed to prevent the Axis powers from fulfilling heavy war production requirements. However, it was distinct in at least two ways. First, it was informed, especially early in the war, by the widely accepted American belief that targeting enemy forces would be the quickest way to erode the ability of the Axis powers to fight. According to Gen. Omar Bradley, deputy commander of Allied forces in Europe during the war,

> While some air commanders may quite honestly have hoped to destroy sufficient German industry to force capitulation without necessity for invasion, there was no American official expression of this view, and more important, the choice of targets for attack by American aircraft was seldom affected thereby. The issue was basic to the employment of air power. If strategic bombardment is preliminary to sea invasion and land fighting, it can most effectively be directed against enemy military capabilities. On the other hand, if air power attempts to win a decision by itself, attack should be carried out not so much against the enemy military establishment (except for air defense), as against the less tangible targets of enemy will to resist, the enemy system of political and administrative controls, or the enemy economy in general. Whatever criticism can be made of details of the air campaign as it unfolded, the underlying premise accepted by the American air forces was sound.[6]

Brodie seemed to have attacks against German military capabilities similarly in mind when he argued that strategic bombing could well have tipped the balance in the Second World War. "One could make out a strong case that our strategic bombing was decisive," he wrote in 1950. "Certainly the fact that from the time of our Normandy landing onward our ground forces did not have to contend with any significant enemy air opposition, while our own planes were making things very rough for the German armies, owes a great deal to our strategic bombing."[7]

A second distinctive feature of the American bombing of the German and Japanese war economies was that it was not aimed against each war economies as a whole but rather at specific elements such as oil, aircraft, chemicals, and rubber.[8] Attacks against the German aircraft industry, and specifically against German fighter plane production (implemented in 1943 and early 1944), seemed a particularly attractive way to reduce German military capabilities.[9] They were in fact the most important part of the early phase of the American daylight bombing program, which sought in 1943, according to the leading American target selection staff organization during the war, "to cut down German strength in the field by diminishing current production of finished armaments."[10]

Brodie endorsed, on strategic and operational grounds, the decision to attack German fighter plane production. "In principle," he wrote in 1959, "the selection of the German Air Force as a target system, and especially of its fighter contingent, was right. It placed first things first according to common sense as well as to the well-known Douhet dictum that command of the air must be won before it can be exploited."[11] He linked that campaign, moreover, to limited American bombing capabilities prior to the Normandy invasion and specifically to "the need for adjusting to limited capabilities by ordering concentration on a single specifically-designated target system."[12]

However, playing down the results of those same attacks, he concluded that

> the attack on airframe production paid dividends—any diminution of enemy strength is a dividend—but they were not in the category of "decisive." They did not bear out what had been promised for a concentrated offensive by air forces of the size we were operating in early 1944. Moreover, we do not know how effectively the German Air Force could have used those "lost" aircraft, in view of shortages in fuel and pilots. The moment we started our attacks upon [German] oil production in May 1944, the Germans began to find themselves with more planes than they could fly.[13]

The ineffectiveness of those attacks he attributed to German resilience. "We now know," he wrote in 1950,

> that the attack upon the German aircraft industry was a failure. The attacks upon aircraft-assembly plants simply induced the Germans to disperse their facilities, which proved relatively easy to do, and the temporary loss of production resulting from the movement of equipment was about all that could be chalked up to the credit of the attacks. At any rate, front-line German fighter strength increased.[14]

The apparent incongruity between Brodie's characterization of strategic bombing as helping to protect Allied armies on one hand and his assessment of the attack against German fighter plane production as a failure on the other appears to have been heavily influenced by USSBS analyses and specifically by USSBS findings that a "dramatic increase in output especially in numbers of [German] airplanes between February and July 1944 [occurred] at the very time when the greatest tonnage of bombs was being dropped on the industry."[15] The USSBS also acknowledged, as did Brodie later on, that Allied air power "helped turn the tide overwhelmingly in favor of Allied ground forces . . . and . . . made possible the success of the invasion."[16]

But other USSBS material cast doubt on the standard Brodie used to evaluate the German aircraft industry attacks. "It is important," noted the USSBS staff, to differentiate between attacks, the principal purpose of which was to reduce the number of airplanes that would be available to the Luftwaffe in the months immediately to follow, and those which were intended to destroy the ability of the industry to produce airplanes six months or more later. The heavy raids on final assembly plants beginning in February 1944 were a part of the pre-invasion effort to weaken the Luftwaffe, and as such should not be judged on the basis of whether or not they crippled the industry. Because they reduced the number of airplanes which the Luftwaffe had operational in June 1944, the airframe assembly plants were wisely selected as targets.[17]

When Brodie critiqued the aircraft industry attacks as "not in the category of 'decisive,'" he seemed to be evaluating them in a manner that would have been more appropriate had the objective of the attacks been, as it never was, to cripple the entire aircraft industry.

Neither Brodie nor the USSBS reports took account of the day-to-day effect of strategic bombing upon ground operations, an effect indispensable in explaining, for example, the unquestioned Allied air superiority at the time of the Normandy invasion. "On D-Day," Bradley pointed out,

> between 0352 and 2340 hours, eighteen groups of Ninth Air Force fighters flew an approximate total of 2300 sorties, accomplishing planned missions of area cover, armed reconnaissance, escort to bombers and troop carriers, and to a lesser degree, close air support. That the fighter cover was adequate is attested to by the fact that during daylight hours of 6 June [1944] only two or three single enemy aircraft were sighted![18]

Brodie's assertion that the aircraft plant attacks had failed was questioned along these same lines by Edward Mead Earle, who had served on the panel that initially recommended German fighter production as a bombing target in 1943. "You say," he wrote to Brodie in 1950,

> "We now know that the attack on the German aircraft industry was a failure. . . . At any rate, front-line German fighter strength increased." Do we know any such thing? The directive on which our target group worked . . . was that we were to give first priority to making possible an invasion of the Continent. If we had failed, the sky should have been full of German aircraft on D-day, whereas the German air force, stronger than ever, flew a grand total of 200 sorties as compared with well over 10,000 of the Allied air forces (as I remember the figures) on the day of the landings. Our first really big strikes against aircraft assembly plants were made in late February 1944, and the German aircraft industry did not recover from them by dispersion or otherwise until long after D-day. . . . But the GAF [German air force] was not short of gas on D-day, but of planes.[19]

In reply, Brodie asserted that the major attacks of late February 1944 against German fighter assembly plants "were rather too recent to have had a substantial effect on front-line availability as of [6 June 1944], and in any case we know the Germans had some thousands of fighters on hand for operations in western Europe."[20]

If the February 1944 attacks were too recent to significantly reduce German aircraft strength in June 1944, production of aircraft begun by February 1944 would also have only marginally made a difference at the time of Normandy. (According to American estimates, more than two months were required to produce a German fighter, and another month to make it operational.[21]) But Earle had in mind that the attacks had delayed receipt of significant numbers of planes by the Luftwaffe that could have been expected to have made a difference at Normandy and that, more generally, the standard for whether attacks against the assembly plants had been successful had to be broader than that of destroying fighter production potential. According to him,

> The statement that German first-line fighter strength increased [during the period of heaviest American attacks] woud be more nearly true if it said that the number of fighter aircraft available to the Luftwaffe increased — strength implies capacity to fly the aircraft available. And the question arises, When? Between February 1944 and June? And if after tha[t], who cares? In fact, we should have paid the Germans to do exactly what they did — to turn out enormous numbers of planes which they couldn't get off the ground. D-day was a D-day for the [American] Eighth Air Force, too, in the sense that thereafter we could really go after oil and let aircraft alone except for certain "policing."[22]

The intensity and duration of American attacks against German fighter aircraft production was sharply debated within the United States Strategic Air Forces (USSTAF) in the spring of 1944, partly because it was difficult for the Americans to know when further loss of German fighters through bombing no longer served American military needs prior to the Normandy invasion. For example, Earle was informed by skeptics in London in May 1944 that "Commanding General Eighth Air Force, still Africa-minded, would continue to hunt out the GAF even under every shrub, and is obsessed with the bombardment of airfields."[23] Had target planners known during the war, as they did afterward, of the major options available to the Germans to compensate for American strikes against the fighter production plants, they would have found such attacks much less attractive, especially given the limited American bombing capabilities when those attacks were first recommended in the spring of 1943. "As late as 1943," James Lowe, a leading civilian in the postwar Air Targets Division of the U.S. Air Force Office of Intelligence, stated in 1947,

> the Chief of the German Air Force told the Commanding General who corresponded to the head of our War Production Board that if the German aircraft industry produced more than three hundred airplanes a month he would not know what to do with them. At that point, the German aircraft industry was operating on an eight hour basis and could just as easily operate on a twenty-four hour basis in case the industry at any point was attacked. In other words, even in the aircraft industry with Germany at war there was pressure to a point where the bombers had to destroy more than two-thirds of the aircraft plant before there would be a single less airplane in the operational unit. Now, if the Air Forces did not have the capabilities to fight through the two-thirds cushion to get into the pay dirt of the industry, the target system would have to be foregone.[24]

This analysis assumed too arbitrarily that every last German fighter being produced had to be destroyed before attacks against fighter assembly plants would be useful.

Moreover, despite the "two-thirds cushion," the bombing of the aircraft plants by early 1944 was successful enough to persuade the Germans to adopt a more efficient mode of aircraft production. According to the chief German war production statistician, Rolf Wagenfuehr, dispersion of some plants and reconstruction of others were not sufficient in 1943 to halt continuous decreases in plane production and in reserves. "In February, 1944," he noted, "these losses became unbearable and the responsible officials of the Air Ministry had to realize that if this situation continued the German aircraft industry and with it the German air defense would be eliminated within a limited space of time."[25] The consequence was that a new centralized "Committee for the Production of Fighter Planes" was established that introduced mass-production methods for fighter planes for the first time, greatly increasing production of fighter and close-support aircraft. In September 1944, Wagenfuehr indicated, Germany produced 2,950 fighter and close-support aircraft, compared with 1,028 the previous February.[26]

Knocking Out the German Economy

When Brodie evaluated bombing attacks against such German economic target systems as steel, petroleum, and transportation designed later in the war to cripple German industry, he found irrelevant any increasing German war production sustained in spite of the bombing. "The often repeated argument," he wrote in 1950, "based on United States Strategic Bombing Survey statistics, that German war production in almost all categories increased drastically between the middle of 1942 and the middle of 1944, is quite beside the point, because the decisive bombing results we are talking about had barely begun by mid-1944."[27] The full fury of the bombing by the last months of the war, Brodie noted, signified that "our strategic bombing knocked the German war economy flat on its back," even though it came too late "to have anything like its full effect on the battlefield."[28] "The fact remains," he observed in 1950, "that the ultimate destruction of the German armies was practically assured at the successful conclusion of the break-out west of St. Lô late in July, 1944, at which time the tangible battlefield results of our strategic bombing, apart from its contribution to suppressing enemy air activities, added up to precious little."[29]

Following the Normandy invasion, long-range bombing for direct support to battlefield activity was de-emphasized relative to the campaign against German war goods production capability. According to Burton H. Klein, referring to the 1944 period, "When their operational capabilities were enormously greater than even a few months before, the U.S. air forces shifted their emphasis from an immediate reduction of the enemy's military production to bringing about a general attrition of his economy."[30] The USSBS staff had concluded that Allied air power "brought the economy which sustained the enemy's armed forces to virtual collapse"[31] and underscored that heavy attacks feasible only following the Normandy invasion had been required to achieve this result. "The campaigns which carried the promise of decisive results began after D-day," the USSBS appraisal continued. "The offensives that started against oil and nitrogen plants in May and June, against the German transportation system in September, and against the Ruhr steel producing area in October, all achieved results fully up to expectations or above them."[32] That same USSBS report also noted, however, that "the full effects of [the German economic] collapse had not reached the enemy's front lines when they were overrun by Allied forces."[33]

Taken in isolation, the redirection of bombing priorities after Normandy seemed to show the full destructive potential of long-range strategic bombing against economic targets with weapons then available and to hint at what atomic weapons could accomplish much more quickly later on. "The complete destruction of [the German] synthetic oil capacity," Joseph E. Loftus wrote, "after allowing a time lag to account for the exhaustion of accumulated reserve stocks of processed oils, spelled the end of the German war machine. An investment of less than two dozen atomic bombs well placed could have rendered the German war machine inoperative after the expiration of the short time in which it would have used up its reserve stocks."[34]

In the campaign against Germany, 555 separate attacks against 135 targets were required to destroy the German synthetic oil industry, detailed examination of which revealed how "under prevailing conditions, a truly tremendous effort was required to deliver a given weight of bombs on damageable [oil-chemical] plant sections."[35] In the campaign against the German oil industry, only one in twenty-nine bombs dropped was subsequently found to have hit structures essential to production.[36]

Brodie seemed to have the same point in mind when he declared in 1952 that "the business of target selection is really the essence of air strategy—what targets you choose and how you go about planning to hit them and in what order"[37]—and that "target selection . . . was a much more critical problem then [that is, in the last war] than it is now."[38] The atomic bomb, he argued,

> reduces force requirements in strategic bombing, so that the force existing at the beginning of a war can be deemed sufficient to carry out a strategic bombing campaign—a very different situation from World War II, and I think an extremely important one. It has thus put a tremendous premium on the logicality of the war plans existing at the outset of the war. As you know, at the beginning of World War II, especially in the Pacific, some of the war plans existing before the event could be torn up and it really didn't make much difference. Certainly our plans for strategic bombing were evolved in the process of the war. But at present we stand committed to a certain procedure on the outbreak of war, and the very fact that in the first few weeks rather than months of the hostilities we will be using up our major asset—namely, the atomic stockpile—means that the plans existing before the event had better be good.[39]

This focus upon logical target selection evidently reflected Brodie's presumption that in the contemporary period no conflict would exist in bombing missions and that planners could concentrate entirely upon reducing the Soviet economy. By contrast, the air campaign against the German war economy reflected continuing conflict over bombing missions and interference of that conflict with strategic logic. For example, ground combat operations retained major claims upon long-range aircraft after June 1944, a situation that raised questions about whether the air campaign against the German war economy should be considered in isolation. According to the official history of the RAF Bomber Command, referring to developments immediately after the Normandy invasion:

> The fact that the allied armies were on the Continent throughout the final air offensive and were, therefore, often able to turn to their own tactical advantage the consequences of these strategic operations did not destroy the fundamental design of the strategic air offensive, though naturally it exerted much influence upon the bombing policy by which the design was to be accomplished. Quite apart from the many supporting and primarily tactical operations which had to be undertaken by the heavy bombers, the aims and the requirements of the armies were important factors in the making of strategic bombing policy. . . . Now, in June 1944, as there had been in May 1940, . . . there was a formidable multitude of tasks which seemed appropriate to the heavy bomber force and there was, therefore, the danger that the effort might be dispersed over too wide a range of defensive, offensive, tactical and strategic roles.[40]

The large priority given to tactical bombing and the relatively small proportion of bombing tonnage directed at targets deep inside Germany make understandable the Bomber Command history's assessment of the strategic air offensive in the summer of 1944 as "an emasculated affair."[41] Later, in December 1944, the Runstedt counteroffensive led to renewed major Allied bombing priority to blunt the German advance and especially to attacks upon German petroleum refineries to interrupt the transport of supplies to the front.[42]

The continuing prominence of battlefield objectives in Allied bombing policy following the Normandy invasion helps explain the delay in reducing the German war economy. But the force of the argument that bombing of the German war economy came too late to have a major effect on the battlefield was lessened, as already indicated, because those interested in using air power for battlefield support gave much higher priority to bombing that would affect existing forces rather than to attacks that would affect Germany's ability to produce war goods. This applied, for example, to the initial American plan by March 1944 to target the German petroleum industry. Walt W. Rostow described the timing of this plan:

> The choice of oil was an obvious next step. It promised, if sedulously pursued, not only to affect the whole German war production structure but also to limit the fighting capacity of the ground and air forces. With D-Day only three months off, this was a decisive consideration. . . . Only a few believed—or still hoped—that the war could be won by the use of air power alone, without the invasion of the Continent. The Army Air Forces had to do everything in their power to contribute to the success of the invasion. But they were in a position to do more: to weaken gravely the enemy's capacity to resist on land and in the air, on every front.[43]

The plan proposed to attack twenty-seven oil installations, based upon evidence that "stocks of finished petroleum products are sufficient only for several months' military operations" and that "the loss of more than 50% of Axis output would directly and materially reduce German military capabilities through reducing tactical and strategic mobility and frontline delivery of supplies."[44] It sharply contrasted with the 555 attacks eventually required on 135 targets to knock out every known operational synthetic oil plant and refinery in Germany. The effectiveness of the initial oil plan, as in the case of attacks against German fighter plane production, would have to be evaluated by standards different from those attached to the large-scale destruction of the German war industry.

In practice, the distinction between the initial twenty-seven target oil plan and the effort to fully destroy the German synthetic oil industry was eroded because the first attacks against the oil system did not occur until May 1944, too close to the Normandy invasion to affect the capacity of German forces in being to resist the invasion. The twenty-seven target plan was rejected by Gen. Dwight Eisenhower in March 1944 because its advocates could not agree on whether its effects would be felt by the first weeks of the Allied invasion.[45] Following the invasion, the growing size of American bombing capabilities and the shift in bombing priorities rendered the twenty-seven target plan obsolete, and the difference between German dependence upon synthetic oil to assist existing military capability on one hand and dependence upon such oil to enhance capability to produce war goods on the other hand was neglected. Yet advocates of attacks against the German synthetic oil industry in the spring of 1944, including Edward Mead Earle, strongly believed that the industry did not have to be totally destroyed for the war to be won within a matter of months. "One can have," wrote Earle in May 1944,

> two objectives in the formulation of a [European] strategy at the moment: first, [to] establish and secure a bridgehead; second, to win the war as a whole. There is no assurance that the second front will succeed or that, if it does succeed, it will win the war this summer. Should, therefore, one have a second sling to his bow? The destruction of the enemy's capacity to wage war through depriving him of his petroleum would almost certainly win the war this summer, even if it did not win it in ninety days.[46]

Hastening Germany's Defeat by Bombing: Improved Target Selection

When Brodie argued for the decisiveness of atomic bombing in contemporary Soviet-American warfare, he had in mind, as we have seen, not the actual bombing experience of the last war but an idealized picture of what that bombing might have been. This picture was drawn in connection with attacks against urban-area targets, in which Brodie insisted that substituting atomic bombs for explosives actually employed in the German campaign would have brought a totally different result. In relation to attacks against specifically economic targets, he seemed equally anxious to dispel doubts that bombing could have been *clearly* decisive.[47] In this instance, however, in which he maintained that bombing results were *already arguably* decisive in practice, his use of the hypothetical past did not incorporate nuclear weapons. Instead of foreseeing revolutionary changes in the bombing of economic targets with contemporary weaponry, Brodie projected incremental changes unrelated to the destructive power of bombing explosives. For example, he seemed to have in mind attacks against economic targets rather than urban-area ones in the Second World War when he contended in 1952 that "the experience of strategic bombing in World War II . . . demonstrated its potentiality to the future."[48]

Specifically, when he applied the hypothetical past to attacks against economic targets in Germany, Brodie contended that the bombing could first of all have hastened German economic collapse. "If the bombing results actually achieved by February and March of 1945 had come six months or so earlier," he argued in 1950, "no one could say that our strategic bombing of Germany had no significant effect upon the outcome of the war."[49] Behind his belief that German economic collapse could have been obtained earlier was his awareness of the inefficiency of the bombing. "We know for a fact," he wrote the same year, "that *the destruction of the German economy was achieved with a minute percentage of the bombs actually dropped on Germany.* We may therefore conclude that given only a moderate improvement in our use of the means at our disposal, the decisive effects of strategic bombing could have come soon enough to make a great, rather than only a marginal, difference in the outcome."[50]

In addition to attacking German ability to produce war goods in the latter stages of the war, Brodie would also have attacked specific economic targets much earlier to affect German forces in being. For example, he would have attacked the German oil industry rather than the German aircraft industry in 1943, so that "the resulting shortages would have been almost immediately felt on the ground as well as in the air."[51] He would also have struck at the German chemical industry, from which nitrogen was required for all German explosives as well as for the production of large quantities of synthetic oil. This target system was actually destroyed, Brodie noted, "as a wholly unexpected bonus" in the Allied attack upon the German oil industry. "Had we elevated [the German chemical industry] to the status of a target system in itself," he concluded in 1950, "we could have demolished it much earlier in the war than we did and with only a small percentage of the bombs ultimately aimed at oil."[52]

These errors Brodie attributed to the neglect of target selection in the United States even up to the initial period of American involvement in the Second World War. "It is remarkable indeed," he wrote in 1950,

that the U.S.A.A.F. [U.S. Army Air Forces] prior to late 1942 had given very little systematic thought to the problem of target selection. Douhet, the prophet of air power, had insisted twenty years earlier that the selection of objectives, the grouping of zones and determining the order in which they are to be destroyed, is the most difficult and delicate task in aerial warfare. Whatever its equipment, however skillful and valorous its crews, an air force can be no more effective than the logic that governs its choice of targets.[53]

Supporting Brodie's assertion was the assessment of Lt. Gen. Ira Eaker, upon taking command of the American Eighth Air Force in Britain in March 1942, that the weakness of American intelligence about German vulnerabilities was his most serious shortcoming.[54]

Selection of economic targets required precise intelligence; however, especially for finished goods industries, intelligence officials were unable to identify all the plants in the industries, to determine the scope of wartime expansion occurring in the industries, or to estimate the likelihood that technical substitutes for plants that were bombed would be found.[55] This ignorance led to important underestimates of the German economic ability to endure in spite of bombing attacks. Neglect of target selection also helped to explain what one careful student of the air campaign against Germany described as "the long time it took the Air Command to learn the decisive strategic importance of oil in the German war economy" and also "a good part of the delay" in the launching of the Allied air offensive against the German synthetic oil industry.[56]

Among the problems associated with attacking economic targets to weaken German forces in being were that the Germans anticipated oil shortages and took offsetting action after initial Allied attacks against the German petroleum industry began in May 1944. According to Walt W. Rostow, the failure of oil attack advocates to predict such a development was a major error. "In calculating the timing of the effect of the attack on oil on German military dispositions," wrote Rostow,

> [Allied oil experts] stuck, rather mechanically, to their measurement of the size of stocks relative to the estimated rate of German military consumption. In fact, the Germans, quite capable of doing arithmetic, began almost immediately to anticipate the consequences on future availabilities of current losses in oil production yielding a much quicker military effect than was initially estimated. In addition the calculations were not sufficiently disaggregated. . . . [A]ircraft fuel was brought down to disastrous levels by June. . . . [I]n failing to dramatize effectively the promptness with which a current and prospective decline in oil production would alter German military plans and dispositions, they reinforced a political situation among the top military commanders which was, in itself, exceedingly costly.[57]

The immediate consequences of the attack against German petroleum paralleled those against the German aircraft industry, stimulating production as well as eroding it. Over the longer term, similar development in other industries interfered with the bombing effort aimed at German ability to produce war goods. "Bombing not only destroyed production capacity," according to the USSBS report *The Effects of Strategic Bombing on the German War Economy*, "but also increased it—in the sense that capacity was utilized which might have been neglected in the absence of bombing. Although bombing caused output losses, it also stimulated rationalization and expansion. It is, of course, impossible to measure the balance of the opposing forces precisely."[58] Thus attacks against the German war economy would be felt only over the long term, giving the Germans a good deal of time to make adjustments unanticipated by Allied intelligence. The Economic Outpost Unit (EOU), an intelligence branch of the U.S. Embassy in London responsible for advising military officials about targets, "emphasized," according to its official history, "the possibilities of evading the military consequences of bomb damage in a mature and resourceful economic system like that of wartime Germany."[59] Yet according to Rostow, an EOU staff member, the EOU underestimated "how far short of full economic mobilization Germany was down to the spring of 1944."[60]

Hastening Germany's Defeat by Bombing: Air Superiority

Another reason pinpointed by Brodie for the inadequate effect of strategic bombing upon the battlefield was what he termed in 1951

> our failure on the provision at an earlier enough date of long range fighting. There was that fatal three year lag between the first production model of the B-17, which I believe came out in 1936, and the first production model of the P-38 and the P-47, which I believe came out in 1939. Now, there seems to be some question . . . as to why there was that tardiness of producing the long-range fighter. I have a feeling[,] though my evidence for it is rather thin, that [it] resulted from some rigid doctrinal or doctrinaire concepts.[61]

For example, Brodie indicated that "the tardy development of long-range fighters . . . is critical for my argument that the results achieved by February and March of 1945 could have been accomplished at least six months earlier."[62] He may have been thinking of how the massive bombing operations to reduce the German economy had sharply affected air superiority requirements by 1944. Maj. Gen. Orvil Anderson, chief operations officer for the Eighth Air Force, complained late in the war that fighter support previously assigned to his command had been withdrawn and assigned instead to support ground operations. In his opinion, described by a USSBS staff member, "the 8th Air Force was engaged in winning a war, rather than a battle, and it should be supported by every type of available aircraft."[63] Anderson then argued as did Brodie that decisive results came too late even after the Allies concentrated on oil and transportation targets and that the delay was due to the difficulties of gaining air superiority over the Luftwaffe.[64]

Anderson's views about fighter support for long-range bombing operations were opposed to those of General Bradley, who wished to employ fighters especially for operations over and around the area of ground fighting; because of their conflicting claims, any mandate to destroy the German war economy more quickly than was actually accomplished would have increased tensions within authoritative American military circles. More broadly, the belief that bombing could have brought about more rapid collapse of the German economy depended on the assumption, implicit in the USSBS report on the German war economy as well as in Douhet's writings, that air power would not be guided by the needs of ground combat,[65] whereas the idea that bombing could have had an earlier effect upon German forces in being conflicted with this assumption.

But operational difficulties would likely have been even more considerable had bombing attacks against German petroleum begun in 1943, as Brodie proposed, when fighter support for American bombers was not yet available. In the most costly American long-range attacks against Germany, strikes against German ball-bearing plants in August and October 1943, the loss rate of 25 percent that had been anticipated could have been maintained with planes and replacement crews, according to the American air force chief of staff, Gen. H. H. Arnold. Yet Arnold acknowledged that unspecified "other factors" had to be taken into account,[66] and the USSBS staff, upon which Brodie elsewhere depended heavily, acknowledged the importance of operational concerns. "As regards the timing of the bomber offensive," the USSBS report on the German war economy stated,

> it can be said that oil production should have been bombed as soon as it became possible operationally to penetrate deep into Germany. This appears to have taken place in February 1944 with the use of P-51 fighter escort. The obliteration of Germany's aviation gasoline production at this time would have clipped the wings of the Luftwaffe three months earlier than it actually occurred.[67]

To be sure, the importance of interdicting the German supply of oil to the front to pave the way for an earlier invasion of Europe from the west might have merited heavy bombing losses. (According to Arnold, the supply of American planes to the European front directly depended on the imminence of an Allied invasion of the Continent.) But the military historian David MacIsaac has insisted that bombing attacks could not be sustained against any target until air superiority was obtained, a condition that was not satisfied until early 1944.

> Throughout the closing months of 1943 and the period of 1944 prior to "Big Week" [that is, the last week of February 1944, when the largest strikes against the German aircraft industry were carried out], the bomber offensive . . . had experienced its darkest hour. The problem had become less that of what targets to strike and more that of whether the means would be found to strike *any* in the context of acceptable air-to-air losses.[68]

Attacks against German aircraft assembly factories in 1943 and 1944 and the initial Allied attacks against German petroleum refineries later in 1944, both aimed at lessening German forces in being, were strategically important for demonstrating and attaining air superiority. The former would blunt anticipated German production of large numbers of new and improved fighters, and the latter would force the Germans to wage an air battle so that Allied control of the skies over Germany could be won.[69]

Furthermore, the bolder the Allies became in their efforts to weaken Germany's capacity to resist, the less important became the need to interdict the German war economy; heavy attacks against the latter logically had to wait until the first was realized. On the other hand, once German resistance in the air and on the ground was greatly diminished, the need for interdicting the German war economy also came into question. Whether the decisive strategic importance of oil for Germany lay primarily in fueling forces in being or in enhancing German capability to produce war goods, and hence whether bombing attacks ought to have been primarily designed to interdict one or the other, Brodie did not state; his aim was to demonstrate the potential of strategic bombing rather than to propose detailed target selection priorities.

Electric Power as a Nuclear Bombing Target:
Immunity to Bombing

Having argued that improved target selection would have ensured a greater impact for strategic bombing against Germany, Brodie failed to discuss one target system never deliberately attacked—the German electric power network, the selection of which authoritative Germans believed would have vividly illustrated Brodie's point. For example, Albert Speer, minister for armament and war production in Nazi Germany, stated to Allied interrogators after the war that a loss of 40 percent of German power capabilities would have been dangerous and that "according to estimates of the Reich, a loss of 60 per cent of the total power production would suffice to lead to a collapse of the whole [power] network."[70] But Brodie was to have a great deal to say about electric power as a nuclear bombing target in the Soviet Union, the official selection of which, reflected in American war plans during the period of Brodie's service for General Vandenberg in 1950 and 1951, seems to have resulted from an assessment of Speer's testimony.

According to James Lowe, civilian director of the ATD, the agency charged by the JCS in the late 1940s and early 1950s with recommending nuclear bombing targets, "the present target system envisions the loss of more than 60% of the total generating capacity of the U.S.S.R. If the lessons of World War II teach us anything they teach us that the loss of more than 60% of the total electric power generating capacity will cause the complete collapse of the war economy."[71] "Jim Lowe," Brodie wrote much later, "had to my knowledge never spoken to Speer, but of course had read what Speer had told our USSBS people. It was on that basis that he was all gung-ho on electric power stations within the Soviet Union as the primary target system."[72] The ATD concluded by 1950 that 64 percent of the Soviet power-generating capacity was produced in 116 of 2,000 power plants known to exist in the Soviet Union.[73] Destruction of the 116 plants would thus exceed the minimum loss of electric power posited by Lowe as necessary to collapse the entire Soviet war economy. A total of 142 targets were allocated to electric power in the target annex proposed by the ATD to the 1951 emergency war plan,[74] taking up nearly half of the approximately three hundred atomic bombs then available for use in the first ninety-day phase of nuclear bombing operations.[75]

Brodie's critique of the priority attached by the ATD to electric power as a target system constituted one of the most important elements of his work for Vandenberg.

He rejected, first of all, the apparent use of Speer's testimony as the primary basis for choosing targets. "I cannot suppress the thought," he wrote in his critique of ATD priorities for General Vandenberg, "that there is a fixation here. Electric power has been recommended by ATD for at least the last two years. If our capability is inadequate for the system now, it was much more so two years ago. It looks like an effort to redeem the supposed lost opportunity of World War II."[76]

This view may have been connected to Brodie's dissatisfaction with those to whom he spoke about targeting matters. "From what I have seen in the Pentagon over the past six or eight months," he declared at the Air War College in May 1951, "and the fact, for that matter, so much less so there in the Pentagon, I should say that the greatest danger to our strategic thinking is rigidity of concepts and that the most dangerous person is the one in the key planning spot who is quite sure that he has all the answers."[77] Brodie's perception of rigidities among those with overall responsibility for the work of the ATD, an agency then housed within the air force but having nominal representation of the army and navy, undoubtedly stimulated him to support changes (which I discuss later) in the procedures for recommending strategic targets to the JCS.

Brodie's critique of electric power as a target was also highly informed by his conception of targeting objectives and especially by his belief that targets should be chosen in part to retard the operation of Soviet forces. In the past, he pointed out, Soviet forces had fought irrespective of drastic losses in electric power. "I might go back," he told his Air War College audience, "to the terrific havoc of the civil war period in Russia where incidentally electric power production was reduced practically to zero and yet the Russian armies continued to operate. What should it teach us? I would say, first of all, it should teach us humility."[78] Brodie's major contemporary concern in this regard was undoubtedly the retarding of a Soviet invasion of Western Europe. "I was and remain a strong deterrence man," he wrote much later when asked to state his views on target selection during his period of work for Vandenberg, "but if pressed at the time I suppose I would have emphasized the importance of industrial concentrations *and* retardation."[79]

If it was important to wear down or deplete Soviet forces in being to retard a Soviet invasion of Western Europe, then destroying the Soviet war economy would hardly be adequate. "The enemy's finished commodities of war," Brodie declared in 1951, "are something that strategic bombing almost by definition cannot touch. The Soviet Union has already a huge stockpile of these and that stockpile is growing a pace [*sic*]. Here is the measure of immunity to a strategic bombing campaign — here is the stockpile that means immunity if anything does."[80] To some extent, immunity to stategic bombing depended on the scale of ground combat. We have seen that in the Second World War, attacks aimed at lessening German forces in being did not require destruction of the German war economy but, as in the case of attacks against aircraft production and petroleum, helped to reduce German stockpiles by supplementing consumption of weaponry in major ground operations. In contemporary warfare, by contrast, the West would be unable to implement major European ground operations at the outset of war against invading Soviet forces; the very limited Western resistance would lessen the effectiveness of stategic bombing compared with what it had been earlier in Germany.

But there might be immunity to strategic bombing, reflected in huge weapons stockpiles, even with major ground operations if bombing targeted the enemy's capability to produce war goods rather than its forces in being. Attacks against electric power that usefully destroyed the war economy but not the enemy's forces in being seemed from this perspective no worse than any other aimed at destroying the former. "We have a characteristic American preoccupation with production and thus with eliminating Russian production," Brodie declared in a 1952 Air War College lecture.

> This preoccupation with production has caused us to give, in my opinion, a fictitious importance to the business of speed in getting the enemy's factories destroyed. If a factory has been turning out guns, tanks, and what have you for ten years or more, what difference really does it make if we get it tomorrow or two months from now? There is already a considerable backlog of production behind them.[81]

Focusing on the issue of speed in implementing a strategic bombing campaign, Brodie neglected the long-term effect on war production of strikes against enemy electric power plants taken into account by the USSBS report *The Effects of Strategic Bombing on the German War Economy.* "Consideration of the desirability of raw materials as a target," that report noted,

> brings into focus the alternative objectives of strategic air attacks, namely the immediate reduction of supplies available for shipment to the front on the one hand or the destruction of the industrial base for military operations on the other. Under the former objective, basic materials obviously have a low priority. Where, however, strategic bombardment has the broad objective of paralyzing the production of military supplies, basic industries provide one of the two general alternative target systems. Attacks can be concentrated against one or more basic industries or against their consumers, the industries producing finished products and components. Steel, coal and electric power were, together with transportation, the primary "general" target possibilities in the German economy. The destruction of any one of them would, sooner or later, have paralyzed war production as effectively as the destruction of a host of specific targets.[82]

But Brodie, having denied the short-term significance of attacks against electric power facilities in instances where prior stockpiling of war matériel had taken place, also denied the long-term strategic significance of *atomic* attacks against war production. "One must not be dogmatic on this issue," he wrote in 1959,

> but one observes how blandly assumptions are made and carried into national policy which seem to envisage a repetition in some future total war of the World War II type of wartime production! This ridiculous and reckless fantasy can be dismissed altogether for an unrestricted war. The duration of the decisive phases of such a war can hardly be more than a few days. It is hard to make a case for any kind of wartime production possessing even a modest degree of military utility.[83]

Recuperation from Economic Attacks

Having argued that attacks against Soviet electric power would not be effective against enemy forces in being and that the strategic importance of collapsing the Soviet war economy was overrated, Brodie stressed the possibilities of recuperating from major losses in the ability to produce war goods. "The Soviet Union," Brodie declared in 1951,

> [lost,] in the first five months of the [Second Word W]ar, territory which had contained forty percent of the country's population, sixty-three percent of the coal output, fifty-eight percent of the steel output, sixty-eight percent of pig-iron output, sixty percent of aluminum output, thirty-eight percent of the grain crop, ninety-five percent of ball bearing production, ninety-nine percent of rolled non-ferrous metals, etc. Now you would say if these losses were a result of the strategic bombing campaign that would be pretty good for a strategic bombing campaign—these are good results. And notice too that after all this was over—after she had sustained these losses—she was obliged to continue fighting great land battles while warring upon a restricted resource land-area. . . . She was to be sure, greatly helped, after a while, by lend lease. Also she did not have to sustain a strategic bombing attack in addition to those losses from the German land invasion. Nevertheless, her comeback after sustaining these losses in productive resources presents a really amazing picture of [resilience].[84]

Similar recuperation, though under the pressure of strategic bombing, took place in Germany during the Second World War. "There was," Brodie declared in a 1952 lecture, referring to the air campaign against Germany, "a well-nigh complete lack of conception of what happens on the receiving end after the bomb is dropped. For example, there was no conception of the resilience of the enemy economy, of the capability of the enemy to repair or circumvent damage. The tremendous German accomplishment in this respect was one of the really important surprises of the war."[85]

It was to prevent such recuperation that conventional wisdom regarded *comprehensive* attacks against electric power facilities as highly desirable. Speer, for example, referring to concentration upon "targets which eliminate a cross section factor of the industry," such as electric power, declared that "the succession of attacks must be accelerated in order to make reconstruction impossible."[86] The USSBS report on the German electric power industry similarly suggested that to deny electric power to Germany through a strategic air campaign, it was preferable "to strike as many plants and substations as possible at one time or within a short space of time."[87] Later, in 1951, after comparing projected effects of strikes at Soviet electric power stations with attacks against other targets, an American panel of outside consultants to the secretary of the air force led by Henry C. Alexander concluded that electric power should be retained as a primary bombing target.[88] That panel also concluded that telescoping the bombing campaign "would greatly increase the effectiveness of the attack."[89]

And there can be little doubt, finally, that the emergency war plan for 1951 contemplated telescoping the attack against electric power, for a JCS-approved hypothesis included in that plan specified that "the initial, three-month, atomic phase of the strategic air offensive will be selected as an integrated program and *will not* depend for major effects upon subsequent phases of the strategic air offensive."[90] This hypothesis was included in the emergency war plan, Lowe reported, because SAC was capable of a ninety-day offensive but not of operations beyond that date, so it was thought prudent "to select a target system that could be destroyed within these 90 days and which would not depend upon subsequent operations for its full effects to be felt."[91] Electric power evidently became the primary target system recommended by the ATD, because it was to be the system slated for destruction within the first ninety days of war, satisfying the JCS directive.

Because plans for comprehensively attacking electric power facilities in the Soviet Union conflicted with the coercive attacks strongly favored by Brodie, he is likely to have opposed selecting electric power as a bombing target for this reason alone. For example, he criticized the ninety-day integrated program hypothesis as reflecting the philosophy "that we must shoot from the hip" and being inconsistent with his preference for coercive warfare and "playing by ear."[92] Citing also what he termed "the inadequacies of a purely hard[ware] approach,"[93] Brodie rejected any plan that sought to destroy the Soviet war economy, proposing to General Vandenberg that "the 142 RGZs [required ground zeroes] now allocated to electric power be supplanted by not more than 60 RGZs on industrial complexes, such complexes to be nominated by SAC and approved in this Headquarters. Such a procedure should take little more than a week. The reasons for reducing the 142 RGZs to 60 can be explained orally."[94]

Brodie's abandonment of a purely hardware approach can be readily understood in political terms. "Maybe the thing to go after," he declared in 1951, "is something of more direct political effect than hardware — than depriving them of so many extra pounds of gun barrels, etc., etc."[95] The more that political considerations were likely to lengthen a nation's endurance in war, as was true for the Soviet Union in the Second World War, the more justifiable was coercive warfare on the part of its adversary and the more compelling the point, argued by Brodie, that the strategic effects of war-making should not be equated with the measures of economic damage.

Brodie's optimistic estimates of the Soviet Union's ability to recuperate from nuclear bombing attacks may have presumed contemporary repetition of Soviet resistance to attack in the Second World War, as when he wrote in 1951, in contrast to advocates of strikes against electric power, that "from the recuperability standpoint, the delivery of any given number of bombs over six months to a year may be about as good as ninety days."[96] The target destruction annex, he maintained in the same vein, "seemed enormously to underrate Soviet capacity for recuperation. . . . [It] greatly exaggerated not only the time required to get a substantial portion of the struck capacity back into operation, but also the importance of that time."[97] But it was difficult to understand how an economy could be resilient without adequate electric power, or how the economic effect of strategic bombing or of territorial losses would not be considerably magnified by the choice of electric power as a bombing target. The centrality of electric power to a war economy depended on evidence that, as noted in a more recent study by Jack Hirschleifer, "power is a vital input into almost every other critical service" and that "there is . . . no practicable substitute for power in most uses, which underlines the importance of this service."[98]

Such evidence apparently informed German targeting specialists during the war when they focused for a time on Soviet electric power facilities. According to Speer,

> A study of an economic committee formed in 1942 showed there was only one economic target that could have been destroyed—the Russian electricity plants in the Ural Mountains. . . . The destruction of these objects would have meant that Russian industry would have been paralyzed [*sic*] for long periods of time. One can say had we been successful, the war with Russia would have ended a short time thereafter.[99]

A retrospective study of the air campaign against Germany and Japan, carried out by Gen. Haywood S. Hansell, Jr., suggested that strikes against electric power would have been equivalent in their economic effects to the much larger and costly destruction of industrial concentrations. "There seemed to be ample time," Hansell wrote, particularly about the Japanese campaign,

> in which to prepare the intelligence and make the target selections for the air offensive against Japanese electric power.
> Unfortunately, electric power was later dropped from recommended Japanese target lists. The decision . . . was made because of inadequate and misleading intelligence. Electric power sources as a selective target system is worthy of reexamination in the light of the USSBS reports. Destruction of the Japanese electric power system would have rendered the great cities of Japan useless as sources of Japanese strength.
> We justified the destruction of the 66 largest cities in Japan on the ground that they contained thousands of small shops which could not be isolated and destroyed. Yet every tool in every shop was completely dependent upon public electric power. . . . In the war against Germany and that against Japan the prizes were so great as to invite our maximum air effort to destroy the electric power system. Yet in each case, the task was dismissed as "much too difficult" before all avenues had been examined.[100]

Brodie did not hesitate, as we have seen, to argue against USSBS conclusions when he analyzed the implications of atomic bombing. With reference to electric power targets, he contended, in contrast to the lessons from the Second World War drawn by Hansell (and directly contrary to the later conclusion of the Alexander panel about bombing the Soviet Union), that more bombs were required in more than half the cases to destroy the Soviet electric power plants than were required for their industrial counterparts. This assessment was challenged by Lowe,[101] indicating that Brodie did not use the ATD data to deal with this question; he may instead have employed data from the Strategic Air Command, whose officials (as we will see) would have agreed with him.[102] But Brodie's target selection preferences did not rest only on intelligence data or on bombing efficiency. As a matter of fact, he sought to play down the economic benefits of bombing economic targets, and inasmuch as striking at electric power afforded economic benefits above all to an attacker, he could be expected to play down also the potential of striking at electric power targets.

The Vulnerability of Electric Power Plants

When Brodie cautioned against the fascination contemporary war planners had with the vulnerability of electric power facilities during the Second World War, he had in mind primarily the limitation of atomic bombs, in sharp contrast to his discussion of morale as a bombing target, which played up the potential of those same weapons. "With the A-bomb," Brodie declared in 1952,

> we have to be concerned with the physical vulnerabilities of the target selected. We know that in World War II there was a tremendous optimism, a very easy optimism, about the vulnerability of targets, reflected in the fact that among other things we used bombs which turned out after the event to have been on the whole much too small. Some people think that a comparable optimism prevails now about physical vulnerabilities. We have today vast and unimplemented assumptions about the collapse which is supposed to follow automatically from placing bombs on certain targets.[103]

He concluded from his tour of duty with General Vandenberg that ATD estimates of the vulnerability of electric power plants to nuclear weapons attack and of the effect of that vulnerability on Soviet war production were inadequate. "The amount of damage we would inflict on the Soviet power grid," he wrote much later,

> had certainly not been thought out. An independent report prepared by one of the think tanks (I cannot at the moment recall its name, though I would recognize it if it were mentioned to me; I think it began with a "B") pointed out that we didn't even know where all the Soviet power stations were, i.e., there were more than we had firm knowledge about. There was also the unresolved question of how many we would hit—and how badly—of those we went after, how much power the S.U. could get along without, etc., etc. These questions did not seem to bother Lowe or his boss, Gen. [C. Pearré] Cabell [director of air force intelligence].[104]

Critically important for Brodie was that the vulnerable portions of those facilities took up a very small area,[105] a point he illustrated with hydroelectric and steam generating plants. "One of the Strategic Bombing Survey's booklets, the one produced by the final division of the Electric Utilities Division," he declared in May 1951,

> talks about the long pipe in a hydro-electric plant which goes down from the surface of the water which may be some high level, down to the power plant below. A pipe usually for a big hydro-electric plant has a diameter of five feet and a thickness of I forget how many inches. Now mark me, if a bomb penetrated that pipe near the bottom that's the end of the hydro-electric plant. Sure, I have the notion that even [if] it would take a pretty heavy and perhaps an armor piercing HE bomb to penetrate that pipe, then it would have to hit right here. Not here. But what we know is that an atomic bomb even one that would explode directly over the pipe [might] do nothing more than shake

the place up. Regarding that report, I feel that all specific vulnerabilities which this report talks about with respect to these kinds of targets do not in the main apply to blast defense with A-bombs.[106]

Perhaps one-fifth of Soviet electric power was generated in hydroelectric plants, two of which were the largest in the world.[107]

Brodie also commented on the difficulty of using atomic bombs against the most vulnerable portions of steam plants and substations. When the USSBS final report on the Japanese electric power industry, evidently informed by the effects of the nuclear attacks against Hiroshima and Nagasaki, concluded that "there is no question that the atomic bomb is by a wide margin the most effective weapon for the destruction of electric utility installations,"[108] it seems to have been referring to steam plants and substations (especially their unprotected transformers and circuit breakers) that, unlike hydroelectric plants, suffered widespread damage in Japan.[109] But Brodie used data about the effect of the atomic explosion at Nagasaki to play down the force of this conclusion. "The Nagasaki power plant," he noted in his report to Vandenberg, "at 5,400 feet from ground zero, had its transformers protected by concrete blast walls and suffered no injury. An electric sub-station in the same city at 2,400 feet from ground zero suffered some damage to switch racks, transformers, and other equipment as a result not of blast but of secondary effects."[110]

This information was unsettling, first, because ATD physical vulnerability calculations were predicated upon the blast effects of atomic explosions rather than upon secondary effects such as incendiary damage;[111] the damage to the power substation would therefore not satisfy ATD damage criteria. Second, to assure the requisite blast destruction of steam generating plants and substations at twenty-four hundred feet from the point on the ground closest to the center of the atomic burst, exceptionally accurate bombing was needed. However, lack of prior American experience in targeting power plants ensured that such plants were relatively unfamiliar contemporary targets. "Our bombing program embraces both strange and familiar targets," LeMay, the SAC commander, wrote in April 1951. "Each strange target presents a unique problem. Evaluation exercises are frequently conducted against the most difficult types of radar targets in which case bombing errors are high and are not representative of errors to be expected under more average conditions."[112]

Strikes against unfamiliar targets required radar as a backup bombing aid, but the use of radar and other navigational and bombing aids in Europe toward the end of the Second World War rendered results about one-fifth as effective as those under visual conditions, according to one informed estimate.[113] On the other hand, visual sighting of hydroelectric power plants in particular was impeded because of their often remote locations and because they lacked easily identifiable characteristics such as smokestacks.[114] According to SAC, 42 of the 142 electric power RGZs contained in the target destruction annex, all of which "lie in or near small communities to which radar navigation would be difficult and where there are no other significant strategic targets," lacked any target material and therefore required visual reconnaissance before strikes could be mounted.[115]

Brodie, who met with LeMay in 1950 and 1951,[116] appears to have underscored for Vandenberg the possibility that assumed bombing accuracy—defined as the circular error probable (CEP), the distance around the target within which 50 percent of bombs aimed at it were expected to fall—might well have been too optimistic for some targets. "Dr. Brodie believes," observed Lowe, in reply to Brodie's critique of the target destruction annex, "that a target system which may be valid under an assumed CEP of 3,000 feet may be wholly invalid if the CEP is actually 5,000 feet or more. I concur fully. In fact it would possibly be invalid if the CEP were raised from 3,000 feet to 4,000 feet."[117] On 23 January 1951, one week after a target panel composed of ATD and SAC representatives decided to approve a three-thousand-foot CEP as a hypothesis guiding selection of target systems for a hypothetical air offensive against the Soviet Union beginning in July 1951, the target panel formally dropped electric power as a target system, "based entirely," according to Cabell, "on operational considerations energetically advanced by the Commanding General, Strategic Air Command."[118]

The ATD Physical Vulnerability Branch, composed of structural engineers, atomic physicists, mathematicians, statisticians, and ordnance experts, with overall responsibility for recommending "appropriate mean points of impact for strategic air attack,"[119] would have considered how assumed CEPs should affect the choice of bombing attack points (AP). For example, limitations in the CEPs might help explain the redrawing of the APs to favor electric power target objectives. "To show you how much they stressed electric power over Government Control," wrote Brodie later, "there was a power station about one mile south of the Kremlin, and the A.P. which had originally been put over the Kremlin had been shifted so that it was halfway between that and the power station."[120] But without SAC data about bombing accuracies against various targets, the air force deputy chief of staff for operations conceded to General LeMay in May 1951,

> We are liable to errors such as the selection of the electric power system which is being corrected only after strenuous efforts on your part and with some embarrassment to us. This particular difficulty is partially attributable to the fact that, without knowledge of SAC capabilities, the target people in this headquarters assumed values based upon their best estimates. A year's effort might have been saved if your data had been available at the outset. Having it now, may save us costly errors in the future.[121]

If the Physical Vulnerability Branch did not doubt that the assumed CEP, included as a hypothesis in the emergency war plan, would in fact be achieved against its specified targets, it may have been because, as Brodie discovered, the ATD and SAC were working with only the most limited interaction. "The only real use of the fund of knowledge at SAC," Brodie wrote to Vandenberg, "has been the contribution of a figure for CEP and SAC's concurrence with the general view that the attack should be concentrated in time."[122] Not surprising, therefore, was Brodie's indication that the ATD "does not have the confidence of the senior officers at SAC who in the event of war will be called upon to execute a plan based on ATD analysis."[123]

He also stressed the minimal participation of high-level general officers in the work of selecting targets. "I had criticized," Brodie recollected later about his evaluation of the target destruction annex, "the fact that the general officers who subsequently comprised the Air Council had met only one afternoon each year to determine the so-called 'hypotheses' for the Emergency War Plan and appended target list. This of course meant that they were not really involved."[124]

Much more difficult to understand, however, was Brodie's unfamiliarity with the work of the bulk of the ATD staff, comprising four hundred people, including the Physical Vulnerability Branch and the Target Research Branch, the latter charged with developing specific target systems to recommend for JCS approval in connection with war plans.[125] "At no time during his short tour," Lowe wrote in March 1951 in response to Brodie's evaluation of the target list,

> has Dr. Brodie been in touch with *any* of the officers who are directly concerned with the selection of targets and target systems. These officers and the civilian staffs with which they get the work done, are physically located in Temporary "U" Building. . . . I seriously doubt that Dr. Brodie knows, even to this day, that Temporary "U" Building is located at 12th and Constitution Avenue, N.W., in Washington, D.C.[126]

Brodie's failure to interact with the ATD staff would not have detracted from his contribution in critiquing target choices insofar as his purpose was to gain a broader view of targeting matters than that to which Lowe or Cabell or their staffs could ordinarily aspire. As Stansfield Turner pointed out, "When managers . . . became so absorbed in the details of current actions, they did not have time to concern themselves with the broader issues, such as the value of what they were doing or its ethics. In my experience a bigger staff does not help such a person step back to look at the big picture; instead, it gives him time to become mired in the details of directing his subordinates."[127]

This failure was nevertheless a disadvantage for Brodie. First, he may have been inclined to greatly overvalue the personal roles of Cabell and Lowe in the process of target selection. This would explain, for example, his statement that "I can find no enthusiasm for the [electric power] system outside the small group of analysts in ATD who recommended it to their seniors."[128] Second, Brodie's assessment that more bombs were required in more than half the cases to destroy electric power targets than the industrial targets corresponding to them was probably affected by his failure to make use of ATD expertise.[129] If, as seems likely, Brodie had taken his estimate from SAC targeting studies or from interviews with SAC officials, his failure to reconcile SAC and ATD data precluded precise comparison of attacks against electric power with those against industrial complexes. Widespread concerns about limited bombing capabilities would have made such a comparison timely.

The Dispute between SAC and the ATD

When he criticized Soviet electric power as a bombing target and advocated area bombing strikes against Soviet industrial complexes, Brodie projected himself into a major dispute between SAC and the ATD in which, he wrote to Vandenberg in 1951, "SAC desires to place primary emphasis on cities as such, while AFOIN [Air Force Office of Intelligence] (or ATD) favors going after vertical systems without regard to the urban or non-urban location of individual targets."[130]

The vertical approach to bombing, reflected in American attacks against Germany, entailed, according to ATD staff member Dan Dyer, that a designated target point, "should be placed directly over each of the installations which collectively constitute a recommended target category . . . regardless of whether a specific installation is located in isolation, in the center of a peat bog or whether it's located in and forms a very integral part of an industrial concentration or a target complex."[131] Attacks against the Soviet electric power system exemplified this type of targeting. As Brodie reported to Vandenberg, such attacks "must for the sake of comprehensiveness include many targets, often small ones, which are in the hearts of cities and surrounded by residential areas" and yet also targets "compris[ing] small structures or groups of structures surrounded by nothing in particular, that is, they may be surrounded by grasslands or by worker's [*sic*] houses."[132]

SAC planners, who "relie[d] on the experience with Japan,"[133] moved in a completely different direction, informing the JCS in April 1951 that "the attack on liquid fuels has been the highest priority target system in war plans for the past few years."[134] Those officials evidently found the Soviet petroleum target system especially attractive for the location of petroleum targets close to other economic targets, as is suggested by the SAC statement in April 1951 that

> at least in the first phases of a war against the Soviet Union, the attack should maximize the destructive power of a scarce weapon. Therefore it is recommended that targets selected be such that the total energy of the bomb will be effective, and whenever possible, selected so that an error in delivery would be compensated for by the destruction of other industry in the vicinity of the selected RGZ.[135]

Brodie recalled later that "cities as such were probably not targeted, though cities would most certainly have been hit (i.e., they contained either the electric power stations that Cabell-Lowe wanted or the industrial concentrations that LeMay seemed to want)."[136]

Rejection of electric power as a target and support for striking at industrial complexes were consistent with Brodie's long-standing interest in making distinctive use of the destructive potential of nuclear weapons. That potential would be smaller when those weapons were aimed at small targets, such as electric power facilities in remote areas. Indeed, the proportion of small targets slated for attack in this way would increase for any vertical target system the wider the coverage given to that system. "It is charcteristic of most 'vertical' systems," he wrote to Vandenberg, "that the more of each system you get the more vital becomes the remaining portion and yet the more absurd as targets for atomic bombs (because smaller) are the remaining installations within that system."[137] Arbitrary target objectives in relation to such targets as electric power could be logically disputed on the ground that an insufficient proportion of Soviet electric power facilities would be destroyed to paralyze the Soviet war economy, but there was no way to expand vertical bombing target coverage without detracting from the distinctive potential of nuclear weapons attack.

Second, targeting Soviet industrial complexes was essential to establishing Brodie's view that the advent of nuclear weapons simplified target selection relative to the experience of the Second World War. For example, when Brodie declared in 1952, in connection with errors in target selection made in that war, that "the problem of target selection . . . was a much more critical problem then than it is now, though it is still an important problem and it is more important now than I suspect it will be in the future,"[138] he seems to have had in mind the ease of destroying particular targets with nuclear weapons, a condition he thought applied much more strongly to area bombing than to vertical target bombing. Thus what Brodie termed "a great deal of confusion" in the Second World War "about the proper selection of aiming points within the target structures" would be ruled out in area attack but not in vertical targeting with nuclear weapons.[139] Such an argument was reinforced by the structure of the Soviet economy. "If you were to take the largest single Russian steel mill," Brodie declared in a May 1951 lecture, "you would find that it accomplished . . . a larger proportion of Soviet steel production than the largest single American steel mill. And I think that can be generalized throughout the economy so that in some respects the Soviet economy is more concentrated than the American — a good deal more so."[140]

An important limitation to area bombing and simplified target selection was that they applied only to what the air force referred to as "the traditional mission of strategic air power"[141] — namely, disruption of the vital elements of the Soviet war-making capacity. They would not apply, for example, to the use of atomic bombs to retard a Soviet invasion into Western Europe and Asia or to the blunting of the Soviet ability to attack the United States and its allies. Both of these missions were apparently specified in emergency war plan hypotheses by 1950, though targets had yet to be developed for them. For example, Brodie wrote much later that "none of the principals I encountered — Vandenberg, Cabell, LeMay, and others — seemed to have the slightest interest in any 'retardation' mission."[142] These same individuals would probably have had little interest in the blunting mission as long as the Soviet Union's ability to deliver an atomic strike against the United States was still very primitive and weak.

Brodie likewise concentrated at this time upon the targets that had already been recommended for the air campaign. "Certainly," he wrote in 1951 with reference to the blunting mission,

> no one is urging any delay whatsoever in going after enemy strategic air capabilities if we know how to reach them. Any accessible target directly connected with those immediate capabilities and promising a reasonable payoff should be attacked at once. But this is a specialized target system rather than a general one, and presumably will account for a minor portion of our indicated targets. What we are concerned with is the ordering of our general strategic bombing program *after* the topmost priorities are accounted for.[143]

Study of retardation and especially of blunting targets would have required Brodie to further refine his concept of nuclear bombing efficiency, a question that later became compelling with the rise of Soviet nuclear capabilities and growth in the American nuclear stockpile. Writing about the immediate needs of high officials at the ATD and SAC, Brodie's observations on area bombing and simplified target selection would become less useful as the other missions of the air offensive assumed greater prominence.

Critique of SAC Ideas

Although his view that bombing with nuclear weapons should use the full destructive potential of those weapons and simplify target selection inclined Brodie with SAC in its target selection dispute with the ATD, he also to some extent criticized SAC's outlook. For example, he argued that the Japanese bombing was not a satisfactory model for a contemporary air campaign, because "the Japanese war-essential industries were already at a low ebb of activity before our strategic bombing ever began, due to the almost complete severance of maritime communications," and that because of the "destruction of her sea and air power, Japan had become completely impotent to wage offensive war and was rapidly declining in ability to erect an effective defense."[144]

By contrast, the American emergency war plan specified by 1950 that Soviet troops would reach the Pyrenees forty days after the start of hostilities, suggesting to Brodie that some atomic bombs should be kept in reserve to target those troops. He could not understand, he recalled later, "why, if the Red Army was going to be at the Pyrenees at D + 40, no nuc bombs were kept in reserve for targets outside the S.U. or Romania."[145] But the idea of a reserve was bedeviled by LeMay's demand that the air campaign had to be launched as soon as possible and in concentrated fashion upon the outbreak of war. "LeMay had no use for any reserve," Brodie recalled, "which in one of my three conversations with him he called a 'violation of the principles of war,' meaning, I suppose, a violation of the principles of concentration. I remember pressing him on this point, asking him why we had to be in such a hurry to deliver ours when the S.U. had virtually none."[146]

Contemporary SAC plans for war with the Soviet Union provided for prompt bombing attacks, partly because of what Brodie referred to in 1951 as "grave risk of diminution or elimination of Strategic Air Command capabilities, through losses of our bases (enemy attack or allied defection), the destruction of our aircraft on the ground, or both,"[147] and partly because other types of American military strength were weak. "If war breaks out in the near future," Brodie declared in 1951, "the bald, inescapable fact, it seems to me, is that we must win primarily through our strategic bombing, and that for the simple reason that we have almost no other kind of genuinely offensive capabilities. We have nothing else."[148]

Interest in speedy bombing operations had earlier disposed LeMay toward attacking Japanese industrial concentrations rather than vertical targets. In that case, Hansell wrote,

> there was an intense concern with 'time,' caused by the arbitrary selection of a November invasion date. But there really should have been no limitation on strategic operations dictated by shortage of time. Time was working to our advantage. The combination of sea blockade, aerial mining, and strategic bombing was bringing Japan nearer to inevitable disaster with every day that passed. . . . It seems to me, in retrospect, that not only were the atomic bombs and invasion unnecessary, but the urban incendiary attacks, which were more devastating by far than the two atomic attacks, could almost certainly have been avoided or their quantity greatly reduced if primary reliance upon selective bombing had been pursued, even if the end of the war were slightly postponed.[149]

The linkage between speedy bombing operations and the choice of area bombing, visible during the Second World War, might also prevail in contemporary nuclear bombing operations, when LeMay's known preference for area bombing would be bolstered by his known interest in implementing bombing quickly. Conversely, relaxing the concern with speed in contemporary bombing would, as in the Second World War, strengthen the case for vertical bombing against such targets as electric power by permitting the filling of intelligence gaps about problematic targets. To be sure, it was by no means clear that the additional time afforded would assure selection of vertical targets; doubts might still persist, for example, on whether atomic strikes would be sufficiently accurate to destroy such targets, and LeMay as bomber commander was likely to advocate area bombing for other reasons as well. But lengthening the time between war outbreak and the implementation of bombing strikes would at least make the relative merits of area and vertical bombing more uncertain.

Once the case for area bombing was weakened by delaying the nuclear bombing campaign, Brodie's criticism of speed in bombing operations came to conflict with his criticism of electric power as a target, whatever the independent validity of each of those points. His failure to address this tension may have been associated with his failure to examine the quality of American intelligence about Soviet targets, an omission hampering determination of the comparative feasibility or efficiency of campaigns directed at a vertical target such as electric power and at industrial concentrations. For example, though Brodie cited for Vandenberg a 1950 report produced on contract to the ATD that stressed shortcomings in intelligence on electric power facilities in the Soviet Union, he found "no basis for evaluating the above estimate and therefore do not identify myself with it, especially as to the figures cited."[150]

Lowe disputed the quality of this report, asserting in response to Brodie that "though the Report was 'based on access to all relevant United States intelligence sources,' it did not reflect that all these sources had been used, and therefore the report itself is not considered as reliable in the Air Targets Division."[151] The ATD's use of "all relevant sources" was presumably what the JCS had in mind when it created the ATD in 1947, as Lowe recalled, "to avoid a repetition of what happened in World War II; namely, that insofar as the war in Europe was concerned, we had to rely 100 percent for our target intelligence on a foreign power and, insofar as the war in Asia was concerned, there had to elapse two or three years before we had anything like sufficient operational target intelligence to lay on a strategic air campaign."[152] Because Brodie does not seem to have carefully considered the quality of the ATD intelligence about Soviet bombing targets, he may have neglected the difference that improved intelligence could make in the choice of targets.

Pressing for Changes in Target Selection Procedure

Brodie not only exposed for Vandenberg shortcomings in the ATD selection of targets but also sought Vandenberg's support to correct them. "If any change is to be made either in the existing plan or existing procedure," he wrote to a correspondent in February 1951,

> it can legally be made only by the J.C.S. And only the Chief can bring the issue up directly with the J.C.S. That simply underlines the necessity of working directly with the Chief, and with him alone, so long as there appears to be any hope at all in his doing something. None of the secretaries can act except through bringing pressure in the first instance upon him.
> Nor do I feel that the hope of his doing something substantial is at all dim.[153]

This attitude undoubtedly reflected the nature of Brodie's relationship to Vandenberg, in which, serving as a special assistant, he seems to have had broad authority to read and comment critically on all targeting proposals crossing the chief of staff's desk.[154] The respect and trust of Vandenberg, who was not likely to engage Brodie without being aware of what his special assistant sought to do and how he sought to do it, was essential to Brodie's effectiveness as a critic of the air staff.[155]

The intensity of Brodie's questioning of the intellectual qualifications of Cabell and Lowe and his criticism of their targeting decisions (notably their choice of Soviet electric power as a primary American bombing target) added to his dependence upon the chief of staff. For example, he wrote much later of his work for Vandenberg that "the experience was certainly a shocking one with respect to what I observed as sheer frivolousness and stupidity with respect to the treatment of the No. 1 strategic problem confronting the U.S. at the time. It also made me skeptical of the net utility of the intense secrecy which served as a shield for the perpetration of such blunders."[156]

If the ATD was indeed in the state that he described, the agency was very unlikely to reform itself. "We are making errors," he declared in his May 1951 lecture to the Air War College,

> I feel quite strongly, some resulting from a mis-interpretation of World War II experience. Others from much too rigid and liberal an observance of World War II experience without making sufficient allowance for change in the character of the enemy and in changes in circumstances and weapons. Above all, it seems to me we are still failing

to grasp the basic complexity of the problem, and are subjecting the pursuit of the answers to an excessively bureaucratic procedure which for my money guarantees only the wrong answers.[157]

In his reference to "an excessively bureaucratic procedure," Brodie may have had in mind how complacence and routine inhibit change. Frequent scrutiny and criticism of existing outlooks and procedures by those who were aware of the imperfections of bureaucracy (such as Brodie) was a good antidote to complacence and routine.

The changes in the target selection procedure proposed by Brodie would have added to the authority of the chief of staff and provided this scrutiny and criticism. For example, Brodie proposed that a JCS decision then in effect, stating that targeting recommendations were to be transmitted directly to the JCS through established JCS machinery—that is, through the ATD—should be changed back to an earlier procedure by which target recommendations were made to the air force chief of staff, who would then transmit them to the JCS.[158] Advocating the personal involvement of the chief of staff in selecting targets and target systems for the air campaign, Brodie adapted toward this end a proposal already made by the secretary of the air force and approved by General Vandenberg—namely, that a panel of four or five highly qualified people be appointed to review on a full-time basis for three or four months the selection of targets and target systems.[159] Brodie recommended that this panel be attached directly to Vandenberg rather than to the director of intelligence, who headed the ATD.[160] Brodie hoped that he would serve on this panel and have a voice in appointments to it.[161]

Whatever the quality of the ATD's work, Brodie's recommendation that a panel of consultants to review targeting decisions be attached directly to Vandenberg was supported by the logic that, as Lowe noted, "the more important a thing is the higher it should be in the echelons of the Air Staff."[162] On the other hand, the intricacy of the ATD organization, the importance of which may have escaped Brodie because of his failure to interact with personnel at the main ATD working location, argued to the contrary. "In a very large organization such as the Air Force," Lowe wrote in evaluating Brodie's recommendation, "it is necessary to organize the efforts of many people, to delegate responsibility where it belongs in the chain of command, and to get the work done within the framework of the organization. Simply because the initial recommendations concerning the selection of target systems is important is no valid reason for ignoring the organization."[163]

When Cabell, whose authority would have been sharply diminished by Vandenberg's acceptance of Brodie's recommendation, protested that it should not be accepted, it may be presumed that he stressed with Vandenberg the importance of working through existing organizational channels. Moreover, as Brodie later pointed out, Cabell was also highly trusted by Vandenberg. "Cabell, who headed Intelligence," he wrote in 1977, "had Vandenberg's ear and confidence, and it was he who was preparing the letters to LeMay for Van. to sign—letters telling LeMay he'd better shape up."[164] It was hardly surprising, therefore, that in such a dispute Cabell would prevail. Brodie wrote in May 1951, about two months after making his views about the review panel known to Vandenberg,

> I saw the Chief last Friday, and while he was as gracious as could be, it was abundantly clear that a certain Major General [notation here in margin in pencil: "Cabell"] had won his fight. In my opinion composition of the group will be determined by him and not by the Secretary and the Chief of Staff. [Asterisk here with footnote at bottom of letter: "I will not be on it."] However, I am not as saddened as you might think.[165]

Conclusions

As did his counterpart work on morale, Brodie's analysis of economic targets systematically critiqued prevailing views on target selection held at the highest levels of the ATD, the chief military planning unit in targeting matters. Particularly in its observations about the choice of electric power as the primary nuclear bombing target, it contained the trenchancy and skepticism for which Brodie was later to become well known. A parallel critique of electric power as a bombing target had been mounted by the SAC commander LeMay during the period of Brodie's work for Vandenberg and before Brodie had written his own report on electric power for the chief of staff. It was LeMay and not Brodie who ultimately brought about a change in targets whereby the electric power system was dropped. But whereas LeMay's criticism appears to have been largely along operational lines, Brodie challenged the choice of electric power on a logical basis, raising the issue of coping with a Soviet invasion of Western Europe, stressing the inability of attacks against war production to adequately cope with such an invasion, and generally arguing for more high-level scrutiny of the ATD's work.

Vandenberg's desire and need for scrutiny of a unit operating within his own headquarters probably illustrated for Brodie the tendency within large organizations for nominally responsible persons to be essentially out of touch with detailed matters of utmost importance. Vandenberg needed but evidently lacked the means to challenge proposals emanating from his own staff,[166] and he would have lacked time and competence to delve into targeting questions, especially in 1950 when his immediate attention was required to coordinate air force participation in the war in Korea and the major buildup of American forces in Europe. At the same time, the perceived danger of war with the Soviet Union associated with hostilities in Korea added to the urgency of considering the adequacy of war plans. These ordinary and extraordinary considerations explain Vandenberg's invitation to Brodie, a strategist committed to strategic bombing but who was not identified with the air force establishment,[167] to review the list of targets proposed by the ATD to be appended to the emergency war plan of 1951, one of the first instances—if not the first—in which an American emergency war plan received examination outside the military establishment.

Unlike Brodie's analysis of morale as a bombing target, which argued importantly for a specific strategy of coupling nuclear bombing with psychological warfare, his work on economic targets was entirely cautionary, acquiescing in attacks against industrial concentrations only as a means to work primarily upon enemy morale. Brodie's ideas about economic targets were supported by references to the compensating effect of national will in overcoming losses in war production, and it appears that those ideas were generally subordinated to his interest in morale as a bombing target. In the broader effects upon his future work, on the other hand, Brodie's analysis of economic targets was perhaps more significant than was his work on morale, because his reaction to what appalled him at the ATD seems to have been directly responsible for his skepticism about strategic bombing.

Thus prior to his work for Vandenberg, in March 1950, he strongly defended bombing as a "way of war" against critics such as John Slessor, who opposed the area attacks of the Second World War and whom Brodie presumed to be challenging bombing in general.[168] However, after completing his work for Vandenberg, Brodie was much more inclined to admit, for purposes of argument, radical critiques of the earlier bombing against Germany. "One of my friends," he told an Air War College audience in 1951,

> is rather a distinguished economist and he served on the Strategic Bombing Survey and . . . has no axe to grind . . . has said to me that he is convinced that the experience of World War II in Germany provides no proof whatsoever that the strategic bombing campaign paid off at all. Now, I don't agree with that. . . . What he means is it couldn't be proved in a court of law. What he means also is that it is not the kind of evidence which a scientist normally accepts as utterly convincing. . . . But I want to point out . . . his opinion simply to say that an unbiased, dispassionate observer can reach such conclusions. I may not agree with it but he can reach it, and it's a conclusion which has to be in a measure respected.[169]

Brodie's willingness to entertain the counterargument that strategic bombing did not pay off may have emanated from newer awareness, supported by sensitive information to which he previously did not have access, that contemporary nuclear bombing capabilities had been for some years inadequate. "Without being able," he wrote in 1953,

> to cite statistics tracing the American nuclear stockpile growth one cannot be dogmatic, but it seems clear to me that whatever the situation is today, it was not possible prior to the end of 1949 for the United States to destroy Soviet military power by strategic bombing attack. . . . [I]f we had initiated a war at that time we would have done little more than bruise the Soviet Union—expending the whole of our then existing atomic stockpile in the process—and they would have taken all of Europe.[170]

Doubts about strategic bombing results would also have been strengthened by his judgment in 1950 and 1951 that errors were being made in the selection of contemporary targets. Such doubts conflicted with his earlier assessment that American nuclear bombing capabilities would probably be adequate at the outset of war to be decisive.[171]

Brodie's newfound skepticism about strategic bombing affected his use of history. Prior to his critique of the emergency war plan target list, his treatment of attacks against economic targets in the Second World War emphasized only the potential of strategically bombing those targets and how faulty selection of targets impeded the use of that potential. For example, he claimed that the bombing of the German war economy, brought about by vertical targeting, was eventually decisive in that it destroyed Germany's ability to fight on the ground but should ideally have done so sooner. Following his critique for Vandenberg, Brodie continued to maintain that bombing in the Second World War had "demonstrated its potentiality to the future," but his primary thrust when dealing with economic targets was that not even atomic bombs could redress the limitations of this earlier bombing. For example, he suggested that combat degradation witnessed in the Second World War remained important in an atomic campaign and that therefore it should be anticipated that prewar estimates of the effect of bombs against specific targets would be overly optimistic. And he criticized the vertical targeting philosophy on the ground that "destroying [any] particular trick target system . . . doesn't make a damn bit of difference whether the Russians take over all of Western Europe."[172]

These shifts were consistent with Brodie's tendency to use history to serve his immediate analytical needs and to caution against applying axioms from one set of historical circumstances to another. Brodie's dismissal of the qualifications of Cabell and Lowe seemed to be above all associated with their refusal to reconsider their uncritical acceptance of Speer's lessons when making recommendations about the electric power targets. And because Brodie played down historical axioms, he found no need, unlike Hansell or the Alexander Committee later on, to examine the importance of electric power in the war economies of Germany, Japan, or the Soviet Union or to discover how an attacker might capitalize on this condition.[173] But though Brodie's recommended use of atomic bombs for psychological purposes was intuitively suggestive since nuclear attacks against urban areas could be expected to have much larger terror effects than attacks with conventional weapons, his critique of using those bombs against electric power facilities seemed counterintuitive, because he was arguing that atomic weapons were *less* efficient against those facilities than their conventional counterparts.

The combination of severe criticism of Cabell, Lowe, and ATD priorities generally and the apparently counterintuitive argument showed the importance Brodie attached to logical criticism and to defending strategic preferences. In this particular instance, they may have caused Brodie to question his own previously unshakable support of strategic bombing and to find better defenses for that view. If so, he may have criticized the ATD study he examined all the more sharply insofar as it exposed but did not permit him to vindicate that earlier view.

However dogmatic were Cabell and Lowe, logical selection of bombing targets could not in practice escape hypotheses set by the JCS to take account of limited bombing capabilities, such as the hypothesis dictating the selection of a target permitting an integrated bombing program in the first ninety-day phase of bombing operations. These were supplemented by other hypotheses derived from intelligence about the Soviet war economy. "Targeting," Dan Dyer of the ATD declared in December 1951,

> must necessarily be done within a framework of hypotheses concerning among other things the nature, the magnitude and the use pattern of all components of war potential. Change these conditions and you change the targets for there's no such thing as a target *pace*, no such thing as a target in an economic vacuum, no such thing as a target without knowing what your hypotheses are. . . . [U]nder different conditions, different target values must be assigned the same plant. The value assigned always depends upon the hypotheses under which you are building your air targeting plan.[174]

We have seen that Brodie rejected the hypothesis dictating an integrated bombing program, because it mandated a comprehensive nuclear attack instead of the coercive attacks he strongly preferred. But because he does not seem to have evaluated the supporting studies of the ATD and yet was so impressed with scarcity in the supply of nuclear bombs, he could be expected to underestimate the contribution that intelligence about the Soviet Union made to decisions about target selection for a nuclear bombing campaign. Neglecting the quality of American intelligence dealing with the Soviet war economy and sidestepping complexities in intelligence, he would recommend choosing targets for which target information was most plentiful, especially target systems struck in the past, to prevent squandering a small atomic stockpile and to minimize the dangers of acting on faulty intelligence. Such an approach might well seem reasonable to a strategist such as Brodie, who was determined to make a small nuclear stockpile count decisively in a Soviet-American war, who would have been conscious of the difficulties of gaining intelligence about a closed society such as the Soviet Union, and who in any event had only a relatively short time to conduct a preliminary analysis of his problem.

This approach was limited in certain respects. First, it dictated a very conservative approach to target selection, in which targeting missions, bombing mode, and type of targets were all a legacy of the experience of the Second World War. "We have yet to develop," Brodie asserted in April 1952, "a target philosophy suited to the Atomic Age. The concepts most often applied are those developed under World War II conditions with HE [heavy explosives]. I am referring to the concern with such categories as cushion depth, etc."[175] Second, the analysis was in some ways too wedded to existing bombing procedures. For example, Brodie's case against electric power was bolstered by the hypothesis established in the 1951 emergency war plan that the first phase of the bombing campaign against the Soviet Union should consist only of atomic strikes. Had the JCS established instead that the first ninety-day phase of bombing included atomic *and* conventional bomb attacks, the case for striking at electric power would have been strengthened.[176] Finally, when not conforming to prescribed routines, the analysis could at times be too simplified, as is suggested by Brodie's contention that the target systems slated for attack could be changed in a week and by his omission of any conditions apart from the narrowness of Cabell and Lowe that would hinder the mating of target selection with strategy.

Brodie's initial analysis of economic targets must be understood in terms of the immediate needs of Vandenberg in 1951 rather than for the long term. As American intelligence about the Soviet Union improved, as the strategic benefits of area bombing with atomic weapons were widely perceived to wane, and as the retardation and blunting missions of the atomic attack grew in importance, analysis of economic targets would not be as easily mated to strategic considerations as it was in Brodie's report to Vandenberg in 1951. On the other hand, his analysis provided a model of how a critical bent could be applied to investigate war plans and to guide such planning. Perhaps the most important long-term consequence of Brodie's analysis of economic targets was that Cabell's successor as director of the Air Force Office of Intelligence, Lt. Gen. John A. Samford, was sufficiently impressed to call upon Brodie to write a book about contemporary strategy to assist war planning. The result of this exercise was the much-acclaimed *Strategy in the Missile Age*.[177]

The immediate follow-up to Brodie's work on economic targets was limited most by that work's trenchancy and candidness, qualities that paradoxically gave it its greatest intellectual strength. Brodie may have had reason to believe that Vandenberg valued those qualities, but they were undoubtedly linked with the sharply critical tone of Brodie's work, which made it inevitable that he would come to be perceived very negatively by Cabell, Lowe, and their associates and that these people would have wished to rebut Brodie's criticism in the strongest possible terms. The tragedy of this portion of Brodie's work may have been that in applying superior intellectual tests to evaluate the quality of the ATD's performance, Brodie probably made himself much less acceptable as a critic.

5 · The H-Bomb: Strategic Air Warfare

In the summer of 1951, American scientists achieved a technological breakthrough on the so-called fusion, or "hydrogen," bomb, which when deliverable would drastically change the character of nuclear war. Perhaps the earliest sustained conceptual study of what this breakthrough implied was carried out by late 1951 at the RAND Corporation in Santa Monica, California.[1] Brodie, who began full-time association with RAND in the summer of 1951, participated in this work. In this chapter, I consider his views on the effect of thermonuclear weapons on strategic air warfare; in the next, I study his application of such weapons to European theater warfare.

Published reports now indicate that fusion weapons consisted at first of an array, or "family," of weapons, but Brodie concentrated entirely on the largest of these, evidently to stress the discontinuity between the two major generations of nuclear weaponry.[2] Brodie's point of departure was that fusion weapons vastly increased the explosive yield of bomb burst relative to older fission devices—a yield one thousand times greater, for example, as between the twenty-megaton yield of the "standard" fusion bomb and the twenty-kiloton yield of the "standard" fission bomb.

Brodie's assumption that H-bombs were revolutionary compared with A-bombs later became widely accepted, both in the unclassified literature and in military circles. Nevertheless, for weapons designers, H-bombs represented only a marginal increase in explosive power over what A-bombs could potentially accomplish. Stanislaw M. Ulam, a key participant in the latest fusion bomb breakthrough, later stated that the results of fusion bombs

> did not seem so qualitatively different from those possible with existing fission bombs. After the war it was clear that A-bombs of enormous size could be made. The thermonuclear schemes were neither very original nor exceptional. Sooner or later the Russians or others would investigate and build them. The political implications were unclear despite the hullabaloo and exaggerations on both sides. That single bombs were able to destroy the largest cities could render all-out wars less probable than they were with the already existing A-bombs and their horrible destructive power.[3]

The consequences of fusion bombs might well have seemed much greater to those sensitive to the political effects of weapons use (such as Brodie) than to people with largely theoretical and abstract interests (such as Ulam). Much of Brodie's prior work had argued persuasively that the advent of new weapons did indeed have important consequences for international politics and that military technology was always changing in often insufficiently understood ways. This was as true of his *retrospective* analyses of the implications of newer weapons, especially in his study *Sea Power in the Machine Age* completed before the nuclear era,[4] as of his *prospective* analyses of those implications in his studies of nuclear weaponry. But the latter were bounded by his tendency, in his pioneering analyses of fission and fusion weapons, to extrapolate use of only standard weapon types. Because of this tendency, Brodie exaggerated the difference between standard fission and standard fusion weapons and failed to give great weight to the profusion of weapon types in each category.

Aware that many kinds of bombs existed, Brodie was surely competent to study the use of any bomb or any collection of bombs that he wished. He may have limited himself to the standard types for purposes of simplification or because it did not seem to him to matter much strategically or politically whether the explosive potential of fusion or fission weapons was more or less than he assumed. But we will see that many of Brodie's conclusions on the subject of fusion weapons followed directly from the enormous yield of those weapons. And other conclusions followed from his exaggeration of the difference between fusion and fission bombs.

It should also be noted that when Brodie considered strategic and political uses for weapons that had not been fully developed — or, in the case of fusion weapons, had not been developed at all — his major contribution did not extend to extrapolating future trends in weapons design. This was understandable, for he was a political scientist and not professionally competent in theoretical or applied modes of designing weapons. He needed to know something about weapons design (his book *From Crossbow to H-Bomb* suggests he knew a great deal about this subject for a nondesigner[5]) and to anticipate shifts in design whenever they bore critically on his work. However, for questions of weapons design, he was likely to consult with those who had major competence in them (for example, Edward Teller, long and closely associated with the thermonuclear bomb program).

Perhaps also because of his relative lack of competence in designing weapons and their antidotes, Brodie characteristically seemed to reach conclusions about strategic weapons that were rather abstracted from and insensitive to changes in weapons technology, *apart from* being explicitly associated with the fission and later the fusion devices that he strongly highlighted. His preoccupation with fission and fusion hardly did justice to the scale of technological progress in weaponry, but Brodie — who was unquestionably impressed by the rapid pace of this progress[6] — took account of it only by seeming in effect to shortchange it, pinning concepts of stability and deterrence on something other than continuing shifts in weapons design. Although he wrote and spoke at length about the "revolution" in nuclear weapons and about the degradation and even obsolescence of older military concepts in the face of it, Brodie did not lead this revolution. He did, however, strain his considerable intellect and imagination to the utmost to comprehend it and to prescribe what to do about it.

As for the strategic and political intricacies of the weapons in which Brodie was most interested, he did not merely master these intricacies for himself but also interpreted (and inevitably simplified) them for others. In seeking and discharging this task, which obviously could not await his expertise on weapons design, Brodie would readily have agreed with Ulam's justification for working on fusion weapons — that is, "It was safer to keep these matters in the hands of scientists and people who are accustomed to objective judgments rather than in those of demagogues or jingoists, or even well-meaning but technically uninformed politicians."[7]

The Novelty of Fusion Weapons

Having accepted the idea that H-bombs were, above all, weapons of enormous explosive power, Brodie concluded that supplementing A-bomb attacks with H-bombs greatly increased the expectation of destroying strategic targets and therefore "the *certainty* of universal destruction."[8] With the new capability, there was no longer any question of optimistic target selection. Brodie, referring to the new weapon, wrote that the "CEP no longer matters — that is, up to two miles it no longer matters. If your CEP is two or three times what the present official estimation of it is, we still get the targets. Physical vulnerability of the target selected no longer matters — at least, not very much. Even the combination of these, physical vulnerabilities and CEP, matter astonishingly little."[9]

Prior to the advent of fusion weapons, much of Brodie's criticism of the hypotheses behind the emergency war plan target list had focused on planners' stubborn adherence to historical experience and their unwillingness to recognize that conduct in the Second World War suitable to defeat Germany and Japan needed to be reexamined in light of more recent strategic developments. Still, the earlier experience could inform target selection even as gravity bombs were replaced for strategic purposes by fission bombs. In contrast, the advent of fusion weapons removed for Brodie any relation between new target selection needs and the Second World War experience. "Ties with the past," he wrote in 1955, "tenuous enough at best, were immediately threatened by the appearance of the modern type of thermonuclear bomb. Among the questions that thereupon became obsolete were most of those concerning the selection of strategic targets."[10]

Adjustments also had to be made to the dramatic increase in operational efficiency in delivering nuclear attack with H-bombs, particularly by permitting smaller force requirements for a strategic bombing campaign than in the past.[11] The argument that fusion bombs permitted smaller nuclear forces paralleled what Brodie had earlier written about fission bombs and was in two parts. First, he asserted that air defenses faced much more difficult requirements to interfere with H-bomb campaigns than they did to impede bombers carrying fission weapons. Previously, the requirement of larger numbers of bombs on target to gain decisive results allowed for "a meaningful air defense, even if not a satisfactory one," but with fusion weapons only a relatively small number needed to be exploded to cause unacceptable destruction.[12] Evidently for this reason Brodie was skeptical about a suggestion from air force secretary Thomas Finletter that (in Brodie's words) "we super the insuperable—that is, make a fighter defense system or some other kind of defense system which really works, and in order for it really to work it would have to extract really high attrition rates, something on the order of 95 per cent or above."[13]

In this skepticism, and in associating successful air defense with very high attrition rates, Brodie had in mind the defense of cities against nuclear retaliation. Inasmuch as he had denied that cities could be successfully defended against fission attack, he not surprisingly maintained the point even more vigorously in discussions about fusion bomb attack.[14] And he linked the attrition problem, from the point of view of the attacker, to the expense of an air campaign and thereby to the same operational attractiveness of fusion weapons that existed for fission ones. This was

a bias, at least for long-range operations, in favor of larger-yield bombs, including perhaps the H-bomb itself. One should rather say it implements a bias already strongly urged by other military considerations which have to do with dependence on intelligence, on bombing accuracy, on the need for re-attack, and on the standard military desire to accomplish decisive results as quickly as possible.[15]

He did not explain how the latter incentives related to the added efficiency of striking at cities provided by H-bombs.

Second, and related to the first argument, Brodie maintained that more potent bombs considerably eased the effects of limited bomb-delivery vehicles that had been acute as fission bomb supplies rapidly grew. "As we leave the era of A-bomb scarcity," Brodie wrote to a correspondent in 1953, "it becomes inevitable that the expensive, the scarce, and therefore the critical item in any strategic bombing campaign is not the weapons stockpile but rather the stockpile of long-range bombers."[16] The degree of bomber scarcity depended to a significant degree on the estimated attrition problem, about which there were considerable differences between Brodie and air force planners,[17] and on the relative importance of preserving bombers (on one hand) and modifying Soviet behavior (on the other).

Impressed by the new operational efficiencies permitted by the H-bomb, Brodie now feared that strategic air war would be waged too efficiently rather than not efficiently enough. Fusion weapons brought, in his estimation,

an efficiency of destruction which is perhaps excessive from the viewpoint of our national objectives. The question tends to be not whether we will be able to carry out our strategic bombing mission, but rather whether we will not carry it out too well, too completely, and too quickly. The term "over-kill" can have political connotations as well as military ones. It may become as important to know what not to hit, as what to hit.[18]

Taking the newfound efficiency of nuclear weapons delivery with fusion weapons into account, it could be argued that the major difficulty with any emergency war plan was no longer deficiencies in the logic of the plan's hypotheses but rather the limitations of even the best logic. Logic could, of course, still be poor, but implementation of the best logic in war planning had become infinitely more difficult, whatever the motives or objectives of nuclear belligerents, as fusion weapons seemed to undermine traditional and useful distinctions between different targets. "Since a thermonuclear bomb," Brodie wrote in a 1955 article entitled "Strategy Hits a Dead End,"

> could not be used on an industrial concentration in or near a city without destroying that city—and since one such bomb will effectively eliminate all the industry associated with that city—there is not much point in asking which industries should be hit or in what order. Whether we like or not, the thermonuclear bomb used strategically is a city-buster.
>
> The same is of course true if we hit air fields near cities. We cannot talk about strategies being aimed against the enemy air force as distinct from the enemy economy or population, unless we actually intend taking deliberate measures to refrain from hitting cities. It cannot matter greatly whether the destruction of cities is a by-product of the destruction of air fields or vice versa.[19]

Brodie had likewise viewed fission weapons as efficient destroyers of cities.[20] The difference with the newer weapons was that it was not necessary to target H-bombs against cities to make them city busters; those bombs could be expected to have excellent "bonus" effect against cities even when detonated accurately elsewhere, and we have seen that many individuals inside the air force wished to capitalize on such an effect. Moreover, accuracy of bomb delivery had greatly improved since the advent of the first atomic bombs, with the result that planners could now take far greater liberties in choosing targets for laying on large nuclear explosions. Still, though planners were no longer subject to operational limitations requiring them to prepare nuclear strikes against urban targets, they were now, ironically, more likely to destroy urban areas if they elected to use fusion bombs. In general, operational and strategic considerations had moved in conflicting directions. Opportunities open to planners—in the past, consisting chiefly of incentives to develop a strategic logic to terminate war more rapidly—were now largely of an operational kind, whereas constraint upon planners, previously largely operational, had become overwhelmingly strategic.

The Problem of Two-Sided Nuclear War

The demonstrated effects of H-bombs strongly argued for restraint in and even abstention from employment of such weapons. But another major argument for restraint in fusion weapons employment was the likelihood of reciprocal use of atomic bombs in a Soviet-American war, a matter Brodie had not considered in his work for Vandenberg. "From now on," Brodie declared in April 1952, "any atomic war is going to be a two-way affair."[21] The H-bomb had still not been openly tested, but Brodie wished to draw attention to the rising stockpiles of fission bombs on both sides and to argue that the utility of the H-bomb could not be considered apart from those weapons. "Whether or not we will beat the Russians to the draw in producing the first H-bomb," he wrote in a paper that grew out of his March 1952 briefings,

> neither we nor they will have anything like the monopoly of destructive power which this nation enjoyed in the years 1948–50, when we had a substantial number of fission bombs and they had either none at all or, at best, a very few test models. Whatever the date at which the pilot model of a deliverable H-bomb appears, it will come at a time when we have a large stockpile of very powerful fission bombs and when they also have a very substantial stockpile of such weapons.[22]

In this same paper, Brodie asked "the question which we have been delaying perhaps too long: How does the threat or actuality of atomic weapons, including H-bombs, being used against *us* affect our entire conduct of the war?"[23]

When he dealt with the strategic implications of H-bombs, and more particularly with the problem of two-sided nuclear war, Brodie emphasized that he was referring to a period of from five to ten years in the future, by which time extreme delicacy would be required upon the outbreak of nuclear war to prevent the fighting from becoming suicidal for both sides.[24] He stressed the ease with which the United States and the Soviet Union, using H-bomb equivalents, could destroy each other. "In the end," he declared in 1952, referring to an H-bomb campaign, "it is numbers of exposed targets rather than numbers of weapons available which becomes [*sic*] the determinant of losses."[25] With reference to American bombing of the Soviet Union,

> some 55 bombs of the kind I have indicated [for example, equivalent to 20 megatons of explosive yield] could eliminate the 50 largest Russian cities, including the practically complete destruction of most of the industry gathered in those 50 largest cities. And after you had done that much destruction, everything else would be quite marginal, in fact useless. Eliminating the 50 largest Russian cities would mean destroying upwards of 35 million people (dead, rather than casualties), assuming that they were in the World War II type of shelters. Notice that this business would literally be done overnight, so that if you didn't want them to escape they probably could not escape.[26]

Brodie was aware of "saturation" levels of the bombing of Soviet cities and industries and took into account fallout effects from bombing operations.[27] He concluded that "the number of targets that it is necessary to destroy is too small, the means of destroying them far too copious," a point he claimed to be able to make using "elementary arithmetic," whatever the "*unpredictability* of the limits of disaster."[28] The same observations could be made from the Soviet side. "I may feel free to use with you a term like 'national suicide,'" Brodie wrote to a correspondent in 1954,

> but with a Congressman I would talk in terms of "X" number of estimated casualties and fatalities and "Y" percentage loss of our productive capacity. For example: It has been estimated that the destruction of our 50 largest cities—which with H-bombs could

be very quickly and easily accomplished—might result in something between 10 million and 30 million *fatalities* and the loss of something like 70 per cent of our productive capacity (better check figures). This, of course, does not represent the limit of the conceivable injury; the next 50 or 100 cities might also go. Are our plans so devised that we could go on fighting after such losses?[29]

Answering this question in the negative, Brodie insisted on acknowledging Soviet damage capability against the United States and on adjusting American war plans accordingly. "Explicitly we accord the Soviets a nuclear capability," he wrote in 1954. "But when it comes right down to drawing the relevant conclusions, it is always we who do the hitting and they who do the suffering."[30] In Brodie's view, the Joint Chiefs, committed since 1951 to the idea that only the prospect of using total war capabilities at the outset of hostilities could deter major Soviet attack, denied that atomic war needed to be reciprocal. "The Joint Chiefs are obviously still thinking of the SAC-nuclear capability in U.S. monopoly terms," he wrote in 1954. "I can think of no greater service the Congress could do than to provoke through the right kinds of questions basic thinking about two-way rather than merely one-way nuclear capabilities."[31]

In the same passage, Brodie indicated he had in mind strategic defenses against Soviet attack rather than an American preemptive strike. The air force, to the contrary, disparaged reliance upon defenses.

> It is obvious . . . that the Air Force does not believe in air defense as a means of stopping the enemy SAC—certainly not when he is carrying nuclear weapons. There is also a strong presumption that it does not want to believe in it, at least not to the extent of spending a lot of money on it. It does *want* to believe in the offensive use of our SAC as a primary means of defending our cities; but *can* it believe in it? I suspect that only the most extreme SACians really can and do believe in it. The rest must wonder whether we can have the necessary initiative, the necessary surprise (which is distinct from initiative) and the necessary intelligence. Above all, with what confidence can we expect to have enough of all three (with whatever else is required) to act as though we really expected to be able to protect our cities through offensive military means.[32]

These defenses were primarily to ensure that some bombers would remain intact after a Soviet attack and so be able to retaliate. Brodie found the objective of protecting retaliatory forces, only then beginning to receive extended study at RAND, to be "unquestionably the greatest single military requirement for security in the atomic age, whether in war or peace."[33]

Brodie evidently believed it was easier to protect retaliatory forces and deter attack in peace than in war, for he counted on the very existence of nuclear weapons to make an attacker pause. "Believe me," he declared in April 1952, "we are entering into an era in which no government, not even a Hitler government if it existed, would undertake this business of war lightly. I myself, concerning the Soviet Union, have never felt the hot breath of imminent war on my back."[34] On the other hand, he admitted the need to protect retaliatory forces to reduce the chances of war even more, which meant reducing "the almost comic opera vulnerability of our military structure."[35] "It is quite conceivable," Brodie wrote early in 1952, "that the existing attachment to the idea of protecting our bombers chiefly through the device of getting them under way against the enemy, even when we postulate enemy initiative in opening hostilities, works against our dedicating the requisite energies to the job of erecting real safeguards against surprise attack."[36]

The cost of strengthening this peacetime deterrent could be paid, Brodie proposed, by the savings in force requirements permitted by the H-bomb.

> The size of the forces necessary to wreak overwhelming destruction to the enemy home front if he transgresses against our rules is clearly reduced. And if the kinds of forces which can have no place in a thermonuclear war are sufficiently cut back, the resulting economies can be devoted to making more effective and also more secure those forces which are appropriate to such a war. It is impossible to disperse our cities or put them underground. No such impossibility attaches to the problem of safeguarding the relatively small forces which are withheld for the single purpose of realizing, when necessary, Operation RETRIBUTION.[37]

Brodie emphasized far more the intrawar aspects of protecting military forces, asking "whether measures adequate to guard against surprise attack at the outset of war would not also be largely adequate for a much longer period."[38] In this connection, his most important concern was to prepare for a war that was other than suicidal — that is, in which large-scale use of fission and fusion bombs against cities was 'avoided. Rejecting the argument that Soviet-American hostilities would begin by "unrestricted strategic air blows with nuclear weapons,"[39] Brodie urged consideration of admissible forms of contemporary warfare. "The dilemma of our age," he declared in 1952, "is that in order to preserve the things we wish to preserve we must stand ready to meet a military challenge, and unless the ensuing business is handled most skillfully, the things we have moved to defend will surely perish. It will require most careful handling to give long life to the atomic age."[40]

High-Value Targets: Soviet Military Installations

When Brodie questioned whether the U.S. Air Force could protect American cities through an offensive bombing campaign, he was expressing skepticism above all about the sufficiency of the "counterweapons" portion of the American emergency war plan. By 1951, prior to the crucial technological breakthrough making fusion weapons development possible, the JCS, determined to prevent Soviet planes from penetrating the American homeland with nuclear payloads, decided to make counterweapons targeting the highest priority of the emergency war plan.[41] This required preemptive American attack to reduce or eliminate at the outset of war Soviet ability to launch attacks against the United States.

Criticizing the objective of protecting American cities through offensive military means, Brodie questioned whether counterweapons targeting was adequate for this purpose. Many in the air force intelligence staff shared his doubts on this score, at least initially. "On the counterweapons system," declared James T. Lowe of the Air Targets Division to a 1951 Air War College audience, "there are x number of air-fields from which the Soviets could take off. Well, we could use the whole stockpile of atom bombs on the x number of airfields. That [*sic*] fact is that we probably wouldn't get any of the airplanes except those who stayed home. They might not have a connection with it." He went on:

> In order to be realistic about the counter weapons target system we have to know two things. I don't think we will ever learn either one of the two things. We have to know, first of all, what is the Soviet plan of attack. That is to say, when the Soviet order to attack the United States with atom bombs is issued and it comes out the Soviet atom bomb carriers will go from a base here, say X, to a place Y to pick up the bombs and then to another place Z, the fuel; then to another place A, which will be a station base. And let's say that they'll arrive at X, Y, Z, and A on Monday, Tuesday, Wednesday, and Thursday. Of course they could make it shorter than that. That's the general idea. Now, we'd have to know when they were going to do this. When they were going to leave X, arrive at Y, arrive at Z, and arrive at A. When they were going to be on the ground, either getting their bombs or loading them or so forth. We'd have to know the Monday, Tuesday, Wednesday, and Thursday timetables. In addition to knowing it, we would have to know it two to five days ahead of time. In other words, Mr. Stalin would have to send General LeMay his operational order dated three or four days ahead of time so that General LeMay could get his bombers in the air and have his bombs over the target at A when they were getting the bombs. I think that's the problem.[42]

Some of the ramifications in Brodie's earlier reference to the "necessary initiative, necessary surprise, and necessary intelligence" in this aspect of the war plan become clear from this passage. Detailed warning of an attack such as Lowe envisioned had often been lacking in the past, and the prospect of obtaining such information must have seemed even more remote because of the intense secrecy and isolation of the Soviet leadership. Though American intelligence of Soviet capabilities and intentions would likely improve over time, the requirements for blunting a Soviet attack must have appeared staggering to someone such as Lowe presiding over what was by all accounts a relatively primitive intelligence network.

Finally, however significant the gains in intelligence, surprise, and initiative, important questions remained throughout the 1950s about whether American military capabilities could adequately implement counterweapons work. For example, the appropriateness of employing nuclear weapons to crater the runways of Soviet airfields, once the airfields vital for the Soviet war plan could be identified in time, was widely doubted. "To use the atomic bomb against airfield targets would be like using heavy artillery to shoot rabbits," one informed study published in 1955 concluded. "It is not only uneconomical, but you are unlikely to have enough shells to kill off most of the rabbits."[43] Counterweapons targeting would also need to take into account that heavily reinforced structures housing weapons facilities might be highly resistant to nuclear explosions in a manner hardly suggested by the magnitude of damage experienced in open cities such as Hiroshima and Nagasaki—even to the point that nonnuclear projectiles might be more efficient than nuclear bombs to destroy them.[44]

Prior to 1951, neither air force planners nor strategists outside the government saw any major need to limit American damage from Soviet attack,[45] but the prospect of thermonuclear attacks made a large difference in this regard. It was evidently one thing to anticipate (as Brodie did in *The Absolute Weapon*) such large Soviet fission attacks against American cities that counterweapons targeting would make relatively little difference to the result; it was another, however, to permit even a very small number of thermonuclear bombs to be exploded with very great disproportionate effects against some of those cities. Preparing a high-priority blunting campaign required giving careful attention to what the Soviets could do to foil the blunting effort. Here it appears from Brodie's criticism of the air force's discussion of "one-way nuclear capabilities" that some air force planners, Lowe notwithstanding, may have been inclined to overestimate the effect of counterweapons work. Relatively small imperfections in the blunting strategy—resulting conceivably from a variety of unrelated factors—might have enormous consequences upon critical American interests in protecting life and treasure. In addition, the blunting strategy might paradoxically increase the chances that cities would be struck quickly, since a nation absorbing a counterweapons attack would likely have such few bombers left over that no other choice of retaliation would make any difference to the outcome of the war. (I have already noted Brodie's view that cities were the most useful targets of opportunity for a state possessing few bombing forces.)

Bonus damage of Soviet cities contributed to the same result. The bonus concept also governed targeting for the blunting mission for much of the 1950s, because initially only a very small number of bombs were allocated to counterweapons targeting, and until 1954 air force intelligence and SAC operations officers governed their counterweapons target system by the proximity of these targets to military-industrial targets—the latter being the favored targets within the air force.[46] In 1954, however, the JCS approved launching strikes discriminately at Soviet military installations in the event of a Soviet attack, a decision that eventually brought about detailed targeting plans that substituted lower yield weapons for higher yield ones and capitalized on more accurate delivery of nuclear payloads to reduce collateral damage to population centers.[47] Insofar as these new plans were based on the objective that he so strongly shared with war planners of sparing cities and cutting out commitment to the bonus concept, Brodie could not, and did not, dissent from them. Nevertheless, he was not as attached to the counterweapons mission as many of his colleagues and for a variety of reasons.

First, Brodie contended that the H-bomb permitted a *reduction* of operational force requirements. Cost effective as this conclusion was during the early 1950s, it worked against the idea of discriminate bombing, because to produce a nuclear force capable of discriminate bombing necessitated increasing force requirements rather than reducing them. Conspicuously missing from Brodie's public or private work is any discussion of how force requirements needed to be adjusted for the blunting mission. By his silence in this regard, it appears that when he anticipated the emergence of nuclear "plenty" in connection with thermonuclear weapons, he did not in fact have in mind an enlarged blunting mission.[48] (His major concern in this argument was instead the attack against Soviet industrial targets and, as will be seen in the next chapter, with Soviet interdiction targets important in a European war.)

Another indication of Brodie's less than complete commitment to the success of the blunting mission was his belief (which I discuss later) that only agreed-upon restraints between the superpowers could prevent a nuclear war from getting out of hand, no matter how discriminate the American targeting capability, and therefore that gaining mutual restraints, which required adroit diplomacy and stringent war-making controls, overshadowed discriminate targeting capability in importance. Third, Brodie was sensitive about whether the Soviets would likewise plan for bombing with reduced collateral damage. Since the Soviets initially gave no indication of doing so,[49] the safest restraint in a Soviet-American war was undoubtedly the holding back entirely of strategic bombing, an objective Brodie had already envisioned. At the same time, he could not readily favor Soviet achievement of a discriminate targeting capability, for such a development might increase the risk of a Soviet surprise attack against American retaliatory forces, about which he and others at RAND became increasingly concerned in the 1950s.[50]

Despite these caveats, Brodie acknowledged that *under certain conditions*, a discriminate targeting capability would be highly valuable and likely to be employed. As the Soviet capability to deliver nuclear weapons increased, he wrote in 1954,

> we may be quite certain that a blunting mission must enjoy at least the same degree of priority among Soviet strategic planners that it does among ours. No conception could be more spontaneously congenial to the military in any country; and besides, knowing where our major and almost exclusive offensive strength lies and knowing also how heavily we rely on it, the Soviets have every possible incentive to adopt the blunting attack idea. Thus, we undoubtedly have a situation where the strategic bombing forces of each side (which, incidentally, will not necessarily be confined to long-range bombers but may include also submarine-launched missiles) plan to eliminate each other at the first sign of war.[51]

Elsewhere Brodie wrote that if a surprise attack *were* able to destroy the enemy's ability to retaliate, "it makes sense to be trigger-happy with one's strategic air power. How could one afford under those circumstances to withhold one's SAC from its critical blunting mission while waiting to test other pressures and strategies?" On the other hand, where a country's retaliatory power could not be removed by a blunting attack, "the restraint that was suicidal in the other situation becomes prudence, and it is trigger-happiness that is suicidal."[52]

Playing up the likelihood of discriminate targeting in some circumstances, Brodie nevertheless was inclined to play down the general chances of success in the blunting mission. "What is most likely," he wrote in 1954, is that "neither side may be able to achieve a successful blunting mission even if it has all the initiative and surprise that it could reasonably hope for. Certainly thermonuclear weapons make it possible for whatever portion of a bombing force survives a surprise attack to wreak tremendous retaliation upon the aggressor. How many H-bombs can any country really stand?"[53]

These views suggested contradictory conclusions about the advisability of refining weapons yields and accuracy to gain better discrimination in targeting. Undoubtedly, much depended on presumptions about whether counterforce attacks could be prevented from evolving into attacks upon cities and about just what constituted "success" in such attacks. If successful implementation of the blunting mission was to be defined as destruction of virtually all Soviet planes on the ground before they could take off, success was indeed remote. But such a demanding criterion could be defended only on the assumption that remaining Soviet planes would almost certainly be directed at American cities in revenge, an assumption challenged by those who believed, to the contrary, that a second strike would still have a choice of military targets if an attacker held back a portion of its forces.[54]

But the main point Brodie tried to make with respect to the blunting mission was that its prospects were never so attractive as to make the best defense synonymous with the best offense.[55] He was not arguing against the blunting mission per se but rather pleading against unqualified dependence upon it.

Lower-Value Targets: Soviet
Industrial Centers and Cities

The counterweapons, or blunting, mission was of course to be supplemented by other missions in the emergency war plan. The second priority in the plan decided upon by the JCS by 1951, the so-called retardation mission, was designed to slow down or stop a major Soviet invasion of Western Europe. Brodie gave major attention to this subject during the 1950s and 1960s, and his work under this heading will be discussed at length in subsequent chapters of this book. Beyond the two top priorities set by the JCS for the emergency war plan were two categories of targets that had previously been most important in Brodie's own writings on strategic nuclear war: Soviet war industries, such as aircraft assembly, petroleum refining, and primary aluminum production plants; and Soviet cities.

Soviet industrial targets constituted the largest number of emergency war plan targets through the mid-1950s.[56] It was these targets that Brodie evidently had most in mind when he complained that using H-bombs might promote "an efficiency of destruction that is perhaps excessive from the viewpoint of our national objectives." He was especially fearful that strikes with fusion bombs at Soviet industrial installations would also have major effects against population centers, for in a large number of cases Soviet war industries were located in the middle of or next to Soviet cities. This was especially convenient to those within the air force who championed destruction of cities as a bonus in the execution of other target missions. Brodie, a determined opponent of the bonus idea, could on the contrary consider striking only Soviet industrial targets with H-bombs on the assumption that Soviet cities would be simultaneously spared. All his writings on using those weapons against Soviet war industries were in fact governed by his strong concerns for protecting Soviet cities, a category of targets to which the JCS by most accounts had come to give the least operational priority in the emergency war plan.

Even when carrying through the assumption that Soviet cities could be spared in a mission against Soviet industrial centers, Brodie was by no means encouraged. "We found," he declared in April 1952, "that . . . picking industrial complexes which were important but which would minimize casualties, would bring the enemy dead down to something like 10 or 11 million [from 35 million]. Of course, this assumes that the enemy will not have a chance to warn his people and that we ourselves will not seek to warn these target populations."[57] Insofar that "as a general rule [with H-bomb use] industrial bombing and urban destruction are inseparable,"[58] many industrial targets presumably would not get hit in a bombing plan of this kind.

Further, of those industrial targets that *could* be hit while sparing population centers, their destruction might not be worth the effort. When Brodie evaluated a possible city-sparing strategy for Soviet leaders, he found that "to get only those relatively few industrial targets which lay well away from major cities would be so unremunerative that to my mind they would not in themselves be worth going after at all."[59] A final difficulty of bombing industrial targets while sparing cities was that even if bombers could somehow operationalize the distinction, enemy leaders would have difficulty perceiving and acknowledging it.[60] However significant the difference between destroying ten million Russians in a city-sparing bombing campaign and destroying more than fifty million in an all-out campaign, it is far from clear that Soviet leaders would absorb ten million dead without assuming that Soviet cities were jeopardized.

Most of Brodie's work on fusion weapons was directed at protecting cities from the effects of those weapons, because he believed, especially for political reasons, that war-making could be politically expedient with such weapons only if cities were spared their effects. His agreement at this time with Clausewitz's contention that war-making should be governed by policy followed logically from this view.[61] He did not categorically reject strategic bombing with nuclear weapons, partly because he conceded that finding ways of avoiding mutual strategic bombing was too drastic and controversial to underlie work done at RAND on strategic offensive forces. (Pertinent here is that advocates of strategic bombing within the air force, including officers at SAC headquarters in Omaha and general officers and planners at air force headquarters, remained totally opposed to any delay in strikes designed to do major damage to Soviet cities.[62]) In early 1953, Brodie defined the central problem of a potential war beginning three years later: "Any effort to fit a strategic bombing program into a meaningful conception of national-objectives-to-be-pursued-through-war approaches close to being a contradiction in terms. Nevertheless, we have to try."[63]

Brodie's strong interest in protecting cities from fusion weapons helps explain why he propounded no theory of target priorities for those weapons. At this time, his major interest was in what *not* to hit, and this interest understandably curtailed his study of the kinds of targets that might have been most usefully exploited for specific political objectives. For example, unlike Robert Oppenheimer, who believed that thermonuclear weapons would be mainly of psychological value,[64] Brodie was now less attracted to employing psychological warfare with H-bombs than he was earlier with fission weapons. He considered warning the Soviet population ahead of time about the effects of H-bombs against cities and utilizing less than comprehensive attacks to demonstrate these effects and to "spare enemy populations while making them fugitives through destruction of their housing and industrial plant."[65] But fusion weapons introduced new questions of the timing of such "sample attacks," for with fission weapons, destruction of enemy physical assets "can be done rapidly enough, and with H-bombs it can, in a very real and literal sense, be done overnight."[66] Brodie complained that "according to our present concepts, this threat value of the atomic bomb is the first thing we plan to throw away the moment that hostilities open. A bomb which has been used no longer has threat value. A city which has been destroyed is no longer worth entering into surrender negotiations for the sake of preserving it."[67] Nevertheless, with the great forbearance in force application required by a sample attack with H-bombs, such an attack would likely be even more strategically awkward to carry out than more massive strikes designed to limit casualties.

If it was not feasible to attack cities with H-bombs even in limited fashion for strategic objectives, the next step was to try to reach agreement with the Soviets on mutual restraint in attacks on cities. Brodie outlined a strategy in which American officials would communicate to Soviet leaders, prior to an outbreak of war, American intent not to bomb Soviet cities in the course of hostilities. The explicit purpose of this communication was to obtain similar restraint from the Soviet side. "What is implied here," Brodie wrote in a formal proposal to this effect,

> is that we should attack enemy cities and industrial establishments only in the event that they attack ours or those of our allies, and that we should make known that intention beforehand and preserve in being a force capable of swiftly executing retaliation in the event they transgress the rules we have laid down and are ready to enforce. The prohibition might extend to cities as such wherever they might be, or to any targets outside the zone of ground battle, or to any reasonable combination of these two principles.[68]

Brodie was not categorical about how this message might be conveyed; the medium was evidently less important for him than the message. In January 1953, he formally circulated at RAND a paper in which he suggested a secret "unilateral declaration" or one in conjunction with the British, possibly at a time "when it was decided that it was no longer possible to defer announcement of the progress towards perfecting the H-bomb" or even earlier when the Allies could assume that atomic weapons used for tactical purposes could "decisively influence the ground battle in Western Europe."[69] The declaration would hold the Soviet government responsible for all attacks on cities, including those of American allies, tailoring retaliation as much as possible to the Soviet behavior provoking it.[70] Rigorous definition of restraint and extended diplomatic discussion of the matter would not be required, for, Brodie believed, "the will is the essential issue. If it is present, the technical problems will prove to be anything but intractable."[71] On the other hand, to choose to abstain from attacking cities was obviously not enough, no matter how logical that choice. *"There cannot be,"* he wrote to Arnold Wolfers in May 1953,

> *mutual restraint* [in the bombing of cities] *unless prior preparation has been made for such restraint by the stronger power, and unless the intention of exercising such restraint has somehow been communicated in advance of hostilities to the opponent.* There are . . . such things as emergency war plans, which have a very high degree of automaticity built into them. When war begins, the existing emergency war plans go into effect in so far as a capability exists for putting them into effect. . . . For us to exercise any kind of restraint means that we have to be prepared in advance to do so, and the purpose of communicating such intentions to the opponent is to suggest to him that he should not make his own plans as though there would be no opportunity on his part for exercising restraint. What the prevailing Air Force doctrine is I leave to your reading of the newspapers. You will understand that there will have to be a profound conversion in some circles before the kind of restraint which you posit as the only rational method of fighting a war becomes at all practicable.[72]

As to Soviet reactions to such a message, Brodie cited three reasons why Soviet leaders might be favorably inclined: First, those leaders had a strong interest in protecting their cities against attack; second, they might be attracted to a proposal that was tantamount to an American rejection of "total victory" as a strategic goal; and third, the benefit of sparing cities was no less valuable for being impossible to guarantee.

The third point Brodie especially stressed. With such a proposal, he argued, "we are offering to leave the Soviet leadership with some degree of control of events even in the event of open war. They can choose whether cities are bombed or not bombed. We may be sure, from what we know of the Bolshevik pattern of thinking, that the one thing they fear most is 'losing control of a situation.'"[73] Perhaps the chief problem of the future, he suggested elsewhere, was to acquire the ability to control events even after the outbreak of war.[74]

The Coercive Use of Fusion Weapons

Preventing fusion weapon attacks against cities requires considerable superpower self-restraint, as well as efforts by each superpower to restrain the other. Brodie was most optimistic that the superpowers might *separately* contribute to bombing restraint when he stressed that, after all, the decision to go to war would not be made by the commanders of strategic bombing forces but rather by the most responsible governmental authorities. He argued that target planners and bomber commanders needed to understand the attitudes of civilian leaders who might be inclined to avoid even the appearance of provocative behavior and who might do their utmost to stave off a war they believed would be enormously destructive. "A military planner ought not to rely for the security of his forces on governmental decisions and actions over which he has no real control," he wrote in *Strategy in the Missile Age*. "When it comes to exercising national military initiative in the thermonuclear age, it cannot be assumed for security purposes that one's own government will act other than deliberately and cautiously."[75] As we will see later, Brodie rejected the idea that authoritative policymakers would be as inclined to employ thermonuclear weapons to deal with diplomatic disputes as they had older modes of forces. If he was correct, his view raised the question of whether a crisis between nuclear-weapons states would be affected more by the fear of national leaders to unleash their states' destructive capabilities or by traditional diplomatic enmities.[76]

Most of Brodie's writing focused on American efforts to gain Soviet restraint in nuclear employment. Virtually alone at the time, he conceptualized — for both American H-bomb monopoly and Soviet-American duopoly — American coercive diplomacy to forestall Soviet attacks against the United States.[77] Brodie believed that an American H-bomb monopoly could be best exploited by avoiding attacks on cities and "would be of large *potential* advantage politically to this country."[78] Feeling that Americans were unaccustomed to making the most out of strategic superiority because they were not sufficiently belligerent, he thought appropriate planning might overcome this obstacle: "Even a temporary monopoly in thermonuclear weapons *could* be used to secure important diplomatic advantages *if* we prepare ourselves in advance for such exploitation. We had such an opportunity with our now-departed fission bomb monopoly, but we were then not even equipped sufficiently to be able to understand the nature of the animal we were dealing with."[79] When he contemplated Soviet-American duopoly in fusion weapons, Brodie admitted that "superiority in numbers and even in means of delivery becomes increasingly meaningless for strategic purposes as numbers of bombs and vehicles increase on both sides," but he argued that "what is objectively true is never as important politically as what people think."[80]

Although Brodie apparently was thinking primarily of situations in which crises might be terminated short of the use of force — or, at the very least, short of the use of strategic force[81] — he was bolder than those who thought that loss of the American H-bomb monopoly critically eroded U.S. ability to threaten the Soviets with such bombs.[82] Separating from the latter group, Brodie searched for ways to stiffen American resolve in future superpower confrontations, though not to the extent of triggering attacks on homelands. This is apparent, for example, in his steady criticism of the American strategy of massive retaliation, a strategy enunciated most notably though not originally by then Secretary of State John Foster Dulles in a speech on 12 January 1954.

This strategy, seemingly based on the American need to prevail over the Soviets in a diplomatic confrontation, gave no sign of adequately supporting such an objective.

The basic idea of the January 12 pronouncement was not new. On several occasions during the previous Administration, one of them a public one before the Committee for Economic Development in New York, Thomas K. Finletter, then Secretary of the Air Force, asserted that the next time we were presented with a Korean-type challenge we should meet it not by local military response but by what he called "diplomatic action." If he meant anything effective by that phrase, he could only have meant an ultimatum to the Soviet Union, or possibly to Communist China, or both. That, of course, must also have been the essence of Mr. Dulles's reference to picking "places and means of our own choosing." Neither Finletter nor Dulles actually used the word "ultimatum," though we cannot doubt such a conception was present in their thoughts. . . .

There are at least two essential questions to ask about the Finletter-Dulles idea. Will our government have the courage to make the necessary ultimatum at the critical time, and will it have the necessary support at home and abroad? As one looks at the history of the Korean War itself and of our more recent handling of the Indo-China affair, one feels disposed to doubt it. If our leaders and our Allies have not yet mustered the courage to be bold, then let us not ask them to have the stomach to be rash. The second question is, If we do manage to screw our courage to the sticking place, are we quite sure the Russians or the Chinese will yield before our ultimatum and halt their local aggressions? If so, then we are basing the argument not on the military needs of concentration and on the evils of dispersion, but on a forecast of Russian and Chinese behavior before our threats.[83]

Brodie evidently had in mind an ability to "negotiate from strength" in those situations, such as diplomatic confrontation, in which there was overriding necessity to negotiate. His point was to prepare American leaders to take risks but also to enable them to control the taking of risks so that unacceptably destructive outcomes might be avoided. (In contrast, Dean Acheson, who as secretary of state had argued in 1951 for the need "to create situations of strength," had advocated postponing serious negotiations with the Soviet government until the United States had obtained effective strength.[84])

Discussing the prerequisites for such a posture, which throughout the 1950s he continued to believe the United States did not satisfy, Brodie made it clear that he was thinking of much more than continued superiority in American military striking forces over those of the Soviets.[85] First, he stressed the need for less-destructive military forces, avoiding so large a dependence upon massive atomic power that diplomats would be frightened and unable to act coercively. "The ultimate argument in diplomacy has usually been the threat of force," Brodie wrote in 1954,

but now the penalties for the use of total force have become too horrible. This means that our present-day diplomacy based on the deterrent value of the great atomic power is in danger of being strait jacketed by fear of the very power we hold. No doubt the enemy himself is in a comparable strait jacket, but all in all the situation is one that puts a premium on nerves. . . . [It] seems unarguable that a diplomacy that concerns itself with aggressions of considerably less directness and magnitude will have to be backed by a more "conventional" and diversified kind of force—a kind that the diplomat can invoke without bringing the world tumbling about his ears. The reciprocity of restraint, whether openly or tacitly recognized, will have to be on the basis of mutual self-interest. Does that sound fanciful? Possibly. Yet the Korean War was fought that way, and inadvertently too.[86]

Presumably, use of diversified forces, and not only those adapted to requirements of general war, would permit prolonging a crisis until sober and rational impulses could bring an end to hostilities. (Such forces are discussed in detail in the next chapter.) Although it might be maintained that coercion was most likely to succeed when the horrors of all-out nuclear war were most strongly implanted on people's minds, Brodie at this point developed the contrasting view that diplomats needed somehow to have their minds eased about these potential horrors. He was, after all, arguing the need to sometimes take large risks, and such risks would realistically be taken only when diplomats rightly or wrongly believed that taking them would not lessen or remove their control of events.

Second, Brodie insisted that any coercive effort had—more obviously than with most strategies—to be governed by policy. This was why, for example, he condemned using the military principle of concentration to underpin "diplomatic action" and insisted instead that diplomatic objectives should in their own right determine how much risk taking was sought.[87] However, having insisted on the need to prepare for major risks in a Soviet-American crisis, Brodie could not identify even one American objective that justified an unrestricted nuclear war, and he seemed to admit that American resolve behind *any* diplomatic objectives would inevitably weaken in proportion to the destruction experienced from nuclear attacks. This was an important qualification to a strategy of coercion and an invitation to accommodate, for no American objective a priori justified forcing the Soviets to accept the American viewpoint. "It is time we left behind us such quaint nineteenth century axioms as that which holds that one goal in war is to win and that the purpose of war is 'to impose one's will on the enemy,'" Brodie wrote in 1953.

> That hoary formula suggests a picture of glowing health and surging strength on the part of the victor, who has both a will to impose and the determination to impose it. It is not pertinent to the case of the desperately and perhaps mortally wounded warrior who has somehow managed to inflict even more grievous hurt on his opponent. If we are all of us really clear that in a future war both sides are likely to receive a degree of hurt which will make even the minimum national objectives which impelled them to war look pathetically irrelevant, we will appreciate how novel a situation we are looking towards.[88]

The more Brodie worried about the vulnerability of cities, the less confident he became about the prospects of acting coercively, because he could not anticipate future American ability to absorb attacks on cities. "Granted that in any case we will have to hit the enemy harder than he is currently hitting us," he wrote in the same paper,

> the degree to which he is hitting and hurting us has a meaning and an importance quite separate from its effects upon our ability to hit back. The latter are the only effects normally considered by the military, or for that matter in most relevant RAND ac-

tivities. . . . Not that there is lacking a good deal of private concern among the groups alluded to about the hurt we may receive, but that concern is normally considered to be strictly extracurricular. Perhaps it is really central to the problem.[89]

Elsewhere Brodie made it clear that standard indicators of strategic superiority had to be discounted in relation to the prospects of urban attacks. "The ascendancy in weapons and delivery techniques which we presently enjoy," he declared in 1952, "is likely to continue for some time — perhaps permanently — but the *significance* of that ascendancy so far as protection of our cities is concerned is bound to diminish rapidly in the future."[90]

Still, attacks on cities by no means removed the importance of coercive military behavior, because short of suicidal behavior, coercion would be a major means of stopping or preventing such attacks. Brodie apparently had urban attacks and coercion in mind when he argued that in a war between two nuclear powers, "our objective should be to get out of the war with the minimum hurt to ourselves and our friends, and on the offensive side to inflict the kind of damage which will make the opponent agree to a termination which is on the whole less favorable to him than to us."[91]

It was unclear where the balance of advantage lay in a nuclear war in which attacks on cities were in progress. Psychologically, such attacks might create vindictiveness or, alternatively, a total unwillingness to carry on; politically, they apparently required diplomatic objectives to be rethought but also accentuated the need for war termination and therefore for coercion toward that end. The uncertainties were highly vexing, for in the early 1950s, strategists had much less confidence than they would later come to have (when they would focus, for example, on the "habit of nuclear nonuse") that strategic nuclear war could be controlled short of suicidal levels. And if, as a means of ending nuclear war short of suicide, it was deemed crucial to establish differences between the ability of Soviets and Americans to absorb attacks on their cities, few could anticipate how far such attack trading would have to progress to demonstrate those differences.

Conclusions

Brodie's analysis of the strategic implications of thermonuclear weapons in some ways recalled his earlier major work on fission weapons; in other ways, however, it was at odds with that earlier work. It reflected the earlier concerns by concentrating on the prevention of nuclear war rather than on the waging of it and by focusing on the implications of new weapons for the protection of cities. It diverged most from that earlier effort by emphasizing the need to bring diplomatic objectives into balance with the likely effects of fusion weapons employment and also by a general unwillingness to predict the form of nuclear war.

We have seen that for Brodie, the need to prevent thermonuclear war rested on the argument that such war might be suicidal — that is, place major population centers easily and quickly in jeopardy. One of Brodie's major contributions in his study of thermonuclear weapons was to argue that once extensive urban damage from thermonuclear explosions had taken place, war-making would retain little or no strategic value commensurate with the losses. Since war-making was presumably all about maximizing strategic value, Brodie's thesis specified that any unleashing of thermonuclear bombs against cities, whether as a by-product of attacks aimed at other targets or through deliberate assault, meant that strategic warfare would have almost certainly gone wrong, no matter how carefully such action was prepared beforehand.

Once it was realized how frequently wars had gone wrong in the past, it could easily be anticipated that war-making might go wrong once again in the nuclear age. On the other hand, if cities were all too easily vulnerable to fusion bomb attacks, that did not necessarily mean that the superpowers had a strong disposition to strike at cities. It was implausible to believe that attacks against adversary cities could be inflicted without such attacks being suffered in turn, and consequently the trading of urban attacks could hardly be attractive to war planners looking to gain strategic advantages at the outset of hostilities. Nor was Brodie very worried that nuclear war would immediately take the form of city trading, for he maintained by early 1953 that

> a considerable measure of deterrence must always exist on the grounds that complete retaliation-denying success can never be guaranteed, that the chances of success are considerably reduced where the intended victim has H-bombs (since even a small surviving delivery capability will suffice for very destructive retaliation), and that success must argue a certain negligence on the part of the intended victim—which unfortunately is not inconceivable for the United States.[92]

We have seen that Brodie expected superpower interest in attacking cities to decline as Soviet and American nuclear arsenals grew.

If Brodie cautioned against suicidal nuclear war, therefore, he evidently was most concerned with the possibility that suicide might occur *in spite of* planners' efforts to prevent it. This was undoubtedly a strong argument for the need to hold back employment of thermonuclear weapons against *any* target and, given what is known about the emergency war plan during the 1950s, was essentially a prescription for avoiding a Soviet-American war altogether.

Yet as we have seen, Brodie had to take into account situations in which a Soviet-American confrontation made war likely, and he argued for avoiding strikes with thermonuclear weapons against cities for as long as possible. "For the sake of deterrence before hostilities, the enemy must expect us to be vindictive and irrational if he attacks us," Brodie wrote in *Strategy in the Missile Age* in 1959.

> We must give him every reason to feel that that portion of our retaliatory force which survives his attack will surely be directed against his major centers of population. A reasonable opposing view, however, is that no matter how difficult it may be to retain control of events in nuclear total war, one should never deliberately abandon control.

If so, how should we cope with an enemy offensive which exercised . . . discriminating restraint [that is, used smaller and cleaner bombs and chose American missile and base targets farther from cities] . . . ? With abundant examples from history to suggest how unrealistic prewar conceptions of impending hostilities can be, it would appear supremely sensible to want to preserve the capacity to make new decisions when the shooting begins. But one of the implications of that statement are [*sic*] that wartime decisions may be very different from those we presently like to imagine ourselves making. To retain control of decisions is to make oneself accessible to coercion concerning those decisions. If that is the course we choose, we should be all the more determined to reduce our general vulnerability, so that we may retain the stance for making strong decisions.[93]

Brodie's defense of diplomacy as a guide to nuclear weapons applications, a dimension completely lacking in his early writings, was worked out in the early 1950s, when prevailing nuclear weaponry did not yet provide adequate subtlety in strategic targeting and when the prospect of Soviet-American nuclear war was by no means remote. It was based on the difference Brodie perceived between nuclear war as it *ought* to happen (including the sparing of cities) and nuclear war as it *might* happen given existing war plans (especially the possibility that it would get out of control). Contemplating the prospect of urban attacks, Brodie understandably wished for diplomats to control the use of force prior to and during war, compensating for a thermonuclear warfare strategy that did not adequately limit employment of nuclear weapons upon the outbreak of hostilities.

An apparent contradiction in Brodie's writings was that although recognizing the inherent limitations of throwing H-bombs against cities, he continued to link the study of strategy with cities. The contradiction is resolvable only in terms of Brodie's conception of diplomacy, for he had come to fix upon the main utility of H-bombs as being not in inflicting destruction but in threat-making. This position—most unorthodox for a strategist in the early 1950s, though much more common since—required giving considerable attention to the diplomatic and psychological consequences of military behavior and to the military consequences of diplomatic and propaganda actions. It also required exploring the distinction between making threats and implementing them, the modes in which threat making is most likely to be respected, and the problem of threats being called.

We have seen that Brodie insisted on the widest latitude for diplomats in these matters and particularly in relating declaratory actions to operational ones. He barely sketched out the relation between diplomacy and threat making, leaving it to others to do a great part of this work.[94] Evidently persuaded that diplomacy most often functioned badly during and prior to those wars with which he was acquainted,[95] Brodie did not have many ideas about how the conduct of diplomacy might be improved operationally, though he may have hoped that operational experience in this regard (an opportunity he was never given) would be conducive to such ideas.

Brodie's sketchiness in discussing diplomacy may help to explain what is perhaps the greatest weakness in his writings about thermonuclear war: his almost complete unwillingness to anticipate how such a war was likely to occur. In contrast to many strategists today who confidently extrapolate nuclear attack scenarios and their consequences,[96] Brodie steadfastly (in contrast to his essays in *The Absolute Weapon*) refrained from making projections of this kind, highlighting instead diverse possibilities and uncertainties. This reticence, however justifiable in light of the obvious changes brought about by nuclear technology and the Soviet-American cold war, was unfortunate in two ways. First, it neglected prior experience that was pertinent to the shaping of nuclear war, a matter of major importance in developing national security studies as a coherent field of study. Put differently, Brodie was giving operational security concerns higher priority than the search for empirically supported generalizations that could support theoretical work in the national security field. This preoccupation with strategy as art rather than science (despite Brodie's earlier effort to outline the study of strategy as a science) still characterizes the great bulk of writing in this field.

Second, Brodie's reticence about making predictive statements about thermonuclear war did not help in facilitating and improving nuclear war plans. In these circumstances, Brodie's unwillingness to forecast the evolution of nuclear war diminished his influence upon those responsible for planning strategic war, because the latter could not suspend the judgments and procedures foreclosing action that Brodie, because of his great concern about diplomatic and strategic flexibility, wished to have the opportunity to reconsider. (Ironically, later on, when far more flexibility had been built into American targeting choices, Brodie questioned whether flexibility alone was adequate to ensure rational war-making.[97]) Given his estrangement from emergency war planners, Brodie would undoubtedly have welcomed the opportunity to ensure through diplomacy that the war plan he so much dreaded would never have to be unleashed.

6 · The H-Bomb: Battlefield Warfare

Brodie was one of the first to study battlefield use of H-bombs as a problem distinct from but affected by the availability of those same weapons for strategic air war.[1] I already noted his perception of the disutilities in strategic warfare with H-bombs and his belief that wide enough understanding of them would lessen the chances of a Soviet-American strategic nuclear war. He supported battlefield warfare with nuclear weapons only on the assumption that strategic air war between the superpowers was ruled out—an assumption strengthened by the potential effects of H-bombs when employed in strategic air war.

Since Brodie continued to associate strategic air war with large-yield thermonuclear weapons and was categorical and consistent in his writing about the effect of H-bombs on strategic air war, his discouragement about the prospect of strategic nuclear warfare became a constant in his thinking, stimulating him to conclude by 1955 that strategy had reached a "dead end."[2] He never varied after 1952 from his position that whatever military gains were to be realized by the strategic use of fusion bombs would be heavily outweighed by the political and moral liabilities of destroying very large numbers of civilians, and that if, as a result, political and moral values were to take precedence over military ones, H-bombs should not be sent to strategic targets except in retribution for an attack.

Brodie's conclusions about battlefield warfare were also highly affected by his decision to study very-large-yield thermonuclear weapons, though he was not unaware of contemporary efforts to think through and develop smaller-yield weapons for battlefield purposes.[3] The same weapons for which, because of their large yields, he could find no rational military target in strategic warfare, he found with little difficulty, because of these same large yields, some very promising tactical uses. Had Brodie relaxed his assumptions about weapon yields, his concerns about the destructiveness of strategic air war might have been allayed and his interest in thermonuclear weapons as tactical warfare tools less vigorous. But Brodie studied large-yield weapons at length, not because he wanted to make a point or deepen his preconceptions of nuclear war but because military leaders valued possession of them, first in the strategic sense for the bonus value they afforded in enlarged bomb damage and later, and far more persistently, to enhance battlefield warfare plans.

It was by no means clear that a given weapon could be confined to one particular mode of warfare, even as it was placed in readiness for use in some other mode; history afforded no examples of such selective restraint.[4] Thus when Brodie discussed the selective application of H-bombs, he was arguing not from an empirical foundation but from political and moral grounds and particularly from his concern that strategic use of H-bombs would be counterproductive politically and morally. But the unparalleled presumption of battlefield nuclear use combined with strategic non-use, Brodie pointed out, was precisely what defined NATO militarily. The NATO alliance was necessary because the "'critical level of exacerbation' at which nations begin threatening to invoke their military power" had been raised by nuclear weapons

> enormously higher than the already high level at which it was, say, in 1938–9. That creates a new dilemma, because inasmuch as we are confused by all sorts of conceptions of war as being necessarily "total" (the experience of a Korean War is for that reason baffling and disturbing rather than enlightening) diplomacy does tend to become isolated from power. But how can it live and have meaning in isolation? What does it have to back it up? In the last few years the official approach to that dilemma has been to create fictitious forms of power, which is what I consider NATO and its military structure to be. It would lose its quality of being fictitious *only if* reciprocal strategic air attack with thermonuclear weapons can somehow be ruled out or circumvented.[5]

One major figure at NATO headquarters who could have been expected to appreciate the problems of NATO diplomacy and defense was Gen. Lauris Norstad, USAF, newly appointed in December 1950 as deputy supreme Allied commander, Europe (SACEur). Norstad, an admirer of Brodie, was one of the earliest ranking U.S. Air Force officials to commission a study of nuclear weapons in tactical warfare.

Early Difficulties in Justifying the Use
of Nuclear Weapons on the Battlefield

Brodie's earliest work (dating from 1951) on the question of allocating atomic bombs to battlefield needs emanated from his view that such allocations should in principle compete with capabilities for attacking the enemy's homeland. "Strategic bombing," Brodie declared in April 1952 in his clearest enunciation of this view, "has been defined as that action which destroys the war-making capacity of the enemy, but I have the feeling that burning up his armies, if you can accomplish it, does the same thing. One may be as easy as the other, and certainly we shouldn't have to do both."[6] The presumption of scarcity in the atomic bomb supply logically encouraged this outlook, insofar as it argued for the need to concentrate atomic bombs on the mission — strategic or battlefield — that most promised decisive results. Since Brodie was initially convinced that strategic bombing would be decisive, his presumption of nuclear bomb scarcity counseled skepticism about employing atomic capabilities to prepare for major ground warfare. It also counseled discounting the contemporary relevance of the relation during the Second World War between Allied strategic bombing of Germany and Japan on one hand and the character of land warfare on the other. According to USSBS reports, with which Brodie was familiar, the effect of the Allied strategic bombing had been increased by the tremendous demands made by land warfare on the military resources of the Axis powers.[7]

The more that the strategic bombing mission was idealized, as it could be by its advocates at the ATD and SAC, the stronger the argument in favor of allocating scarce atomic bombs to implement that mission. In practice, Brodie wrote subsequently, none of the most important air force general officers he encountered in the course of his target selection work for General Vandenberg "seemed to have the slightest interest in any 'retardation' mission."[8] Strategic bombing advocates commonly contended that destroying enemy field armies was both difficult and expensive and that bombing the enemy's homeland was more efficient militarily to end hostilities early and favorably. "A B-36, with an A-bomb," said air force secretary Stuart Symington in 1949 in a typical expression of this viewpoint, "can take off from this continent and destroy distant objectives which might require ground armies years to take — and then only at the expense of heavy casualties. The B-36 could do the job within 16 hours . . . — all this at the risk of only 16 American lives."[9]

Brodie's earliest appraisal of the strategic value of the NATO alliance, which also appeared in 1949, further highlighted the conflict between the long range and large payload of the B-36 on one hand and the expectation that the United States would assist in defending NATO allies from invasion on the other. "From the point of view of the 'victory through air power' theory," he asserted,

> the North Atlantic Pact is destined to remain a military liability not only over the short term but over the long term as well. For it would oblige us to commit our resources and forces in a way that basically compromised the strategy which would otherwise commend itself as most economical and effective. Even if we decided that although engaged on land we would adopt a defensive strategy there and leave the offensive to air power, the costs to the offensive power would be incalculable. For it is characteristic especially of a land front — and we are talking in this instance of long land fronts — that it is bound to suck in incalculably large resources.[10]

Maintaining a battle front was indispensable if troop landings on the Normandy pattern — which could be seriously undermined by atomic bomb attacks at embarcation points — were to be avoided.[11]

A major issue here was Soviet superiority over the Western powers in the number of ground troops deployed in Europe — according to Brodie, "the one respect in which the Soviets have had us at an apparently permanent disadvantage."[12] The earliest short-term NATO defense plan, unable to cope with this Soviet advantage, provided upon a Soviet invasion for a major retreat of Western forces, the purpose of which, according to Roger Hilsman, was principally to save as many of the troops as possible in the event of war. It amounted to little more than assignments to withdrawal routes, the authority to commandeer ships in British and Allied ports to be used for evacuation, and perhaps a desperate hope—which was never expressed—that [Spanish president Francisco] Franco might let the Allied troops pass through Spain or even stand with them in an attempt to hold at the Pyrenees."[13]

Brodie cited the negative outlook in such plans as a persuasive reason why a Soviet invasion of Western Europe should not be resisted by scarce atomic bombs. "The tactical air mission and the tactical by-product sought for in the strategic air mission has usually been summed up by the word 'retardation,'" Brodie declared in April 1952. He continued:

> I tried for a long time last year [1951] to find out what retardation meant, especially retardation for what? If the purpose of retardation was to delay the progress of the Russian armies to the Pyrenees by something like ten to fifteen days, assuming they would stop at the Pyrenees, I didn't quite see the point. I finally gathered that the function of retardation was to permit a retreat, a withdrawal first from the battlefield and then presumably the continent.
>
> Such a prospect, of course, does not provide an attractive investment for any substantial proportion of our scarce resources in both atomic weapons and delivery aircraft. The Air Force was quite right, in my opinion, in looking with a jaundiced eye upon the allocation of any substantial part of the limited atomic stockpile for tactical use.[14]

Brodie had difficulty conceiving, prior to the development of fusion weapons, how atomic bombs could retard a Soviet invasion, other than what he perceived to be ineffective use in the demolition of stockpiles and logistical points valued by an invader. "As a planner," he declared in May 1951, "I would regard any results of demolitions squads in the kind of [European] war we would likely have if one broke out in the near future . . . as sheer boners—something not to be expected . . . to enter the war plan."[15]

Of course, NATO might not have to rely on nuclear bombs to retard a Soviet invasion of Western Europe. Brodie in May 1951 acknowledged this point, declaring that "what would be above all desirable in order to make our present strategic bombing capability really effective would be 60 good divisions in Western Europe. That is what we obviously haven't got and are not going to have soon."[16] Nevertheless, NATO planners, evidently presuming that the nuclear bomb scarcity under which they were laboring would continue, had already begun drafting a force requirement plan permitting NATO contingents to stand their ground (at least to some extent) inside Germany without employing nuclear bombs. This plan, entailing an on-line force of thirty-five to forty divisions, an expansion to eighty-six divisions by thirty days after the start of hostilities, and a tremendous buildup from the available twelve on-line divisions in 1951, was ultimately to be approved by NATO political leaders in Lisbon in February 1952.

Supporting the requirements, decided upon following the attack against South

Korea in 1950, was the military argument that obstacles to Normandy-type landings necessitated repositioning troops at defensible points, or at least quickly airlifting them to these points, to defeat a massive invasion by Soviet forces. But the requirements plan, known as the Lisbon force goals, was deficient because it was determined on the basis of the economically attainable and not the militarily desirable. Thus the planners gave up some measure of defense against an attack in favor of deterring one. "From the earliest discussions both European defense planning and military assistance programs have been bedeviled by the conflict between the desirable and attainable," then Secretary of State Dean Acheson wrote many years later, "or—putting it another way—by the attempt to clothe the attainable in respectable strategic theory. . . . The result attainable would be a force in Europe that would preclude quick victory by sudden marches, backed up by an American capability for punishing blows against an aggressor's home territory. This placed the emphasis on deterrence."[17] Military deficiencies of the Lisbon force goals were matched by political difficulties in implementing them. "The process of scaling down the goals and stretching them out in time began almost immediately after the Lisbon meeting had closed," wrote Roger Hilsman.[18]

An idealized conception of strategic bombing and the emergency war plan would only be affirmed by the military and political difficulties of preparing an adequate defense of Western Europe. But as Brodie became fully determined in the course of his work for Vandenberg *not* to treat the emergency war plan and its strategic bombing mission in idealized fashion, he seems to have become more receptive to the tactical use of atomic bombs. Following completion of his critique of the ATD's target selection, he argued that if the particular strategic target systems espoused within the air force (electric power, for example) were illogical and unfounded, as he claimed, this "might suggest more sympathy than exists in some circles for the practical [that is, tactical] use of the atomic bomb."[19]

Brodie recognized, moreover, that if the emergency war plan neglected battlefield warfare entirely and no significant resistance took place to a Soviet invasion of Western Europe, the consequently reduced Soviet demand for military equipment would also reduce the criticality of American strategic bombing with atomic weapons. "We should have tried," he declared in 1951, "to devise a target system and a technique of [strategic] bombing which would be effective in the absence of a ground war, which I suspect we have not succeeded in doing."[20] On one hand, planners for the strategic bombing mission seemed to have assumed, in drafting hypotheses about the emergency war plan target list, that prolonged ground battles in Europe similar to those of the Second World War would erode Soviet mobilized military strength and heavily burden the Soviet war economy. On the other hand, committed by air force doctrine to prepare for strategic bombing in any event, they did not think extensively about how such a contemporary land war would occur and failed to allow that it might not happen.

A third point weighing in favor of the battlefield use of nuclear bombs was that if defense of Western Europe were indeed vital for the United States, the most immediate problem was that Allied military divisions in Europe—then consisting almost entirely of occupying forces in Germany—were vulnerable, without adequate supply lines, and highly exposed to Soviet ground attack. This problem, which could be remedied only by holding back *some* bombs from the strategic bombing mission, evidently preoccupied Brodie while he worked for Vandenberg. "The [air force] Emergency War Plan for FY1951 called for the Red Army to be at the Pyrenees at D plus 40," he later wrote. "I remember no talk, certainly no emphasis, on a counter-invasion. . . . I do remember asking why, if the Red Army was going to be at the Pyrenees at D + 40, no nuc bombs were kept in reserve for targets outside the S.U. or Rumania. The answers ranged from unsatisfactory to ludicrous."[21]

Finally, the issue of battlefield nuclear use would become inescapable, even in a period of atomic bomb scarcity, once nuclear weapons adaptable to the battlefield were introduced into American forces in Europe. This development, which in the summer of 1952 came only a few months after announcement of the Lisbon force goals,[22] contributed to a scaling-down and stretching-out of the Lisbon goals and thrust into central importance the role of nuclear weapons in NATO war planning.

Two Defenses for the Employment of Thermonuclear Weapons on the Battlefield

Not until his studies of fusion weapons in 1952 did Brodie justify battlefield use of nuclear weapons, using two not fully consistent rationales. The first stressed the battlefield role of fusion weapons in contributing to nuclear plenty, while the second dwelled on the destructive potential of fusion bombs against strategic as well as battlefield targets. When he stressed the operational potential of fusion weapons on the battlefield, Brodie took account of the strategic consequences of bombing of this type cited in USSBS reports of the experience of the Second World War. According to this view, diametrically opposed to competitive strategic and battlefield nuclear use, vigorous battlefield warfare usefully *supplemented* strategic bombing. "*If* the allocation of larger increments of our growing weapons stockpile to the ground battle," he wrote in 1952,

> can at some point make the difference between success and failure in that battle, then that chance of success is worth a very large investment. The ability to maintain a fighting front in Europe would not only be enormously valuable in its own right, politically *and* militarily, but would also greatly enhance the effectiveness of any strategic bombing campaign—by forcing the enemy to use up those military commodities for which our strategic bombing is denying him replacement.[23]

Whereas the idea that strategic and battlefield capabilities were competitive presumed scarce bombing capabilities, the view that the two supplemented each other relaxed this presumption. I already noted Brodie's attention, in his earliest writings on fusion bombs, to the rising stockpiles of fission bombs that accompanied fusion bomb development.[24] The same theme was evident in his 1954 statement that "certainly 40-odd American atomic test explosions suggest that the weapon can no longer be regarded as exceedingly scarce or costly."[25] And his confidence that bomb scarcity was a thing of the past was reflected in his conception, in the same 1954 article, that "liberal use of nuclear weapons must contribute vastly to the effective fire power of ground forces" and that it was unwarranted "on *a priori* grounds [to] exclude thermonuclear weapons from tactical use, where they may indeed prove to have even greater comparative utility than in strategic bombing."[26] In an informal RAND paper that developed from a Washington briefing he delivered in March 1952, Brodie indicated that he had in mind three hundred to five hundred large bombs for the mission of resisting a Soviet invasion of Western Europe.[27]

Highlighting the new overall condition of nuclear bomb plenty, Brodie in his private writings sought (as will be seen) to give maximum scope to the potential afforded by this condition for facilitating the retardation portion of the emergency war plan. In doing so, he was undoubtedly more advanced than those SAC and ATD planners deeply committed to the strategic bombing mission. But the freedom of those planners to consider target selection from the point of view of that mission alone was being circumscribed in any event. By March 1951, pressured by widespread anticipation of a European war growing out of the hostilities in Korea, the JCS had decided that retarding a Soviet invasion of Western Europe had a priority for the Strategic Air Command second only to striking at counterweapons targets. It determined that "a certain number of atom bombs will be allocated to the theater commanders to be used by them on targets designated by them in an effort to retard the ground advance of enemy troops and SAC will be the delivery agent and is on call."[28]

In all of the foregoing, the prospect that fusion weapons could be used on the battlefield by no means detracted from the continued importance of the strategic bombing mission or from the presumed allocation of bombs and bombers adequate to accomplish that objective. In a hypothetical Soviet-American war, the simultaneous implementation of the retardation and strategic bombing missions enhanced the value of the latter because of the demand effect of heavy ground battles on Soviet war production and was necessary to demonstrate the emergence of nuclear bomb plenty. But Brodie also put forward a defense of tactical warfare with H-bombs to check the tendency of war planners to depend too heavily on such bombs to implement the strategic air campaign. Simply by making full use of the operational efficiencies obtainable by fusion bombs—for example, by exploiting the bonus effect of such bombs—a strategic bombing campaign could quickly bring about far greater destruction than political objectives warranted. Because Brodie feared that virtually any use of fusion bombs in a strategic air campaign would invite suicidal warfare, he wished to prevent it *irrespective* of the potential of fusion bombs against battlefield targets. But he also viewed attractive battlefield targets as incentives to planners to hold back strategic air war.

According to this justification for nuclear use on the battlefield, choices for planners persisted between the strategic bombing and retardation missions despite the emergence of nuclear plenty. Nuclear bombs, Brodie declared in 1952,

> have of course increased in efficiency and also in specificity for military use.
> Now, military planning can anticipate these changes in at least two ways. We can find more and more targets in the strategic bombing category on which to expend our greater numbers of bombs, or we can allocate an increasing proportion of them to tactical usage. . . . [C]ertain projections . . . which I have seen (not war plans but studies) really anticipate the growing number of A-bombs by a more than comparable growing number of required targets in the strategic category. One drawback among several to adding targets in the strategic category . . . is that after a certain point, rapidly drastic diminishing returns must set in. The term "overkilling" can have strategic implications as well as purely physical ones.[29]

Brodie's contribution under this heading was to find a way for air force planners to escape the operational problem that fusion bombs might be too much of a good thing for certain strategic targets and that the falloff in fusion bomb efficiency against those targets counseled diverting some of the weapons to the retardation mission. This depended heavily on the presumed effect of fusion weapons in making possible concerted NATO resistance to a Soviet invasion of Western Europe.

Operational Justification of Nuclear Weapons Use

Through 1951 at least, American appreciation of the distinction between battlefield targets for nuclear weapons and strategic targets for those same weapons was very inadequate. "In the fall of 1951 I received a separate briefing in Europe," Brodie later recalled, "in Wiesbaden I believe, explaining what they would do with the 25 nuclear weapons then assigned to USAFE [United States Air Force in Europe] for retardation [of an advance of Soviet ground troops]. Considering *their* targets, it was a good thing they didn't have more."[30]

In the summer of 1951, General Norstad proposed that major study be given to applying atomic weapons to "the tactical problem," that this study move beyond "accepted operational conceptions," and that it take account of "the developments in the atomic weapon field with which we have recently been acquainted."[31] Brodie's earliest work on the tactical implications of H-bombs followed Norstad's outline, and the resemblance was almost certainly not accidental, for Norstad, who had initially sponsored (as air force deputy chief of staff) Brodie's work for Vandenberg on target selection, again requested Brodie's services after transferring to NATO headquarters.[32]

In his discussion of the tactical implications of fusion weapons, one of the series of briefings he gave in March 1952 on the implications of fusion weapons, Brodie argued for H-bomb use against Soviet military forces in a European war and for integrating H-bomb use into NATO war plans.[33] This prescription lessened the need for a major buildup in NATO conventional forces. His point was that by taking advantage of large-yield thermonuclear bombs as battlefield weapons, NATO could gain an excellent defense against a Soviet attack at relatively little cost.

Some of Brodie's arguments on tactical matters derived from his understanding of the effectiveness of H-bombs against strategic targets. I already noted Brodie's view that H-bombs permitted a reduction in strategic force requirements. Another implication of this reduction was that it liberated bombers for the tactical mission, which they could implement without the extensive resistance anticipated from Soviet air defenses in deep-penetration bombing runs against Soviet strategic targets. According to Brodie, "The differential attrition rates as between deep and shallow penetrations, especially where the large size of the plane makes it more readily identifiable as a dangerous bomb carrier, will mean that a given number of available aircraft will cover a larger number of delivered bombs in tactical use than in strategic."[34] In his critique of assumptions behind strategic targets, Brodie had played down on operational grounds the safety of bombers, terming them sacrificeable for the results of bombing; now, in arguing on behalf of tactical warfare capabilities, he paid considerable deference to these same bomber safety concerns.[35]

But Brodie's most important point in this work was the effectiveness of fusion bombs against nonstrategic targets. In his judgment, battlefield use of thermonuclear weapons would permit firepower sufficient to provide "the chance of success in not merely retarding but actually holding the Soviet armies."[36] We have seen that H-bombs were primarily useful as area weapons. "Provided only that the area desired to be covered is large enough to warrant its use at all," Brodie argued, fusion weapons "will be both very much cheaper and more effective than the fission bombs required to cover the same area."[37] But this meant that fusion weapons were especially suitable against battlefield targets. "In strategic or interdiction targets," Brodie wrote,

> the useful area of destruction tends to be limited by the spatial extent and conformation of a fixed target. In use against ground forces the more area covered the better, because enlargement of the area of destruction anticipates to a degree the target's capacity to move and to spread itself. And in the process of dispersing it is inevitably yielding up its offensive capabilities against friendly ground forces.[38]

To illustrate the major military effects feasible with H-bombs, Brodie furnished examples from the past in which such weapons would have been suitable to neutralize major enemy troop concentrations. He wrote of one such example from the Korean War:

> The outstanding case for the use of a very large-yield bomb seems to have occurred between 27 and 29 December 1950 in the Pyongyang-Chorwon-Kumhwa area, when some 65,000 to 95,000 CCF [Communist Chinese Forces] troops were gathered in a roughly equilateral triangle measuring about 20 km. on each side. ORO [Operations Research Office] considers that this concentration would have been a juicy target for six to ten closely spaced 40 KT A-bombs (which probably can be translated into one H-bomb) had we been permitted to use these bombs and had we known of the concentration at the time, which we did not.[39]

The force of this example presumably extended prospectively to the major path of Soviet invasion in Western Europe, the North German plain, which had a width of about four hundred miles. The limited size of this area would pose difficulties to an invader forced by nuclear explosions or the threat of them to disperse his forces.

> If we accept the various radii of destructive effects conservatively outlined today, and if we assume an effectively available number of bombs of say three to five hundred, it becomes inconceivable, in view of the restricted spaces involved, that the Russians can launch across Europe anything like the forces presently available to them. If they must cut those forces greatly in size and resort to tactics which minimize concentration both in time and place, then our own potentially available ground forces begin to look more than respectable.[40]

Although NATO forces were widely thought to be greatly outmanned by their Soviet counterparts, Brodie found that, reminiscent of other cases in which firepower and mobility had been employed to neutralize troop shortages, "superiority in numbers of troops will count for less than it has before—except to provide juicier targets with respect both to the troops themselves and to their equipment and supply trains."[41] In this case, Brodie wrote, "enemy concentrations will often reveal themselves most conspicuously by the force of their attack . . . [and] heavy attack remains a useful index of when to launch an atomic weapon on the enemy's rear, on the assumption that the attack usually betokens a considerable deployment of enemy force in depth to support and exploit the attack."[42] Nuclear weapons, including fusion bombs, might, according to Brodie, even "be a great leveller of opposing ground forces," favoring the defense once proper tactical defensive adjustments were made. Attacking forces on the move would generally not be able to gain protection against such bombs in massive underground shelters, but defending forces could do so; the latter would gain "a great *comparative* advantage" over the offense by reintroducing the Maginot Line of fortification as "many individually small and scattered or at least discontinuous strong points, supported by highly mobile and mechanized forces organized to be self-contained in relatively small units."[43]

One major liability of the employment of large H-bombs on the battlefield, Brodie thought, was psychological: It was unclear how soldiers would react to bombs of this magnitude. Panicked troops might decide the military result, or perhaps anticipation of panic might discourage the use of substantial numbers of Soviet troops and effectively prevent a massive European invasion. A second liability—potential Soviet use of similar weapons against American field targets—Brodie dealt with by assuming "a decisive or at least significant" American lead in nuclear weapons, including both fission and fusion types, along with "at least parity in air power and superiority in the mode of using both."[44] His point was that by permitting the United States to demonstrate in advance that it would win a major military battle in Europe, military superiority would "add . . . a powerful increment to those factors which presently deter the Soviet Union from launching aggression."[45]

Evaluating Brodie's Ideas on the Effects
of Nuclear Use on the Battlefield

Brodie's discussion of how a nuclear-armed defender could stop a ground attack seems to suggest that only a few large bombs would suffice to stop a Soviet invasion since no battlefield commander could accept dramatic losses at precisely the point of what had been his greatest source of strength in past campaigns. If only a small number of H-bombs were at issue, if the Soviets lacked a significant retaliatory capability, and if no other mode of resisting Soviet advances was available, use of those weapons might be acceptable. "Presumably," one qualified authority wrote, "in wars in which the Russians would use no or a very few nuclear weapons, not many of ours would be needed to redress our numerical inferiority in troops. Consequently, the damage inflicted by use of nuclear weapons in the theater might be so small that for the West it would compare favorably with the devastation that would otherwise be inflicted by Soviet invasion."[46] But Brodie's observations about the possible drastic alteration of land warfare—perhaps the most startling prediction he made in regard to thermonuclear weapons—can only be understood in light of his assumption about liberal nuclear use.

The advantage he had in mind from tactical nuclear use—the neutralization of Soviet superiority in military manpower—justified for Brodie a rather buoyant attitude about the opportunities for nuclear weapons use on the battlefield. To convince those responsible for preparing the strategic air campaign that they should not neglect tactical war requirements, Brodie needed to demonstrate that fusion weapons would be fully effective against key battlefield targets. On the other hand, he did not explain why, if thermonuclear weapons were as potent on the battlefield as he argued, it might be necessary to use so many of them to repel a Soviet attack.[47] He implied that the Soviets would be very stubborn upon launching a ground campaign and would by no means be easily repulsed, even though very aggressive behavior on the part of the attacker would merely play into the hands of an H-bomb-equipped defending force. Such a Soviet Union was certainly far more disposed to take risks than was the Soviet Union outlined in his plea for restraint in urban attacks. In the end, the combination of an attacker willing to take great risks and a defender willing to take equal risks in opposition would mean suicide on the battlefield for armies targeted in air war. "The growing abundance of nuclear weapons on both sides," Brodie wrote in 1955,

> may . . . force us to the ultimate conclusion that under their unrestricted use tactically no substantial forces will be able to live in the field at all. If organized bodies of troops cannot exist above ground in the field—or at any rate, cannot operate effectively there—it would seem that they must be either under ground or in the air. In either case we must think in terms of greatly reduced numbers; and, as for airborne forces, we must remember that in nuclear war usable air fields will become quickly scarce, and that small combat aircraft competing for the use of surviving fields can carry nuclear bombs.[48]

This conclusion suggested to him "the same result in considering unrestricted tactical war in the future that we get in unrestricted strategic war. In each case the conclusion tends toward the nihilistic."[49]

Arguing on the basis of military and technological logic rather than historical experience, Brodie was not dismayed. "If we are forced," he wrote in a RAND informal paper, "to the ultimate and nearly absurd conclusion that with the reciprocal use of thermonuclear weapons *no* substantial forces can live in the field — offensive or defensive — that is of course all right with us too. Our defensive objectives in Western Europe are thereby attained."[50] His reasons for advocating battlefield nuclear use were not inconsistent with those military and technological considerations that, in the words of another RAND staff member, were "forcing . . . tactical fission weapon yields to higher levels." The latter included (1) the prevailing design philosophy in tactical nuclear weapons sent to Europe during the 1950s that "generally involved extracting the maximum nuclear yield that could be achieved in a given warhead size and weight"; (2) conservative military requirements for physical destruction of tactical targets and for a high probability of such destruction; and (3) concerns about scarcity of fissionable materials, which overrode concerns about collateral damage.[51]

Brodie pioneered by anticipating nuclear plenty at the battlefield level — a condition reminiscent of Brodie's projections much earlier in *The Absolute Weapon*, in which numbers of nuclear weapons were large relative to their targets and in which the destructive potential of the newer weapons was stunningly displayed. But just as the logic could be questioned in the earlier instance on the ground that no country was likely to accept destruction associated with unrestricted strategic nuclear use, so in this case the logic was vulnerable to the assertion that no country would accept unrestricted tactical nuclear use no matter how successful it was in stemming a Soviet invasion.

Those such as Brodie who highlighted the unique value of large-yield battlefield nuclear weapons apparently were content to stop a Soviet invasion by destroying the invading forces, even if this meant making battles between armies obsolete. Others such as Roger Hilsman maintained that battlefield nuclear capabilities would not impair the traditional function of armies, because defensive forces would need to be repositioned over a wide European area before the start of hostilities.[52] This second group, evidently envisioning nuclear weapons to *protect* armies, would have established controls on the kinds of nuclear weapons employed on the battlefield, distinguishing between smaller nuclear weapons for tactical purposes and larger ones for strategic uses. Brodie criticized this idea, observing that

> before this particular habit [of distinguishing tactical and strategic weapons by size] becomes too firmly established, we might ask whether there is any basis for it other than the obvious one — that it is easier to imagine ground forces operating in not too unaccustomed a fashion if the nuclear weapons they use and contend with are small and relatively few in number. But the enemy may not be so accommodating.[53]

Soviet officials and NATO commanders alike denied during the 1950s that strategic and tactical uses of nuclear weapons could be distinguished.[54] This made it unlikely that agreement over the kinds of bombs to be used would be reached quickly after the start of hostilities. Moreover, the effectiveness of the nuclear bombing of battlefield targets without thermonuclear bombs remained in question. Those less interested in or opposed to the use of large nuclear bombs for battlefield purposes did not publicly explain how large battlefield purposes did not publicly explain how large battlefield targets would be destroyed in other ways. I have already noted that thermonuclear bombs served the same purposes in strategic warfare as did large fission bombs; Brodie understood that this same relation also held for tactical warfare.

> By the very broad reach of its destructive power the thermonuclear bomb may anticipate and negate the tactics which ground combat forces might adopt as a counter to the smaller fission bomb, that is, distribution into smaller, more widely dispersed units— which cannot in any case be carried too far without forfeit of offensive power. It would also reduce dependence on precise enemy rear area intelligence, which in any rapidly moving campaign is almost always woefully inadequate.[55]

Collateral Damage and Threats to European Cities

Brodie cited "avoidance of destruction to non-targeted personnel or equipment near the specified target" and especially "avoidance of injury to one's own people and equipment in battle line areas" as constraints upon battlefield use of fusion bombs.[56] These constraints presumed that suitable targets for such bombs could be distinguished operationally from targets such as cities, against which use of those bombs would be disastrous. Brodie never took this distinction for granted, because of his strong fear of large nuclear bombs being employed against cities.

Thermonuclear attacks against Soviet troop concentrations in relatively compact areas would cause comparatively little collateral damage, because the force of the nuclear explosion would be absorbed mostly by enemy forces. But there were other targets for fusion bombs associated with battlefield warfare—including such interdiction targets as bridges—posing a much greater likelihood of major collateral damage. Against targets where, according to Brodie, "there is a high strategic value in getting [critical targets] eliminated quickly and for sure," fusion weapons strikes would be undertaken to ensure speed and to compensate for bombing inaccuracy.[57] Brodie conceded that such attacks, in which the size of the target might constitute only a relatively small portion of the area affected by bomb destruction, would be an exception to the rule that H-bombs would be used only where expected results were larger than those from an equivalent number of fission bombs. According to Samuel T. Cohen, some early NATO nuclear targeting requirements studies in which he participated not uncommonly "pose[d] a warhead yield requirement to destroy a key bridge which would also have totally destroyed the city or town at or near the bridge."[58]

Interested in the effective use of fusion weapons, Brodie at first had little to say about collateral damage to European cities, wishing primarily to prevent the uncoiling of the American emergency war plan in response to a massive Soviet invasion of Western Europe. He emphasized instead that NATO nuclear attacks against both troop concentrations and interdiction targets were compatible with superpower agreement to abstain from attacking their respective cities. "Our use of atomic weapons," he wrote in a paper circulated at RAND in 1953, "against his [that is, Soviet] troops in the field and against interdiction targets could be coupled with the use of 'conventional' weapons against the transportation system of Western Russia. If these operations can be carried off successfully, there is no need or purpose in destroying Russian cities or any industrial facilities in or near those cities."[59] The greater the damage that forces under the command of SACEur could inflict upon their Soviet counterparts, the more remote would be SACEur's recommendation to launch attacks upon the Soviet homeland. However, NATO success in blunting a Soviet invasion would presumably mean very-large-scale warfare, which in turn added to the need for a no-cities agreement beforehand.

For Brodie, potentially unrestricted warfare on the battlefield or against superpower homelands meant that "for any war among the major powers we cannot henceforward consider air strategy, naval strategy, and land strategy (or the political objectives they are supposed to secure) in separate categories — *unless* there is some form of deliberate restriction on the use of nuclear weapons."[60] But avoiding attacks against Soviet and American cities would hardly be enough if intensified warfare in Europe brought about collateral damage to European cities.

Brodie was preoccupied most by the vulnerability of European cities to *Soviet* employment of nuclear bombs against them, perhaps to redress military shortcomings on the ground. Indeed, the better Brodie made nuclear use on the battlefield seem, the more serious was the possibility that Soviet leaders would also capitalize on large-yield nuclear weapons, but to place European cities in jeopardy. Summarizing in 1954 the arguments favoring battlefield use of large-yield bombs, Brodie concluded: "All this would seem to present the NATO Powers with a great net military gain vis-à-vis the Soviet Union, *provided always the former can stand up as well as the latter to the threat of destruction of their cities*, and provided also that reasonable precaution is taken against surprise nuclear attack on our tactical air forces."[61]

Defending against a Soviet invasion seemed militarily easy since NATO's H-bombs were highly useful for that purpose; but defending against threats to NATO's cities was militarily impossible, because for that purpose NATO's H-bombs were of no help. Protecting European cities would be harder if weakness in Soviet ground forces encouraged the Soviets to use scarce nuclear bombs against targets of greatest opportunity, which in Brodie's mind consisted especially of European cities. "If we assume R to conclude that U will hit his cities anyway," he wrote to Arnold Wolfers in 1953, "what better targets could he have for a small number of bombs — besides the ports you mention — than the major cities of our NATO allies in order to induce them to leave the war. What will the mere threat of utterly destroying Paris (and a few other cities) do to the French will to fight?"[62]

Elsewhere Brodie wrote of the effect of Soviet blackmail in *keeping* the NATO allies out of a Soviet-American war, not just in forcing them out of such a war.

"The awful vulnerability of our Allies to atomic weapons," he wrote privately in 1953,

> is something which our strategic bombing planners tend to lose sight of. We are inclined to forget that every fourth Englishman is a Londoner, and that most of the other British also live in large cities. The destruction of Paris would involve a lesser proportion of Frenchmen, but would be equally unacceptable to all the French, who have other large cities as well to worry about. Our planning for the use of foreign bases in a strategic bombing campaign simply ignores the fact that our Allies would in a crisis be utterly unable to face up to the threat of atomic weapons being used strategically against them, and the growth of atomic stockpiles with the inclusion of thermonuclear weapons is not going to make them more disposed toward such a fate. We are very conscious of the peacetime utility of our atomic stockpile as a deterrent to Soviet aggression, but all too disregardful of the increasing potentiality of the growing Russian stockpile as an instrument of blackmail.[63]

To keep the European allies together once a Soviet-American war broke out, American officials needed to make known to the Soviets their desire for a bilateral agreement to spare American, Soviet, *and* European cities. Above all, American leaders apparently could not afford to have their Soviet counterparts believe that Soviet cities would be struck in any event, for the conditional American promise of keeping Soviet cities intact was perhaps the only leverage available to the United States in protecting European (as well as American) cities. We have already seen that American policy beginning in the early 1950s was not to hit Soviet cities at the outset of a war (though this by no means prejudged the procedures in effect at SAC headquarters); accordingly, little would have been lost by conveying this fact to the Soviets.[64]

Assuming that a Soviet-American no-cities agreement could be extended to European cities as well, the question remained how this would affect NATO strategic needs, especially for time-urgent targets, in blunting a Soviet invasion. Advocating fusion weapons use at this early stage to help blunt such an invasion, Brodie did not draw the connection between the unwanted collateral effects of battlefield bomb use and the arguments supporting effective use of such bombs.[65] In addition, failing to explicitly consider European attitudes about collateral damage, he did not appreciate how European dissatisfaction on this score could undercut the military advantages to NATO of fusion bomb use and increase the political benefits to the Soviet Union of Soviet threats to attack Western cities.

Conclusions

In this chapter, I have emphasized the differences between Brodie's discussion of strategic air war and his discussion of battlefield nuclear war, but for Brodie these two subjects fit into a general strategy. Underlying this strategy was the prevention of nuclear weapons use against cities in particular and against Soviet and American homelands in general, since attacks on homelands might progress to destruction of cities. The application of nuclear weapons in land combat was to be a substitute for strategic air war, and it was only in this guise that the former had any major interest for Brodie. Here, as in his later writings, he tended to look beyond battlefield nuclear warfare to the implications of such hostilities for the likelihood of Soviet-American strategic warfare.

Under the restricted terms in which Brodie investigated the feasibility of using fusion weapons for European land combat, he gave tactical allocation of fusion weapons the widest sanction. Full license for battlefield nuclear war was evidently to be the price in his mind for full exclusion of strategic air war, perhaps because the use of fusion weapons against military targets in Europe seemed less horrible to Brodie than their use against American and Soviet homelands. Touting fusion weapons as a boon to the NATO alliance, he maintained that deploying them would "for the first time enable the masses of Europeans to think seriously about the contribution they might make to the common defense, because it would make defense meaningful."[66] He was slow to concede, however, that the use of large-yield weapons could provoke major political difficulties in NATO.

Perhaps Brodie thought that effectively stopping a Soviet invasion was the only realistic way to prevent a third world war and that some collateral damage was a minor price to pay for avoiding a still more intensified and dangerous war. Or he may have trusted General Norstad (and his SACEur superior) not to sanction fusion weapons use in Western Europe in situations in which collateral damage to European cities would be heavy. Norstad would be far more constrained than, say, SAC officers by the problem of collateral damage, because many of the attack points he would approve for targeting Soviet forces would presumably be located inside NATO countries. But Brodie's difficulty was that he had a good idea—applying large-yield nuclear weapons to resist a Soviet invasion—that could be fully judged only with reference to particular hypothesized situations. He apparently had not investigated these situations in detail, and without such work, his idea was largely abstract, lacking standards to determine when the idea had outlived its usefulness. When nuclear weapons stationed in Europe expanded greatly in number and dependence upon them increased, the idea could not be sustained without additional refinement.

One indication of how much Brodie's ideas about battlefield war depended on his outlook on strategic air war was his amazing lack of interest in European diplomacy. NATO's diplomatic importance, he maintained, depended on the rejection of all-out Soviet-American war, but a Soviet invasion of Western Europe contained too many uncertainties for him to assume that homeland attacks against the Soviet Union and the United States would not ultimately follow such an invasion. Since any European war *could* lead to a wider Soviet-American war, there was not much need to inquire about the views of American allies or to give attention to NATO as an independent decision-making body; there was plenty of reason, however, to view a European war as largely a bilateral superpower matter.

To be sure, Brodie highlighted—perhaps better than anyone at the time—the political weakness of the NATO alliance in the face of the threatened use of weapons of mass destruction.[67] Fusion bombs — by one account, not available to NATO in sufficient numbers through 1953 to be depended upon to stop a Soviet invasion[68] — would hardly suffice even in significant numbers to resist Soviet coercion. Impressed as Brodie was with the use of H-bombs to aid NATO military objectives, he was just as impressed with the way the Soviets could use H-bombs politically to undercut those same objectives. But this problem was similar to the one (examined in chapter 5) of American cities being hit by nuclear weapons. In each case, Brodie doubted whether the national will would withstand major hardship and dislocation, actual or potential.

Differences among NATO members about resisting the Soviet Union might well be traceable, in the event of a European war, to differences in urban damage experienced by the Allies in the Second World War. As long as the United States was spared such destruction following the outbreak of war, American diplomacy would probably need to strengthen the will to endure of the European governments that had suffered or might suffer attacks upon their cities. American diplomatic support might also be required to reassure NATO allies if collateral damage resulted from NATO's own weapons. Finally, American policymakers presumably would have to give much attention to the needs of NATO allies *before* the outbreak of hostilities to protect the integrity of the alliance *during* the war.

All this pointed once again to an agreement with the Soviets to spare cities in a nuclear war, an agreement Brodie believed needed to be the basis for controlling warfare. But a no-cities agreement would certainly be imperiled by the major use of large-yield fusion weapons in a European war. As fighting in Western and Central Europe approached what Brodie termed the "nihilistic," Western political leaders would be hard pressed to interpret such warfare as consistent with superpower interest in war-making restraint, even if SACEur's major military needs were thereby satisfied and even if Soviet and American strategic targets had not yet been struck.

Even if a no-cities agreement existed, the outbreak of a European war, as well as the launching of reciprocal Soviet-American nuclear strikes, would place an enormous burden upon diplomats to control the violence rapidly enough to prevent a third world war. The use of H-bombs in a European war unquestionably would add to this burden, but, as Brodie now saw it, so also would the decision not to use H-bombs in these circumstances. In either case, the problem for Brodie was that although logic might forecast the outbreak of "nihilistic" or suicidal warfare, a strategy that produced such a result must be wrong-headed.[69]

Committed to rectifying the mistakes in national policy from which suicidal warfare might emerge, Brodie could be expected to later reconsider (which he did) the arguments and assumptions underlying his support of H-bomb use on battlefields. Thus these early arguments should be understood as having a certain tentativeness. With respect to the more enduring concerns of students of national security affairs on the other hand, Brodie raised especially the question of the extent to which strategy depended on satisfying demands for producing particular military effects.

Finally, Brodie used his logical, analytical skills to satisfy two major constituencies with differing interests. He assured American civilian leaders that all-out nuclear war would not necessarily occur in the event of major hostilities, and he showed American and Allied military commanders and planners that lesser forms of warfare were viable. Some of the weaknesses in his reasoning undoubtedly resulted from his efforts to please divergent audiences — obviously, there are limits to a strategist's ability to be logical when he also tries to be sensitive to the immediate and specific needs of diverse constituencies. If preventing a third world war depended in part on widespread acceptance of war-making limitations, a politically chaotic world was bound to create difficulties for even the most reasonable argument.

7 · Limited War

Favoring fusion weapons use in tactical warfare but not in strategic bombing, Brodie had outlined a strategy of limited war tailored to the existence of nuclear weapons. Although not originating the study of limited war,[1] he was among the earliest to conceptualize it as "wholly different in motivation and character from the 18th century variety, where the limitations were usually due to unwillingness or inability to mobilize the full resources of the state."[2] The problem for the nuclear-armed superpowers, Brodie argued, was to withhold from war already fully mobilized forces and, "insofar as there must be confrontation or actual hostilities, to 'bring war back to the battlefield.'" As this suggests, he wished not just to protect cities from war but to deflect war from them, preserving war-making limitations once cities had initially been spared.

In his writings on this subject, the earliest of which seems to have stimulated important work by others,[3] Brodie continually maintained that war-making was most reliably limited by keeping hostilities clearly demarcated geographically. "At the beginning of 1952," he wrote later in explaining what he had in mind,

> when some of us here at RAND heard that a thermonuclear weapon would be tested the following November and would probably work[,] . . . I proposed that strategic bombing be interdicted altogether (at that time strategic bombing already meant something given exclusively to nuclear weapons). I was not going to have them bomb any targets, whether airfields or anything else, within the homeland of the Soviet Union, but sought to confine targets strictly to battlefield zones, and to disallow the larger cities even there. My reason was . . . [that] a line like a river or frontier is something relatively easy to distinguish in exercising limitations. I thought then, and still think, that it would be easier to preserve a limitation founded on gross distinctions of geography than to distinguish between military and civilian targets within enemy territory, especially since the two types might in many instances be in very close juxtaposition to each other.[4]

Sparing superpower homelands entirely was not popular with those sympathetic to striking at high-value SAC targets inside the Soviet Union, but Brodie doubted war could be limited once high-value SAC targets were struck.[5] Instead he had in mind limitations similar to the "self-imposed barrier at the Yalu River" during the Korean War. "*If* the struggle [in Korea] was going to be contained regionally," he wrote in 1954, referring to the Yalu barrier, "*some such* arbitrary line was the simplest and therefore the most reliable way of delimiting it."[6] Such demarcations allowed relatively easy monitoring of the observance of restraints, and they could shape policymakers' expectations about abiding by or breaking those restraints. Believing that efforts prior to war to gain mutual war-making limitations needed to be backed by the threat of "sanctions comprising retaliation in kind," Brodie expected Soviet leaders to be restrained when put on notice that their decision to attack the American homeland would be followed by the destruction of Soviet cities.[7]

Another important contribution made by Brodie to limited-war thinking was to maintain that war in Europe could be localized, without the launching of SAC forces upon a Soviet attack.[8] He was one of the first to suggest that a European war would not have to lead to general war between the superpowers and that the belligerents might be strongly disinclined to escalate to general war levels. In this respect, however, Brodie's ideas were soon to shift. Having early on rebutted the argument that all war needed to be total war, Brodie by 1955 was complaining that too many people were accepting the conclusion that war would be limited if policymakers intended it to be so. "I am alarmed at the readiness with which people are now assuming that an unrestricted general war cannot happen because both sides are agreed on its absurdity," he wrote in October 1955, elaborating on a recently published essay that referred to possible "nihilism" in a European war.

> The fact is that we need to discover and develop sanctions to keep limited any military action that occurs, because we know of powerful pressures to make them unlimited. The sanctions which operated in the case of Korea were of a quite special kind and would probably not be repeated, but they are nevertheless extremely interesting to examine from the point of view of the general problem I have just mentioned.[9]

The "pressures" helping to make war unlimited, Brodie believed, were nonrational and emotional. "We must get away from thinking about war and peace in terms of all or nothing," he declared in February 1956.

> Such is the sweet voice of reason. But what we come up against immediately is the fact that passion and fear are also inseparable from war, that the resort to arms is itself enough to stimulate in those who do so a powerful flow of adrenalin. . . . War, in other words, does have an inherent and almost necessary tendency to be orgiastic. But that does not argue that we must always surrender to that tendency, or that we must use our reasonable moments during peace to concoct doctrines that justify lack of reason in war.[10]

Earlier, Brodie had stressed the Bolshevik code's prescription (as outlined by Nathan Leites) against Soviet leaders' losing control of a situation, when he argued that those leaders would probably wish to avoid urban attacks with nuclear weapons. He had also subscribed to the idea that nuclear weapons had considerably increased the "critical level of exacerbation" at which states would go to war with each other. Now, in highlighting "orgiastic" tendencies in war, he played down by implication the restraints that in his earlier work he believed stabilized nuclear deterrence and warmaking, but he did not justify this conceptual shift.[11]

We have seen that Brodie's earliest work on the H-bomb endorsed seeking military advantage in warfare within the European theater but rejected it in relation to strategic targets within the American and Soviet homelands. In subsequent work during the 1950s, his concerns about the expansion of war increasingly led him to stress mutual military restraint rather than military opportunity in limited war. (His formulation for mutual military restraint—namely, "a more or less tacit agreement among the belligerents to keep the hostilities confined to a particular area, an agreement based upon other than 'strictly military considerations'"[12]—was consistent with his no-cities proposal described in chapter 5.) Eventually he rejected his earlier reliance upon large fusion weapons—or indeed *any* nuclear weapons—in stemming a Soviet invasion of Western Europe, asserting to the contrary that any battlefield nuclear use made limiting war more difficult. These changes in view were part of an effort to rationalize war limitations on something more enduring than the characteristics of a single type of weapon. However, they did not emanate from any critical examination of the expansion of war, which Brodie engaged in only later in the 1960s.

The Uniqueness of Contemporary Limited War

Brodie's emphasis on historical discontinuities in his work on limited war recalled his early work on fission and fusion weapons. "In using the term 'limited war' today," he wrote in 1957,

> we are not talking about a return to something. We are talking about something quite new. If wars were limited in ages past, the reasons why they were so have on the whole little relevance for us today. Apart from the existence of moral and religious scruples, wars were kept limited by the small margin of the national economic resources available for mobilization, as well as by the relatively small capabilities for destruction that could be purchased with those narrow margins. Today, on the contrary, we speak of limited war in a sense that connotes a deliberate hobbling of a tremendous power that is already mobilized and that must *in any case be maintained at a very high pitch of effectiveness*—for the sake only of inducing the enemy to hobble himself to like degree. No problem like this one has ever presented itself before. The problem of modern limited war is the problem of sanctions for keeping out of action, even though in being, precisely those instruments which from a strictly military point of view are the most efficient.[13]

The thrust of that statement was that whereas limitations in capability had significantly restrained war-making in the past, capabilities were no longer effectively limited for the nuclear superpowers, for whom restraints upon war-making would now depend overwhelmingly on the will to avoid weapons use. But Brodie, who did not systematically explore war-making limitations effective before nuclear weapons, failed to show the link between shortcomings in military capabilities and prior instances of limited war. On one hand (as he subsequently pointed out), "demonstrated limitations in capability" helped widen target areas for strategic bombing during the Second World War, especially insofar as inaccuracy of night bombing encouraged area bombing of cities.[14] But elsewhere, limitations in capability have inhibited warfare, as in the Spanish Civil War, where the absence of a Soviet naval capability in the Mediterranean and of an effective Italian bombing capability against the Spanish Republicans helped discourage wider belligerence.[15]

Brodie associated control and limitations upon contemporary warfare with strategy and policy, as when he cited Clausewitz's maxim that wars should be fought as a continuation of policy and therefore as "planned violence and therefore controlled."[16] He had first emphasized the importance of strategy when studying the awesome power of thermonuclear weapons.[17] But it might be asked why such an emphasis was not also (or equally) fruitful in understanding war limitations prior to 1945.

To be sure, war limitations will never depend on strategy alone. Michael Howard argued that war by definition is controlled and limited, the major issue being whether controls and limitations can be derived from "criteria other than those inherent in sound strategy and the requirement for 'good order and military discipline.'"[18] One of the other criteria cited by Howard — "the categorical imperatives derived from the general value-systems of the culture concerned" — was probably responsible for the great fear of general war that grew up in the aftermath of particularly bloody wars and was accentuated in more recent decades by the buildup of awesome mobilized strategic forces, such as (prior to the nuclear age) the Royal Air Force (RAF).[19] Fear of this kind within the British government seems to have worn off within a year following the outbreak of the Second World War, when a decision was made to attack German cities in order to provoke similar German attacks and to take pressure off the RAF. In that instance at least, cultural values were a casualty of strategic interests. "Little could be done," wrote Howard, "to mitigate the totality of wars when that totality was caused by the deliberate policy of the belligerents. But if destructiveness is the consequence not of the object aimed at but of the means employed, then military and moral restraints are not necessarily incompatible."[20] Brodie's earliest writings on H-bombs did not criticize employment of such weapons per se but particular *objects* aimed at with them.

Wars are restrained by strategic considerations — for example, when aggressors hold back some forces in the hope of being able to achieve their goals at the least cost to themselves and their acquisitions. Aggressor states may indeed assume that their adversaries will also abide by force limitations,[21] but the weakness of such an assumption was demonstrated during the Second World War, when bombing limitations lasted nine months before targets in cities were struck. On the other hand, if a nuclear war was short, as many expected, duration of limitations would evidently be less crucial than events at the outset of hostilities — in particular, whether an aggressor could calculate that a limited attack would not lead at once to an all-out war and whether a defender could wait to gauge the intentions of the attacker before deciding to abandon all limits. In general, Brodie assumed that if the Soviets were intent on limited war in Europe they would act to make this intent clear; this was what he meant when he wrote that "we will not be the ones who will choose to fight the one big war" and that "the choice of big or little war would rest with the USSR."[22] But whether the Soviets would somehow modify their military behavior—"hobbling" their capability (beyond nonuse of the Soviet Strategic Air Command [SUSAC]), to use Brodie's phrase—to convey interest in limitations or whether such intent could be otherwise perceptible remained uncertain.[23]

When in previous eras military capabilities had been less potent, signaling restraint with them had been situationally harder, and yet the requirements for waging total war in prior eras were not so very great. Brodie's statement, for example, that warfare had been limited in the past by (among other things) "the small margin of the national economic resources available for mobilization" could be criticized on the grounds that even very small economic margins were historically sufficient to permit total warfare and that these already small margins were often further narrowed by the exploitation of conquered lands.[24] Again, although moral and religious scruples *might* contribute to limiting war, it was not clear why they would not also (in any era) contribute to inflicting massive punishment upon an aggressor who had, in the eyes of the defender, violated some moral code.[25]

Although there is greater wisdom today than in the past about avoiding total war, greater commitment to avoid such war, and greater explicit advance effort to prepare for war-making limitations, situational difficulties in controlling hostilities obviously remain, even assuming that SAC and SUSAC can be "hobbled." First of all, risk taking, which Brodie merely touched upon, is likely to be important in limited war, and at least some failures ought to be anticipated in connection with it. The second and larger point has to do with the ability of national leaders to sustain moral and political moderation in the aftermath of political and military failures, including breakdowns in efforts to prevent hostilities. Since national and personal prestige suffer from such failures, keeping wars limited will depend to a great degree on the success of policymakers in subordinating prestige interests to still more vital war-limitation objectives.

Regional Limitations and Military "Hobbling"

In one respect—the mode in which wars might be usefully limited—Brodie found history had much to say about contemporary problems. "The history and rationale of attempts to limit wars," he wrote in 1954,

> suggest that limitations on the character and use of weapons, wherever they have been attempted, always stand up best in wars that are also limited regionally. Of wars limited regionally by deliberate intent of both parties there is a long catalogue in history. Even wars within Europe have been geographically circumscribed by great-power participants, as for example the Spanish Civil War that preceded the Second World War and the Greek

Civil War that followed it. However, history suggests that Europe is a good place *not* to have a war if one wants to keep it reasonably manageable.[26]

Brodie was defining regional limitations by the degree to which great powers could restrain their military involvements. In Europe, this restraint seemed particularly difficult to achieve since "the great powers tend to get directly involved in what they consider to be the great issues, whereas outside of Europe they either do not get involved directly at all or can regard the issues as being of a colonial character or of peripheral rather than central importance."[27]

Of course, wars that are regionally limited could still be big wars for reasons largely unrelated to the size of the terrain on which they are fought, as in the First World War and in Brodie's own early projection of a thermonuclear war in Europe utilizing three hundred to five hundred bombs. (The Spanish Civil War, though not large by the standard of international military participation, was unlimited in character within Spain and was fought over terrain not much smaller in size than the land combat area on the western front in the First World War.[28]) Brodie addressed this difficulty with the idea that limited war entailed in addition a hobbling of military capability (as the First World War assuredly did not), and he connected military hobbling with geographically demarcated boundaries for warfare by introducing the concept of "sanctuaries" in Soviet and American territory. The latter, evidently suggested by war-fighting restraints adopted in Korea, ruled out the use of strategic air power for homeland (and especially high-value target) attacks.[29]

The effect of hobbling military force (that is, of steering clear of militarily efficient targeting) remains poorly documented. Perhaps superpower belligerents would in some cases concede certain military advantages to create a climate for restraint conducive to, and even necessary for, negotiation toward a rapid conclusion to the war. "It is often argued," wrote Henry Kissinger in defending the idea of limited war,

> that since limited wars offer no inherent guarantee against their expansion, they may gradually merge into all-out war. On purely logical grounds, the argument is unassailable. But it assumes that the major protagonists will be looking for an excuse to expand the war whereas in reality both sides will probably grasp at every excuse, however illogical, to keep a thermonuclear holocaust from occurring. This . . . happened in the Korean War. . . . We refused to retaliate against the Manchurian air bases from which enemy planes were attacking our forces. And the Chinese made no effort to interfere with our aircraft-carriers, or with our bases in Japan, or even to launch an attack against our only two big supply ports, Pusan and Inchon.[30]

But it is unclear that the examples Kissinger referred to constituted a hobbling of military force, as Brodie understood the term. The failure to bomb north of the Yalu was reportedly supported by field commanders, who feared that enemy bombing behind UN lines would interfere with Allied military operations and lessen the effects of attacks against Manchurian targets.[31] At the same time, Communist planes taking off from Manchuria were by no means hurting the Allies, for they were—as Brodie indicated later—being effectively destroyed by Allied fighters.[32]

Even if "illogical" military behavior had not limited war in the past,[33] it might still do so, particularly if, as Kissinger also argued, "illogical limitation is often particularly effective in conveying self-restraint to the other side."[34] Illogical military behavior might be preferable to traditional diplomacy for communicating with the adversary in at least two cases in which the parties are highly desperate; both have been documented by Thomas C. Schelling.[35] In the first case, one or both antagonists act coercively in the belief that the adversary lacks comparable resolve, but coercive diplomacy fails to bring accommodation. Thus to be effective in gaining accommodation, illogical military behavior (hobbling the use of force) must somehow be clearly distinguished from the prior search for military advantage that supported the initial risk taking; this in turn lessens the risk taking. In such an instance, one side's hobbling of its force can be taken advantage of by an opponent still inclined to take major risks. (We will see later that when SAC became more hobbled in the 1960s as protected long-range ballistic missiles removed the need to launch strategic forces to protect them, Brodie and Schelling agreed that the superpowers would be more inclined to take risks if war broke out between them.) Brodie in general did not study risk-taking ventures of this kind; his writings suggest that he would have subordinated such risk taking to the search for ways to terminate hostilities once they had begun.

The second case in which unconventional communication would seem to be important is where a situation seems dangerous to the belligerents not because they have wished it so but because they are not able to adequately control the drift of events.[36] Highly sensitive to this second case, Brodie recommended thinking through beforehand diplomatic action in such a situation and preparing war plans demarcating war-making as much as possible. But irrespective of these commonsense preparations, using intrinsically implausible steps to communicate interest in restraint evidently will yield only limited benefits, as will bargaining upon the onset of superpower hostilities. Many war-making restraints will be sensitive not to bargaining but to military developments,[37] and even when military hobbling and tacit bargaining occur, belligerents are not likely to want to immediately stop fighting at any cost.

The Special Case of Europe

Mostly skeptical about the applicability of pre–nuclear era events to the contemporary limited-war problem, Brodie was also ambivalent about the significance of the Korean War in this respect. On one hand, he declared in 1956 that "if it had not been for the Korean War . . . , it would probably be hardly possible for us today even to envisage such a thing as modern limited war."[38] Here Brodie evidently had in mind the hobbling of military force in Korea. On the other hand, he declared shortly afterward that "our handling of the Korean War can hardly be put forward today as a model of what modern limited wars must be like."[39] This second idea must now be considered, for it indicates that Brodie's conception of limited war was not strongly grounded in experience; he would accordingly be swayed more than usual in his ideas on this subject by later policy and force developments.

First, he did not initially wish to recommend nonuse of nuclear weapons on the Korean model to the problem of defending against a Soviet invasion of Western Europe. "My own feeling," he wrote in 1954, "is that we cannot in the future have 'alternative military plans for carrying on non-atomic warfare' unless we are speaking only of small wars like Korea or Indo-China."[40] It appears that Brodie conceptualized so-called peripheral wars wholly on the basis of Korea. They would occur "on the margins of Soviet power," and the United States

> will be *in support of* some local regime or nation. In a sense we have to be invited in. Usually the area in question will have no intrinsic strategic value to us (just as Korea did not), but our intervention will be part of our general containment (bad word?) policy. All this means that we do the purpose of our intervention no good if we simply rub out the people we are avowedly trying to help. Certainly our military manners will affect future invitations. Those manners are very much bound up in the question: "what kinds of weapons do we use?"[41]

Where American interests were vital, as in Europe, "invitations" to assist threatened countries might be prearranged; but where American interests were nonvital, there was evidently doubt whether invitations would in fact be issued. In the latter instances, if an invitation was issued, much thinking about the specific needs of the regime to be protected and about military logistics would need to be done rather quickly.[42]

Planning for peripheral wars encouraged thinking about war limitations, because military circles (as Brodie reported) insisted on the "terrible . . . hazard involved in attempting to limit any war which is not clearly a peripheral affair,"[43] and because such wars seemed to readily exclude hostilities against Soviet and American homelands. Planning for war in Europe did not initially stimulate such thinking, because Europe was anything but peripheral to the interests of the great powers. Although the use of large nuclear weapons on the battlefield would have been sufficient to make a European war "big," the vital interests over which the powers could fight (as in the two world wars) would have made such a war large irrespective of the weapons employed.

It would have been surprising had the Korean War suggested nuclear weapons nonuse in Europe, for the outbreak of that war stimulated development of nuclear weapons of all types. The availability of newer varieties of nuclear weapons, together with American frustration at fighting in Korea without using these weapons, led the National Security Council (NSC) to authorize the JCS in 1953 to base its war planning on the assumption that tactical and strategic nuclear weapons would be employed whenever militarily convenient.[44] Also in that year, NATO approved new force goals based upon early authorization of nuclear weapons to meet a Soviet attack.[45]

Moreover, American leaders had apparently considered using nuclear weapons early in the Korean War. Brodie later condemned as "uninformed . . . about the uses of nuclear weapons" the recommendations of American commanders during the Korean

War "that there were no suitable targets for n[u]clear weapons in Korea."[46] Asserting that nuclear weapons might have effectively interdicted Chinese forces in Korea, Brodie seems to have overridden this point with another — namely, that once nuclear weapons had been used "from aircraft operating from our own South Korean air bases," those bases would then not be immune from Soviet nuclear counterattack.[47] This last point Brodie did not raise in his initial advocacy of thermonuclear bombs use in Europe, possibly because he had not yet become concerned about the rising battlefield nuclear capabilities of the Soviets, and possibly because in regard to Europe he had in mind defense of vital American interests, whereas in Korea he found only the defense of prestige interests to be at stake.[48]

The second drawback to using the Korean case as a model was that whatever was useful in that war was unplanned. "In view of the fact that ideologically we were completely unprepared for the [Korean] experience (remember that before then it was axiomatic that in modern times all wars are total wars)," Brodie declared early in 1958,

> it seems to me that the overall direction of that war deserves much more praise than blame. . . . Yet we more or less blundered into an adoption of all the major constraints necessary to keeping a war limited, including willingness to settle for goals representing a considerable degree of compromise with the enemy and thus readiness to enter into and maintain negotiations with him while the hostilities were still going on. That was historically a very novel situation, at least, for us. Certainly totally unlike the two world wars.[49]

Major planning during and after the Korean War was directed toward the outbreak of war in Europe. But the question raised in Brodie's work was whether governments could usefully plan for limited war if plans restricted military and political flexibility. Brodie above all did not want the American government to be encumbered by interests, plans, or prior dispositions pressing it one way or the other or closing it off from the nuances of a situation. But limited war may not contribute to flexibility. Those directing the fighting of such a war would obviously need to master much information in a short period while also concentrating upon details of the war and adversary attitudes. Biases could be dangerous in such circumstances, and yet openness to new ideas and skepticism about traditional notions of warfare could not fully substitute for biases.[50]

In addition, traditional ideas were likely to impede flexibility, because they had contextual importance. For example, military force decisions made at any moment would affect freedom of diplomatic maneuver at some later time and, as Brodie noted in 1956, "decisions have been made and are being made now which will determine whether limited wars can be pursued at all and, if so, under what circumstances and with what constraints."[51] In this connection, pursuit of Clausewitz's idea that "war is an instrument of national policy" required "absolute integration" between military planning and foreign policy, yet it was doubtful that such integration existed in the mid-1950s.[52]

Brodie's third problem with the Korean experience was with the political gain American policymakers sought from it. "Korea is a very bad example of a limited war," he declared in 1952,

> because the objectives there appear to be so limited that they sometimes become extremely difficult to detect. But I hope that does not reflect on the general category of limited war. It seems to me that had we raised our sights just a little bit about what we were trying to achieve, it would have been an excellent example indeed of really valuable objectives being accomplished.[53]

Brodie's boldness about American political aims in Korea implied he was satisfied that war limits were not in danger of being broken in that case, because he believed that making the limitations stick was more crucial than the political considerations. "If you try to keep war limited," Brodie wrote in 1954,

> it is because you want to avoid disaster to yourself. In that event, conceptions of "minimum goals" might get terribly in your way. What you want is simply the most you can get *short of* a disastrous breakdown of restrictions. Our settlement in the Korean war, incidentally, was definitely not the most we could have got even under the circumstances of a limited war.[54]

Brodie applied the "hypothetical past" to Korea to suggest that greater political activism might be possible in future limited wars. Others, including Gen. Matthew B. Ridgway, commander of UN forces in Korea, emphasized instead the military costs of unifying the Korean peninsula, particularly in lengthening the supply lines of UN forces and in exacting additional forces to hold a wider battlefront at the Yalu, costs to which American political leaders would have been sensitive.[55] For Brodie, these costs would not have been so important, because they did not bear upon limiting war to the Korean peninsula, and Brodie sought to make force serve political objectives (and not the other way around) within established war limitations. He also hoped for tangible gain to justify the unparalleled American decision to hold back general war forces and to legitimate limited war. But the fear of general war that had governed American behavior in Korea from the start of hostilities was not easily overcome. Having erred by assuming that Korea could be unified without Chinese opposition, American officials became all the more determined to sustain clear-cut limitations, a cautious attitude suggesting that fear of general war could contribute, in the words of Robert Osgood, to "a kind of paralysis of reason and will, [helping] to magnify the risk of measures short of massive retaliation beyond the objective indications of existing military and political conditions."[56]

In a limited war, the greater the perceived risk of general war—or at least the more incalculable and uncertain this risk seemed—the poorer the political imagination of the leaders was likely to be.[57] Playing down the search for one-sided advantages in a Soviet-American war in Europe, Brodie came out against another Clausewitzian maxim that the object of war was to impose one's will on the enemy, rejecting this view "at least for any opponent who has a substantial nuclear capability behind him."[58] But we have seen that Brodie was not as interested in defining rules of conduct for limited war as he was in maximizing flexibility in modes of fighting and in political aspirations.

Early Dissent to NATO Ideas about Limiting War

Brodie had connected tactical use of nuclear weapons to war in Europe with two partly conflicting arguments. First, he presumed, particularly when reflecting on the broader implications of the Korean War, that nuclear weapons ought to be employed to serve vital interests and that the great powers would be engaged in Europe as they had been earlier. Second, Brodie proposed tactical nuclear use to help limit a Soviet-American war since he was convinced that other weapons would not suffice for this purpose. Yet the more strongly engaged vital interests became in a European war, the greater the difficulty in limiting it, *irrespective of the weapons employed.* Brodie did not address this point directly in his writings, but by 1955 he had reconsidered his earlier support for tactical use of nuclear weapons in Europe, mainly on the ground that nuclear use would *weaken* efforts to keep a European war limited. Undoubtedly concerned about the sharply growing Soviet nuclear arsenal aimed at Western Europe, Brodie was equally worried about military inflexibility in the conduct of war, a problem independent of the choice of weapons. If military leaders did indeed receive "a powerful flow of adrenalin" during war, caution in diplomacy was even more important, whether or not nuclear weapons were used.

When Brodie rejected reliance on the tactical use of nuclear weapons, he cited, first of all, the operational difficulty of keeping nuclear war limited. In this connection, he seems to have been sensitive to the prompt as well as the delayed effects of nuclear weapons explosions, in contrast to his earlier writings on the effects of fusion weapons on the battlefield, which were concerned about prompt effects alone.[59] The BRAVO thermonuclear test of March 1954, which killed a Japanese fisherman more than one hundred miles from the point of explosion and revealed to scientists the full magnitude of delayed radiation (fallout) effects,[60] led to further studies of these effects and to upward revision of RAND damage estimates of Soviet bomb attacks against Western Europe. The RAND studies underscored NATO's need to detonate bombs farther east, relying upon wind patterns to sweep nuclear fallout away from friendly populations.[61]

Fallout complicated the protection of friendly military forces from nuclear explosions, but coping with delayed nuclear weapons effects was not altogether different from coping with prompt nuclear damage.[62] Prompt damage, which military planners almost exclusively concentrated upon, was extensive enough in some NATO nuclear war plans of the early 1950s to bring into question NATO's political ability to continue fighting. For example, in the "Carte Blanche" military exercise held in Europe in June 1955, 335 nuclear bombs were "dropped" on airfields and air stations, supply sources, and communications systems in a forty-eight-hour period over an area comprising the Low Countries, part of France, and all of western Germany.

By unofficial calculations, the exercise produced more than five million German "casualties."[63] "The soldiers faced with these sums [of casualties] during 'Carte Blanche,'" Nigel Calder wrote,

> began marking "nuclear fire zones" on their maps, areas that might contain farms and hamlets, but no large concentrations of civilians, and where nuclear weapons might be used with the minimum of self-injury. In the densely populated plains and valleys of Central Europe the nuclear soldier finds himself badly cramped. As one of them complained to me, with legitimate hyperbole, "German towns are only two kilotons apart." He meant that only the smallest nuclear weapons can be used in the gaps between them without killing the inhabitants of the towns.[64]

It was obviously worth considering whether a nuclear war in Europe could be limited at levels whose effects were politically acceptable as well as militarily useful. For example, one informed military estimate found a three-to-five-kiloton weapon optimum for close support missions, apparently since larger weapons might have unintended effects against NATO's own forces. (The same source reserved his demands for larger weapons for targets behind enemy lines.[65]) "In theory," a civilian analyst wrote, "a nuclear war in Europe could be conceived in which *both sides* agree to use only battlefield weapons of very low yield and to attack only targets where collateral damage can be avoided. This type of war ought not to result in damage much higher than in previous wars, and could allow a politically sensible defence."[66] At one point, Brodie seemed to concur in this opinion, asserting in 1955 that "there is plenty of open space between towns so that if you really wanted to refrain from hitting cities while nevertheless attacking the Soviet army with atomic weapons, you could do so. After all, to hurt us he [sic] has to move."[67]

If Calder was correct about the collateral damage prospects, and Brodie wished to keep collateral damage to cities low, the latter would have to accept only limited-size nuclear bombs for the battlefield purposes envisioned. Still, much depended on the nature of the military target. At the time he referred to "plenty of open space between towns," he reiterated his skepticism about limiting tactical nuclear warfare to small-yield weapons.[68] His early position had been that there was no military reason to be content with small-yield bombs, but now Brodie's interest in satisfying military requirements seemed to interfere with his interest in limiting a Soviet-American war. That is, satisfying NATO military commanders seemed to add to the danger that a European war could not be kept limited, given the commanders' interest in military efficiency and Brodie's own understanding of the collateral effects to be expected in such a war. As in his initial proposal for war limitations, when he argued against the SAC bombing mission, Brodie now gave the goal of preserving limitations a higher priority than NATO commanders' interest in effective military use. He condemned, and with some justification, the too-easy attraction of the commanders to large-yield bombs.

It must be stressed that in the 1950s, NATO war-making would probably have been governed by considerations other than that of limiting collateral damage. NATO

planners, then unwilling to impose arbitrary limits upon the size or numbers of nuclear weapons used, provided for the use of some large nuclear bombs. For example,
the prevailing view at NATO headquarters, similar to Brodie's earlier outlook, was
that nuclear weapons exchanges would decide any European war and that the defense
would be advantaged by the need of attacking forces to concentrate.[69] As Brodie
noted, the denser the target, as in the case of concentrated attacking forces, the
greater the military justification for using large-yield nuclear weapons against it.

High-yield nuclear strikes might not in themselves lead to high collateral damage,
as in the case of dense concentrations of Soviet troops, but the Soviets might deny
such excellent targets to NATO. Brodie had noted earlier that by avoiding heavy
troop concentrations, Soviet forces would be proportionately weakened in their attacking strength, but this was true only in a traditional war of fixed battle lines;
many believed that nuclear weapons had rendered a war of this kind obsolete.[70] For
example, the Soviets might divert their forces to major Western European cities,
hoping NATO nuclear strikes against such cities would be ruled out.[71] Collateral
damage would probably be extremely heavy if such strikes were nevertheless implemented and especially if elusiveness of enemy personnel required them to be
indiscriminate.[72]

Another possibility was that the Soviets might preempt use of nuclear weapons
to support troop movements. By 1954 they apparently had introduced battlefield
nuclear capabilities into their European armies and had begun to train their forces
in East Germany to attack in dispersed fashion in terrain in which they would not
present effective targets for atomic weapons.[73] The danger of Soviet preemptive use
of nuclear weapons grew as the Soviets developed nuclear-tipped intermediate-range
ballistic missiles (IRBMs) targeted against NATO, which, with high accuracy, became "the almost ideal counterforce weapon."[74] If NATO nuclear forces were destroyed in a Soviet nuclear attack, SAC might then be launched from American bases
against Soviet homeland targets, either in all-out fashion, in accordance with a 1956
NATO Council policy directive, or against military targets alone, as suggested in
a proposal put forward by Richard Leghorn.[75]

For all these reasons, a Soviet attack against Western Europe that spared economic
and urban targets was by no means sufficient to ensure that such a war would be
kept limited. The Soviets might in fact attack those economic and urban targets.
The NATO war plan of 1955 assumed such targets were safe since the Soviets would
wish to capture NATO economies intact,[76] but Brodie nevertheless questioned hing-
ing the NATO war plan so heavily on such an assumption. "If we use large weapons
against the enemy," Brodie argued in 1955, "we must expect him to reply in kind
up to the limits of his capability. We certainly could not rely on his voluntarily re-
fraining from doing so. When we are talking about a war in which weapons of
the magnitude described are actually being dropped in large numbers in Europe, we
are talking about a war in which rationality as an inhibiting factor has already been
left far behind."[77]

In this statement, Brodie seems to be giving far more weight than he had earlier to the side effects of nuclear weapons explosions and to growth in the Soviets' military strength and their willingness to use it and far less weight to the prospects of an agreement to confine the use of nuclear weapons to targets other than cities. As to why the Soviets would employ nuclear weapons to the "limits of their capability" (which presumably meant attacking cities) even if NATO should attempt to refrain from such attacks (the only reasonable basis for the assumption that the Soviets would also refrain), Brodie may have believed that apart from the military utility of attacking cities full of soldiers, it was not self-evident that Soviet interests would support the limitations NATO planners hoped for. Nor did Brodie anticipate such limitations, for his concept of hobbling military force did not include limitations *within* the battle theater; it was only the geographic *widening* of the theater that Brodie wished to avoid.

If NATO planners assumed Soviet war-making restraint without providing incentives to the Soviets to conform to that expectation, any NATO effort to limit nuclear war in Europe would be fragile.[78] On the other hand, Brodie never urged full NATO rejection of the high-yield nuclear bombs whose use he feared might lead the Soviets to abandon the restraints he valued. His understanding of the military arguments for nuclear use on the battlefield and his anticipation that nuclear weapons would be exploited for their full combat value after all ironically contributed to his subsequent disinclination to use battlefield nuclear weapons, much as his earlier strong awareness of the military effectiveness of strategic bombing contributed to his rejection of such bombing.[79]

More NATO Ideas and More Brodie Dissent

Brodie's trenchant critique of NATO strategy was greatly at odds with his earliest advocacy of tactical warfare less than four years earlier. Then, confident of limiting war, he looked to nuclear weapons as a major indispensable resource of NATO war-making, emphasizing the battlefield destruction potential of nuclear bombs and the political gain for the alliance in its newfound ability to hold the Soviet army. By 1955 Brodie had become highly worried about reciprocal use of nuclear weapons in a European war. Again, in 1952, he had been privately concerned about the vulnerability of Western European cities to Soviet coercion as a weak point of the NATO alliance without, however, doubting the usefulness of H-bombs to the NATO defense problem. Three years later, by contrast, he had concluded that the two matters were more closely interconnected — that is, that use of large nuclears by NATO would likely affect Soviet propensity to attack Western European cities. And whereas in 1954 Brodie claimed that American ability to stay ahead of the Soviet Union in all types of bomb production, once exercised, assured major NATO advantages on the European battlefield, a year later he failed to cite anything that might contribute to comparable military benefits.

In the interval, Brodie had become convinced of the delicacy of war-making limitations, and since he had already made war limitations a matter of the highest priority, all his attitudes about European war-making were bound to shift. Much of his 1955 critique of NATO strategy was traceable to his differences with NATO commanders and planners over the priority to be attached to limiting war. In this controversy, Brodie may have overstated the dangers of war expansion in Europe and for two reasons. First, he appeared to neglect the intervention of NATO's political leadership in the conduct of a European war. A coalition as unwieldy as NATO might well decide upon war more slowly and more contentiously than would, say, a government in Washington or in London; this was an important price for subjecting NATO war-making to supreme political authorization and governance.[80] (That such governance would not be merely nominal is strongly indicated by the popular outcry that followed publication of the results of exercise Carte Blanche.) To be sure, European political leaders had repeatedly expressed opposition to war-making limitations, but their statements to this effect were part of an understandable effort to deter war and might seem much less appropriate once war had broken out.

Second, Brodie implied that the will of NATO's military staff to limit war counted in practice for nothing. Of course, even the best NATO war plan might not succeed in reconciling demands for military restraint with inevitable pressures to employ nuclear weapons for military advantage. Further, irrespective of the strength of the military will to restrict war, limitations might be impossible if NATO civilian leaders—on whose shoulders presumably lay the largest responsibility for conveying intent to limit war to the Soviets—lacked a comparable attitude.[81] (Having already spoken negatively on this subject in the 1950s, the civilians would presumably have a difficult time conveying more benign intent following a major Soviet attack.) When Brodie referred to the "orgiastic" tendencies of war, he seems to have had in mind most of all a weakened personal and collective will to limit war, but he could not have been fully describing the motives of governments or their military advisers to expand war, for accompanying any orgiastic tendencies from the start would also probably be considerable agony within policymaking circles at the rapidly mounting destruction. As Brodie himself pointed out in discussing large-scale attacks on cities in the United States, such sentiment would add greatly to political pressures to terminate hostilities.

In subsequent years, there was to be no lack of thinking at NATO headquarters and outside it about how to enforce limitations in a European war. The concept developed by General Norstad, after he succeeded in 1956 to the position of SACEur, was to prepare for an initial holding period following a Soviet attack, before the SACEur would recommend use of major retaliatory forces against the Soviet Union. "I propose," he declared in 1957, "to hold long enough to force the Soviets to consider the effect of this retaliatory force which will lead to their destruction, and if they start the war I think we can hold until the effect of our retaliatory force is felt. . . . I am confident that given the forces we have indicated we require . . . we can hold for this purpose."[82]

Whether a pause was possible, and for how long, would obviously depend on the scale of the Soviet attack. For example, a small Soviet attack, which was possibly a precursor to a major one, might lead to a decision to supplement NATO's conventional forces with a few small nuclear weapons against specific targets.[83] Coral Bell remarked that the pause concept "is obviously designed to meet the ambiguities of a situation in which the distinction between a negotiable border clash and the prelude to general war would not necessarily be immediately apparent."[84] She meant that the pause was designed to clarify the purpose behind relatively minor Soviet military incursions; it would have little to do with massive attacks, the motive for which would probably be unambiguous. The difficulty, however, was that expanded force requirements approved for NATO for the late 1950s and early 1960s were geared much more for large-scale war in Europe than for the minor incursions against which the pause would be helpful. (The bulk of NATO war planning had in fact been to prepare for a deliberate, massive Soviet attack in Europe.[85]) NATO document MC 70 (a study examining the period 1957–1962) proposed that NATO forces balance the Russian forces based in East Germany, Poland, and Hungary and that battlefield nuclear weapons be used to prevent reinforcement of those forces. Satisfying and probably exceeding this requirement, American intermediate-range ballistic missiles (IRBMs) and additional nuclear weapon stockpiles controlled under a double-veto system were sent to Europe. Under the new conditions,

> the definition of "tactical" was such that the Supreme Allied Commander, Europe (SACEUR) was to be able to destroy all Soviet weapons aimed at Europe. The nuclear arsenal in Europe thus included some weapons of a range and destructiveness indistinguishable from those in the arsenal of the Strategic Air Command (SAC). They could be called "tactical" only in the sense that they were stationed in Europe and not in the United States and that they were controlled by SACEUR rather than the commanding general of SAC.[86]

Accepting Norstad's pause concept, Brodie nevertheless questioned the need for the new NATO force requirements. These requirements, helping to proliferate nuclear weapons and nuclear force missions, were justified by the perceived vulnerability of SAC to a Soviet attack, which some believed weakened the protection afforded by American strategic forces to Europe's defense.[87] Brodie presumably had SAC vulnerability in mind when he wrote in 1959 that "it is obvious that the larger the conflict, the more pressure there must be for abandoning limitations."[88] He obviously wished to keep a European conflict at the lowest possible level, an objective seemingly unaided by multiplying nuclear forces in Western Europe. The new NATO forces were attractive targets for Soviet missiles stationed along the western border of the Soviet Union and, as they were vulnerable especially to major nuclear attack, they undercut the value of the pause. They were also likely to strengthen predispositions within NATO headquarters to use nuclear weapons to defend Western Europe.[89] Whether flexibility offered at levels of major war by NATO's nuclear weapons could be as small as the flexibility offered by the American emergency war plan under comparable conditions is not clear, but at those levels the outlook for keeping war limited may not have appeared good in any case.[90]

Criticizing the NATO force goals from the perspective of limiting warfare, Brodie emphasized instead the distinction between nuclear and nonnuclear weapons, because "it is bound to be easier to distinguish between use and non-use of nuclear weapons than between the use of a 10 KT weapon and one two or three times as large. If there are going to be sanctions against violations, the violations must be unequivocal. The need for simplicity in discrimination is paramount. The problem of keeping wars limited will be at best difficult enough."[91] Brodie believed that the salience of this distinction was critical, for mutual understanding of the limits "will almost certainly have to be tacit rather than explicit."[92] The recent popular tendency to distinguish nuclear from nonnuclear weapons use, he argued, even though produced by nonrational feelings, "ought not be blandly waved aside as unimportant."[93]

The distinction between nuclear and nonnuclear weapons also has technological justification, for nuclear bombs become more efficient only at higher yields, whereas conventional explosives are more efficient at lower yields.[94] But this rationale was unlikely to contribute to war limitations. Since fighting in Europe without nuclear weapons was so inefficient for NATO, a European war would presumably persist in that form only if the alliance obtained compensating advantages, such as rapid end to the fighting or Soviet abstinence from nuclear weapons use or more generally from capitalizing on major military opportunities.

Brodie seems to have favored compensating for military inefficiencies in Europe by threatening reprisal attacks—with American homeland forces out of range of Soviet IRBMs—against military targets inside the Soviet Union; in other words, some Soviet aggression in Europe would be discouraged and met by alerted American strategic forces.[95] As in his earlier work, Brodie was substituting threats for the actual use of force, making of coercion a limited war technique without spelling out the process that such threat making would take. In this case, furthermore, he played down the dangers of Soviet reprisals by suggesting that if the Soviets really did contemplate major war with the United States, they assuredly would concentrate on attacking American strategic forces instead of exploiting NATO's weaknesses in Europe. "What gives a modest number of NATO divisions the chance of coping with the Soviet Army," he wrote in *Strategy in the Missile Age*,

> is not their capacity to use nuclear weapons, which the Soviet Army also enjoys, but the fact that a massive intervention of Soviet ground forces is unlikely except with a Soviet decision to wage total war. As we have already indicated, so long as the United States seems to be committed to retaliate massively to such intervention, the Soviets would have to anticipate our reaction by a strategic bombardment of the United States. A limited-war capability in Europe should be considered as having very little to do with that kind of war. . . . NATO troops in Europe that are openly dedicated to limited-war strategies and functions are likely to have a stabilizing influence precisely because they will tend to discourage the proclivity for probing and testing which is so characteristic of Soviet military diplomacy.[96]

If major Soviet aggression in Europe were tantamount to a Soviet decision to wage total war, there would obviously be little room for reprisals against Soviet military targets. This was hardly the most interesting case, but the strategists were divided about what was of most interest to them in the event of war in Europe. The staunchest advocates of counterforce hoped to use the threat of reprisal to stiffen NATO resolve; they seemed to believe that counterforce attacks were practicable even after major, though nonnuclear, Soviet aggression in Europe.[97] Brodie, evidently not among these advocates, was less interested in validating the use of counterforce than in establishing the prior importance of the intent behind the Soviet aggression.

A Dissent to Advocates of Conventional War in Europe

Not all strategists sympathized with the idea of repairing European conventional force inadequacies primarily by expanding general war capabilities. Those such as Brodie who focused more on the political aspects of crisis decision making rather than on the military concerns tended to take a different tack. But where Brodie in the late 1950s rather complacently rested his case against NATO nuclear rearmament on the idea that the Soviets would in all likelihood reject anything that could lead to total war, others concentrated on problems associated with NATO diplomatic behavior toward the Soviet Union. In particular, the NATO European allies, who had earlier opposed waging limited war in Europe, also paradoxically demonstrated themselves in practice to be very fearful of the risks of general war. For example, the three-year crisis over Berlin that began in 1958 was characterized by the mild and sometimes divided response of the major allies to Soviet threats to sign a separate peace treaty with East Germany.

Some, especially Malcolm Hoag, traced this relatively unassertive response to fears that resolute opposition to the Soviet initiatives would raise the risks of general war too high. Anxious to enhance NATO's political initiative, they dissented from the view (supported by Brodie and others) that nuclear capabilities — in the form of reprisals against Soviet homeland targets — were needed to shore up NATO's political will. Without rejecting counterforce initiatives entirely, they proposed to narrow them in the main to situations in which the Soviets had already used nuclear weapons tactically in a European war but without striking at SAC.[98] The necessary political backbone for the alliance, they maintained, should be provided by building up NATO conventional forces to withstand, primarily with those forces, maximum Soviet conventional forces (including reserves) that could be brought against them until superior American military potential could be brought to bear.[99] This view was ultimately accepted by the American government, which decided in 1960 and 1961 that a strengthening of NATO conventional forces would have priority over that of battlefield nuclear weapons.

Hoag wished to ease the "agonies" of NATO decision making by offering alternatives to "the fateful nuclear decision."[100] Brodie was unconvinced of the connection between *larger* forces and political backbone — he pointed out that during the Berlin crisis, some at NATO headquarters (including Norstad) had opposed military action for reasons other than timidity and that some in NATO would oppose such future action even once alliance forces were strengthened. Brodie was also unconvinced that the "firebreak" between nuclear and nonnuclear weapons was *invariably* the best cutoff point for war-making limitations.[101] In his view, "strong and firm resistance to a local and limited aggression" could clarify to the Soviets the resolve of the NATO alliance and, though "there is less chance of that demonstration going out of control if nuclear weapons have not in the meantime been used," conventional warfare could also get out of hand. *"There is no basis in experience,"* Brodie wrote in 1962, *"and very little in logic for assuming that the increase in level of violence from three divisions to thirty is intrinsically a less dangerous form of escalation than the introduction of nuclear weapons."*[102]

Worried about escalation, Brodie was nevertheless basing his strategy upon threatening it, for he wished to deter a less than all-out Soviet attack in Europe without the prospect of an adequate capability to defend against it. Presumably, such threat making would change the minds of Soviet leaders before relatively weak NATO conventional forces would be overwhelmed by a Soviet attack. (Instead of taking pressure *off* of NATO, he wished to pile it *on* Soviet leaders, impressing them with the awesome prospects of initiating war in Europe.) If the Soviet attack were large scale, the opportunity for changing Soviet intentions under Brodie's strategy would be minimal or nonexistent, and I have already noted Brodie's belief that such an attack would sooner or later involve major attacks against vulnerable superpower strategic forces. Trying to affect Soviet intentions was therefore important for him only when the attack was relatively minor. Hoag, on the other hand, advocated conventional defense against a major Soviet attack, presumably to provide a longer opportunity for Soviet leaders to change their war-making assessment.

The two strategists, moreover, conceptualized Soviet behavior differently. Hoag contended that NATO's lack of a conventional force option was exploitable by an enemy who refused to quit fighting "because he is winning and pressures for NATO capitulation are high. It is the weak side at whatever level war is being fought which bears the greater burden of decision, because it is the side most driven to escalation risks that nobody can calculate confidently."[103] Brodie played down this point because he believed that Soviet leaders, prior to launching an attack in Europe, would have to reckon anyway with the prospect that nuclear weapons would probably be used, and therefore "the prospect of fighting a large land battle in Europe without nuclear weapons may well look simply too bizarre to the Russians to be taken seriously."[104]

It followed that too much was being asked for the conventional forces strategy in gaining Soviet reassessment following a major Soviet premeditated attack.

Where is the inducement to the Soviet Union to play the game that way? We have made as clear as we can (because we really mean it) that we will not accept a loss. We may in fact think differently after a limited loss, or the enemy may think we will, which is one of the things wrong with the philosophy [of stemming for a time an all-out Soviet nonnuclear attack with NATO conventional forces] and certainly one important reason why Germany, for example, is not likely to accept it. Reassessment is a two-way street, and if we think we are immune to it our allies, and our enemy, may not. But if we mean what we say and do what we mean, we will be ready to bring in our nuclear weapons—not in tactical but in discriminate strategic action. . . .

[T]he Russians . . . will either refrain from large-scale aggression altogether, or they will proceed towards it in something other than a U.S.-preferred way. And if they refrain, which is what we want them to do, it is of course our strategic nuclear forces, not our local conventional forces, which have obliged them to do so. That is exactly where we stand now. What then will we have gained by the further conventional buildup?[105]

Conclusions

In this chapter, I have noted the large uncertainties to be found in limited war and Brodie's sensitivity to them. Much of Brodie's work during the 1950s was to expose what he believed to be the insufficient attention given, especially by military staffs, to these uncertainties, which were both military and political. Militarily uncertain in limited war were battlefield targets, the scope of fighting limitations accepted by the adversary, and the effect of acting on one's own side to take full advantage of military opportunities. Politically uncertain were how to gain fighting limitations from the other side and how to use force to achieve vital national interests. Military and civilian planners needed to allow for these uncertainties by incorporating a wide range of assumptions into studies about military and political dispositions, anticipating alternative war-expanding and limitation-preserving scenarios.

Brodie was prepared to sacrifice much to ensure that limitations would stick, though since he was in no position to narrow the uncertainties about limited warfare, he inevitably emphasized the virtues of caution and deliberation. He was gloomiest about the feasibility of enforcing limitations, as when he anticipated orgiastic warfare and when he contended that "the larger the conflict, the more pressure there must be for abandoning limitations."[106] Without citing empirical justification for this outlook, he used it to justify making heavy concessions in military and political values for the sake of keeping war limited and especially to seek those limitations most likely to be respected by the adversary.

Much of Brodie's writing on limited war pertained to politicians charged with the overall direction of war. For example, enforcing war limits with threats of war expansion, as Brodie recommended, was a political responsibility that presumed an awareness of the need to hobble use of force at the outset of war. In addition, the most important contributor to expanded war, particularly in Europe, was likely to be the vital political interests over which the war had begun.

On the matter of Western threat making, much obviously depended on whether NATO had adequate will and unity to make such threats, on whether the Soviets might anticipate such NATO threat making prior to attacking, and finally on whether the Soviets would indeed attack after anticipating the higher risks of an escalated war. To the extent that Soviet leaders were uncertain about retaining war limitations, they might hesitate to go to war, but these uncertainties might be overridden in time of tension by severe "pressure of events" considerations. Bold action by NATO might have a telling effect upon Soviet leaders, particularly if they did not expect it, but there was little in NATO's experience to suggest that the alliance was prepared to take risks of this kind, however effective they might be.

Brodie went beyond stressing the uncertainties inherent in limited war, but he nowhere outlined a coherent strategy for it, in part because he was not of a single mind on how such wars might develop. For example, his idea that the Soviets would yield in the face of NATO threats was not fully consistent with his view that wars did, after all, tend to expand orgiastically. He clearly wished to control limited war-making as much as possible, which necessarily entailed manipulating threats and risks, but he also wished to keep risks as small as possible by avoiding the use of battlefield nuclear weapons entirely. One or the other might be successful, but Brodie did not point the way to a sense of priorities between them or to the consequences of trying them both.

On the second political question — determining the vital interests over which war in Europe would be fought — Brodie depended heavily on strictures about making war the servant of political objectives, which he had gleaned from Clausewitz and which he applied mainly to his analyses of limited war. Here again, however, he was of two minds. He initially argued that military values ought to be sacrificed for the sake of political ones, but later, especially when critiquing NATO plans for limited war, he seems to have treated the hobbling of force as a problem in itself. If, as in this second perspective, military forces were the major concern, it was crucial to make whatever concessions in political objectives were necessary for strategic forces to stay hobbled. Depending on the perspective chosen, war limitations could either be governed by political objectives (as in Korea) or be torpedoed by them, and Clausewitz would not be falsified in either case.

It was for the military planners and commanders, however, rather than the political leaders that Brodie directed his harshest criticism in his work on limited war. He became skeptical of the ability of responsible military officials to think adequately about limitations and saw their war plans as the source of potentially orgiastic warfare. This helps explain why Brodie changed his views about how to keep war in Europe limited and proposed neutralizing all nuclear weaponry for battlefield combat. Ironically, upon changing his views he criticized a military outlook at NATO headquarters that he himself had recommended in 1952. In coming a rather long way from his earliest relatively uncritical support of nuclear weapons use in European combat, Brodie probably set his expectations unrealistically high in holding planners and commanders to the same chastened views about European nuclear war that he came to have.

Brodie no doubt feared what NATO military commanders could do with the forces at their disposal, particularly with large-yield bombs, which he associated with the highest nuclear-striking efficiencies. The same concern with large-yield bombs that informed his analyses of thermonuclear weapons also colored his estimate of the potential for nuclear war in his writing on limited war later in the 1950s.[107] He would not exclude the large nuclear bombs from war-making, apparently because he was sensitive to the needs that military commanders had for them; but his later argument against using any nuclears in a European war depended heavily on his fear of large-yield weapons being used. Part of the problem was undoubtedly Brodie's use of large-yield weapons as a standard of military efficiency—a somewhat wooden standard since technical efficiency depended on targets struck as well as on the attributes of particular weaponry. Another aspect of the problem was Brodie's failure to study operational war-making carefully. For example, once he excluded nuclears from tactical warfare, he failed to discuss to his own satisfaction what weapons would replace them, an issue particularly urgent for military professionals frustrated by the exclusion of nuclear capabilities from the Korean War.[108]

In one sense, given all too little knowledge about how to keep war limited, the least amount of fighting was wisest; on the other side, however, the risks of excluding the best military muscle for the sake of war limitations were considerable. Brodie's most lasting major contribution in his earliest writings about limited war (as in much of his other work) was to substitute ideas about diplomatic subtlety for the satisfaction of military requirements.[109] How much diplomatic wisdom could indeed offset the lack of adequate defensive capabilities in Europe was not clear, and Brodie did not study this question in detail. It was not irrational in principle to depend on political action to limit war in Europe, but in practice Brodie had advocated placing the primary burden for defending Europe on the politicians while denying them adequate tactical military support. If they failed to show the requisite political imagination in these circumstances, they stood to lose a great deal.

8 · Escalation

Brodie's work on limited war during the 1950s was linked to his assumptions about escalatory tendencies in war, because policymakers needed resolve and skill to combat those tendencies in order to preserve limitations on hostilities. But the contrasting situation of a breakdown of limitations—what Brodie termed "orgiastic" warfare[1]— might develop in spite of policymakers' attempts to prevent it, which is to say that diplomatic and military efforts to combat escalatory tendencies would be present even in that case. Those efforts were likely to be intense, given the widespread appreciation of the enormous consequences attending contemporary Soviet-American failure to make war limitations stick and—especially once nuclear weapons had been employed—would almost certainly overshadow attempts to prevent orgiastic wars of the past. Little or no work had been done by the early 1960s on escalatory tendencies in war, one reason being the dominant concern with surprise attack among strategic analysts during that decade.[2] This concern, stimulated by vulnerable strategic forces, implied that it would be difficult indeed to stop escalation of a Soviet-American war. Overshadowing Brodie's interest in and elaboration upon the concept of limited war during that decade was his sharing of this concern about the surprise-attack problem; studies on the basing of air power under way at RAND had highlighted this problem in relation to the vulnerability of long-range retaliatory forces. "In a world in which there was," Brodie wrote in 1959,

> very little incentive on either side, or at least on the Soviet side, for surprise strategic attack . . . we should have much less reason to fear the quick spiraling upward of the level of violence. Some means of controlling that level for the local area would still have to be found, but the problem would nevertheless be of much more moderate dimensions than the one we face now, when the "balance of terror" is far from stable.[3]

Another, related reason for the neglect of escalation in strategic analysis was the overwhelming preoccupation of strategists at the time with major nuclear war, in which efforts to avoid escalation would presumably be unimportant or unavailing. Brodie, who had described the military and political consequences of nuclear weaponry with the largest explosive yields, defined escalation as the "unintended spread of limited wars"⁴ and focused upon major escalation occurring all at once. The rationale was that the great pressure to send strategic bombers to their targets to remedy their vulnerability could outweigh superpower reluctance to start a third world war. Such reluctance was for Brodie the basis for all ideas about limited war.⁵ "The chief problem in any limited war," he wrote in the same 1959 study, "will be, not how to fight it conveniently, perhaps not even to assure ourselves a decisive local victory, but rather how to make sure that it stays limited—more particularly, how to make sure that it does not erupt into that total war which starts disastrously with our receiving the first blow."⁶ If escalation could come quickly, render all earlier war-making insignificant, and dwarf all peacemaking efforts, it was all the more deserving of study. Not surprisingly, however, the preoccupation with "eruption" of hostilities predisposed strategists to concentrate "on avoiding the outbreak of war, rather than the escalation that we feared must surely follow an outbreak."⁷

This pessimism was at odds with Brodie's pioneering work on limited war and with his belief that escalatory threats could be manipulated to control a European war.⁸ By the 1960s, however, his anticipation of newfound strategic stability associated with large numbers of protected ballistic missiles signified for him an opportunity for more flexibility in European war and for refining the concept of escalation to reflect that flexibility. "In its most common use," Brodie wrote in 1962, " 'escalation' usually refers to a change from limited to general war. However, the term itself connotes the idea that the progress from one condition to the other can be by stages, which may, however, be traversed rapidly."⁹ With this refinement, the importance of "unintended" escalation wasa critically diminished.¹⁰ Second, at this same time, the American massive retaliation strategy was replaced by one endeavoring to diminish reliance upon nuclear weapons in a war with the Soviets. In the early 1960s, Brodie's thinking about escalation became intertwined with his opposition to a major component of this new strategy—namely, the conventional force buildup in Europe.

The Effect of General War Forces on Limited War

I have already noted in this study Brodie's long-standing view that limited war preparations could not be pursued or evaluated on their own but rather depended on strategic force strengths and dispositions. A corollary of this view was that strengthening American limited war priorities—widely urged by the late 1950s—required prior adjustment in general war forces. "The more effectively we do our job in the area of total war responsibilities," Brodie wrote in 1960, "the greater the range of possible cases for the application of limited force. In other words—and the paradox of it should not worry us too much—we have to spend more on total war in order to have good reasons for spending more on limited war."¹¹

It seemed self-defeating, to be sure, to spend heavily on limited war forces if the risks of escalation were high, as they were in the 1950s with super-alerted strategic bombers and their very short reaction time to a warning of attack.¹² These features, accentuated by American plans for counterforce attacks against the Soviets—were especially dangerous because, according to Brodie,

> in periods of intense crisis we are probably as capable as the Russians of acting out what may seem to be the imperatives of the moment. And our conceptions of what we are compelled to do will be molded, like theirs, by a range of rational, semi-rational, and non-rational judgments or impressions, all coming out of human beings charged with emotion, including emotions of which the possessors are not even conscious.
>
> The decisive factor, however, is that we have commitments which may force us to take intransigeant [sic] and even menacing positions. We live in a world in which many things have changed and are continuing to change drastically, above all methods of waging war, but in which the basic patterns of diplomacy have changed relatively little. Those patterns continue to place a very heavy reliance on threats of force, implicit or explicit, to maintain existing positions or to change them for the better.[13]

This instability to which he referred was linked in his mind to limited war, for he indicated that "any outbreak of hostilities which involves or threatens to involve members of the communist world against members of the non-communist world will have the feel of a crisis situation."[14]

At one extreme, strategic instabilities could be so high that limited war forces would be unable to control any hostilities. The concept of escalation held during the 1950s, which allowed for only two levels of war-making, seemed based on a condition not far removed from this extreme case. Yet Brodie, who insisted that manipulating the threat of general war was possible even in that instance, once limited war forces were employed, critically depended on the assumption that *some* strategic stability would permit risk taking; whatever small degree of stability strategic forces then afforded could help inhibit escalation.[15] To be sure, manipulating the threat of general war under such conditions also invited mutual provocation once localized hostilities started.[16] Brodie understood this to be a perceptual problem, in which biases were likely to affect decision making and increase the chances of miscalculation. "I should like to suggest," he wrote in a 1959 paper entitled "Provocation Works on People,"

> that we must avoid a go–no go criterion for what is provocative. If we define as provocative only that action of ours which will directly induce the Soviet Union to attack us (even if the attack itself should be somewhat delayed) then admittedly almost no action of ours would be provocative. We are all agreed that if we do things which convince them that we are planning an immediate attack upon them, they will try to preempt us. However, we are also interested in the cumulative effect of lesser acts, and in lesser responses than total war. . . . But above all, inasmuch as we seem to have rejected preventive war, we presumably want deterrence to last a very long time.[17]

At the other extreme, also with negative consequences for limited war forces, the threat of general war could inhibit *all* warfare. This situation evidently presumed significant one-sided military superiority, such as that which the United States exercised over the Soviet Union in the late 1950s, in which the threatening power could be bolder than its adversary. Brodie's primary rationale for limited war forces during the 1950s was that one-sided situations did not remove the risks of escalation completely. Because of those risks, Brodie asserted, relying wholly on the threat of general war to discourage lesser aggression would be acceptable only if the threat of general war reduced the chances of aggression "almost to zero." However, he went on,

> if we accept this [massive retaliation] argument at face value, we must still be concerned with the degree to which the low probability of war credited to this policy falls short of being zero. The probability of war does not have to be high to impel us to hunt for alternatives to *total* war. We might be willing to accept a much higher probability of wars breaking out if we could confidently expect to keep them limited.
>
> Our problem of choice is easier, however, if we are persuaded that the massive-retaliation policy does not in fact minimize the probability of small wars.[18]

Neither full instability in general war forces nor full military superiority in such forces encouraged wider study of escalation. Nor did two broad and axiomatic generalizations that Brodie, asserting they were grounded in history and human psychology, put forward on this subject in 1961. The first of these specified that "a new and higher level of violence introduced by one side in a conflict is highly likely to be *at least met* by the other side, so long as the latter possesses the appropriate capabilities and is not ready to relinquish its position."[19] The other contended that "in war, levels of violence tend almost always to move upwards, rarely downward, until the actual ending of the conflict." Silent about stopping the escalatory dynamic, the primary objective of any escalation strategy, these propositions left unclear how analysis of this subject would yield policy benefits.

What Brodie termed a "crucial change . . . in the general strategic environment"[20] — that is, the fortuitous deployment of protected long-range ballistic missiles on land and sea, that permitted local war in Europe without raising alarmingly the chances of a third world war — critically improved the outlook for escalatory strategy.[21] Brodie viewed relatively invulnerable long-range missiles as mainly a deterrent force whose purpose was defeated once they were fired. In this instance, such forces promised to deter a general war begun either by a strategic nuclear attack against the opposing superpower or through escalation of a lower-level European conflict. "Attractive counterforce targets," Brodie wrote in 1964 in connection with the problem of strategic nuclear attack, "promise to become scarce because of hardening and concealment [of missiles]"; moreover, "the withdrawal of the enemy's forces from accessibility does *not* make his cities a more attractive target but rather a much more dangerous one. Neither side can fail to understand that."[22] In addition, the greater difficulty of implementing a counterforce attack promised also to dampen war-expanding impulses, lessening the risks of an escalation strategy. In this way, as with the development of fusion bombs, apparent frustrations in strategic target selection directed attention toward limited warfare.

Escalation in a Limited Nuclear War

Believing that lessened risks of general war permitted the employment of limited war forces in a larger variety of situations, Brodie at first saw that opportunity as lessening the inhibitions associated with introducing nuclear weapons into hostilities. "If one side or the other sees some advantage in introducing tactical nuclear weapons in a limited war," he wrote in 1962, "it has the bracing assurance that both sides recognize it to be clearly and deeply in their interests to refrain from going to a strategic exchange. In short, stability at the top may work against stability at lower and intermediate levels."[23] This same development not only suggested a lessened fear of escalation and the newer significance of deliberate war expansion but also the "unintended spread of limited war" that he had conceptualized as late as 1960. The former, and the accompanying possibility of exercising far more control over war-making than in the past, Brodie distinctively highlighted when playing down the dangers of war expansion. In particular, he came to stress that some escalation could actually work against further expansion of war and be less dangerous than, for example, rapid, major conventional force increases in war. "It is interesting," Brodie wrote in 1962,

> that the standard argument in favor of larger conventional forces in Europe not only tends to assume considerable ease of escalation in the size of forces committed but, even more, seems on examination to be willing to make it *easy* for this kind of escalation to take place. It does so by attempting to suppress the threat that increase in scale of commitment will trip use of nuclear weapons. If escalation in size of forces is in fact (especially in Europe) a very dangerous as well as intrinsically destructive kind of escalation, it might be well to seek means for inhibiting rather than encouraging it; one way to discourage it would be to threaten to bring in nuclear weapons relatively early, or actually to do so. In this respect the threat or actual use of tactical nuclear weapons may be counter-escalatory.[24]

Developing the idea of counterescalatory nuclear weapons use, Brodie for the first time distinguished nuclear weapons committed to the battlefield from those committed to homeland attacks, attributing this change in outlook to the fact that "there can be large differences in sizes and types of weapons, in the manner of use and means of delivery, and certainly in the targets that might be attacked. Also one has to think of vast differences in quantities used."[25] These differences helped to insulate the battlefield area from Soviet and American homeland targets. But his main point was that the dangers associated with introducing nuclear weapons were not easily acceptable. "There is no doubt," he wrote in 1962, "that the use of nuclear weapons tactically would add gravely to the dangerousness of limited war. That may indeed be its major purpose. But who today considers any war between the super-powers not to be serious? Who will take the first step if he is so appalled at the thought of taking the second?"[26]

Most analysts continued to be preoccupied with the dangerousness of automatic escalation. "It is obvious," Brodie wrote in *Escalation and the Nuclear Option*, that views attributing a powerful and automatic escalatory stimulus to nuclear weapons — views not the less firmly advanced for being based entirely on intuition — have been of critical importance in molding attitudes toward appropriate strategies in the event of limited war, especially in any conflict between the United States and the Soviet Union or China. These views have thereby greatly affected force postures, recommended and realized, for ourselves and for our allies. The ramifications of these attitudes, and the disagreements they engender, affect the whole gamut of national defense policies.[27]

This difference focused on whether war-expansion increased the dangers of general war. For example, during the 1960s, military planners stressed the vulnerability of battlefield nuclear weapons systems and the need to launch them to limit vulnerability. "Most of the major systems used in tactical nuclear warfare are highly vulnerable," Alain C. Enthoven and K. Wayne Smith asserted,

> particularly ground forces, aircraft, short-range nuclear delivery systems, target-acquisition capabilities, command and control facilities, lines of communication, and logistic support systems. Moreover, these systems tend to be highly interdependent. If one major component of the over-all complex collapses, other components are in danger of becoming inoperative.
>
> One implication of these vulnerabilities and interdependencies is that the duration of any kind of controlled tactical nuclear battle is likely to be, at most, a few days. Another is that this vulnerability produces immense pressures for further escalation.[28]

Moreover, because most of the Soviet nuclear delivery capability allocated against Western Europe was based in the Soviet Union, Soviet and American homelands would most probably not be safeguarded in such a case.[29] "Beyond the limited demonstrative use of a few weapons," Enthoven said, "there is no such thing as a tactical nuclear war in the sense of sustained purposive military operations. Studies showed that the first spasm of destruction would destroy airfields (usually near cities), headquarters and troop concentrations. General breakdown and paralysis would ensue."[30]

"Breakdown and paralysis" in European war seemed to fit not only Brodie's critique of NATO nuclear war plans in the 1950s but also his points that "passion and fear are . . . inseparable from war" and that war tended to be "orgiastic." In the 1960s, he still emphasized that "war itself invariably and deeply involves the emotions, especially . . . anger and fear," and that "the very outbreak of hostilities generally argues some strong irrationality somewhere."[31] Envisioning the use of only a small number of nuclear weapons against battlefield targets, he cited inevitable superpower concern "with the most vital of their vital interests — their very existence" — to argue that independent reduction of the risk of general war would encourage reason and moderation to inhibit war expansion.[32] But for those who foresaw only a very short period for controlled tactical nuclear use, the decisive consideration was the anticipated strategic employment of nuclear weapons — a decision they dreaded making. "Nuclear weapons were obviously important in helping to deter aggression — even aggression limited to the European theater," explained a 1960s study summarizing newer thinking in the Office of the Secretary of Defense.

But what if deterrence failed? If the war began with an all-out Soviet attack on targets that included our cities, the answer was simple. We would reply in kind. But what if the war started with less than an all-out attack? What if the Soviets used only conventional forces? Would we still respond with a nuclear spasm? As [Secretary of Defense Robert S.] McNamara repeatedly noted: "One cannot fashion a credible deterrent out of an incredible action." Strategic nuclear weapons had a role, but it was intrinsically a limited one.[33]

This was the kernel of the thinking that led by 1960 to JCS approval of a major NATO conventional forces buildup and initiatives to forestall as much as possible a decision by the secretary of defense to recommend to the president use of battlefield nuclear weapons in a European war.[34]

Brodie's point that fear of strategic warfare would eventually retard war expansion may have been ignored in the Pentagon studies, along with the possibilities that fear of strategic warfare offered for threat making.[35] Not well adapted to planners' needs of protecting their own military forces, for example, was Brodie's point that the major source of stability in a European war was the mutual fear of moving toward general war. Furthermore, whether a European war could be terminated short of threatening general war and thereby increasing the likelihood of it was in doubt. Thomas Schelling, who focused on the *absence* of controls on limited war, argued that manipulating the threat of general war was an indispensable ingredient in defusing more limited hostilities.[36] For his part, Brodie depended heavily on ensuring restraint during war through mutual confidence in nuclear retaliatory capabilities, notwithstanding that intrawar deterrence was inherently more difficult to implement than deterrence in peacetime.

Threats associated with specific actions that expanded war were not wholly a military issue, though how well diplomats and civilian leaders dealing with the nonmilitary implications of those threats would be insulated from war-expanding passions was unclear. Even if they remained independent of those passions, agreement between adversaries might prove elusive, precisely because strategic nuclear war was regarded as unlikely in any event. As Coral Bell noted, "The balance of terror, if it is assumed to be stable, clearly makes successful negotiation less likely, rather than more likely. If the incentive to agreement in international politics is the fear of the consequences of disagreement, then the down-grading of this fear must also downgrade the prospect of agreement."[37] On the other hand, Brodie may have too easily presumed that the emotional impulses of American officials deciding upon battlefield nuclear use, as well as Soviet leaders whose attitudes would affect the outcome of American first use of nuclear weapons, would be fully contained upon deliberate escalation. To be sure, American nuclear use would be designed to compel Soviet leaders to put aside whatever misconceptions and emotional impulses had led them to initiate hostilities and to soberly alter their intentions. At the same time, the shock value Brodie sought from nuclear use could and would inevitably trigger new emotions and passions in place of older discarded ones.

Modes and Purposes of Tactical Nuclear Use

Brodie initially was noncommittal about the kind of nuclear use he preferred. "One could make," he wrote in 1962,

> a good case for and also a strong case against providing forward echelons with small weapons like the Davy Crockett and its brothers. Certainly forward deployment of such weapons (as against rear-area deployment of larger weapons) would seem to favor undesirably the early use of nuclear weapons in a local conflict, but against that effect one would have to weigh their possibly important added deterrent effect on the local outbreak of hostilities.[38]

He emphasized military utility in nuclear use. "I want to make clear," he wrote in May 1964, "that by demonstration use I do not mean token use. A demonstration use has to be militarily effective or it is likely to demonstrate the wrong things."[39] Large-yield nuclear weapons would obviously be the most militarily effective, and Brodie had insisted throughout the 1950s, anticipating early use of many such weapons in a European war, that large-yield weapons had important battlefield uses. He did not at first attempt to reconcile their early use with efforts to limit war — even apart from vulnerable Soviet and American strategic forces. By the 1960s, however, believing that strategic developments favored controlling hostilities, he had become interested in adapting nuclear use to prevent further escalation. "We ought not to be talking," Brodie wrote in 1966,

> certainly not initially, about using a great many nuclear weapons; that is a possibility that occurs only after a conflict has already graduated to large proportions and corresponding intensity. We should be interested mainly in seeing how it can be prevented from ever reaching such proportions. We are interested, in other words, in the prevention, through deterrence, of escalation — though not for one moment are we less interested in the comparable prevention of initial hostilities.[40]

Brodie considered using large- and, alternatively, small-yield weapons according to this standard. On one hand, he wrote of using "two or three substantial [nuclear detonations] as a demonstration of resolve — though with the understanding that the best way to demonstrate resolve is to use any bombs detonated with the highest possible degree of military effectiveness."[41] On the other hand, small-yield weapons seemed better adapted for threatening Soviet leaders with further escalation. "*Vis-à-vis* the Soviet Union," Brodie wrote in 1966,

> we can no longer effectively threaten general war as an *initial response* to anything other than a direct strategic attack upon us. However, our strategic nuclear capabilities cannot fail to play an important role in any serious crisis. What we can and no doubt will threaten in such an instance will be some move or action which, so long as it spells violence, *could* escalate. We have to leave to the opponent in his next move the choice of making the situation more dangerous or less so, though we can of course massively influence the choice he will make.[42]

Asserting that "large-scale tactical war in Europe, if it occurs at all, must come about through escalation from Soviet probing actions,"[43] Brodie expressed himself as strongly favoring small-yield weapons use that would place the onus for escalating to "large-scale tactical war" upon Soviet leaders.

The weapons Brodie had in mind for this purpose, "which are specifically intended for possible tactical use and would rarely if ever be considered for strategic use,"[44] were smaller than those introduced into the American arsenal up to that time.[45] This view was not far from General Norstad's orientation for dealing with a limited Soviet attack in Europe. "The enemy may not necessarily be using atomic weapons," declared Norstad in 1966,

> but if he indicates in a big way that they will be coming this would really make the decision for us. But there are some areas, perhaps short of that, where a decision would have to be made. . . .
>
> . . . Assume there is a small attack in a certain area and forces of a certain size move across and this is the beginning of an effort to spearhead a major attack, and intelligence supports this. You might, under these circumstances, decide you can't meet this with conventional forces. One of the several plans for dealing with the situation would certainly contemplate the use of some limited number of small atomic weapons against carefully selected targets. This might be five weapons. Maybe that would be satisfactory. You might have 100 or 200. We are talking in that range. You would find a starting point in that range.[46]

Brodie and Norstad, highly sensitive to the need to limit nuclear destruction, held very measured views about nuclear use in light of NATO's rapidly growing land-based nuclear weapons stockpile. Totaling about three thousand weapons in 1961, the stockpile increased to about seven thousand in 1967.[47]

But whereas Norstad, conceiving of using small-yield nuclear weapons against "carefully selected targets," evidently had in mind militarily effective attacks against fixed points of importance to the Soviet offensive, such as supply lines and bases, Brodie in advocating use of nuclear weapons of *very* small yield—evidently against enemy tanks, for example—was prepared to sacrifice more immediate military potential for the sake of seeking major political effects in the inhibiting of further escalation. Illustrating how limited war was "inefficient war,"[48] this was not designed to turn the military tide but rather to shock the enemy. NATO plans likewise entailed military restraint. Milton Leitenberg wrote that such plans provided for informing the Soviet government of NATO's interest in restraining the extent of hostilities and in sparing Soviet command and control systems, thereby allowing enemy commanders to remain in control of their forces.[49] Both interdiction and shock objectives dictated limiting civilian casualties,[50] and NATO plans apparently included weapons use for shock value.[51] But Brodie was imaginative and evidently distinctive in recommending the use of minimal numbers of nuclear weapons *primarily* to shock Soviet leaders, and with the threat of inexorable increases in civilian casualties, to force an end to the fighting; it was, after all, the prospect of much higher civilian casualties that most made nuclear war dangerous.[52] Some strategists, notably Thomas Schelling, had shock aspects of this kind in mind when they dwelled upon the consequences in a European war of breaking down the "firebreak," or threshold, between nuclear and nonnuclear weapons.[53]

On the other hand, if shocking Soviet leaders was also desirable, then, as Schelling pointed out, "there is no cheap, safe way of using nuclears that scares the wits out of the Russians without scaring us too."[54] Whether NATO members would approve nuclear use was perhaps more critical for the war-making utility of nuclear weapons in Europe than the explosive effects of those weapons. Use of only a few nuclears was probably situationally and dispositionally easier in a crisis than use of a very large number and therefore more conducive to standing firm in a confrontation than the latter.[55] But Brodie, aware that fearfulness might lead policymakers to reject employing even a few nuclear weapons, did not pursue this point. "Do strong mutually-shared inhibitions against going to general war inhibit also the use of nuclear weapons in limited war?" he asked in 1962. "We can see one constraint operating in that direction, namely the fear that use of nuclear weapons may prompt escalation even to a mutually disastrous general war."[56]

Elsewhere, however, Brodie indicated his belief that the shock of nuclear use would probably be overshadowed by the shock associated with the initiation of hostilities. "From what we can presently sense," he wrote in 1962,

> it seems probable that the most dangerous single event that can happen in Europe is not escalation to total NATO involvement, or even the first use of nuclear weapons, but rather the *initial outbreak of unmistakable hostilities*. Our wholly justified concern with the special emotions (as well as physical destruction) released by the first use of nuclear weapons has caused a quite unjustified depreciation of what it means to start fighting! Pearl Harbor was not less shocking than Hiroshima, and the emotional and political consequences of Pearl Harbor would have been little diminished if the scale of the attack had been a third as great as it was. To be sure, that attack was at once comprehended to be premeditated and thus to herald the onset of a great war. But a clash of comparable scale in the future is not going to be less foreboding.[57]

Gauging Soviet Intent in a Limited War

Brodie distinctively hinged the need for using nuclear weapons in a European war on Soviet intent rather than on superior Soviet military strength, using two conceptions of Soviet risk taking he had distinguished by the late 1950s. The more encouraging of the two for limiting a Soviet-American war was the concept of Soviet probing and testing, which fit what Brodie believed was prevailing Soviet military and political restraint. He had this profile in mind, for example, when he wrote that limited war forces would dampen "the proclivity for probing and testing which is so characteristic of Soviet military diplomacy."[58] The view of Soviet intentions as belligerent, which suggested potentially dangerous Soviet miscalculation of Western intentions, was not based on Soviet behavior but rather on the conventional explanation for the Japanese attack against Pearl Harbor.[59] For instance, when discussing a massive Soviet attack in Europe, Brodie invariably pointed out that the Soviets would have to count on a massive response comparable to the response made earlier against the Japanese, which no Soviet leader would wantonly risk.[60]

The question of whether Soviet intent was belligerent underlay Brodie's whole treatment of the issue of whether a European war was likely to escalate. Where the Soviets were not belligerent, and war was therefore not premeditated, he believed there was no serious danger of escalation. "It would seem," he wrote in 1962, "to be a safe conclusion that a large-scale non-nuclear attack by the Russian field army would in all likelihood be premeditated. The chance that such a state of affairs would merely be the adventitious outgrowth of a small testing action may be more than trivial, but it is hardly worth putting large bets on it."[61] Brodie evidently assumed that if war was unpremeditated or accidental, the Soviets would not let hostilities get out of hand or be unaware of Western commitments. In particular, the idea of Soviet probing and testing seemed to suggest that the Soviets were primarily interested in retaining control over any confrontation with the West;[62] if they kept such control and were not interested in a direct challenge to Western commitments, escalation was unlikely to arise from superpower confrontation.[63]

Ironically, despite Brodie's interest in cultivating nuclear options to save manpower, he emphasized that part of NATO military planning which needed to cope with commitment by the Soviets of fewer rather than larger numbers of forces in unpremeditated hostilities not calling for a nuclear response. "If there were serious errors in NATO planning," Brodie wrote in *Escalation and the Nuclear Option*,

> they seemed to me (and to various others) to be posed not in terms of *how* best to meet a massive Soviet attack but rather in terms of whether that was the kind of crisis we really ought to be chiefly worrying about as compared to much lesser crises. On the other hand, in so far as we do have to have some concern with it in planning terms — from the point of view of SHAPE, considerable concern with it — it has always seemed to me the condition that posed practically no difficulty *in advance* between adopting a nuclear or a non-nuclear tactical posture. . . . [T]hat part of my opposition to the conventional war idea about which I feel the least doubt concerns its applicability to a massive, and thus deliberate, Soviet attack.[64]

Problems that Brodie believed required limited war forces in the first place, such as "border probings and . . . periodic testings of our readiness to meet force with force, as well as with genuine accidents in the form of unpremeditated local flareups," he associated with war not precipitated by deliberate attack.[65] In this category, military use of limited war forces became as important as the political use of such forces; only when Soviet intent was nonbelligerent was Brodie optimistic about staving off nuclear use, citing "the great lack of certainty (to put it mildly) that we *could* keep anything larger than a border skirmish non-nuclear."[66]

As the Soviets committed fewer forces to war, NATO's nonnuclear defensive capability would count for more, but only if its conventional forces were already substantial. Brodie, mainly interested in resisting the current American proposal to build

NATO forces from twenty-four to thirty divisions and in highlighting the nuclear option as a substitute for it, indicated at one point that NATO conventional capabilities might be increased, presumably to manage unpremeditated warfare. "None of the above arguments," he wrote in a 1962 article that extensively criticized the conventional forces buildup proposal,

> should be construed as an attack on the idea that it is a good thing to have troops with strong non-nuclear fighting capabilities. The United States may indeed need more such forces than it has, and it might also be a very good thing if NATO were substantially stronger in such forces than it presently is. The intrinsic utility of such troops, or the deficiencies of present and projected deployments, have not, after all, been examined in this paper. What has alone been examined is the argument that specifically hinges the requirement for such troops on the alleged desirability of being able to stop even the whole Soviet Army with conventional arms.[67]

On the other hand, a massive Soviet attack, Brodie wrote in 1959, would indicate premeditated Soviet aggressiveness;[68] NATO's use of battlefield nuclear weapons would be designed to sharply convey to Soviet leaders the dangerousness of their actions. In this case, larger NATO conventional capabilities were less critical in Brodie's mind, because early nuclear use was an effective substitute. In fact, a token conventional force might be all that was required. Thus, when discussing the NATO pause concept, designed to give the Soviet adversary an "opportunity for reassessment and reconsideration of his intentions," Brodie wrote that "it is hard to see why the time for the pause should come after 30 divisions are involved rather than after, say, three. The risks may in fact be much smaller by opting for the lower threshold, because the discriminate use of nuclear weapons is also an earnest of determination."[69] It was in reference to this strategic view that Brodie seemed to accept, as he had earlier, a NATO "doomed to a continuing, gross inferiority" in numbers of ground forces in relation to the Soviet Union and its allies[70] — the logical consequence of his presumption that battlefield nuclear capabilities were substitutes for manpower shortages.

By not assuming an unvarying Soviet calculus, Brodie was implicitly arguing for diplomatic refinement and for intelligence gathering to detect Soviet motives, prevent Soviet leaders from miscalculating Western intent, and ultimately control escalation. However, aggressive Soviet intent rendered diplomatic cooperation to control escalation problematic. Although Soviet aggressiveness might be softened by fears that general war might grow out of more limited hostilities, it might also be reinforced in the course of the fighting. The Pearl Harbor episode, not decisive in this regard, illustrated the failure of established American military commitments to deter attack,[71] as well as exaggerated American estimates of Japanese aggressiveness. NATO efforts during the 1950s to deter a Soviet attack in Europe, conceptualized along the lines of Pearl Harbor, may have overlooked both of these aspects of the attack.[72]

Even if adversaries wished to cooperate, the context of their warfare might interfere with their ability to gauge and communicate intent. In this sense, wartime diplomatic cooperation depended upon and would be validated by battlefield developments. The latter might be inconclusive for gauging Soviet intent, especially if each side's war plans initially underplayed the effect that capabilities other than standing armies had on the outcome of the fighting. Ambivalent military results in a European war would be another major source of difficulty in gauging adversary intent, and through it, attempting to terminate or contain hostilities.[73]

The Cuban Missile Crisis and Brodie's
Reaffirmation of Nathan Leites

Following the Cuban missile crisis of 1962, Brodie's ideas about escalation became more categorical, primarily, it appears, because he believed the crisis had affirmed Nathan Leites's earlier depiction of the prescription in the Soviet operational code toward the probing and testing of Western intentions. "For a moment," Brodie wrote in reference to the crisis,

> a curtain was lifted, giving us the means of checking some old hypotheses about the Soviet Union—and about ourselves—as well as a burst of new insights. True, it is only a single case with inevitably special characteristics, but, fortunately or unfortunately, we are not vouchsafed many such cases for exploration, and there is much to be learned from this one. . . .
>
> We already know a great deal about Soviet operational precepts for their political maneuvering. About a dozen years ago, one of our colleagues, Dr. Nathan Leites, published his pioneering *Study of Bolshevism,* an outline summary of which was published separately as *The Operational Code of the Politburo.* His insights on Soviet attitudes toward political advances and retreats provided us with an interpretation of Soviet conduct last October that appeared to fit all the known facts far better than any alternative interpretation known to us.[74]

Brodie seems to have been unusually confident all along about peaceful settlement of the crisis, on grounds that the Soviets were by all accounts inferior to the United States "in every important branch of arms" and that Soviet leaders knew it.[75] On the other hand, like most others he seems to have been surprised by the quickly favorable resolution of the crisis. "I think no one would have gamed the Cuban crisis of 1962 as it actually turned out," Brodie declared in a 1964 lecture, "with Red yielding after Blue's first move."[76]

The Cuban crisis, as is now well known, occurred when the Soviet Union introduced—in disregard of American warnings—intermediate-range ballistic missiles and bombers into Cuba, and it ended when the Soviets complied with American demands to remove those forces.[77] The results of the Cuban crisis convinced him that the Leites study of the Soviet operational code, and not the RAND gaming exercises, had predicted correctly Soviet interest in avoiding war with the United States. In particular, Soviet leaders' determination to avoid war, and their removal of the weapons from Cuba, seemed to reflect their acceptance of the requirement in their operational code that (in Brodie's words) they "must advance against the opponent wherever opportunity affords" and, "on the other hand[,] . . . must at no point subject to grave hazard the basic achievement already consolidated."[78] Finding basic similarities between Soviet restraint in the Cuban case and prior Soviet caution in the Berlin blockade of 1948/49, Brodie generalized that there had probably been no "really dangerous crises" between the superpowers since the Second World War, in part because "the Russians were so determined not to have a war that we can hardly imagine what kind of blundering on our part might have produced one."[79]

Insofar as Brodie ascribed Soviet restraint wholly to American efforts to contain or block Soviet expansionist tendencies, he was validating not only the view (expressed earlier by George Kennan as well as Leites[80]) that the Soviet threat to Western interests was limited to low-risk probes and tests of Western intentions but also the feasibility of Western efforts to deter a range of Soviet actions. Brodie himself stressed after the Cuban crisis that efforts to strengthen the status quo by deterring attack were likely to succeed and, in contrast to his earlier view that "stability at the top may work against stability at lower and intermediate levels," posited more optimistically that a "strategic nuclear umbrella" could have a "deterrent effect on all war, not merely the strategic exchange."[81]

Since the outlook for deliberate escalation depended (as he saw it) on the workability of deterrence, Brodie's optimism about deterrence added to his optimism about the feasibility of deliberate escalation in a European war.[82] First, the more he believed deterrence would work in practice, the less he could conceive of a premeditated Soviet attack in Western Europe (representing a deterrence failure) calling for a NATO nuclear demonstration or larger nuclear response. Second, if an attack nevertheless led to a nuclear demonstration, Brodie, relying on his older idea that the "critical level of exacerbation" (at which nations deliberately decided upon general war) had gone up, was convinced that "spontaneous escalation" to general war would not result.[83] "Unless we are dealing with utter madmen," he wrote in *Escalation and the Nuclear Option*,

> there is no conceivable reason why in any necessary showdown with the Soviet Union, appropriate manipulations of force and threats of force, certainly coordinated with more positive diplomatic maneuvers, cannot bring about deterrence. That is one respect in which the world is utterly different now from what it was in 1939 or 1914, when deterrence, however effective temporarily, had the final intrinsic weakness that one side or both did not truly fear what we would now call general war.[84]

Third, Brodie now chose to understand emotions such as rage or fear as having collective rather than idiosyncratic expression and thereby as deterrable even in their most belligerent manifestations. "We can also say of humiliation what we can say of reactions of rage," he wrote, "that governments, even Communist dictatorships, tend today to be corporate entities in which the emotional feelings of individuals, however highly placed, are likely to be moderated and contained by the counsels of their advisers. The Hitler regime was different and exceptional in this respect."[85]

Optimistic about deterring Soviet efforts to escalate war, Brodie believed that the strategy's success depended on American and allied leaders' acceptance of the "frightening prospect" of future nuclear weapons confrontation. "If a President of the United States could face up last October to a maneuver that entailed in his mind some risk of general war," Brodie wrote in May 1963,

> there is little reason why he or an equally staunch successor could not do the same in a like situation five or ten years hence.
>
> The fact that it is *"some"* risk is what makes it possible. We rarely have to threaten general war. We threaten instead the next in a series of moves that seems to tend in that direction. The opponent has the choice of making the situation more dangerous, or less so. This is all pretty obvious when stated, but so much of the theorizing that has been going on about the inapplicability of the nuclear deterrent to the future overlooks this simple fact.[86]

Brodie seems to have assumed that crises would occur from Soviet violation of the status quo, the latter being an internationally legitimate standard by which the West could be expected to define its vital interests (as it had over Cuba). Because the West would risk war with the Soviets to defend this standard, the Soviets could be made to respect it.

This view, as much as Brodie's acceptance of Leites's thesis about the Soviet operational code, apparently made Brodie oppose the slightest hint of American yielding to Soviet views, including the "face-saving" solutions in the Cuban case.[87] But his most important reason for anticipating that the United States would prevail in such crises was his belief that American military superiority over the Soviet Union would remain as clearly perceptible to Soviet leaders as it had been in 1962. He did not define this superiority (as had others) as "credible first-strike capability"—that is, an impressive ability to strike at Soviet military targets without triggering general war—but rather as "simple" or intuitive force superiority. "One of the reasons I think that the simple kind superiority still matters," Brodie wrote in 1963, "is that no amount of sophisticated argument can shake the basic feeling that in the clutch it's better to be the man with more rather than the man with less, especially when more means lots more."[88] With such superiority, there was no need in his view to worry about Soviet nerve and toughness. "We will still have in 1970," he wrote,

> that simple but tangible kind of strategic superiority demonstrated impressively by the fact that no one free to choose would prefer the opponent's posture to ours or even be indifferent to the choice. Why, then, do we assume, as many in the Administration do seem to assume, that the opponent will have a superiority of toughness and of nerve to compensate for his inferiority in weapons?[89]

Evaluating Brodie's Reaction to the Missile Crisis

Not surprisingly, Brodie was building a strategy on what he regarded as the weakest link in Soviet military capability—namely, the lack of Soviet nerve in high-risk situations.[90] The usefulness and feasibility of such a strategy were certainly strengthened by indications that the Soviets wished to avoid hazardous situations. However, Brodie implied that the lack of Soviet nerve demonstrated during the Cuban missile crisis was an *immutable* weakness and that nothing could compensate for it. He uncharacteristically failed to make any allowance for Soviet actions that (in the language of a 1953 paper of his) were "genuinely embarrassing or even disconcerting"[91] and instead described a Soviet Union so well postured to control escalation that to him escalation problems largely dissolved.[92] On one hand, lack of Soviet nerve seemed to rule out the deliberate Soviet attack of Europe that the West had partly sought to deter through the threat of a nuclear response; the nuclear threat, impressing Soviet leaders with the risks of deliberate attack, was thereby in Brodie's mind the best war preventive. (He discounted local forces in Europe as a prerequisite for Western boldness, implying that he was depending wholly on nuclear threats for this purpose.[93]) Here the major question was whether the Soviets could ever summon up enough nerve to make a Soviet-American confrontation truly dangerous. On the other hand, Brodie dismissed as unlikely inadvertent or accidental warfare in Western Europe, finding no examples of war resulting from probing action brought about by miscalculation of the defender's resistance or from unauthorized actions of military personnel.[94] He neglected how, even with low initial force commitment, bad war planning could make terminating hostilities more difficult.[95]

Soviet leaders may be said to have generally acted so as not to "subject to grave hazard the basic achievement already consolidated." However, highly belligerent Soviet behavior is not the only conceivable precipitant of American deterrence failure. Cautious Soviet challenges of American commitments have also caused such failure,[96] as in the Berlin crises of 1958 and 1961 (over Soviet threats to conclude a peace treaty with East Germany) and the introduction of offensive weaponry into Cuba. Brodie was particularly concerned about the Cuban case, writing that "our behavior in the Bay of Pigs episode [in 1961] and thereafter apparently led the Russians to expect that, despite our words to the contrary, we would accept the missiles and bombers in Cuba as we had accepted the earlier phases of their military build up. . . . We should not have let them think they could get away with it."[97]

Leites discussed Soviet dispositions, whereas the question of whether American deterrence would work depended also on many situational factors, including how the Soviets perceived American will and capability to implement deterrent threats in particular instances.[98] Low-risk behaviors, including those by the Soviet Union, may be situationally harder to deter than high-risk ones, irrespective of any operational code, because even if a country were persuaded to avoid actions it defines for itself as high risk, it would also, for deterrence to fully succeed, need to avoid those actions that *other* countries define as high risk. (In this sense, deterrence may be impeded by governments' inability or unwillingness to comprehensively communicate their plans for action in specific situations.[99]) Brodie's high confidence that the Soviets really would give way when confronting the United States depended on his understanding of the Soviet disposition, and on instinctive views about how international norms and military superiority could be brought to bear upon a crisis. But this confidence was not backed by an analysis of how, despite original discrepancies between Soviet and American outlooks on risk in specific situations, those outlooks could come to coincide.[100]

Those advising the president during the Cuban crisis were probably encouraged by estimated American force superiority over the Soviets to seek removal of Soviet missiles and bombers from Cuba but were much less confident than was Brodie—who had the same estimates—about a peaceful resolution. American officials had not expected deployment of Soviet missiles and bombers in Cuba, and American Soviet specialists, already mistaken about the deployment, were likely to be especially careful in projecting possible Soviet reaction to specific American force and diplomatic initiatives. First, some Soviet responses could not be easily anticipated at all. "President Kennedy's last letter to Nikita Khrushchev had, after all, been a shot in the dark," wrote Elie Abel about the diplomatic ultimatum that climaxed the crisis. "The President had eagerly accepted a proposition the Russian had never formally offered. And the Soviet Ambassador had warned Robert Kennedy that, in his opinion, the Kremlin was far too deeply committed to accept."[101] Elsewhere, shifts in Soviet outlooks seemed more impressive than the unknown. Having first suggested that the Soviets might be looking for a way to save face in the crisis, the ranking State Department expert on the Soviet Union seemingly reversed himself following a tough Soviet message when he warned that the Soviet government was likely to regard a trade between the Cuban missiles and American missiles in Turkey and Italy as a sign of weakness.[102] Such inconsistencies are inevitable during crises, because diplomats search for more refined interpretations of events and because crises especially highlight changes in positions without, however, establishing how critical they are.

Finally, in at least one respect Brodie read the Cuban missile crisis ambivalently. Insisting *after* the crisis that the nuclear umbrella was stronger than ever, he also had felt confident *during* the crisis that American force superiority over the Soviets *in all categories* would help head off war, and he conceded subsequently that the Cuban case was at least one success for limited war ideas emphasizing nonnuclear local force dominance.[103] But in this respect as in others, Brodie probably learned too much from the Cuban case. Albert and Roberta Wohlstetter, who stressed more than Brodie the utility of nonnuclear threats during the crisis, appropriately cautioned against generalizing that lesson. "This single [Cuban] encounter," they wrote, "where the United States had both the capability to dominate in a conventional conflict and also to inflict overwhelming nuclear damage could not demonstrate once and for all that conventional superiority will always have a major utility; still less could it show that it might easily be dispensed with."[104]

However, Brodie's main point was that too much efficacy for the use of conventional forces alone should not be derived from the Cuban episode.[105] He questioned, as we have seen, whether bold behavior required conventional buildups and, apart from his concern that such buildups could dramatically increase defense burdens if adversaries took offsetting action, he implied that they could help proliferate security commitments uncritically.[106] Brodie seemed to be suggesting, in this last sense, that the limited war idea encouraged proliferating commitments by enlarging capabilities to support them and that these growing commitments added to the risk of war. This idea evidently concerned him even with respect to the NATO alliance, which most informed Americans believed was vital to American defenses. "Western Europe is not *really* vital to our home defense," he wrote in a 1963 RAND unpublished paper, "but we have scarcely asked how vital it is in view of our confidence that we could preserve it without undue risk."[107] In Brodie's view, advocacy of limited war contributed to American involvement in Vietnam and shared responsibility for its failure.[108]

American war-making in Vietnam does appear to be an unfortunate outgrowth of an unwillingness to ask whether the cost of American commitment was justified. However, statesmen do not commonly determine risks by comparing the costs that war would bring with the objects that could be gained by war, and they would have difficulty if they tried to do so.[109] Inasmuch as difficulties of balancing commitments and capabilities exist irrespective of the currency of military forces being fitted to the equation, it was not immediately evident why the worst consequences of far-flung commitments should be attributed to a strategy of relying more heavily on conventional forces and the best consequences to reliance upon nuclear forces. Furthermore, irrespective of how governments determined what was vital, much depended on whether they wished to reduce the chances of confrontation or to see a confrontation through.[110]

Conclusions

Brodie's work on escalation shared with its predecessors three major features: an interest in force restraint and coercive behavior; detachment from existing military plans to which he presumably had access; and a preoccupation with a critical technological development — in this instance, the deployment of protected ballistic missiles — as the basis for a new strategic analysis. However, this work — in its optimistic conclusions about the prospects for controlling war in Europe, an optimism that supported Brodie's fundamental values — was very different from what had preceded it.

Brodie did not discuss numerous escalatory options but merely made the case for one such option — a nuclear weapons demonstration. His silence on operational matters associated with nuclear use and on requirements for fighting different hypothesized wars implied that he thought they were secondary to the political and moral problems of resisting a Soviet invasion and of implementing that resistance in controlled ways. By definition, the smaller the noncoercive application of force, the larger the role for wartime diplomacy. Brodie's new estimate of the controllability of a European war was not based on any demonstration that diplomats would be equal to the challenge. But his analysis drew attention to the indispensability of effective diplomacy in making possible mutual superpower appreciation of their respective intentions.

It is doubtful whether more systematic empirical work on this subject would justify categorical findings. First, whatever the prior escalatory tendencies in war, much
obviously depended on the present-day war-making circumstances out of which the
threat and actual use of nuclear weapons could be conceived. Further, whatever the
interests of the contemporary belligerents in intrawar deterrence and whatever their
diplomatic and military preparations toward that objective, uncertainties of all kinds
would probably grow in proportion to the number of nuclear weapons employed
in a European war. Those such as Brodie who argued from a more abstract political
standpoint and those who took an operational viewpoint could agree on the need
to keep the use of nuclear weapons in a European war as circumscribed as possible,
for otherwise the unforeseeable would increasingly complicate diplomatic solutions
as well as weapons effectiveness. This was not to prescribe making better military
plans but rather to find more adroit diplomatic ways of ending a European war
sooner. For those advocating a major conventional forces buildup in Europe, a European war would probably have already gone on too long by the time nuclear weapons
were used; for Brodie, who favored earlier nuclear use, the war would have gone
on too long once the Soviets responded in kind. Neither side in the escalation
controversy seems to have given adequate attention to the consequences of a war
going on long enough for uncertainties to affect the result or how those uncertainties could be allowed for in advance.

Second, an adequate theory of escalation evidently would need to take into account a broader range of variables and considerations than anyone appears to have
done in the 1960s. What seems to have forestalled such broad analysis is a tendency,
reflected in Brodie's work, to factor problems into component parts and to probe
the part that was closest to the analyst's own specialization and background. Fac-
tored analysis of this kind invariably understated that uncertainties in war-making
are not localized. In this case, however, there were special problems associated with
fragmented analysis, for diplomats and military planners—each anticipating a part
of the escalation dynamic—were at the very least taking each other for granted.[111]
Brodie, who stressed demonstration use of nuclear weapons, believed such a demonstration could help stop the fighting, but he seemed oblivious to the possibility that
battlefield problems would not be adequately coped with by first nuclear use. Those
problems, even if they did not count as much as the diplomacy of war termination,
might still adversely affect that diplomacy. In contrast, operational planners seemed
to underplay the requirements of diplomacy as they acted to satisfy military needs,
neglecting that diplomatic objectives almost certainly would affect the course of war-
making once nuclear weapons were used.

Military planners, preoccupied by "automatic" escalation, may have failed to conceptualize *enough* limitations in a European war, but Brodie, because he failed to
allow (following the Cuban missile crisis) for instances in which a European war
might get out of hand, may have conceptualized *too many* such limitations. The
qualities of nerve and resolve, unless carefully controlled, could threaten those limitations, either by stimulating provocative military activity or by lessening diplomatic

moderation. During the Cuban crisis, by one account, the requirement of "toughness" in dealing with the Soviets seemed to diminish the priority of straightforward diplomacy in gaining the removal of the missiles and bombers from Cuba; at that time, only a series of military plans received detailed consideration by American leaders.[112] Whether toughness can be demonstrated without giving such prominence to military plans or whether such plans once set in motion lead to immoderate diplomacy in certain instances seems to have received insufficient study.

Brodie's differences with some of his colleagues, particularly after the Cuban missile crisis, arose because they tried to do different things. But the differences also seemed to be accentuated by a certain unsparing quality that came to characterize Brodie's work and by his confusing his role as a critic—which he had always relished and now pursued vigorously—with his role as a conceptual and policy integrator. In the past, as I have noted, he had successfully widened popular discussion in carrying out his role as an integrator but only by understating his role as a critic. (The reader of Brodie's *Strategy in the Missile Age*, for example, receives little or no enlightenment about major differences of opinion on strategic questions then existing inside the RAND Corporation.) At this point, his vigorous criticism of his colleagues tended to distort his analysis, narrowing his substantive focus and limiting his own analytic contribution. For example, the only military scenario Brodie examined was the one outlined by those who wished to build up NATO conventional forces from twenty-four to thirty divisions. Consisting of all-out Soviet conventional attack in Europe (the "Hamburg grab" invasion), it was ironically also the strongest justification in Brodie's mind for his own proposed demonstration use of nuclear weapons. However, though using it to argue for his prescriptive nuclear strategy, Brodie also criticized the realism of that same scenario, thereby limiting the utility of his own prescription. His proposed nuclear demonstration could for this reason hardly be a panacea, however concentrated the attention he gave to it.

Another narrowing feature of his analysis was parodoxically his interest in finding strategic justification for battlefield use, which meant linking forces for limited war with those for general war.[113] The nuclear use Brodie had in mind was not a sufficient rationale for the thousands of nuclear weapons introduced into the NATO arsenal by the early 1960s or for the size of the already large NATO conventional forces. In a 1963 informal RAND paper directed at a prior discussion of the conventional forces buildup issue, Brodie complained that "the question of *how much* never got mentioned at the meeting the other day. Instead the same old straw men were dragged out, to be slain again."[114] But in fact Brodie's own strategic approach prevented him from discussing the issue of conventional force size in all but the most general way. "Since we have to keep five plus divisions in Germany for demonstration purposes, for the sake of the German and the Russian audience," he wrote in 1964 to a RAND colleague, "that sort of sets the stand. But these are not strategic considerations except by the widest possible construction."[115]

In this sense, his work gave no guidance to planners engaged in thinking about deterrence failure, and it supported a reliance upon demonstration use that was militarily abstract. Where deterrence did succeed, of course, plenty of opportunity might be afforded for diplomatic subtlety, but where it did not — and certain situations would be more than usually conducive to deterrence failure — diplomacy might be significantly impeded, particularly if national leaders were laboring under considerable strain.

9 · On Strategy and Strategists

Brodie's most mature work addressed the political core of strategy and the over-valuation of narrower military and technical approaches to war-making. "We may . . . expect," he wrote in 1968, "in any strategic analysis, a heightening of the importance of the political environment with respect to the total governance of any military operations."[1] He had in mind here, first, the absence of any newly projected technological breakthrough comparable to fission and fusion weapons and the difficulty of overcoming already large Soviet and American nuclear arsenals with newer technology to gain decisive military advantage; and, second, the fitting of military instruments to national objectives. Although informed strategic analysis commonly allowed for prospective changes in nuclear weapons technology, it attended much less to national goals.[2] Brodie's critiques of the theories of contemporary defense economists and the French strategist André Beaufre and his favorable review of the writings of the nineteenth-century German strategist Carl von Clausewitz sought to repair that neglect.

That politics was central to strategy Brodie had learned from Clausewitz when, following news of the first projected test of fusion weapons, he was persuaded of the political futility of strategic nuclear war. "We must . . . proceed," Brodie wrote in January 1954, "to rethink some of the basic principles (which have become hazy since Clausewitz) connecting the waging of war with the political ends thereof, and to reconsider some of the prevalent axioms governing the conduct of military operations."[3] In his later works, especially *War and Politics,* he applied war-making to political interests as Clausewitz had done, taking account of contemporary experience.

Concentrating upon political objectives, Brodie had followed a very different approach from that taken in his *Guide to Naval Strategy* and in his essays in *The Absolute Weapon,* explaining in 1955 that "I feel the new weapons require that one bring to the center of attention in any strategic discourse subjects which the older treatises on strategy could easily ignore, like questions of national objectives, etc."[4] This approach was unorthodox for a strategist in any era, and Brodie pioneered in it as Clausewitz had earlier. Unlike Clausewitz, however, Brodie's political conception of strategy depended on a very optimistic evaluation of the stability of the contemporary great power relationship.

A Critique of Cost-Effectiveness Studies

By the mid-1960s, Brodie had set himself apart from most strategic analysts in describing his training as primarily in political science, "with a leaning towards economics," whereas "a majority of those who have made their mark today as theorists in strategy have been trained as economists, or at least have more than a bowing acquaintance with the concepts and principles in that field."[5] He had in mind in this connection the training of contemporary economists in mathematics and other quantitative techniques,[6] noting in 1968 that "perhaps the contemporary strategists contrast most sharply with the old precisely in their different attitude toward quantification."[7] Another contrast drawn by Brodie between himself and economists (to be discussed in the next two sections) was that "economists as a group seem to be rather more at home in the world of technology than do members of other branches of the social sciences."[8]

Earlier, by contrast, in a much-remarked-upon 1949 analysis, "Strategy as a Science," Brodie fully associated himself with the application of economic concepts to the study of strategy. He argued that such concepts as marginal utility and opportunity costs were highly relevant to what he termed "problems involving economy of means, i.e., the most efficient utilization of potential and available resources to the end of enhancing our security," and that using them would help free strategy "from addiction to the slogan."[9] Fifteen years later, in 1964, he conceded this earlier argument was "confirmed by events to a degree which the author never expected" and that the proficiencies of economists "fit one peculiarly well for grappling with certain characteristic problems of strategy, especially in what we call 'cost-effectiveness' analysis," as in choosing between competing designs of weapons systems according to a common standard.

Yet he stressed at that time the limitations of economists' output on strategic issues. "There is always," he wrote, reviewing the accomplishments of contemporary strategists, "the larger context—often with its special political and psychological overtones—into which the weapon systems must be fitted. In fact, the more strategic or political a problem becomes, as compared with the merely tactical, the more we tend to outrun the limits of usefulness of cost-effectiveness analysis."[10] The price of economists' analytical elegance, he argued, was a tendency to neglect wider political and historical concerns. "The usual training in economics," he pointed out in 1964,

has its own characteristic limitations, among which are the tendency to make the possessor insensitive to and often intolerant of political considerations which get in the way of his theory and calculations. We have already noted how weak he tends to be in either diplomatic or military history. One is sometimes amazed at how little some of the best-known strategic analysts of our times may know about conflicts no more remote in time than World War I, let alone earlier wars. . . . It is not that they have no time for history but rather that the devotees of any highly developed science — and economics is clearly the most highly developed of the social sciences — tend to develop a certain disdain and even arrogance concerning other fields. It is a grave intellectual fault, but a very common one.[11]

The limitations of economists were evidently illustrated for him in the course of his dispute with those who most pushed in the 1960s to build up NATO's conventional forces strength, because the four persons Brodie had in mind who led that drive were all trained economists.[12] "The intellectual leaders of that movement in the 1960s," Brodie related later,

> to force an enormous American and NATO buildup of conventional armaments, in order, they thought, to circumvent use of nuclear weapons, were all systems analysts, with no basis in their training or preoccupations for claiming special political insight of any kind. This despite the fact that they rested most of their arguments on what they considered to be political considerations. They were trained to be highly scientific in one area of limited application, but that did not incline them to be comparably scientific or even wordly [sic] wise in the larger area where ends become more meaningful than means and where it becomes important to consider motivations and emotions as well as mechanics.[13]

A concern for policy ends was by no means absent from Brodie's 1949 essay, which distinguished between strategy "in the narrower military sense," or application of mobilized resources to achieving victory in a particular war, and broader "security policy," in which "strategy anticipate[d] the trials of war, and by anticipation [sought] where possible to increase one's advantage without unduly jeopardizing the maintenance of peace or the pursuit of other values."[14] Brodie wished to broaden military analysis beyond strategists' traditional concern with fighting wars to victory. The same point was suggested by his 1968 assertion that "while the primary problem for strategists in the past was to assemble and effectively utilize superior strength, in the contemporary period the more frequent problem is how to make the available power relevant to objectives likely to be in dispute."[15] But Brodie in the 1960s seemed particularly anxious to stake out his own special competence in "the larger area where ends become more meaningful than means" and especially where, as in enlightened leadership to prevent or limit war-making, "'good judgement,' that is, intuition based on experience and insight, remains of enormous and indeed supreme importance in the decision-making process."[16]

Systems analysts, such as C. J. Hitch, who studied cost-effectiveness questions conceded that "every systems analysis is shot through with intuition and judgement."[17] As they defined what should be studied, such qualities would likely in the end be more important than quantification, insofar as, according to E. S. Quade, systems analysis "is associated with that class of problems where the difficulty lies in deciding what ought to be done — not simply how to do it — and honors go to people who have the ability or good fortune simply to find out what the problem is. The total analysis is thus likely to be a more complex and less neat and tidy procedure, one seldom suitable for quantitative optimization."[18] Judgment could be employed only with assumptions about a specific problem, about the time frame for that problem, and about opportunities and limitations in coping with that problem, all likely to be affected by a strategic analyst's primary focus.

However, Brodie's choice of analytical assumptions depended more on his critical attitude toward conventional wisdom and particularly toward what he termed "assumptions or 'hypotheses' offered by the Air Force concerning strategic needs to be met by the weapon systems to be examined." Early work at the RAND Corporation relied heavily on those assumptions, Brodie noted, and only a small proportion of the RAND staff questioned them.[19] Having distinguished himself at air force headquarters and in his first years at RAND by critiquing dominant air force assumptions in very broad, wide-ranging analysis, Brodie later diverted this intellectual energy to his fellow RAND staff members, endorsing in 1964 "clipping the wings supporting some of the freer flights of fancy of our colleagues."[20]

In some cases, judgment—conforming to or challenging air force standards—could accomplish what systems analysis purportedly had been most useful in accomplishing—namely, "the invention of better systems."[21] But it was not likely to do so in an area in which the problem was not adequately appreciated or defined, a condition that often prevailed and that dictated collaborative work among analysts with different competences. "We trust a man's intuition in a field in which he is expert," declared Hitch in a lecture on systems analysis.

> But in complex problems of military force composition or development, we are dealing with a field so broad that no one can be called expert. A typical systems analysis depends critically on numerous technological factors in several fields of technology; on military operations and logistics factors on both our side and the enemy's; on broad economic, political, and strategic factors; and on quite intricate relations among all these. No one is an expert in more than one or two of the subfields; no one is an expert in the field as a whole and the interrelations. So, no one's unsupported intuitions in such a field can be trusted.[22]

Intuition and judgment would also tend to be less reliable when, as in the NATO forces buildup case, major differences among strategic analysts increased the difficulty of collaborating to define the problem.[23] Brodie, who did his best work independently, was not inclined to collaborate with those with whom he sharply disagreed.

Hitch's evaluation of the work of systems analysts seemed to suggest that narrowing the conceptualization of a problem—either by prior definition or by subsequent study—facilitated success in that work, for he observed that "the case for analysis in broad context problems is comparatively unproved."[24] Brodie, by contrast highly interested in the broad context for strategic choices, would have been intellectually and temperamentally unwilling to delimit arbitrarily his consideration of that context. His strongest endorsement of systems analysis work was directed at one feature that broadened it—namely, the introduction of multiple contingencies. He wrote in 1964, for example, that where the "tendency [of the 'scientific strategists'] used to be to try to find the optimum method of dealing with a single most-expected contingency, the realization that the enemy might play the game differently from the way in which we think we ought to play it has prompted us instead to seek that mixture of solutions which does rather well over a complex of contingencies."[25]

Discounting the Impact of Changes in Weapons Technology

Emphasis upon applying power to disputed objectives supported not only Brodie's critique of the omissions of economists in the strategic field but also his discounting of one apparently fruitful aspect of their work—namely, the study of problems associated with contemporary weapons innovation. Stating as "reasons for expecting that strategic thought will be much less concerned with technological developments than in the score of years following World War II," he cited first of all in 1968 "ceilings on meaningful effectiveness" of newer weapons systems.[26] "In various important categories of technology," he wrote in 1971 in his broadest elaboration of this argument,

we may expect that future improvements even of the most ingenious kind will not have social and political consequences remotely comparable to those achieved in the past. There is, in other words, a kind of asymptote of influence in any category of technology beyond which change becomes more or less free-wheeling, interesting to engineers and often to economists but not to political scientists. . . .

The asymptotic factor applies even to the effective changes in the nature of war. . . . After the coming of nuclear weapons, which changed everything, no new weapons technology could quite matter as much politically—unless it cancelled out nuclear weapons, a highly unlikely development. True, nuclear weapons became thermonuclear, missiles of increasing accuracy replaced aircraft as the primary delivery vehicles, the numbers and technological sophistication of both weapons and delivery systems increased considerably, and now we have the ABM. All these changes have been significant and certainly costly. Still, the big political event was Hiroshima, and most of what has happened since simply confirms and underlines that fact.[27]

When Brodie retrospectively evaluated the impact of nuclear weapons technologies upon world politics, he argued that superpowers wielding nuclear arsenals would surely pause for moral, political, and psychological reasons even while aware of the great strategic advantages available in attacking first. For example, evaluating Albert Wohlstetter's influential 1959 article, "The Delicate Balance of Terror," which argued that American SAC bombers were very vulnerable to Soviet air and especially ballistic missile attack, Brodie contended that the Wohlstetter article,

as is characteristic of so many writings on military technological affairs, took no account whatever of the inhibitory political and psychological imponderables that might and in fact *must* affect the conditions implied by that word *delicate*. Many things are technologically feasible that we have quite good reason to believe will not happen. It has in fact become abundantly clear since the Wohlstetter article was published, and indeed since the dawn of the nuclear age, that the balance of terror is decidedly *not* delicate.[28]

The same perspective suggested to him the excessive insecurity and belligerence of those who studied military and technological developments. Thus he argued in 1973 that "often the total political context will indicate to the politically sensitive a much smaller risk in postponing a decision than the weapons-oriented technologists are conditioned to believe."[29] And he faulted systems analysts for giving primary weight to Soviet capabilities rather than to Soviet intentions. Failure of such analysts to explicitly consider enemy intentions, he contended, "clearly favors a bias toward increasing armaments, the more so because those who advance it most vigorously are habitually insensitive to the way one's own armaments programs may look to the opponent. It is, in short, the doctrine which powers armaments races."[30]

These observations were sharply at odds with Brodie's earlier concern about the difficulty of adjusting strategic concepts to changes in nuclear weapon capabilities. "Changes, even marginal ones, in the inherent potentialities or limitations of the machines with which war is waged," he wrote in 1949,

> may affect not merely the handling of those machines but a whole strategic concept. Principles may still survive those changes intact, but if they do it will be because they have little applicability or meaning for the questions that really matter. The rules fathered by Jomini and Clausewitz may still be fundamental, but they will not tell one how to prepare for or fight a war.[31]

It was precisely because strategy seemed so unsettled that what Brodie then called "the absence of the habit of scientific thinking" explained for him "the incredible and sometimes disastrous lag of tactical and strategic concepts behind developments in materiel."[32] Here and in his comment in *Strategy in the Missile Age* that "technological progress could . . . push us rapidly towards a position of almost intolerable mutual menace,"[33] he seemed to share the concern of systems analysts such as E. S. Quade that "technological considerations, in particular the rapid rate of change in weapons and their almost exponential increase in complexity, are now fully as important as the traditional political, economic, and military factors."[34]

The scope of this problem, but not its solution, was underscored for him by historical experience. "In the past," he wrote in 1954,

> with technological changes of far lesser moment and degree than those we are witnessing now, the military have usually proved themselves conceptually behindhanded at the onset of each major war. Because of the nature of the enterprise in which this behindhandedness has been manifested, the national cost has often been hideous and tremendous. These thoughts are so far hardly novel. . . .
>
> Because of the nature of the technological changes occuring [sic] today, the lag between concept and reality is bound to be both far greater in degree and far costlier in effects than any similar lag in the past.[35]

Brodie had the First World War in mind as an earlier instance of conceptual behindhandedness. In 1959 he wrote that "World War I was . . . a war which, because of technological changes of much lesser degree than those which are new to us now, completely baffled the military leaders who had to fight it."[36]

By no means did Brodie slight political and psychological forces in this earlier work. As James King pointed out, Brodie in *Strategy in the Missile Age* argued against preventive war and first-strike strategies on moral and political grounds, even as he proclaimed that nuclear weapons had logically introduced conditions in which "offensive-mindedness" (as Brodie put it) and "seizing the initiative and carrying the fight to the enemy" became the basis for the most efficient strategy.[37] Nor did Brodie afterward neglect the hardening, concealment, and dispersal of intercontinental ballistic missiles (ICBMs), which supported his 1973 assumption that "I do not see the United States (or the Soviet Union) on the verge of a position where its retaliatory force ceases to deter or even undergoes serious diminution in its deterrence value."[38] But this last argument was less weighty in relation to an intense crisis than in ordinary circumstances. In particular, both psychological and strategic incentives to attack preemptively would increase sharply in a crisis once the opponent appeared to be preparing to attack, and it was unlikely that shifts in force dispositions during the crisis would be satisfactorily able to conceal belligerent intentions. As Paul Bracken observed in an incisive analysis, the potential instabilities of Soviet-American crisis periods are magnified by contemporary technological developments. "In certain respects," Bracken wrote,

> American and Soviet strategic forces have combined into a single gigantic nuclear system. What cements the coupling is the warning and intelligence networks of each side. . . .
>
> This mutual coupling occurs because a threatening Soviet military action or alert can be detected almost immediately by American warning and intelligence systems and conveyed to force commanders. The detected action may not have a clear meaning, but because of its possible consequences protective measures must be taken against it. . . . [T]his action-reaction process . . . in more ominous circumstances . . . may be seen as a jockeying for positions before the first salvo of an all-out war. . . .
>
> In addition to the improved American (or Soviet) ability to monitor enemy forces that has led to faster counterreactions, intelligence systems now have the ability to monitor not only enemy military units but also enemy warning and intelligence systems themselves. In addition the possibility exists that each side's warning and intelligence systems could interact with the other's in unusual or complicated ways that are unanticipated, to produce a mutually reinforcing alert. Unfortunately, this last possibility is not a totally new phenomenon; it is precisely what happened in Europe in 1914. What *is* new is the technology, and the speed with which it could happen.[39]

Interested in the political will of states, Brodie concentrated not surprisingly on the more subtle aspects of their intentions during crises. "Our capabilities, and the opponent's," he wrote in *Escalation and the Nuclear Option,*

> are important less for determining who would win a major nuclear conflict—which neither he nor we will care to see proceed to any conclusive test—than for their bearing . . . on the questions that immediately arise concerning any projected crisis: What will the opponent be likely to *do* under certain contingencies? How will he respond to what we do? What, under these considerations, can we bring ourselves to do?[40]

But this neglected that the exercise of self-control by countries might well be impaired by the need for quick reaction and that in any event stability would especially in the most dangerous cases depend heavily on technological conditions that he failed to examine.

A second problem pertained to Brodie's assertion that those specializing in technological requirements were insensitive to adversary reactions and therefore contributed to arms races. For example, he noted that proponents of deploying a defense against ballistic missile attack, such as Donald Brennan, neglected why "the Soviets [should] not respond to our BMD [ballistic missile defense] buildup by instituting one of their own *plus* a considerable added number of offensive missiles—a pattern which we would then have to copy."[41] That such competition was unnecessarily intensified followed from Brodie's view that "we have long become accustomed to the fact that each 'answer' has its own reply."[42] Elsewhere, however, when discussing the growing size of nuclear forces rather than their technological improvement, he maintained that military buildups *contributed* to contemporary strategic stability. "With nuclear weapons especially," he wrote in *War and Politics,*

> there could be a meaningful competition in quantities even while there was an extremely fast rate of change in technology. The Russians seemed content not to push the pace until about 1965, when they embarked on a program showing determination to achieve something like parity with us in strategic nuclear weapons.
>
> Unfortunately, such a program lends itself to all kinds of interpretations in the rival country, and those with a low threshold of alarm, like former Secretary of Defense Laird, became too readily certain that what the opponent intends is not "parity" but a "first-strike capability." . . . Others, including this writer, while accepting the need to be watchful and to maintain a secure retaliatory force, see a situation where very wide gyrations in force levels may have little real effect on the strategic balance. . . .
>
> [T]he kind of nuclear race that was going on through the 1950s and 1960s could hardly be considered to be contributing to anyone's bellicosity. . . . The more both sides built up, the less possibility there was that either could achieve that first-strike capability which in any case would remain uncertifiable. Thus, the strategic situation between the Soviet Union and the United States became profoundly stable. Here is a case, in other words, of an arms competition producing stability rather than the reverse.[43]

The Political Standard for Weapons Use

Brodie's second argument for discounting the study of weapons technology—the unsuitability of highly destructive nuclear weapons in war for what he termed "*any* conceivable political objectives"[44]—echoed his earliest reaction to fusion weapons and led him to give extended treatment to the ideas of Clausewitz. "Clausewitz is probably as pertinent to our times as most of the literature specifically written about nuclear war," he wrote in an essay accompanying a new translation of Clausewitz's *On War.*

Among works of the latter genre we pick up a good deal of useful technological and other lore, but we usually sense also the absence of that depth and scope which are particularly the hallmark of Clausewitz. We miss especially his tough-minded pursuit of the idea that war in all its phases must be rationally guided by meaningful political purposes. That insight is quite lost in most of the contemporary books, including one which bears a title that boldly invites comparison with the earlier classic, Herman Kahn's *On Thermonuclear War*.[45]

Using Clausewitz to argue for the political irrelevance of attacking with thermonuclear weapons, Brodie, like Clausewitz, understood that war would not invariably serve "meaningful political purposes." Clausewitz conceptualized what he termed "absolute war," characterized by the absence of restraint on the pattern of the Napoleonic wars. "One might wonder," Clausewitz wrote,

> whether there is any truth at all in our concept of the absolute character of war were it not for the fact that with our own eyes we have seen warfare achieve this state of absolute perfection. After the short prelude of the French Revolution, Bonaparte brought it swiftly and ruthlessly to that point. War, in his hands, was waged without respite until the enemy succumbed, and the counterblows were struck with almost equal energy. Surely it is both natural and inescapable that this phenomenon should cause us to turn again to the pure concept of war with all its rigorous implications.[46]

Brodie noted in his analysis of *On War* that Clausewitz had "witnessed some of the worst horrors in the long grim history of war, including the disastrous crossing of the Berezina River by the French in their retreat from Moscow, which he saw with his own eyes from the Russian side and which he described with the most deep-felt, shuddering anguish in a letter to his wife."[47] For his part, Brodie believed that the First World War, which he termed in 1959 "the purposeless war, which no one seemed to know how to prevent and which, once begun, no one seemed to know how to stop,"[48] most notably negated Clausewitz's precept that war should be governed by political considerations. That case may well have alerted him to the dangers inherent in other instances in which political guidance was not appropriately exercised over war-making; for example, reacting to the Clausewitzian concept of absolute war in his analysis of *On War*, he wrote that Clausewitz "insists and reiterates that war is always *an instrument of policy* because he knew, and we know today, that the usual practice is rather to let war take over national policy."[49] Brodie's assertion in the 1950s that war once begun had an inherent tendency to become "orgiastic," the starting point for his effort to strengthen war limitations, is especially compelling from this same perspective.[50]

Brodie also shared with Clausewitz an understandable abhorrence of absolute war and the view that guiding warfare by political considerations protected best against the tendency of war to become absolute.[51] Following Clausewitz, Brodie wrote in *War and Politics* that "unless it is in pursuit of a reasonable political objective, any nation resorting to war is simply perpetrating wanton destruction of life and goods on a vast scale. The appearance of order imposed on the process by the use of military organization and method only makes the destruction greater and more efficient."[52] But unlike Clausewitz, who studied war of his day at its most abhorrent,

Brodie by 1952 was no longer able to check his revulsion of major nuclear war sufficiently to examine that subject. Instead his acceptance at that time of Clausewitz's
precept of guiding war-making by political objectives and his belief that major nuclear war was unsuited to any of those objectives enabled him to avoid studying it.

Clausewitz could not have anticipated contemporary technologies permitting massive warfare at the outset of hostilities. He merely alluded briefly to the possibility
of such conditions when he wrote that "if war consisted of one decisive act, or of
a set of simultaneous decisions, preparations would tend toward totality, for no omission could ever be rectified."[53] In reference to conditions of his own time (the early
nineteenth century), Clausewitz cited the existing social climate and imperfect military organization of states as impeding the waging of absolute war.

Brodie played down superpower inclination to seek "a single solution" to their
disputes but not because of the difficulties in seeking such a result, for he argued
in *War and Politics* that "strategic thermonuclear war is indeed possible."[54] Rather,
he seems to have had in mind superpower agreement that nuclear war could not
appropriately advance political objectives. But as Michael Howard showed, the moral
imperative of guiding warfare by political aims became vastly more important as
newer technologies facilitated waging absolute war.[55] By failing to consider the dynamics of contemporary absolute warfare in his later work, Brodie could only understand the contemporary relevance of Clausewitz's absolute warfare concept in an abstract way. For example, he treated that concept theoretically in *War and Politics*
when, elaborating upon "the dialectical character of Clausewitz's presentation," he
noted that Clausewitz "first insists that the use of force is theoretically without limits and then goes on to explain why it must in fact be limited. He also frequently
invokes the images of philosophical idealism, no doubt also derived from Hegel, as
when he speaks of 'absolute war,' meaning an abstract idea akin to Plato's ideas and
not something to be witnessed on earth."[56]

Elsewhere Brodie noted Clausewitz's view that warfare in the Napoleonic era ap-
proximated absolute war, but when he understood absolute war as an abstract concept he weakened the moral imperative for using Clausewitz's precept of guiding
war by the choice of political objectives. In general, the more Brodie in his later
writings stressed the improbability of major nuclear warfare and the wrongheaded-
ness of excessive preoccupation with it and the technologies making it possible, the
more he shifted attention away from the essential question of the attractiveness of
Clausewitz's precept to public officials. For example, if he was correct that "the usual
practice is . . . to let war take over national policy," such an imperative might not
be very persuasive even during an intense Soviet-American crisis. On the other hand,
the favorable comments of both Lenin and Stalin on using war as an instrument
of political objectives could help dispose their political heirs to the same view.[57] More
widely, J. F. C. Fuller, conceding that the First World War reflected a breakdown
of the Clausewitzian precept, concluded that Brodie's generalization was incorrect.
"The point to note," he wrote in 1946, "is that up to 1914 all England's wars were
political instruments, as were the wars of other nations, for the aim of each was

a more profitable peace to the victor, and even in the most aggressive of these wars the aggressor's aim was to annihilate the enemy by obliterating his country."[58]

A second problem for those such as Brodie who took the view that general nuclear war could not usefully support political objectives was that, as Donald Brennan pointed out, NATO war plans provided strong evidence to the contrary. Criticizing a statement by Michael Howard that following the Korean War "it became almost impossible to visualize any political objective for which the use of such [nuclear] weapons would be appropriate,"[59] Brennan noted that the security of the NATO allies has been widely regarded as having "been protected (in the obviously limited sense involved) by the threat of such use ever since the period mentioned," and he argued that "there is not the slightest doubt that Clausewitz would have condemned this [that is, Howard's] mode of thought out of hand."[60] Brennan had in mind what he considered to be the very large destruction from nuclear attacks envisioned in NATO War Plan MC-14/2, prepared in 1957, the triggering of which he evidently believed necessitated political agreement in the alliance.[61]

Still more problematic was whether the assertion that major nuclear war could have no political utility and the adoption of a rigorous political context to examine the utility of nuclear weapons stultified development of nuclear strategy, a result highly ironical for those such as Brodie and Howard asserting the contemporary relevance of Clausewitz. If the major task of present-day superpower statecraft was to select and protect defensible national objectives in light of the risk of hostilities, strategy could be overshadowed by crisis management. "The most conspicuous milestone" for such a development, Coral Bell observed,

> is a remark of Mr. McNamara's, in the aftermath of the Cuban missile crisis, that "There is no longer any such thing as strategy, only crisis management." This rather arguable dictum crystallizes the main anxiety, to my mind, behind the notion: the anxiety that, in situations of crisis, political ends should maintain ascendancy over military means. . . .
>
> The emotional — indeed the moral — impulse behind the search for a theory or a technique of crisis management has been the belief that political considerations *must* maintain ascendancy over military ones in the nuclear age.[62]

Still, that same political standard handicapped strategists in adjusting to critical technological developments. According to Herman Kahn,

> The invention of the atomic bomb . . . seemed to end any constructive thinking about strategy and tactics. Nuclear war was simply unthinkable — both literally and figuratively.
>
> This phenomenon, known as psychological denial, meant that while one side (ours) did little or no thinking about nuclear weapons, the other side simply regarded them as "bigger bombs," or "higher-quality weapons," and also did not undertake any fundamental rethinking of classical political and strategic assumptions.[63]

This condition, attributed by Kahn to the feeling "even among professionals and scholars . . . that strategy and tactics as they [understood] them, had come to an end," was once again demonstrated when the advent of fusion weapons interrupted what he called a "partial awakening" in the discussion of strategic options. He specifically cited in this connection Brodie's 1955 article "Strategy Hits a Dead End" as "a block in strategic thinking."[64] In the early 1960s, after initial study of how thermonuclear war could be fought and ended to suit the prevailing American strategic forces advantage, Kahn wrote that "discussion now seems again to be dying down with the growing belief that, as both sides develop relatively or absolutely invulnerable forces, strategy and tactics *really* do come to a dead end; war really is obsolete."[65]

Detailing weaknesses for contemporary strategy of a political perspective that dramatized the horrors of nuclear war, these ideas ignored the contribution of that same perspective to analyzing noncentral war concerns. For example, Brodie's earliest studies of fusion weapons had warned of the excessive destructiveness of those weapons for any political objective and challenged the prevailing view that all Soviet-American war must be total. With respect to strategic nuclear war, Brodie's first work on this subject was hardly characterized by psychological denial, and his interest by 1949 in coercive warfare helped to widen informed discussion of strategic bombing options.[66] But Brodie's later retrospective argument that atomic weapons reached their "asymptote of influence" with the Hiroshima attack of 1945 suggested a very different state of affairs than did his earlier ideas responding to post-Hiroshima technological developments.

A Critique of André Beaufre

Having split with economists by emphasizing the political dimension of national security affairs, Brodie also challenged the view, argued forcefully by the contemporary French strategist Gen. André Beaufre, that such research should aim at comprehensive study and generalization. "My own bias," he declared in an August 1965 review of two of Beaufre's books,

> rears itself in the view that, strategy being essentially the pursuit of success in certain types of competitive endeavour, a pragmatic approach is the only appropriate one. The basic pragmatic principle is, I suppose, that "Truth is the idea that works." Thus, one weighs a strategic concept or idea by investigating as thoroughly as possible the factors necessary to its successful operation as well as the question whether those factors do in fact exist or are likely to exist at the appropriate time. This inevitably involves one in a good deal of detailed study, preferably over the whole range of relevant and important variables — political, technological, geographic, etc.[67]

This position — affected, Brodie conceded, by his undergraduate training in the "distinctively and characteristically American" philosophy of pragmatism and echoing his frequent references to the importance of circumstance in the development of strategy — emanated from his view that strategy should be treated as a branch of politics. "Strategic thinking," he wrote in *War and Politics,*

> or "theory" if one prefers, is nothing if not pragmatic. Strategy is a "how to do it" study, a guide to accomplishing something and doing it efficiently. As in many other

branches of politics, the question that matters in strategy is: Will the idea work? More important, will it be likely to work under the special circumstances under which it will next be tested? These circumstances are not likely to be known or knowable much in advance of the moment of testing, though the uncertainty is itself a factor to be reckoned with in one's strategic doctrine. . . .

Strategy is a field where truth is sought in the pursuit of viable solutions. In that respect it is like the other branches of politics and like any of the applied sciences, and not at all like pure science, where the function of theory is to describe, organize, and explain and not to prescribe.[68]

Prescriptive analysis of strategy would deal with ambiguous, contradictory, and uncertain detail and urge correct and prescient appreciation by leaders of their circumstances;[69] explanatory analysis such as Beaufre's would develop abstract concepts to make otherwise incongruous data more intelligible and stress leaders' understanding of those concepts. Moving from the general to the particular to develop strategic concepts, Beaufre argued that he did not neglect facts but asserted that "what was lacking was clear ideas on the central scope of strategy," reacting in this respect against his own formative experience. He wrote in response to Brodie's review that

I have lived many years under the iron rule of pragmatism that Marshal Pétain had imposed upon the French General Staff: one proceeded always from the particular (the tactical realm) but never reached the general (the strategic realm) which was taken as futile. This pragmatism has not been very successful. I feel that today it is rather the opposite which is true: without an overall outlook no detail of application is valuable. What it is necessary for us to discover and to master is the means of reasoning in a simple and fair manner over the larger unities. Contemporary strategic phenomena have become so important, complicated, and subtle that it is indispensable to clarify and synthesize them if one wants to understand anything about them. Otherwise, one is lost in the forest.[70]

The idea that strategy was "futile" came, Beaufre believed, from erroneous lessons drawn in France from the First World War. "The static warfare of 1914–18," he wrote in his *Introduction to Strategy,*

was held to be proof of the "bankruptcy of strategy," whereas in fact it demonstrated only the bankruptcy of one particular strategy. It was primarily in France (but France was very influential at the time) that strategy was held to be an outdated science, a thought process concerned with war but no longer abreast of developments; evolution appeared to give pride of place to material over ideas, to war potential over operational manoeuvre and to industry and science over philosophy. This view wore the cloak of realism; as a result "strategists" were held to be pretentious and behind the times; all efforts were concentrated upon tactics and equipment. Yet in view of the speed of developments this was precisely the moment when foresight of a particularly high and perspicacious order was required—and only strategy could have produced it. The result was the military defeat of France in 1940 but equally Germany's failure to consummate her victory; both were due to mistaken appreciations of the situation because both had appreciated [*sic*] on too narrow a basis.[71]

But Beaufre also believed that no strategy could succeed without what he called "the guiding principle, a philosophy,"[72] and he argued that philosophy and strategy were two distinct disciplines,"

> necessary and misunderstood over a number of decades in France. By philosophy, I understand as does everyone what the Greeks called philosophy, "love of wisdom," the sense of life. By strategy, I understand "the art of employing force or constraint for realizing fixed goals by policy," and I add that the choice of this goal by policy is enhanced to an extent by philosophy which animates it. I have never meant to speak of a "philosophy of strategy," which would not make any sense.[73]

For example, he asserted that "lack of philosophy" had contributed to the French defeat in 1940, whereas the British and American rebound in Europe from 1942 to 1945 was attributable to the presence of philosophy and strategy.[74]

Brodie and Beaufre typically addressed strategy decided at the most authoritative levels of government, which would ordinarily have the widest impact. In addition, they both understood strategy as multifaceted and not of narrowly military interest. This is what Beaufre had in mind, for example, by the term "total strategy," which reflected that "war today is total . . . carried on in all fields, political, economic, diplomatic and military. Such, with all its varying shades of emphasis, is the pattern of the cold war (which I referred to as 'War in Peacetime' in 1939). Equally therefore strategy must be total."[75] Finally, both strategists concentrated on the intangible elements of their subject. Beaufre, having distinguished five strategic concepts and maintained that "there will be a special strategy to fit each situation,"[76] emphasized the contemporary importance of what he referred to as the "indirect approach," most suitable for countries whose freedom of action was limited and whose military forces were insufficient to threaten decisively (in contrast to the strategy of deterrence). Here the emphasis needed to be upon political and diplomatic pressure rather than upon military threats; as Beaufre put it, "The psychological factor . . . becomes dominant" and "force is required to exploit (or threaten to exploit) the situations created by psychological manoeuvre."[77] This was reminiscent of Brodie's interest in the political and psychological bases for military behavior and of his insistence on the unwillingness of present-day superpowers to fight to a final showdown.

Brodie parted from Beaufre in depreciating the importance of philosophy as a guide to strategy and as an explanation of strategic outcomes. Assuming that Beaufre defined philosophy as a kind of axiomatic thought, Brodie, with reference to the aphorism "fire kills" (which he attributed to Marshal Pétain), wrote, "What is a philosophy worth that misses the booby traps?"[78] And he criticized Beaufre's assertions about the importance of philosophy during the Second World War. "The English Channel," he wrote, "British stubbornness, and vast American resources were certainly among the essential factors determining the differences between the French performance and that of the 'Anglo-Saxons.'"

A second difference between Brodie and Beaufre was over the application of strategic insights. Evidently believing that Beaufre wished to seek generalizations applicable to all situations, Brodie doubted that such generalizations would excite much policy or analytic interest. "I do not deny," he contended, "that there are certain propositions that override all these differences and changes, such as that men fear violent death, or that uncertainty may magnify dangers otherwise considered small (to mention only some of the ingredients of deterrence), but these, if they manage to be meaningful and true, are usually not very novel."[79] Even as he discounted the importance of military technology, Brodie still viewed technological developments as impeding generalizations about strategic behavior, as when he wrote in 1976 of Herman Kahn's major study, *On Thermonuclear War,* that "Kahn . . . based his main argument — that the United States could survive and therefore ought not too much fear a thermonuclear war with its chief rival — on technical premises which are certainly obsolete today, whether or not they were realistic when his book was published in the not-so-distant year of 1960."[80] Brodie had in mind the growing stockpile of Soviet nuclear forces and its impact on defending American urban populations.[81]

Beaufre for his part wished to demonstrate the applicability of strategic concepts to more than one historical era rather than generalize over many historical situations. For example, taking the view that the "gigantic technological race . . . in progress" was a new form of peacetime strategy "of which the phrase 'arms race' used prior to the old great conflicts is hardly more than a faint reflection,"[82] he compared that technological rivalry to the attrition effect of the battle of Verdun in the First World War and the German Russian campaign and Allied air bombardment of Germany in the Second World War.[83] Similarly, he compared contemporary indirect strategy to the one Hitler followed from 1936 to 1939, which employed military force but moved "in a series of bounds interspersed with political negotiations."[84]

Beaufre's method of analysis was in this respect much closer to that of Clausewitz than was Brodie's, for Clausewitz wished to find out "how one thing is related to another, and keep the important and the unimportant separate. If concepts combine of their own accord to form that nucleus of truth we call a principle, if they spontaneously compose a pattern that becomes a rule, it is the task of the theorist to make this clear."[85] Without expecting to find absolute truth, the theorist would aim, Clausewitz believed, "to analyze everything down to its basic elements, to incontrovertible truth,"[86] requiring in turn what Peter Paret referred to as "the logical extreme, the philosophic ideal, which alone could provide a reliable basis for measurement and analysis,"[87] meaning, evidently, a concept whose applicability transcended its fit with particular situations.

Clausewitz's absolute war concept was a case in point. Paret and James E. King pointed out that Clausewitz, after showing how warfare had fallen short in many cases of extreme effort and violence and thereby defied strictly logical reasoning, wrote that "theory must concede all this; but it has the duty to give priority to the absolute form of war and to make that form a general point of reference, so that he who wants to learn from theory becomes accustomed to keeping that point constantly in view, to measuring all his hopes and fears by it, and to approximating it *when he can* or *when he must.*"[88] Brodie's own disinterest in theory may help explain, as King pointed out, his failure to discuss this use by Clausewitz of the absolute war concept. However, "as a deep admirer of the work of Clausewitz," Brodie wrote in response to Beaufre,

> I can hardly be opposed in principle to the pursuit of basic generalizations which may help us to integrate intelligibly the facets of the military problems we have to deal with. However, I also believe that to do under modern conditions what Clausewitz — and he almost alone — succeeded in doing under the simpler conditions of his time would be a work of colossal difficulty, and not useful to attempt unless one is going to do it supremely well.[89]

Clausewitz and the Use of History

Notwithstanding Brodie's discounting of interesting regularities in strategic behavior, other recent writings encouraged their documentation. "It is slightly surprising, in retrospect," wrote Alexander George and Richard Smoke in an influential book about contemporary applications of deterrence strategy,

> how many of the concepts of contemporary deterrence theory — commitments, and how to reinforce or escape them, signaling, comparatively fine calculations of opposing forces, the fear of escalation and the use of that fear as a deterrent, the mutual assumption of rationality — were implicitly part of the diplomatic practice of the balance-of-power system, without being articulated in this kind of terminology.
>
> Indeed, eighteenth- and nineteenth-century diplomatic and military history provides the politico-military analyst with a rich lode of empirical material for the expansion and refinement of contemporary concepts.[90]

Those inquiring about historical parallels to contemporary conditions could be expected to be especially interested in less intense forms of war. Michael Howard, for example, found that historically the threat to use weapons has been effective even when such use was regarded as unnecessary, as in present NATO strategy in Europe. "As in the days of pre-Napoleonic strategy," Howard contended in a 1973 essay,

> the movement of forces once again becomes part of the bargaining process, an indicator of resolution or of willingness to consider accommodation. To that extent classical models have relevance for nuclear as for non-nuclear powers, but the models must be those, not that of Napoleon with his decisive battles nor those of Napoleon's successors with their total wars of attrition, but of Napoleon's eighteenth-century predecessors: men who had much to lose and little to gain from war, who fearfully committed their forces to battle and manoeuvred them cautiously; men with limited resources and often a divided public opinion within their domains.[91]

Such parallels brought into question widely accepted notions. "Traditional strategy," Howard wrote, assumed that in any conflict the antagonists were in complete control of their national resources and that their governments commanded a total consensus of national will. Violence between states was considered to be totally crystallized into those manifestations of it and controlled by governments."[92] The traditional view was logically supported by the introduction into war-making in the Napoleonic age of public opinion and of a broadened scope of governments and also by the tendency of governments from the time of Napoleon to wage war as a direct test of strength. At present, by contrast, not only were such tests of strength ruled out between major nuclear powers, but the division between publics and governments often precipitated war. "Operational techniques and technological tools were now as ancillary to the main socio-political conflict as the tools of psychological warfare had been to the central operational and logistical struggle in the two World Wars," Howard argued.

> In those conflicts, fought between remarkably cohesive societies, the issue was decided by logistic attrition. Propaganda and subversion had played a marginal role, and such successes as they achieved were strictly geared to those of the armed forces themselves. Conversely, in the conflicts of decolonization which culminated in Vietnam, operational and technological factors were subordinate to the socio-political struggle. If that was not conducted with skill and based on a realistic analysis of the societal situation, no amount of operational expertise, logistical backup or technical know-how could possibly help.[93]

Both types of strategic orientation distinguished by Howard were analyzed in Clausewitz's *On War*, which made prominent reference to the Napoleonic campaigns as well as the much more limited, strategically defensive but operationally offensive campaigns of the Prussian king Frederick II during the Seven Years War. When he discussed Napoleon's battles, Clausewitz contributed to the traditional view of strategy through his celebrated references to what he termed "a paradoxical trinity" of forces in war, including natural forces, such as hatred and enmity (which concerns the people), probability and chance (which relates to the commander and his army), and subordination as a reasoned instrument of policy (a responsibility of government).[94] But when he concluded that in the later years of the Seven Years War Frederick's military successes came from defensive operations and spelled out the Prussian king's wish to avoid serious losses in battle and his concern that now "even victories cost too much," Clausewitz was suggesting the political utility of force in the absence of military engagements.[95]

Brodie, discounting the possibility and the value of theorizing about strategy, did not distinguish these two strategic orientations in his commentary on *On War*, making no reference to Clausewitz's trinity concept and terming Clausewitz's main discussion of war limitation "dated."[96] His lack of interest in generalizing about strategy discouraged the conceptual refinement required for it, but from a war-fighting standpoint Brodie's interest in Clausewitz was more abstract than practical. "What Clausewitz tries to tell us," he wrote,

> is mostly how to study war rather than how to fight it—specifically, how to absorb with discrimination and profit the enhanced understanding that can come from the copi-

ous reading of good military history. Those chapters of practical advice on the handling of battles and campaigns which one does find in *On War* are by and large the least interesting and the least "Clausewitzian" in the work; certainly they are the most dated, though they will retain interest for the military historian.[97]

Instead of approaching Clausewitz from a theoretical or war-guidance perspective, Brodie used him to caution against tolerating extremes, distinguishing as did Clausewitz between total and less than total war-making efforts for a given purpose. He cited Clausewitz when arguing that total effort would ensure (in Clausewitz's words) that "all proportion between action and political demands would be lost."[98] And he recalled "the problem the United States faced in Vietnam" from reading Clausewitz's exhortation that

> to discover how much of our resources must be mobilized for war, we must first examine our own political aim and that of the enemy. We must gauge the strength and situation of the opposing state. We must gauge the character and abilities of its government and people and do the same in regard to our own. Finally, we must evaluate the political sympathies of other states and the effect the war may have on them.[99]

This formulation, which strongly guided Brodie's critique of twentieth-century warfare in his last book, *War and Politics,* might have been addressed to any war. It implied the popular unity and governmental control behind war-making specified in the traditional conception of strategy that Howard had dismissed for contemporary warfare, as well as the need for the wariness, caution, and rejection of highly intensive combat reflected in Frederick's behavior.

Brodie, like Howard, depended heavily on mastering what Clausewitz referred to as "the faculty of using judgment to detect the most important and decisive elements in the vast array of facts and situations."[100] Yet the approaches of the two strategists were in some ways quite different. By using a more differentiated historical approach, Howard was better able to generalize about strategic behavior and to employ history as a guide to contemporary problems. For example, having highlighted the relevance of pre-Napoleonic war-making as a model for *contemporary* warfare, Howard criticized Liddell Hart's application of pre-Napoleonic warfare to the era of the Second World War.[101] Brodie referred to history in a merely illustrative way without modifying his guiding concepts, which were loose enough to permit him, for example, to radically change his position about waging war in Vietnam.[102] On at least one important issue—that of limiting war—Brodie's concepts sharply diverged from those of Clausewitz, as he insisted that contemporary war limitations required deliberate withholding of arms from battle rather than modification of political aims.[103] Finally, because of Brodie's strong preoccupation with the difficulties great powers would have in making war, he could be expected to define highly demanding and even practically unattainable war-making standards.

Emotional Motivations for Making War

Brodie accepted Clausewitz's rational equation between war-making and political objectives because he was as committed as Clausewitz was to logical strategy and to combating axiomatic views. But he was also very favorably inclined to a second, subordinate theme in *On War*—the importance of emotional motivations behind warfare, which he treated as opposed to the first theme. "Clausewitz . . . acknowledged, at the very beginning of his book," Brodie wrote in *War and Politics,* "the inevitable and indeed necessary involvement of aggressive emotions in any act of force, an involvement that grows with 'the importance and duration of the hostile interests'; but it is not compatible with statecraft to permit such emotions to dominate the choice of means, let alone ends."[104] But Clausewitz also made reference to emotional motivations when explaining, as Brodie noted, "why there is so great a gap between the pure concept of war and the concrete shape which war generally assumes." In his guide to *On War,* Brodie cited in full Clausewitz's statement that "logic comes to a stop in this labyrinth [of war]; and those men whose habit in great things and small is anyway to act on particular dominating impressions or feelings rather than according to strict logic are hardly aware of the confused, inconsistent, and ambiguous situation in which they find themselves."[105] "Impressions or feelings" could help assure that war was not one "in which [according to Clausewitz] two mutually destructive elements collide, but one of tension between two elements, separate for the time being, which discharge energy in discontinuous, minor shocks,"[106] and that hostilities were accordingly dampened rather than intensified.

Finally, Brodie cited the balanced treatment given by Clausewitz to psychological forces, as in the latter's discussion of "military spirit," the collective effect that morale contributes to the efficiency of an army. Brodie specifically had in mind Clausewitz's contention that "military spirit" was not indispensable for an army's fighting effectiveness—a contention he asserted "only Clausewitz would [argue] among all the classic writers on strategy."[107] "It cannot be maintained," he quoted Clausewitz, "that it is impossible to fight a successful war without these qualities. We stress this in order to clarify the concept, so as not to lose sight of the ideas in a fog of generalities and give the impression that military spirit is all that counts in the end. . . . The spirit of an army . . . is a tool *whose power is measurable.*"[108] By "measurable," Brodie believed, Clausewitz meant that the importance of this as of other very significant concepts could be exaggerated.

The originality of Clausewitz's references to emotion-based behavior in his study of strategy was pointed out by Peter Paret, who observed that

> since antiquity writers had stressed the importance of emotion in war; but beyond listing desirable and undesirable characteristics, they had done little with the subject. More recently, in the train of the Revolutionary Wars, some authors had emphasized the importance of the irrational, linked it with the power of chance, and concluded either that the psychology of the soldier was too obscure or that war was too anarchic to be subject to scientific analysis. Clausewitz took the decisive step of placing the analysis of psycho-

logical forces at the very center of the study of war. In accord with Kantian philosophy he acknowledged that some things could not be fully understood; but that did not mean that they should be ignored. *On War* made the psychology of the soldier, his commander, and the society they served an essential part of the theory of war.[109]

As did Clausewitz, Brodie alternately inflated and deflated the importance of psychological forces in war, striving for balance but not identifying any regularities. He was also likely to borrow in this area from Clausewitz, first, because Brodie believed that "in matters psychological Clausewitz is always the keenest and also the most measured of observers,"[110] and, second, since Brodie depended heavily on Clausewitz for a logical standard of war-making, he would likewise depend on him for instances in which that standard had been or might be violated in order to establish its practical strength. Moreover, Brodie was deeply interested in psychological and psychoanalytic interpretations of behavior as a result of his close acquaintance with colleagues at RAND trained in psychoanalytical techniques as well as of his own experience under analysis in the 1950s and 1960s.[111]

Brodie particularly stressed emotional motivations for war when he judged logical standards inadequate. For example, in the late 1950s, he tried to counter a "tendency, perhaps on both sides, to over-rationalize the actions of the adversary, that is, to exaggerate the degree to which his actions are consistently ruled by a sober, detached evaluation of self-interest. How can anyone even tell what such a sober, detached evaluation ought to be?"[112] Brodie maintained that rational behavior could be overrelied upon for deterring superpower attack, because

the intrusion of emotions, conscious and unconscious, in Soviet decision-making about deterrence or the like is not merely a possibility but a certainty—regardless of their injunctions to the contrary—simply because the Russians are human beings and not computing machines. Naturally, the same is true of our own decisions. . . .

When I say that emotions, conscious and unconscious, must affect the high state decisions of the Soviet leader or leaders, I mean by "emotions" something not to be identified merely with excitability nor confined to conspicuous manifestations either of rage or euphoria. . . . The precept not to yield to one's "emotions" (in this same popular sense) in important policy decisions is after all a universal one, being familiar also in our own society. The fact that the Bolsheviks give it very special emphasis would suggest, as it did to [Nathan] Leites, that the culture in which they were reared predisposed them to being weak in this respect, or at least to fearing weakness.[113]

Assertions that the Soviets would act with considerable rationality, he continued, seldom referred to the individuality of Soviet leaders, reflected for example in the "constantly distorted perception of reality" of Stalin on the eve of the Nazi invasion of the Soviet Union in 1941 and in the "something akin to plain anger" stimulating President Truman's decision to go to war in Korea in June 1950.[114] Finding Nathan Leites's depiction of the operational code of Soviet leaders, in *The Operational Code of the Politburo,* not fully satisfactory in this regard, Brodie went on to say that "it is now a clinical commonplace that precepts concerning behavior, however earnestly and sincerely adopted, are not only helpless against the unconscious components of one's thinking and behavior, to which they have little if any access, but are also notoriously weak against those conscious thoughts and emotions which are derived from or strongly affected by the unconscious ones."[115] Finally, he linked "the issue of 'provocation' as a by-product of certain aspects of our military posture" with intuitions about Soviet leaders' emotional reaction to American behavior.[116]

Some years later, Brodie completely shifted his thinking on the intrusion of emotions into decisions about war, highlighting the group basis of decision making as a more appropriate focus of analysis than the study of specific individuals. "In the decision-making process that accounts for the political behavior of states," he declared in a 1964 paper,

> we observe conspicuously at work many factors that greatly modify the emotional and other psychological elements which so directly influence individual behavior, including the behavior of the statesman. Most obviously, the actions of states stem characteristically from decisions reached by groups rather than by individuals. . . .
>
> Perhaps most important of all, governmental behavior is modified not only by the cultural milieus but also by the national traditions and by the distinctive political precepts which may characterize each of the parties to the confrontation. . . . [O]ne of the major precepts of behavior in the Bolshevik code is that personal feelings, whether of fear, rage, humiliation and the like, must be utterly controlled and rejected as influences upon one's political conduct. . . .
>
> All this is not to say that the psychological makeup of our own policy-makers, especially those of the top level, is unimportant. It is only to say that we must beware of generalizing too easily from the area of personal behavior to that of government.[117]

This statement, affected by Brodie's interpretation of superpower decision making during the Cuban missile crisis of 1962, supported his criticism of the widespread view that a low-intensive Soviet-American war in Europe would quickly escalate to a major nuclear war. It suggested that political understanding, with consequences for institutional behavior, was more important for international stability than was psychological insight.[118]

Both of these broad points of view found a place in *War and Politics,* where Brodie used them to suit his argument. For example, in his discussion of the "fierce dedication to the goal of victory" during the First World War, Brodie concluded that "we are . . . confronted not with simple greed but with some deep psychological need expressed on the national rather than the personal level."[119] Again, referring generally to "the more emotionally evocative symbols" in diplomacy and war, Brodie stressed the

> realization that man is by nature deeply emotional, and that the real issue is not his inclination to feel and express indignation but rather what it is that he becomes indignant about. . . . [T]heories of international relations that assume certain motivations to be rational, or at least perennial, merely because they are familiar are likely in a swiftly changing era like our own to fall very wide of the mark.[120]

Elsewhere in *War and Politics,* on the other hand, he indicated the importance of

group decision making and, in a discussion of the psychological causes of war, asserted that psychological theories "do not easily adjust" to the changes humans have
made more recently in the character of war, including the fact that "nuclear weapons
have clearly made a critical difference in man's proclivity for war."[121] In the same
vein, he played down the difference for international stability potentially brought
about by improved understanding of human emotions. "It is a pertinent question,"
he wrote, "whether our having a better knowledge of what emotions, hidden or
otherwise, are at work during wars and during crises that may lead to war would
make the least difference in our handling of the next crisis that comes along. Very
likely not."[122]

These statements suggest that without explicitly studying the strategic effect of
human emotions, Brodie used awareness of emotional motivations as a control for
his commitment to logic in strategic analysis while also using the latter as a control
for endorsing the application of psychological insights to such analysis. This protected him against overarguing his case, but his points on one side weakened the
effect of his observations on the other. Moreover, in one key respect he may have
oversimplified his distinction between logical and emotional behaviors. Although
depending on Leites's insights about the Soviet operational code to illustrate the
former, he seems to have overlooked that some of those insights could be explained
with reference to the emotions of Soviet leaders. Brodie neglected a point suggested
in a passage from *On War* that emphasized self-control as "strength of mind, or of
character," in the waging of war. "We mean," Clausewitz wrote, with reference
to these concepts,

> the ability to keep one's head at times of exceptional stress and violent emotion. Could
> strength of intellect alone account for such a faculty? We doubt it. Of course the op-
> posite does not flow from the fact that some men of outstanding intellect do lose their
> self-control; it could be argued that a powerful rather than a capacious mind is what
> is needed. But it might be closer to the truth to assume that the faculty known as *self-
> control* — the gift of keeping calm even under the greatest stress — is rooted in tempera-
> ment. It is itself an emotion which serves to balance the passionate feelings in strong
> characters without destroying them, and it is this balance alone that assures the domi-
> nance of the intellect.[123]

Limiting Clausewitz's study of psychological forces, however suggestive, was the
primitive character of the discipline of psychology in his day.[124] It was therefore not
surprising that, as Paret explained in reference to Clausewitz, "his enumeration of
psychological traits remains conventional; his speculations on their relevance to war,
although full of common sense and marked by flashes of brilliance, suffer, as he himself admits, from the same impressionistic defect that he condemns in the writings
of other theorists."[125] If the backwardness of psychology as a discipline limited the
quality of Clausewitz's linking emotions to war, the considerable contemporary advance in that discipline facilitated it.[126] Brodie, however, was inhibited by his disinterest in theory from taking full advantage of this advance. In addition, because he
was not competent to employ psychological and psychoanalytic insights, he neces-

sarily deferred to those who could relate such insights to the political problems that concerned him, even as their fund of ideas was not immediately adaptable to his satisfaction. Writing in *War and Politics,* for example, that "psychoanalysis is an abstruse science,"[127] he blamed the difficulties on lack of knowledge psychoanalysts and political scientists displayed about each other's concerns.

Psychological and Psychoanalytical Interpretations of Clausewitz

Interested in Clausewitz primarily for his contribution to strategic concepts, Brodie also studied him at length from a psychological and psychoanalytic point of view. This latter work depended heavily upon a 1971 popular biography of Clausewitz by Roger Parkinson, until that time the only book-length account of Clausewitz's life available in English.[128] Parkinson found evidence in prior writing that Clausewitz, who never held a senior command position, had been ambitious but later in life saw himself as a failure, had frequently been melancholy and depressed, and had broken his melancholia only when anticipating war and participation in battle. Summarizing his argument, Parkinson wrote:

> The factors which had made Clausewitz so unhappy throughout his life, especially in recent [that is, his last] years, had had an accumulative and accelerating effect: the lack of appreciation from the King and his ministers; the belief that he could do far more if only he were given the chance, the conviction that war with France was inevitable, and that too few preparations were undertaken for it. Perhaps there was disappointment, too, that hostilities with France had not already begun.[129]

Arguing that "one should be able to recognize deep depression as a morbid symptom" and suggesting that "Parkinson seems to be unaware of the significance of what he is reporting,"[130] Brodie seemed attracted to Parkinson's presentation by his own deeply intuitional understanding. As he explained in a letter to Peter Paret in 1973:

> Granted that one should not hang too much on a single letter, or even three or four. Still, a single letter can sometimes betray a capability—for madness or genius or anything else—that does not require other letters to implement it. Now Parkinson may be unreliable; he certainly is careless. But he seems to know something of the German language, and he clearly is not a fool. I am impressed with the fact that despite his naivety or innocence about psychoanalysis or even psychology, he came up with some remarkable letters or statements that certainly ring some kind of bell.[131]

Brodie made a series of deductions about Clausewitz's character from statements in *On War,* each echoing Parkinson's findings. For example, from Clausewitz's contention that no emotions inspiring men to battle can "substitute for a thirst for fame and honor," Brodie suggested that "in this respect introspection might have got the better of his objective judgment, for there is no doubt that Clausewitz is describing a thirst which affected him deeply."[132] This was consistent with a letter by Clausewitz stating that "I would rather have won fame at the front of a company of soldiers, with sword in hand."[133]

Elsewhere, to Clausewitz's observations that "as a rule most men would rather believe bad news than good" and that military commanders should suppress personal convictions if they did not have buoyant dispositions, Brodie commented that Clausewitz "was not of a 'buoyant disposition,' and perhaps for that reason he was as a senior officer invariably in a staff rather than a command position."[134] Brodie may have had in mind a letter quoted by Parkinson that Clausewitz had written from Potsdam in 1821. In it, Clausewitz recalled an earlier visit to that city, when he was left by his father at age twelve to begin his military service:

> Potsdam always tends to remind me of many sad and serious things. It was always so, and it is natural enough, since I always feel strange and lonely here. . . . I still have the same sadness which so filled my heart at that time, and which has never really left me. I admit that Fate so often smiled upon my life that I took it for granted. Yet, for all that, I have certainly never been quite free from that sadness.[135]

This thought, Brodie asserted, reflected "depression . . . almost consciously tied to a sense of abandonment."

Finally, Clausewitz discussed the quality of boldness at the command level, advocating boldness as essential to a distinguished commander, yet finding it "at a disadvantage only in an encounter with deliberate caution." Here Brodie found Clausewitz to have "a quite unwonted ambivalence . . . [and to be] struggling with his own temperament"; yet of the latter's advocacy of boldness, Brodie found it "remarkable that he should have been able to pay such tribute, albeit modestly qualified, to a quality he probably knew he did not possess."[136] Clausewitz's characteristic caution is reflected in the Parkinson volume,[137] and Brodie may have associated Clausewitz's lack of command appointments with this particular character trait.

When he went beyond assertions about character traits to more boldly probe Clausewitz's unconscious motivations, Brodie depended even more upon Parkinson's materials. Thus, impressed by Clausewitz's apparent attraction to battle, Brodie concluded that

> we must confront the fact that this man, who had seen so much of the worst horrors of war, whose face still bore the marks of the frostbite he had acquired in the Russian campaign, had been brought from chronic depression into positive exultation at the thought of going to war again, especially against the French. When he found this was not to be, that there was going to be no war at all, he was plunged back into the deepest gloom. Again there were endless "premonitions" of death.[138]

Terming this "an extraordinary demonstration," Brodie suggested that the taste for violence it showed

> is by no means to be considered normal. It argues some inner rage—repressed, unconscious, but alive. . . .
> The bloody phrases so often quoted out of context from [Clausewitz's] great posthumous work burn with their own fierce fire. They are kindled by something within.

They are indeed countered and, on intellectual balance, overcome with other words in which the intellect is at work rather than passion; and the intellect in this case is tremendously strong. This intellect is guided by a firm honesty, so that he will not refrain from going where it directs him and from expressing every thought that it brings to him. But the destructive passion against which that intellect is working is also strong.

We are dealing here with a deep internal conflict, and there can be no doubt that this conflict is directly linked to his growing depression.[139]

The idea that intellect and passion were in tension, which Brodie also applied to his analysis of *On War,* becomes understandable only if it is believed — as Brodie apparently did in his psychological and psychoanalytical interpretations of Clausewitz and in his interpretations of Clausewitz's ideas about strategy — that passion is associated with "destructive" forces. But just as emotions such as self-control can be constructive (as Clausewitz noted) and contribute to stability, so too could what Brodie referred to as Clausewitz's "neurosis"[140] have been in some sense constructive, as it has been with other writers.[141] Brodie conceded that Clausewitz's depression did not prevent him from developing his great ideas and that in spite of Clausewitz's having looked forward (in one of his letters) to the end of "a weary and paralyzed life," Clausewitz

> was not paralyzed in actuality. Perhaps the fact that the writing was always about war gave him the needed release. Just as Machiavelli's great work was inevitably a projection of himself acting as a prince, . . . so Clausewitz's was a projection of himself acting not as chief of staff but as a field marshal, and the occupation contemplated was not statecraft but war. In his case, however, the slaughter and destructiveness inherent in war were made good by the fact that a superb intelligence was guiding everything towards a politically wise end. Slaughter can at least be dedicated to statecraft, and the use of intelligence can achieve economies in the necessary acts of destruction.[142]

Brodie conjectured that Clausewitz's neurotic passions produced the first draft of *On War,* since "the first draft is 'from the heart,' or from wherever it is that the emotions reside." That draft, Brodie pointed out, deals mostly with winning wars, in contrast to the final version, which had been revised to highlight war as policy by other means.[143]

Satisfying as this explanation may be for that portion of Clausewitz's passions associated with the yearning to participate in war, it seems inadequate for Clausewitz's depression, remarked upon by Parkinson and Brodie as characterizing his life at other times. Brodie may have found it difficult to correlate Clausewitz's depressive state with *On War,* inasmuch as he seems to have accepted the view that depression impairs creativity. However, considerable recent evidence has challenged the thesis that Clausewitz was depressed, which Peter Paret termed "a cliche in the Clausewitz literature" that Parkinson, heavily dependent on previously published sources about Clausewitz, merely reiterated.[144]

In his major work on Clausewitz, published in 1976, Paret pointed out that Clausewitz had been promoted to junior rank much faster than almost all his contemporaries, that he was suitably decorated for a valued officer, and that as chief of staff of the army mobilized in 1830 he held one of the most important positions in the Prussian army.[145] "Almost to the last day of his life," Paret wrote to Brodie in 1973,

> Clausewitz was active, productive, and self-confident, and . . . we have no reason to believe that he was a depressed human being (by which I [mean] that he was suffering from a severe, chronic depression). He had a difficult life, but he was very happily married, he had very close and long-lasting friendships, he enjoyed being a soldier, he enjoyed research and writing, and his creative life was characterized by steady, constant productivity. The feverish note that is so pronounced in a Dostojevsky or a Kafka is entirely lacking.[146]

Whatever sadness Clausewitz felt from his experiences, Paret argued, he continued to have the desire to live and work. For example, in an 1821 letter in which, after referring to the sadness he had experienced when he left home to enter the army, Clausewitz continued:

> Now things are slowly and gently going downhill, and the tomb, which still may be far off, appears closer to me because nothing seems to separate me from it. But I simply cannot reconcile myself to that. I believe the curve of my life will ascend again, it will reach a higher point of culmination even if only so that you could say: un beau mourir toute la vie honoré. In short, I have not labored enough to rest, and I don't feel sufficiently tired to go to sleep.[147]

From these and other similar Clausewitz observations, Paret concluded that "evidently whatever discouragement [Clausewitz] sometimes felt was temporary rather than permanent and did not run deep."[148]

A Debate about Psychohistory

Drawing different conclusions about Clausewitz's emotional state of mind, Brodie and Paret disagreed even more fundamentally about Brodie's enthusiasm for interpreting Clausewitz's life and work psychoanalytically. I have noted Brodie's persistence in probing Clausewitz's personality even as he conceded there was little evidence to support this, but Paret, known to Brodie to have a sympathetic interest in Freudian psychoanalysis, ironically took the position that "I don't believe the psychological analysis of a historical figure is useful unless it is based on more than a few scraps of evidence."[149] Remaining skeptical on this point as he completed his major study of Clausewitz, Paret wrote to Brodie in 1973 of having "scraped together everything that can be found on Clausewitz's background, on his childhood, his relationship to his father and his brothers, etc., all of which seems to me essential for a psychological interpretation, but even so I continue to be very reluctant to proceed to such an interpretation."[150]

Paret's denial that Clausewitz suffered from severe or chronic depression and his affirmation instead of "the impression of a strong, essentially healthy psychological constitution"[151] were psychological interpretations, as was his assertion, in reference to Clausewitz's "own aggressive impulses," that they "appear to have been sublimated to a considerable extent in his writings on war."[152] In the latter instance, at least, Paret's interpretation seemed to agree with that of Brodie. "If I . . . do devote several sections throughout [my] book on interpretation of various facets of Clausewitz's personality," Paret wrote to Brodie, "it is because on certain aspects the material seems to me to be adequate if it is integrated with detailed analysis of certain episodes of his career which can be copiously documented. But even then I warn the reader that we [are] proceeding on thin ice."[153]

Paret's reluctance to pursue such analysis about Clausewitz came primarily from his belief that insufficient data existed about the childhood sources of Clausewitz's adult attitudes. For example, noting Clausewitz's preference to delay publication of his larger study on strategy until after his death and his unwillingness to have his ideas reviewed or criticized by educated people or experts, Paret observed that

> it would not be difficult to speculate on the psychological elements and their dynamic that underlie and create such attitudes. But we know far too little about Clausewitz's childhood to do so with any sense of assurance. Because the evidence for many episodes in his life and work is obviously incomplete, this study has tended throughout to under-interpret the data, rather than force conclusions from them. The available material is almost always suggestive but so very fragmentary that its [sic] seems preferable to point to the implications and let the reader draw his own conclusions. If firm patterns of thought and behavior nevertheless emerge clearly in Clausewitz's life, this is not surprising in a man who took ideas seriously enough to explore them as thoroughly as he could and who also attempted—instinctively and often consciously as well—to integrate his ideas completely with his feelings and actions.[154]

Brodie, very respectful of Paret's appreciation of psychoanalytic methods, evidently expected Paret to make more explicit use of it. "I must say in all candor," he responded to Paret, "that I really think you go too far—too far in rejecting the sensitivity you are endowed with and the knowledge of human nature that you have accumulated in your exceptional exposure to and training in psychoanalysis."[155] Subsequently, reviewing *Clausewitz and the State*, Brodie remarked that "Paret's interest . . . is centered more on the man's thought and on his overt behavior than on the man himself. The man is indeed fleshed out, some would say in considerable detail. But the dimensions are nevertheless somewhat compressed." He went on to note that the Parkinson biography of Clausewitz

> does make contact with a more deeply sensitive person, both artistically and emotionally, than the Clausewitz portrayed by Paret. It is most often simply a matter of what letters the respective authors think worth quoting, and also what events they choose to dwell upon. To give but one out of numerous possible examples: though Paret shows a superior comprehension of Clausewitz's role in the campaign of 1812, he omits any mention of the remarkable letter, which Parkinson quotes, in which Clausewitz describes to his wife his horror at witnessing the human disasters to the retreating French in their river crossing at the Berezina.[156]

Clausewitz's reaction to the French retreat at the Berezina, which Paret did indeed cite in his study, was perhaps sufficient to convey Clausewitz's deeply emotional sensitivity, but Brodie and Paret seemed to approach that sensitivity differently. Brodie, convinced that Clausewitz experienced a strong inner tension between his emotions and his highest caliber intellect, viewed him in psychological terms as primarily wrestling with his emotions, whereas Paret, believing Clausewitz to be emotionally healthy, portrayed the theorist as understanding and accepting the challenge of integrating his ideas with his feelings.

Paret's definition of psychic health, moreover, was the Freudian one of possessing the ability to live and the ability to work.[157] But the dispute for Paret was not over what in Clausewitz's letters and events should be emphasized, as Brodie suggested; it was whether the analyst should above all retain a sense of detachment and skepticism in analytical work or become emotionally involved in it. In this instance, Brodie seemed to reverse roles: Skeptical in virtually all of his other work, he was here committed to making particular deductions that intuitively impressed him. Paret, on the other hand, adopted in those instances in which he could not be conclusive the approach so characteristically and fruitfully employed by Brodie in the past.[158] As Brodie noted in reference to *Clausewitz and the State,* Paret's concluding assessment of Clausewitz's character and personality was "mostly to refute what he regards as unfounded assertions by others."[159]

In this instance, as elsewhere, Brodie adjusted his views. Evidently believing that depression is generally incompatible with creativity, he decided to solicit comments from two psychoanalysts of his acquaintance about his interpretation of Clausewitz, furnishing the psychoanalysts with a short biographical account of Clausewitz, "with its small package of quotations and other data, all derived from Parkinson."[160] One of the analysts affirmed his interpretation, but the other, distinguishing two separate sources of depression, arrived at a different conclusion that Brodie came to accept. According to this latter view, depression could be produced by internalized rage, which was inhibiting because of the guilt that it generated, but it could also be produced by the feeling of having failed to make oneself important. The latter type of depression, one of disappointment that did not inhibit creativity because it led to a determination to gain recognition, seemed to this analyst to be at work in Clausewitz's case.[161]

As to why Brodie should have focused so tenaciously on Clausewitz's depression, it may be conjectured that because he so much admired Clausewitz as a writer on war, he probably focused upon parallels he saw between himself and Clausewitz in this and other areas. Among the confirmable parallels between the two men were their distinctive roles as critics of conventional wisdom and recognized authority,[162] their focus upon what Paret termed "ultimate issues" in strategy,[163] their major but unsuccessful efforts to gain larger recognition for their ideas and contributions, and their interest in the impact of emotions upon war-making. Inasmuch as Brodie is known to have been aware of these parallels and is known, furthermore, to have been depressed in his last years,[164] he may well have presumed that Clausewitz's character was in this respect similar to his own. On the other hand, whether Brodie's readiness to revise his views and accept that Clausewitz's depression did not inhibit creativity can also be understood in the same fashion is less clear; it may be doubted that Brodie's depression interfered with his writing, but existing information does not permit one to ascertain whether Brodie was preoccupied with the inhibiting effect of his own depression.

Conclusions

In critiquing the systems analysts and Beaufre and in much of his writing on Clausewitz, Brodie strongly defended for the first time his characteristic judgmental, interpretive style of analysis underappreciated by those strategic analysts seeking primarily objectively verifiable insights. When analysts tended to aim at making assertions that were objectively verifiable, as at RAND, for example, differences in judgment were likely to be insufficiently identified and debated.[165] Moreover, strategic analysts would tend to neglect political objectives and the emotional state of civilian and military leaders as they shied away from conjecture. For example, urging reflection at RAND "on the differences in psychological and emotional tension between the game environment and the real world," Brodie wrote that "it is remarkable how little — practically nothing — has been written on that subject."[166]

Gaming had been used extensively at RAND to test hypotheses about crisis behavior, but little evidently had been done there to study perceptual aspects of international conflict.[167] Moreover, avoidance of conjecture in analysis would have discouraged attention to the subjective manner in which objective analysis was likely to be received by policymakers and policy staff officials, for whom, as Henry Kissinger noted, "the *status quo* has at least the advantage of familiarity."[168] Such individuals generally wished to receive endorsement rather than criticism and tended to be suspicious of analytical frameworks leading to conclusions critical of their proposals and actions.

We have seen that Brodie's focus upon the political and psychological aspects of strategy was dictated by his assumption that strategic nuclear war had become politically unacceptable. In establishing the importance of these aspects and the unacceptability of nuclear war, Brodie's writings were highly relevant to the foreign policymaking structure, which, as Gary Sick pointed out, "searches for points of leverage and control rather than contemplate[s] massive destruction."[169] On the other hand, the relation between force employment and political objectives was most critical in wartime and focusing upon it invited concentrating on situations most characterized by, or conducive to, violent activity. To such situations, Brodie gave less attention, because he had faith in the deterrent effect of nuclear weapons, which he believed extended to attack begun with conventional weapons.[170]

As in the past, Brodie's views often matured in the process of arguing with others. For example, when he criticized the defense economists on the excessive narrowness of systems analysis, Brodie emphasized the wider potential of strategic thinking; but when he urged that Beaufre dismount "from that intellectual high horse that Beaufre has thus far felt it necessary to ride,"[171] he seemed to be addressing instead the inherent limitations of strategic thinking. Whereas Brodie categorically condemned Beaufre for abstracting himself from policymakers' interests, his criticism of the defense economists stressed more balanced, comprehensive analysis. "We certainly need to stress the superior importance of the political side of strategy to the simply technical and technological side," he asserted in 1971. "Preserve and cherish the systems analysts, but avoid the genuflections."[172]

Understandable in terms of his earlier repeatedly reflected critical outlook, this last statement must also be understood at a deeper personal level, namely, Brodie's dissatisfaction—probably from a period prior to his first published criticism of the defense economists—at not being given more deference by RAND colleagues and clients, a feeling perhaps to be expected from a highly respected individual who sought greater political influence. "With RAND itself," Brodie wrote in 1971, "there was a quiet but strongly-felt status differential between those who knew how to handle graphs and mathematical symbols, especially if they also knew how to manage teams of similarly equipped young men, and those who merely knew how to probe political issues."[173] Contributing to this situation, he believed, was the tendency of air force officials to be impressed by team rather than individual research.[174]

Nonintellectual concerns also intruded upon Brodie's strong personal identification with Clausewitz, shown most clearly in his friendly debate with Peter Paret, which rendered him sympathetic to an intuitive belief that Clausewitz's life should be explained psychoanalytically and to an uncharacteristic support of conventional wisdom. They also were very likely reflected in his steadfast belief in the political unacceptability of nuclear war. In this last instance, he seems to have been unable to avoid conforming to his own characterization, reached in 1955 with "evidence from the first decade of the atomic age both here and abroad," that "emotions of fear which awareness of the new gadgets engender tend to cause *repression* of any review of their implications rather than the reverse."[175]

Condemning abstraction indulged in by others, Brodie was at times unable to escape it in his own insistence on a political focus in strategic affairs, as in his argument that the Hiroshima atomic attack was the most important *political* event associated with nuclear weapons and that the political importance of subsequent nuclear weapons development could easily be overstated. Whatever the declining political importance of nuclear technological developments after Hiroshima, policymakers would not ordinarily be expected to discount them—for the same reason that their predecessors had not discounted the importance of the development of fission atomic bombs. Abstraction is also reflected in Brodie's insistence upon Clausewitz's assertion that war must be considered as politics by other means, because, in spite of being inspired by the belief that major nuclear war could not usefully contribute to the political interests of states, it was unaccompanied by consideration of the feasibility of limiting war capabilities and objectives once fighting had started.[176] Reference has also been made, finally, to the abstract manner in which Brodie dealt with Clausewitz's concept of absolute war.

The tendency toward abstraction in these instances may have resulted in part because, although Brodie sought to unpin his analyses from the effect of any specific change in nuclear weapons technology, he did not wish to neglect the overall impact of nuclear weapons on contemporary political conditions. The latter could obviously not be determined without a study of technological developments subsequent to Hiroshima. A second source of abstraction seems to have been Brodie's practice of employing his political and psychological approaches in the broadest fashion, leaving many pertinent details necessarily unstudied. This may have been the reason, for example, that he neglected the value of narrower systems analysis to deal with specific social and psychological problems encountered in force planning.[177] Finally, as in Brodie's failure to study absolute war, emotional impulses were also conducive to abstraction.

In other cases, views Brodie developed later on came to coexist with older ones with which they were in apparent conflict. For example, one of his major arguments in *War and Politics* was the tendency of emotion-based arguments to contribute to wider and lengthier war, yet he cited the dampening effect upon such emotion of collective decision making during the Cuban missile crisis, without pointing up the implications of this last case for his main argument. In addition, having cataloged in the same study a large number of errors in the conduct of war that he traced to faulty intuition, he did not reconcile those errors with his own defense of intuition in analysis when he critiqued the defense economists. Elsewhere, on the other hand, Brodie sharply revised his working hypotheses to suit his reading of more recent events, as in his treatment of President Truman's decision to go to war in 1950. Having cited in 1959 the "something akin to plain anger" motivating this decision, he wrote in 1964 (following the Cuban missile crisis) that "it is correct to say that some degree of anger played a part in determining the policy actually pursued, but it would be not only a libel against President Truman but also a great historical error to say that he acted only or even predominantly out of anger."[178] Such tensions and shifts suggest that Brodie's usually forceful argumentation was of limited value in strengthening his own position.

10 · Conclusions

In this volume, I have identified important continuities in the focus and character of Brodie's strategic thinking since 1945. With regard to focus, I noted his persisting interest in (1) the likelihood of strategic nuclear war; (2) the unique consequences of nuclear weapons for superpower interests; (3) the potentially tremendous destructiveness of nuclear weapons; (4) the limitation of superpower hostilities if they should occur; and (5) the shared interests of opposing superpowers to avoid strategic nuclear war. The character of Brodie's thinking has also been reflected repeatedly in his methodical logic, intellectual breadth, and independence. In these respects, Brodie's legacy to the now highly popular field of strategic studies is considerable.

In this book, I also challenged conventional wisdom about Bernard Brodie as a strategic thinker. For example, he is often counted among the strongest advocates of deterring nuclear attack, an important element of what has been termed the "stable balancer" school of thought.[1] He accepted limits to the utility of nuclear weapons and to the expansion of nuclear force levels, two corollaries of this outlook. But especially from the 1960s on, Brodie did not subscribe to other "stable balancer" views — namely, that first use of nuclear weapons would eventually spiral into general war, that a Soviet attack upon Western Europe was best deterred by conventional forces, or that marginal superiority in nuclear capabilities under conditions of mutual assured destruction had little political significance. Rather, he would have subscribed in this same period to the contrasting "war fighting" school of thought, arguing that deterrence would help control escalation following the outbreak of war and that marginal nuclear superiority had political importance.

Second, Brodie's views suggest that the field of strategic studies may be less mature than commonly realized. This is partly because of omissions in subject matter occasioned by security sensitivity and personal discretion. For example, none of Brodie's published works elaborated at length on the coercive use of nuclear force or on nuclear weapons targeting, concerns generally neglected until recently in the nonclassified literature yet known to be important to Brodie and discussed in some of his private writings.[2] In addition, Brodie, like most other contemporary strategic analysts, was at best incisive and suggestive but not comprehensive or detailed in his work. Taking revolutionary technological developments as his starting point, he did not ordinarily anticipate how comparable developments in the future might undermine his views or how more evolutionary changes in weapons technology would also have important military and political consequences. Moreover, because of Brodie's disinclination for detailed analysis and because of the vigor of his argumentation, his writing—like other writing in this field—was subject to imprecision and discrepancies. Another point with wider implications is that timeliness and originality (Brodie is justly celebrated for both) are often in tension in this field. Brodie was perhaps most famous for criticizing conventional wisdom, but at times he also borrowed uncritically from consensus viewpoints. The latter may be defended on the ground that it permitted him to provide timely analysis, but it did so at a price that has been underappreciated.

Third, in this study of Brodie's ideas, I have pinpointed different types of strategic analysis and probed the strengths and weaknesses of each. In particular, Brodie worked alternately as a critic of military and civilian thought; an advocate of the unique strategic potential of nuclear weapons through his use of the "hypothetical past"; a student of politics and an advocate of the need to make strategic employment of nuclear weapons proportionate to political objectives; and a conceptualizer and distinguisher of different projected situations suitable for the employment of a nuclear force. Elaborating on these preoccupations will be helpful in evaluating Brodie's work.

Critiques for Military Audiences

Brodie contributed most to the development of nuclear strategy in a lengthy series of critiques of military thinking, in which, extremely skeptical of employing weapons of mass destruction efficaciously, he urged reexamination of the potential scope of strategic nuclear war, the resources to control it, and, most broadly, the political and military rationale of war plans. He criticized, first of all, dogmatic and often principled assertions such as General LeMay's belief in concentrated nuclear attack; General Cabell's rigorous commitment to striking at economic targets in the Soviet Union; the belief of LeMay, Cabell, and their associates that nuclear war should be won militarily at any cost; and the air force view that "all modern war is total war."

Brodie also criticized arguments that incompletely or wishfully weighed narrower elements of a particular scenario: (1) the early prevailing assumption of the air force that damage from Soviet attacks against the United States could be neglected in plans for war with fusion weapons; (2) the assumption of military planners that politicians would overcome their fears and approve major retaliatory nuclear strikes against economic targets in and near enemy cities; (3) the assumption of military planners that the unintended effects of nuclear strikes over European, American, and Soviet territory could be neglected; (4) the assumption of NATO planners in the 1950s that a war in Europe could remain limited even after large numbers of European targets had been struck by nuclear weapons; (5) the assumption of advocates of a nuclear buildup in Europe in the 1950s that plans specified for those forces would not trigger attacks against Soviet and American homelands; and (6) the optimism military planners had about the recuperability potential of countries subjected to major nuclear attacks.

Brodie's characteristic scorn and impatience with inadequate planning assumptions dated from his disillusionment while working for General Vandenberg with the quality of military staff work. "I know that I can learn much from you," wrote Hans Speier, then head of the RAND Social Science Division, to Brodie in November 1954.

> You disappoint me whenever I seem to learn less than expected merely because you are engrossed in scolding some uninteresting people with well-known names. It is only natural, I suppose, that I should expect your influence on your military audience as well to be even greater than it is if you chided them less often. The response to stern and frequent chiding by an outsider will depend not only upon their intelligence but also upon their pride.[3]

Much later, in 1973, Brodie forcefully spelled out his lack of respect for what he termed the "military mind," writing that "the talents [the military] are chiefly seeking are not intellectual. It follows that officers sometimes get a reputation for being 'brilliant' who in a more intellectually demanding milieu would not have that reputation."[4] In the same vein, he stressed that military professionals stood for purposes fundamentally different from those about which he most cared. "We see," he stated, "that the whole training of the military is toward a set of values that finds in battle and in victory a vindication. The skills developed in the soldier are those of the fighter, and not of the reflector on ultimate purposes. . . . All this is fitted into a simplistic vision of the world and of what makes it function."[5]

Brodie strongly sought influence inside the military establishment, observing to Speier in 1954 that "my own best and most careful work has always been done for military audiences."[6] But it appears that he did not succeed in reconciling his aspirations for power inside the military establishment with the critical detachment that could be expected to be strongest for an outsider. For example, Brodie insisted in 1973 that his negative portrayal of the "military mind" and of the distinctive orientation of the military professional could only be made by someone outside the military establishment.[7] Moreover, as an outsider Brodie did not seem to have worried that his aspirations for power may have been blunted by his strong criticism; he recollected in 1973 — in the same study in which he vented his most trenchant published criticism of military attitudes — that "my own reception by the armed services has on the whole been extremely generous over a long span of years despite my often expressing criticism of their views, though their approval was especially warm when my views coincided with theirs."[8]

Brodie surely had reason to be pleased at the positive reception his views gained with such high-ranking air force general officers as Norstad and Samford and at the numerous yearly invitations he received to lecture at American war colleges. Yet his disdain for his military audiences — which may well have been produced by the lack of approbation given to his ideas by influential general officers such as LeMay and Cabell — would not have encouraged him to think extensively about improving the receptivity to his ideas. He seemed to demand more in approval from military audiences than his broad depreciation of their intellectual potential suggested was likely to be summoned up.

For his part, Brodie, in spite of his strident tone, had no difficulty gaining the analytical balance he sought, for his analytical conclusions shifted as he came into contact with a wider circle of authoritative general officers whose views he abhorred.[9] Indeed, the best index of Brodie's determined pursuit of analytical balance was his willingness to change his views and emphases as he enlarged his contacts within the military profession, and in doing so he almost invariably reached conclusions that were *at odds with* those of his new contacts. This was the case, for example, following his encounters with LeMay, Cabell, and officers at NATO headquarters during the mid-1950s. In these cases, the stridency of Brodie's critiques seemed to stem from his perception of the inflexible manner in which his interlocutors reasoned. On the other hand, Brodie's own attitude toward the military profession may have interfered with his search for analytic balance by preventing him from being objective about the qualifications of military professionals as a whole and by depriving him — through his alienating of officers such as Cabell — of sources of information that might have deepened his understanding of the strategic issues he investigated.

Brodie's concern for analytical balance would in any event have been much less appreciated and useful inside the military establishment, where loyalty and shared viewpoints are routinely prevalent, than it was outside. Those characteristics would, after all, contribute most to the conventional wisdom that Brodie was committed to combat. In addition, Brodie's devotion to analytic balance required some abstraction from military needs irrespective of the strident tone of his criticism. Hedley Bull wrote that "a great deal of argument about military strategy . . . postulates the 'rational action' of a kind of 'strategic man,' a man who on further acquaintance reveals himself to be a university professor of unusual intellectual subtlety."[10] But from the point of view of many military professionals, an outsider such as Brodie might well not appear analytically balanced and would therefore be dismissed out of hand whatever the logical weight of his ideas. This at any rate was the response of the Air Targets Division, over which Cabell had jurisdiction, to a key memorandum Brodie wrote for Vandenberg.

Critiques for Civilian Audiences

Supplementing Brodie's critical writings for military planners was criticism directed at persons outside the military establishment. The instances of the latter that I referred to in this book are (1) Brodie's challenge in 1949 to the prevailing RAND view that enemy morale was not a suitable atomic bombing target system; (2) his challenge of the assumption held by the advocates of the threat of massive nuclear retaliation that diplomats would hold fast when defending vital interests even though they had only a large-scale military option with which to defend those interests; (3) his challenge in 1957 of P. M. S. Blackett's pessimistic estimates of the number and weight of atomic weapons required to inflict decisive damage; (4) his questioning in the late 1950s of the widespread view that Soviet behavior would be invariably rational and predictable and his linkage of nonrational Soviet behavior to international instability; (5) his challenge in 1962 of Malcolm Hoag's proposal to lessen NATO dependence upon the threat of counterforce attacks against the Soviet Union to defend Berlin and West Germany more generally from Soviet encroachments; (6) his related questioning at about the same time of the conventional forces buildup in Europe to cope with the "Hamburg grab" scenario; (7) his critique of the systems analysis methodology and his insistence upon the central importance of political and psychological concerns in military decision making; (8) his dispute with Thomas Schelling in the 1960s about the likelihood of a general Soviet-American war when superpower retaliatory forces consisted primarily of protected long-range ballistic missiles, and about whether some danger of nuclear war was indispensable for threatening escalation in limited war; (9) his critique of General Beaufre's assertion that strategic analysis should aim at generalizations from which detailed analysis applicable to any set of circumstances could be deduced; and (10) his critique of Peter Paret's failure to rely more heavily on psychoanalytical insights in his work on Clausewitz. These writings, like Brodie's criticism of military ideas, illustrated his tendency to develop his own views while thoroughly criticizing the views of others, convincing himself as he argued with them. Second, both types of criticism were associated with full intellectual detachment and broad-gauged analysis. Third, Brodie made explicit in both instances the political and psychological components of military behavior, the importance of which he believed had been enhanced by the advent of atomic weapons.

However, at least four differences may be cited between the two types of critique, the first being one of substantive focus. Brodie did not have to fight rigidities of thinking as intensively or plead as strongly for restraint in nuclear force employment among, for example, RAND colleagues as he did when taking aim at the military establishment since the former would already have considerable respect for the logic sustaining such analysis. In the actual case, he directed his criticism at the more problematic aspects of logical analysis, including overrefinement and excessive advocacy of logical policy positions. Among critiques of overrefinement are Brodie's arguments against overrationalizing Soviet behavior, overgeneralizing modes of strategic behavior, magnifying manipulation of risks in superpower crisis, and overstressing the consequences of shifting military technology for superpower relations. He focused upon immoderation in his criticism of the omission of enemy morale as a target for nuclear weapons and of the proposed conventional forces buildup in Europe.

Second, whereas Brodie in his critiques of the views of the military especially stressed overweddedness to older outlooks, his critiques addressed to civilians dwelled more frequently on the opposite error of too hasty or extreme support of newer policies and capabilities, as in his disapproval of massive retaliation and the proposed conventional forces buildup in Europe.[11] These two critiques in particular, separated by nearly ten years, had more in common than merely going against the prevailing policy emphasis of the time, for Brodie had always supported the massive retaliation strategy *with respect to Europe.* He used massive retaliation as a major part of his argument against the very large conventional forces buildup contemplated in the 1960s while criticizing massive retaliation with respect to the protection of peripheral American commitments such as defense of South Korea. At the same time, he had by the 1950s supported strengthening NATO ground combat forces *to some extent,* later making an issue of that strengthening only when it appeared to be designed as a substitute for threatening nuclear retaliation.

A third difference between the two types of critique was that whereas Brodie chastised military professionals for their lack of imaginative planning — a shortcoming he associated with intellectual weakness — he came in the 1960s to criticize some RAND civilian analysts for excessive imagination. "I am all in favor of people being imaginative," he wrote in 1964 to J. M. Goldsen, the new head of the RAND social science staff, "and in dreaming up the widest range of contingencies that could conceivably occur. Nevertheless, I think that we in [the RAND] Social Science [Staff] have a responsibility for introducing some conception of probability into the speculation. I think we are usually too inhibited on that score, possibly because no one likes to be tagged 'unimaginative.'"[12] Part of this difference seems explainable by Brodie's changing orientation toward the Soviet-American strategic balance. His strongest chastisements of the military establishment in the early 1950s were based on his belief that military planners were far too sanguine of the costs and consequences of a Soviet-American war. By the 1960s, and especially after the Cuban missile crisis, he became much more complacent about superpower relations and worried more about civilians who did not seem to recognize the stability of those relations than about war plans.

Fourth, Brodie completely altered his posture toward other civilian analysts in the 1960s, directing his strongest criticism during those years to other RAND staff members, including but not limited to advocates of the conventional forces buildup in Europe. The result of this shift was that his criticism of civilian analysts came to resemble the categorical character of his earlier criticism of the military establishment. The shift evidently had personal as well as intellectual sources, as Brodie, in sharp contrast to his orientation during the previous decade, had set himself apart from other well-known members of the RAND staff. I have already mentioned Brodie's view that status as an outsider was essential to his criticism of the military establishment. Such a status seems to have characterized Brodie's own role in the 1960s at RAND, and his experience shows that the role of an outsider — so apparently useful for trenchant criticism — is significantly self-defined. Whatever Brodie's qualifications as a critic and whatever his reasons for perceiving himself as an outsider (a plausible reason he gave was mentioned in the previous chapter), his changed view of himself was likely to quicken his propensity to criticize others at RAND and to become more intellectually isolated there.

During the 1950s, when Brodie accepted the risks of being unpopular with military audiences, he played down and even suppressed differences with other members of the RAND staff, such as over his 1952 contention that thermonuclear weapons justified withholding strategic nuclear bombing except as a last resort — an idea, Brodie recalled later, that was regarded at RAND as "crackpot"[13] — and over his criticism of the population "bonus" concept of nuclear weapons strikes, accepted by most at RAND outside the Social Science and Economics divisions.[14] His critical outlook toward the military establishment at that time — an outlook Brodie hoped to institutionalize at RAND with the assistance of his colleagues — made it especially important for him to develop consensus and avoid excessive controversy within the corporation. Indeed, in at least three documented projects between 1951 and 1956 — on the spacing of air strikes in a strategic air war, on force employment guidance in such a war, and on tactical air power — Brodie and other members of the RAND staff collaborated on critiques of inadequate military planning.[15] But by the 1960s, the inadequacies that most preoccupied Brodie were less with the uniformed military than with civilians, and so it was controversy rather than consensus at RAND that he came to seek.

Revolutionary Technology: Strategic Foundations

Much of what Brodie had to say about the obsolescence of strategic ideas in the contemporary period was linked to the obsolescence of older weaponry. Thus his earliest treatment of atomic bombs argued that preventing war had become more important than winning it, because of the potential destructiveness of a two-sided nuclear war. His earliest writings on fusion weapons argued that such weapons rendered general war between the superpowers obsolete by undermining the meaning of victory and also compelled attention to the relation between military instruments and political objectives. Finally, his earliest evaluation of protected ICBMs and SLBMs pointed out that they reduced the superpowers' incentive to strike first, thereby decreasing pressures toward escalation in limited war.

Unifying these ideas was Brodie's belief that the new bombing destructiveness and newer means of delivering nuclear explosives should be devoted mostly to reducing the likelihood of war. Inasmuch as weapons of the past had not been introduced primarily for this purpose and as states and people had suffered tremendously when putting newer weaponry to the test of seeking victory in war, a strong case could be made that nuclear weapons revolutionized strategic doctrine. At the very least, they no longer legitimated, as newer weapons had done in the past, strategies employed earlier.

And yet, despite his call for reorienting the substance of strategy and the method of arriving at it, Brodie in practice did not reject all his prior assumptions but rather adapted uncritically older concepts and assumptions to new conditions. In connection with the advent of atomic bombs, he presumed that nuclear-equipped belligerents would willingly escalate to all-out war irrespective of their political goals, much as states had done in the two world wars, and that cities would be massively hit with atomic bombs as they had been hit earlier with conventional ones. Later, rejecting strategic bombing with fusion weapons, he argued for employing such weapons coercively against the Soviet Union, much as he had for using fission weapons coercively. Finally, he continued in the early 1960s as he had earlier to rely upon the threat of massive retaliation with nuclear weapons to deter massive nonnuclear attack by Soviet forces in Europe.

These carryover views make it apparent that Brodie had in mind a doctrinal revolution only in connection with his central concerns, the limited scope of which is explained partly by the rapidity by which he completed his pioneering studies of the technological shifts that preoccupied him. Thus he completed the initial draft of his study of fission weapons less than three months after the attacks against Hiroshima and Nagasaki, his study of the political and military implications of fusion bombs about three months after being informed of the impending fusion weapons test, and his earliest study of escalation within five months. These studies, yielding categorical conclusions within a relatively short period, depended upon firm initial reactions, enormous logical skills, and wide-ranging thinking. More systematic analysis over a longer time might well have revealed a less categorical picture about the feasibility of attack with fission and fusion bombs and about the stability of mutual deterrence with relatively invulnerable missiles. Brodie might have highlighted situations in which defenses against nuclear attack — particularly one directed against an enemy retaliatory force — could lessen or undermine the revolutionary potential of nuclear weaponry.[16] And beginning in the 1960s, he might have given attention to the opposite possibility — that the growing potential of a strategic nuclear attack could undermine the security provided by long-range ballistic missile delivery systems.

To define the critical questions of others and to make clear the dangers of being behindhand in strategic thinking, Brodie needed to make his views known quickly and widely. But as I noted, he was not a leader in harnessing nuclear weapons technology. As a conceptualizer, he was taxed to the utmost in comprehending revolutionary technological shifts, and inevitably he simplified their complexities.[17] For example, behind his concentration upon nuclear attacks against urban centers was not only a fear of the effects of a two-sided war but also evident difficulty in appreciating a nuclear bombing campaign directed against a variety of targets. Concentrating on the bombing of cities alone highlighted most of all the revolutionary strategic consequences of fission and fusion weapons, the value of keeping cities hostage to nuclear retaliation, and the difficulty or impossibility of defending against strategic bombing.

As a result, Brodie was invariably most categorical about the use of bombs against cities, even as he continually played down the likelihood of that eventuality. "The trend in weapons," Brodie wrote in 1959, "with their ever-larger yields and greater potentialities for fallout, has certainly increased the life-destroying capability of an aggressor who wishes to use it."[18] Yet even without protected retaliatory forces, Brodie saw nuclear weapons contributing at best a stability based upon mutual fear — evidently from widespread concern with protecting cities hostage to attack. "I do not at all think [the risks of Soviet attack] are substantial," he wrote in the same year, "but I think they are not altogether nil either. Certain respected and very well-informed specialists in the field rate them higher than I do. Although I do not accept their estimate, I have to recognize that they have a view which *could* be right."[19] Brodie apparently assumed that the likelihood of war was reduced by the desire and ability of Soviet and American leaders to keep political control in a crisis and by their widespread expectation that any Soviet-American war would be extremely difficult to keep limited.

The development of protected missile delivery forces eased both the fear and the likelihood of general war, by discouraging the prospects of attack aimed at counterforce targets and consequently also the prospects for a dramatic escalation of nuclear war. "Oddly," Brodie wrote in *Escalation and the Nuclear Option,* "the same bomb that caused the fears of the fifties . . . has caused also the more relaxed attitude of the sixties; and it has not only been a matter of getting used to it, though that helped."[20] This change supported Brodie's complacence about Soviet-American affairs and his criticism of those who he believed did not give sufficient attention to the stability of the balance of terror.

The view that the balance of terror is stable was sharply criticized in the 1980s by those anticipating future technological shifts toward defenses able to safeguard democracies from nuclear threats.[21] But Brodie's major contribution to nuclear strategy and his more mature complacence about the risks of nuclear war stemmed from his confidence about the narrower but equally important area of what the superpowers ought *not* to do with nuclear weapons. Further shifts in nuclear technology or in nuclear strategy did not, in his view, assure reducing the chances of major nuclear war beyond what they were in the 1960s, then quite acceptable by his standards. On the other hand, considering strategy as something negative was at odds with the spirit of Brodie's well-known definition of strategy in *War and Politics* as "a 'how to do it' study, a guide to accomplishing something and doing it efficiently."[22]

Revolutionary Technology: Targeting Efficiency

The most striking examples of Brodie's tendency to depend on older conceptions and scenarios was his use of the hypothetical past to rationalize the value of atomic weapons, thereby defending the decision to develop and deploy them. In these cases, without identifying any new targeting concept, Brodie relied upon newer atomic weapons, and specifically the much larger scale of destruction permitted them, to redeem conceptions already known to him. Four such instances have been cited in this study: his argument that large-scale strategic bombing employing fission bombs would be quickly decisive against the kinds of targets struck during the Second World War; his contention that smaller-scale bombing with fission weapons would rehabilitate the targeting of enemy morale from its failure in the war against Germany, because of the unique effect of A-bomb attacks directed against cities; his endorsement of C. J. Hitch's view that the A-bomb reduced force requirements in strategic bombing, making an in-being force sufficient for a bombing campaign; and his defense of employing fusion bombs in battlefield warfare against targets available earlier in the Korean War.

Comparing contemporary weaponry with prior opportunities was an important check against historical determinism, and I have noted Brodie's continual alertness to changes in the "boundary conditions" when learning from historical experience.[23] At the same time, the hypothetical past offered the opportunity to sidestep detailed study of *real* history and generate contemporary insights in spite of lingering uncertainties about the past. To narrow those uncertainties through detailed study would delay the work of rationalizing a nuclear force arsenal and, since policymakers were not likely to employ nuclear weapons without being convinced those weapons could make a political and military contribution, would thereby undermine the utility of that arsenal.

Use of the hypothetical past also permitted Brodie to give full play to his view that nuclear weapons were more advantageous for war-making than their predecessors. Each of the hypothetical past assessments showed how the added feasibility of destroying specified targets contributed to war-making objectives and, by doing so, opened a defense of nuclear use in other, more exacting scenarios. The weight of this justification may have depressed Brodie's known fear of general war, explaining why despite that fear he never argued that strategy or stability were best served by abolishing nuclear weapons.

Brodie's earliest studies of nuclear weaponry, including his essays in *The Absolute Weapon,* gave more attention to how destructive nuclear bombs upset prior strategy than to adapting those weapons for meaningful purposes. He did not develop a nuclear strategy until he tackled the assumption of scarcity in the nuclear bomb stockpile, a matter that became most important for him when as a consultant to Vandenberg he evaluated the employment of nuclear bombs against predetermined targets. His strong dissatisfaction with the air force's emphasis upon target destruction and his later inability to find any worthwhile objective for bombing with fusion weapons led to heavy concern about tension between strategic results in a nuclear war and the feasibility of nuclear bomb strikes.

By 1951 this tension was one of Brodie's chief preoccupations, which meant that he was no longer primarily interested in justifying a nuclear bomb arsenal. "We have to prove first of all to ourselves and to others," he wrote in a 1951 RAND essay, "that such spacing of attacks as will result from deliberate prolonging of the campaign need not unduly hazard or excessively reduce our overall delivery capabilities."[24] Later in the same essay, however, he suggested that operational concerns might in some cases have to be sacrificed. "If we have to pay a somewhat higher price for one kind of campaign rather than another," he declared, "we should not only seek to determine the price disparity between the two but we should also leave the planner free to gauge the payoff in each case against the cost. The ultimate payoff is the thing that counts, the forces involved being a means to that end (and an expendable one at that)."[25]

As we have seen, by 1952 Brodie's analyses focused more on what not to hit with nuclear bombs, notably American and Soviet homelands, than on potentially attractive targets. In such thinking, the logic of the hypothetical past moved counter to strategic imperatives, all the more so since Brodie found force requirements for successful strategic bombing with fusion weapons further reduced "by a large factor" from what they had been with fission bombs.[26] Far from rejecting scenarios of the hypothetical past under these new conditions, however, Brodie still seemed heavily committed to them, as when he repeatedly stated that the decisive stages of nuclear war should be quite short.

For example, he wrote in *Strategy in the Missile Age* that, contrary to the bombing of Germany in the Second World War, enemy economic collapse "would occur within days or hours of the onset of [nuclear] attack"[27] and that "the duration of the decisive phases of [nuclear] war can hardly be more than a few days."[28] With such statements, Brodie presumably had in mind that in connection with fission bombing the ability of nations to absorb punishment "seems to vanish in the face of atomic attack."[29] But whether strategic bombing would come all at once, as this implied, was disputable; Brodie on several occasions strongly criticized the air force's penchant for speed in implementing a strategic bombing campaign.[30] Suggesting nevertheless that decisive bombing would be very condensed in time, he seems to have reverted to the hypothetical past and its justification of nuclear weaponry as his point of reference without defending the legitimacy of such conduct.

Restraining the Use of Force

Arguing that nuclear weapons could more efficiently destroy enemy assets than their predecessors, Brodie also warned that capitalizing illogically and passionately upon force efficiency could be suicidal. Ironically, as military efficiency increased tremendously through an in-being force capable of exerting decisive effect at the outset of war, a development Brodie strongly supported, logical planning and decision making became proportionately more important. In at least four instances, he argued in favor of restraining the efficient use of nuclear force: employing a small fission bomb supply to hasten war termination on favorable terms; employing a large nuclear arsenal to discourage major attack; using a nuclear arsenal to enforce restraints in limited war; and employing nuclear weapons to serve political objectives commensurate with the cost of war-making.

Whereas Brodie's preoccupation with nuclear force efficiency began full blown in 1945, his interest in the political and psychological dimensions of nuclear weapons, especially in alternatives to unlimited violence early in nuclear war, progressed only gradually. His first shift in this direction occurred subsequent to his initial awareness late in 1948 that the nuclear bomb stockpile would remain relatively small for an extended period. He then sought to gain disproportionate coercive value from a relatively scarce nuclear bomb supply, an interest deepened by his examination of the emergency war plan of 1951 and his suggestion that military planners were insensitive to American political interests toward the Soviet Union. Finally, his new awareness of fusion weapons late in 1951 undermined his earlier belief that contemporary war-making would probably overshadow the political concerns that inspired it. The destructive potential of fusion weapons led Brodie to acquiesce in and even insist upon preparing to wage war in a militarily *inefficient* manner, giving coercive warfare primacy over the physical use of force.

Along with his discussion of the hypothetical past, Brodie's treatment of force restraint highlighted the unique potential of nuclear weapons. Unlike his use of the hypothetical past, however, Brodie's interest in force restraint was not at all grounded in military history. This is evident, first of all, in the ad hoc shifts in his views. Two stages in this transformation, associated with the smaller-than-expected size of the fission bomb arsenal and the advent of fusion weapons, were brought about by largely unpredictable developments; the third stage, Brodie's experience as a consultant to Vandenberg, was responsible for his greatest shock as a strategist. In addition, Brodie's discussion of force restraint typically used history as a fund of examples of how not to fight—for instance, the use of excessive force (the First World War), the exercise of faulty political reasoning (the decision to target German morale in the Second World War), or the incorrect application of force to political objectives (the Second World War and the Korean War). Some of his most powerful and best-known criticism was directed at what he perceived to be the grievous errors of earlier wars; unlike the hypothetical past, such errors made enlargement of "boundary conditions" meaningless.

On the other hand, just as Brodie slighted historical detail and nuance in favor of the broad strategic picture in his treatment of the hypothetical past, so also he slighted details and highlighted broader considerations of the practice of force restraint. For example, he attached considerable importance to constancy in forward commitments in crisis, as illustrated by his support of the massive retaliation doctrine in the late 1950s to deter major Soviet aggression in Europe. "It is customary to blame most policy failures on weaknesses in intelligence," he wrote in 1959, "but actually the deficiencies are generally to be found in the alertness and resolution of the leaders."[31] Little appreciated thus far has been Brodie's willingness to take large risks in crises, a view evidently based on his belief that risk could be manipulated to prevent war, partly through American exploitation of superiority in the balance of strategic forces.[32] He may also have had in mind the widely conceded legitimacy of protecting existing lines of commitment.[33]

More detailed analysis would not expect to find the same level of political resolution in all cases of crisis but would distinguish instances when strategic forces were less protected against attack (the 1930s and 1950s) from those cases in which strategic forces were well protected against attack (the 1960s). Diplomacy in the former case would tend to be more cautious, and in the latter case more bold. Even if there were a larger premium on political resolve in highly risky situations, detailed analysis of crisis experience might find such resolution to be in shortest supply paradoxically when it was most needed.[34]

I have already stressed Brodie's own regard for the contribution that protected second-strike forces made to international stability. This same development also affected what he had to say about the prospects for military restraint once Soviet-American hostilities began. For example, when Brodie denied in the early 1960s that war-making restraints would be weakened by the losing side's rejection of force limitations,[35] he was assuming that strategic stability would lower escalation and ensure coordination in diplomatic and military behaviors. By contrast, during the 1950s, he worried about "the quick spiralling upward of the level of violence" and about whether "use of nuclear weapons will not make it critically more likely that a limited war will erupt into total war."[36]

Concerned about whether force limitations would prevail at the start of war, he warned that any agreement to maintain cities as sanctuaries in limited war would have to be enforced, which meant in effect "presenting an ultimatum, especially where there is a high probability that it will be accepted as a challenge."[37] Whether the ultimatum would be challenged, and whether expansion of the fighting would occur, partly depended on whether diplomacy would be inflexible. Brodie's alertness to the dangers of limited war in the 1950s was presumably informed by the assumption of inflexible diplomacy, which makes it understandable why he should associate war limitations with diplomatic accommodation. "It is of course true and important," he wrote in 1959, "that we cannot have limited war without settling for limited objectives, which in practice is likely to mean a negotiated peace based on compromise. Clausewitz's classic definition, that the object of war is to impose one's will on the enemy, must be modified, at least for any opponent who has a substantial nuclear capability behind him."[38]

Only a negotiated peace would, after all, ensure that the nuclear power that had lost military engagements in limited hostilities would decide not to escalate.[39] At the very least, Brodie would probably have wished to preserve the option of flexibility to protect against the failure of coercion to have its intended effect. But because he did not draw out detailed diplomatic implications of extending war limitations, he left unclear the proper balance between diplomatic flexibility and diplomatic resolve. The choice of political tactics depended on this balance, for if flexibility was sought, diplomacy ideally would need time to succeed without being constrained by military pressure, while diplomatic resolution would presumably be assisted by appropriate military maneuvers.

Apart from the absence of detail, Brodie's definition of the problem of force restraint was circumscribed by his assumptions. For example, his interest in using atomic bomb attacks against cities to induce Soviet surrender in a Soviet-American war was based on the nondiplomatic notion that the Soviet government, like its Nazi counterpart in the Second World War, would undertake last-ditch resistance and never agree to peace terms. This assumption, generating a requirement for larger strategic bombing and for inducing popular revolt against an insufferable Soviet regime — unlike limited war requirements or fighting for political objectives — Brodie does not seem to have investigated carefully. Later, by contrast, when he had lost interest in strategic bombing because of its potential destructiveness, he incorporated massive retaliation, limited war, and Clausewitz's principle of fighting for political objectives into his writing. At this point, his assumption that fusion bombs would be the mainstay of a strategic bombing plan led him to dismiss entirely the coercive value of strategic attacks.

Sensitivity Studies

Distinctive in Brodie's work for their detail were two early analyses that tested assumptions against hypothesized developments: his 1949 study of how hypothesized changes from nuclear scarcity to nuclear plenty and from American bomb monopoly to Soviet-American duopoly affected American security; and his 1952 study of the effect upon American security of the change from American monopoly to Soviet-American duopoly in fusion weapons. In these writings, Brodie illuminated the trade-offs in strategic choices more sharply than he did elsewhere, as when he observed in 1949 that loss of a fission bomb monopoly meant that withholding bombs to deter attack "would of course nullify the offensive significance of our [bomb] superiority" unless the bombs were withheld only conditionally.[40] This observation challenged at the margin his prevailing belief in the decisiveness of strategic bombing with fission weapons. Also challenging that view was Brodie's observation, made at the same time, that amassing sufficient numbers of American bombs to cover targets in the Soviet Union might still not assure nuclear plenty, because of insufficient numbers of planes to deliver the bombs. He gave due respect in this connection to the possibility that requirements of air superiority, prepared ahead of the bombing campaign in order to protect atomic carriers, made decisive atomic bombing feasible only with a gigantic logistic effort comparable to that of the bombing campaign in the Second World War.[41] The realism of this possibility is indicated by a statement by General Vandenberg in 1953, cited earlier, to the effect that thirty bombers would have to be sent along to protect the atomic mission against the Soviet Union;[42] the desire to head off that possibility spurred Brodie's advocacy in 1947 of an in-being force to ensure decisive nuclear bombing at the start of hostilities.[43]

These observations also brought home, finally, the great value of a coercive bombing campaign—as Brodie put it, "a bolder use of even a small number of atomic bombs"[44]—and of relaxing the planning requirement, understandable for a period of nuclear scarcity, that each bomb needed to be delivered to its intended target. Yet even as demands for targeting reliability were eased, shifting bomb employment to coercive warfare could transform an apparently scarce bombing force to one plentiful enough to be decisive, taxing further Brodie's initial assumption that nuclear bombs were likely to render a bombing campaign decisive and creating a paradox: a larger bomb supply might be inadequate and a smaller supply adequate enough to be decisive. Study of targets, which Brodie carried out most incisively in his critique of the Soviet electric power target system in the 1951 American emergency war plan, suggested that it was not nuclear bombs per se that made bombing decisive but rather their logical employment. This conclusion departed from his earlier reasoning in *The Absolute Weapon*, which dwelt upon the opportunities served by the use of atomic bombs but not upon the constraints of such use.

The role of diplomacy, missing in much of Brodie's early writings on fission weapons, became prominent in his sensitivity studies of atomic duopoly. Diplomacy—supported mainly by mutual fear of general war—became central, he argued, when American military capabilities could not force an end to a Soviet-American war; in this case, diplomacy had somehow to be reconciled with war plans.[45] (This situation was the opposite of the wholly one-sided one that Brodie had in mind when he endorsed strategic bombing to undermine the Soviet regime.) Later, in his study of fusion bombs, Brodie stressed that the reciprocal fear of surprise attack added considerably to the burdens upon diplomats and that protecting Soviet and American homelands from attack necessitated Soviet-American agreement to restrict wartime use of fusion bombs even before the Soviets perfected such weapons.[46]

The more Brodie acknowledged operational constraints, the more useful his work became to military planners, who always labored under specified constraints. To be sure, those constraints were of secondary importance to Brodie compared with his interest in the strategic effects of bomb attacks. However, for planners more deeply concerned about scarce resources, the constraints were of primary importance in the selection of targets. But Brodie in his sensitivity studies was serving as his own devil's advocate in pinning down the limitations of his beliefs and assumptions—that is, doing the work that he expected military planners to perform. In this area, Brodie's conceptual refinement ideally complemented the tendency of military planners to specialize in limited aspects of a war-making campaign and to apply arbitrary assumptions (some imposed upon them) to incremental changes in war-making conditions.

Second, in his sensitivity studies, Brodie proposed using the hypothetical past as a research tool and not merely to broadly justify a nuclear force arsenal. This was the case, for example, when he addressed the need to anticipate Soviet acquisition of nuclear weaponry and in particular to reconcile the value of military concentration with the vulnerability of concentrated forces to atomic attack. "No doubt," he wrote in the 1949 study, some ways can be found of achieving the degree of concentration necessary to a tactical end while minimizing the vulnerability of that concentration to atomic bomb attack. . . . It is by no means too early . . . for our strategists to start rethinking the campaigns of the recent war with the assumption that the enemy had had a few atomic bombs to use at critical places. Some very important conclusions would no doubt follow from such exercises.[47]

Directing attention to an adversary's ability to react intelligently and in timely fashion to American dispositions and plans, sensitivity studies would take account of accommodative as well as malevolent enemy intentions and would test the adequacy of older strategies in the face of newer technological developments.

As to why Brodie did not do more of this work, he was first of all temperamentally more comfortable with broader political and psychological aspects of strategy, not extensively studied by sensitivity and systems analysts, than he was about matters of detail. Second, sensitivity analyses of greater interest to Brodie would have had to highlight political concerns for which hard data were lacking and for which the hypothetical past appeared to provide little or no guidance. For example, they might have usefully identified how American force postures, excelling in noncrisis situations, were likely to perform during intense crises such as war. To perform such a study, however, Brodie would have had to construct measures of risk and danger, take into account the various orientations of national leaders, make a detailed study of various force dispositions in "normal" and crisis periods of history, and choose many arbitrary assumptions to make his study manageable, pinning down and constraining his analyses far more than he found congenial.

Third, Brodie was mainly interested in doing in war and in crisis what the superpowers were doing prior to those eventualities — that is, maintaining controls on the use of force. He was not interested in using sensitivity analysis to confirm what his conjectures told him was correct. Fourth, and perhaps most important, Brodie's horror at any strategic bombing that employed fusion weapons appears to have prevented him from studying the consequences of such bombing and the political developments conducive to it.

Coping with Deterrence Failure

Amid the many shifts in Brodie's analytical priorities and substantive views, the most important continuity in his thinking was his advocacy of using nuclear weapons to deter general war, beginning with his famous 1946 statement that "thus far the chief purpose of our military establishment has been to win wars. From now on its chief purpose must be to avert them. It can have almost no other useful purpose."[48] By the advent of fusion weapons, the priority Brodie gave to deterrence was informed by his view that "total nuclear war is to be avoided at almost any cost."[49] To be sure, he had in mind that "if deterrence fails we shall want enough forces to fight a total war effectively,"[50] but he was much less worried than others that giving primacy to deterrence would impair the search for unilateral advantage in nuclear war. "What we have done," he concluded in 1959, "must convince us Thucydides was right, that peace is better than war not only in being more agreeable but also in being very much more predictable. A plan and policy which offers a good promise of deterring war is therefore by orders of magnitude better in every way than one which depreciates the objective of deterrence in order to improve somewhat the chances of winning."[51]

Envisioning that general war was best discouraged by the threat of responding massively to a Soviet attack against the United States or against NATO allies, Brodie took the view that "only if [the enemy] feared to strike at us first could our striking force deter the enemy from massive attack upon an ally."[52] This implied that deterring the latter depended upon deterring the former. Yet he never stated categorically what should be done if the Soviets attacked the United States in spite of American threats of massive retaliation. "We assure the enemy," he wrote in 1959,

> by assuring ourselves (long-term security about our intentions being very undependable), that we will not reconsider the matter in the event he attacks us. We will hit back with all our surviving power at his cities and, especially if that power contains a fair number of missiles, he can count on losing those cities. It should not be difficult, if we make the appropriate effort beforehand, to assure him that, come what may, he will lose thirty, fifty, or more of his largest cities. This prospect should give him grave pause.
>
> The rub comes from the fact that what looks like the most rational *deterrence* policy involves commitment to a strategy of response which, if we ever had to execute it, might then look very foolish. The strategy of deterrence ought always to envisage the possibility of deterrence failing.[53]

This dilemma would be framed most starkly if the Soviet Union struck with nuclear weapons at American military targets but avoided attacks against American cities or against military targets close enough to cities to cause heavy civilian casualties. "For the sake of deterrence before hostilities," Brodie went on, "the enemy must expect us to be vindictive and irrational if he attacks us. We must give him every reason to feel that that portion of our retaliatory force which survives his attack will surely be directed against his major centers of population."[54] American historical conduct might well help shape such expectations, for American leaders, Brodie noted,

> have in the past proved themselves capable of acting irrationally or unreasonably, either because of inadequate forethought about consequences or because accepted and accustomed modes of behavior seemed to leave no choice (e.g., actions constrained by concepts of "national honor"), and in both kinds of cases positive constraint usually had behind it a very strong charge of emotion in the form of anger or fear or both.[55]

Finally, Brodie cited the difficulty of retargeting surviving American weaponry against Soviet forces held back in the first wave of attacks. "It is not at all clear," Brodie observed, "that over time we can pretend one objective and plan another, or that we will have enough flexibility to change our target list after the enemy attacks."[56]

The other response suggested by Brodie to a Soviet attack was to avoid irrationality, rethink prewar threats, and preserve as much American control over wartime decision making as possible.[57] He took note of analysis done at RAND that "suggests powerfully that even in a strike second attack no other group of targets is likely to make as much sense as those comprising the enemy's remaining strategic offensive strength."[58] And, anticipating in 1959 that retaliatory forces would become well protected, he wrote that in such a case, "certainly an American president is going to find it very much harder to give a signal which will result in the almost certain destruction of fifty or more of the largest American cities than he would if he faced no such penalty."[59]

During the 1960s, when protecting long-range retaliatory forces for deterrence purposes inspired the American concept of mutual assured destruction (MAD), Brodie asserted that the very low likelihood of general war created "a strong inducement to go-for-broke on deterrence."[60] On the other hand, the MAD concept was little suited to a vindictive response if deterrence failed; Brodie, who downplayed the importance of irrationality and emotion as contributors to war following the Cuban missile crisis, no longer was concerned about implementing an apparently irrational nuclear threat.[61] Instead he argued that since some risk of general war inhered in any Soviet-American diplomatic confrontation (a point he believed was impressed upon some American leaders during the Cuban missile crisis), massive retaliation did not have to be threatened.[62]

Had Brodie highlighted the problem of deterrence failure in this context, he might well have undercut his own "go-for-broke" attitude toward deterrence and raised questions about the foundations of his strategic thinking; the categorical nature of his arguments, at this time unconventional among strategists, tended to direct him away from matters he regarded as of secondary importance. Yet inasmuch as Brodie continued to argue that thermonuclear war remained *possible*,[63] his avoidance of the issue of deterrence failure lent abstraction to his views, divorcing them from an important area of concern to decision makers and military planners. Second, his strong views now led him to shift his emphasis away from the threat of massive retaliation that had ensured deterrence and toward less risky behaviors that would not have catastrophic consequences. Brodie apparently was reinforced in his optimism about avoiding catastrophe by his belief that important wider inhibitions were at work. "It is obvious," he wrote in 1959,

> that many inhibitions against initiating thermonuclear total war exist apart from the certainty of retaliation—otherwise we should have a general war before now—and it therefore seems reasonable to suppose that building even a modest amount of protection into the retaliatory capabilities of both sides will have disproportionate effects on the preexisting inhibitions.[64]

A strong case could surely be made for excluding thermonuclear war from a humane value perspective alone, and Brodie's horror of thermonuclear war was fully consistent with his emphasis on strengthening inhibitions against such a war. But if the threat of irrational retaliation had become less important than in the past for making deterrence work, requirements for nuclear deterrence became more debatable. Furthermore, Brodie's avoidance of the problem of deterrence breakdown may have lessened his ability to criticize his own operating assumptions and contributed to a reifying of his own value outlook upon national leaders.

Brodie's Critics: Jonathan Schell and Colin S. Gray

We have seen that Brodie's emphasis upon stability in Soviet-American relations was grounded since the 1960s in his view that Soviet strategic attack upon the United States was very improbable and irrational. By the early 1980s, this view had been challenged from two very different premises, both informed by the belief that a nuclear attacker's doubt about the victim's willingness to retaliate against the attacker's cities would increase the chances of war. These challenges, by Jonathan Schell and Colin S. Gray, will now be briefly reviewed. Schell, who diverges sharply from Brodie in his conclusion that nuclear weapons do not contribute to international stability, accepts Brodie's long-standing views that the major military fact of nuclear weapons is that they enabled belligerents to target each other's cities and thus bring about a war of annihilation and that winning wars cannot be the appropriate foundation for contemporary nuclear forces. But he concludes that employing nuclear weapons to deter attack is self-contradictory. "Nuclear deterrence," he wrote in *The Fate of the Earth,*

> requires one to prepare for armed conflict not in order to "win" it if it breaks out but in order to prevent it from breaking out in the first place. But if armed conflict breaks out anyway, what does one do with one's forces then? In pre-nuclear times, the answer would have required no second thought: it would have been to strive for the decision by arms — for victory. Yet nuclear deterrence begins by assuming, correctly, that victory is impossible. Thus, the logic of the deterrence strategy is dissolved by the very event — the first strike — that it is meant to prevent. Once the action begins, the whole doctrine is self-cancelling. In sum, the doctrine is based on a monumental logical mistake: one cannot credibly deter a first strike with a second strike whose *raison d'être* dissolves the moment the first strike arrives. It follows that, as far as deterrence theory is concerned, there is no reason for either side not to launch a first strike.[65]

Schell also rejects the idea that nuclear war can occur without triggering annihilation. "Victory does not suddenly become possible," he wrote,

> simply because it offers a solution to the logical contradiction on which the mutual-assured-destruction doctrine rests. The facts remain obdurately what they are: an attack of several thousand megatons will annihilate any country on earth many times over, no matter what line of argument the strategists pursue; and a "nuclear exchange" will, if it is on a large scale, threaten the life of man. . . . This "solution" is therefore worse than the error it sets out to remedy. It resolves the contradiction in the deterrence doc-

trine by denying the tremendous new reality that the doctrine was framed to deal with. . . . Consequently, this "solution" could lead us to commit the ultimate folly of exterminating ourselves without even knowing what we were doing.[66]

Colin Gray, by contrast, aims his criticism not at nuclear weapons but at faulty war-making strategies and concepts. Whereas Schell cites the defender's self-deterrence to support his assertion that strategic nuclear attack might be plausibly launched, Gray points to the defender's self-deterrence to bolster his contention that nuclear attack will not bring mutual annihilation. "Orthodox deterrence thinking," he writes, with Brodie's ideas clearly in mind,

> discounts totally the intra-war self-deterrent implications of the vulnerability of American assets. Foreign policy, in good part, is about freedom of action. Mutual assured destruction thinking, which still lurks in our declaratory policy and, presumably, in our war plans, virtually ensures self-deterrence and denies us the freedom of strategic-nuclear action that is a premise of NATO's strategy of flexible response.[67]

But Gray also believes that alternatives to such deterrence thinking and to self-deterrence are needed to obtain what he believes is an indispensable American objective of political victory over the Soviet Union—by which he means the demise of the Soviet state.[68] "If there is no theory of political victory in the U.S. SIOP [Single Integrated Operations Plan]," he argues, "then there can be little justification for nuclear planning at all."[69] Seeing "grave danger" in Brodie's judgment that a contemporary military establishment can have "almost no other useful purpose" than preventing war, Gray observes: "This is a prime example of a good idea becoming a poor idea when it is taken too far; at worst, it is a doctrinal formula for losing wars."[70]

Taking aim at Brodie's ideas, neither Schell nor Gray seem aware that their views have antecedents in Brodie's less widely regarded and unpublished work. For example, Schell's insistence that wars would lead to major attacks against cities matches Brodie's image of nuclear war contained in his *Absolute Weapon* essays, which presumed that contemporary policymakers would be as short-sighted in their war-making decisions as their predecessors were in the Second World War. I have argued in this study that because nuclear annihilation *could* occur so quickly and because policymakers are known to be fearful of that prospect, the assumption that nuclear war would quickly become uncontrollable cannot be accepted uncritically. On the other hand, Gray's assertion that deterrence strategies are incompatible with winning wars is rebutted in Brodie's endorsement from 1949 to 1951 (notably in his work for Vandenberg) of the strategy of threatening more attacks to come and of the objective of destroying the Soviet political regime. Brodie modified both these views when he took account of two-way war with fusion weapons, insisting then on the need to slow the pace of war-making and to reduce the scope of war-making objectives in order to sustain war limitations.

The prevalence of what Brodie would have considered atavistic thinking in the current debate about nuclear weapons is not altogether surprising, for we have seen in his own writings that apparently new ideas have been difficult to separate analytically from older, more traditional views about the function of modern-day weaponry. The imaginative potential of analysts to propound innovative uses for new weapons should not be exaggerated, a conclusion that raises important questions about the effective novelty of those weapons. As Brodie's earliest analyses made clear, the most horrendous potential of the new weapons was also devoid of any strategic or political meaning, which meant that this potential had relatively little or nothing to recommend it.

Among the first to understand this potential, Brodie was at his best as a strategic analyst when seeking alternatives to scenarios in which the unlimited killing power of nuclear weapons was likely to be displayed. When doing this, however, he made pioneer reference to a major dimension of nuclear strategy played down or neglected entirely by both Schell and Gray—namely, the coercive use of nuclear weapons. Coercive use could well diminish the chances of self-deterrence once a nuclear attack took place, because it was associated with both restraint in the application of force and boldness in resisting the attacker's intentions. Brodie presumed that leaders were much more likely to summon up the requisite boldness to respond to attack if they were persuaded that they were self-restrained than if their only choice was to retaliate in the most massive fashion.

If Brodie's analyses of the physical use of nuclear weapons were generally weaker than his discussion of their coercive use, it may have been because he invariably assumed weapons yields that were uniform, large, and too unwieldy for any strategy apart from the coercive. War-winning scenarios that depended upon attacks by a diverse arsenal against a diverse array of targets would have required detailed, problematic, and elaborate studies less suited to Brodie's prevailing approach to nuclear strategy. But Brodie did not neglect war-winning strategies altogether; he merely associated them with the coercive use of nuclear weapons, in which visible restraint in force employment was the key ingredient.

Two Levels of Strategic Analysis

This book, which affirms Brodie's definition of strategy as "a 'how to do it' study, a guide to accomplishing something and doing it efficiently," argues for distinguishing strategy and strategic analysis at two levels. On a very broad level, strategy integrates political objectives and military strength to prevent war or to gain victory in war. Strategy at this level, sometimes referred to as "grand strategy," provides conceptual unity, as Brodie wrote forty years ago, "adequate not only as a base of departure for specific strategic plans but also as a means of weighing one plan against another."[71] The need for such unity was made manifest for him by the "extraordinarily broad range" of circumstances affecting Soviet-American conflict. Brodie pioneered at this level by highlighting the political and psychological aspects of contemporary superpower relations, especially the shared interests between superpower opponents brought about by the introduction of weapons of mass destruction. Rather than guide policymakers in their particular circumstances, Brodie wished as did Clausewitz to sharpen the ability of policymakers and planners to apply their prevailing dispositions to military problems.[72]

A second level of strategy assumes realistic or hypothetical constraints upon political and military choices in specified circumstances and attempts to clarify and operationalize strengths and interests in those circumstances using war planning, net assessments, systems and contingency analyses, and game exercises.[73]

Instead of aiming at a conceptual unity, strategy at this level is defined differently at different echelons of command,[74] both political and military, in the internal as well as the external political environment.[75] Some of Brodie's best work is found in his outlining at a relatively early time the differences for the military positions of the superpowers between atomic bomb scarcity and plenty and between American bomb superiority over the Soviet Union and mutual nuclear plenty. From a particularist standpoint, these differences depended upon an individual's or an agency's functional responsibility. Again, Brodie's 1951 critique of the Air Targets Division appendix to the emergency war plan was likely to be the only radical criticism that plan would receive and hence was necessary for the accountability of the air staff in its choice of strategic targets.[76]

Although Brodie in this work and also in his *Absolute Weapon* essays masterfully gleaned major strategic insights from a large amount of detailed information, his analyses were generally driven less by detail, which he tended to use illustratively and retrospectively, and more by his values and his search for analytic balance. Contributing to this approach was his shocked reaction to the unintellectual, principled, and narrow attitudes of Cabell and LeMay and his assumption that "to construct the details" would subject him to inevitable error.[77] He used detail to organize the general direction of his analyses, as in his citing of the RAND study of the warning of target populations prior to bombing attacks and the detailed RAND evaluation of the lethal radii of fusion bomb attacks; to adjust the weight of his arguments, as in the results of the interrogation of North Korean and Chinese prisoners of war and the results of the Cuban missile crisis; and to bolster pre-existing arguments, as in his discussion of strategic bombing in the Second World War and of grand strategy in both world wars.

During his first decade at RAND, most notably in *Strategy in the Missile Age,* Brodie depended heavily on particularistic analyses done by other members of the RAND staff.[78] The distinctive value of Brodie's work must be judged in part by the absence of any major RAND institutional interest in questions of basic strategy, but his building upon particularistic RAND analyses indicates he also understood that important questions about strategy can only be answered in terms of explicit assumptions about strengths, intentions, and circumstances and that some of the best strategic analysis emanates from rigorous respect for constraints posited in the analysis. By contrast, Brodie's subsequent criticism of his RAND colleagues for neglecting broader political and military concerns seemed to shortchange the value of particularistic analysis, underestimating the aid that constraints—whether arbitrary or realistic—can make to imaginative solutions.[79]

The weaknesses of strategic study at the broader level of analysis are also evident in this book. First, as Brodie himself noted with his references to conceptual behind-handedness, major changes in the operational environment can render the analyst's predispositions inadequate. Although Brodie emphasized the consequences for those cases in which the inadequacy went unperceived, almost as problematic is the requirement of reconstructing a strategic foundation after the analyst has become aware that his or her premises have been undermined. One of the perils of broadly inclusive analysis, apparently, is that its striving for consistency and foundation foster preconceptions that are vulnerable to the unforeseen. The only way to ensure that analysis will not be undermined in this way is to strive for greater abstraction that renders analysis less related to technological developments or to the practical difficulties of constrained behavior. For example, Brodie's insistence by the 1960s in the strength of deterrence of general war protected him against any further rethinking of his ideas yet was abstracted from the operational problem of preparing for general war.

The second problem at this level is the difficulty of distinguishing strategy from militarily effective behavior. In practice Brodie never conceded that the use of force should be anything other than militarily effective, though he indicated at several points that the most efficient weapons employment would be inconsistent with broader strategic requirements and especially with the pursuit of diplomatic objectives. If a case could be made on the basis of diplomatic values for less-efficient warfare, too much was being made of the broad virtues of atomic weapons as decisive, because they distracted analysts from the more serious and complex problem of inconclusive warfare justified by political goals, the tyranny of which came to be appreciated only in the course of the Vietnam war.[80]

A third difficulty with broad strategic thinking is that it must aim at a more refined and coherent consensus of ideas even as it needs to be alert to flaws in prevailing views. For example, when Brodie worked at the instigation of General Samford, the air force director of intelligence, to develop a basic air-power doctrine, he was endeavoring to assemble a framework of ideas to serve as a defensible consensus; on the other hand, when he worked in the role of what has been termed "crude navigation," he undermined consensus views. Brodie did as much as anyone to critique premature and superficial attitudes by refocusing debate about military priorities, the purposes that nuclear weapons should most appropriately serve, levels of perceived threat, and levels of acceptable risk.[81] His enormous self-assurance and refinement in debate might have sufficed in this regard, but Brodie arguably made a still larger contribution by his commendable willingness to rethink his own views.[82]

Brodie appears to have been less successful in assisting the development of strategy. Whether he might have done more to develop grand strategy is unclear; he was certainly qualified to do so, but we have seen that he was hard-pressed to adapt his views to the major technological changes of the contemporary period.[83] Whereas in his *Guide to Naval Strategy* Brodie built upon ideas about strategy articulated by others and upon prior experience of war at sea, in the contemporary period he endeavored to develop a wholly new strategic framework centered around nuclear weapons and based primarily on the aim of preventing war. In light of the difficulties he is known to have experienced in completing this latter project,[84] account should be taken of the possibility that aspiring for a coherent unified strategy may be unrealistic in peacetime if it is to be elaborated around a wholly unique weapons system whose wartime use has been almost entirely hypothetical.[85]

But to argue, as does Robert Jervis, that "very little new has been said since 1946. . . . Forty years of thought have not taken us very far,"[86] is to weigh too heavily Brodie's earliest postwar contributions in *The Absolute Weapon* and neglect his subsequent work, including his writings on fusion bombs and his newer views about strategic coercion, diplomacy, limited war, and escalation. By 1973 Brodie was inclined, as was Jervis, to stress the prescience of his 1946 essays in arguing for the uniqueness of nuclear weapons and the centrality of deterring general war.[87] And yet his writing in the intervening period repeatedly made reference to adapting basic strategy to changes in international situations.

To be sure, the importance of novel ideas depends on the strategic problem being discussed. For example, Brodie had relatively little new to say about the problem of preventing any deterrence failure during the intervening period, and it was in relation to this same problem that the lengthening tradition of nuclear weapons nonuse strengthened the case beyond what it was in 1955 (when Brodie first argued it) — that strategy had reached a "dead end."[88] He also had little to say about strategic targets, because his concentration on the destructive potential of fission and then fusion weapons dictated a preoccupation with cities as targets for nuclear weapons. On the other hand, once strengthening deterrence of general war and strengthening deterrence of hostilities at other levels were distinguished, the value of deterrence *in* war, highlighted by Brodie beginning with his writings on fusion weapons, becomes especially important.[89] And Brodie did sharply distinguish, by 1949 but not in 1946, coercive use of nuclear weapons from purely physical employment of them, a refinement critical for military restraint in a major war and for applying nuclear warfare to political objectives.

But Jervis's statement is also inadequate because examining strategic thought very broadly, as Brodie had done, it does not take into account the particularistic level of strategic analysis. A major conclusion of this book is that the particularistic level is understudied and underappreciated, a situation traceable in part to Brodie's success and authority as a conceptual thinker, his growing impatience with detailed operational studies, and his insistence that detailed analysis was distinct from strategy. Undoubtedly this general situation has had other causes as well: Intuitively, most students of strategy admire the elegant, critical, incisive writing for which Brodie was so reputed and much important operational study is off-limits because of its security sensitivity. Still, to the extent that Brodie influenced strategic studies, the popular depreciation of detailed analysis is part of his legacy. I argued here that studies yielding more insightful and more subtle predispositional attitudes should inform, and be informed by, studies of constrained behavior in particular circumstances.

Appendix:
Bernard Brodie—A Chronology

Born, Chicago, Illinois	20 May 1910
Ph.B., University of Chicago	1932
Marries Fawn McKay	28 Aug. 1936
Second World War begins	1 Sept. 1939
Ph.D. (in international relations), University of Chicago	1940
Fellow, Institute for Advanced Study	1940/41
First book, *Sea Power in the Machine Age,*	1941
Japanese attack Pearl Harbor	7 Dec. 1941
Instructor, Dartmouth College	1941–43
A Layman's Guide to Naval Strategy	1942
Enlists in Naval Reserve	29 Dec. 1942
Begins active duty as lieutenant (junior grade) at General Ordnance School, Washington Navy Yard	6 Jan. 1943
Assigned to Navy Bureau of Ordnance	Mar. 1943–Jan. 1945
Temporary duty, Office of Chief of Naval Operations	Jan.–Oct. 1944
Allied invasion of Normandy	6 June 1944
Assigned to State Department Executive Office	Jan.–Mar. 1945
Special assistant to secretary of the navy	Mar.–July 1945
Temporary duty with director, Office of Special Political Affairs; State Department technical expert on U.S. delegation to the San Francisco Conference establishing the United Nations	Apr.–June 1945
German surrender; V-E Day	8 May 1945
Hiroshima A-bomb attack	6 Aug. 1945
Japanese surrender; Second World War ends	14 Aug. 1945
Resigns active naval duty as first lieutenant	4 Sept. 1945
Joins Yale University Department of International Relations as associate professor and director of graduate studies	Fall 1945
The Absolute Weapon, edited by Brodie	1946
Member of First Resident Faculty group, National War College	1946/47
Senior Specialist in National Defense, Legislative Reference Service, Library of Congress	1946/49
Begins annual Air War College lecture series	Spring 1947
Resigns navy commission	21 Oct. 1947
Outbreak of the Korean War	25 June 1950

Special assistant to air force chief of staff	Aug.–Sept. 1950
Chinese intervene in the Korean War	Oct. 1950
Special assistant to air force chief of staff, acting as RAND Corporation consultant (on leave from Yale)	Nov. 1950–June 1951
First successful lab test of fusion	8 May 1951
Becomes full-time RAND senior staff member	Aug. 1951
Participates in numerous Washington briefings on implications of fusion weapons	Mar. 1952
Director of air force intelligence arranges for Brodie to work at RAND on a major new study of air-power doctrine	Apr. 1952
First fusion weapon explosion	31 Oct. 1952
Korean War armistice	27 July 1953
Massive retaliation strategy publicly outlined by John Foster Dulles	12 Jan. 1954
First Soviet test of an ICBM	Aug. 1957
Strategy in the Missile Age	1959
Carnegie Corporation Reflective Year Fellowship spent in Paris	July 1960–July 1961
From Cross-Bow to H-Bomb (with Fawn Brodie)	1961
Cuban missile crisis	Oct. 1962
Limited Test Ban Treaty signed	25 July 1963
La Guerre Nucléaire, edited by Brodie	1965
First American marines arrive in South Vietnam	6 Mar. 1965
Resigns from RAND and becomes professor of political science at the University of California, Los Angeles	Aug. 1966
Escalation and the Nuclear Option	1966
War and Politics	1973
Vietnam War armistice	23 Jan. 1973
Appointed faculty research lecturer at UCLA	1975
Retires from UCLA, becoming Emeritus Professor	1977
Death, Los Angeles, California	24 Nov. 1978

Notes

Chapter 1. Introduction and Overview

1. Robin Higham, *The Military Intellectuals in Britain: 1918–1939* (New Brunswick, N.J.: Rutgers University Press, 1966), 246.

2. "In the few years since the first hydrogen bomb was test-exploded," wrote S. L. A. Marshall in a review of Brodie's *Strategy in the Missile Age*, "more books have been written and published on the military strategy of the future than were given to that subject during the gunpowder millenium. [*sic*]. Few, if any, of these books were authored by generals on active duty who were concerned with problems of strategy." "Strategy in Missile Age Is Largely Guessing Game," *Riverside Enterprise* (Calif.), 10 September 1959, in a file of offprints and reviews of *Strategy in the Missile Age*, Box 5 (Folder 3), Bernard Brodie Papers, Collection 1223, University Research Library, University of California, Los Angeles (henceforth referred to as "UCLA Collection").

3. Brodie's dissertation is referred to in Quincy Wright's *A Study of War* (Chicago: University of Chicago Press, 1968, first published 1942), appendix I. For some of Jacob Viner's views about scholarship, which seem to coincide with Brodie's, see David A. Baldwin, *Economic Statecraft*, (Princeton, N.J.: Princeton University Press, 1985), 373.

4. This seminar's best-known efforts culminated in a path-breaking volume, *The Makers of Modern Strategy*, edited by Edward M. Earle (Princeton, N.J.: Princeton University Press, 1943). This project is recalled by Peter Paret in a successor volume, *Makers of Modern Strategy: From Machiavelli to the Nuclear Age*, edited by Paret (Princeton, N.J.: Princeton University Press, 1986), 4. Virtually forgotten is a somewhat later pioneering study by Earle and this seminar on the subject of strategic bombing of economic targets.

5. According to Thomas C. Schelling, the term "layman's" was dropped in the third edition of the book in 1944 so that the book could be deemed suitable for distribution within the navy. Obituary notice by Schelling for Bernard Brodie in *International Security* 3 (Winter 1978/79): 2.

6. On his editing role, see Brodie to Edward Mead Earle, 23 September 1943; Edward Mead Earle Papers, Seeley G. Mudd Manuscript Library, Princeton University, Princeton, N.J., Box 3 (B Folder) (henceforth referred to as "Earle Papers). On his speechwriting, see Brodie to Earle, 7 October 1943, ibid. On his function as a commentator, see memorandum, "Comment on Some Portions of Attached Document" (a review of a statement by the vice chief of naval operations), from "Ad5" to "A" (signed by Brodie), 10 April 1943, enclosed in Brodie to Earle, 11 May 1943, ibid. The last of these responsibilities matched one later exercised by Brodie as a special assistant to Air Force Chief of Staff Hoyt Vandenberg.

In a review of *A Layman's Guide to Naval Strategy*, by Capt. Charles C. Gill, USN (*U.S. Naval Institute Proceedings*, November 1942), Brodie is identified as having been appointed by the Navy Department to write, beginning in January 1943, a wartime history of the Bureau of Ordnance. And the previous September, Brodie was touted by his publisher as the "official historian of the

Bureau of Ordnance." Datus Smith to Ralph A. Bard, 4 September 1942 (photocopy). Both of these documents are found in Clippings Scrapbook, UCLA Collection, Box 5 (Folder 2).

7. On this contribution, see Brodie to Earle, 7 October 1943; Earle Papers, Box 3 (B folder). On Brodie's move to the Office of the CNO, see Brodie to Earle, 11 November 1943, ibid., in which he stated: "I am now hard at work with three other men on the King Report, and will be responsible for the Introduction, the section on the Battle of the Atlantic, the ordnance material, and for the general over-all editing of the whole." In all likelihood, Brodie was here involved in the preparation of the first of three reports prepared by Adm. Ernest J. King for the secretary of the navy, completed 27 March 1944 and published 23 April 1944. For the text of all three King reports, see Ernest J. King, *U.S. Navy at War, 1941–1945: Official Reports to the Secretary of the Navy, by Fleet Admiral Ernest J. King, U.S. Navy* (Washington, D.C.: U.S. Navy Department, 1946). Pages 1–93 of this volume comprise the first of the King reports.

8. Brodie to Earle, 11 November 1943, Earle Papers, Box 3 (B Folder).

9. The summary report of the work of section 16-W includes the following: "For about one year, an officer served on the staff on a loan arrangement effected by Admiral Yarnell. This officer had a Ph.D. in political science, and had acquired a considerable reputation as a writer on naval affairs. He contributed much to the Norden broadcasts and to the Sea War Annex. This was particularly helpful because the other specialists in the branch were less familiar with this general field." *U.S. Naval Administration in World War II: CNO, Office of Naval Intelligence*, vol. 3 (pt. 14: Special Warfare [W Branch]), 1369. Microfilm copy, Navy Department Library, Washington Navy Yard, Washington, D.C. According to this report (ibid., 1376), the "War at Sea" memos were sometimes the only authentic reports received by the Office of War Information about naval events, and Admiral King had been sympathetic to their production and helped draft guidelines for them.

Independent confirmation of Brodie's service in section 16-W of the navy is to be found in William T. Golden to Sidney Souers, 23 November 1951, personal collection of William T. Golden, New York City (folder: Bernard Brodie). Henceforth referred to as "Golden Papers."

10. *War and Politics* (New York: Macmillan, 1973), 450f. Italics in original.

11. Ibid.

12. Brodie to Earle, 3 April 1945 (postscript), Earle Papers, Box 5 (folder: Brodie, Bernard). Donald Blaisdell had earlier contacted Earle about the possibility of Brodie joining his division at the State Department. Earle to Brodie, 28 March 1945, UCLA Collection, Box 5 (Folder 2).

13. Information obtained from Brodie's Navy Personnel File, National Personnel Records Center, St. Louis, Missouri.

14. *A Layman's Guide to Naval Strategy* Princeton, N.J.: (Princeton University Press, 1942), ix.

15. Ibid., 114.

16. Ibid., 15. He gave as an example of the perils of ignoring "age old verities" and "long-tested doctrines" the failure of the French high command in the summer of 1940.

17. Ibid., 5.

18. Ibid., ix. Schelling has observed that the *Layman's Guide* "contains some of the best early 'systems analysis' I ever saw." Schelling obituary notice for Bernard Brodie, 2.

Of considerable interest is an exchange of memoranda by members of Earle's seminar, including Brodie, regarding the definition of the term "strategy." Brodie, rejecting what he termed "excessive inclusiveness," proposed a definition that some considered the narrowest of all the seminar members. "The most comprehensive reference acknowledged by Webster (first sentence)," he wrote, "is far more restricted in meaning than the definitions proposed. It is, in his words: 'The science and art of *employing* the *armed strength* of a *belligerent* to secure the objects *of a war.*'" Italics added by Brodie. *"Memorandum Regarding the Term 'Strategy,'"* n.d. *[1940 or 1941]*, Earle Papers, Box 25 *(folder: Strategy)*.

19. "Strategy as a Science," *World Politics* 1 (July 1949): 477.

20. This quotation and the next are from "Must We Shoot from the Hip?" 4 September 1951,

RAND Informal Working Paper, in *The Development of American Strategic Thought: Writings on Strategy, 1945–1951*, edited by Marc Trachtenberg, vol. 2 of *The Development of American Strategic Thought, 1945–1969*, edited by Trachtenberg (New York: Garland, 1987–1988), 247–248. Italics in original. This volume is cited henceforth as *Development of American Strategic Thought, 1945–1951*.

21. *Layman's Guide*, 10.

22. Michael Howard, *The Causes of Wars* (Cambridge, Mass.: Harvard University Press, 1983), 42.

23. "In your last letter," a correspondent wrote to Brodie, "you wrote that you preferred to work on strategy in its 'pure' state, and I wish I could discuss this with you" (Eileen Galloway to Brodie, 31 October 1955, UCLA Collection, Box 3 [folder 2]). Responding to this letter, Brodie wrote in a postscript: "I hope you did not take too literally my comment that I was interested only in strategy in its 'purest' state. All I meant was that there are a lot of items in any military budget which have to be of interest to some people but which interest me less than . . . questions I have alluded to above" (Brodie to Galloway, 8 November 1955, ibid.).

24. Higham, "The Dangerously Neglected—The British Military Intellectuals, 1918–1939," *Military Affairs* 29 (Summer 1965): 83. In a letter to Brodie giving an appraisal of Brodie's *Strategy in the Missile Age*, Richard Rovere, the respected Washington correspondent of *The New Yorker*, wrote that he was stimulated by "what I can only call the *spectacle* of your reasoning [in that book]. I got a kind of esthetic satisfaction from the book as well as instruction and stimulation. And this quite apart, or so it seemed, from the merits of the case" (Rovere to Brodie, n.d. [notation by Brodie as having been received 17 February 1960], UCLA Collection, Box 2 [R Folder]: italics in original).

25. "Strategy as a Science," 484. Italics in original. Brodie's statement that "formerly the need for [such method] was not great" is difficult to understand.

26. Ibid., 473.

27. *War and Politics*, 457. Donald Cameron Watt, in a study of European military ideas during the interwar period, documents instead the widespread belief in the superiority of the defense. He cites Liddell Hart, who propagated this view extensively in Britain, as arguing that "it is common assumption that attack has usually paid in the past. This is contrary to the balance of evidence. Analysis shows that in the majority of battles which are engraved on the pages of history the loser was the army which was the first to commit itself to the attack" (*Too Serious a Business* [Berkeley: University of California Press, 1975], 70–71).

28. Higham, *Military Intellectuals in Britain*, 244.

29. *War and Politics*, 457. Liddell Hart points to the French assumption in 1940 that the Ardennes was impassable as "one of the most striking examples in recent history of how a body of professional experts can continue under the influence of a fixed idea handed down from one generation to another without re-examining it" (*The Liddell Hart Memoirs*, vol. 1 [New York: G. P. Putnam's Sons, 1965], 237).

30. "Strategy as a Science," 476. In a footnote to this statement, Brodie wrote: "I am trying desperately here to restrain the bias of the academician that effort of writing is an almost indispensable catalyst to the production of original thoughts" (ibid., 476n). Higham has observed that "it is extremely difficult for a man in the Services to write much. Tradition is against it. It is liable to censorship. It must be non-controversial or anonymous" (*Military Intellectuals in Britain*, 237).

31. "Strategy as a Science," 479–480. Italics in original.

32. *War and Politics*, 448. Brodie made no mention of Clausewitz in his 1949 article "Strategy as a Science."

33. *Liddell Hart Memoirs*, 168–169.

34. Ibid., 240.

35. On the military backgrounds of interwar British thinkers other than Liddell Hart, see Higham, "The Dangerously Neglected," 82.

36. *War and Politics*, 462–463.

37. Higham, "The Dangerously Neglected," 73.

38. Colin S. Gray, "What RAND Hath Wrought," *Foreign Policy*, no. 4 (Fall 1971): 119.

39. Bernard Brodie was widely recognized, at least through the early 1960s, as being the most prolific of all contemporary strategic analysts. See Roy E. Licklider, *The Private Nuclear Strategists* (Columbus: Ohio State University Press, 1971), 18. For more information on the strategic thinkers at the RAND Corporation, see Fred Kaplan, *The Wizards of Armageddon* (New York: Simon & Schuster, 1983).

40. See, for example, "War Department Thinking on the Atomic Bomb," *Bulletin of the Atomic Scientists* 3 (June 1947): 150–165; "Navy Department Thinking on the Atomic Bomb," *Bulletin of the Atomic Scientists* 3 (July 1947): 177–180; "A Critique of Army and Navy Thinking on the Atomic Bomb," *Bulletin of the Atomic Scientists* 3 (August 1947): 207–210.

41. Brodie to David A. Rosenberg, 22 August 1977, UCLA Collection, Box 9 (Folder 21).

42. *Strategy in the Missile Age* (Princeton, N.J.: Princeton University Press, 1959), xi–xii.

43. "The Morale Factor in STRAP Planning," 5 August 1949, *passim*, UCLA Collection, Box 11 (Folder 17). "STRAP" was evidently an acronym for "Strategic Attack Plan."

44. "Tactical Effects of H-Bombs," 7 November 1952, RAND Informal Working Paper, in *The Development of American Strategic Thought: Writings on Strategy, 1952–1960* (vol. 1), edited by Marc Trachtenberg, vol. 3 of *The Development of American Strategic Thought: Writings on Strategy, 1945–1969*. This volume is cited henceforth as *Development of American Strategic Thought, 1952–1960 (1)*. See also *War and Politics*, 65.

45. *Strategy in the Missile Age*, 330. Italics in original.

46. *War and Politics*, 463.

47. H. Stuart Hughes, *Consciousness and Society* (New York: Alfred A. Knopf, 1958), 10.

48. "Strategy as a Science," 469.

49. "Must We Shoot from the Hip?" 242f.

50. Ibid., 256.

51. *War and Politics*, 463.

52. Hughes, *History as Art and as Science* (New York: Harper & Row, 1964), 102–103. Hughes had in mind de Toqueville and de Gaulle.

53. Relatively few policymakers have written thoughtfully about their experiences, though the proportion has grown in recent years. However, Brodie was generally discreet in his writings about his professional activities and about policy matters.

54. "Implications for Military Policy," in *The Absolute Weapon: Atomic Power and World Order*, edited by Bernard Brodie (New York: Harcourt, Brace, 1946), 76.

55. Ibid., 88.

56. Higham, "The Dangerously Neglected," 76.

57. "Morale Factor in STRAP Planning," 13.

58. "The Warning of Target Populations in Air War: An Appendix of Working Papers," by members of the Social Science Division of the RAND Corporation, Research Memorandum RM-275, November 1949. This work, cited henceforth as "RAND Warning Papers," was alluded to by Brodie, for example, in "Changing Capabilities and War Objectives," Air War College lecture, 17 April 1952, in *Development of American Strategic Thought, 1952–1960 (1)*, 79. (Also in the UCLA Collection, Box 12 [Folder 15]). A clean transcript of this lecture, incorporating corrections (evidently in Brodie's hand) displayed in the copy reproduced by Trachtenberg, is in the U.S. Air Force Historical Research Center (henceforth cited as AFHRC), Maxwell Air Force Base, Montgomery, Alabama, catalog no. K239.716252-105.

59. "Must We Shoot from the Hip?" 266.

60. As I noted above, Brodie had been unwilling to be swayed earlier by the SAC argument that nuclear attack against the Soviet Union should be initiated quickly upon the outbreak of war to forestall American "collapse" from Soviet bombing.

61. "The Influence of Mass Destruction Weapons on Strategy," Naval War College lecture, 6 February 1956, 22, UCLA Collection, Box 14 (Folder 7).

62. "Unpublished, Unclassified Notes—1955," on file at the RAND Corporation.

63. *Strategy in the Missile Age*, 331.

64. *Escalation and the Nuclear Option* (Princeton, N.J.: Princeton University Press, 1966), 33. Italics in original.

65. Ibid., 101.

66. "Political Impact of U.S. Force Postures," 28 May 1963, RAND Informal Working Paper, in *The Development of American Strategic Thought: Writings on Strategy, 1961–1969, and Retrospectives*, edited by Marc Trachtenberg, vol. 6 of *The Development of American Strategic Thought: Writings on Strategy, 1945–1969*, 243. This volume is cited henceforth as *Development of American Strategic Thought, 1961–1969*.

67. Conference transcript, "Theater Nuclear Forces," undated but attached to Brodie paper outline entitled "Factors Bearing on TNW Decision," [May 1967], 31, UCLA Collection, Box 7 (Folder 6). It should be noted that the concept of limited war is an American one; such a war would not be limited by European standards.

68. One of Brodie's reports to Vandenberg alluded to the so-called Friendship Resolution (Senate Concurrent Resolution 11, 1951, reproduced in full in *Congressional Quarterly Almanac*, 1951, 240). See James T. Lowe, "Memorandum for Record," 9 March 1951, 3. This memorandum, which quotes liberally from this Brodie report, is filed in Record Group 341 (Records of the Chief of Staff, U.S. Air Force), Entry 214 (Operational Files of the Air Force Directorate of Intelligence), Box 56 (Folder: Document nos. 2–18900 to 2–18999), Modern Military Branch, National Archives, Washington, D.C. This memorandum is cited henceforth as "Lowe Critique" and the collection in which it is included as "National Archives USAF Intelligence Collection."

69. "Changing Capabilities and War Objectives," 63–64.

70. "Political Consequences of the H-Bomb," 7 November 1952, RAND Informal Working Paper, *Development of American Strategic Thought, 1952–1960 (1)*, 33. Italics in original.

71. Ibid., 35. He had in mind at this point two-sided fusion bomb capabilities.

72. *War and Politics*, 25.

73. "U.S. Political Objectives in a Context of Strategic Bombing," 19 February 1953; RAND Informal Working Paper, in *Development of American Strategic Thought, 1952–1960 (1)*, 117. See also "Political Consequences of the H-Bomb," 25.

74. "U.S. Political Objectives in a Context of Strategic Bombing," 117.

75. "New Techniques of War and National Policies," in *Technology and International Relations*, edited by William F. Ogburn (Chicago: University of Chicago Press, 1949), 167. The larger portion of this article was delivered, with minor changes, as an Air War College lecture, "A-Bombs and Air Strategy," 24 March 1949; the lecture transcript is on file at AFHRC, K239.716249-13(R).

76. "Changing Capabilities and War Objectives," 87.

77. Brodie to Quincy Wright, 18 November 1959, UCLA Collection, Box 2 (W Folder). He went on to say: "Although I do not accept their estimate, I have to recognize that they have a view which *could* be right." Italics in original.

78. "Morals and Strategy," *Worldview* (September 1964): 7. Italics in original. See also *War and Politics*, 407f.

79. A short Brodie paper — "The Issue of Strategic Superiority: A Comment" (19 July 1963) — which circulated as a RAND Informal Working Paper, raised the question (p. 1) of "whether or not we are now, or are likely to become in the foreseeable future, willing to yield up to the Soviets that old-fashioned kind of superiority which is best described simply as possession of a lot more strategic weapons than the opponent has, preferably also of better quality and better protected." Brodie answered this question in the negative.

Earlier, in 1959, he had written more obliquely that "large forces look more impressive than small ones — for reasons which are by no means entirely irrational — and in some circumstances such impressiveness may be important to us" (*Strategy in the Missile Age*, 277).

80. "Strategy," in *The International Encyclopedia of the Social Sciences*, edited by David L. Sills (New York: Macmillan & Free Press, 1968), 15:287. See also *War and Politics,* passim.

81. *War and Politics*, 380. Italics in original. The Wohlstetter article was published as "The Delicate Balance of Terror," *Foreign Affairs* 37 (January 1959): 211–234.

82. *Strategy in the Missile Age*, 239 and 225.

83. Ibid., 281.

84. Ibid., 185n. and 355n.

85. See *Strategy in the Missile Age*, 331.

86. *War and Politics*, 380. Italics in original. In this instance, Brodie reinforced his view retrospectively according to his interpretation of a formative event.

87. "Political Impact of U.S. Force Postures," 237.

88. *Escalation and the Nuclear Option*, 85.

89. "Political Consequences of the H-Bomb," 29. For detailed study offering such a conclusion, see Hans Speier, *German Rearmament and Atomic War*, RAND Report R-298, February 1957. In 1959, however, Brodie played down the danger of Soviet atomic blackmail, observing that "it would be difficult to establish that we have seen much evidence of it yet. . . . It is not a foregone conclusion that they are going to do so in the future, or that, if they do, we are bound to be victimized by it" ("Strategic Objectives and the Determination of Force Composition," 9 June 1959, RAND Informal Working Paper, in *The Development of American Strategic Thought: Writings on Strategy, 1952–1960* (vol. 3), edited by Marc Trachtenberg, vol. 5 of *The Development of American Strategic Thought: Writings on Strategy, 1945–1969*, 77. This volume is cited henceforth as *Development of American Strategic Thought, 1952–1960(3)*.

90. *Strategy in the Missile Age*, 239.

91. Ibid., 239–240.

92. "Political Impact of U.S. Force Postures," 237. In 1954, Brodie wrote to Eileen Galloway that "diplomacy, in so far as it involves political pressures of any kind . . . is essentially inseparable from military power." Brodie to Galloway, 21 October 1954, UCLA Collection, Box 3 (Folder 2).

93. "The Missing Middle—Tactical Nuclear War," 9 April 1964, revised on 8 May 1964, RAND Informal Working Paper, in *Development of American Strategic Thought, 1961–1969*, 259.

94. Brodie to Rosenberg, 22 August 1977, UCLA Collection, Box 9 (Folder 21).

95. Brodie's two-stage assignment as special consultant to Vandenberg, beginning in August 1950 and ending in June 1951, was apparently instigated by Gen. Lauris Norstad, air force vice chief of staff until December 1950 and an admirer of Brodie's earlier writing who would have known of the latter's wartime service with the navy. These dates are different from Brodie's 1977 recollection to David Rosenberg, accepted as fact by Rosenberg in "The Origins of Overkill: Nuclear Weapons and American Strategy, 1945–1960," *International Security* 7 (Spring 1983): 17ff. Brodie had evidently forgotten details of his first stage of work for Vandenberg, the report of which is cited in chap. 4 of this book.

96. *War and Politics*, 63–64.

97. Ibid., 64f. It is difficult to reconcile this episode with Brodie's 1952 statement (noted above) that he had "never felt the hot breath of imminent [Soviet-American] war on my back." Possibly Brodie did not agree with the intelligence estimate in the 1950 episode, or, if he did, he may later have repressed that belief when it proved false.

98. On the "Delta" mission of a strategic bombing campaign, see *Strategy in the Missile Age*, 338f.

99. On planning factors behind war planning, see *War and Politics*, 462f.

100. See Lowe Critique, 5.

101. The surface point immediately under the center of bomb burst is "ground zero." See *Strategy in the Missile Age*, 125ff.

102. See Maj. Gen. C. P. Cabell to Lt. Gen. Curtis E. LeMay, 5 April 1951, National Archives USAF Intelligence Collection, Box 56 (Folder: Document nos. 2–19000 to 2–19099).

103. Cited in Lowe Critique, 10.

104. Reference to RAND critiques of air force assumptions and hypotheses is in "The American Scientific Strategists," RAND Paper P-2979, October 1964, 19.

105. Cited in Lowe Critique, 5.

106. Ibid.

107. In 1956, Norstad was named supreme allied commander for Europe; he remained on friendly terms with Brodie.

108. Howard, "The Classical Strategists," first published in 1969 and reproduced in Howard's *Studies in War and Peace* (New York: Viking, 1971), 159–160.

109. Cited in *War and Politics*, 377. Italics reproduced from *Absolute Weapon*, 76.

110. Mandelbaum, *The Nuclear Question: The United States and Nuclear Weapons, 1946–1976* (Cambridge: Cambridge University Press, 1979), 19.

111. Ibid., 19–20.

112. Ibid., 50.

113. Ibid., 206. Mandelbaum went on, quoting McNamara: "'When both sides have a sure second-strike capability,' [McNamara] had said in an interview in late 1962, 'then you might have a more stable balance of terror.' McNamara shied away from stating bluntly and unequivocally that a nuclear stalemate was in prospect. He was sensitive to the political risks of acknowledging that the Soviet Union was, for all practical purposes, the nuclear equal of the United States. But if he was hesitant to admit it publicly, there can be little doubt that he understood privately that the Soviets could assemble a nuclear striking force as 'survivable' as its American counterpart." For more recent thinking by McNamara along these lines, see Roman Kolkowicz's introduction in *The Logic of Nuclear Terror*, edited by Kolkowicz (Boston: Allen & Unwin, 1987), 5.

114. Jervis, "MAD Is the Best Possible Deterrence," *Bulletin of the Atomic Scientists* 41 (March 1985): 43. Later, in more careful study, Jervis conceded that, "of course, not all the basic ideas were on the table by the end of 1946. . . . I think the development of three concepts in the 1950s fleshed out the earlier ideas. Wohlstetter's distinction between first- and second-strike capability, Snyder's clarification of the problem of extended deterrence, and Schelling's discussion of the reciprocal fear of surprise attack—what is now called crisis stability—were crucial in providing the conceptual tools for our current strategic thinking. They added sophistication and nuance to the positions associated with Brodie and Borden but left the basic arguments unchanged" ("Strategic Theory: What's New and What's True," in Kolkowicz, *The Logic of Nuclear Terror*, 49).

115. Jervis, *The Illogic of American Nuclear Strategy* (Ithaca, N.Y.: Cornell University Press, 1984), 41.

116. Howard, *Causes of War*, 133–135. By contrast, Jervis has written that "Brodie's views were certainly incorrect when he first enunciated them because nuclear weapons were scarce and, by today's standards, small" ("Strategic Theory: What's New and What's True," 48).

117. The reader should remember this point when evaluating Jervis's appraisal of Kissinger's writing alluded to earlier.

118. For a useful exhortation to examine the merits of strategic analysis, see Stephen M. Walt, "The Search for a Science of Strategy: A Review Essay on *Makers of Modern Strategy*," *International Security* 22 (Summer 1987): 160–162. This interest is missing from the writing of at least three people venturing to document and comment upon the evolution of strategic ideas who have in recent years highlighted Brodie's contribution: Gregg Herken, Fred Kaplan, and David Rosenberg. For various reasons, alluded to elsewhere in this study, the writing of these individuals about Brodie has been less than satisfactory.

Of other broad, critical studies of the evolution of contemporary strategic ideas, the best thus far is Lawrence Freedman, *The Evolution of Nuclear Strategy* (New York: St. Martin's, 1981), which is heavily drawn upon in Freedman's essay, "The First Two Generations of Nuclear Strategists," in Paret, *Makers of Modern Strategy*, 735–778. New analysis of the significance of a large amount of strategic writing, much of it only recently available to the general public, is in Marc Trachtenberg, "Strategic Thought in America, 1952–1966," in *Development of American Strategic Thought, 1961–1969*, 443–484. Also useful is Colin S. Gray, *Strategic Studies: A Critical Assessment* (Westport, Conn.: Greenwood Press, 1982); and Henry S. Rowen, "The Evolution of Strategic Nuclear Doctrine," in *Strategic Thought in the Nuclear Age*, edited by Laurence Martin (Baltimore: Johns Hopkins University Press, 1979), which does not refer to Brodie.

119. Because Sam Cohen, the inventor of the neutron bomb, was then a RAND colleague, Brodie was certain to have known early in the 1960s about the successful development of this weapon system.

120. This point has been gleaned from interviews.

121. This problem has at least two important facets. First, the widely perceived need to protect sensitive information appears to have operated to keep discussions to a broad, general level—that is, to the level at which Brodie characteristically adhered in his postwar work—when interagency exchanges of sensitive information could not be easily expedited. For example, Brig. Gen. William M. Garland, assistant director of air force intelligence, referring in 1952 to information Brodie had requested prior to arriving for a visit at air force headquarters, informed him: "The studies covering the subject in which you are interested [are] in such a state of acceptance and approval by the various staff agencies that we are not in a position to release them for review. . . . It is my personal opinion that discussions such as you held with [Lt.] General [John A.] Samford and myself provide the medium through which broad concepts may be explored and investigated. The same principle also applies to this type briefing which your [that is, RAND] people gave recently to members of the Air Staff" (Garland to Brodie, 4 April 1952, UCLA Collection, Box 1 [G folder]).

A second facet of the discretion problem would have been the tendency to keep discussion of sensitive topics informal, without transcripts. For example, in an important Air War College lecture in 1951 Brodie is recorded as saying the following when discussing the "inadequacies of a purely hard[ware] approach" to strategic bombing: "Maybe the thing to go after is something of more direct political effect than hardware—than depriving them of many extra pounds of gun barrels, etc., etc. Now, that, to me, is a very intriguing subject and I shall try to enlarge upon it next week." "Air Power in an Overall Strategy," Air War College lecture, 23 May 1951, 17, AFHRC, K239.716251-26. No confirmation or record of the follow-on talk exists, an omission notable in light of the many fully recorded Air War College lectures by Brodie.

122. Consistent with the hypothesis that Brodie was inhibited in this fashion are three pieces of otherwise unrelated information. First, only two formal oral debates were documented between Brodie and other members of the RAND staff over the fifteen-year period of Brodie's tenure at RAND. The first debate occurred in 1954 with John Williams, then head of the RAND Mathematics Department, in the RAND "Strategic Objectives Committee" over a preliminary draft of a report ("The Next Ten Years") on which Brodie had collaborated with Charles Hitch and Andrew Marshall. This debate was followed by an exchange of memoranda. The second oral debate, evidently before a larger RAND audience, took place in the early 1960s with Malcolm Hoag over intensifying plans for a conventional war in Europe (the "Hoag Doctrine"). It was reflected in RAND Informal Working Papers and is summarized in chapter 7 of this book. See especially Brodie's "A Critique of the Doctrine of Conventional War in Europe (CWE)," 24 September 1962, RAND Informal Working Paper, in *Development of American Strategic Thought, 1961–1969*, 159–183.

In five other debates involving Brodie for which a written record exists—with Gershon Cooper, C. J. Crain, Vince Taylor, Robert Levine, and another with John Williams—no evidence has surfaced of formal oral interchange.

Second, in at least one instance, Brodie drafted a paper in part because he was dissatisfied with his oral contribution on a prior occasion. See, for example, "Afterthoughts on CWE from the Meeting (with Herr Erler) of April 16," 22 April 1963, UCLA Collection, Box 18 (Folder 2). In this paper, he wrote (p. 3) that his remarks at the meeting in question about "the distinction between deterrence on the one hand and the problems of actually fighting a war on the other . . . were very inept for expressing my meaning."

Finally, although there is evidence that Brodie could be scathingly critical in writing even of colleagues or former colleagues, there is no evidence that he employed such strong criticism in oral exchanges. A published critique that Brodie privately characterized as "mean" can be found in "The McNamara Phenomenon," *World Politics* 17 (July 1965):672–686. For this characterization, see the postscript of Brodie to Gen. Pierre M. Gallois, 10 September 1965, UCLA Collection, Box 1 (G folder).

Should Brodie's restraint in oral argument be confirmed by further study, the combination of this restraint and the vigor of his critical writing might suggest that he compensated in the latter for the frustrations and inhibitions he experienced in interpersonal relations with other strategic analysts.

123. This tendency is illustrated by Brodie's later account of the effects of his dispute with Cabell over one of the reports he had written for Vandenberg. The report, Brodie wrote, "must have been relayed on to Cabell, who was of course incensed that I should have been so critical of the work being done under his jurisdiction. Anyway, my employment for Vandenberg was rather abruptly terminated (I was then on my way from Yale to RAND anyway)." Brodie to Rosenberg, 22 August 1977, UCLA Collection, Box 9 (Folder 21).

Brodie was indeed apparently headed for RAND irrespective of his work for Vandenberg. The start of his full-time association with RAND coincided with his second period of work for Vandenberg, when he took a leave of absence from Yale at the end of the fall 1950 academic term. Nevertheless, Brodie's prior move to RAND did not alter the fact that termination of his employment for Vandenberg had been a major defeat for him.

124. Evidence is put forward in this study for Brodie's frequent intellectual indebtedness to the work of his colleagues.

125. Brodie to DeWeerd, 20 October 1952, UCLA Collection, Box 1 (D folder).

126. Ibid. Inasmuch as this is a recruitment letter, it should be viewed carefully. In it, elaborating on his prior situation at Yale, Brodie wrote: "I was tired of being a maverick among my academic colleagues. I was interested in military and strategic questions and none of my colleagues were, either at Yale or in the profession generally." This statement is difficult to understand, since there are known to have been a number of Yale faculty members with interests in military questions, including Arnold Wolfers.

27. Satisfactory portrayal of the depth and extent of intellectual ferment at RAND, particularly in the 1950s, has yet to be written. See, however, Bruce L. R. Smith, *The RAND Corporation: Case Study of a Non-Profit Advisory Corporation* (Cambridge, Mass.: Harvard University Press, 1966), and Kaplan, *Wizards of Armageddon*.

128. It is for this reason, argues H. Stuart Hughes, that intellectual history is never definitive (*Consciousness and Society*, 6–7).

Chapter 2. Using the Absolute Weapon

1. "Implications for Military Policy," 76. Italics in original. For another contemporary view that peace in the atomic age would need to depend on fear and, in particular, that "fear of retaliation in kind is the surest deterrent against the misuse of atomic energy by an aggressor nation," see Ernest L. Woodward, "The Development of International Society: Approach through Law and Institutions," lecture delivered at the Princeton University Bicentennial Conference, 1946, 2. A copy of the Woodward paper has been found among the Earle Papers, Box 24 (Folder: Princeton Bicentennial Conf.).

2. "The Atomic Bomb as a Weapon," National War College lecture, 6 September 1946, 8–9. Lecture transcript on file at, Air University Library, Maxwell Air Force Base, Montgomery, Ala., M-33507-C.

3. "Implications for Military Policy," 71. A Brodie outline, "Strategic Consequences of the Atomic Bomb," n.d., refers to "threatened brevity of wars." Earle Papers, Box 5 (Folder: Chicago University—Atomic Energy Meeting).

4. "War in the Atomic Age," in Brodie, *Absolute Weapon*, 29. Brodie probably had in mind the effects to morale resulting from the use of the atomic bomb, but he did not make that point

explicit at this time. For an argument that the "horror of the atomic bomb" might not have such an impact, see P. M. S. Blackett, *Military and Political Consequences of Atomic Energy* (London: Turnstile Press, 1948), 56. Blackett wrote that "the power of human beings to 'stick it' is immense; a determined folk will learn to stand atomic bombardment, if that is their fate, just as Germans learnt to stand ordinary bombing." See also note 28 below.

5. "Implications for Military Policy," 71.

6. See "The Morale Factor in STRAP Planning," 5 August 1949, 8 (UCLA Collection, Box 11 [Folder 17]).

7. See especially Jacob Viner, "The Implications of the Atomic Bomb for International Relations," *Proceedings of the American Philosophical Society* 90 (January 1946): 53–58; see also Kaplan, *Wizards of Armageddon*, 47.

8. "Implications for Military Policy," 80. Italics in original.

9. Ibid., 89.

10. Ibid., 77.

11. *Strategy in the Missile Age*, 98.

12. "The war has demonstrated beyond the shadow of a doubt," Brodie wrote in 1946, "that the sky is much too big to permit one side, however superior, to shut out enemy aircraft completely from the air over its territories" ("War in the Atomic Age," 45). This observation glossed over the potency of a bombing force and whether this potency could be reduced by prior bombing attack. A more incisive statement about this problem was made by Brodie in 1952, when he commented upon the "almost comic opera vulnerability of our military structure," which, among other things, allows "our target weapons [to] be stored in three or four sites, the locations of these being very well known to the enemy and each one individually being very slightly guarded." See "Changing Capabilities and War Objectives," in *Development of American Strategic Thought, 1952–1960 (1)*, 87. Pioneering work on the vulnerability of strike-back forces was led by Albert Wohlstetter in the 1950s.

13. Ernest L. Woodward, *Some Political Consequences of the Atomic Bomb* (London: Oxford University Press, 1945), 9.

14. Ibid., 16.

15. As to why, for example, Germany did not begin the Second World War by bombing London and Paris, it appears that the German air force was not designed for bombing cities (see Blackett, *Military and Political Consequences of Atomic Energy*, 9–11). Even had it been designed for city bombing, however, such bombing would not have been inevitable at the start of the war. In a study entitled *Bombs Bursting in Air* (New York: Reynal & Hitchcock, 1939), G. F. Eliot wrote: "Germany's great present advantage is her superiority in the air. If she risks the whole of that air force in a mighty attempt to overwhelm Britain by bombing, it will be the greatest gamble ever undertaken by a major power since Napoleon's invasion of Russia. If it fails, Germany, or at any rate Nazi Germany, is doomed" (65). On the other hand, he argued, a partial bombing effort was unlikely because it would probably not demoralize the English and French populace. Cited from Eliot by Edward Mead Earle in notes entitled "Air Power in International Politics," n.d., Earle Papers, Box 23 (Folder: Theories of Air Power—General).

16. See Alexander L. George and Richard Smoke, *Deterrence in American Foreign Policy: Theory and Practice* (New York: Columbia University Press, 1974).

17. "Implications for Military Policy," 88. Brodie seems to have accepted Robert Oppenheimer's view that atomic bombs, "if they are ever used again . . . may well be used by the thousands, or perhaps by the tens of thousands" (cited in ibid., 73). Oppenheimer believed that atomic bombs would in all likelihood be used for aggressive purposes and by surprise. Brodie presumed that Oppenheimer meant that an aggressor employing such weapons would not have to fear retaliation (ibid.). In the statement quoted here, Brodie accepts that retaliation *would* occur, which leaves unclear why such a war should ever happen.

18. "The Problem of Integrating the Factors of National Strategy," Air War College lecture,

17 March 1950, 2–3 (transcript in AFHRC, K239.716250–12[R]). The same quotation, minus the reference to Clausewitz, was published slightly earlier in "Strategic Implications of the North Atlantic Pact," *Yale Review* 39 (December 1949): 203–204. "I felt," Brodie subsequently declared, "that modern war, modern total war, is much too big, much to [*sic*] violent to fit into any concept of a continuation of diplomacy. I felt that war by its very outbreak must create its own objective— in modern times, survival—in comparison with which all other objectives must hide their diminished heads" ("Changing Capabilities and War Objectives," 64).

An early draft of Brodie's contribution to *The Absolute Weapon* endorsed the Clausewitzian idea of war as a tool of policy. "A nation," he wrote in November 1945, "which had inflicted enormous human and material damage upon another would find it intolerable to stop short of eliciting from the latter an acknowledgment of defeat implemented by a readiness to accept control. Wars, in other words, are fought to be terminated, and to be terminated definitely. Regardless of technological changes, war remains, as Clausewitz put it, an 'instrument of policy,' a means for realizing a political end" (*The Atomic Bomb and American Security*, Yale Institute of International Studies Memorandum 18, 1 November 1945, 9f). The final version ("Implications for Military Policy," 92) deleted the third of these sentences and reproduced the first two sentences, only substituting "definitely" for "decisively." It may be deduced from the omission that Brodie, wholly preoccupied in 1946 with military results in total war, viewed nuclear weapons rather than diplomatic objectives as the key determinant of war termination.

19. On the political objectives of Churchill and Stalin in the Second World War, see Brodie, *War and Politics*, 40–42; on certain political objectives that guided Roosevelt, see John Lewis Gaddis, *Strategies of Containment: A Critical Appraisal of Postwar American National Security Policy* (New York: Oxford University Press, 1982), 4–9; on Hitler's political objectives, see F. H. Hinsley, *Hitler's Strategy* (Cambridge: Cambridge University Press, 1951).

20. Brodie's views on total war, quoted above, seem especially close to those he later ascribed to Douhet (in *Strategy in the Missile Age*, 98–99): "Every war *must* be a total war, regardless of the character of the power waging it, the causes of the conflict, or the original objectives of the statesmen who have let themselves be drawn into it. In fact there can be no meaningful objectives other than survival through the elimination of the threat-posing rival" (italics in original). When he summarized Douhet's views—following development of the hydrogen bomb—Brodie sharply criticized them. Earlier, however, though his own views about atomic warfare at the time seemed to bear a strong resemblance to those of Douhet, there is no record that Brodie ever mentioned Douhet in connection with them. However, his views at this point were not influenced only by those of Douhet. As Brodie repeatedly stated later, the dominant view at air force headquarters at that time was that "modern war means total war" (*Strategy in the Missile Age*, 307). For ideas of strategists (including Douhet) generally, see Earle, *Makers of Modern Strategy*.

21. For essays that provide a political analysis of the atomic bomb, see the contributions of Arnold Wolfers, Percy E. Corbett, and William T. R. Fox to *The Absolute Weapon* and also Ernest L. Woodward, "Development of International Society" and *Some Political Consequences of the Atomic Bomb*.

22. Without the atomic bomb, Brodie wrote, "strategic bombing would, as was certainly true against Germany, influence or determine the decision mainly through its effects on the ground campaigns" ("Implications for Military Policy," 70).

23. Brodie did not make this point as categorically in *The Absolute Weapon* as he did a few years later. In "War in the Atomic Age," he wrote of his belief that the bomb "will not be scarce enough to spare any nation against which it is used from a destruction immeasurably more devastating than that endured by Germany in World War II" (59). In "Implications for Military Policy," he wrote, "All that is being presumed here is the kind of destruction which Germany actually underwent in the last year of the [S]econd World War, only telescoped in time and considerably multiplied in magnitude" (90). His most categorical statement on atomic bombing is in "New Techniques of War and National Policies," in Ogburn, *Technology and International Relations*, 156ff.

24. "Sea Power in the Atomic Age," Naval War College lecture, 19 January 1949, 7 (Naval Historical Collection, Naval War College Library, Newport, Rhode Island, catalog no. 6890–7770; transcript dated 9 March 1949).

25. "The Atom Bomb as Policy Maker," *Foreign Affairs* 27 (October 1948): 25–26. For the view (cited by Brodie in the same article) propounded in ignorance of the atomic bomb, that a Soviet-American war would likely end in stalemate—because "the points of direct [Soviet-American] contact [are] so few and inaccessible [and] the centers are widely separated"—see William T. R. Fox, *The Super Powers* (New York: Harcourt, Brace and Co., 1944), 102–103, 106. Fox speculated that widespread awareness of this condition would discourage Soviet-American hostilities.

Deterrence of attack can come from an inability to make war as well as (especially today) from a fear about its consequences. But the major difference between these two types of deterrence is that the first says practically nothing about strategy, whereas the second requires placing strategy at the center of political preoccupations.

26. For a case in which new weapons had not been properly integrated among existing ones at the start of war, see Michael Howard, *The Franco-Prussian War* (New York: Macmillan, 1981), 36.

27. "Strategy as a Science," *World Politics* 1 (July 1949): 485f.

28. *Strategy in the Missile Age*, 6. Jacob Viner made Brodie aware of Adam Smith's point that "there is a great deal of ruin in a nation." See Viner to Brodie, 4 May 1954, UCLA Collection, Box 2 (V folder). Although there were other reasons (I discuss later) for initially focusing on cities as atomic targets, the attempt to take into account Smith's point was probably also a factor.

29. Brodie wrote in 1955: "The fact that the emphasis continued to be on strategic bombing is certainly not proved wrong by the experience of World War II, . . . but it does recall Samuel Johnson's observation on the second marriage of a widower as representing 'the triumph of faith over experience'" ("Some Notes on the Evolution of Air Doctrine," *World Politics* 7 [April 1955]: 365).

Brodie obviously attached the highest importance to strategic bombing in the first years after Hiroshima, but not because he knew a great deal about such bombing. "If war breaks out in the near future," he declared in a 1951 lecture, "the bald, inescapable fact, it seems to me, is that we must win primarily through our strategic bombing and that for the simple reason that we have almost no other kind of genuinely offensive capabilities. We have nothing else" ("Air Power in an Overall Strategy," Air War College lecture, 23 May 1951, 4 [AFHRC, K239.716251-26]).

30. *Atomic Bomb and American Security*, 2f. This statement does not appear in *The Absolute Weapon*, which took account, as the earlier draft did not, of an interim stage of scarcity of nuclear bombs. Compare with note 69 below.

31. David Rosenberg, "The Origins of Overkill: Nuclear Weapons and American Strategy, 1945–1960," *International Security* 7 (Spring 1983): 7. Italics in original.

32. Ibid., 14.

33. Compare Brodie's later observation that the first nuclear bombs were as much tactical as strategic weapons (*Strategy in the Missile Age*, 325).

34. "New Techniques of War and National Policies," 155.

35. Ibid., 165. This point seemed to suggest potential diplomatic use for atomic weapons, but in a 1950 lecture, Brodie was not optimistic about such use. "Concerning the relations of military posture to diplomacy and vice versa," he observed, "I think we run into great danger of exaggeration. I hold that the relationship of foreign policy to military strength is indirect and, so far as day to day decisions are concerned, quite irrelevant. Military power is a guarantee of our ability to meet the final challenge which any or all of . . . our policies may provoke. Our military strength gives us room for policy maneuver. But that is a very different thing from insisting, as it has now become fashionable to insist, that our foreign and our military policies are two aspects of the same thing" ("The Problem of Integrating the Factors of National Strategy," 4).

For Brodie's suggestion that "it is easy to be oversubtle concerning the political consequences of our present monopoly of the bomb," see "Atom Bomb as Policy Maker," 29.

36. "New Techniques of War and National Policies," 167 (italics in original). "The burdens

of diplomacy" that Brodie had in mind are not fully clear. The role of diplomats in preventing war, which required diplomatic coercion and threats, needed to be distinguished from the free hand given diplomats by widespread fear of war. Presumably, the case under discussion here highlighted the latter.

Brodie did not seem to allow that a state lacking military superiority over its rival could coerce it. Since, according to him, two rivals relatively equal in military strength lacked coercive capability over each other, they had good reason to act cautiously.

37. "Implications for Military Policy," 73. For this idea he cited Viner's "Implications of the Atomic Bomb" (see note 7 above).

38. Initial discussions of the atomic bomb seem to have focused on the bomb's destructive potential rather than on its threat value. See, for example, note 23 above.

Blackett contended in 1948 that "much of the earlier discussion of atomic bombs and their effect on warfare . . . seems to have been vitiated by an exaggerated idea of the military results of a few bombs dropped on the civilian population of cities" *(Military and Political Consequences of Atomic Energy,* 80). But the threat value of atomic bombs, if any, would have to be taken into account when calculating the "military results" of bomb attacks.

39. "Implications for Military Policy," 94–95.

40. "War in the Atomic Age," 58–59. Oppenheimer indicated (cited in Blackett, *Military and Political Consequences of Atomic Energy,* 80f) that perhaps two years would be required to accumulate a thousand bombs if a country knew how to make them and manufactured them in peacetime in atomic plants.

41. "War in the Atomic Age," 59.

42. "Atom Bomb as Policy Maker," 28. In fact, because the Atomic Energy Commission, regulator of bomb production, worried that a higher production rate might push up the bomb's unit cost, the rate was apparently no higher than about three a month in the middle of 1948 (Brodie, *War and Politics,* 64f; Rosenberg, "Origins of Overkill," 14).

"In 1951," Herman Kahn wrote later, "there was still much talk of the scarcity of uranium, a view which was reinforced by most of the technical people. Few people in or out of government thought of the atom bomb as soon being plentiful; nobody realized that practical and convenient thermonuclear bombs would be available before long" ("The Arms Race and Some of Its Hazards," in *Arms Control, Disarmament, and National Security,* edited by Donald G. Brennan [New York: George Braziller, 1961], 110).

43. "New Techniques of War and National Policies," 158.

44. Ibid. In 1946, when Brodie anticipated larger atomic bomb stockpiles, he estimated ("War in the Atomic Age," 43) that five hundred bombs would be necessary to eliminate enemy industrial plants and that up to five thousand bombs would cover heavy wastage in a bombing attack. The wastage would offset the effects of enemy defenses (which Brodie stressed), as well as bombing inaccuracy (which he neglected). In the later estimate mentioned here, Brodie did not provide a higher figure to cover wastage; it appears instead (especially from the discussion above) that he intended the figure of one hundred bombs to include wastage.

If the one hundred bombs included wastage, the remaining number of bombs that would reach their targets could be quite low. Presuming that Soviet defenses enjoyed the effectiveness against incoming bombers postulated by Brodie in 1946, and provided that some bombers were sent as decoys to distract Soviet defenses, only thirty out of three hundred or forty out of four hundred attacking bombers would survive. The surviving bombers would not all be atomic carriers. Further diminution of bombing effectiveness would occur from inaccurate bombing or heavy Soviet fighter and antiaircraft resistance.

Finally, adequate reckoning of overall bombing effects also had to take account of formidable bomb delivery problems never considered by Brodie. In 1948, for example, shipping bomb assemblies abroad in medium-range B-29 bombers upon the outbreak of war was an enormous problem. In addition, as Gregg Herken noted, "the number of atomic bombs that could be used in a single attack was one hundred, but the government as of fall 1948 still lacked sufficient bomb-assembly teams to prepare that entire number at one time" (*The Winning Weapon: The Atomic Bomb in the Cold War, 1945–1950* [New York: Vintage Books, 1982], 386f). For all these reasons, the actual destruction obtainable from a relatively small three-figure bomb stockpile did not support optimism about the decisiveness of such destruction, at least in relation to damage caused to Germany and Japan in the previous war.

However, it is not likely Brodie would have put forward his three-figure threshold without having thought about the explosive effect of a relatively small number of bombs. He remained as confident in 1949 as he was in 1946 — even when faced with a wide variety of estimates about bomb production (see, for example, "Sea Power in the Atomic Age," 7) — that atomic bombing would be decisive. But this confidence would have had to be supported by evidence of nonmaterial bombing effects; information below confirms that Brodie did have these effects in mind in this regard.

45. "Atom Bomb as Policy Maker," 31.

46. "Sea Power in the Atomic Age," 7.

47. "Atom Bomb as Policy Maker," 31.

48. "As long as the truth of the atomic arms race is buried in a very few informed minds (and often pushed back out of daily consideration even by those who know the truth), there is no possibility of framing policy in such a fashion as to take due account of the national danger" (McGeorge Bundy, "Early Thoughts on Controlling the Nuclear Arms Race: A Report to the Secretary of State," January 1953, in *International Security* 7 [Fall 1982]: 20).

49. See note 29 above.

50. In such circumstances, planners would understandably think of nuclear weapons largely in terms of weapons of the past. But Brodie saw them as entirely *distinctive* and not appropriately measured in terms of their predecessors.

51. "New Techniques of War and National Policies," 153–154. In another 1949 lecture ("Sea Power in the Atomic Age," 15), Brodie cited as "perhaps most important" among the consequences of the atomic bomb, when compared with its predecessors, "the matter of psychological impact, the terror effects of the atomic bomb, the proportion of which we can scarcely begin to predict." According to Kaplan (*Wizards of Armageddon*, 50), Brodie had been among those at Yale who in 1949 "had done some consulting work on psychological warfare for the RAND Corporation."

52. "War in the Atomic Age," 25n.

53. "Navy Department Thinking on the Atomic Bomb," *Bulletin of the Atomic Scientists* 3 (July 1947): 179.

54. Ibid. These sentences imply that Brodie did not anticipate that bombers carrying atomic bombs would be accompanied by fighters. He also did not seem to have allowed that a very large bomber buildup would make these technological handicaps less pressing in bombing operations. I discuss both of these points later.

55. Asher Lee, "Trends in Aerial Defense," *World Politics* 7 (January 1955): 251.

56. Harry R. Borowski, *The Hollow Threat* (Westport, Conn.: Greenwood Press, 1982), 104–105.

57. "Changing Capabilities and War Objectives," 70. On expected attrition rates from bombing operations, see Anthony Cave Brown, ed., *Dropshot* (New York: Dial Press/James Wade, 1978), 24–27.

58. Lee, "Trends in Aerial Defense," 254.

59. Ibid., 252–253. The basis for Lee's 25 percent figure is unclear.

60. Ibid., 248.

61. Blackett, *Military and Political Consequences of Atomic Energy*, 54.

62. Borowski, *Hollow Threat*, 164–165.

63. "A Critique of Army and Navy Thinking on the Atomic Bomb," *Bulletin of the Atomic Scientists* 3 (August 1947): 207–208. For Brodie's calculation underlying this wastage level, see note 44 above. The residual number of bombs would have to be directed at preventing enemy retaliation in kind, Brodie noted, but he did not explain how enemy air forces would also be destroyed in

air attacks aimed at enemy cities. In all probability, Brodie would not have been able to do so, for the large wastage that he accepted seems to depend on the assumption that atomic bomb attacks would cause heavy damage to cities. See below.

That nuclear weapons capabilities made decisive bombing feasible, even with high bomber attrition, was argued by Maj. Gen. Orvil A. Anderson, who headed the military advisory committee of the Pacific division of the U.S. Strategic Bombing Survey (USSBS). See Robert F. Futrell, "Air Power in World War II," in Monro MacCloskey, *The United States Air Force* (New York: Praeger, 1967), 40. Brodie claimed to have spoken with Anderson on the subject of strategic bombing. See Brodie to Earle, 15 August 1950, Earle Papers, Box 10 (B folder).

64. This was implied, for example, by Brodie's insistence ("War in the Atomic Age," 34) that the atomic bomb, once introduced, would probably not be met by adequate defensive adjustment.

65. "New Techniques of War and National Policies," 158 (italics in original). He seems, for example, to have had in mind cities as targets when he declared in a 1949 lecture that "the amount of damage effected by one atomic bomb is so much greater than that effected by conventional explosives . . . [and] you have so much greater acceptable cost per sortie that you have a situation where it is not necessary to get back the planes which have successfully dropped the atomic bomb. In other words, you can accept 100 percent losses in planes" ("Sea Power in the Atomic Age," 13–14).

66. Kahn, "Arms Race and Some of Its Hazards," 110.

67. "Implications for Military Policy," 99.

68. "New Techniques of War and National Policies," 153. By 1948, however, the view that "the atomic bomb in its minimum efficient size is necessarily of 'city buster' destructiveness" was being undermined by weapons tests, notably the Sandstone series in 1948, which reportedly demonstrated that atomic bomb yields could be made smaller than those exploded at Hiroshima and Nagasaki. This would also permit the development of vastly increased numbers of nuclear bombs by economizing on fissile material. These tests, of which Brodie was apparently not at first aware, soon altered American planners' estimates about projected bomb stockpiles. Results from the Sandstone tests not only permitted the development of highly varied and smaller-yield bombs and more selective targeting but also undermined Brodie's earliest assumptions about easy mating of large bombs and large targets. See Rosenberg, "Origins of Overkill," 19.

Insofar as he maintained that "everything about the atomic bomb is overshadowed by the twin facts that it exists and that its destructive power is fantastically great" ("War in the Atomic Age," 52), Brodie would have had difficulty discussing substandard-yield nuclear weapons.

69. "We can see at once," Brodie wrote, "that it does not require the obliteration of all its towns to make a nation wholly incapable of defending itself in the traditional fashion. Thus, the number of *critical* targets is quite limited, and the number of hits necessary to win a strategic decision— always excepting the matter of retaliation—is correspondingly limited. That does not mean that additional hits would be useless but simply that diminishing returns would set in early; and after the cities of, say, 100,000 population were eliminated the returns from additional bombs expended would decline drastically" ("War in the Atomic Age," 48; italics in original).

70. See p. 35.

71. See note 23 above.

72. At the extreme, very large numbers of atomic bombs might be viewed "as just another and better kind of ammunition" (Bundy, "Early Thoughts on Controlling the Nuclear Arms Race," 10). But a plentiful bomb supply had to be distinguished from a plentiful supply of bombers, the attainment of which, as I noted, caused far greater long-term problems.

73. Some planners were so optimistic about these operations that they were unconcerned about bombing losses. See, for example, Bob Considine, "3,000-Man Raids Tie Up Millions of Foes, 55% of Nazi Fighters," *Washington Post*, 12 September 1943 (included in Earle Papers, Box 21 [folder: Air Power]). "We could have lost every bomber and every man on the Regensberg raid," Considine quoted an unnamed general as saying, "when we knocked out 35 per cent of Germany's Messer-schmidt fighter production, and yet it would have been a victory for us—so great was the damage

done to the enemy." See also David Irving, *The War between the Generals* (New York: Congdon & Lattes, 1981), 67.

According to Robert F. Futrell, "During the late 1940's and early 1950's, air leaders would believe that they could safely ignore Soviet defenses and plan to attack targets without first attaining control of the air" ("Air Power in World War II," 41). Only later, according to Futrell, did they give primacy to destroying the enemy air force.

74. "New Techniques of War and National Policies," 158. Compare this quotation with Futrell's observation in note 73 above. In other writings (for example, "Sea Power in the Atomic Age," 9), by "bolder use" of bombs, Brodie meant more wasteful use. On his discussion of wasteful bomb use, see above.

75. "Strategy as a Science," 478. Elsewhere, Brodie associated this idea with the strategist Douhet. See, for example, "Strategic Bombing: What It Can Do," *Reporter* 3 (August 1950): 30.

76. "Strategy as a Science," 478.

77. "Changing Capabilities and War Objectives," 71.

78. "Strategy as a Science," 474–475.

79. "Strategic Implications of the North Atlantic Pact," 205–206.

80. "Strategic Bombing: What It Can Do," 31.

81. The same point was made by Brodie about the writings of Douhet. See "Some Notes on the Evolution of Air Doctrine," 350–351.

82. "I say we must confine ourselves to broad outlines because we are likely enough to be in error even if we do so, and are *bound* to be in error if we try to construct the details as well" ("Sea Power in the Atomic Age," 23; italics in original).

83. By contrast, Brodie's later analyses of fusion weapons focused so much on the tremendous destructive potential of those weapons that he questioned whether *any* security interests of nuclear powers justified their use.

84. Kaplan, *Wizards of Armageddon,* 29.

85. See note 20 above.

86. "Changing Capabilities and War Objectives," 71–72.

87. "Post-War Strategy," in *The Soviet Air and Rocket Forces,* edited by Asher Lee (New York: Praeger, 1959), 100.

Chapter 3. Using History: Morale as a Bombing Target

1. Secretary of Defense James Forrestal sought to repair this deficiency when he requested the Joint Chiefs of Staff (JCS) in October 1948 to examine the "psychological aspects of atomic bombing on the Soviet will to wage war." Kenneth W. Condit, *The History of the Joint Chiefs of Staff: The Joint Chiefs and National Policy,* vol. 2 (1947–1949) (Wilmington, Del.: Michael Glazier, 1979), 382.

2. Reference to Brodie's participation in this work is in Kaplan, *Wizards of Armageddon,* 50. For Brodie's prior work in the U.S. Navy's Psychological Warfare Staff organization during World War II, see chap. 1, n. 9. Konrad Kellen, who also participated in psychological warfare operations during the Second World War, has written: "I prefer not to dwell on the incomparably stronger effect Sykewar has had on those who conducted it than on those who were subjected to it. Those who conducted it—exposed as they were to the most gruelling type of self-suggestion—have never been the same afterward. For them, their job was a psychological Hiroshima" (cited in Daniel Lerner, *Psychological Warfare against Nazi Germany* [Cambridge, Mass.: MIT Press, 1971, first published 1949], 313).

3. RAND Warning Papers. Gen. Lauris Norstad, who as air force vice chief of staff had recruited Brodie for service within the Air Staff, used this RAND research as the basis for his 1950 decision on behalf of the air force to issue warnings to enemy populations prior to attacking Korean

cities (included in a listing of "Examples of RAND Payoffs," in "Memo of General Information on Project RAND," 24 February 1955, 4. Authorship uncertain; declassified and released to the present writer from the files of the Air Force Directorate of Intelligence, Headquarters Air Force Intelligence Agency, Fort Belvoir, Virginia.

Evidently aware of this decision, Brodie specifically pointed to the goodwill potential "inherent in the accuracy of our bombings in [Korea] and the fact that we frequently issued warnings prior to attacks on urban areas" (cited by William T. Golden in Golden to Sidney Souers, 11 May 1951, Golden Papers [folder: Sidney Souers]).

4. Brodie, "Strategy as a Science," 473–474. "You never fail to point out," Paul Kecskemeti wrote to him in spelling out this interest, "that one cannot put past to profit unless he makes a determined effort to allow for changes in the 'boundary conditions'" (Paul Kecskemeti to Brodie, 29 May [1953?], UCLA Collection, Box 1 [K folder]).

5. Lowe Critique, 5.

6. Cited in Kaplan, *Wizards of Armageddon*, 47–48. In a 1982 article, Kaplan contended that Brodie, by the time of his service for General Vandenberg, was seeking city-sparing strategies for nuclear weapons attack ("Strategic Thinkers," *Bulletin of the Atomic Scientists* 38 [December 1982]: 52).

Brodie by no means advocated sparing cities altogether, as will be seen, but he sometimes played down the destruction entailed in use of the threat of more attacks to come. In an unpublished fragment, "Schlesinger's Old-New Ideas," undated but evidently written in 1974 when Secretary of Defense James R. Schlesinger made important statements on nuclear weapons targeting, Brodie wrote very summarily: "It happens that I contributed in a report to General Hoyt Vandenberg, then Chief of Staff of the Air Force, the suggestion that we should slow down the proposed delivery rate of nuclear weapons—after all, the Soviet Union at that time had virtually none—on the ground that there was more strategic leverage in holding cities hostage than in making corpses." He went on to say that this proposal "could not make much headway with the military, particularly with a General LeMay, who argued that the 'principles of war' required concentration of effort in time as well as space. In those days the military were the academics, not the professors" (this fragment, a copy of which is found in the UCLA Collection, Box 33 [Folder 8], was kindly given to me by Prof. Fawn Brodie).

7. "Strategic Implications of the North Atlantic Pact," *Yale Review* 39 (December 1949): 206.

8. Brodie, "Strategic Air Attacks on Enemy Morale: Present Meaning of World War II Experience," 6 January 1953, 9, RAND Informal Working Paper, in "Fourteen Informal Writings from the Unpublished Work of Bernard Brodie, 1952–1965," a collection of internal working papers assembled by the RAND Corporation, 1980. This paper is cited henceforth as "Strategic Air Attacks," and the collection in which it is included as "Fourteen Informal Writings."

The RAF bomber commander Arthur Harris wrote similarly that "in the last months of the war [against Germany] the loss of production resulting from the destruction of cities became really disastrous" (*Bomber Offensive* [New York: Macmillan, 1947], 262).

9. Brodie, "Strategic Bombing: What It Can Do," *Reporter* 3 (August 1950): 30.

10. Ibid.

11. Brodie, "The Morale Factor in STRAP Planning," 5 August 1949, UCLA Collection, Box 11 (Folder 17), 3. Inasmuch as the first page of this memorandum indicates Brodie was affiliated with the RAND Corporation, and since it roughly fits the time at which the psychological warfare study was done at Yale for the RAND Corporation (see Kaplan, *Wizards of Armageddon*, 50), the memorandum may have represented Brodie's contribution to this study. A copy of this paper apparently does not exist in the records of the RAND Corporation.

For the basis of these ideas, see *The Effects of Strategic Bombing on German Morale*, USSBS Report no. 64b (European War) (Washington, D.C.: Government Printing Office, 1947), 7 and 42ff; reproduced in *The United States Strategic Bombing Survey*, edited by David MacIsaac, vol. 4 (New York: Garland, 1976). The latter edition is henceforth cited as "MacIsaac Collection."

12. Harris, *Bomber Offensive*, 191–192.

13. *Effects of Strategic Bombing on German Morale*, 1. See also ibid., 65.

14. Charles Webster and Noble Frankland, *The Strategic Air Offensive against Germany, 1939–1945*, vol. 1 (London: Her Majesty's Stationery Office, 1961), 296–297.

"The policy underlying the RAF attacks," declared a member of the British target selection staff during the war, "particularly in the early days, was that cities should be the target, and if you dehoused people, you would prevent them working in factories, and thus lower the rate of production. The effect of the RAF raids on housing was very severe, because they set out to attack the centers of cities, which are more apt to be the [*sic*] residential and commercial in character, with the industrial area on the outskirts. "The typical German city, like the typical British or American city, consists of a downtown city center, surrounded by the residential area, and the factories are apt to be located around the margin of the city. Therefore, the typical RAF raid will do more non-industrial than industrial damage" ("Damage Caused by Strategic Bombing," lecture delivered by Dr. Barger to the USSBS staff in Washington, D.C., 19 December 1944, 4, in Record Group 243 [Records of the United States Strategic Bombing Survey], General Correspondence, catalog no. 314.7 [USSBS Division Histories, 1944], Box 25, National Archives. This collection is cited henceforth as "USSBS Records").

15. Webster and Frankland, *Strategic Air Offensive against Germany*, 1:281. British evaluation of German air attacks against Britain early in the war contributed to this error. "In the [1940] attack on Coventry," Harris wrote, "which seemed to the enemy so successful that they proposed to make it a standard of all bombing and call any city 'Coventrated' if it had endured similar damage, about one hundred acres in the centre of the town were devastated. Coventry was a large and important town, with the great majority of its inhabitants engaged in war industries; the light engineering industries of Coventry were almost indispensable to the production of a great range of weapons and war equipment. On the day after this attack production in all the war factories of the town was one-third of what it had been before. Some damage had been done to the factories themselves, but it was very slight compared with non-industrial damage. The loss of production was almost entirely due to the interruption of public utilities, the dislocation of transport, and absenteeism caused by the destruction of houses, and many other causes. There was very heavy damage, for example, to sewers, water supply pipes, electric cables, gas pipes and so forth, and this had an immediate effect on production. Output was back to normal again in about two months, but there were special circumstances which led us to believe that production would not recover so quickly in Germany as in England. War industries in Britain were not fully expanded at the time of the German attacks on us, and there was therefore much labour to spare for the work of repair" (*Bomber Offensive*, 86–87).

The first RAF attack based on this conception was the thousand bomber raid upon Cologne in May 1942, an episode unprecedented not only for the scale of the attack but also for the decision to broaden the scope of the attack to include the center of a German city as well as industrial concentrations at the periphery. The attack, aimed at economic supports for industry rather than war production per se, appears to have done relatively little damage to German war production (Webster and Frankland, *Strategic Air Offensive against Germany*, 1:485–486).

16. Martin Middlebrook, *The Battle of Hamburg* (New York: Charles Scribner's Sons, 1981), 280.

17. Galbraith, *A Life in Our Times: Memoirs* (Boston: Houghton, Mifflin, 1981), 205–206. According to Speer, area bombing against Hamburg (and also Cologne in the same year) assisted his efforts to gain more thorough economic mobilization, including the closing of civilian plants (see Burton H. Klein, *Germany's Economic Preparations for War* [Cambridge, Mass.: Harvard University Press, 1959], 232).

When Brodie observed in 1959 (*Strategy in the Missile Age*, 121) that "there was immense destruction and damage wrought on the buildings in German cities, and it is really surprising that the war industries gathered in those cities should have suffered so little impairment or loss of production," he evidently meant that those implementing the RAF air campaign were surprised. Compare his appraisal of the American bombing of Japan below.

18. *The Effects of Strategic Bombing on the German War Economy*, USSBS Report no. 3 (European

War) (Washington, D.C.: Government Printing Office, 1945), 14; reproduced in the MacIsaac Collection, vol. 1.

19. Brodie does not appear to have commented on the German morale collapse of 1918, which seems to have strengthened RAF determination to aim at the same result. In the earlier case strategic bombing was not important (see Harold D. Lasswell, *Propaganda Technique in the World War* [New York: Alfred A. Knopf, 1927], and George G. Bruntz, *Allied Propaganda and the Collapse of the German Empire in 1918* [Stanford, Calif.: Stanford University Press, 1938]).

20. *Effects of Strategic Bombing on the German War Economy*, 39.

21. Ibid., 159–161.

22. See "Area Bombing and Direct Morale Effects" below.

23. "Morale Factor in STRAP Planning," 9–10, 12–13.

24. *Strategy in the Missile Age*, 123. Italics in original.

25. Harris, *Bomber Offensive*, 265. Presumably, the size of the bomber force could have been significantly reduced from that which Harris thought was required had atomic bombs been available for his projected air campaign.

26. *Strategy in the Missile Age*, 121.

27. Harris, *Bomber Offensive*, 88.

28. Ibid., 87.

29. Almond, "The Size and Composition of the Anti-Nazi Opposition," n.d., 18, in USSBS Records, catalog no. 64.b.t.(8), Box 77. Almond noted in this connection the "special severity of the bombing of Cologne, a Catholic city never fertile soil for Nazism," which received twice the overall tonnage of bombs in proportion to area and population as did Hamburg. The bombing of Cologne, he observed, "appears to have created hostility toward the Allies. The question on all sides was, 'Why should Cologne, a city in which the Nazis had one of their weakest footholds, suffer the most severe and most continuous bombing of all?'"

30. For example, an RAF staff memorandum in August 1944 noted that few able-bodied men in Germany between the ages of seventeen and forty-five were outside the army or the police and that the police were able to quell public dissatisfaction "even in areas where morale has been greatly affected for a time by prolonged and intensive air attacks." The memorandum concluded, therefore, that "it is unlikely that fluctuations in civilian morale will have any decisive influence upon the [German] High Command until its authority has already been greatly weakened by other causes and the machinery of repression has begun to break down" (Webster and Frankland, *Strategic Air Offensive against Germany* 3:54). On the other hand, even if morale were not decisive in itself, it was generally believed that morale attacks could hasten victory gained in other ways (ibid., 54–55).

31. *Strategy in the Missile Age*, 121.

32. Solly Zuckerman, *From Apes to Warlords* (London: Hamish Hamilton, 1978), 362. The major weapon in RAF attacks against cities was the four-pound incendiary bomb (Harris, *Bomber Offensive*, 161).

Martin Middlebrook cited as "probably the most important single development in the part played by the R.A.F. in the bombing war" the use of low-level target marking, which "opened up immense possibilities" through greater bombing accuracy. By adding to RAF concentrated attack, low-level target marking undoubtedly facilitated more destructive bombing of German cities (Middlebrook, *Battle of Hamburg*, 362).

33. For the failure of a bombing attack against Chemnitz, which followed up the attack against Dresden, see Middlebrook, *Battle of Hamburg*, 154ff.

34. Ibid., 322–323. Harris wrote after the war, "It was in point of fact a physical impossibility for Bomber Command, at this stage of its expansion and equipment [that is, in the period following the attack against Hamburg], to do what, in Speer's opinion, would have brought the war quickly to an end. Even with all the luck in the world, we could not have hoped to destroy in a brief space of time six more great cities as effectively as Hamburg had been destroyed" (*Bomber Offensive*, 180).

35. Webster and Frankland, *Strategic Air Offensive against Germany*, 1:392.

36. According to the official Bomber Command history, "From the Lübeck attack, . . . though the defences at the target were light, twelve Bomber Command aircraft failed to return. Anti-aircraft fire was intense on the route. . . . From the observations of returning crews, it was estimated that flak had brought down seven of the missing aircraft. It was also noticed that night fighters were 'unusually active.' No fewer than fifteen attacks and thirteen interceptions were reported. In these encounters ten bombers were damaged and it seemed likely that at least three more were destroyed.

"The missing rate in this attack on a particularly easy target was, therefore, rather more than five per cent of the sorties despatched and this was a casualty rate which Bomber Command could not afford to sustain for many months if it was to remain an effective fighting force. . . . Bomber Command losses . . . were gradually increasing and . . . were approaching the dangerous level which towards the end of 1941 had temporarily checked the offensive" (ibid., 398–399).

37. Harris, *Bomber Offensive*, 83.

38. "The Problem of Integrating the Factors of National Strategy," Air War College lecture, 17 March 1950, 2 (transcript in AFHRC, K239.716250-12[R]). In this unpublished lecture, Brodie characterized the British area bombing method in stronger terms than in his published work, terming it "inhumane" as well as "militarily wasteful."

39. "Strategic Bombing: What It Can Do," 31.

40. Zuckerman, *From Apes to Warlords*, 362–363.

41. F. M. Sallagar, *The Road to Total War: Escalation in World War II*, RAND Report R-465-PR, April 1969, 161–162. Klein concluded in *Germany's Economic Preparations for War* that "the mistake of Sir Arthur Harris and his followers is simply that they anticipated history in imputing to their blockbusters the destructive power of atomic bombs" (235).

42. David Irving, *The Destruction of Dresden* (London: William Kimber, 1963), 158. See also ibid., 45.

43. Ibid., 154. Italics in original.

44. I discuss this later in the chapter.

45. See chapter 2, note 29.

46. *Strategy in the Missile Age*, 138. See also note 69 below.

47. Herken, *Winning Weapon*, 266.

48. Thomas H. Etzold and John Lewis Gaddis, eds., *Containment: Documents on American Policy and Strategy, 1945–1950* (New York: Columbia University Press, 1978), 362.

49. "Strategic Implications of the North Atlantic Pact," 206 (italics in original). For detailed discussion of the coordination of the air offensive with land operations, see chapter 4 in this book. According to a conference memorandum found in the USSBS records, "Mass raids on industrial centers, as conceived by some theorists, appeared to Army Air Corps officers to require very great forces at [*sic*] aircraft in order to achieve significant results. The sustaining sources of enemy military strength, it was felt, might be critically impaired by the destruction of key targets in various industrial systems. It was thought that this form of attack would require fewer numbers of aircraft than area attacks; on the other hand, it necessitated the development of the long-range heavy bomber, the precision bomb sight, defensive fire power and of the necessary techniques to reach and attack the objectives" ("Memorandum for the Vice Chairman, U.S. Strategic Bombing Survey, Re: Conference with Major General Muir S. Fairchild, U.S.A.," 28 October 1944, 1–2, in USSBS Records, General Correspondence, catalog no. 337 [Conferences, Military, Naval, and Other], Box 37).

One plausible reason for the requirement of heavier attack in area raids than in attacks against specific industrial systems was that the latter depended much more than the former on target intelligence. I discuss this point in chapter 4.

50. "Morale Factor in STRAP Planning," 1.

51. Brodie, "Must We Shoot from the Hip?" (see chap. 1, n. 20), 262 (italics in original). In a letter to Col. Richard Weller, 18 September 1953, (UCLA Collection, Box 9 [Folder 17]), Brodie wrote of disagreeing with four economists who had served on the USSBS staff and who disputed

the view that the Allied bombing of Germany "made a really significant contribution to the winning of the war." "When I talked with these persons," he wrote, "I argued the opposite point of view from theirs and suggested to them that they were biased in favor of purely economic results." See also Weller to Brodie, 14 September 1953, ibid.

52. See David MacIsaac, *Strategic Bombing in World War Two: The Story of the United States Strategic Bombing Survey* (New York: Garland, 1976), 101. For further analysis of Allied bombing of German economic targets, see chapter 4 in this book.

53. *Effects of Strategic Bombing on German Morale*, 30.

54. Ibid.

55. See, for example, "U.S. Concentrations of Industry and Population as Target Systems," Air Staff memorandum prepared for assistant chief of staff, G-2 Intelligence, U.S. Army, 14 September 1951, in National Archives USAF Intelligence Collection, Box 60 (folder: document nos. 2-2100 to 2-21199). "It cannot be said for certain," indicated this memorandum, "that the total population merits a high priority as a target for air attack with atomic bombs. Preliminary studies by the Allied Vulnerability Branch indicate that population *per se* is an extremely costly target even for atomic attack to destroy a sufficient percentage to physically affect the national war potential. It is a fact that in each metropolitan area the number of workers in manufacturing are [*sic*] on the order of 10 to 20 per cent of the total population."

This memorandum failed to consider how nuclear explosions could affect people without killing them. By contrast, American atomic scientists admitted to having underestimated, in their work prior to Hiroshima, the psychological effect of the very great light emitted from nuclear explosions, a phenomenon that some speculated might have been adapted to an atomic demonstration as an alternative to the actual Hiroshima attack (Alice Kimball Smith, *A Peril and a Hope* [Cambridge, Mass.: MIT Press, 1965], 49).

56. 'Strategic Air Attacks," 9.

57. "Morale Factor in STRAP Planning," 11.

58. "Strategic Air Attacks," 15–16. "I have argued," he recollected in 1957, "in print, as early as 1950, that a big and successful atomic blitz might very well incapacitate the government of the target state to the degree that it was unable to surrender" (memorandum, Brodie to George K. Tanham, 31 July 1957, UCLA Collection, Box 1 [B folder]). It remains unclear which of his writings Brodie had in mind in this observation.

59. "New Techniques of War and National Policies," in Ogburn, ed., *Technology and International Relations*, 152. The same point is made in "Sea Power in the Atomic Age," Naval War College lecture, 19 January 1949, 9–11 (Naval Historical Collection, Naval War College Library, Newport, R.I., catalog no. 6890-7770; transcript dated 9 March 1949). Compare Lewis Ridenour, "The Bomb and Blackett," *World Politics* 1 (March 1949): 397.

60. In his Tanham memorandum (see note 58 above), Brodie wrote: "It seems to me clear that the incidence of casualties relative to property damage will be disproportionately higher—and very much so—for atomic bombs as against HE [heavy explosives]. I have in mind not only the radiation factor, but, and perhaps more importantly, the warning factor. With HE and incendiaries it took at best several hours to bomb a city that could now go up in a single instant." He went on to state in a footnote that "because of its duration, in other words, HE bombing can never be wholly without warning."

Not easily reconciled with this statement was Brodie's assertion that there was general agreement in RAND, in connection with the question of whether people or industrial facilities should be targeted in atomic attack, "that some measure of warning is likely even if the attacker does not offer it" ("Must We Shoot from the Hip?" 262). But in 1949 he observed that "so long as the atomic bomb is carried in a single aircraft the problem of providing adequate warning of impending attack must be far greater than in the case of HE attacks, even if we assume that in many if not most cases the A-bomb carrying plane will have to be escorted by several decoys and perhaps fighter planes" (Morale Factor in STRAP Planning," 9). See also *Strategy in the Missile Age*, 158.

61. According to one account, the population of Hiroshima, put at three hundred twenty thou-

sand before the city was attacked in August 1945, dropped to five or six thousand by the week afterward. See Mark Gayn, *Japan Diary* (New York: William Sloane Associates, 1948), 267.

62. Kecskemeti, "Dispersal of Populations in Germany, 1944–1945," 17 June 1949, included in RAND Warning Papers, D-32.

63. See "The Value of the Threat of More Attacks to Come," below.

64. "Morale Factor in STRAP Planning," 13.

65. He was interested in finding out in 1949 "how much . . . the structural integrity of the Russian Communist system depend[s] upon personal identification with the top leadership" and whether "the top leadership [was] unavoidably committed, as was Hitler, to last ditch resistance in the event of total war" (ibid., 6).

66. Brodie, "Air Power in an Overall Strategy" Air War College lecture, 23 May 1951, 15 (AFHRC, K239.716251-26).

67. "Must We Shoot From the Hip?" 240. "The Air Force, or at least those who believed in the emergency target list," he wrote much later about that period, "simply expected the Soviet Union 'to collapse' as a result of the bombing campaign called for in the [E]mergency [W]ar [P]lan. People kept talking about the 'Sunday Punch.' I remember asking Gen. 'Pre' Cabell whether anybody could structure the process of collapse for me, i.e., explain how it would come about through the bombing, and he seemed to think it was a bizarre question" (Brodie to David A. Rosenberg, 22 August 1977, UCLA Collection, Box 9 [Folder 21]).

A member of Air Targets Division at that time with an excellent memory, whom I interviewed, had no recollection of the "Sunday Punch" phrase. Brodie could have been introduced to that phrase in his conversations at SAC headquarters during the same period.

68. Cited in Lowe Critique, 4. See also note 55 above.

69. "The duration of the decisive phases of [an unrestricted nuclear] war can hardly be more than a few days" (*Strategy in the Missile Age*, 215).

70. "Must We Shoot from the Hip?" 263.

71. Ibid., 259.

72. Ibid.

73. Ibid., 260. Italics in original.

74. Ibid.

75. "Morale Factor in STRAP Planning," 13. For the general idea of capitalizing on the fear of more attacks to come, Brodie may have been indebted to the work of Herbert Goldhamer. "Goldhamer stresses," Brodie wrote in 1951, "that the threat of calamity, of impending disaster, rather than past attacks and present misery, is most conducive to political behavior. Moreover the threat must continue for a long enough time to produce the desired effect" ("Must We Shoot from the Hip?" 268; the latter part of this paper is taken up by a critique of a Goldhamer memorandum on the subject of strike spacing).

76. "Morale Factor in STRAP Planning," 13.

77. Cited in Lowe Critique, 8.

78. Herken (*Winning Weapon*, 286) cites air force war plan TROJAN as providing a total of three hundred bombs to be used in an initial attack upon the Soviet Union in early 1950. He also cites (ibid., 386) a JCS memorandum giving the bomb stockpile in fall 1948 as one hundred.

79. "Must We Shoot from the Hip?" 251. Already by 1949, the JCS review group, chaired by Lt. Gen. Hubert Harmon, USAF, had concluded that "atomic bombing would validate Soviet propaganda . . . stimulate resentment against the United States, unify these people and increase their will to fight" (Herken, *Winning Weapon*, 294).

80. "Must We Shoot from the Hip?" 264.

81. Davison, "Bombing and Resentment in Germany," 22 August 1949, included as Appendix G in RAND Warning Papers, G-21 and G-22.

82. Ibid., G-24 (italics in original). Compare the views of Donald N. Michael, n. 91.

83. Davison, "Some Effects of Various Patterns of Bombing on German Morale," 18 July 1949, included as Appendix I in RAND Warning Papers, I-4.

84. Ibid., I-2, 8. This statement supports Freeman Dyson's contention that "as bombing becomes heavier, people rapidly adapt themselves to it and learn how to stay alive" (*Weapons and Hope* [New York: Harper & Row, 1984], 18). For other data on this subject, see Irving L. Janis, *War and Emotional Stress* (New York: McGraw-Hill, 1951).

85. "Strategic Air Attacks," 10–11. Some of Brodie's writing in this passage paralleled earlier writing by Davison on the same subject. To illustrate his point that Germans who believed they had already experienced the worst bombing showed little apprehension about future bombing, Davison wrote: "For example, the police cited a case of a man in Hamburg who wanted his wife to come back to the city from the country because 'there is nothing left to destroy'" ("Some Effects of Various Patterns of Bombing on German Morale," I-8).

In bombing operations, the threat of more attacks to come appears to have especially spurred German evacuation following the heaviest attacks, such as those against Hamburg and Dresden. The most important effect of that threat in the European theater, however, was probably in war tactics, though Brodie did not acknowledge this fact. For this effect on the western front, see Cyril Falls, *The Nature of Modern Warfare* (New York: Oxford University Press, 1941), 15. For its still greater effect on the eastern front, see *Effects of Strategic Bombing on German Morale*, 70; and Kecskemeti, "Dispersal of Populations in Germany," D-14 and D-15.

For analysis of the trekking phenomenon in Britain brought about by the German bombing of British cities, see Richard M. Titmuss, *Problems of Social Policy* (London: Longmans, Green, 1950), 306ff and 341ff, and T. H. O'Brien, *Civil Defense* (London: Longmans, Green, 1955), passim.

A study by Davison, "Rumors Concerning Advance Warnings of Air Attacks as Reported by German Security Police," 7 July 1949, included as Appendix C of RAND Warning Papers, concluded that some rumors of attacks were based on actual warning leaflets dropped over German cities, but the study lacked detailed information about leaflet drops.

86. *The Effects of Strategic Bombing on Japanese Morale*, USSBS Report no. 14 (Pacific War) (Washington, D.C.: Government Printing Office, 1947), cited in Janis, *War and Emotional Stress,* 112.

87. *Effects of Strategic Bombing on Japanese Morale*, 134–135. Brodie's use of this idea is found in "Strategic Air Attacks," 18.

88. "Summary of Twentieth Air Force Operations, 5 June 1944–14 August 1945," Office of Statistical Control, Twentieth Air Force, Document SC-CS-41, 1 October 1945, 7. This document was found among the Earle Papers, Box 24.

89. "Strategic Air Attacks," 16.

90. Ibid. See also *Strategy in the Missile Age*, 142. According to Victor Hunt, a member of the RAND social science staff who studied the Japanese evacuation, the official Japanese figure of eight and a half million "is certainly too low" ("Warnings and Dispersal in Japan," 29 July 1949, included as Appendix B in RAND Warning Papers, B-7). By the time the warning leaflets were initiated, virtually all large Japanese cities had already been bombed and, Hunt noted, "the raids on the medium and small cities and even towns came as a tremendous shock to the Japanese. The phrase 'effects of the intensified raids on medium and small size cities' recurs again and again in the interviews with officials" (ibid., B-14). Hunt also pointed to police reports of "the effects of refugee stories in starting evacuation" (ibid., B-17).

Brodie's comparison of evacuations in Japan with those in Germany did not refer to important differences between two cases. First, in Japan, unlike Germany, the government did not assist the evacuations following the start of heavy bombing (ibid., B-20). Second, dispersal was not a major objective in the war against Germany (Kecskemeti, "Dispersal of Populations in Germany," D-7). A final difference appears to be that in Germany no major urban evacuations traceable to bombing occurred in advance of raids ("Dispersal of Populations in Germany," D-11).

Against Germany, nearly six billion leaflets were dropped during the entire course of the war, and somewhat less than three billion from late June 1944 to the end of the war. In the latter period, it appears, the leaflets were coordinated especially with ground combat operations; between a third and a half of these "tactical leaflets" were appeals to German soldiers. Among those classified as "strategic leaflets" were ones described as "Civilian Instructions," that is, "warnings to

specified communities, evacuation orders, instructions on how to save town by surrender, on eva-
sion of *Volksturm* etc." The latter were evidently intended to ease the advance of the Allied armies.
(George C. McDonald, *The Contribution of Air Power to the Defeat of Germany*, 7 August 1945,
Document KO-45112, Appendix M, 138–141, prepared for the commanding general, U.S. Strategic Air Forces, Europe. This document was kindly supplied to me by Joseph E. Loftus. The pages
cited compose Section Five ["Leaflet Dropping"] of Appendix M to this report, entitled "Miscellan-
eous Aspects of Air Attack.")

Nearly fifty million leaflets were dropped over Japan in the last three and a half months of the
Pacific war ("Summary of Twentieth Air Force Operations," 31).

91. "Strategic Air Attacks," 8. Attaching considerable importance to forced evacuation, Brodie
may have assumed that the adversary government would wish to prevent such evacuation and therefore that bombing would promote popular tension between public demands and regime intentions.
If so, he did not take into account the point made by the USSBS that "had there been no [evacua-
tion] program, as was the case in Freiburg, confusion and demoralization of the civilian population
would have been much greater than they were" (*Effects of Strategic Bombing on German Morale*, 70).

Other analysts acknowledged psychological effects from bombing in the Second World War
but failed to clearly make allowance for the effects of evacuation. "The USSBS surveys," wrote
Donald N. Michael, "indicate that food shortages are especially likely to lead to considerable discon-
tent and hostility toward the home agencies—not toward the enemy. Hostility toward home agencies and the powers that be appear to be a frequent delayed consequence of disasters generally.
The agency that fails to provide protection rather than the agency of attack is generally, but not
exclusively, the object of hostility. The wartime data from both Japan and Europe show this to
be the case as do data from peacetime disaster studies both here and abroad" ("Civilian Behavior
under Atomic Bombardment," *Bulletin of the Atomic Scientists* 11 [May 1955]: 176).

Major studies of the effect of German bombing on the British population categorically deny
that sizable evacuations from such cities as London reflected poor population morale (Titmuss,
Problems of Social Policy, 342; and Zuckerman, *From Apes to Warlords*, 143–144). According to Titmuss, the British tended to employ attendance at work immediately after a bombing incident as
an estimate of group morale. They found that absence from work for personal reasons "was closely
associated with the amount of house damage. No other factor was important" (*Problems of Social
Policy*, 341).

92. According to the official history of the U.S. Army air forces, the decision was designed
to "lessen the stigma attached to area bombing" (Wesley F. Craven and James L. Cate, eds., *The
Army Air Forces in World War II* [Chicago: University of Chicago Press, 1983], 5:656–657).

93. "Strategic Air Attacks," 18. Brodie preferred the leaflets dropped over Japan that were written by the staff of Adm. Chester Nimitz, which emphasized "the humanity of the American
attacker and his desire to save lives." The warning leaflets did lead many Japanese, who were frightened into evacuation and who realized that American bombing could have been still more devastating in absence of the warnings, to subsequently credit the Americans with humane impulses. See
Victor Hunt, "Japanese Reactions to Warnings of Air Attacks," 26 July 1949, included as Appendix A in RAND Warning Papers, A-9.

Hunt also notes, however, that "during the war, resentment against Americans because of bombing was widespread and often bitter among Japanese" and that this resentment was greater than
noted in the USSBS report on Japanese morale ("Bombing and Resentment in Japan," 4 August
1949, included as Appendix E in RAND Warning Papers, E-21).

94. Hunt, "Warnings and Dispersal in Japan," B-20 and B-21.

Examples of how ineffective bombing attacks undermined the threat of more attacks to come
were afforded by the bombing campaigns of the First World War, termed by Lasswell "propaganda
of the deed . . . that is, some isolated act of violence which is intended to produce a powerful
impression." In that case, Lasswell wrote, "the dropping of bombs upon enemy cities was less
for immediate military and strategic purposes, than for propaganda purposes. It was supposed

that civilian morale would crack under the strain of perpetual fear. This, besides the propaganda of frightfulness and other acts of frightfulness, was supposed to produce discouragement and defeatism. . . . On the whole, its chief result was to stiffen the determination of the people to defend themselves" (*Propaganda Technique in the World War*, 199).

95. *Strategy in the Missile Age,* 129.

96. Ibid., 130–131. It could be argued, on the other hand, that Germany had also "already lost the battle of production" by 1944, considerably before the time that Brodie asserted German morale had most deteriorated—that is, by the last days of war.

97. Herbert Feis, *Japan Subdued: The Atomic Bomb and the End of the War in the Pacific* (Princeton, N.J.: Princeton University Press, 1961), 38. Having psychological effects in mind, the planners of the two atomic attacks believed that the second bomb should be used quickly after the first, "so that [in the words of the director of the Manhattan Project, Leslie M. Groves (brigadier general, USA)] the Japanese would not have time to recover their balance" (Groves, *Now It Can Be Told: The Story of the Manhattan Project* [New York: Da Capo Press, 1983; first published 1962], 342).

98. "Must We Shoot from the Hip?" 250. For subsequent writings by Brodie on the subject of weapons demonstrations, see "Military Demonstration and Disclosure of New Weapons," *World Politics* 5 (April 1953): 281–301.

99. Haywood S. Hansell, Jr., cited in Futrell, "Air Power in World War II," in MacCloskey, ed., *United States Air Force,* 54; see also Haywood S. Hansell, Jr., *Strategic Air War against Japan* (Washington, D.C.: Government Printing Office, 1980), 60.

100. *The Strategic Air Operations of Very Heavy Bombardment in the War against Japan (20th Air Force),* USSBS Report no. 66 (Pacific War) (Washington, D.C.: Government Printing Office, 1946). Included in vol. 9 of the MacIsaac Collection, 12.

101. MacIsaac, *Strategic Bombing in World War Two,* 204f.

102. General LeMay's Commanding General's Diary for 23 January 1951, Curtis E. LeMay Papers, Box B-64, Manuscript Division, Library of Congress.

103. Ropp, *War in the Modern World,* rev. ed. (New York: Collier, 1962), 380.

104. In Germany, urban bombing targets were also being rapidly depleted by the last months of the war. On 1 November 1944 (that is, prior to the bombing of Dresden), Harris noted that within eighteen months, the RAF had virtually destroyed forty-five out of the sixty leading German cities (Irving, *Destruction of Dresden,* 89).

105. Dyer, "Horizontal Approach to Target Analysis," Air War College lecture, 12 December 1951, 7, AFHRC, K239.716251-55.

106. Desmond Ball, "U.S. Strategic Forces: How Would They Be Used?" *International Security* 7 (Winter 1982/83): 55.
Brodie later wrote of this early period that a nuclear attack point had "originally been put over the Kremlin" (Brodie to Rosenberg, 22 August 1977).

107. "Must We Shoot from the Hip?" 265.

108. Ibid., 265–266.

109. "Must We Shoot from the Hip?" 255.

110. *Strategy in the Missile Age,* 131.

111. Indeed, as historian Kent Roberts Greenfield noted, the Americans had already made such a decision in the latter stages of the war against Germany: "To overcome the interruptions imposed on their offensive by the weather over Europe the Americans adopted the techniques of the Royal Air Force for bombing through overcast. This was blind bombing and hardly less indiscriminate than area bombing at night." American bombers also participated in area attacks against Dresden and Berlin in 1945. Greenfield, *American Strategy in World War II: A Reconsideration* (Baltimore: Johns Hopkins University Press, 1963), 116. See also Robert C. Batchelder, *The Irreversible Decision: 1939–1950* (Boston: Houghton, Mifflin, 1962), chap. 15 ("The Evolution of Mass Bombing").
One indication that the RAF was moving toward American bombing conceptions is afforded by the official history of Bomber Command, which states that by 1944, "the strategic arguments

in favour of general area bombing of German towns had . . . been largely abandoned by the Air Staff" (Webster and Frankland, *Strategic Air Offensive against Germany*, 3:57). Instead, the Air Staff was increasingly interested in applying area bombing selectively to towns in which key ball-bearings, aircraft, and later oil production was also under way. Reference has already been made (see note 15 above) that the RAF occasionally attacked the peripheries of German cities as well as city centers.

112. Hansell, *Strategic Air War against Japan*, 61.

113. LeMay leveled such a critique, for example, at the selection by air force headquarters in 1950 of Soviet electric power installations as a target system for American nuclear weapons attack. For this critique, see chapter 4.

114. "Must We Shoot from the Hip?" 244.

115. Ibid., 264.

116. Ibid., 241–242.

117. Ibid., 272.

118. "Strategic Air Attacks," 5. See also "Air Power in an Overall Strategy," 15. "No reasonable observer can deny," wrote Brodie in 1953 about the American campaign against Japan, "that the aerial bombardment greatly hastened the end of the war and sufficed to make invasion unnecessary. But what should be denied for the sake of clarity in strategic thinking is that this process operated to any important degree through changes in public morale" ("Strategic Air Attacks," 15).

The Japanese emperor's quarters and compound had been spared from destruction thoughout the American bombing, a decision made before the first Doolittle raid against Japan from China in 1942. James Doolittle had been in Britain in 1940 when a German attack damaged Buckingham Palace: he recalled that the incident infuriated the British people more than did the destruction of their own homes. He believed that the Japanese fought hard enough without the greater defiance that he feared would be created by targeting the emperor's quarters. Lowell Thomas and Edward Jablonski, *Doolittle: A Biography* (Garden City, N.Y.: Doubleday, 1976), 173–174.

119. Kecskemeti, *Strategic Surrender* (Stanford, Calif.: Stanford University Press, 1964), 208 (italics in original). Kecskemeti did not study specifically the American bombing of Japan.

120. Craven and Cate, eds., *Army Air Forces in World War II*, 5:644. President Roosevelt and Prime Minister Churchill first approved of the demand for unconditional surrender as Allied policy at the Casablanca Conference of January 1943 but do not seem to have discussed it with their chiefs of staff beforehand. On the latter point, see John Slessor, *The Central Blue* (New York: Praeger, 1957), 447–448.

121. Cited in Lerner, *Psychological Warfare against Nazi Germany*, 315.

122. "Must We Shoot from the Hip?" 251–252 (italics in original).

123. Ibid., 259–260.

124. "Strategic Air Attacks," 4–5 (italics in original).

125. Leites, *The Operational Code of the Politburo* (New York: McGraw-Hill, 1951), passim.

126. Lerner, *Psychological Warfare against Nazi Germany*, 316–317. Lasswell pointed out earlier that an essential ingredient in Germany's collapse in the First World War had been the rhetoric of Woodrow Wilson, whose "matchless skill . . . in propaganda has never been equalled in the world's history" and whose "speeches were one prolonged instigation to revolt" (*Propaganda Technique in the World War*, 216–217).

127. By 1948 a National Security Council (NSC) study envisioned that the Soviet Union would not be required to surrender unconditionally (Herken, *Winning Weapon*, 276).

In his essay on the British orator and politician John Bright, who vigorously criticized his country's participation in the Crimean War, A. J. P. Taylor wrote that "Bright underrated what a Power will agree to when it has been defeated" ("John Bright and the Crimean War," in *Essays in English History* [New York: Pelican Books, 1976], 100).

128. The best-known distinction between the intentions of Nazi Germany and those of the Soviet Union was provided by George Kennan (see "The Sources of Soviet Conduct," *Foreign Affairs* 25 [July 1947]: 566–582).

129. "Must We Shoot from the Hip?" 270.
130. "Morale Factor in STRAP Planning," 6.
131. Ibid., 7.
132. "Air Power in an Overall Strategy," 21.
133. Ibid., 2.
134. "Must We Shoot from the Hip?" 266.
135. Kennan, *Russia and the West under Lenin and Stalin* (New York: New American Library, 1961), 365. See also Herken, *Winning Weapon*, 315, which indicates that Kennan had linked an earlier critique of comprehensive atomic attack with a presumption of H-bomb use.
136. According to Paul M. A. Linebarger, "The sound psychological warfare operator will try to get enemy troops to believing that the enemy is not themselves but somebody else—the King, the Führer, the elite troops, the capitalists. He creates a situation in which he can say, 'We're not fighting you.' (This should not be said too soon after extensive use of bombs or mortars.) 'We are fighting the So-and-so's who are misleading you.' Some of the handsomest propaganda of World War II was produced by the Soviet experts along this line. Before the War was over, Soviet propaganda created a whole gallery of heel-clicking reactionary German generals *on the Russian side*, and made out that the unprofessional gutter-snipe Hitler was ruining the wonderful German Army in amateurish campaigns. Joseph Stalin's ringing words, 'The German State and the German *Volk* remain!' gave the Russians a propaganda loophole by which they implied that Germany was not the enemy—no, not Germany! just the Nazis. This was superb psychological warfare, since the Russians had already built up the propaganda thesis that the common people (workers and peasants) were automatically—by virtue of their class loyalty—on the side of the workers' country, Russia. That left very few Germans on the other side" (*Psychological Warfare* [Washington, D.C.: Combat Forces Press, 1954], 50–51; [italics in original]). Linebarger evidently had ignored the great popular anxieties created by the advance of the Soviet army on the eastern front.
137. Cited in Lowe Critique, 6. The measure to which Brodie referred, sponsored by Sen. Brien McMahon (Dem.-Conn.), was intended to convey, "without intervention and distortion of the Politburo if possible, the basic friendship of the American people and government toward the Russian people." For the text of this "Friendship Resolution" (Senate Congressional Concurrent Resolution 11, 1951), see *Congressional Quarterly Almanac*, 1951, 240.
For a critique of American efforts to distinguish the Communist regime in mainland China from the Chinese people following the victory of the Communists in the Chinese civil war, see John Stoessinger, *Why Nations Go to War*, 3d ed. (New York: St. Martin's Press, 1982), 76–77.
138. Etzold and Gaddis, *Containment*, 362.
139. Testimony before the Harmon Committee, 11 February 1949 (Tab A), included in Record Group 218 (Records of the Joint Chiefs of Staff), Box 38, CCS 373 (10-23-48), bulky package, pt. 1A, National Archives.
Herbert Goldhamer wrote that "it is probably a safe rule for psychological and political warfare that when possible its campaigns should be waged and its objectives achieved well before their full benefits are to be reaped or are required" ("Communist Reaction in Korea to American Possession of the A-Bomb and Its Significance for U.S. Political and Psychological Warfare," RAND Research Memorandum RM-903, August 1952, 56).
140. Edmund Taylor, *The Strategy of Terror* (Boston: Houghton, Mifflin, 1940), 263. It was for this reason, Taylor went on, that "Allied propaganda has not been able to achieve the single-mindedness which is the fundamental condition of any really effective propaganda" (ibid., 263).
141. Kecskemeti, "Dispersal of Populations in Germany," D-34 and D-35.
142. Cited in "Must We Shoot from the Hip?" 270.
143. Schelling, "Comment," in *Limited Strategic War*, edited by Klaus Knorr and Thorton Read (Princeton, N.J.: Princeton University Press, 1962), 254–255.
On the warning of enemy cities prior to attack, see also two articles by Leo Szilard: "Disarmament and the Problem of Peace," *Bulletin of the Atomic Scientists* 11 (October 1955): 297–307; and "The Mined Cities," *Bulletin of the Atomic Scientsts* 17 (December 1961): 407–412. For later syste-

On the warning of enemy cities prior to attack, see also two articles by Leo Szilard: "Disarmament and the Problem of Peace," *Bulletin of the Atomic Scientists* 11 (October 1955): 297–307; and "The Mined Cities," *Bulletin of the Atomic Scientists* 17 (December 1961): 407–412. For later systematic work on the coercive uses of nuclear weapons, see Thomas C. Schelling, *Arms and Influence* (New Haven, Conn.: Yale University Press, 1966).

144. Kennan, *Russia and the West under Lenin and Stalin*, 366.

145. Soviet terrorist tactics during the Second World War were reflected notably in the shooting of deserters. I am indebted to Ross N. Berkes for this point.

146. Brodie subsequently wrote that the supposed estrangement between the Russian people and their leaders "may be easily overstressed," a point he bolstered by his interpretation of the German case: "German disillusionment with the Nazi regime was quite far advanced by the beginning of 1944, but at no time before the war ended was any large group of Germans convinced that—apart from the cessation of the air raids themselves—they would be any better off under the dominion of the Allied governments than they were with their own. Quite the contrary" ("Strategic Air Attacks," 10).

147. I am indebted in this section to James E. King for several very helpful suggestions.

148. Compare what Brodie had to say on this subject in his *Layman's Guide to Naval Strategy*, which is discussed in chapter 1.

149. "Must We Shoot from the Hip?" 248.

150. "Dispersal of Populations in Germany," D-35. To a RAND audience in 1951, Brodie maintained that it was better to ask questions about the work of planners "to which we could essay only tentative and contingent answers" than to leave planners undisturbed with questions unasked ("Must We Shoot from the Hip?" 248).

151. Brodie to Rosenberg, 22 August 1977. Evidence that Brodie met with LeMay and his staff at least twice at SAC headquarters in the course of his service for Vandenberg—on 20 December 1950 and 1 March 1951—is provided in General LeMay's Commanding General's Diary, LeMay Papers, Box B-64. There is no evidence that Brodie met with LeMay before this tour of duty. On the significance of being exposed to the target list, Freeman Dyson described what the same opportunity meant to J. Robert Oppenheimer: "I once asked him [Robert Oppenheimer] long after he had lost his security clearance, whether he regretted having fought so hard for tactical nuclear weapons. He said, 'No. But to understand what I did then, you would have to see the air force war plan as it existed in 1951. That was the goddamnedest thing I ever saw. Anything, even the war plans we have now, is better than that'" (*Weapons and Hope*, 137). William T. Golden related that on 26 February 1951 Oppenheimer "told me he had talked with Bernard Brodie several times within the last few days when he was in Washington" (Golden memorandum, "Conversation with Dr. J. Robert Oppenheimer," 26 February 1951, included in "Government Military-Scientific Research: Review for the President of the United States, 1950–1951," bound volume, Golden Papers). Dyson seems to go astray, however, when he concludes that "the 1951 war plan was, in short, a mindless obliteration of Soviet cities" (*Weapons and Hope*, 137).

152. Brodie's constant adjustment to suit his needs as a critic was evidently not unusual for abstract thinkers, for whom, physicist Pyotr Kapitsa noted, "the process of argument is a way of thinking" (cited in George W. S. Trow, "The Harvard Black Rock Forest," *New Yorker* 60 [June 1984]: 95).

153. Arguing in 1951 against "betray[ing] ourselves into devising a specific schedule of [nuclear bomb] delivery" and in favor of leaving that responsibility to the air staff, Brodie wrote that "we will be making a sufficient but necessary contribution if we simply jar the prevalent complacency on the doctrine of shoot-from-the-hip-and-empty-the-magazine" ("Must We Shoot from the Hip?" 247–248).

Chapter 4. Using History:
Economic Targets

1. Brodie to David A. Rosenberg, 22 August 1977, UCLA Collection, Box 9 (Folder 21). Referring to Norstad, Brodie wrote that "he always let on that he was a great admirer of mine, which perhaps he was." Professor Rosenberg has made extensive use of this letter in his own published work, most notably "The Origins of Overkill: Nuclear Weapons and American Strategy, 1945–1960," *International Security* 7 (Spring 1983): 17ff. Unfortunately, he did not take into account that Brodie's recollection of his service for Vandenberg dimmed with the passage of more than twenty-five years (see note 2 below). Another account of Brodie's tenure with Vandenberg is in Gregg Herken, *Counsels of War* (New York: Alfred A. Knopf, 1985), 27ff. Herken's study suffers from his uncritical dependence on other sources, including Rosenberg and an earlier, much superseded version of the present study; from his tendency to make hasty judgments on the basis of those sources; and from a series of inexplicable errors in reproducing material from his sources.

2. Brodie's own recollection of this work was most clearly stated in his letter of 22 August 1977 to David Rosenberg: "I worked as a special assistant to General Hoyt Vandenberg, then C.S., from about the middle of December 1950 to about the end of March 1951. . . . General Vandenberg asked me to have a look at the target list of the emergency war plan and tell him what I thought about it. . . . The finished product was in two reports, a short one handed to Vandenberg at the end of my first two weeks, and a longer one at the end of March or in early April [1951]. . . . I commented exclusively on the target list appended to the Emergency War Plan. Note that this target list had never been officially approved by the JCS, but was nevertheless considered to be in force for want of any other plan."

Information about the titles and dates of the two major reports Brodie wrote for Vandenberg were supplied to me from the RAND Corporation classified document log in Santa Monica, California. The two citations are as follows: "(1) 1 page memo with 36 page enclosure of papers presenting views and findings from B. Brodie to Lt. Gen. Norstad and Gen. Vandenberg re: 'Observations Resulting from Review of U.S. Strategic Bombing Plans with Special Reference to Selection of Target Systems,' dated 9/15/50. (2) 2 page memo with 41 page annex and 1 page Table of Contents from B. Brodie to Gen. Vandenberg re: 'Report on Mission to Study Target Plans and Procedures with Recommendations,' dated 3/6/51." Copies of these two reports, evidently brought by Brodie to RAND in 1951 when he began his tenure at that institution, were routinely declassified many years later and then destroyed in a periodic housekeeping operation. I am indebted to Malcolm Palmatier and to Claude Culp of the RAND Corporation for this information.

Item 1, nearly as lengthy as item 2, does not seem to match the "shorter report" referred to by Brodie; moreover, it falls outside the time period Brodie later recollected as having worked for Vandenberg. The most important source of information about the contents of item 2 in the RAND classified log is a memorandum by James T. Lowe, civilian head of the Air Targets Division (ATD) in 1950 and 1951, cited here as "Lowe Critique," which comments on and quotes liberally from a Brodie memorandum, "Target Plans and Procedures, with Recommendations." (In the Lowe Critique, paraphrases and quotations from the Brodie report are underlined; the underlining is omitted here.)

The Lowe Critique indicates that Brodie was evaluating a "study" prepared within the ATD recommending targets to the JCS. From other documents in Record Group 341, it appears that this study was numbered 245 in the list of ATD studies and was also numbered in the records of the Joint Strategic Planning Committee as JSPC 877/131. A memorandum, "Target Selection," 27 January 1951, from C. P. Cabell to the director of plans, deputy chief of staff for operations, refers to "the revision of the plan SHAKEDOWN (AIS #245, 'Target Systems Submitted for Consideration in Fulfilling the Objectives of the Joint Outline Emergency War Plan, FY 51')" (National Archives USAF Intelligence Collection, Box 54 [folder: document nos. 2-18100 to 2-18199]. The letters "AIS" apparently signify "Air Intelligence Study").

Although the list of targets in AIS 245 remains classified, a list of the hypotheses governing the selection of targets in this study and an outline of information projected for inclusion in its target appendixes may be found in "Extract from Air Targets Division Action Summary 264/FY 51, 'Target Systems Submitted for Consideration in Fulfilling the Objectives of the Joint Outline Emergency War Plan, Fiscal Year 1951,'" Tab A attached to a memorandum, "Recommendations and Estimates for Preparation of Certain Appendices for Revision of Plan OFFTACKLE, FY 51," E. Moore to Intelligence Division, General Staff, U.S. Army, 17 May 1950 (National Archives USAF Intelligence Collection, Box 50 [folder: document nos. 2-13100 to 2-13199]). See also note 118 below.

3. See chapter 3 of this book.

4. Brodie to Rosenberg, 22 August 1977.

5. For the historical sources on strategic bombing during the Second World War employed by Brodie, see the introduction to chapter 3.

6. "Effect of Air Power on Military Operations: Western Europe," prepared for the use of the U.S. Strategic Bombing Survey (USSBS) staff by Gen. Omar N. Bradley and the Air Effects Committee, 12th Army Group, [1945] 1, in Earle Papers, Box 24. Cited henceforth as "Bradley Report."

7. "Strategic Bombing: What It Can Do," *Reporter* 3 (August 1950): 29.

8. David MacIsaac, "General Introduction," in MacIsaac Collection, 1:xxii. This point was also made in the *Over-all Report*, USSBS Report no. 2 (European War) (Washington, D.C.: Government Printing Office, 1945), 37 (reproduced in MacIsaac Collection, vol. 1).

9. For example, according to the War Diary of the Economic Outpost Unit (EOU) of the Office of Strategic Services (OSS), located in London: "To put the matter baldly, if the entire G.A.F. were knocked out of the air, the loss would eliminate the equivalent of only 4 months' production; and conversely the loss of 4 months' production is equivalent to the entire first-line strength" ("Economic Outpost with Economic Warfare Division," vol. 5 of War Diary, Research and Analysis Branch, Office of Strategic Services, London, 39–40, in Record Group 226 [OSS Records], Entry 91 ["History of the OSS in London], Box 8, National Archives, Washington, D.C. Cited henceforth as "EOU Report").

10. Ibid., 41.

11. Brodie, *Strategy in the Missile Age*, 117.

12. Ibid.

13. Ibid., 118.

14. "Strategic Bombing: What It Can Do," 30.

15. Brodie to Edward Mead Earle, 5 August 1950, Earle Papers, Box 10 (B File).

16. *Summary Report*, USSBS Report no. 1 (European War) (Washington, D.C.: Government Printing Office, 1945), 16 (reproduced in MacIsaac Collection, vol. 1).

17. *Aircraft Division Industry Report*, USSBS Report no. 4 (European War) (Washington, D.C.: Government Printing Office, 1947; first published 1945), 53 (reproduced in MacIsaac Collection, vol. 2).

18. Bradley Report, 92. Air superiority, critically important for the invasion of Europe, depended not only on long-range attacks against aircraft plants inside Germany. "The achievement of air supremacy," Bradley wrote after the war, "was a necessary precondition of successful invasion. Defensively, the German air force had to be prevented from attacking Allied ports, marshalling areas, shipping, depots, beachheads, and movement. . . . Offensively, dominance of the air was required to bring the full weight of Allied air power against the enemy as he attempted to defend the beachhead and, later, to prevent the uncoiling of Allied land power" (Bradley Report, 2–3).

19. Earle to Brodie, 13 August 1950, Earle Papers, Box 10 (B File). More exact figures were provided by Earle in "Notes on Conversations with Generals Brereton and Schlatter (D-Day, June)

and S. E. Anderson (June 7, 1944)" (Earle Papers, Box 24 [untitled envelope]). He wrote: "We flew a record 13,000 sorties on D-Day with negligible losses. 9,000 the following day, ditto, but with 102 Germans shot down. We lost only 15 aircraft out of more than 9,000 which participated in airborne landings, according to General Brereton."

20. Brodie to Earle, 15 August 1950, Earle Papers, Box 10 (B File). Brodie cited the opinion of Maj. Gen. Orvil A. Anderson, military adviser to the USSBS staff, that Allied attacks against airfields in France had been decisive in this respect; according to Anderson, Allied bomber forces had incapacitated most airfields around Paris and northeast of it prior to the invasion and struck the remaining ones on D-Day. Gen. Ira Eaker, commander of the American Eighth Air Force, which carried out the attacks against the aircraft plants, was unable later to reconcile the weak German resistance at D-Day with the small losses of German fighters to Allied attacks claimed by the Germans (Thomas M. Coffey, *Decision over Schweinfurt* [New York: David M. McKay, 1977], 338).

Addressing the reported German statistics showing large-scale fighter production in 1944, the USSBS Military Analysis Division found "unquestionably . . . a discrepancy between claimed new production when compared to losses and the strength in units of the GAF" (*Defeat of the German Air Force*, USSBS Report no. 59 [European War] [Washington, D.C.: Government Printing Office, 1947; first published 1945), 39: reproduced in MacIsaac Collection, vol. 3).

21. EOU Report, 42.

22. Earle to Brodie, 13 August 1950.

23. "Memorandum of Conversations with Colonel Richard Hughes and General Frederick K. Anderson, at Widewing, 1 May 1944," Earle Papers, Box 24 (untitled envelope). Having advocated attacks against aircraft plants in 1943, Earle worried by May 1944 that such attacks might already have fulfilled their purpose. Conferring with military planners in Britain, Earle was told, as he put it, by the senior U.S. Air Force target planning officer in Britain that "we are bombing ourselves out of targets (cf. [The] German aircraft industry, which he considers a dead or at best a sick horse not worth further flogging — except for the few large remaining establishments)" (ibid.).

24. Lowe, "The Intelligence Basis of Selection of Strategic Target Systems," Air War College lecture, 13 November 1947, 15, in AFHRC, K239.716247–50. A similar condition seemed to operate on the Allied side. "Parenthetically," Earle wrote in summarizing one of his conversations in England in May 1944, "General Williams told me . . . that he doubted if we could despatch more bombers to Germany even if we had them because the force would spread over so many miles that fighter coverage would be an almost hopeless problem with any forces we are likely to have" ("Conversations at Second Division, May 18–19, 1944," Earle Papers, Box 24 [untitled envelope]. General Williams is not further identified.

25. Rolf Wagenfuehr, "The Rise and Fall of the German War Economy: 1939–1945," [1945], 45. This unpublished manuscript, by the head of the Statistical Department of the German Ministry of Armament and War Production, was discovered and translated by the USSBS staff. A copy of it was kindly provided to me by Joseph E. Loftus.

26. Ibid.

27. "Strategic Bombing: What It Can Do," 28.

28. Ibid.

29. Ibid., 29.

30. Klein, *Germany's Economic Preparations for War*, 230.

31. *Over-all Report*, 107.

32. *Effects of Strategic Bombing on the German War Economy*, 12.

33. *Over-all Report*, 107. This view appears to have been strongly argued by Maj. Gen. Orvil A. Anderson (MacIsaac, *Strategic Bombing in World War Two*, 142). Brodie claimed to have communicated with Anderson about strategic bombing in the last war (see chapter 2, note 63). See also note 20 above.

34. Loftus, "Strategy, Economics, and the Bomb," *Scientific Monthly* 68 (May 1949): 318.

35. *Oil Division Final Report*, USSBS Report no. 109 (European War) (Washington, D.C.: Government Printing Office, 1947; first published 1945), 121 (reproduced in MacIsaac Collection, vol. 3). See also *Strategy in the Missile Age*, 111.

36. *Oil Division Final Report*, 121.

37. Brodie, "Changing Capabilities and War Objectives" (see chap. 1, n. 58), 71.

38. "Implications of Scientific Advances to Military Strategy," Air War College lecture, 9 April 1952, issued as a RAND Informal Working Paper, 7 November 1952, 14. (included in "Fourteen Informal Writings from the Unpublished Work of Bernard Brodie, 1952–1965," a collection of internal working papers assembled by the Rand Corporation, 1980).

39. "Changing Capabilities and War Objectives," 69–70. This statement is not fully reconcilable with Brodie's criticism elsewhere of the American neglect of target selection prior to late 1942, which, he argued at that point, *did* have costly effects in the European theater in helping to prolong the war. (I discuss this in more detail later in the chapter.)

40. Webster and Frankland, *Strategic Air Offensive against Germany*, 3: 42–43. "If our air forces," Brodie wrote in 1955, "were guided by a consideration of their greater successes as against their lesser successes in World War II, they would today favor emphasizing tactical as against strategic bombing" ("Some Notes on the Evolution of Air Doctrine," *World Politics* 7 [April 1955]: 365). According to David Irving, "During July and August 1944 the reality of the flying bomb and the threat of the V-2 successfully attracted 40 percent of the R.A.F. Bombing Command effort from other target systems" (*The Mare's Nest* [London: William Kimber, 1964], 308).

41. *Strategic Air Offensive against Germany*, 3:48.

42. Walt W. Rostow, *Pre-Invasion Bombing Strategy* (Austin: University of Texas Press, 1981), 67, 69.

43. Ibid., 31, 37.

44. Cited in ibid., 34, from EOU planning studies.

45. I discuss this later in the chapter.

46. "Memorandum of Conversation with Colonel Kingman Douglas, at the Air Ministry, 17 Monck Street, 4 May 1944," Earle Papers, Box 24 (untitled envelope).

47. Some former members of the USSBS staff made known to Brodie their view that the strategic bombing of Germany was not at all worthwhile (see note 169 below). As far as is known, however, Brodie did not publicize this divergence until he had worked for Vandenberg and taken a more critical view of strategic bombing results based on his reading of contemporary bombing plans.

48. "Implications of Scientific Advances to Military Strategy," 13. See also Brodie's comments on J. F. C. Fuller (note 168 below) and compare the ideas of Joseph E. Loftus (p. 84).

49. "Strategic Bombing: What It Can Do," 29–30.

50. Ibid., 31 (italics in original). A year later, Brodie acknowledged as an answer to this point "that the Germans made at least comparable mistakes in their air defense and that if we are going to presume a situation in which we had not made any of the errors I have [al]luded to, we must also[,] to be fair to our analysis, presume a situation in which the Germans had not made their particular brand of errors" ("Air Power in an Overall Strategy," Air War College lecture, 23 May 1951, 10, AFHRC, K239.716251-26).

51. Strategic Bombing: What It Can Do," 30.

52. Ibid. On the German chemical industry, see *Over-all Report*, 49ff; *Oil Division Final Report*, 42–43; and *Effects of Strategic Bombing on the German War Economy*, 85.

53. "Strategic Bombing: What It Can Do," 30. The targeting doctrine taught at American Air Corps schools in the interwar period was, according to historian James L. Cate, "dedicated to the principle that the German war potential could be paralyzed by the destruction of a limited number of strategic targets, vulnerable only to daylight precision bombing—'pickle-barrel bombing' it was optimistically called" ("Development of United States Air Doctrine, 1917–41," in *The Impact of Air Power: National Security and World Politics*, edited by Eugene M. Emme [Princeton, N.J.: Van Nostrand Company, 1959], 190). The army air forces staff was established in the spring

of 1941; its Plans Division was composed of former instructors of the Air Corps schools. Hardly grounds for satisfaction from Brodie's perspective was Cate's opinion that the first American plan for air war "gave a preview of the European phase of the war which was in most important respects remarkably accurate" (ibid.). For a summary of AWPD-41, "Munitions Requirements of the Army Air Forces," 9 July 1941, the first comprehensive effort by the army war planners to anticipate bombing operations and calculate aircraft requirements to carry out those operations, see Theodore Tannenwald, Jr., "Air Warfare Plans Division, 1941 (AWPD-41)," Tab A of "Memorandum on Bombardment Planning Documents," by Tannenwald, USSBS Secretariat, 30 March 1945. I am indebted to Joseph E. Loftus for a copy of the Tannenwald memorandum.

Targeting recommendations made in 1943 by the Committee of Operations Analysts (COA), established by order of the air force chief of staff in December 1942, discussed targeting priorities for actual and anticipated numbers of American bombers rather than for some ideal bombing capability and therefore required a much more systematic comparison of bombing prospects against particular categories of targets. The full COA report, dated 8 March 1943, is contained in "History of the U.S. Strategic Bombing Survey (European Theater), Appendix of Supporting Documents, 1944–45," at the Center of Military History, Washington, D.C. I am indebted to John E. Taylor, of the Military Archives Division of the Modern Military Headquarters Branch of the National Archives, and to Hannah M. Zeidlik, of the Center of Military History, for a copy of the COA report. See also Arthur B. Ferguson, "Origins of the Combined Bomber Offensive," in Craven and Cate, eds., *Army Air Forces in World War II*, 2:348–368.

54. Alfred P. Goldberg, "Establishment of the Eighth Air Force in the United Kingdom," in Craven and Cate, eds. *Army Air Forces in World War II*, 1:624. In his final report as commanding general of the army air forces in the United Kingdom, 31 December 1943, Eaker wrote that "almost no information regarding targets in Germany, strength and disposition of G.A.F., etc. or target material, pictures, maps, etc. was available in the U.S. In effect, we had no intelligence information and material about Germany and her occupied territories" (cited in Victor H. Cohen, "Air Intelligence," unpublished U.S. Air Force Historical Study no. 106-87, chap. 13 ["Target Intelligence"], 6. This document is available on AFHRC, microfilm reel K1021).

55. Carl Kaysen, *Notes on Strategic Air Intelligence in World War II (ETO)*, RAND Report R-165, October 1949, 11ff.

56. Loftus, "Strategy, Economics, and the Bomb," 318. These points suggest that American errors in selecting precision bombing targets paralleled those of the RAF in the selection of area targets. The official Bomber Command history, taking account of faulty British estimates of German economic strength and the manner in which those estimates exaggerated the anticipated effect of area bombing, observed that in this respect "the error was mainly as regards the nature of the German economy and not as regards the effects of bombing upon it" (Webster and Frankland, *Strategic Air Offensive against Germany*, 2:247).

American target analysts initially depended heavily on RAF target intelligence about Germany. However, because British area attacks against German cities did not require the precision sought by the Americans, U.S. analysts spent little time studying RAF data about German cities (Kaysen, "Notes on Strategic Air Intelligence in World War II [ETO]," 11).

57. Rostow, *Pre-Invasion Bombing Strategy*, 76–77.

58. *Effects of Strategic Bombing on the German War Economy*, 157.

59. EOU Report, 49–50; Rostow, *Pre-Invasion Bombing Strategy*, 23.

60. Rostow, *Pre-Invasion Bombing Strategy*, 23.

61. "Air Power in an Overall Strategy," 8.

62. Brodie to Earle, 15 August 1950.

63. "Conference at Pine Tree, 13 November 1944," memorandum by Guido R. Perera, 14 November 1944, 4, USSBS Records, Box 37, catalogue no. 337 (Conferences, Military, Naval, and Other)."

64. MacIsaac, *Strategic Bombing in World War Two*, 142.

65. The USSBS report on the effect of bombing on the German war economy neglected the effect of bombing on ground combat and also the shifts in the day-to-day selection of bombing targets.

66. Arnold, *Global Mission* (New York: Harper, 1949), 495.

67. *Effects of Strategic Bombing on the German War Economy*, 495.

68. MacIsaac, *Strategic Bombing in World War Two*, 26 (italics in original). Gen. Carl Spaatz, commanding general of the USSTAF during the war, stated afterward that air superiority was "the absolutely necessary prerequisite for sustained strategic bombing" ("Strategic Air Power: Fulfillment of a Concept," *Foreign Affairs* 24 [April 1946], 11).

69. Spaatz judged that the Luftwaffe would more likely rise to defend oil plants, which he proposed to hit, for example, than to defend rail centers (Rostow, *Pre-Invasion Bombing Strategy*, 4). By the middle of 1943, intelligence indicated the existence of ambitious plans in Germany of increasing German air power, and it was feared that unless prompt preventive measures were taken, new improved fighters, capable of devastating attacks against heavy bombers, would soon come off the production lines and destroy Allied air superiority (*Effects of Strategic Bombing on the German War Economy*, 3).

70. Cited in *German Electric Utilities Industry Report*, USSBS Report no. 205 (European War) (Washington, D.C.: Government Printing Office, 1947; first published 1945), 46 (reproduced [without most of the exhibits] in MacIsaac Collection, vol. 6). MacIsaac referred to German electric power as "the target that never happened," inasmuch as it was given a prominent place in AWPD-41 but was later dropped from American targeting priorities. See MacIsaac's introduction to volume 1 of the MacIsaac Collection, xxxv.

According to the EOU Report, 36, the Ruhr power plants were considered as a target in the winter of 1943.

71. Cited in the Lowe Critique, 10.

72. Brodie to Rosenberg, 22 August 1977.

73. Dan B. Dyer, "Generation of Target Systems," Air War College lecture, 7 April 1950, 8, AFHRC, K239.716250-22(S). This document was consulted on microfilm reel K2729 at the Air Force History Office, Bolling Air Force Base, Washington, D.C.

74. The Lowe Critique, 11, quotes Brodie as writing to Vandenberg of "the 142 RGZs now allocated to electric power." RGZ signifies required ground zero—that is, the target to be destroyed.

75. On the three-hundred bomb figure, see chapter 3 of this book.

76. Cited in the Lowe Critique, 10.

77. "Air Power in an Overall Strategy," 3.

78. Ibid., 17.

79. Brodie to Rosenberg, 22 August 1977 (italics in original).

80. "Air Power in an Overall Strategy," 17.

81. "Changing Capabilities and War Objectives," 72.

82. *Effects of Strategic Bombing on the German War Economy*, 67. This statement neglected, as did Brodie, that attacks against electric power might have helped blunt enemy forces in being during the Second World War. Specifically, attacks against electric power generating stations servicing production of the German V-1 rocket might have blunted German ability to launch the rockets even as direct attack against the factory producing them or against their deployment sites had failed. According to an unpublished USSBS document, "Report of U.S.S.B.S. Field Team no. 43 on Underground Factory Niedersachswerfen (Nordhausen), Germany," 8 May 1945, the underground Nordhausen factory assembling the V-1 was served by overhead transmission lines from power stations at Bleicherode and Sondershausen ("Construction Data on Underground Armament Factory, Nieder-Sachswerfen, Germany," 4, contained in the Niedersachswerfen USSBS report). I am grateful to Joseph E. Loftus for sharing a copy of this report with me. See also Irving, *Mare's Nest*, 312.

83. *Strategy in the Missile Age*, 215.

84. "Air Power in an Overall Strategy," 16. The lecture transcript has Brodie citing for this

data the "Soviet economist Verenige," whose "views have been accepted as accurate and reliable by U.S. intelligence," but he may have been referring to the economist Eugen Varga.

85. "Implications of Scientific Advances to Military Strategy," 14.

86. *German Electric Utilities Industry Report*, 46.

87. Ibid., 52.

88. Thomas K. Finletter, "Memorandum for General Cabell," 30 July 1951, National Archives, USAF Intelligence Collection, Box 59 (folder: document nos. 2-20300 to 2-20399). "I must say," wrote Finletter, then secretary of the air force, "that the consultants make a very strong case for the inclusion of electric power" (ibid.).

89. Ibid.

90. Cited in the Lowe Critique, 5 (italics in original).

91. Ibid.

92. Ibid.

93. "Air Power in an Overall Strategy," 17.

94. Cited in the Lowe Critique, 11. See also note 74 above.

95. "Air Power in an Overall Strategy," 17.

96. Cited in the Lowe Critique, 5.

97. Ibid.

98. Hirshleifer, "Disaster and Recovery: A Historical Survey," RAND Research Memorandum RM-3079-PR, April 1963, 9.

99. *German Electric Utilities Industry Report*, 46–47.

100. Hansell, *Strategic Air War against Japan*, 78–79.

101. Lowe Critique, 9.

102. See note 129 below.

103. "Changing Capabilities and War Objectives," 71–72.

104. Brodie to Rosenberg, 22 August 1977. In the Lowe Critique, 9, the think tank in question is given as the Battelle Memorial Institute, and the date of the report as 26 April 1950. See also below.

105. *Strategy in the Missile Age*, 121f.

106. "Air Power in an Overall Strategy," 23. On the vulnerability of hydroelectric plants, see *The Electric Power Industry of Japan (Plant Reports)*, USSBS Report no. 41 (Pacific War) (Washington, D.C.: Government Printing Office, 1947), 89. On the vulnerability of steam electric power plants see *The Electric Power Industry of Japan*, USSBS Report no. 40 (Pacific War) (Washington, D.C.: Government Printing Office, 1945), 34.

107. T. L. Zolotaryov, "Hydroelectric Stations (Principles of Engineering Policy)," in *Electric Power Development in the U.S.S.R.*, edited by Benjamin I. Weitz et al. (Moscow: INRA Publishing Society, 1936), 269. (According to this volume, the two stations—at the Dnieper and Perm rivers—were under construction in 1936.) I am indebted to Joseph E. Loftus for this volume. According to the Zolotaryov essay, the ratio of the output of hydroelectric stations to the total power generated in the USSR was 7.3 percent in 1932, but this ratio was to be raised to nearly 20 percent by 1937 (ibid., 268).

108. *Electric Power Industry of Japan*, 28.

109. Japanese hydroelectric plants, usually camouflaged, were largely untouched. See *Electric Power Industry of Japan (Plant Reports)*, passim.

110. Cited in the Lowe Critique, 9. The most comprehensive evaluation of the atomic attack against Nagasaki is *Effects of the Atomic Bomb on Nagasaki, Japan*, 3 vols. USSBS Report no. 93 (Pacific War) (Washington, D.C.: Government Printing Office, 1947).

111. USSBS staff damage assessment of Japanese electric power plants discounted the effect of incendiary bombing upon steam generating plants and substations constructed with fire-resistant materials, except for plants and substations located within urban-area conflagrations (*Electric Power Industry of Japan*, 28; *Electric Power Industry of Japan [Plant Reports]*, 3).

112. LeMay to Gen. Nathan Twining, 26 April 1951, Record Group 341 (Records of the Chief

of Staff, U.S. Air Force), Entry 3 (Office of the Chief of Staff, Classified Numerical Correspondence File), Book, 18-A (case nos. 14180–15928), case no. 14768, National Archives, Washington, D.C.

113. According to Lt. Gen. James Doolittle, as described in Perera, "Conference at Pine Tree, 13 November 1944," 2.

114. See *German Electric Utilities Industry Report*, 29–30; *Electric Power Industry of Japan*, 31; and *Electric Power Industry of Japan (Plant Reports)*, 90.

115. "Strategic Air Command Comments and Recommendations on the Target Destruction Annex for Plan SHAKEDOWN (Enclosure to JCS 2056/9)," 4, attached to "Memorandum by the Chief of Staff, U.S. Air Force, for the Joint Chiefs of Staff on the Target Destruction Annex for Plan PINWHEEL," 9 April 1951, National Archives USAF Intelligence Collection, Box 56 (folder: document nos. 2–19100 to 2–19199). In his memorandum to Vandenberg, Brodie noted that sixty-eight of the assigned electric power targets (that is, about 48 percent) required visual photography prior to air strikes, whereas ATD data indicated that only thirty-one of the targets (about 22 percent) required visual photography (Lowe Critique, 3). Brodie's source of information for his contention is unclear, but the divergence between the ATD and SAC in this respect indicates that the two agencies had different systems for classifying targets on their need for prestrike visual photography and also for the difficulty of detecting them by radar. See also Cabell to LeMay, 5 April 1951, National Archives USAF Intelligence Collection, Box 56 (folder: document nos. 2–19000 to 2–19099).

116. See chapter 3 in the book.

117. Lowe Critique, 2. When he pointed out that acutal CEPs could diverge from assumed ones, Brodie was informed by the bombing experience of the last war. "Our World War II experience,' he declared in April 1952, was that when we tested an equipment, let's say a radar equipment, in this country . . . we got a certain CEP, and then when we sent in the same equipment abroad and used it over Germany, with either the same crews or crews of comparable training, our CEP rose by two or three times. That was something we called 'combat degradation.' Now, is that one of the lessons of World War II? Some hold not—that combat degradation is non-existent" ("Changing Capabilities and War Objectives," 71). In "Implications of Scientific Advances to Military Strategy," Brodie traced the underestimate of force requirements in the last war partly to "an exaggeration of the accuracy that would be achieved in bombardment. We didn't know then about such things as combat degradation of bombing accuracy" (13).

118. Cabell, "Comments on Memorandum by Dr. Brodie on Target Plans and Procedures," 23 March 1951, forwarded to deputy chief of staff/operations and to the chief of staff, National Archives USAF Intelligence Collection, copy attached to the Lowe Critique. A much lengthier earlier draft of this letter, which made very extensive use of critical responses found in the Lowe Critique to rebut Brodie's arguments, pointed out that the commanding general of SAC "had determined previously (5 July 1950) that the Strategic Air Command had the operational capability of destroying the electric power targets." A copy of this draft, dated 15 March 1951, is also attached to the Lowe Critique.

A summary account of the target panel meeting of 23 January 1951, referred to by Cabell, is provided in LeMay's Commanding General's Diary, LeMay Papers. The account indicates that LeMay was highly concerned—as was Brodie at this time (see note 117 above)—with combat degradation in bombing accuracy, insisting (according to the paraphrase in the summary) that "any target system picked that failed to reap the benefits derived from urban area bombing when a larger circular error is encountered than planned was wasteful and for that reason the basic target system of electric power was felt to be wrong." LeMay agreed with the other members of the panel that petroleum and atomic weapons should have priority but also believed that industry itself should be attacked (see also note 135 below). On the question of the current list of targets, the summary went on to say: "General LeMay had in his office at the time of the meeting a letter from the Air Force requiring that he adopt system 245 in his current war plan. Primary system in this plan was electric power. General LeMay clearly stated that he did not want to adopt this plan for aforementioned reasons and asked that this letter be rescinded. This was done and plan OFFTACKLE, later called SHAKEDOWN, is still in effect."

When the JCS on 26 February 1951 approved the Target Destruction Annex specified in study 245, it did so even though the air force general officers had already rejected that list of *specific* targets in favor of a list of target *systems* in the OFFTACKLE plan approved by the JCS on 24 October 1949 (Cabell et al., "Memorandum for General Vandenberg: [Regarding] the Target Destruction Annex for Plan PINWHEEL," 14 April 1951, National Archives USAF Intelligence Collection, Box 56 [folder: document nos. 2–19100 to 2–19199]). As far as can be determined, this discrepancy was never officially brought to the attention of the JCS.

119. The responsibility of the Physical Vulnerability Branch, according to a memorandum explaining the work of the ATD, "is to recommend appropriate mean points of impact for strategic air attack, to determine the optimum types and qualities of bombs to be employed, and to estimate the number of bombs required on target to achieve the optimum balance between physical destruction and production loss" ("Personnel Engaged in Target Work" n.d., 4, Record Group 341, Plans and Operations Division, 1942–1954 (special file: Strategic Air Offensive, Sec. 1). This document indicates that "approximately 270 persons in the Air Targets Division of the Directorate of Intelligence, Headquarters, U.S. Air Force, are the nucleus of personnel directly concerned with the selection of targets for strategic air attack." According to Ed Coffee, of the Modern Military Headquarters Branch of the National Archives, to whom I am indebted for finding this document, it was an enclosure or appendix to another paper dated April 1950. Another memorandum found in the National Archives USAF Intelligence Collection, 25 September 1950, refers to "the combined effort of the 270 Air Force and Navy civilians and officers now engaged in target analysis; these represent the entire analytical effort of the Government in this field" (Target Programs Branch, ATD, "Memorandum for Colonel William S. Steele, Executive Officer to Mr. Finletter," Box 52 [folder: document nos. 2–15500 to 2–15599]).

120. Brodie to Rosenberg, 22 August 1977.

121. Edwards to LeMay, 18 May 1951, Record Group 341, Entry 3, Book 18-A (case nos. 12029–17700), case no. 14768, 1950.

122. Cited in the Lowe Critique, 12.

123. Ibid., 11.

124. Brodie to Rosenberg, 22 August 1977. The very infrequent meetings of target panels deciding target hypotheses certainly reflected poor communication between general officers at air force headquarters and those at SAC headquarters, since a target panel would ordinarily comprise the most authoritative persons from each location. But it may be questioned whether this same condition reflected the lack of involvement of those individuals in the determination of target hypotheses. Those persons (such as the five air force officials cited in LeMay's Commanding General's Diary as composing the target panel that met on 23 January 1951 (see note 118 above), including LeMay, Cabell, Deputy Chief of Staff Nathan Twining, Director of Plans Truman H. Landon, and the assistant to the director of intelligence for production, Ernest Moore) would have been thoroughly briefed by their staffs, would occasionally have had strong views of their own (as we have seen) on the subject, and would generally tend to take their responsibilities seriously.

125. Lowe Critique, 3 (italics in original). Compare with note 119 above. According to a document describing ATD personnel, "There are sections [in the Target Research Branch] dealing with atomic energy and chemicals, petroleum and power, munitions, transportation, metals and equipment, and political and social problems. These sections are divided into units, and each unit is responsible for designated segments of industry. Each unit consists of eight to twelve highly experienced target analysts and trained industrial engineers" ("Personnel Engaged in Target Work," 2).

126. Lowe Critique, 8 (italics in original). A draft of "Changing Capabilities and War Objectives," evidently edited by Brodie, contains, immediately after the point that "the business of target selection is really the essence of air strategy," the following sentence crossed out in its entirety: "That idea has apparently not made much headway in the Pentagon, because the business of target

selection is put into a little corner of the Air Intelligence Directorate" (71). The version of this lecture found in the AFHRC files, presumably the one Brodie actually delivered, does not contain this sentence.

A study reviewing "D/I, USAF Plan for Effective Exploitation of Special Intelligence Information (SII) in the Light of Developments and Experience since the Original Plan Was Approved in October 1949," by Capt. W. M. Nation, USN, Lt. Col. R. A. Gould, USAF, and L. Canfield, [May 1950], referring to a reorganization of the Directorate of Intelligence on 1 April 1950, indicated that under the existing plan, "both the Evaluation Divison and regrouped Air Targets Division [in the Directorate of Intelligence] are physically split between the Pentagon and Temporary 'U' Building. In the Air Targets Division, only the Division Office, the Target Programs Branch and a segment of the Target Research Branch are located in the Pentagon" (attached to Capt. R. M. Nation et al., "Memorandum for Record," 3 May 1950, National Archives USAF Intelligence Collection, Box 50 [folder: document nos. 2–13100 to 2–13199]).

127. Stansfield Turner, *Secrecy and Democracy* (Boston: Houghton, Mifflin, 1985), 202.

128. Cited in the Lowe Critique, 8. In his generally negative appraisal of Brodie's memorandum, Lowe tried to attach the maximum significance to Brodie's neglect of the ATD staff in Temporary 'U' Building. "Dr. Brodie's entire period of duty with AFOIN [Air Force Office of Intelligence]," he wrote, "was spent outside the Air Targets Division in consultation with certain elements in SAC who object to the electric power target system allegedly because of operational considerations. It is not surprising, therefore, that Dr. Brodie could find no enthusiasm for the target system when he spent all his time 'outside the small group of analysts in ATD who recommended it to their seniors'" (ibid.). Brodie depended in his critique of electric power on SAC attitudes but hardly spent *all* his time away from AFOIN.

Brodie's belief that target selection matters could be managed at the highest level of the air force may have been informed by his apparent impression that the target selection staff inside the air force making recommendations to the JCS was relatively small. See note 126 above.

129. According to Lowe, toward the end of February 1951, Brodie asked for "some elementary statistical data" from the ATD that evidently dealt with the proportion of electric power targets requiring visual photography and those difficult or impossible to detect by radar. Lowe asserted (Lowe Critique, 3) that Brodie did not call for this information until after he presented his memorandum to Vandenberg.

130. Cited in the Lowe Critique, 6.

131. Dyer, "Horizontal Approach to Target Analysis," Air War College lecture, 12 December 1951, 5–6, AFHRC, K239.716251-55.

132. Cited in the Lowe Critique, 8.

133. Ibid., 6.

134. "Strategic Air Command Comments and Recommendations on the Target Destruction Annex for Plan SHAKEDOWN (Enclosure to JCS 2056/9)," 5.

135. Ibid., 4–5. A target panel established late in 1950, consisting of members of the ATD and SAC and working to determine concepts and guidance to select targets to support the Joint Emergency War Plan for war beginning after 1 July 1951—that is, for fiscal year 1952—was asked to include in its guidance a new hypothesis at the request of the Strategic Air Command to the effect that "the target complexes nominated for atomic attack should be such that the full force of each atomic bomb will be utilized to obtain maximum effective physical destruction" ("Target Systems Which Could Be Destroyed by the (Strategic) Air Offensive Initiated in Support of the Joint Emergency War Plan, Fiscal Year 1952," 29 December 1950, attached to C. P. Cabell, "Memorandum for Members, U.S.A.F. Target Panel—Subject: Meeting of Target Panel," 3 January 1951, National Archives USAF Intelligence Collection, Box 54 [folder: document nos. 2-17800 to 2-17899]).

136. Brodie to Rosenberg, 22 August 1977.

137. Cited in the Lowe Critique, 7.

138. "Implications of Scientific Advances to Military Strategy," 14. See also above.

139. Brodie may have had in mind here the point cited earlier by Joseph E. Loftus about the use of atomic bombs against petroleum installations.

140. "Air Power in an Overall Strategy," 20. As Dyer noted in 1951, "Clustering of industry is perhaps one of the most significant characteristics of the industrial side of the Soviet Union" and "following this policy of concentration . . . the Soviets have . . . [simplified] the SAC bombing problem" ("Horizontal Approach to Target Analysis," 6–7 and 9).

141. "Target Systems Which Could Be Destroyed by the (Strategic) Air Offensive, Fiscal Year 1952," 2.

142. Brodie to Rosenberg, 22 August 1977.

143. "Must We Shoot from the Hip?" (see chap. 1, n. 20), 243–244 (italics in original). Brodie's failure to consider what JCS guidance for war planning referred to as "the counter atomic offensive mission" and termed "of greatest urgency" beginning with the SHAKEDOWN plan was probably associated with his failure to consider the antecedents in the Second World War for the contemporary blunting mission, including the Allied campaign against the German V-1 and V-2 programs and the German campaign against RAF bases in England.

144. Cited in the Lowe Critique, 6. See also chapter 3 in this book. Lowe, in a typically negative reaction to Brodie's report, observed that "this type of thinking is atavistic, i.e., it is a reversion to an earlier type of thinking, wherein all the Air Force accomplished in bringing about the defeat of Japan was inpede [*sic*] the progress of the Navy." Lowe cited the USSBS conclusion that, to the contrary, "the program was transformed from one of slow strangulation to a relatively quick knock-out by strategic bombing. . . . [T]he air offensive against Japan proper was the major factor determining the timing of Japanese surrender" (*The Effects of Strategic Bombing on Japan's War Economy*, USSBS Report no. 53 [Pacific War], 2 and 59, cited in ibid., 6–7). But we saw in chapter 3 that Brodie never criticized the American bombing of Japan.

145. Brodie to Rosenberg, 22 August 1977. The Lowe Critique quotes Brodie as writing that target systems then approved for selection were based upon the assumption that "we must not under any circumstances use atomic bombs on targets outside the Soviet Union or what are now satellite countries (nor even withholding a reserve tagged for that purpose)" (3). Disagreeing with this contention, Lowe responded that "the satellites, and countries presently occupied by the U.S.S.R., . . . are deemed appropriate countries within which targets may be selected for destruction with atomic bombs" (3–4). He provided as evidence for his view the following sentence in "the study 'analyzed' in [Brodie's] Memorandum, . . .on the first page of the study in paragraph 2d": "The U.S.S.R., its satellites, and countries presently occupied by the U.S.S.R. will be deemed enemy countries in which targets may be selected for strategic air attack in the initial phase; targets selected in areas outside the U.S.S.R. proper must either have reasonably immediate effects on the Soviet war-making capacity or be of such overall importance that failure to destroy them would jeopardize the total strategic offensive" (cited in ibid., 3).

If, as surmised in note 2 of this chapter, Brodie examined ATD Study no. 245, "paragraph 2d" of that study is likely to have been included as one of the hypotheses governing the selection of target systems. That it was in fact one of the war plan hypotheses is suggested by another document, "Target Systems Which Could Be Destroyed by the (Strategic) Air Offensive, Fiscal Year 1952" (see note 135), in which all the hypotheses for the war plan are included under paragraph 2. But though the hypothesis *permitted* selecting targets in the satellite countries in Eastern Europe, the targets actually selected may have been entirely within the Soviet Union.

146. Brodie to Rosenberg, 22 August 1977.

147. "Must We Shoot from the Hip?" 241.

148. "Air Power in an Overall Strategy," 4.

149. *Strategic Air War against Japan*, 90–91. In the European theater, the RAF area bombing of Germany was similarly constrained by the need for speed in mounting bombing operations. And on the American side in that theater, the initiative of General Spaatz, the Eighth Air Force commander, to initiate attacks against German petroleum refineries shortly after a decision had

been taken by Eisenhower to attack a totally different set of targets also seems to illustrate this point. By the middle of April 1944, according to the British Bomber Command history, even before General Eisenhower had prepared a directive summarizing his decision to bomb German rail targets in advance of the Normandy invasion, "the oil offensive had already begun, and before the allied soldiers went ashore in Normandy, it had already achieved some significant effects. Before the break-out from the beachheads Bomber Command had followed the American initiative and was also embarked upon an oil plan. All this took place without any mention of it in a directive and it was largely the result of the initiative taken by General Spaatz" (Webster and Frankland, *Strategic Air Offensive against Germany*, 3:46).

150. Cited in the Lowe Critique, 9. The report in question is the same as that referred to in note 104 above.

151. "More than that," Lowe went on to say, "the shortcomings in the report are so vast that it was not considered necessary or desirable to renew the research contract with the Battelle Memorial Institute" (ibid., 9–10).

152. Lowe, "Intelligence Basis of Selection of Strategic Target Systems," 1.

153. Brodie to J. Robert Oppenheimer, 26 February 1951, J. Robert Oppenheimer Papers, Box 192 (folder: Strategic Air Warfare), Library of Congress.

154. This is strongly suggested, for example, by Fred Kaplan, (*Wizards of Armageddon*, 47–48), who cites a Brodie comment to a December 1950 internal Air Staff memorandum. For this comment, see chapter 3 in this book.

155. Vandenberg made a point of knowing the dispositions of people he engaged on special assignment prior to their engagement. For an example of this, in connection with members of the Alexander Committee of Target Consultants, see Vandenberg telephone diary, entry of 25 May 1951, Hoyt S. Vandenberg Papers, Box 2, Library of Congress. Suggestive of the same point is a Brodie postscript to a 28 November 1950 letter to Vandenberg. "'Keeper of the King's Conscience' was an ancient title," Brodie wrote, "but Keeper of the Chief's Disbelief is a new function under the sun, and I am proud to have it" (Vandenberg Papers, Box 17).

156. Brodie to Rosenberg, 22 August 1977.

157. "Air Power in an Overall Strategy," 10.

158. As indicated in the Lowe Critique, 2.

159. Reference to negotiations starting in December 1950 to establish a targeting panel is contained in "Comments on Memorandum by Dr. Brodie on Target Plans and Procedures." Creation of this panel was evidently decided in February 1951 by Louis Ridenour, chairman of the Air Force Science Advisory Board, and Thomas K. Finletter, secretary of the air force, who had then asked J. Robert Oppenheimer to participate in it ("Conversation with Dr. J. Robert Oppenheimer," 26 February 1951, included in "Government Military-Scientific Research: Review for the President of the United States, 1950–1951," bound volume, William T. Golden Papers). Cabell, in "Comments on Memorandum by Dr. Brodie on Target Plans and Procedures," indicated that Finletter, on the recommendation of Vandenberg, had on 9 March 1951 selected Henry C. Alexander to organize such a panel.

160. Lowe Critique, 1.

161. A memorandum from Vandenberg to Brodie, 23 March 1951, is cited by Fred Kaplan (*Wizards of Armageddon*, 48–49) for his observation that Vandenberg initially appointed Brodie to direct a special advisory committee on strategic bombing objectives. If this committee coincided with the one decided upon by Louis Ridenour and Thomas Finletter (note 159), Brodie's appointment is not immediately reconcilable with the selection on 9 March 1951 by Finletter, on recommendation of Vandenberg, of Henry C. Alexander to organize such a panel. Perhaps Vandenberg intended that Brodie direct the panel's work and that Alexander chair the panel, a division of responsibility reflected in the earlier massive USSBS project of which Alexander had been vice chairman.

Apart from his own intentions to participate in the panel, Brodie worked to ensure that J. Robert Oppenheimer would participate. Accompanying a letter from Brodie to Oppenheimer, found among the Oppenheimer Papers, is a copy of a prospectus, "Proposed Study of Strategic Air Warfare," whose purpose was to enhance generally the effectiveness of the strategic air force. Oppenheimer had at this time upset Vandenberg and Norstad by urging very conservative technical estimates of the feasibility of developing thermonuclear weapons, contrary to the prevailing thinking at air force headquarters. For Oppenheimer's activity in this respect and Cabell's awareness of negative air force feelings toward Oppenheimer, see *In the Matter of J. Robert Oppenheimer: Transcript of Hearing before Personnel Security Board and Texts of Principal Documents and Letters* (Cambridge, Mass.: MIT Press, 1971; first published in 1955), especially 682–696.

162. Lowe Critique, 1.

163. Ibid.

164. Brodie to Rosenberg, 22 August 1977.

165. Brodie to William T. Golden, 21 May 1951, Golden Papers. Brodie remained for a time optimistic about the effects of his work, writing to Golden on 26 June 1951 (Golden Papers) of "hearing of more and more developments which indicate that my work had a success far beyond my previous expectations. So I really don't feel at all badly about it." A marginal Golden notation to this letter states: "Quite different attitude, still based on incomplete data, on Aug. 4/51."

Writing much later of the two reports he wrote for Vandenberg, Brodie noted: "I don't know that they had any effect on Vandenberg, who at my pressure read them rather hastily one afternoon while I waited outside his office. They must have been relayed on to Cabell, who was of course incensed that I should have been so critical of the work being done under his jurisdiction. Anyway, my employment for Vandenberg was rather abruptly terminated (I was then on my way from Yale to RAND anyway). I don't know what the immediate consequences, if any, of my report [*sic*] were" (Brodie to Rosenberg, 22 August 1977). It was to the successor group chaired by Henry C. Alexander that Cabell recommended, and Vandenberg approved, that Brodie's March 1951 report to Vandenberg be referred. As already indicated, this group reached conclusions in the summer of 1951 diametrically opposed to those of Brodie on the selection of electric power targets, but there is no indication that it directed itself to Brodie's criticisms of the electric power targets.

166. Stansfield Turner describes an analogous experience he had as director of the Central Intelligence Agency (CIA). "I simply didn't have the levers to pull to ensure a team effort," he wrote of his decision making on technical collection questions. "Whenever I tried to deal directly with the person who had the information I needed, it always seemed necessary to call for one more person. Often there wasn't time to do that. I was astounded, for instance, that I was expected to make decisions about renting Red Baron aircraft or dispatching a CIA intercept team at a morning conference when most of the people present were not qualified to compare the relative capabilities of overhead reconnaissance and civilian aircraft on hire. I constantly found myself confronted with advocates for one system, but never anyone who had analyzed the advantages and disadvantages of the alternatives" (*Secrecy and Democracy*, 228).

167. One individual I interviewed, a member of the Air Staff in 1950 and 1951, pointed out that it was understood within the Air Staff that Brodie's prior work for the navy provided him with "objectivity" in his work for Vandenberg.

168. "The Problem of Integrating the Factors of National Strategy," Air War College lecture, 17 March 1950, 2, AFHRC, K239.716250-12(R). He was referring to Fuller's argument "about the strategic bombing of Germany as something which did nothing to win the victory but which 'knocked the bottom out of the peace.'" Noting that Fuller had in mind "the destruction of cities in area bombing," Brodie contended that "Fuller's statement as applied to the future is a misreading of World War II experience." "Incidentally also," he went on to say, "it is true that only a small part of our present problems in Germany derive from the results of our strategic bombing" (ibid.). For J. F. C. Fuller's ideas on this subject, see his *The Second World War, 1939–1945* (New York: Duell, Sloan, and Pearce, 1949).

169. "Air Power in an Overall Strategy," 13. In "The Heritage of Douhet," *Air University Quarterly Review* 6 (Summer 1953): 126, Brodie wrote: "Yet today there are intelligent and relatively

unbiased persons who have made a close study of the data and have concluded that there is no incontrovertible evidence to prove that the Allied bombing of Germany made a really significant contribution to the winning of the war." When questioned about who had arrived at this conclusion and on the basis of what data, Brodie referred in a letter to four civilian economists on the USSBS staff who, he asserted, were "biased in favor of purely economic results" (see, for this letter, chapter 3, note 51). Brodie continued: "This [the economists] admitted, but erected telling counter-arguments. That generally was why I used the phrase 'no *incontrovertible* evidence'" (italics in original).

In "Air Power in an Overall Strategy," he declared that "throughout the whole of our strategic bombing offensive . . . we continued to devote the major proportion of our bombs on purely ur-ban bombing which in the end we had every reason to believe simply did not pay off. But on the contrary, presented . . . a great many post-war problems that we are still faced with" (9). (The lecture transcript includes three words omitted here from the last sentence of this quotation, "a lack of," before the words "a great many," which seems to be a transcription error.)

170. "A Commentary on the Preventive War Doctrine," 11 June 1953, RAND Informal Working Paper, included in *Development of American Strategic Thought, 1952–1960* (1) (see chap. 1, n. 44), 143. Brodie went on, in rather authoritative fashion, to write the following: "The implementation of this statement (which at best must involve certain subjective judgements) would require a review not only of the development of our atomic weapons stockpile between the years 1945–1949 but also of target systems — those actually adopted and the available alternatives. The prohibitive classifi-cation of these data is obvious. Naturally, the introduction of attrition and navigation and bombing error calculations and the like would have been necessary (though still inadequate) to a comprehen-sive picture, but I am persuaded of the correctness of the proposition I have made in the text above even if one were to assume all our available weapons delivered to the 'proper bomb release point'" (ibid., 143f). Nothing suggests that Brodie would have been in a position to make such an in-formed assessment prior to the time of his service for General Vandenberg.

171. See, for these earlier assessments, chapters 2 and 3 of this book.

172. "Air Power in an Overall Strategy," 17. This view seemed to coincide with that of Arthur Harris, the British bomber commander in the Second World War, whose views on area bombing Brodie had sharply criticized. See chapter 3 of this book.

173. Electric power targets were struck by American bombers during the Korean and Vietnam wars. See Robert F. Futrell, *The United States Air Force in Korea, 1950–1953*, rev. ed. (Washington, D.C.: Government Printing Office, 1983), 193–194; and James R. McCarthy and George B. Al-lison, *Linebacker II: A View from the Rock* (Washington, D.C.: Government Printing Office, 1979).

174. "Horizontal Approach to Target Analysis," 18–19.

175. "Changing Capabilities and War Objectives," 70.

176. Another otherwise promising target seemingly excluded by the war plan hypotheses was the Soviet transportation system. "Notice," Brodie declared in 1951, "that the atomic bomb is relatively ineffective against some kinds of targets — against which HE bombs are highly effective. For example, transportation. . . . [A]tomic bombs don't look like the right kind of weapon for attacks on transportation. This is exceedingly unfortunate in view of the fact that transportation is really the weakest link of the whole Soviet economic system" ("Air Power in an Overall Strategy," 19–20). In the same lecture, he observed that "it seems to me that [attacks upon] transportation would have been the means of causing the collapse of Germany without the necessity of a great land campaign. I don't know what other target systems would have fulfilled that objective" (13).

177. "Some time later," Brodie wrote to Rosenberg, addressing the effect of the reports he wrote for Vandenberg, "Lieut. Gen. John A. Samford, who had meanwhile become head of that tri-service intelligence agency (I forget what it was or is called, but you will know; I understand it has been or is about to be liquidated) told me that he had obtained copies of my reports and had read them through very carefully at least three times" (Brodie to Rosenberg, 22 August 1977). As director of air force intelligence, Samford proposed in April 1952 to the president of the RAND Corporation that Brodie study air power in war to assist development of an adequate U.S. Air

Force basic doctrine, for which "the Air Force ha[d] been feeling around . . . for a long time" (Samford to Frank Collbohm, 18 April 1952, UCLA Collection, Box 2 [S Folder]).

Chapter 5. The H-Bomb: Strategic Air Warfare

1. Smith, *RAND Corporation: Case Study of a Non-Profit Advisory Corporation*, 87. Brodie telephoned William T. Golden on 3 August 1951 to inform him that he had already had a number of conversations with Edward Teller, the most distinguished and persistent advocate of the fusion bomb program (Golden, "Memorandum for the File," 3 August 1951, Golden Papers [folder: Bernard Brodie]). According to a 24 February 1955 "Memo of General Information on Project RAND" (see chap. 3, n. 3), which listed study of the implications of H-bombs as one of "Five of the Most Important RAND Projects of the Past Three Years," the RAND briefing on this subject — known to have been given by Brodie of the Social Science Division, Ernest Plesset of the Physics Division, and Charles Hitch of the Economics Division — was given at least eight times in March 1952 to the Air Council, the JCS, the joint secretaries, the secretary of defense, the Undersecretary and other top officials of the State Department, a Committee of the NSC including the secretary of state, the undersecretary of defense, the chairman of the Atomic Energy Commission, the National Security Resources Board, and the president. A summary report of the briefing was issued as *Implications of Large-Yield Nuclear Weapons*, RAND Report R-237, 10 July 1952 (released in sanitized form at my instigation). Brodie's contribution to the briefing of special interest for this chapter was "Political Consequences of the H-Bomb" (see chap. 1, n. 70). The next chapter focuses especially on another Brodie contribution to this briefing, "Tactical Effects of H-Bombs" (see chap. 1, n. 44).

Thermonuclear principles were first tested on 8 May 1951, and an actual thermonuclear device exploded 31 October 1952; an H-bomb was not dropped from an aircraft until May 1956. David A. Rosenberg, "American Atomic Strategy and the Hydrogen Bomb Decision," *Journal of American History* 66 (June 1979): 87f. See also Roger Hilsman, "NATO: The Developing Strategic Context," in *NATO and American Security*, edited by Klaus Knorr (Princeton, N.J.: Princeton University Press, 1959), 24. For Teller's role, see Herbert York, *The Advisors: Oppenheimer, Teller, and the Superbomb* (San Francisco: W. H. Freeman, 1976).

2. Brodie was certainly aware of bomb types other than those regarded as "standard." In a 1954 paper, he wrote that "the thermonuclear weapon, when and if it comes, will be only the latest and largest of a potential *family* of weapons" ("Nuclear Weapons: Strategic or Tactical?" *Foreign Affairs* 32 [January 1954]: 220; italics in original). For a reference to "fractional crit" (smaller critical masses of fissionable material required to produce a nuclear explosion than those associated with the standard 20-kiloton atomic bomb), see "Tactical Effects of H-Bombs," 7. Finally, in an April 1952 lecture, he referred to the possibility of making thermonuclear bombs comparable to the energy field of the standard atomic bomb, in which case the physical effects of the thermonuclear bomb would be identical with its fission predecessor except for the greater gamma radiation in a fusion explosion ("Changing Capabilities and War Objectives" [see chap. 1, n. 58], 78). Among the Brodie Papers at UCLA is the text of a speech by Gordon Dean, then chairman of the Atomic Energy Commission, dated 17 September 1952 ("The Atom in National Defense"), in which Dean states that it was then possible to have "a complete 'family' of atomic weapons" for use not only by strategic bombers, but also by ground support aircraft, armies and navies." Attached to Ken Mansfield to Brodie, 19 September 1952, UCLA Collection, Box 2 (M folder). See also *In the Matter of Oppenheimer*, 492–498 and 503–504. The extent of Brodie's competence in matters of nuclear weapons technology prior to his joining RAND is indicated by the award to him of a certificate for completing the staff officer orientation course at Sandia Base, New Mexico, 3–6 April 1951 under the auspices of the Armed Forces Special Weapons Project, UCLA Collection, Box 2 (Folder 2).

3. Ulam, *Adventures of a Mathematician* (New York: Charles Scribner's & Sons, 1976), 222–223. In 1946, in "War in the Atomic Age," in Brodie, *Absolute Weapon,* 60–61, Brodie noted that because the efficiency of energy release increased with the size of nuclear bombs, "there is a theoretical optimum size for the bomb which has perhaps not yet been determined and which may very well be appreciably or even considerably larger than the Nagasaki bomb." But he then questioned whether this potential increase was likely to occur.

4. *Sea Power in the Machine Age* (Princeton, N.J.: Princeton University Press, 1941).

5. *From Crossbow to H-Bomb,* rev. ed. (Bloomington: Indiana University Press, 1973), co-authored with Fawn Brodie.

6. See especially "Implications of Scientific Advances to Military Strategy," Air War College lecture, 9 April 1952, issued as a RAND Internal Working Paper, 7 November 1952, 4–6 (included in "Fourteen Informal Writings").

7. *Adventures of a Mathematician,* 222.

8. "Political Consequences of the H-Bomb," 24 (italics in original).

9. "Changing Capabilities and War Objectives," 78–79. The implication is that when the CEP *does* matter—and the great effort in recent years to improve the CEP in nuclear delivery systems carrying much smaller yield weapons suggests that it does—the utility of high-yield H-bombs diminishes to the vanishing point. Brodie, in contrast, had emphasized the importance of the CEP for fission bombs (ibid., 11).

10. "Strategy Hits a Dead End," *Harper's* 211 (October 1955): 34.

11. "Political Consequences of the H-Bomb," 24. For this point, Brodie cited Charles Hitch of the RAND staff.

12. Ibid. See also "Strategy Hits a Dead End," 34.

13. Brodie continued: "But what are the stakes and what are the odds of success? I leave that to you" ("Changing Capabilities and War Objectives," 82–83). About a year later, he downplayed using strategic defenses to lessen or eliminate vulnerability to nuclear attack. "To be sure," he observed, "high attrition rates imposed on the attacker may be relatively good enough for some time to come, but the further in the future we go, the more nearly perfect must the defense become to be really meaningful" ("U.S. Political Objectives in a Context of Strategic Bombing" [see chap. 1, n. 73], 123).

14. For Brodie's full endorsement of passive hardening of retaliatory forces, see below. More controversial and less authoritative was Brodie's downplaying of active defenses of military targets. For example, a Washington discussion of air defenses attended by Brodie in November 1957 led, according to a summary supplied to Brodie by James E. King, another participant, to "precisely the 'more and bigger' conclusions for SAC that you were among the first to challenge. And the crux of the argument turns on your high confidence with regard to the value of the first (surprise) strike. You gave full credit to the effect of 'hardening,' but seem quite unaware of the real potential of the defense." King went on to say that Brodie's "flat statement" that the defense can "always be saturated" raises critical qualifications, each one of which introduces uncertainties of the kind King spoke about. King had in mind, for example, the possibility of jamming the electronics of air to ground missiles and that defenses were no longer based on interceptors. "The bomber," he wrote, "is now being opposed by a defense that is one big phase ahead of it in the technological revolution" (King to Brodie, 12 November 1957, UCLA Collection, Box 1 [K Folder]). Responding to King's assertions, Brodie disclaimed great competence in the technological aspects of the issue but wrote of his feeling that "from the non-technological point of view, the odds are overwhelming against a successful active defense. I have in mind, for example, the fact that a learning period during hostilities has in the past always been more important for the defense than for offense, and that such a learning period is denied by the size of the weapons we are dealing with" (Brodie to King, 21 November 1957, ibid.). Brodie's presumption that war with fusion weapons overwhelmingly favored an attacker over the defender was supported by his view that the offensive side was always engaged in exploiting weaknesses in defensive capabilities (*Strategy in the Missile Age,* 202). Perhaps because of the strength of his presumptions, or because of his

preoccupation with the offensive-mindedness of atomic planners, Brodie does not seem to have acknowledged that an attacker might *inadequately* exploit H-bomb capabilities.

In practice, Brodie rejected spending huge amounts on defenses whose workability seemed subject to very large technological uncertainties. This point is made in a 24 September 1954 letter sent by Brodie to Klaus Knorr (UCLA Collection, Box 1 [K Folder]), in which Brodie distinguished "rational" and "irrational" grounds for spending additional money on strategic defenses. Admitting that irrational grounds were at that point dominant in the United States, he explained his reluctance on rational grounds to support greater efforts on defenses. "Progress in weapons so far has been such as to discourage projections for defense," he wrote to Knorr. "A policy which looks fairly adequate one year tends to look grossly inadequate the next. Proposals for dispersion . . . have been particularly hard hit by certain recent developments. . . . It seems to me at present impossible to predict the upper limits of catastrophe in the event of war beginning two or three years hence, or later. All efforts which you and I have seen to specify numbers of casualties in such an event are based on arbitrary and usually optimistic assumptions. It may be that the best we can do in defenses will not save more than a minority—unless *defenses help to discourage attack*" (italics in original). (His observation about dispersion referred to the greater power of fusion over fission bombs and the death of a Japanese fisherman exposed to fallout from American atomic tests in the Pacific.) Brodie's best-known essay on the problem of strategic defenses is chapter 6 of *Strategy in the Missile Age*, "Is There a Defense?"

15. "Nuclear Weapons: Strategic or Tactical?" 222–223.

16. Brodie to Arnold Wolfers, 26 May 1953, UCLA Collection, Box 2 (W Folder). With regard to the expense of bomber stockpiles, Brodie wrote in January 1954 that "every year our strategic air force costs us an amount not far short of the entire sum we have thus far spent on atomic weapons," estimating the latter figure to be ten billion dollars ("Nuclear Weapons: Strategic or Tactical?" 221, 222).

17. SAC officials apparently remained highly concerned about attrition rates from Soviet defenses even with H-bomb delivery by SAC planes. Their concerns created skepticism within some air force circles about whether the introduction of thermonuclear bombs would permit a reduction of requirements at all. General Vandenberg, for example, was quoted in June 1953 as stating that "it would be a mistake to believe fewer bombers were required to deliver atomic or hydrogen bombs over an enemy target even though their destructive effect was many times greater than that of conventional high-explosive bombers." His logic was that although two airplanes carrying atomic bombs could accomplish what thirty planes could do with conventional high-explosive bombs, it was necessary to send thirty bombers along to protect the atomic mission (cited from the *New York Times* by Arnold Wolfers, in "Superiority in Nuclear Weapons: Advantages and Limitations," *Annals* 290 [November 1953]: 8f). In the previous chapter, I noted Brodie's criticism of operational concerns of this kind, which were evidently based on the assumption that protecting American planes was both vital and highly difficult; clearly, an attrition rate of far less than 95 percent was highly worrisome to air force operational planners.

18. "Political Consequences of the H-Bomb," 31.

19. "Strategy Hits a Dead End," 34.

20. See above, and also "War in the Atomic Age," 24ff. According to Arnold Wolfers, "In the early postwar years when in everybody's mind atomic warfare was closely associated with the image of Hiroshima and Nagasaki—the only experience the world had had with it—it was generally assumed that in a nuclear war large cities would constitute the primary target. The American monopoly of atomic bombs supported this notion because city-busting appeared as a sure means of ending a war in a matter of days as it had done in the case of Japan. Today, with the near certainty that city-busting would be a two-way affair, urban population centers as targets have had to be subjected to a new look and as a consequence have dropped to the very bottom of any rational priority list" ("Could a War in Europe Be Limited?" *Yale Review* 45 [Winter 1956]:220).

21. "Changing Capabilities and War Objectives," 81.

22. "Political Consequences of the H-Bomb," 23.

23. Ibid., 32 (italics in original).

24. Ibid., 34; "Changing Capabilities and War Objectives," 81.

25. "Political Consequences of the H-Bomb," 34.

26. "Changing Capabilities and War Objectives," 79. For RAND staff calculations about damage from thermonuclear attacks, see *Implications of Large-Yield Nuclear Weapons* (note 1 above).

27. On "saturation" levels in bombing, see Brodie to Eileen Galloway, 19 April 1954, UCLA Collection, Box 3 (Folder 2); on fallout effects, see Brodie to Eileen Galloway, 21 October 1954, UCLA Collection, Box 3 (Folder 2).

28. Brodie to Galloway, 2 November 1954, UCLA Collection, Box 3 (Folder 2). Italics in original.

29. Brodie memorandum, 27 April 1954, with notation "sent to Mrs. Galloway", UCLA Collection, Box 3 (Folder 2) (italics in original). In 1952, he had declared that "there is really no use talking about large-scale *reciprocal* use of fission and thermonuclear weapons against cities as being anything other than national suicide for both sides" ("Political Consequences of the H-Bomb," 33 [italics in original]; see also "Changing Capabilities and War Objectives," 82).

30. Brodie memorandum, 27 April 1954. Questioning whether air force authorities could be so sure that "*absolute* air supremacy . . . can be won *so abruptly* upon the outbreak of hostilities that devastation with thermonuclear bombs would remain completely one-sided," Brodie called air force assurance on this point "another example of the age-old but presently exacerbated military disease of ferociousitis, the chief symptom of which is 'extreme delight in exclusive and preclusive contemplation of damage inflicted on the enemy'" (Brodie to Galloway, 20 April 1954, UCLA Collection, Box 3 [Folder 2]; italics in original).

31. Brodie to Galloway, 19 April 1954.

32. Ibid. (italics in original). Brodie did not deny that *some* warning of Soviet attack could be anticipated. He wrote much later: "However, I do support fully the belief implicit in the Air Force position that some kind of political warning will always be available. Attack out of the blue, which is to say without a condition of crisis, is one of those worst-case fantasies that we have to cope with as a starting point for our security planning, but there are very good reasons why it has never happened historically, at least in modern times, and for comparable reasons I regard it as so improbable for a nuclear power as to approach virtual certainty that it will not happen, which is to say it is not a possibility worth spending much money on" ("The Development of Nuclear Strategy," *International Security* 2 [Spring 1978]: 68–69). Others, however, have questioned whether political warning would be useful. Joseph E. Loftus argued that "all warning signals are essentially equivocal and will always remain so; and since they are such, one can perceive a warning signal or combination of them that because of their essential equivocality will either paralyze the observer, or precipitate a disastrous reaction or series of reactions that will end up in a war situation." He asserts the truth of this "whether the system is designed solely to provide a basis for taking strictly defensive measures only; or more horrendous, taking offensive action." Surprise attack can occur, he notes, where a good deal of "political warning" is available, as in the Pearl Harbor episode. Loftus, "Brodie on Deterrence," unpublished paper dated 26 June 1980, kindly furnished to me by the author.

33. "A Slightly Revived Proposal for the Underemployment of SAC in an H-Bomb Era," 23 January 1953, RAND Informal Working Paper (an introductory note indicates that it was actually prepared and delivered to the RAND staff in February 1952 but circulated in written form only the following year), in *Development of American Strategic Thought, 1952–1960 (1)*, 100. This point is also made in "Political Consequences of the H-Bomb," 35; and *Strategy in the Missile Age*, 185.

34. "Changing Capabilities and War Objectives," 87.

35. Ibid.

36. "Slightly Revived Proposal" 100. See note 33 above.

37. Ibid.

38. Ibid.

39. Brodie to Galloway, 1 December 1954, UCLA Collection, Box 3 (Folder 2). He was appraising a view of Viscount Montgomery.

40. "Changing Capabilities and Military Objectives," 81.

41. James T. Lowe, "Last 5 Minutes of Discussion Period," Air War College transcript fragment, 1 March 1951, 2, AFHRC, K239.716251-184.

42. Ibid., 4–5.

43. Asher Lee, *Airpower* (London: Gerald Duckworth, 1955), 23. According to Lee (ibid., 20), each atomic bomb cost nearly one million dollars.

44. Lee wrote that "analysis of atomic bomb damage in Nagasaki, Hiroshima and at the postwar atomic bomb trials at Bikini and New Mexico has shown that against certain resistant targets of concrete and steel, the atomic bomb can be less efficient than a series of rocket or armourpiercing bombs. In an attack on submarine pens heavily reinforced with concrete or on underground aircraft or other factories, the atomic bomb may be very wasteful. Modern steel and concrete cities will not suffer as Hiroshima and Nagasaki did, especially if there is a disciplined passive defense force to deal with the emergency" (ibid., 22–23). This argument is reminiscent of Brodie's earlier criticism of using atomic bombs against electric power installations.

45. See, for example, Brodie's "Commentary on the Force Employment Study," 9 January 1953, RAND Informal Working Paper, kindly provided to me by Malcolm Palmatier. In this paper, a critique of an Air Staff study, Brodie pointed to the lack of Air Staff consideration of the consequences of a Soviet surprise attack against the United States.

46. For the second clause in this sentence, see Henry S. Rowen and Albert Wohlstetter, "Varying Response with Circumstance," in *Beyond Nuclear Deterrence: New Aims, New Arms*, edited by Johan S. Holst and Uwe Nerlich (New York: Crane, Russak, 1977), 233. The remainder I obtained from a personal interview.

47. By 1954, a new American intelligence estimate that the Soviets had begun to build bombers as capable as the latest American models boosted the dormant blunting mission. On this new intelligence estimate, see Allen Dulles, *The Craft of Intelligence* (New York: Harper & Row, 1963), 162ff. If and when completed, a major Soviet buildup in advanced strategic bombers would enormously increase the threat to the safety of the American strategic bomber force, and the prospect of such a buildup raised the need of offsetting American adjustments in targeting of forces if not in bomber production.

48. This point is strengthened by two other considerations. First, by 1952 Brodie listed as a drawback to adding strategic targets the idea that "after a certain point, rapidly drastic diminishing returns must set in" ("Changing Capabilities and War Objectives," 75). This did not apparently take into account that Soviet forces might grow in the interval. Second, Brodie argued that "usually, where a small weapon is good, a larger weapon is better" ("More about Limited War," *World Politics* 10 [October 1957]: 118; *Strategy in the Missile Age*, 325). Using largest yield weapons was a most awkward way to go about the blunting mission, but Brodie apparently never criticized this viewpoint from the blunting mission perspective. We have already seen how earlier, in 1951, Brodie endorsed the blunting mission without examining it in detail (see chapter 4 of this book).

49. "More about Limited War," 117f.

50. On Brodie's concern about Soviet surprise attack, see *Strategy in the Missile Age*, 355–56 and 355f, and note 45 above.

51. "Unlimited Weapons and Limited War," *Reporter* 11 (November 1954): 17. In an unpublished earlier draft of chapter 8 of *Strategy in the Missile Age*, Brodie, in contrast, referred to "the tradition which holds that extra from a delivered bomb is always a 'bonus'—a tradition which is probably as strong on the Soviet side of the military fence as it is on our own" ("Alternative Strategic Policies II," 27 March 1958, RAND Informal Working Paper, 28). This draft was kindly provided to me by Roman Kolkowicz.

52. "Unlimited Weapons and Limited War," 18. The same point is made in "The Influence of Mass Destruction Weapons on Strategy," Naval War College lecture, 6 February 1956, 23–24, UCLA Collection, Box 14 (Folder 7); the end of the quotation in the lecture transcript is followed by an exclamation point.

53. "Unlimited Weapons and Limited War," 18.

54. See, for example, Henry S. Rowen, "The Future of General War," in *American National Security: A Reader in Theory and Policy*, edited by Morton Berkowitz and P. G. Bock (New York: Free Press, 1965), 71.

55. Brodie to Galloway, 19 April 1954.

56. Rowen and Wohlstetter, "Varying Response with Circumstance," 233.

57. "Changing Capabilities and War Objectives," 79.

58. Brodie to Wolfers, 26 May 1953.

59. Ibid.

60. Ibid.

61. Perhaps his earliest statement of this argument is in "Changing Capabilities and War Objectives," 64.

62. A deletion was made from the VISTA report, a major study on tactical warfare in Europe completed in 1951, of a conclusion supporting the withholding of the American SAC attack on Soviet cities until American cities had been attacked (*In the Matter of Oppenheimer*, testimony of Luis Alvarez, 770).

63. "U.S. Political Objectives in a Context of Strategic Bombing," 111.

64. *In the Matter of Oppenheimer*, 407. See also chapter 3, note 55, of this book.

65. "Political Consequences of the H-Bomb," 32. For Brodie's earlier work on this subject, see chapter 3 of this book.

66. "Political Consequences of the H-Bomb," 32. The term "sample attack" was used at RAND. The RAND Social Science Division had by September 1951 considerably thought about, and was rather confident of, in Brodie's words, the idea that "pursuit of psychological or direct political objectives calls for techniques which inevitably require a certain deliberate prolongation of the attack" ("Must We Shoot from the Hip?" [see chap. 1, n. 20], 239). Despite this view, there had as yet not been, Brodie pointed out, any study within the Air Staff of the "strike-timing" problem (ibid., 240). According to Brodie, the sample attack strategy was "abortively discussed within RAND during the days of the American atomic monopoly, but it was taken for granted, no doubt too easily, that the termination of the monopoly situation ended the possibilities of war by sample attack" ("Strategic Objectives and the Determination of Force Composition" [see chap. 1, n. 89, 93).

67. "Changing Capabilities and War Objectives," 88.

68. "Slightly Revived Proposal," 95. For a briefer suggestion of this idea, see "Changing Capabilities and War Objectives," 89.

69. "Slightly Revived Proposal," 96–97. Later, in December 1953, Brodie suggested that the idea of avoiding city attacks be put forward in a different form as the cornerstone of a public proposal at the ongoing major power negotiations on nuclear disarmament. Writing to the deputy of Adm. Lewis Strauss, who as chairman of the Atomic Energy Commission had been instructed by President Dwight Eisenhower to develop new arms limitation proposals, Brodie wrote: "Supposing it were possible to call the Russian bluff—or to meet them half way—by proposing a qualitative kind of prohibition in use. . . . I fail to see why a partial prohibition scheme which avoids 'irritating' inspection and which leaves us with plenty of bombs in case of enemy violation is altogether inferior to a disarmament *cum* inspection plan (which I submit has no chance of being both accepted by them and genuinely acceptable to us). And since we normally assume that if and when war comes the enemy will strike first, I don't see that it makes much difference to our *retaliatory* power whether or not we have agreed to some kind of partial outlawing scheme. Of course, if we want to remain free to *initiate* atomic strategic bombing regardless of Soviet acts or intentions during war, then we must reject both restrictions on use, and, even more, atomic disarmament.

And what is the potential price for such freedom?"; Brodie to William T. Golden, 15 December 1953, UCLA Collection, Box 1 [G Folder] italics in original). But Brodie had already been apprised by Golden that the AEC chairman had decided to move in a different direction—to a plan that still depended on inspection and that became known as the "Atoms for Peace" Program (Golden, "Notes on Control of Atomic Energy," 13 October 1953, copy sent by Golden's secretary to Brodie, 27 November 1953, UCLA Collection, Box 1 [G Folder]).

70. "Slightly Revived Proposal," 103.

71. Ibid., 95. Elsewhere he cited the Korean War as an example in which rules for restrained warfare were laid down in the unilateral manner he had in mind ("Nuclear Weapons: Strategic or Tactical," 228). Later, however, he complained there had been too much restraint followed by the United States in the Korean conflict (*War and Politics*, 91ff).

72. Brodie to Wolfers, 26 May 1953 (italics in original).

73. The three points are discussed in "Slightly Revived Proposal," 104. For the idea that the Soviets would value American support to keep control of a situation, Brodie appears to be indebted to Nathan Leites, a member of the RAND staff, for his outlining of the Bolshevik operational code. See Leites, *A Study of Bolshevism* (Glencoe, Ill.: Free Press, 1953). Brodie was evidently familiar with Leites's ideas from their inception (see Brodie to Leites, 17 August 1951, UCLA Collection, Box 1 [Folder 14]). See also chapter 7, note 11, of this book.

74. "Political Consequences of the H-Bomb," 36.

75. *Strategy in the Missile Age*, 183.

76. Some indication of this problem was afforded to Brodie by President Eisenhower's decision, taken early in 1960 prior to his planned visit to the Soviet Union, to cancel the SAC airborne alert. The president, wrote Brodie, obviously thought the alert was repugnant and incongruous with the planned summit conference ("The Rejection of Airborne Alert: Another Facet of the 'Provocation' Problem," 8 February 1960, RAND Informal Working Paper, UCLA Collection, Box 17 [Folder 11]). He felt the president's action should have been taken into account in earlier evaluations of the SAC alert, even though Eisenhower's attitude would not have been much affected by a careful study of the chances of an "unauthorized act" occurring as a result of the alert.

77. Coral Bell was impressed, on the basis of her reading of the Oppenheimer hearings, "by the absence of optimism, even on the part of those who were strongly 'for' the [thermonuclear] bomb, that its possession could readily be transmuted into diplomatic advantage" (*Negotiation from Strength* [New York: Alfred A. Knopf, 1963], 33).

78. "Political Consequences of the H-Bomb," 24 (italics in original).

79. Ibid., 27 (italics in original). Shortly afterward, Brodie played down the significance of a fusion bomb monopoly. Writing to Arnold Wolfers in May 1953, he declared that "I think the distinction between a monopoly and the absence of it has been overdone. There is of course a certain unique advantage in monopoly possession *per se*. For example, even with a very few bombs the Russians would have a blackmail potential, especially against our NATO allies, which might be out of all proportion to the real military value of their small stockpile. On the other hand, militarily the question of monopoly versus multilateral possession cannot be divorced from considerations of quantity. We were no doubt relatively stronger atomically than the Russians a year after they produced their first bomb than we were at the moment they did so, and it is even conceivable that our relative advantage may be greater right now than it ever has been before. . . . It is true that the geometric ratio of advantage over the opponent which the stronger power enjoys is bound to decline with time even if the latter's production remains much greater" (Brodie to Wolfers, 26 May 1953).

80. The first statement is in "Slightly Revived Proposal," 97; the second statement is in "Political Consequences of the H-Bomb," 24.

81. This same focus characterized Brodie's book *Strategy in the Missile Age*, in which he pleaded for controlling implementation of the strategic air offensive and for planning for alternatives to such an offensive.

82. Coral Bell wrote of Dulles's strategy of "massive retaliation" that "a policy debatably appropriate in a world still lit by the glare of the first American H-bomb looked a good deal less reasonable in a world that contained a Soviet weapon of the same sort" (*Negotiation from Strength*, 154). And James E. King observed in 1957: "It is notable how much of recent discussion of United States military and foreign policy has been devoted to our alleged lack of determination to use the advantages we are assumed to have in nuclear power, and how little to the question whether we really have such advantages, and what we should do about it if we do not have them, or if, having them temporarily, we are about to lose them" ("Nuclear Plenty and Limited War," *Foreign Affairs* 35 [January 1957]: 240).

83. "Unlimited Weapons and Limited War," 20.

84. Bell, *Negotiation from Strength*, 6ff.

85. I already discussed his concern for protecting strategic retaliatory forces.

86. "Unlimited Weapons and Limited War," 18–19.

87. Ibid., 20–21.

88. "U.S. Political Objectives in a Context of Strategic Bombing," 127–128.

89. Ibid., 124. One scientific panel concluded in 1949 that the United States was more vulnerable to very-large-yield nuclear weapon attacks than was the Soviet Union (*In the Matter of Oppenheimer*, testimony of Oppenheimer, 253).

90. "Political Consequences of the H-Bomb," 34 (italics in original).

91. "U.S. Political Objectives in a Context of Strategic Bombing," 128–129. Roger Fisher wrote that a group of military officers to whom he outlined the problem of stopping a European war "found it hard to draft a fair cease-fire that didn't sound like a unilateral Western ultimatum" ("Preventing Nuclear War," *Bulletin of the Atomic Scientists* 37 [March 1981]: 12).

92. "U.S. Political Objectives in a Context of Strategic Bombing," 122–123.

93. *Strategy in the Missile Age*, 293–294.

94. Especially important has been the subsequent work of Thomas Schelling.

95. See especially *War and Politics*.

96. Among such persons are Paul Nitze and Edward Luttwak.

97. See "Development of Nuclear Strategy."

Chapter 6. The H-Bomb: Battlefield Warfare

1. "What I have in mind," wrote Brodie in this connection to a correspondent in November 1953, "is this: the prevailing assumption is that a new war will begin a la Pearl Harbor, that is, with an overwhelming nuclear attack on our cities and other targets in the interior, as well as on our allies. Such an action I should regard as an unambiguous signal for retaliation—whatever good such retaliation would do. And I have implicitly argued that our present publicized policies and attitudes encourage and even coerce the Soviet Union to just such a form of initiation of war if they choose to launch one. But wars may begin in all sorts of ways and by all sorts of actions, such as might involve the movement strictly of ground troops. Do we then 'retaliate' against that with a nuclear air strike, and thereby oblige the Russians to retaliate in kind against ourselves? So far as I know, this is the kind of question that is not being asked, let alone answered, anywhere" (Brodie to Hamilton F. Armstrong, 18 November 1953, UCLA Collection, Box 1 [A Folder]).

2. "The old concepts of strategy, including those of Douhet and of World War II, have come to a dead end" ("Strategy Hits a Dead End," *Harper's* 211 [October 1955]: 36).

3. See chapter 5, note 2, of this book.

4. Those working to develop atomic weapons for use in the Korean War were optimistic on this score. "During the doldrums of the H-bomb," Oppenheimer later recalled, "the war in Korea broke out, and a large part of GAC's and other committee's [*sic*] attention was, as I say, devoted to the very immediate and the very obvious, and, I would say, to using an atomic explosive

not merely in a strategic campaign but also in a defensive or tactical campaign, and I think the record will bear out that that is what we were spending most of our time worrying about. That is . . . the origin of the exercises which led to the development of a tactical capability in Europe, the origin of one at least of the threads, one at least of the reasons for the very great expansion in the atomic energy enterprise to support a much more diversified use of weapons, even leading some people to suggest—I think this was Gordon Dean—that maybe the atomic weapons on the battlefield would be so effective that it would not be necessary to use them strategically" (*In the Matter of Oppenheimer*, 83). The GAC was the General Advisory Committee of the Atomic Energy Commission (AEC), and Gordon Dean was then chairman of the AEC. Since Brodie is known to have held a number of discussions with Oppenheimer during the first year of the Korean War, he is likely to have been aware of the priority being given at that time to developing nuclear weapons for tactical uses and the rationale for that priority. See also chapter 7 of this book.

5. Brodie to Galloway, 21 October 1954, UCLA Collection, Box 3 (Folder 2); italics in original. Brodie's idea that "diplomacy, in so far as it involves political pressures of any kind . . . is essentially inseparable from military power" (ibid.), is closely related to his view (examined in the last chapter and to be discussed in chapters 7 and 9 as well) that war ought to be governed by political objectives.

6. "Changing Capabilities and War Objectives" (see chap. 1, n. 58), 81. In 1952 Brodie wrote that "so far as the Air Force is concerned, tactical requirements for both nuclear weapons and aircraft will always be competitive with requirements for strategic bombing, at least in terms of original resources" ("Tactical Effects of H-Bombs" [see chap. 1, n. 44], 3).

7. "Air Power in an Overall Strategy," Air War College lecture, 23 May 1951, 11, AFHRC, K239.716251-26.

8. Brodie to David A. Rosenberg, 22 August 1977, UCLA Collection, Box 9 (Folder 21).

9. Cited in Henry A. Kissinger, *Nuclear Weapons and Foreign Policy* (New York: Harper & Brothers, 1957), 154. See also Brodie, "Slightly Revived Proposal" (see chap. 5, n. 33), 98.

10. "Strategic Implications of the North Atlantic Pact," *Yale Review* 39 (December 1949): 199.

11. Ibid., 196.

12. "Nuclear Weapons: Strategic or Tactical?" *Foreign Affairs* 32 (January 1954): 226; "Changing Capabilities and War Objectives," 80. Alain Enthoven and George Kennan (the latter by 1950) have pointed separately to a tendency within the American government to exaggerate the land combat strength of the Warsaw Pact. See Milton Leitenberg, "Background Materials in Tactical Nuclear Weapons (Primarily in the European Context)," in *Tactical Nuclear Weapons: European Perspectives*, assembled by the Stockholm International Peace Research Institute (SIPRI) (New York: Crane, Russak, 1978), 23–24. There is no evidence that Brodie ever examined Warsaw Pact capabilities critically.

13. Hilsman, "NATO: The Developing Strategic Context," in Knorr, ed., *NATO and American Security*, 14. According to Hilsman, this plan was discarded, evidently in favor of a medium-term defense plan, when SHAPE (Supreme Headquarters, Allied Powers, Europe) was established in 1951.

14. "Changing Capabilities and War Objectives," 73–74. See also "Air Power in an Overall Strategy," 18.

15. "Air Power in an Overall Strategy," 19. Earlier (in 1948) he had written, with reference to a Soviet attack against Western Europe, that "small powers have only marginal strength to contribute at best, and they may decide that surrender even to Russian occupation—which they will hope to be temporary—is preferable to demolition by atomic bombs" ("Strategic Implications of the North Atlantic Pact," 195).

16. "Air Power in an Overall Strategy," 19.

17. Acheson, *Present at the Creation: My Years in the State Department* (New York: W. W. Norton, 1969), 308. Omar Bradley, then chairman of the JCS, subsequently criticized the Lisbon force goals for not providing an adequate European defense, but he acknowledged to Acheson that "the

forces recommended were better than what we had, were the best we could get, and, taken together with our nuclear capacity, would have a strong deterrent effect upon any desire to test their adequacy" (ibid., 623).

18. Hilsman, "NATO: Developing Strategic Context," 21.

19. "Air Power in an Overall Strategy," 18. See also chapter 4 of this book.

20. "Changing Capabilities and War Objectives," 74.

21. Brodie to Rosenberg, 22 August 1977.

22. Leitenberg, "Background Materials," 13. The first nuclear weapons were delivered to NATO in the summer of 1952 (ibid., 12), but some nuclear weapons had been placed under the jurisdiction of American air force officials in Germany earlier (see below).

23. "Tactical Effects of H-Bombs," 5 (italics in original). In this same paper, Brodie wrote that "the addition of H-bombs to the arsenal of weapons used tactically may profoundly affect the Allied chances of stopping the Soviet armies, especially if these have been combined with a successful strategic bombing campaign" (6). Compare "Changing Capabilities and War Objectives," 73 and 81. David A. Rosenberg has documented how early American progress in strategic weaponry was fueled significantly by what military planners and leaders perceived to be insufficient American conventional force strength, particularly in relation to forces of the Soviet Union in Europe. As early as January 1950, for example, JCS chairman Gen. Omar N. Bradley informed the secretary of defense that fusion weapons would likely have "high tactical value in special situations . . . against such targets as . . . massed enemy forces might provide" (Rosenberg, "American Atomic Strategy and the Hydrogen Bomb Decision," *Journal of American History* 66 [June 1979]: 83). Not surprisingly, air force officers were slower to grasp this argument than their army counterparts. See below.

24. See chapter 5 of this book.

25. "Nuclear Weapons: Strategic or Tactical?" 222.

26. Ibid., 225.

27. "Tactical Effects of H-Bombs," 14.

28. James T. Lowe, "Last 5 Minutes of Discussion Period," Air War College transcript, 1 March 1951, 3, AFHRC, K239.716251-184. David A. Rosenberg reported that the JCS's endorsement, late in 1949, of the use of nuclear weapons and SAC to retard a Soviet invasion of Western Europe was a distinct mission of the American strategic bombing campaign being planned against the Soviet Union (Rosenberg to Brodie, 13 May 1977, UCLA Collection, Box 9 [R Folder]; Rosenberg, "American Atomic Strategy and the Hydrogen Bomb," 82). The document that generated study 245 as the list of targets for the strategic offensive in connection with the fiscal year 1951 war plan projected another study of targets, "The Vulnerability to Strategic Air Attack of the Advance of the Soviet Army and Supporting Elements into Western Eurasia." No evidence has yet come to light to indicate that Brodie critiqued the contents of this study. Altogether, fifteen studies or appendixes to the emergency war plan were to be carried out. See "Extract from Air Targets Division Action Summary 264/FY 51, 'Target Systems Submitted for Consideration in Fulfilling the Objectives of the Joint Outline Emergency War Plan, Fiscal Year 1951,'" Tab A attached to a memorandum, "Recommendations and Estimates for Preparation of Certain Appendices for Revision of Plan OFFTACKLE, FY 51," E. Moore to Intelligence Division, General Staff, U.S. Army, 17 May 1950 (National Archives USAF Intelligence Collection, Box 50 [folder: document nos. 2-13100 to 2-13189]).

29. "Changing Capabilities and War Objectives," 75. See also chapter 5, note 48, of this book.

30. Brodie to Rosenberg, 22 August 1977 (italics in original). Compare General Bradley's assessment of fusion bombs in note 23 above.

31. Norstad to Vandenberg (telephone conversation), 25 August 1951, RL 332, Vandenberg Papers, Box 86 (Redline folder). Acknowledging that many army and air force groups had considered applying atomic weapons to "the tactical problem," Norstad observed that many had tried to prove some preexisting conviction, with the result that atomic weapons had been considered

"as little more than heavy artillery since they have normally worked on the basis of enhancing our capacity to work within operational conceptions." He went on: "The developments in the atomic weapon field with which we have recently been acquainted may change materially our approach to the problem. It is possible that we should work on the basis of new concepts rather than concentrate our efforts on [improving] the old ones. It is also possible that the size and composition of forces of all services might be affected by the [result] of an objective and comprehensive study made in an atmosphere that eliminates the inhibitions and limitations which govern our thinking [as] long as we remain within the boundaries [of] conventional tactical doctrine."

Norstad proposed that an ad hoc working group be established as an urgent matter under the auspices of his headquarters "to consider the application and effect of atomic weapons on the defense of Western Europe." For study purposes, Norstad recommended use of the assumptions "that numbers are not a limiting factor; that physical specifications be made to conform with the capabilities of the carrying vehicle[;] and that bombs generally of Nagasaki power are involved." (Inasmuch as Norstad wished to analyze "bombs generally of Nagasaki power," it may be presumed that the newer atomic weapon developments that Norstad had in mind pertained to the greater adaptability of later versions of atomic bombs for battlefield use.) Brodie's work diverged only from the last assumption; he considered thermonuclear weapons for the tactical war mission, because, in his opinion, only weapons of that magnitude when added to fission weapon applications would be adequate to make "traditional arguments against the use of nuclear weapons against troops in the field fall to the ground" (see "Changing Capabilities and War Objectives," 80; compare with ibid., 76). Norstad's project was distinct from another major effort, code named VISTA and under way under contract from the three military services at the California Institute of Technology at about the same time, that inquired into defending Western Europe as soon as possible under the assumption that American nuclear weapons would be used for this purpose (*In the Matter of Oppenheimer*, 48ff, and chapter 5, note 62, of this book).

32. Telephone interview with Gen. Lauris Norstad, 16 May 1980.

33. In the list of briefings spelled out in chapter 5, note 1, this subject would have been particularly appropriate for the Air Council, the Joint Chiefs of Staff, and the secretary of defense. One briefing session, before the Air Staff, is referred to in Brig. Gen. William M. Garland to Brodie, 4 April 1952, UCLA Collection, Box 1 (G Folder). General Garland is known to have directed an early study of the retardation problem, still classified, in the Air Force Office of Intelligence. Brodie's briefing on H-bomb use in European war, "Tactical Effects of H-Bombs," which brought up the key planning question of whether to "discover more and more targets for the strategic bombing campaign, or . . . consider the allocation of large *proportions* of our growing stockpile [of nuclear weapons] to tactical uses" (italics in original), did not find fault with strategic bombing. This was in contrast to his briefing "Political Consequences of the H-Bomb," which presented the case for restraint in H-bomb use against Soviet and American cities (detailed in chapter 5 of this book).

34. "Tactical Effects of H-Bombs," 6.

35. "The question for the present and immediate future," declared Brodie in April 1952, "is: Will not the attrition rates which our aircraft will suffer in deep penetrations over Russian territory result in a large part of our weapons stockpile becoming essentially ineffective because we don't have the vehicles to carry them?" ("Changing Capabilities and War Objectives," 76). Such a question was evidently directed especially at those air force officials in Washington and at SAC headquarters in Omaha who believed, contrary to Brodie's other writings, that the H-bomb did not permit savings in nuclear bombs and in bomb carriers.

36. "Tactical Effects of H-Bombs," 5. In "Changing Capabilities and War Objectives," Brodie referred to "a fantastic augmentation of firepower" (80).

37. "Tactical Effects of H-Bombs," 9.

38. Ibid., 14. In January 1954, Brodie wrote that the limits of tactical nuclear use "are imposed only by the locations of people whom one does not want to hit; and so long as these can be pro-

tected or removed, the more area covered the better" ("Nuclear Weapons: Strategic or Tactical?" 225). He did not explain how these people were to be "protected or removed."

39. "Tactical Effects of H-Bombs," 13.

40. Ibid., 14.

41. Ibid., 16.

42. Ibid., 9–10.

43. Ibid., 17–18 (italics in original). The resemblance of these ideas to the much later writings of Steven Canby on NATO tactical defense should be noted (see Canby, *The Alliance and Europe, Part IV: Military Doctrine and Technology*, Adelphi Paper no. 109 [London: International Institute for Strategic Studies, 1974/75]).

44. "Tactical Effects of H-Bombs," 3. See also Canby, *The Alliance and Europe*, 16 and 19.

45. Ibid., 3.

46. Malcolm Hoag, "The Place of Limited War in NATO Strategy," in Knorr, ed., *NATO and American Security*, 117.

47. See chapter 2 of this book for a similar criticism of Brodie's anticipated use in 1946 of large numbers of atomic bombs against Soviet cities in a Soviet-American war.

48. "Strategy Hits a Dead End," 36.

49. Ibid. For another estimate of the implications of a "nihilistic" scenario of large-scale use of nuclear weapons on the battlefield, see note 65 below.

50. "Tactical Effects of H-Bombs," 18 (italics in original).

51. Samuel T. Cohen, *The Neutron Bomb: Political, Technological, and Military Issues* (Cambridge, Mass.: Institute for Foreign Policy Analysis, n.d.), 3–4.

52. "Although it is as yet too early to tell for sure," wrote Roger Hilsman in 1956, "there seems to be nothing in the facts of nuclear weapons, or in the attempts to work out the military doctrines appropriate to those facts, to indicate that fewer men will be needed on the ground rather than more. If the enemy is to be forced to concentrate sufficiently to form a target for nuclear weapons, troops will be needed all across the front in just about the same quantities, so far as anyone can now tell, as they would in conventional war. Of course, the defender in conventional war never needed to match an enemy man for man, and there is no reason to believe that nuclear war would differ in this respect. But the defense of any given theater of operations against an enemy who is rich in manpower is still likely to require a certain number of divisions, determined by the length of front, terrain and natural obstacles, and density of road and rail networks. No one can name an exact number; still, the general level of forces needed for a given piece of terrain in [sic] usually rather obvious. . . .

"Besides needing just as many forces in a nuclear war, we also probably need to have a higher percentage of these forces ready and in position before a war starts. . . . All this means that, far from reducing the burden of military preparations, nuclear weapons have probably increased it" ("Strategic Doctrines for Nuclear War," in *Military Policy and National Security*, edited by William W. Kaufmann [Princeton, N.J.: Princeton University Press, 1956], 72 and 74). Gen. Matthew B. Ridgway, then army chief of staff, apparently made parallel arguments in attempting to counter army cutbacks proposed under the Eisenhower "New Look" defense budget (Glenn H. Snyder, "The 'New Look' of 1953," in *Strategy, Politics, and Defense Budgets*, edited by Warner R. Schilling et al. [New York: Columbia University Press, 1962], 447). For an opposing view paralleling Brodie's, see Kissinger, *Nuclear Weapons and Foreign Policy*, 153.

Qualified Soviet writers agreed with Hilsman at this time that battlefield atomic warfare would make more rather than fewer soldiers necessary (Bell, *Negotiation from Strength*, 156f and 175). Early military exercises anticipating deployment of nuclear weapons for tactical purposes in Europe underscored Hilsman's ideas while casting doubt upon Brodie's views. See Wolfgang Heisenberg, *The Alliance and Europe, Part I: Crisis Stability in Europe and Theatre Nuclear Weapons*, Adelphi Paper no. 96 (London: International Institute for Strategic Studies, 1973), 1; and Harvey A. DeWeerd, "Atomic Weapons and Ground Combat: The Search for Organization and Doctrine," RAND Paper

P-497, 1954, 4f and 6, cited in Uwe Nerlich, "The Political Choices," in *New Conventional Weapons and East-West Security, Part II,* Adelphi Paper no. 145 (London: International Institute for Strategic Studies, 1978), 12. When Brodie revised his ideas on this subject (see chapter 7 of this book), he gave much more prominence to Soviet capabilities and intentions than he had in his 1952 "tactical effects" paper.

53. "Strategy Hits a Dead End," 36.

54. For the Soviet view, see, for example, Cyril E. Black and Frederick J. Yeager, "The USSR and NATO," in Knorr, ed., *NATO and American Security,* 45; and Brodie, "More on Limited War," *World Politics* 10 (October 1957): 117f. The NATO view is discussed in the next chapter.

55. "Nuclear Weapons: Strategic or Tactical?" 225.

56. "Tactical Effects of H-Bombs," 7.

57. Ibid. Brodie's idea that large-yield fusion bombs were to be used against such critical targets to compensate for inadequate CEPs fits in with his argument, referred to in chapter 5, that fusion bomb yields were so large that they made CEPs inconsequential. But we may note again his view, detailed in the previous chapter, that fusion weapons might be used *too* efficiently for satisfaction. This point Brodie initially refrained from developing in regard to tactical warfare, though his analysis of a strategic air war employing fusion weapons was critically based upon it.

58. Cohen, *Neutron Bomb,* 4f.

59. "Slightly Revived Proposal," 94–95.

60. "Strategy Hits a Dead End," 36 (italics in original).

61. "Nuclear Weapons: Strategic or Tactical?" 226 (italics added).

62. Brodie to Wolfers, 26 May 1953, UCLA Collection, Box 2 (W Folder). During the 1950s, Soviet leaders pointed out to the European members of NATO that the Soviet Union was less vulnerable to nuclear weapons than were the latter with their more concentrated populations and resources (Black and Yeager, "USSR and NATO," 55–56).

63. "Slightly Revived Proposal," 102. See also "Political Consequences of the H-Bomb," 29; and Brodie to Wolfers, 26 May 1953.

64. There is no public indication that such an initiative was ever undertaken. An initiative of this kind would have been at odds with the spirit of the *declared* American "massive retaliation" strategy of deterring aggression by a willingness and ability "to respond vigorously at places and with means of [our] own choosing" (see Brodie, *Strategy in the Missile Age,* 248ff). According to Wolfgang Heisenberg, however, Dulles "several times qualified his 'massive retaliation' statement of 12 January 1954 by stating—as seemed more likely anyway—that nuclear weapons would first be used on a selective basis against military targets" ("The Alliance and Europe," 3).

65. Malcolm Hoag wrote: "If we seek to exploit our nuclear superiority tactically at a time when absolute levels of stockpiles are very high, we must be prepared for the explosion of a great deal more fissionable material in combat. If this occurs, and if the fissionable material is so packaged that both we and the Soviets get great weapon effects per unit of fissionable material—the crude direct way of maximizing military effects—then total damage in any tactical theater rises enormously. 'Taking war back to the battlefield' is a fine slogan, but if it is used to rationalize unlimited theater employment of atomic weapons, it becomes a mockery to allies over whose territory they are being employed. The battlefield will be deep, because rear-located tactical air bases and missile launch sites are obviously prime targets, and logistic supply lines may well be. Hitting them hard and early is terribly important. And military commanders have compelling reasons to use big weapons rather than little ones to compensate for inaccuracy in their delivery" ("Place of Limited War in NATO Strategy," 117).

66. "Slightly Revived Proposal," 102. In his writings, Brodie did not take account, for example, that greater NATO reliance upon battlefield nuclear weapons made equity in member-state contributions to the alliance more difficult to realize since only the United States could readily supply such capabilities.

67. An indication of how little inherent cohesion Brodie saw in NATO at this time is found

in his worry that American announcement of progress in H-bomb development, unless carefully prepared beforehand, might add to European divisions about the value of the alliance ("Political Consequences of the H-Bomb," 30).

68. Hilsman, "NATO: The Developing Strategic Context," 24.

69. Brodie, "Strategy Hits a Dead End," 36. See also my conclusions in the previous chapter.

Chapter 7. Limited War

1. For an earlier analysis, see B. H. Liddell Hart, "War, Limited," *Harper's* 192 (March 1946): 193–203. In a letter to Liddell Hart, 26 April 1957, UCLA Collection, Box 1 (L Folder), Brodie wrote that he had been "in effect a follower" of Liddell Hart when he learned in 1952 that a thermonuclear weapon would be tested the following autumn and would probably be successful.

2. This quotation and the next are from "Learning to Fight a Limited War," *Los Angeles Times*, 3 December 1967, G-7. The idea of bringing war "back to the battlefield" has also been associated with J. Robert Oppenheimer (see Mandelbaum, *Nuclear Question*, 100, and chapter 6, p. 4 of this study).

3. I am referring especially to the work of Richard Leghorn and William W. Kaufmann. Brodie later wrote that "I do happen to have been the first person in RAND to have urged (at the beginning of 1952) consideration of limited war and development of special capabilities for it" (Brodie to Alastair Buchan, 21 January 1964, UCLA Collection, Box 6 [Folder 3]). According to James E. King, who subsequently chronicled the development of ideas about nuclear strategy, a study by Klaus Knorr, *The War Potential of Nations* (Princeton, N.J.: Princeton University Press, 1956), advanced many of the ideas about limited war found in Brodie's work at the time (King to Brodie, April 1972, UCLA Collection, Box 8 [K Folder]).

4. Brodie to [Thomas] C. Schelling, 9 January 1957, UCLA Collection, Box 2 (Folder 11).

5. Brodie himself wrote that his ideas on this subject were regarded as "somewhat crackpot," ascribing this skepticism to the then "deeply entrenched . . . axiom that 'all modern war is total war'" ("Learning to Fight a Limited War," G-7). For another, more popular view of war-making limitations, see Richard Leghorn, "No Need to Bomb Cities to Win War," *U.S. News and World Report*, 28 January 1955, 78–94. Leghorn proposed that the United States prepare to respond to a nonnuclear Soviet attack against the American homeland or against NATO "by using tactical nuclear weapons to destroy his attacking units in the battle zone and the military installations in his immediate rear areas" (ibid., 79). Referring to Leghorn's article, Brodie wrote later that "I feel I have a certain paternal relationship to that article." He went on: "In February, 1952 I wrote a paper, classified, presenting essentially the same argument as Leghorn's, though not developed in as much detail. This paper had some circulation within the Air Force, and I also used it in some lectures I gave at various of the war colleges. Leghorn must have known that paper or its derivatives, because in sending his manuscript to some of my friends at RAND for review, he asked specifically that I read and comment on it, which I did—sparcely [*sic*]. However, I must add that I never was as positive about the matter as Leghorn seems to be, and I am much less positive about it now [than] I was formerly. . . . [I]f you really want to avoid strategic bombing you also have to refrain from going after the enemy's strategic air force. So far this notion seems extremely difficult for our people to grasp or accept, which is one reason why I no longer have much faith in the feasibility of the whole proposal" (Brodie to Stephen Jones, 25 February 1955, UCLA Collection, Box 1 [J Folder]). The 1952 paper to which Brodie referred may be a precursor of Brodie's RAND paper, "Slightly Revived Proposal" (see chap. 5, n. 33). Brodie and Leghorn may have disagreed about the feasibility of keeping war limited once strategic targets had also been attacked. Brodie apparently was referring here to U.S. Air Force officials' unwillingness to distinguish more limited attacks against Soviet bombing forces from more general strategic bombing. See also note 9 below.

6. Brodie to W. L. Borden, 20 October 1954, UCLA Collection, Box 1 (B Folder); italics in original.

7. "Slightly Revived Proposal," 96.

8. See chapter 6 of this book. According to G. C. Reinhardt, early studies of nuclear weapons use in limited war assumed the belligerents would be strongly disinclined to move to general war, but the studies did not consider Europe as the battlefield ("Nuclear Weapons and Limited Warfare: A Sketchbook History," RAND Paper P-3011, November 1964, 9).

9. Brodie to Paul Davis, 4 October 1955, UCLA Collection, Box 1 (D Folder).

10. "The Influence of Mass Destruction Weapons on Strategy," Naval War College lecture, 6 February 1956, 22, UCLA Collection, Box 14 (Folder 7). The origin of Brodie's interest in human emotions as a contributor to the expansion of war is likely to have been the work and interests of some other person or persons at RAND, where in 1954 the research staff included, according to Brodie, "nuclear physicists, mathematicians, and social scientists whose training includes a measure of psychoanalysis" (memorandum, Brodie to Hans Speier, 23 November 1954, UCLA Collection, Box 4 [Folder 19]). Specifically, the most important source was probably the work of Nathan Leites. In 1968, Brodie wrote that he had earlier co-authored with Leites "a semi-psychoanalytic interpretation of [Gen. Curtis E.] LeMay's personality"; for "institutional reasons," all copies except Brodie's were recalled and destroyed (Brodie to Knorr, 25 January 1968, UCLA Collection, Box 6 [K Folder]). No trace of this study has been found. Brodie was not likely to have written "that the resort to arms is itself enough to stimulate in those who do so a powerful flow of adrenalin" without having some person or persons in mind, and the reference may be to LeMay. Brodie's earliest published comment on the psychoanalytic method in social science research is a book review, "A Psychoanalytic Interpretation of Woodrow Wilson," *World Politics* 9 (April 1957): 413–422. See also *Strategy in the Missile Age*, 266f; chapter 8, note 31; and chapter 9 of this book. Brodie himself began to undergo psychoanalysis in 1957, and he remained in analysis for an extended period (see Brodie to Robert Dahl, 21 May [1962?], which responds to a note from Dahl to Brodie dated 3 May 1962, UCLA Collection, Box 1 [D Folder]).

11. In a letter to Donald Brennan dated 30 November 1966 (UCLA Collection, Box 6 [B Folder]), Brodie recalled writing at RAND a "cautionary note against over-rigid subservience to a pattern of views which in general I hold in high respect," indicating that he meant Nathan Leites's *A Study of Bolshevism*. (The paper about which he was being questioned by Brennan is entitled "Provocation Works on People: SOFS — Strategic Objectives — 9," dated 12 June 1959; this paper is discussed in chapter 8.) Brodie went on to say that "while I had over time tended to be somewhat less respectful of the Leites discoveries or formulations, the Cuban missile crisis brought me back into line." However, Leites worked on diverse subjects, and we have seen (note 10 above) that his influence upon Brodie was not limited to his writings on the Soviet leadership.

12. Brodie to Stephen B. Jones, 25 February 1955. See also "Slightly Revived Proposal," 97–100. Here again Brodie seemed to diverge from such commentators as Richard Leghorn, who wished to limit war in militarily defensible ways. Brodie was evidently more interested in the political foundation of war limitations than was Leghorn. According to James E. King, the idea that "limited war is 'inefficient war'" may have originated with Hans Speier (King, "Airpower in the Missile Gap," *World Politics* 12 [July 1960]: 631). Speier headed the RAND Social Science Division for much of the 1950s, and Brodie could be expected to be very familiar with his work.

13. "More about Limited War," *World Politics* 10 (October 1957): 114–115 (italics in original). See also "Influence of Mass Destruction Weapons on Strategy," 20.

14. Brodie to Schelling, 16 May 1962, UCLA Collection, Box 2 (Folder 11).

15. Richard Smoke, *War: Controlling Escalation* (Cambridge, Mass.: Harvard University Press, 1977), 66.

16. "Changing Capabilities and War Objectives" (see chap. 1, n. 58), 63–64.

17. See chapter 5 of this study.

18. Michael Howard, "*Temperamenta Belli*: Can War Be Controlled?" in *Restraints on War: Studies in the Limitation of Armed Conflict*, edited by Howard (Oxford: Oxford University Press, 1979), 4.

19. Donald C. Watt, "Restraints on War in the Air before 1945," in Howard, ed., *Restraints on War*, 65. See also Michael Howard, "Military Power and International Order," *International Affairs* (London) 40 (July 1964): 397–408.

20. Howard, *"Temperamenta Belli,"* 12.

21. Liddell Hart, "War, Limited," 201. See also George H. Quester, *Deterrence before Hiroshima* (New York: John Wiley & Sons, 1966).

22. The first of these assertions is in Brodie, "Unlimited Weapons and Limited War," *Reporter* 11 (November 1954): 21; the second is in Brodie to Stephen B. Jones, 25 February 1955, which was stimulated by a series of questions asked by Jones about the *Reporter* article. See Jones to Brodie, 22 February 1955, UCLA Collection, Box 1 (J Folder).

23. Thomas Schelling wrote: "In the event of an effort to fight a restrained nuclear war, there may be only a brief and busy instant in which each side must decide whether limited war is in full swing or full war has just begun; and twelve hours' confusion over how to make contact might spoil some of the chances for stabilizing the action within limits" ("Bargaining, Communication, and Limited War," *Journal of Conflict Resolution* 1 [March 1957]: 34). Elsewhere Schelling wrote that "one of the functions of limited war . . . is to pose the deliberate risk of all-out war," an idea that presumes widespread distinction between limited and all-out war levels as well as accurate perception of threats (Schelling, *The Strategy of Conflict* [New York: Oxford University Press, 1960], 193–194). See also Schelling, "Nuclear Strategy in Europe," *World Politics* 14 (April 1962): 421–432.

24. Klaus Knorr to Brodie, 1 July 1957, UCLA Collection, Box 1 (K Folder). Brodie wrote that "I always have you in mind as the person from whom I originally got the idea about the margins of resources available for war purposes in the 18th century and earlier being very limited. As I recall, you put it to me once that those people were living on a near-subsistence basis, and not much could be squeezed out of them for war purposes even if we could imagine government as efficient for the purpose as those we know today" (Brodie to Knorr, 9 July 1957, UCLA Collection, Box 1 [K Folder]). In *War Potential of Nations*, Klaus Knorr quoted the economist Adam Smith on this point: "'In modern war the great expense of fire-arms gives an evident advantage to the nation which can best afford that expense; and consequently, to an opulent and civilized, over a poor and barbarous nation. In ancient times the opulent and civilized found it difficult to defend themselves against the poor and barbarous nations. In modern times the poor and barbarous find it difficult to defend themselves against the opulent and civilized.'" (36). Brodie himself, somewhat inconsistently with his own definition of the limited war problem, chose to emphasize in *Strategy in the Missile Age* Smith's view that "there is a great deal of ruin in a nation" (6). This last point Brodie initially heard much earlier from Jacob Viner, who cited for it Sir John Sinclair's *Recollections* (Viner to Brodie, 4 May 1954, UCLA Collection, Box 2 [V Folder]).

25. Another military historian observed that "long . . . before the development of aircraft made long-distance strategic bombing possible, the juridical (or legalistic) theory to justify it and the national passion to demand it were both already there" (Geoffrey Best, "Restraints on War by Land before 1945," in Howard, ed., *Restraints on War*, 31).

26. "Unlimited Weapons and Limited War," 20 (italics in original).

27. Brodie to Jones, 25 February 1955.

28. On the unlimited character of the Spanish Civil War, see Smoke, *War: Controlling Escalation*, 50.

29. How long belligerents abstained from homeland attacks in limited war depended in part on how long their adversaries avoided putting the sanctuary areas to military use. According to Brodie, "Limited war of necessity implies the existence of a great sanctuary area in the rear of each major contestant. Keeping the war limited may depend on not using that sanctuary area as a base for attacking the other with nuclear weapons" (*Strategy in the Missile Age*, 329). For a similar formulation, see William W. Kaufmann, "The Crisis in Military Affairs," *World Politics* 10 (July 1958): 596. (It may be inferred that when Kaufmann demonstrated at RAND in the late 1950s the

feasibility of counterforce attacks against the Soviet Union, he anticipated, among other things, that the Soviets *would* put their sanctuary to military use during a limited war.) In a manuscript, Brodie strongly implied that the popularity of the sanctuary concept rested on the assumption that a limited war would not involve a two-way use of nuclear weapons. "If we give the adherents of sanctuary the benefit of each doubt," he wrote, "some impressive instances of sanctuary observance are found in the Korean experience. As a result, our war games players have relied very heavily on the concept. Most of their neatly arranged plays for limited war with nuclear weapons would be impossible without it" ("Alternative Strategic Policies II," 27 March 1958, RAND Informal Working Paper, 65). See also *Strategy in the Missile Age*, 328–329.

30. Kissinger, *Nuclear Weapons and Foreign Policy*, 143–144. See also Morton Halperin, *Limited War in the Nuclear Age* (New York: John Wiley & Sons, 1963). Kissinger seems to have neglected in this context the widening of the Korean War that resulted from the United Nations (UN) advance to the Yalu River in 1950.

31. Arnold Wolfers to Brodie, 27 July 1954 (first letter), UCLA Collection, Box 2 (W Folder). For this view, Wolfers cited his discussions with U.S. Army and Air Force officers. The major advocate of bombing north of the Yalu was Gen. Douglas MacArthur, commander of UN forces in Korea until April 1951, who pushed it to gain UN political objectives in Korea with fewer casualties and, as Robert Osgood noted, "with more chance of avoiding a third world war" (*Limited War* [Chicago: University of Chicago Press, 1957], 174). Although MacArthur seems to have had a doctrine of limited war that was different from Brodie's, Brodie gave much more attention to MacArthur's conduct than to his ideas (see *War and Politics*, chap. 3).

32. Brodie later wrote that "we spared the Communist bases north of the Yalu largely because the tactical aircraft operating from them were not seriously hurting us. On the contrary, they were mostly presenting targets to our own fighter aircraft and being shot down at a ratio of twelve to fourteen of theirs to one of ours" (*Strategy in the Missile Age*, 329).

33. No instance of such behavior is noted in Richard Smoke's study of escalation, possibly because in no case examined by Smoke was the fear of general war large enough to engender it.

34. Kissinger, *The Necessity for Choice* (New York: Harper & Brothers, 1961), 63. Kissinger cites the writings of Thomas Schelling on this point.

35. Schelling, *Strategy of Conflict*, especially chap. 8.

36. "When some signal is desperately needed by *both* parties and both parties know it, even a poor signal and a discriminatory one may command recognition, in default of any other. Once the contingency is upon them, their interests, which originally diverged in the play of threats and deterrents, substantially coincide in the desperate need for a focus of agreement" (Schelling, "Bargaining, Communication, and Limited War," 35; italics in original).

37. Smoke, in *War: Controlling Escalation*, 245ff, emphasizes the importance of contextual and nonbargaining factors.

38. "Impact of Weapons of Mass Destruction on Strategy," 21.

39. "The Case for Limited War," Air War College lecture, 5 June 1958, 8–9, AFHRC, K239.716258-1, Reel K2738.

40. Brodie memorandum, "sent to Mrs. Galloway," 27 April 1954, UCLA Collection, Box 3 (Folder 2).

41. Brodie to Eileen Galloway, 12 January 1956, UCLA Collection, Box 3 (Folder 2). Italics in original.

42. Brodie reports that he represented a widespread RAND viewpoint when he urged in 1955 "the necessity of moving rapidly from the general to the specific, even in the realm of doctrine. We felt that a peripheral war would be governed by the geography of the area involved—which must therefore be studied intensively—and by the political and military circumstances of the moment. These circumstances had to be conceived in some detail through the preparation of scenarios. We were also convinced of the utility of 'the gaming principle,' not necessarily in the sense of some elaborate technique but merely in the sense of bringing in the devil's advocate, the man or

group who is obliged to take the enemy's point of view and capabilities and force them upon our consciousness" ("Unpublished, Unclassified Notes—1955," on file at the RAND Corporation). For what Brodie may have had in mind in coupling limited war study with "the gaming principle," see M. G. Weiner, "War Gaming Methodology," RAND Research Memorandum RM-2413, July 1959. Weiner's study outlines the logic and procedures behind the SIERRA project, a major ongoing 1950s RAND study of limited war in Southeast Asia, the Far East, and the Middle East.

43. Brodie to Jones, 25 August 1955, UCLA Collection, Box 1 (J Folder). See also note 8 above.

44. Leitenberg, "Background Materials," in SIPRI, *Tactical Nuclear Weapons*, 12.

45. According to Coral Bell, the new force standard provided that a European war "would inevitably be nuclear, that the peak of destruction would occur in the first days, that the outcome of the conflict would be determined by forces in being, and that first strikes would be at potential retaliatory forces rather than centres of population" (*Negotiation from Strength*, 152). Supporting this concept, NATO conventional force goals were extensively cut, with the bulk of the cuts coming in forces previously slated to be mobilized after the outbreak of hostilities. On these cuts see Hilsman, "Strategic Doctrines for Nuclear War," in Kaufmann, ed., *Military Policy and National Security*, 73f.

46. "Case for Limited War," 10.

47. *Strategy in the Missile Age*, 329. In his letter of 25 February 1955 to Stephen Jones, Brodie added that "the revulsion which such use would have undoubtedly caused in the world" might also have discouraged nuclear use in Korea. Brodie was to attach much meaning to this latter point soon afterward, when he noted the significance of a "habit of nuclear non-use" and the importance of strengthening it (see below), though still later he was to drastically play down that same point. Brodie's letter to Jones may be the first in which he noted the special political liabilities that might arise if nuclear weapons were used.

48. For Brodie's reference to prestige interests, see "Case for Limited War," 6. Brodie's concern about national objectives, triggered by the advent of fusion weapons (see chapter 5 of this book), pushed his major 1950s air-power study (to become *Strategy in the Missile Age*) in a direction different from his older *Guide to Naval Strategy*, on which he had originally modeled it. For an elaboration of this point, see chapter 9 of this study.

49. "Case for Limited War," 9–10.

50. On the problem of controlling biases, see Robert Jervis, "Hypotheses on Misperception," *World Politics* 20 (April 1968): 454–479.

51. Brodie, "Scientific Progress and Political Science," *Scientific Monthly* 85 (December 1957): 318.

52. Eileen Galloway, "Memorandum to the Joint Chiefs of Staff," 18 February 1954, shown to Brodie and found in UCLA Collection, Box 3 (Folder 2). This memorandum, by a staff member of the Legislative Reference Service, was prepared at the request of Rep. Lawrence H. Smith, who chaired the Subcommittee on National Security of the House Foreign Affairs Committee.

53. "Changing Capabilities and War Objectives," 68. Brodie was referring to the decision to relax the American offensive against Chinese forces and accept overtures from the Communist side for discussions about a diplomatic settlement. This aspect of the Korean conflict seems to have underlined for Brodie the importance of the association between ends and means in warfare, a matter that disposed him to give new prominence in his own thinking by 1952 to the writings of Carl von Clausewitz and on which he was to do his own major thinking later. "The Korean war uncovered a deep and pervasive confusion on the matter of ends and means," he wrote in 1957. "The politicians restrained the soldiers' use of means because they spontaneously recognized that the true objects of American intervention required such restraints. On the other hand, largely because of the novelty of the situation, the political leaders were so inept at formulating and explicating those objectives that they made basic and even elementary errors of direction—above all, the error of arresting their military pressure at the first moment that the Communists showed an interest in negotiations." ("Scientific Progress and Political Science," 317–318). The associating

of ends and means in warfare, arguably Brodie's most pervasive contemporary concern, was first used by him to justify limited war. Later, he applied this idea as a standard by which to evaluate all wars (see *War and Politics,* passim).

54. Brodie to W. L. Borden, 20 October 1954 (italics in original). The last point in this quotation, stated by Brodie undeviatingly and with the greatest assurance through several transformations in many of his other major ideas about limited war, depended entirely on the unpublished work of Herbert Goldhamer. Brodie wrote in 1964: "One of my RAND colleagues, Dr. Herbert Goldhamer, happened to be in Korea at the time of the armistice, where he was interrogating Chinese prisoners. His interrogations led him to conclude that the Chinese Communist army had been on the verge of collapse when our offensive was halted. There were great numbers of defections and surrenders, and there would have been many more had we made it easier to surrender. He made this information available in a memorandum that was carried at least as far as Ridgeway [*sic*], and which was apparently greeted as a revelation. He was then asked to serve as an informal advisor to the American military officers who were negotiating the final settlement with the Chinese. He has written up this experience, but because of the sensitivity of his remarks about people still living the circulation of this classified document has been severely limited. Anyway, my feelings about the event stem largely from my having read this document and also having discussed his experiences with Goldhamer at some length.

"He tells me that during the early period of the negotiations we were able to get the Chinese to move on one or two occasions by threatening to resume our offensive. However, after a time this threat became unavailable. He agrees with me absolutely that the failure to keep the offensive going is what accounted for the extremely long drawn-out negotiations. Apparently the American military officers on the spot thought so too" (Brodie to Alastair Buchan, 7 April 1964, UCLA Collection, Box 6 [Folder 3]). See also chapter 1, p. 3.

Apparently, Brodie fused Goldhamer's observations to Clausewitz's idea of governing warmaking by specific political objectives, for in the Korean instance both sources justified going beyond the status quo ante. But on another level the two were not so easily reconcilable. Goldhamer's conclusion had been that political leaders should weigh militarily significant field developments more heavily before deciding to ease military pressure; the idea Brodie valued in Clausewitz, on the other hand, was that the views of political leaders should prevail over those of military field leaders.

Dean Acheson, who noted in his memoirs the unprecedented unity within the American government about Korean War strategy and tactics at the start of the armistice negotiations, defended the early search for an armistice on the ground that "experience had taught a costly lesson: to push the Chinese back upon their border — their source of reinforcement and supply — only increased their strength" (*Present at the Creation,* 529; see also 651). Denying that the difficulties in the armistice negotiations were due, at least in 1951, to relaxation of military pressure, Acheson attributed the problem to the shock experienced by the Russians and Chinese "when at the start of a negotiation to restore, as they thought, the *status quo ante* they found us demanding a new line for our sphere of influence, not only more militarily significant but involving considerable loss of prestige for them" (ibid., 536). In an earlier case, weaknesses in Japanese military capabilities at the end of the Second World War by no means were associated by American leaders with any significant decline in Japanese resistance potential. In addition, resumption of the Korean offensive was not the only source of leverage in coercing the Chinese to negotiate; threats of American nuclear weapons use were also conveyed to the Chinese.

55. Osgood, *Limited War,* 185.

56. Ibid., 182.

57. This helps to explain the attraction of simple bargaining solutions. See Schelling, "Bargaining, Communication, and Limited War," 33.

58. *Strategy in the Missile Age,* 313.

59. Because the fallout effects of nuclear explosions were a closely guarded secret following the first American nuclear test in 1945, it is not possible to infer from Brodie's silence on this

subject that he was not aware of those effects. However, in a letter dated December 1951 to a contact at Sandia Base, the major American military center for research on nuclear weapons effects, Brodie asked for information on "radiation effects in Roentgens at various distances from ground zero (or was it center of burst) at the bottoms of fox holes of various depths" (Brodie to Col. C. S. Maupin, 19 December 1951, UCLA Collection, Box 2 [M Folder]). He did not refer in this letter to delayed radiation damage. There is no evidence that Brodie ever spelled out fallout effects when discussing the prospects of cities withstanding direct Soviet-American war. Brodie's knowledge of nuclear weapons effects largely depended upon information supplied to him by highly competent nuclear physicists and military planners. His omission of fallout in his initially classified writings may therefore have reflected the failure of those persons to discuss fallout effects with him, perhaps because of their underestimation, prior to 1954, of the danger from delayed nuclear radiation. On the fallout question, see Ralph Lapp, *Atoms and People* (New York: Harper & Brothers, 1956), chap. 7. I am also indebted on this matter to Berend D. Bruins. (See chapter 5, notes 14 and 27, of this book.) "Until two weeks ago," Brodie wrote in February 1955, "I would have said that there was only one piece of really basic information vital to an appreciation of the strategic problems of the future that was still being withheld – that concerning 'fallout.' Now even that information is in the public domain" (Brodie to Joseph E. Johnson, 28 February 1955, UCLA Collection, Box 1 [J Folder]).

60. Lapp, *Atoms and People*, 114ff.

61. References by Brodie to the BYSTANDER project, which had studied fallout effects in a European war, and to the asserted need to take account of wind directions in NATO nuclear war planning are in Brodie's paper, "Unpublished, Unclassified Notes – 1955."

62. Foxhole defense, anticipated by Brodie against prompt nuclear effects (see note 59 above), would suitably shield troops against delayed effects as well (Lapp, "Fallout, Civilian Defense, and the Test Ban," *Bulletin of the Atomic Scientists*, [May 1959]; reprinted in *The Atomic Age*, edited by Morton Grodzins and Eugene Rabinovitch [New York: Basic Books, 1963], 307). And although fallout would add to the difficulties of friendly force movement, including occupation of territory (Lapp, *Atoms and People*, 132), Brodie was more interested in keeping Soviet forces ineffective than in claiming new real estate for the NATO allies.

63. On the Carte Blanche exercise, see Osgood, *Limited War*, 305; and Gordon Craig, "NATO and the New German Army," in Kaufmann, ed., *Military Policy and National Security*, 225.

64. Nigel Calder, *Nuclear Nightmares* (New York: Penguin Books, 1981), 32–33. It should be reiterated that, as suggested by Brodie's observations, smaller nuclear weapons would add to intelligence and target selection requirements. For one skeptical discussion of using only small-yield nuclear weapons to fight a nuclear war in Europe (silent however about intelligence and target selection problems), see Malcolm Hoag, "Place of Limited War in NATO Strategy," in Knorr, ed., *NATO and American Security*, 118.

65. Brodie, "Unpublished, Unclassified Notes – 1955." Edward Teller believed that military commanders would prefer small-yield nuclear weapons over their larger counterparts. See "Alternative Strategic Policies II," 62f.

66. Wolfgang Heisenberg, *The Alliance and Europe, Part I: Crisis Stability in Europe and Theatre Nuclear Weapons*, Adelphi Paper no. 96 (London: International Institute for Strategic Studies, 1973), 8–9 (italics in original).

67. Brodie to Jones, 25 February 1955. Brodie had been asked what the NATO allies would do if the Soviet army "use[d] cities for 'cover', advancing from town to town as rapidly as possible, using the towns and cities as camps and supply bases" (Stephen B. Jones to Brodie, 22 February 1955, UCLA Collection, Box 1 [J Folder]). Brodie and Jones evidently presumed that Soviet troops could reach their destinations before nuclear weapons were used against them. Political delays in gaining authorization for using nuclear weapons (which had been observed in war games) could allow Soviet troops to reach those destinations (Reinhardt, "Nuclear Weapons and Limited Warfare," 10).

68. Brodie to Jones, 25 February 1955. In this letter, Brodie also noted: "It seems to be a developing custom to distinguish between 'tactical' and 'strategic' weapons according to size, the former presumably being restricted to the fission variety of modest size. I happen not to agree with this classification or the reasons for it, but mine is one still, small voice. My guess is that Leghorn is adopting conventional thinking in this respect."

69. Brodie, "Unpublished, Unclassified Notes—1955." In this paper, the largest military requirement cited was for a half-megaton bomb to disable an airfield; in his earliest writings advocating battlefield use of thermonuclear weapons, Brodie and envisioned bomb yields of one megaton.

70. Kissinger, downplaying the lessons of the Carte Blanche exercise, wrote in 1957: A "limited nuclear war would approach all-out war in destructiveness only if it should be conducted with the tactics of World War II, with fixed lines, massive attacks on communication centers and an attempt to wipe out the enemy industrial potential. The lessons of 'Carte Blanche' are therefore deceptive. In the near future—as strategic doctrine goes, within ten years—the massive attack on opposing air installations will become strategically unproductive or unnecessary. With the advent of missiles and vertical take-off aircraft there will be no need to drop some three hundred atomic devices within forty-eight hours [as in Carte Blanche]. The key goal in a limited nuclear war should not be to eliminate enemy communication centers but to prevent an enemy from controlling territory by keeping him from concentrating large bodies of troops in the contested area. A limited nuclear war should not be compared to a ground war in the traditional sense" (*Nuclear Weapons and Foreign Policy*, 309).

71. During the Second World War, cities were extensively damaged in order to dislodge enemy troops from them and to overcome the protection that cities afforded such forces (William R. Van Cleave and S. T. Cohen, *Tactical Nuclear Weapons: An Examination of the Issues* [New York: Crane, Russak, 1978], 35). It has also been noted that "in all past wars in Europe a large fraction of the population, and in particular the urban population, did not remain in cities but traveled along roads to other areas. Yet refugee casualties are rarely included in theatre nuclear war considerations" (W. K. H. Panofsky, "Science, Technology and the Arms Buildup," speech cited in the *Congressional Record* [Senate] for 11 June 1981). See also note 67 above.

72. Samuel T. Cohen wrote that "as I view the problem, collateral damage in non-PGM [precision-guided munitions] warfare results not so much from warheads that miss their targets but rather from warheads that are—better yet, have to be—applied indiscriminately because the targets (enemy personnel) can't be acquired and, moreover, are protected by the urban structure they occupy" (memorandum, Samuel T. Cohen to James Digby, 4 April 1975, commenting on a RAND paper by Digby; a copy of the Cohen memorandum was sent to Brodie and is now in the UCLA Collection, Box 7 [Folder 6]).

73. Alastair Buchan, *NATO in the 1960's* (London: Weidenfeld & Nicolson, 1960), 86–87.

74. George W. Rathjens, Jr., "NATO Strategy: Total War," in Knorr, ed., *NATO and American Security*, 79.

75. In 1956, the NATO Council approved a policy whereby, except in the case of very-small-scale attack, the period of conventional or tactical nuclear warfare would be very short and would soon escalate into all-out hostilities (Leitenberg, "Background Materials," 14). This decision was consistent with the "trip-wire strategy" adopted by the NATO alliance in the 1950s. Leghorn, in his 1955 essay (see note 5 above), wrote that "if the Soviets, or any nuclear-equipped aggressor, employ nuclear weapons, 'hot pursuit' would be our announced reaction. In this event, we would attack instantly and massively all the nuclear stocks, forces, and bases of the aggressor nation. In destroying its nuclear capabilities, we would make clear that no cities would be attacked unless those of our ally were first attacked" (85).

76. Brodie, "Unpublished, Unclassified Notes—1955."

77. Ibid. Later on, Brodie felt differently, believing that a major Soviet attack would come with nuclear weapons whatever the NATO dispositions. "Fortunately, I have an extremely low expectation of a Soviet attack [in Europe]," he wrote to Stansfield Turner in 1976, "or I should

lose much sleep over this matter. But if they did decide on a full scale attack, I would expect them not to resort to strategic bombing but to use tac nucs from the start.

"That is the way their military philosophy seems to run—they clearly have not bought our curious doctrine—and anyway, they would be utter idiots to do otherwise. I should expect tactical nucs to be used on land and sea—after all, what better targets are there for such weapons than our nice, big aircraft carriers?" (Brodie to Turner, 16 January 1976, UCLA Collection, Box 9 [T Folder].)

78. Arnold Wolfers summarized for Brodie a *New York Times* article, dated 25 July 1954, about a report by the NATO headquarters staff, "worked out under Al Gruenther," that had been forwarded to the United Kingdom Joint Chiefs. The report declared that the first nuclear targets would be the "enemy's forces not major centers of population." Wolfers concluded that he and Brodie had a new ally, namely, "fear of European neutralism which is said to be growing because war is identified with A & H bomb attacks against major cities" (Wolfers to Brodie, 27 July 1954 (second letter), UCLA Collection, Box 2 [W Folder]).

The delicate distinction between tactical and strategic nuclear weaponry was not always made clear. "It seems to me certain," declared P. M. S. Blackett in 1956, "that the planning going on at S.H.A.P.E. [Supreme Headquarters, Allied Powers in Europe] must be based on the assumption that atomic weapons can be used tactically without precipitating their strategic use. For unless this assumption is made, their planning makes nonsense. Can one really believe that S.H.A.P.E. envisage waging a land battle with tactical atomic weapons in Europe when, say, London, Paris, Brussels and the Ruhr cities have been destroyed by atomic bombs in the first week? It is clear that S.H.A.P.E. planning must assume that this will not happen. Now, since active defence will not stop all the atomic bombers, the only way to keep these cities functioning is not to attack similar Soviet targets. So if S.H.A.P.E. is really planning for at least a defensive victory, it must be planning not to initiate strategic atomic bombing" (*Atomic Weapons and East-West Relations* [Cambridge: Cambridge University Press, 1956], 22–23).

79. This in turn suggests that Brodie had become less opposed to nuclear use per se in a European war than with the manner in which such weapons would be employed and with the difficulty of establishing that such use would succeed without provoking all-out war. In *Strategy in the Missile Age*, chap. 9, Brodie resisted battlefield nuclear use more strongly, relying heavily on the point that it would inevitably lead to a wider war. On this last point, see below.

80. Leitenberg, "Background Materials," 20–22 and 27. Recall in this connection Brodie's remarks, noted earlier, on the strong likelihood that the launching of SAC would be controlled by the American civilian leadership and not by SAC commanders. For further discussion of this point, see below.

81. Western European governments were reluctant to permit a limited ground war in Europe and to provide less than massive forces for deterring or coping with limited attack. See, for example, Denis Healey, "Britain and NATO," in Knorr, ed., *NATO and American Security*, 217–218. Malcolm Hoag wrote that a NATO political directive in force in the late 1950s "explicitly forbids limited war" ("1962 Unclassified Notes," kindly supplied by Hoag to me).

82. Cited in Bell, *Negotiation from Strength*, 157. The purpose of this new force evidently was to enable the alliance, in Norstad's words, "to meet less-than-ultimate threats with a decisive, but less-than-ultimate response" and to provide "essential political and military maneuverability." Cited in *Strategy in the Missile Age*, 337.

83. Leitenberg, "Background Materials," 29.

84. Bell, *Negotiation from Strength*, 158.

85. Brodie, "Some Considerations Governing Escalation," RAND Informal Working Paper, 4 September 1964, 38. This paper, shown to me by Malcolm Palmatier, was the initial draft of Brodie's *Escalation and the Nuclear Option*.

86. Henry A. Kissinger, *The Troubled Partnership* (New York: McGraw-Hill, 1965), 97. Norstad proposed, consistent with these force requirements, deployment of a NATO IRBM system known as "Missile X." This proposal was ultimately rejected.

87. Alastair Buchan, for example, wrote in 1960 that "SAC is now becoming primarily an instrument for deterring attack on North America rather than a means of maintaining the overall strategic balance" (*NATO in the 1960's*, 74).

88. *Strategy in the Missile Age*, 335. Unmentioned by Brodie during the 1950s was the possibility that the shock effect from using nuclear weapons might serve to sober up policymakers, restraining them and strengthening their determination to end hostilities. This point was to be important for him in the 1960s.

89. Brodie wrote in 1959: "The conclusion that nuclear weapons *must* be used in limited wars has been reached by too many people, too quickly, on the basis of far too little analysis of the problem. Decisions of great moment have stemmed and continue to stem from that conclusion, decisions which work to deprive us of a capability for fighting even a small war without nuclear weapons. Once we are in that position, the original proposition, however mistaken to begin with, appears to be proved right, for the fact that we cannot fight without nuclear weapons argues cogently that we should not attempt to do so" (*Strategy in the Missile Age*, 330; italics in original). This argument apparently was meant in part as a criticism of Henry Kissinger's 1957 study, *Nuclear Weapons and Foreign Policy*, which made a strong argument for battlefield use of nuclear weapons. One person I interviewed emphasized the great disquiet produced at RAND by the publication of Kissinger's book. For his part, however, Brodie seems to have played down that part of Kissinger's contribution that most taxed others, for he argued (in contrast to James King, for example) that Kissinger stressed having a nuclear capability for limited war more than he did the point that nuclear weapons needed to be used (Brodie to King, 31 October 1956, UCLA Collection, Box 1 [K Folder]). For Brodie's short published review of *Nuclear Weapons and Foreign Policy*, see *Scientific Monthly* 85 (October 1957): 206–207.

90. This was at any rate Brodie's view; but compare Henry S. Rowen, "The Future of General War," in Berkowitz and Bock, eds., *American National Security*, 74ff. Writing in 1956, Gordon Craig observed that "if we can believe the utterances of some of its representatives, NATO has only one strategical plan. Whether the aggressive Eastern force is composed of the massed armies of the Soviet Union or only of the *Kasernierte Volkspolizei* of East Germany, whether it employs atomic weapons or restricts itself to conventional arms, once hostilities commence the NATO forces become mobile and start firing atomic cannon. In the event that the attacking force is not using atomic weapons, the allies thus—as General Ridgway pointed out in the persuasive letter which he wrote before retiring as Chief of Staff of the U.S. Army—incur the onus of resorting to their use and leave the enemy 'no choice but to respond in kind'" ("NATO and the New German Army," 231).

91. "Alternative Strategic Policies II," 60. Compare *Strategy in the Missile Age*, 323. For another effort, made about the same time, to distinguish nuclear and nonnuclear weapons in this way, see Thomas C. Schelling, "Nuclear Weapons and Limited War," included as Appendix A in *Strategy of Conflict*, 258–266. Wide variation in tactical nuclear force requirements might well interfere with the detection of restraints. "I have talked to a wide number of persons," Brodie declared in 1958, "about bomb-sizing [tactical nuclear weapons] at different wars and the estimates for maximum size range from one or two kilotons to several [megatons]" ("Case for Limited War," 20).

92. *Strategy in the Missile Age*, 322.

93. Ibid., 324. Brodie later relaxed this view considerably. "Why do people talk about nuclear weapons never having been used," he wrote to Thomas C. Schelling on 8 December 1964, "as though Hiroshima and Nagasaki were simply a bad dream? I have no clear idea what that previous use portends about the future, but it was not a casual use. As I stated once before, the 'tradition of non-use' has to be weighed against the fact that Korea is the only war we have been in since Nagasaki [where] there was even a chance of its being used" (UCLA Collection, Box 2 [Folder 11]). Amplifying these remarks somewhat earlier to Schelling, Brodie wrote: "In short, we have not used nuclear weapons largely because there has been little or no occasion to use them, a fact that probably has something to do with the fact that nuclear weapons exist. I think that the tradi-

tion of non-use *could* become quite too encrusted, and I say that because I believe, as I am sure you do too, that there are some enormous potential benefits to be derived from having nuclears around (to compensate for the disagreeable *necessity* of their being around) such as the rather good chance of permanently avoiding major war and of doing with a lot fewer minor wars as well" (Brodie to Schelling, 9 October 1964, ibid.; italics in original). The difference between these two views seems largely a result of a changed interpretation of events; Brodie does not seem to have studied in detail the questions affecting his interpretation.

94. This point was made by Thornton Read: "Ten-ton high-explosive bombs could be used in ground combat, . . . the military pressures are all against doing so because such weapons would be outrageously unwieldy and inefficient. The pressure would be to distribute the high explosive in smaller and more efficient packages. The reverse would be the case for a nuclear weapon having a yield of 10 tons, because a small increase in the weight of a low-yield fission weapon gives a large increase in explosive yield, and hence in area of destruction. Therefore, the pressures are first to package a limited supply of fissionable material into larger bombs (as, in fact, the Soviets, whose supply of critical material is more limited than ours, appear to have done), and secondly to use these larger bombs in combat in preference to smaller and less efficient ones.

"In short, the technical characteristics of weapons produce strong military pressures driving one down the scale of conventional explosives and up the scale of nuclear explosives. The conventional-nuclear boundary is thus a watershed with a precipitous slope on the nuclear side" ("Limited Strategic War and Tactical Nuclear War," in Knorr and Read, eds., *Limited Strategic War*, 74–75). Compare Malcolm Hoag, who wrote in 1959 that "it is the great improvements in guidance that make missiles not only feasible in conventional warfare, but perhaps revolutionary. . . . It would be a pity if our natural concern with nuclear weapon developments leads us to neglect the technological changes that can be incorporated to our advantage in preparing for conventional war" ("The Place of Limited War in NATO Strategy," in Knorr, ed., *NATO and American Security*, 122–123).

95. For one reference to this view, see note 105 below. On this point, Brodie stood rather apart from most other strategists. During the 1960s, he became more skeptical of counterforce efforts because of the importance he attached to attempts by the superpowers to protect their retaliatory forces (see chapter 8 of this book). Others, in contrast, made their support of reprisal strikes (such as against the Soviet Baltic or Black Sea Fleet) contingent upon the same protection of retaliatory forces. On the latter viewpoint, see Klaus Knorr, "Aspects of NATO Strategy: A Conference Report," appendix in Knorr, ed., *NATO and American Security*, 314 and 325.

96. *Strategy in the Missile Age*, 341–342.

97. See, for example, Rowen, "Future of General War," 74–75.

98. Hoag, "1962 Unclassified Notes."

99. Brodie also noted how "a limited war, especially one fought with non-nuclear weapons, would permit the expansion and mobilization of our industrial war potential in the style of the Korean War" (see *Strategy in the Missile Age*, 335).

100. Hoag, "1962 Unclassified Notes."

101. For the first part of this sentence, see Brodie, "A Comment on the Hoag Doctrine," 17 July 1962, RAND Informal Working Paper, included in Trachtenberg, *Development of American Strategic Thought, 1961–1969*, 107–108. For the second part of the sentence, see page 105 of the Trachtenberg reproduction of this same paper, on which Brodie cited approvingly in this connection Thomas Schelling's view that "the *purpose* of introducing nuclears in a tactical war that we would otherwise lose . . . is to make the war too painful to continue" ("Nuclear Strategy in Europe," 431; italics in original). This view is sharply at odds with Brodie's prior worries about the tactical use of nuclear weapons (see also chapter 8, note 36, of this volume). The "1962 Unclassified Notes" furnished to me by Malcolm Hoag appear to be a response to "Comment on the Hoag Doctrine."

102. Brodie, "Critique of the Doctrine of CWE" (see chap. 1, n. 122), 175. Italics in original.

103. Hoag, "1962 Unclassified Notes."

104. Brodie, "Critique of the Doctrine of CWE," 174.

105. "Comment on the Hoag Doctrine," 102–103. See also "Critique of the Doctrine of CWE," 177. The second of these papers, written somewhat later than the first, contains a passage that coincides with much of the portion quoted here but states instead: "We will be ready to bring in our nuclear weapons—*either* in tactical or *even* indiscriminate strategic action" (italics added). For the reasons behind this shift, see chapter 8 of this book.

Recognizing that the conventional war doctrine was "closely bound up with a desire to see greater inter-allied equalization of the defense burden" ("Critique of the Doctrine of CWE," 165), Brodie nevertheless played down this objective. This was partly because he was inclined to stress the difficulty of realizing Hoag's preferred goal of thirty well-equipped and full-strength divisions in Europe ready for war. "The question of whether we are really 'almost there' is quite crucial," Brodie wrote. "Our conventional-strategy advocates tend to exaggerate enemy inherent weaknesses and to gloss over our own" ("Comment on the Hoag Doctrine," 100). Partly also it was because he invariably saw a tough fight ahead when decisions about shaping alliance forces had to be made. "The cost *to us* of divisions raised by the U.K. *et al.* (apart from dependence on military assistance) is the political credit we use up in pressing the issue," Brodie wrote in 1962, "which may be quite considerable, and, more to the point, may be and I think is likely to be quite futile. Perhaps this is too pessimistic a view, but all our allies except the Germans have been dragging their feet on almost every major commitment they have made, and this large built-in resistance to further efforts is not going to be alleviated by a philosophy which they find it hard to accept. Moreover, I should want to be sure *I* can accept it before I were to begin to proceed urging it upon them" ("Comment on the Hoag Doctrine," 99–100; italics in original). See also chapter 6, note 66.

106. *Strategy in the Missile Age*, 335.

107. Brodie declared in 1958 that "the problem of limited war is the problem of determining how much restraint we want and how we are going to keep it pegged at that level. What are the sanctions for mutual enforcement? Talk of quality weapons and of efficient versus inefficient weapons are somewhat beside the point. Because in limited war we already decided not to use the most efficient instrument of all, at least, not in the most efficient way. In other words, we have recognized that weapons can be too efficient for our purposes; that strategic bombing can be too efficient for our purposes" ("Case for Limited War," 20).

108. The major problem in determining acceptable tactics in the absence of nuclear weapons use, Brodie wrote in one of his very few forays into this subject, was that careful judgment had revealed by the late 1950s that the interdiction campaign in Korea had been a total failure. "If we did not use nuclear weapons," he wrote in a draft chapter of *Strategy in the Missile Age,* "we should have to abandon the idea of using a small part of our SAC, operating from home bases, to put down outbreaks of aggression anywhere in the world. We should have to return to the type of operation symbolized by Korea, where fairly large numbers of aircraft operated from within the local theater in direct and indirect support of large numbers of friendly ground forces. One can understand why the prospect does not look attractive to anybody, especially to airmen.

"The interdiction campaign attempted in Korea simply did not work well under the conditions of that war. One reason is that for long periods the lines were too static, and hence the enemy troops were not being forced to use up enough munitions. Another is that interdiction carried on almost exclusively by day is not going to work well with any resourceful enemy, especially where he disposes of large quantities of coolie labor. But it had not worked in Italy either, where the Germans had succeeded in supplying twenty-five very active divisions on a front that was anything but static.

"Yet, if the atomic bomb had not been invented, or if it were simply not considered available for general tactical use, we would now be working out new tactics and new doctrine for air tactical operations in order to make them effective. Under those circumstances the air forces would not be maintaining that they had no significant tactical capability" ("Alternative Strategic Policies II," 70–71; omitted in *Strategy in the Missile Age*).

We have seen that irrespective of whether nuclear weapons would be used in Europe, superpower and European governments disposed their armies in anticipation of such use, avoiding concentrated forces and static lines. In general, as tacticians applied themselves over the long term to neutralize the effect of radically new weapons, those weapons might not so easily be applied to produce decisive military results. It was not quite clear from Brodie's remarks, finally, whether protection of American tactical bombers or interdiction of tactical targets was the most sensitive part of the tactical military problem.

109. Another major strategic analyst who was comfortable with this substitution was Thomas C. Schelling. See especially Schelling's 1966 work, *Arms and Influence*, 105ff.

Chapter 8. Escalation

1. See the introduction of chapter 7 in this book.

2. Herman Kahn remarked that during the 1950s, the possibility that Soviet-American war might be the outgrowth of a crisis was "almost completely ignored" (*On Escalation: Metaphors and Scenarios* [New York: Praeger, 1965], 152).

3. *Strategy in the Missile Age*, 331.

4. Brodie to Dean S. Lucal, 16 March 1960, UCLA Collection Box 2 (Folder 2). Albert and Roberta Wohlstetter wrote that "a process of escalation is usually thought of simply as an increase in violence growing out of a limited conflict in which an adversary may act to stave off his loss or an opponent's prospective success. The aspect of 'escalators' that inspired its use in this connection, we suspect, is the fact that moving stairways carry a passenger on automatically without any effort of his will" (*Controlling the Risks in Cuba*, Adelphi Paper no. 17 [London: International Institute for Strategic Studies, 1965], reprinted in *The Use of Force: International Politics and Foreign Policy*, edited by Robert J. Art and Kenneth N. Waltz [Boston: Little, Brown, 1971], 263).

5. *Strategy in the Missile Age*, 339.

6. Ibid., 334.

7. Brodie, *Escalation and the Nuclear Option*, 33.

8. The latter idea was consistent with a massive retaliation strategy, which entailed a threat to escalate low-intensity conflicts (George and Smoke, *Deterrence in American Foreign Policy*, 563). Herman Kahn noted that "strategies that emphasize the possibility of escalation or eruption are associated with the term 'brinkmanship'" (*On Escalation*, 7); the latter term is associated with John Foster Dulles, who also first articulated the massive retaliation strategy. Brodie was attracted to the massive retaliation strategy only with respect to war in Europe, writing in 1963: "As one of the first who argued that the old massive retaliation doctrine lacked credibility for the cases for which it seemed to be devised—which I still wholeheartedly believe—I should like to suggest that the tactical situation in Europe is a horse of a completely different color" ("Afterthoughts on CWE from the Meeting (with Herr Erler) of April 16," 22 April 1963, 6, UCLA Collection, Box 18 [Folder 2]). He added in a published paper that "we are not talking about massive retaliation anyway, but tactical nuclear defense" ("What Price Conventional Capabilities in Europe?" *Reporter* 28, 23 May 1963, reprinted in *Problems of National Strategy*, edited by Henry Kissinger [New York: Praeger, 1965], 321).

9. "Some Preliminary Observations on Escalation," 13 September 1962, RAND Informal Working Paper, in Trachtenberg, *Development of American Strategic Thought, 1961–1969*, 137.

10. Brodie, "Some Considerations Governing Escalation," RAND Informal Working Paper, 4 September 1964, 44.

11. "How Probable Is General War?" 19, UCLA Collection, Box 17 (Folder 25). (A lecture with this title was delivered by Brodie in 1961 [April?] at the NATO Defense College in Paris.) This paper was subsequently published in revised form as "Defense Policy and the Possibility of Total War," *Daedalus* 91 (Fall 1962): 733–748.

12. *Strategy in the Missile Age,* 176 and 190.

13. "How Probable Is General War?" 16.

14. *Strategy in the Missile Age,* 355. He went on to say: "It will intensify anxieties about being 'caught on the ground' and increase sensitivity to alarms, false and otherwise. Even in a limited war, nuclear bombs may start to fall. General anxiety will be sharpened into fear, which will stimulate the urge to get the strategic air force under way" (355).

15. Reference has already been made (chapter 1) to Brodie's belief that the balance of terror was not delicate.

16. On these instabilities, see Thomas C. Schelling, "Surprise Attack and Disarmament," in Knorr, ed., *NATO and American Security,* 176–208. In developing the idea of a "reciprocal fear of surprise attack," Schelling may have been indirectly criticizing work being done at RAND on counterforce strategies.

17. "Provocation Works on People," 12 June 1959, RAND Informal Working Paper, 19–20, UCLA Collection, Box 17 (Folder 2); italics in original. A copy of this paper was kindly furnished to me from the personal collection of Robert Jervis.

18. *Strategy in the Missile Age,* 349–350 (italics in original).

19. This quotation and the next are in "Some Preliminary Observations on Escalation," 139 and 140, respectively.

20. *Escalation and the Nuclear Option,* 65.

21. "As soon as people sensed the possibility that we could have a war even with the Soviet Union that might stay limited," Brodie wrote later, "then escalation, which is to say the erosion or collapse of limitations, became quite appropriately the object of special attention" (ibid., 33). James King pointed out, in a review of Brodie's *Strategy in the Missile Age,* that Brodie did not immediately conceive of long-range missiles in this way. King argued that Brodie did not adequately distinguish in that study between strategy under conditions of ballistic missiles and strategy under conditions of air power. By not making this distinction, King contended, Brodie seemed to be suggesting that with missiles as well as with bombers, "the offensive strategy of preventive war is the best *military* strategy for *both* the great nuclear powers" ("Airpower in the Missile Gap," *World Politics* 12 [July 1960]: 629; italics in original). King then disputed this conclusion for the missile age. Brodie by the early 1960s had come to fully accept King's earlier views about ballistic missiles, but in *Strategy in the Missile Age* he had discussed "strike-second" forces almost entirely in abstract fashion.

22. Brodie to Leonard Beaton, 18 September 1964, UCLA Collection, Box 6 (Folder 3). Italics in original.

23. Brodie, "Critique of the Doctrine of CWE" (see chap. 1, n. 122), 178.

24. "Some Preliminary Observations on Escalation," 138 (italics in original). Brodie attributed the idea of counterescalation to Thomas C. Schelling, referring to Schelling's "Nuclear Strategy in Europe," *World Politics* 14 (April 1962): 421–432. See also note 36 below.

25. Brodie to Fred C. Iklé, 22 October 1965, UCLA Collection, Box 1 (I Folder). "In World War II," he wrote some years later, "there was no problem in distinguishing between tactical and strategic bombing, and in avoiding the latter where it seemed politically desirable to do so. It is not self evident that the distinction would be more difficult when nuclear weapons are involved, especially if we shift to smaller tactical nuclear weapons than those that are presently deployed in Europe—which we should want to do anyway" ("Lecture 7," 1–2, included in "Drafts of Japan Lectures," [1978?], UCLA Collection, Box 33 [Folder 5]).

26. "Critique of the Doctrine of CWE," 178.

27. *Escalation and the Nuclear Option,* 34–35.

28. Alain C. Enthoven and K. Wayne Smith, *How Much Is Enough? Shaping the Defense Program, 1961–1969* (New York: Harper & Row, 1971), 126. Desmond Ball emphasized particularly the vulnerability to attack of command and control systems in Western Europe. See his *Can Nuclear War Be Controlled,* Adelphi Paper no. 169 (London: International Institute for Strategic Studies, 1981), 9.

29. Enthoven and Smith, *How Much Is Enough?* 127.

30. Cited in Walter Pincus, "During Cold War, U.S. Did as It Pleased with A-Bombs in Europe," *Washington Post*, 20 November 1981.

31. "Some Preliminary Observations on Escalation," 135–136. From July 1960 to July 1961, Brodie took up a Reflective Year Fellowship awarded him from the Carnegie Corporation and, residing in Paris, studied "the subject of neurotic factors in political decision-makers that tend to make for international conflict rather than peace" (Brodie to William M. Marvel, 27 September 1961, UCLA Collection, Box 3 [Folder 7]).

32. "The Missing Middle—Tactical Nuclear War" (see chap. 1, n. 93), 256.

33. Enthoven and Smith, *How Much is Enough?* 124.

34. John C. Garnett, "Limited 'Conventional' War in the Nuclear Age," in Howard, ed., *Restraints on War*, 90; Hoag, "1962 Unclassified Notes." Robert McNamara later observed that "the level at which nuclear weapons might be used," under the "flexible response" strategy adopted in the early 1960s when he was secretary of defense, "was raised so high that it was, in effect, the equivalent of mutual assured destruction" (Robert Scheer, "Fear of a U.S. First Strike Seen as Cause of Arms Race," *Los Angeles Times*, 8 April 1982). This supports Brodie's point, made in 1964, that "there exists today no concept or strategy of a controlled use of nuclear weapons tactically" ("Missing Middle—Tactical Nuclear War," 248).

35. In 1964, Brodie criticized an American official who denied the existence of "so-called limited nuclear war" as having "the apparent assumption that with the first use of nuclear weapons of whatever size against whatever targets, one or both of the contestants will immediately abandon all discretion" ("Missing Middle—Tactical Nuclear War," 256).

36. See chapter 7, note 101, of this book. Brodie broke with Schelling, however, in denying that the likelihood of general war needed to be increased once strategic stability had been obtained. "It may also be true," Brodie wrote in 1962, "as Professor Schelling asserts in his article ["Nuclear Strategy in Europe"], that the purpose of using nuclear weapons in a limited war is not to affect the local tactical situation so much as to give more earnest warning of a threat of general war. Under present conditions that proposition certainly makes much sense, but under stable standoff conditions of mutual strategic deterrence it would be less applicable" ("Critique of the Doctrine of CWE," 181).

37. Bell, *Negotiation from Strength*, 219–220.

38. "Critique of the Doctrine of CWE," 181–182. The Davy Crockett warheads were introduced into the NATO stockpile in 1961 and withdrawn in 1970.

39. "Missing Middle—Tactical Nuclear War," 258. This distinguished Brodie from others who envisioned employing limited numbers of nuclear weapons purely for shock value, such as detonating a low-yield nuclear weapon either at a sufficiently high altitude to cause little damage on the ground or in uninhabited areas at the start of a large-scale Soviet conventional attack. For these demonstration uses of nuclear weapons, see Bernard Gwertzman, "Haig Cites a Standing NATO Plan Envisioning a 'Warning' A-Blast," *New York Times*, 5 November 1981; and Cecil B. Currey, "NATO's Old Planning for Nuclear Warfare," *New York Times*, 24 November 1981. Kahn (*On Escalation*, 89) sets forward the concept of "barely nuclear war" but does not apply it to battlefield nuclear warfare.

40. *Escalation and the Nuclear Option*, 73–74.

41. "Some Considerations Governing Escalation," 47. In the published version of that essay (*Escalation and the Nuclear Option*, 124), the term "substantial" was omitted.

42. *Escalation and the Nuclear Option*, 28–29.

43. Ibid., 73.

44. Ibid., 22.

45. Ibid., 23. He was evidently referring to "mini-nukes," including fission bombs with reduced blast and radiation and/or fusion bombs with reduced blast and enhanced radiation, the latter known as the "neutron bomb." Both types were well known to the classified defense com-

munity by the early 1960s but had still not been deployed by the late 1970s. One source (William van Cleave and Samuel T. Cohen, *Toward a New Defense for NATO: The Case for Tactical Nuclear Weapons*, National Strategic Information Center Agenda Paper 5 [New York: NSIC, 1976], 44) indicates that a decision was taken in the early 1960s not to develop clean tactical nuclear weapons on "political," not strategic, grounds. See also Samuel T. Cohen, *Neutron Bomb*. The Davy Crockett had a yield in the "tens of tons of TNT, not kilotons" (Herbert Scoville and Herbert York, cited in Leitenberg, "Background Materials," in SIPRI, *Tactical Nuclear Weapons*, 50).

46. Cited in Leitenberg, "Background Materials," 29. Whether these detonations would come before or after the well-known NATO "pause" was not fully clear, but this may have depended on the magnitude of the Soviet attack. According to J. Miettinen, "In the battlefield the employment of [NATO] theatre weapons is planned in 'packages' of specified number and yields for a specified area. For a given 'package' release is given within a limited time-frame, typically hours. The 'package' is employed within the time frame in a short time span—typically tens of minutes—to achieve a shock effect and to synchronize the use with other military actions" ("'Mini-Nukes' and Enhanced Radiation Weapons," in SIPRI, *Tactical Nuclear Weapons*, 234.

Theo Sommer, a West German journalist and strategic thinker, wrote in 1966 that "the 'guidelines' laid down for the use of nuclear weapons by the ministerial meeting of the NATO Council in Athens in 1962 defined the obvious and left the ticklish decisions open: massive nuclear retaliation against massive nuclear attack; tactical nuclear riposte against massive conventional or tactical nuclear attack after proper consultation, if time allows; employment—after consultation—of tactical nuclear weapons against small attacking forces that cannot otherwise be stopped" ("The Objectives of Germany," in *A World of Nuclear Powers?* edited by Alastair Buchan [Englewood Cliffs, N.J.: Prentice Hall, 1966], 44).

47. Leitenberg, "Background Materials," 8 and 16–17.

48. See chapter 7, note 12, of this volume.

49. Leitenberg, "Background Materials," 30.

50. Advocates of battlefield nuclear weapons use have argued that "to make a nuclear-emphasis defense acceptable to our allies, the goals for minimizing expected collateral damage must be set at levels at least equal to and preferably even lower than would be associated with a conventional defense" (W. S. Bennett, R. R. Sandoval, and R. G. Shreffler, "A Credible Nuclear Emphasis Defense for NATO," *Orbis* 17 [Summer 1973]; cited in Frank Barnaby, "The Irrationality of Current Nuclear Doctrines," in SIPRI, *Tactical Nuclear Weapons*, 218).

51. Refer also to the statement by J. Miettinen in note 46 above.

52. See Schelling, "Nuclear Strategy in Europe," 430.

53. "I happen to like the firebreak," Schelling wrote, referring to the term commonly employed to distinguish conventional from nuclear forces, "because . . . nuclears when needed will be so much more dramatic if we do not downgrade them ahead of time. I would hate to waste the first nuclear weapon on a second rate emergency. It should be the most dramatic military event since Pearl Harbor, and the date will probably be remembered as long, and I would hate to see the extraordinary potential impact dissipated on an unworthy objective. We may waste the shock effect of nuclears by pretending that their effect is limited to blast, heat, and radiation" (Schelling to Brodie, 30 September 1964, UCLA Collection, Box 2 [Folder 11]).

54. Cited in Fred C. Iklé, "When the Fighting Has to Stop: The Arguments about Escalation," *World Politics* 19 (July 1967): 699.

55. For Brodie's earlier doubts that Western leaders would have the fortitude to stand fast, being able to threaten only massive responses, see chapter 5 of this book. Compare Brodie's statement in note 8 above.

56. "Critique of the doctrine of CWE," 178. It may have been one of the weaknesses of Brodie's proposal that European members of NATO seemed not to agree upon any working procedures for escalating a war. This point comes through in Brodie's writings. "In short," he wrote in 1962, "the Europeans seem to want to settle for deterrence on the tactical level as well as on

the strategic. It is not true that they eagerly accept tactical nuclear war because they fail to under-stand its full implications. They accept it in the same way and for the same reasons that we accept the necessity of maintaining large forces for strategic deterrence. In fact, deterrence on the tactical level means for them exactly what deterrence on the strategic level means for us" (ibid., 180). The trouble was that preparations for escalation needed to take into account that deterrence, whether at the tactical or the strategic level, might fail.

A later study, evidently based on thorough familiarity with leading NATO opinion, assigns a distinctly subordinate role to escalation in NATO strategy. "Nuclear defence strategies," it finds, "are by their nature de-coupling. After all, their aim is to deter attack by presenting unacceptable odds on the ground, not by the risk of escalation" (Gregory Treverton, *Nuclear Weapons in Europe*, Adelphi Paper no. 168 [London: International Institute for Strategic Studies, 1981], 12). "It is widely recognized," Treverton observed, "that, given the way forces are currently configured, NATO could well be worse off after an exchange of battlefield nuclear weapons. On that score, a decade and a half of NATO studies of low-level TNF [tactical nuclear forces] have made a dif-ference" (ibid.). He concludes that for this reason, though NATO battlefield nuclear weapons are largely located for early use, "responsible political leaders in the West simply will not authorize the use of nuclear weapons early in a conflict (unless the other side fires them first), or delegate responsibility for weapons to *anyone else* (much less to field commanders)" (ibid.; italics in original). Brodie later sought to overcome NATO political leaders' fears about escalatory use of nuclear weapons.

57. "Critique of the Doctrine of CWE," 176–177 (italics in original). In the same paper, Brodie raised the possibility that "in Europe the most dangerous eruption between the super-powers is the one that commits the first brigade or division" (182). This point constituted a major portion of Brodie's critique in the 1960s of the firebreak idea. "You say you 'would hate to waste the first nuclear weapon' (meaning, no doubt, after Nagasaki) on a second-rate emergency," he wrote to Thomas Schelling in 1964, "well, so would I, but one needs to know what you mean by 'a second-rate emergency.' You then say the use of such nuclear weapons would be: 'the most dramatic mili-tary event since Pearl Harbor . . . '.But one of my major points has been that massive aggression, too, is dramatic, at least equally dramatic, and let's not forget it. . . .

"It all seems to come down to a question of scale, to what separates the worthy from the unwor-thy objective. All of us seem to want to avoid being specific, but let me make one trial sortie into specificity. I have long felt, and have said in writing, that it was political wisdom on the part of our government to refrain from using nuclear weapons during the Korean War. I am un-changed in that opinion, though I am now rather less sure about it than I used to be. However, let me add that I feel quite sure that we should not again engage in another war with China on anything like that scale without using nuclear weapons, preferably small ones, tactically. I think that to avoid using them would thenceforward seriously compromise the worldwide deterrent ef-fect of our nuclear power" (Brodie to Schelling, 9 October 1964, UCLA Collection, Box 2 [Folder 11]).

Elsewhere, in criticizing the idea of a conventional forces buildup in Europe, Brodie pointed to the incentives to the Soviets in some cases to employ nuclear weapons first in a European war: "Clearly, the proposed [CWE] strategy offers no inducement to the Russians to stay non-nuclear in an all-out premeditated attack with their ground forces. Proponents of the CWE philosophy repeatedly assert that we will not allow ourselves to be beaten. Since, in tactical operations with nuclear weapons, first use is extremely important—for example, by accomplishing the quick destruction of the opponent's supporting air forces—our determination to introduce such weapons rather than accept defeat tells the enemy, if he believes us, that *he* must introduce them. It is one thing to propose an armaments restraint to which we promise to adhere, come what may, as long as the opponent does too; it is quite another to offer such restraint with the proviso that we will abandon it as soon as it clearly seems to interfere with the serious business of winning" ("What Price Con-ventional Forces in Europe?" 322; italics in original). See also chapter 7, note 77, of this volume.

58. *Strategy in the Missile Age*, 342. Probing and testing could be taken as merely one aspect of Soviet interest in acting in minimally risky ways. When Brodie focused on the minimal risk

element, however, he sometimes used Leites to show how the Soviets could decide upon surprise attack rather than probing and testing. For example, he used Leites as his authority for the "moral imperatives that impel a Bolshevik to exploit to the fullest whatever opportunities come his way" and that encourage full-scale aggression if Soviet leaders "should ever decide that by a surprise attack they could confidently count on destroying our strategic retaliatory force" (ibid., 355f and 356). In *Escalation and the Nuclear Option* (53–54), in which he tried to argue that accidental war had been practically nonexistent historically, Brodie took special care to distinguish probing and testing actions from a major deliberate attack.

59. Brodie's lengthiest statement on the Pearl Harbor episode appears in "Provocation Works on People," in which he agreed with Roberta Wohlstetter's view (*Pearl Harbor: Warning and Decision* [Stanford, Calif.: Stanford University Press, 1962]) that (in his terms) the Japanese decision "is . . . not explicable in rational terms." Brodie tried to show that alternatives to the Pearl Harbor attack were intolerable for Japanese leaders "in view of the emotional needs that the military leaders (who controlled the government) had developed by that time . . . [including] victory and the expansion of hegemony *for their own sakes* ("Provocation Works on People," 8; italics in original).

60. Brodie's explanation of Japanese action at Pearl Harbor with reference to nonrational motives suggested a linkage of emotional outlooks with belligerent behavior. At other times, however, Brodie tried to establish the importance of the emotional bases for provocative behavior *irrespective* of whether a country's leaders (such as those of the Soviet Union) were constrained by an operational code to act cautiously and carefully. For example, when writing about the unintended provocative effect of otherwise prudent security actions, he linked emotional impulses to "miscalculation of serious proportions," claiming the latter to be "not simply an occasional but rather a constant element in Soviet appraisal both of our intentions and of the respective capabilities of both sides" ("Provocation Works on People," 3). It was in this context that he noted that bias, which often leads to miscalculation, "almost always has an emotional underpinning" to which people sensitive to operational codes may be oblivious (ibid., 5, and "How Probable Is General War?" 14). But he also applied the point to American leaders ("Provocation Works on People," 7).

61. "Critique of the Doctrine of CWE," 179. This is in sharp contrast to the fashionable view in NATO headquarters in the early 1960s. Writing about NATO strategy from about 1959, for example, Gen. André Beaufre observed that

> the fear of another Pearl Harbor had disappeared, but in its place came a new obsession: fear of *accidental war*, caused by an originally fortuitous incident which, by the reciprocal interaction of the two adversaries, would bring about what has since been called an automatic "escalation." It is certain that the anti–Pearl Harbor arrangement necessitated quick counteraction at the first sign of attack and that extremely dangerous machinery might be activated on the basis of insufficient information. (*NATO and Europe* [New York: Alfred A. Knopf, 1966], 59; italics in original).

Compare *Escalation and the Nuclear Option*, 34–35. Addressing the problem of accidental war in 1962, Brodie wrote that "we should distinguish sharply between accidents of circumstance by which and within which crises are developed, and the so-called 'accidental war,' which connotes an outbreak of conflict that neither side has desired or really wants to press (e.g., local bluffs being unexpectedly called, etc.). To say that accidental war is a possibility worth a good deal of thought is not the same as saying that a conflict breaking out in Europe is more likely than not to be of the accidental variety. The latter proposition, which is made frequently, deserves to be very carefully examined, because the whole concept of limitation and escalation is greatly affected by it" ("Some Preliminary Observations on Escalation," 142).

62. This idea is also an important theme in Arnold L. Horelick and Myron Rush, *Strategic Power and Soviet Foreign Policy* (Chicago: University of Chicago Press, 1965).

63. Brodie denied that states continually engaged in tests of resolve, a point consistent with

his own conception of Soviet testing insofar as it suggested that the Soviet government would act with caution and restraint (Brodie to Schelling, 18 December 1964, UCLA Collection, Box 2 [Folder 11]).

64. *Escalation and the Nuclear Option*, 14–15 (italics in original).

65. *Strategy in the Missile Age*, 341–342.

66. "Afterthoughts on CWE," 5 (italics in original).

67. "Critique of the Doctrine of CWE," 182–183. Again, in 1963 he wrote that "At this late date there is no difference within RAND—and I suspect relatively little outside—as to whether the U.S. and its allies should have substantial conventional capabilities. The question is rather *how much*, particularly how much more than we already have—especially since this question has apparently become a matter of dissension between us and some of our allies and a source of misgivings to them" ("Afterthoughts on CWE," 1; italics in original).

68. *Strategy in the Missile Age*, 339.

69. "Critique of the Doctrine of CWE," 175.

70. See chapter 6 of this book.

71. "The generalization 'war is the result of miscalculation' is at best a partial truth," argued Alexander George and Richard Smoke in a later major and influential study on this subject. "Other historical cases besides Pearl Harbor fail to support the hypothesis that deterrence failures are the result of initiator's belief that a credible deterrence commitment is lacking. In many of the case studies presented . . . clear U.S. commitments did not prevent serious encroachments of various kinds" (*Deterrence in American Foreign Policy*, 525).

72. Beaufre, *NATO and Europe*, 54ff.

73. Brodie may have been in a minority at RAND when he distinguished different levels of Soviet threat-making. In some crisis games at RAND, for example, those acting as Western political decision makers "believed that the ambiguity of the enemy's intent could sometimes be the basis for an attempt to resolve the crisis, while [they] prepared appropriate retaliatory action in the event the attempt failed" (H. Averch and M. M. Lavin, "Dilemmas in the Politico-Military Conduct of Escalating Crises," RAND Paper P-3205, August 1965, 11).

74. "Political Impact of U.S. Force Postures" (see chap. 1, n. 66), 236.

75. "Morals and Strategy," *Worldview* (September 1964): 7. The Soviets did not order a full missile alert during the crisis (Edward Klein and Robert Littell, "Shh! Let's Tell the Russians," *Newsweek*, 5 May 1969).

76. "Missing Middle—Tactical Nuclear War," 252. At first Brodie seemed to fault gaming procedures per se in this connection. He wrote: "We should really begin to adjust to the Soviet opponent not as he appears in a war-gaming room—where he is always alert, aggressive and without biases or fixations other than those we share with him—but as our experience refined by close study tells us that he really is, which is to say, among other things, always deeply respectful of our power" ("Political Impact of U.S. Force Postures," 242; see also "What Price Conventional Capabilities in Europe?" 320).

Later, after RAND colleagues took favorably to his suggestion that the game exercises be modified to incorporate the rapid settlement of the Cuban missile crisis (David Novick to F. R. Collbohm, 10 March 1964, UCLA Collection, Box 2 [Folder 15]), Brodie seemed to take a softer appraisal of the game technique. After making the point about "Red yielding after Blue's first move," he went on to write, "Nevertheless it is by no means hopeless to examine the problem systematically, and some of us in RAND are now attempting to do just that. It may indeed require simply a variation of the game technique, but the essential question to ask at each point is *why* is each side doing what it does? What are the emotions as well as the considerations guiding it? We are attempting to analyze just how and by what steps a local and limited war could develop into a general war. What conditions would favor such a progression? Are those conditions likely to exist, and if so what could we prudently do to modify them? Above all we must bring into play our very considerable knowledge based on a long and fairly intimate experience, of our two major Communist opponents, especially the Soviet Union" ("Missing Middle–Tactical Nuclear War," 252–253; italics in original). He also wished to exclude the "well-known 'Hamburg Grab' gambit of the war games," which, he wrote, "is a monument to the degree to which political models can get out of line with political experience" (ibid., 261).

77. Among the extensive writings on the Cuban missile crisis, see especially Elie Abel, *The Missile Crisis* (New York: Bantam, 1968; first published 1966); Herbert S. Dinerstein, *The Making of a Missile Crisis: October 1962* (Baltimore: Johns Hopkins University Press, 1976); and Albert and Roberta Wohlstetter, *Controlling the Risks in Cuba.*

78. "Political Impact of U.S. Force Postures," 237.

79. Brodie to Schelling, 18 December 1964, UCLA Collection, Box 2 (Folder 11). For example, Brodie insisted that during the Berlin blockade of 1948/49, "the United States was completely bluffed concerning ground access" to Berlin, and "Stalin was clearly determined to avoid getting into hostilities with the United States over the issue and in fact never made any threat of the use of force to deny us such access" ("The McNamara Phenomenon," *World Politics* 17 [July 1965]; 682f).

80. The classic Kennan article is "The Sources of Soviet Conduct," *Foreign Affairs* 25 (July 1947): 566–582.

81. Conference transcript, "Theater Nuclear Forces," attached to "Factors Bearing on TNW Decision," [May 1967], 31, UCLA Collection, Box 7 (Folder 6).

82. He did not, moreover, expect refined Soviet testing of Western deterrent efforts. "When we erect a deterrent posture for the present or project one for the future," Brodie wrote in 1963, "subtle minds can always discover certain flaws in it; but we may be sure that the leaders of the Soviet Union will be not at all anxious to explore those flaws. It is one thing for us in the Air Force and at RAND to study the present and pending weaknesses or inadequacies in our posture and to correct those that we can correct. It is quite another for the nation to retreat because of them to a secondary and inferior line of defense. Such retreats are altogether unnecessary and unwise" ("Political Impact of U.S. Force Postures," 243–244). In 1959, he wrote much more pessimistically that "enemy planners are bound to be constantly searching for the weakest link in our retaliatory system, and ready to fix their attention upon it, as they did in the Pearl Harbor attack" (*Strategy in the Missile Age*, 222).

83. In 1963, Brodie criticized the "unfounded assumption that we cannot use or threaten to use on any level of fighting any kind of nuclear weapons, because such use or threat of use will set off escalation to the limitless destruction of general war — as though the conspicuous superiority in weaponry and in skill that we can continue to enjoy on all tactical levels, and which is not excluded for the future even on the strategic level, counts for nothing" ("Political Impact of U.S. Force Postures," 243).

84. *Escalation and the Nuclear Option,* 74.

85. Ibid., 123. For the most elaborate statement of this position, see Brodie, "The Intractability of States: A Distinctive Problem," September 1964, reproduced as an appendix in ibid., 135–148.

86. "Political Impact of U.S. Force Postures," 240–241 (italics in original). In this regard, Brodie allowed for crises in which the Soviets made counterthreats, as they did not do in 1962.

87. Brodie to *New York Times*, 13 November 1962, UCLA Collection, Box 17 (Folder 26); "Morals and Strategy," 7–8.

88. "The Issue of Strategic Superiority: A Comment," 19 July 1963, RAND Informal Working Paper, 1. See also memorandum, Nathan Leites to Brodie, "Our Discussion of July 30 Concerning Your D-11536," 30 July 1963, UCLA Collection, Box 1 (Folder 14). In *Strategy in the Missile Age*, Brodie wrote that "large forces look more impressive than small ones — for reasons which are by no means entirely irrational — and in some circumstances such impressiveness may be important to us" (277).

89. "Political Impact of U.S. Force Postures," 241–242. Note also Brodie's view that "crisis situations appear to induce on both sides regression to relatively primitive evaluations" (*Escalation*

and the Nuclear Option, 76). During the Cuban missile crisis, V. V. Kuznetsov, then a Soviet deputy foreign minister, is reported to have told John J. McCloy, who was negotiating with him on behalf of the president over the removal of Soviet weapons from Cuba, that although the Soviet Union would give way in this instance, it could not be expected to do so on the next such occasion. See John Newhouse, *Cold Dawn: The Story of SALT* (New York: Holt, Reinhart, and Winston, 1973), 68.

90. "If the aggressor is right in assuming his nerve is superior to ours," Brodie wrote in 1964, "we have had it" ("Missing Middle–Tactical Nuclear War," 259). Today, Robert Scheer pointed out ("Fear of a U.S. First Strike Seen as Cause of Arms Race"), many who question whether the United States can deter Soviet strategic attack are actually questioning American nerve.

91. "Commentary on the Force Employment Study," 9 January 1953, RAND Informal Working Paper, 1.

92. When discussing more than ten years earlier Soviet intentions from the same perspective outlined by Leites, Brodie seemed to focus on Soviet advantages and American vulnerabilities. "We have very good and strong reasons to believe," he wrote in 1952 (citing Leites in this connection), "that the attitude of the Soviet leaders towards power and the use of force is a good deal less ambivalent than our own, and on the whole much easier to examine and analyze. They are not beset by qualms concerning its use as we are, by plaintive reflections on how sweet the world would be if the east-west tensions were liquidated once and for all, and especially by voluptuous contemplation of power-substitutes which are much less costly than shooting hardware and which look very much like charity-plus-6-per-cent. They look upon power not only as something which one naturally maximizes for oneself at almost any cost but also as something which one applies without hesitation and without restraint to gain even small ends so long as one can do so without undue risk. How wonderfully straight-forward this is, and how effective! How much more effective it would be if they only believed their eyes—which their dogma fortunately prevents their doing—at the confusion they behold in the opposite camp" ("Attitudes towards the Use of Force," RAND Paper P-360, December 1952 [revised December 1953], 7; a copy of this paper was kindly provided to me from the personal collection of Prof. Robert Jervis.

93. *Escalation and the Nuclear Option*, 52. Compare the ideas of Malcolm Hoag outlined in chapter 7 of this study.

94. Ibid., 53.

95. To prevent war, Fred C. Iklé wrote, "expectations regarding the [war] outcome must not only look worse than the price for peace, they must also clearly govern all the decisions and dynamics through which military violence might be unleashed. It is not enough that those who can deliberately start a war should at no time come to believe that their nation, or their 'cause,' would be better served by going to war than if peace were maintained. For even if this condition is met, it will not be sufficient if wars can be started by technical accidents, or started by leaders who fail to think coherently how the fighting will end, or who, in some perverse stubbornness, no longer care if it ends in disaster for their own country.

"Many wars in this century have been started with only the most nebulous expectations regarding the outcome, on the strength of plans that paid little, if any, attention to the ending. Many began inadvertently, without any plans at all" (*Every War Must End* [New York: Columbia University Press, 1971], 108).

96. *Deterrence in American Foreign Policy*, passim. "We must avoid confusing an occasionally necessary confrontation with failure of deterrence," Brodie wrote in 1966 (*Escalation and the Nuclear Option*, 52).

97. *Escalation and the Nuclear Option*, 48–49.

98. See, for a discussion of the importance of situational context, Klaus Knorr, "Failures in National Intelligence Estimates: The Case of the Cuban Missiles," *World Politics* 16 (April 1964): 455–467.

99. A case in point is the Soviet invasion of Afghanistan in December 1979. Thomas J. Watson,

then American ambassador in Moscow, reflected later that Soviet leaders "understand most poorly how we may react to any given situation. It would have been relatively easy for you or for me to say what would happen if they suddenly moved into a neutral border nation. . . . I find it very hard to believe [that] the Soviets would have risked a wounded Olympics, loss of grain, complete interruption of business relations and a delay in the SALT treaty. I don't think they were prepared to put that on one side of the scale, Afghanistan on the other, and say Afghanistan outweighed those things" ("Envoy Watson Leaves Moscow—and 15 Months on the Razor's Edge," *Los Angeles Times,* 18 January 1981).

100. On force of events considerations, see Oran Young, *The Politics of Force: Bargaining during International Crises* (Princeton, N.J.: Princeton University Press, 1968).

101. Abel, *Missile Crisis,* 180–181.

102. The shifting views of Llewellyn Thompson, American ambassador to the Soviet Union, who participated in executive decision making during the Cuban crisis, are noted in ibid., 165–168. Robert Kennedy wrote that the president "wished to hear from Tommy Thompson . . . whose advice on the Russians and predictions as to what they would do were uncannily accurate and whose advice and recommendations were surpassed by none (*Thirteen Days: A Memoir of the Cuban Missile Crisis* [New York: W. W. Norton, 1971], 94).

103. Brodie, "Defense Strategy in Its Political Context," lecture at the Fifth International Wehrkunde Conference, Munich, February 1968, included in *The Political Dimension in National Strategy: Five Papers by William P. Gerberding and Bernard Brodie,* Security Studies Paper no. 13 (Security Studies Project, University of California, Los Angeles, 1968), 41, kindly provided to me from the personal collection of Prof. Robert Jervis. Albert and Roberta Wohlstetter, in their well-known essay on the Cuban crisis, wrote: "The main risks were of a local, non-nuclear action involving the United States and Russian forces. The possibilities of isolating a limited conflict have seldom been clearer. The situation is very different from Berlin. . . .

"What was threatened was a local non-nuclear action, a measure of very limited violence, only the boarding of ships" ("Controlling the Risks in Cuba, 258).

104. "Controlling the Risks in Cuba," 259.

105. "In view of the lessons we must draw from the Cuban crisis of 1962 concerning our position in Berlin," Brodie wrote in 1963, "it is a mischievous interpretation to hold that the outcome was determined *mostly* by our local conventional superiority. If local superiority in conventional arms made all the difference, why did not Khrushchev make some face-saving retaliation in places where he was superior, as in Berlin? ("What Price Conventional Capabilities in Europe?" 324; italics in original).

106. On the first point, Brodie wrote to Max Singer in 1964: "It seems to me quite obvious that when we compete with the Russians in conventional forces we compete in an area in which they have a minimum disadvantage—as is certainly true also of the Communist Chinese. I also happen to believe that the Russians have a positive advantage *vis-à-vis* the NATO powers in peacetime in providing conventional forces. . . . I think that if we were to succeed (which I am quite sure we will not) in substantially raising NATO conventional contributions to the Central Front, the Russians would also raise theirs. By the way, I hope I am making clear that I am not talking about what may or may not be the exact situation at present, but about what could happen in a conventional race" (Brodie to Singer, 11 November 1964, UCLA Collection, Box 4 [Folder 11]).

On the second point, he declared in 1968 that prodigality in American commitments "resulted at least in part from the tendency to distinguish so sharply between limited and general war and from the confidence that we Americans know how to control escalation. There was also confidence that we had or could easily create enough conventional forces to achieve our military purposes without any special dependence on nuclear weapons—except insofar as the latter helped to prevent escalation" ("Defense Strategy in Its Political Context," 41).

107. "Afterthoughts on CWE," 4–5 (italics in original).

108. Brodie's earliest observation that the Vietnam war represented a failure of limited war, is

in "Defense Strategy in Its Political Context." He complained in that lecture that "we have been essentially locked in . . . able neither to escalate nor to de-escalate in any meaningful fashion" (43). Less than three years earlier, in a letter to the *New York Times* (4 May 1965, UCLA Collection, Box 2 [N Folder]), Brodie argued strongly in favor of the bombing of North Vietnam as necessary pressure to bring the North Vietnamese to negotiate. And in his study *Escalation and the Nuclear Option*, he wrote that "the possibility that imaginative use of special types of nuclear weapons much earlier in the [Vietnam] campaign might have gone far toward defeating the Viet Cong without the commitment of large numbers of American ground forces ought to be recognized, even if one accepts that under the political circumstances prevailing it would probably have been unwise policy" (17f). It cannot be established, finally, whether Brodie's major effort to gain draft exemption for his draft-age son during the war affected his views or to what extent. Documents describing this effort are in the UCLA Collection, Box 6 (G Folder).

Brodie's lengthiest critical treatment of the Vietnam war is in *War and Politics*, chaps. 4–5.

109. See Warner R. Schilling et al., *American Arms and a Changing Europe: Dilemmas of Deterrence and Disarmament* (New York: Columbia University Press, 1973), 172–173. Compare note 95 above.

110. In *War and Politics* (341ff), Brodie stressed the emotional reasons behind the selection of vital interests.

111. In August 1965, Brodie wrote to the head of the Rand Social Science Division, pointing out "how little substantive communication we in the Social Sciences have thus far succeeded in establishing with members of other disciplines. . . . Our interdisciplinary approaches have thus far accomplished no miracles of understanding and empathy between the Departments" (memorandum, Brodie to J. M. Goldsen, 18 August 1965, UCLA Collection, Box 2 [Folder 15]).

112. Adam Yarmolinsky, *The Military Establishment* (New York: Harper & Row, 1971), 127. I am indebted for this reference to James A. Nathan and James K. Oliver, *United States Foreign Policy and World Order* (Boston: Little, Brown, 1976), 330.

113. As we will see in the next chapter, this interest also separated him from his RAND colleagues who sought a buildup in NATO's conventional forces strength, because Brodie was inclined at this time to highlight his credentials as a strategist and play down theirs.

114. "Afterthoughts on CWE," 1 (italics in original). See also note 67 above.

115. Memorandum to E. Vandevanter, Jr., 5 March 1964, UCLA Collection, Box 4 (Folder 22). Brodie indicated in this letter that "unless we really plan to defend Europe by conventional means against a large-scale conventional assault (which I consider the least likely of all imaginable contingencies, less likely by much than general war), I would on an off-the-cuff basis much prefer a package which contained say ten *good* highly mobile divisions, considerably behind the front where they could be moved around easily, to thirty divisions on the line" (italics in original). He further indicated he might boost this number considerably after more study.

Chapter 9. On Strategy and Strategists

1. Brodie, "Strategy," in *International Encyclopedia of Social Sciences*, 287.
2. Brodie, *Strategy in the Missile Age*, 388.
3. Brodie, "Nuclear Weapons: Strategic or Tactical?" *Foreign Affairs* 32 (January 1954): 229.
4. Brodie to Herbert S. Bailey, Jr., 8 February 1955, UCLA Collection, Box 1 (B Folder). See also Brodie to Gen. John A. Samford, USAF, 29 April 1952, UCLA Collection, Box 2 (S Folder); and Brodie to Gen. Truman Landon, USAF, 9 May 1952, UCLA Collection, Box 1 (L Folder).
5. Brodie, "The American Scientific Strategists," RAND Paper P-2979, October 1964, 20–21.
6. Ibid., 21–22.
7. Brodie, "Strategy," 284.

8. Brodie, "American Scientific Strategists," 22.

9. Brodie, "Strategy as a Science," *World Politics* 1 (July 1949): 472 and 478. The 1964 statements in the remainder of this paragraph are from "American Scientific Strategists," 20 and 22, respectively.

10. Brodie, "American Scientific Strategists," 24.

11. Ibid., 22.

12. Brodie, *War and Politics*, 475f. The four people listed by Brodie were Alain Enthoven, Malcolm Hoag, Henry Rowen, and Albert Wohlstetter.

13. Ibid., 475–476.

14. Brodie, "Strategy as a Science," 477.

15. Brodie, "Strategy," 287.

16. Brodie, "American Scientific Strategists," 24.

17. C. J. Hitch, "Analysis for Air Force Decisions," in *Analysis for Military Decisions*, edited by E. S. Quade (Chicago: Rand McNally, 1966), 21.

18. Quade, "Introduction," in ibid., 7. In some cases, a problem might need to be studied whose variables were difficult to quantify. Herbert Goldhamer noted in a RAND paper as early as 1950 on the efficient use of combat personnel in military operations that the difficulty of providing accurate estimates or promising modes of investigation did not free psychologists and social scientists of responsibility for dealing with that problem (Goldhamer, "Human Factors in Systems Analysis," RAND Research Memorandum RM-388, April 1950, 24).

19. Brodie, "American Scientific Strategists," 19.

20. Memorandum, Brodie to Joseph M. Goldsen, 13 February 1964, UCLA Collection, Box 2 (Folder 15).

21. Hitch, "Analysis for Air Force Decisions," 17 (emphasis omitted).

22. Ibid., 23. "One accomplishes much by bringing representatives of the several relevant disciplines together to work jointly on the same problems," Brodie wrote in 1964, "along with physicists, engineers, and other technologists. This broad method of approach is one of the distinctive values of institutions like RAND. But the inter-disciplinary exchange of insights is not always easy to accomplish" ("American Scientific Strategists," 22).

23. In such cases, differences in temperaments would tend to become more of a barrier. For an earlier case in which differences among strategic analysts added to the difficulties of deciding upon a course of action, see Elting E. Morison's review of the dispute between advocates of convoys and advocates of search and attack to meet the submarine threat in the Second World War, in Morison, *Men, Machines, and Modern Times* (Cambridge, Mass.: MIT Press, 1966), chap. 4. See also the concluding section of this chapter.

24. Hitch, "Analysis for Air Force Decisions," 23. In *War and Politics* (464), Brodie recounts Hitch's view that systems analysis appeared more appropriate to managing traffic over the George Washington Bridge than to solving foreign policy problems.

25. Brodie, "American Scientific Strategists," 28–29.

26. Brodie, "Strategy," 287.

27. Brodie, "The Impact of Technological Change on the International System: Reflections on Prediction," in *Change and the Future International System*, edited by David S. Sullivan and Martin J. Sattler (New York: Columbia University Press, 1972), 4–6: first published in 1971 in the *Journal of International Affairs*. Some years earlier, Brodie was much less complacent on this matter. "We have already referred," he wrote in 1968, "to the difficulties resulting from the fantastic speed with which military technology is presently changing. We have no real reason to foresee a future state of equilibrium even in the factors of most elementary importance, such as the nuclear weapons themselves. The layman feels that after a nuclear bomb has reached a certain level of power, a further increase in its power or other change in its characteristics is likely to be of little importance. In some categories of weapons that view is indeed justified, but if we are seeking to use a weapon as the warhead on a missile, we may be critically concerned with reducing its over-all weight with-

out sacrificing yield. As the opponent installs and augments passive protection around his missiles, we not only have to make our own missiles more accurate but we may also have to fit them with more powerful warheads. . . .

"However, to consider any one category of weapons or instruments inevitably over-simplifies the problem. It is a broad spectrum of weapons in which change is occurring at so alarming a rate — alarming because of all the elements of uncertainty, with resulting fallibility, that are bound to be introduced" ("American Scientific Strategists," 27–28).

28. Brodie, *War and Politics*, 380 (italics in original).

29. Brodie, "Impact of Technological Change on the International System," 3.

30. Ibid., 3f.

31. Brodie, "Strategy as a Science," 471.

32. Ibid., 473.

33. *Strategy in the Missile Age*, 304. In a preliminary version of chapter 8 of *Strategy*, Brodie put this point more strongly, writing that "technological progress *is* pushing us rapidly towards a position of almost intolerable mutual menace" ("Alternative Strategic Policies II," 27 March 1958, RAND Informal Working Paper, 37; italics added).

34. Quade, "Introduction," 6. Brodie noted that RAND was founded primarily to provide technological assistance ("American Scientific Strategists," 18).

35. Brodie to Hans Speier, 23 November 1954, UCLA Collection, Box 4 (Folder 19).

36. *Strategy in the Missile Age*, 56.

37. Cited in James E. King, Jr., "Airpower in the Missile Gap," *World Politics* 12 (July 1960): 630. See also chapter 8, note 21, of this book.

38. *War and Politics*, 392.

39. Bracken, *The Command and Control of Nuclear Forces* (New Haven, Conn.: Yale University Press, 1983), 59–60; italics in original.

40. Brodie, *Escalation and the Nuclear Option*, 87–88. Italics in original.

41. Brodie, "The Argument Against Proceeding with the BMD: An Aspect of Strategy, Politics, and Arms Control," 14, prepared for the U.S. Arms Control and Disarmament Agency under Contract ACDA/WEC-126, Security Study Project, University of California, Los Angeles, 19 June 1968, Kindly supplied to me from the personal collection of Robert Jervis.

42. *War and Politics*, 391.

43. Ibid., 321–322. If the balance of terror were as stable as Brodie indicated, stimulating technological developments on so-called worse-case assumptions would be unnecessary; however, Brodie did not address the opposite argument (Albert Wohlstetter, "Rivals, But No 'Race,'" *Foreign Policy*, no. 16 [Fall 1974]: 75; and Samuel P. Huntington, "Arms Races: Prerequisites and Results," in *Public Policy* 8, edited by Carl J. Friedrich and Seymour E. Harris [Cambridge, Mass.: Harvard University Press, 1958]) that technological changes increased stability by dampening the quantitative nuclear force buildup.

44. "Strategy," 287 (italics in original).

45. Brodie, "The Continuing Relevance of *On War*," included in Carl von Clausewitz, *On War*, edited and translated by Michael Howard and Peter Paret (Princeton, N.J.: Princeton University Press, 1976), 51. All further references to *On War* are to this edition unless otherwise indicated.

46. *On War*, 580.

47. "A Guide to the Reading of *On War*," included in ibid., 643. See *War and Politics*, 443f, for pertinent quotations from this letter. At one point (*War and Politics*, 254), Brodie included the savage partisan warfare that occurred in Spain and Portugal during the Napoleonic wars as an aspect of absolute war.

48. *Strategy in the Missile Age*, 55.

49. "Guide to *On War*," 645–646 (italics in original).

50. See chapter 7 of this volume. Brodie's references to orgiastic tendencies in war may have had their origin in his reading of Clausewitz's concept of absolute war. According to this reading,

all interstate violence tended to eventually displace the political objectives that initially guided it. James King pointed out that such a reading of absolute war "is to risk making of it an Aristotelian 'final case,' that is, an *end* of 'pure' or 'perfect' war towards which all actual wars 'tend' or 'move,' in other words, a teleological construct" ("On Clausewitz: Master Theorist of War," unpublished manuscript, 161; italics in original). I am grateful to Professor King for letting me read this manuscript, which is a review essay of the Howard-Paret edition of *On War* and of Peter Paret's *Clausewitz and the State* (New York: Oxford University Press, 1976). On pages 21–22 of a condensed version of this manuscript with the same title, published in *Naval War College Review* 30 (Fall 1977), and also in that portion of the unpublished manuscript which addressed Brodie's ideas at much greater length, King argued that although some of Clausewitz's writings did suggest such a meaning for absolute war, the correct significance of that concept was as a point of reference to guide theorizing on the subject of war. For an extended discussion of Clausewitz's theoretical interests that was fully in agreement with King on this point, see Paret, *Clausewitz and the State*, 356ff.

51. "Guide to *On War*," 706. See also *On War*, 607.

52. *War and Politics*, 6.

53. Cited from *On War* (book 1, chap. 1, sec. 8), 79. I am indebted here to Michael Howard's essay "War as an Instrument of Policy," included in *Diplomatic Investigations: Essays in the Theory of International Politics*, edited by Herbert Butterfield and Martin Wight (London: Allen & Unwin, 1966), 195.

54. *War and Politics*, 425.

55. Howard, "War as an Instrument of Policy," 195.

56. *War and Politics*, 11f. The source for Brodie's assertion that absolute war was "not something to be witnessed on earth" may have been the following passage from book 8, chap. 3A, of *On War* (p. 582): "Within the concept of absolute war . . . war is indivisible, and its component parts (the individual victories) are of value only in their relation to the whole. Conquering Moscow and half of Russia in 1812 was of no avail to Bonaparte unless it brought him the peace he had in view. . . .

"Contrasting with this extreme view of the connection between successes in war, is another view, no less extreme; which holds that war consists of separate successes each unrelated to the next as in a match consisting of several games. The earlier games have no effect upon the later. . . .

"The first of these two views of war derives its validity from the nature of the subject; the second, from its actual history. Countless cases have occurred where a small advantage could be gained without an onerous condition being attached to it. The more the element of violence is moderated, the commoner these cases will be; but just as absolute war has never in fact been achieved, so we will never find a war in which the second concept is so prevalent that the first can be disregarded altogether."

James King suggests that the "nature of the subject" associated with the first view described here refers to the theory of war, and that Clausewitz was proposing "two unattainable poles, one absolute (unlimited?) and one something else (limited?), between which actual wars are to be found" ("On Clausewitz: Master Theorist of War," unpublished manuscript, 213). See also King's review essay cited in note 50 above. Brodie, not generally interested in the theory of war, seems to have concentrated on the second Clausewitzian view. And because he had in mind especially the political objectives envisioned in war, he referred instead to Clausewitz's point (in the same *On War* chapter) that "the closer . . . political probabilities drive war toward the absolute, . . . the more imperative the need not to take the first step without considering the last" ("Guide to *On War*," 702). I am indebted to King for the contrast between his and Brodie's formulations on this point.

57. For Lenin's and Stalin's favorable attitudes toward Clausewitz's precept, see Raymond L. Garthoff, *Soviet Military Doctrine* (Glencoe, Ill.: Free Press, 1953), 53ff. Brodie commented (*War and Politics*, 42) that Stalin followed Clausewitz's precepts in August and September of 1944 when he halted the Red Army before Warsaw to permit the Germans to quell the Warsaw uprising then taking place.

Donald Brennan, in a review of the Howard-Paret edition of *On War*, went on to write that "the Soviet Union—through Lenin, a student of Clausewitz—has thoroughly assimilated Clausewitzian perspectives. Many specific items of evidence, ranging from doctrinal writings to its extensive civil-defence activities, indicate that such Clausewitzian modes of thought permeate the Soviet defence establishment. It is to the peril of the West that we largely ignore them" ("Review of Clausewitz's *On War*," *Survival* 20 [January/February 1978]: 39). Brennan's elaboration of this point, omitted from *Survival*, may be found in his uncut "Review of Clausewitz's *On War*," Hudson Institute document HI-2713-P, October 1977.

58. Fuller, *Armament and History* (London: Eyre & Spottiswoode, 1946), 200.

59. Howard, "The Influence of Clausewitz," in *On War*, 43. In a 1981 essay, Howard questioned, as Brodie had earlier, the apparent neglect of political thinking in American scenarios about nuclear war. "Has not the bulk of American thinking," he asked, "been exactly what Clausewitz described—something that, because it is divorced from any political context, is 'pointless and devoid of sense'?" ("On Fighting a Nuclear War," reprinted in Howard, *Causes of War*, 141. For the Clausewitzian phrase "pointless and devoid of sense," see *On War* (book 8, chap. 6B), 605. Given his skepticism that *any* political objective was worth a nuclear war, Howard's major concern seemed to be not with the exclusion of Clausewitzian thinking from nuclear war scenarios but rather with the appropriateness of such thinking in those scenarios.

60. Brennan, "Review of Clausewitz's *On War*" (*Survival* version), 38.

61. In a letter to Michael Howard, 19 May 1978, a copy of which was sent to Brodie (UCLA Collection, Box 33 [Folder 5]), Brennan wrote that if Howard thought Dulles sounded "bloodthirsty" he should read the NATO 1957 War Plan MC-14/2. Although it is not certain that Brodie read this plan, he was probably aware of its broad outlines, and his assumptions about the nuclear war being anticipated in Europe in the late 1950s (see chapter 7 of this book) could well have flowed from War Plan MC-14/2. If so, Brodie's questioning of those assumptions may also be viewed as criticism of the plan. Whether Plan MC-14/2 illustrated Clausewitz's precept of guiding war by the choice of political objective remains unclear. Another informed observer of the NATO alliance, pointing out that "there is no monolithic *political* strategy for the NATO community with which the allegedly recalcitrant generals could be forced to align themselves," observed that alliance military leaders drafted ground rules and tactical plans as a way of coping with the lack of defense guidance (E. Vandevanter, Jr., "NATO's Man on Horseback," RAND Paper P-2841-1, February 1964, 18, UCLA Collection, Box 35 [Folder 2]; italics in original).

62. Coral Bell, *The Conventions of Crisis: A Study of Diplomatic Management* (London: Oxford University Press, 1971), 2–3; italics in original. For the argument that crisis management underpinned the contemporary international system even before the Cuban missile crisis, see Gordon A. Craig and Alexander L. George, *Force and Statecraft* (New York: Oxford University Press, 1983), 118ff.

63. Herman Kahn, *Thinking about the Unthinkable in the 1980's* (New York: Simon & Schuster, 1984), 90.

64. Kahn, *On Escalation*, 197–198. In describing the "reawakening," Kahn referred to "initial discussion of the various options open to a potential nuclear attacker," including "threats he might make and the appropriate tactics if threats failed[,] . . . counteroptions available to the defender, . . . rationality of irrationality, withholding tactics, various mixtures and levels of counterforce and countervalue targeting." Brodie's contribution to some of these issues was not mentioned by Kahn.

65. Kahn, *On Escalation*, 199 (italics in original).

66. See chapters 2 and 3 of this volume.

67. Brodie, Review of Beaufre, *Survival* 7 (August 1965): 208.

68. *War and Politics*, 452–453 (italics in original).

69. Ibid., 35–36.

70. Translated from the enclosure in André Beaufre to Brodie, 6 October 1965, UCLA Collection, Box 6 (B Folder). This enclosure, published in the original French in *Survival* 7 (December

1965): 342–343, is henceforth referred to as "Beaufre Response." I am indebted to Prof. Alain Marsot for assistance in the translation.

71. André Beaufre, *An Introduction to Strategy*, translated by R. H. Barry (New York: Praeger, 1965), 20.

72. Cited in Review of Beaufre, 208.

73. Beaufre Response, 342.

74. Cited in Review of Beaufre, 208–209.

75. Beaufre, *Introduction to Strategy*, 13–14.

76. Ibid., 13.

77. Ibid., 129. I am indebted to Michael Carver, "Conventional Warfare in the Nuclear Age," in Paret, ed., *Makers of Modern Strategy*, 789, for drawing my attention to these sentences. The term "indirect approach" originated with the strategist B. H. Liddell Hart, whose influence Beaufre acknowledged. See Liddell Hart, *Strategy: The Indirect Approach* (New York: Praeger, 1954).

78. This quotation and the next are from Review of Beaufre, 208 and 209, respectively. Beaufre seems to have meant by "philosophy" the opposite of what Brodie initially presumed, for he wrote to Brodie that he had in mind by it "love of wisdom" (Beaufre Response). This suggested an intellectual openness evidently missing at the time Marshal Pétain's aphorism became popular. "Rigidity of doctrine," Brodie wrote in 1959, "we have always with us" (*Strategy in the Missile Age*, 41).

79. Review of Beaufre, 209.

80. "Continuing Relevance of *On War*," 51.

81. As related in Brennan, "Review of Clausewitz's *On War*" (*Survival* version), 38. Three years earlier, in *War and Politics*, Brodie wrote of Kahn's "courage to explore as thoroughly as his exceptional ability and knowledge permitted the character of a 'general war' with thermonuclear weapons" but observed that "while Kahn cared well enough where he was going, he was helped along by an optimism that has in some critical respects turned out to be unwarranted" (420). Brennan pointed out in *Survival* that Kahn's civil defense studies leading up to his *On Thermonuclear War* assumed hypothetical Soviet attacks to a total yield of 80,000 megatons—a figure several times larger than that deliverable by the late 1970s. Brodie's point is also difficult to understand by his own logic, because by 1952, when he first dwelled on a Soviet-American war with fusion weapons, he insisted that massive vulnerability of cities to fusion weapons attacks was the fundamental reason why thermonuclear warfare was politically absurd (see chapter 5 of this volume). It is not clear how the rising Soviet nuclear stockpile altered the technological premises behind this logic.

82. Beaufre, *Introduction to Strategy*, 77.

83. Ibid., 40 (table: "Parallels between Types of Strategy").

84. Ibid., 44. Evidently because Beaufre depended upon Liddell Hart's reading of Clausewitz, he failed to see that indirect strategy such as that followed by Hitler could also be traced to *On War*. Hans Rothfels summarized this portion of Clausewitz's ideas: "Limited warfare has occurred and will occur again in two cases: first, whenever the political tensions or the political aims involved are small; second, whenever the military means are of such a character that the overthrow of the enemy cannot be conceived of at all, or can only be approached in an indirect way" ("Clausewitz," in Earle, ed., *Makers of Modern Strategy*, 109). For Liddell Hart's negative association of Clausewitz with the concept of "absolute war," see Howard, "Influence of Clausewitz," 39–41; compare Beaufre, *Introduction to Strategy*, 42.

85. *On War* (book 8, chap. 1), cited in Paret, *Clausewitz and the State*, 356.

86. *On War* (book 2, chap. 5), 156. See also King, "On Clausewitz," *Naval War College Review*, 17.

87. Paret, *Clausewitz and the State*, 358.

88. *On War* (book 8, chap. 2; italics in original), cited in Paret, *Clausewitz and the State*, 358; and in King, "On Clausewitz" (unpublished manuscript), 160.

89. Brodie rejoinder to Beaufre, *Survival* 7 (December 1965): 343. James King, in his evaluation of Brodie's interpretive guide to *On War*, pointed out that "in consonance with his insistent

pragmatism, Brodie examines "all the subjects discussed for what they tell about war, or about Clausewitz's views on war, not for what they tell us about Clausewitz's theory of war" ("On Clausewitz" [unpublished manuscript], 162).

90. George and Smoke, *Deterrence in American Foreign Policy*, 14.

91. Howard, *Causes of Wars*, 99. This essay, "The Relevance of Traditional Strategy," was first published January 1973.

92. Ibid., 88.

93. Howard, *Causes of Wars*, 108–109.

94. *On War* (book 1, chap. 1), 89.

95. "Gradually his operations became more passive," Clausewitz wrote, referring to Frederick. "Realizing that even victories cost too much he tried to manage with less. His one concern was to gain time, and hold on to what he had. . . . His letters . . . show how keenly he looked forward to winter quarters and how much he hoped he would be able to take them up without incurring serious losses in the meantime" (*On War* [book 8, chap. 8], 615).

96. For Brodie's omission, I am indebted to James King, "On Clausewitz" (unpublished manuscript), 162f. Brodie's characterization of Clausewitz's discussion of war limitation is in "Guide to *On War*," 707.

97. Brodie, "In Quest of the Unknown Clausewitz: A Review of *Clausewitz and the State* by Peter Paret," *International Security* 1 (Winter 1977): 67.

98. *On War* (book 8, chap. 3B), cited in "Guide to *On War*," 702.

99. Ibid.

100. Ibid.

101. Howard, *Causes of Wars*, 204–205.

102. For Brodie's 1965 argument endorsing the bombing of North Vietnam as necessary to force the North Vietnamese regime to discuss peace terms, see chapter 8, note 108, of this book. In *War and Politics*, by contrast, he wrote that "the main reason we failed in Vietnam was also the reason why it was impossible from the beginning to succeed. We were supporting a government that not only did not deserve that support but which could not benefit from it" (173).

103. See chapter 7 of this volume.

104. *War and Politics*, 9–10. See also "Guide to *On War*," 643.

105. *On War* (book 8, chap. 2), cited in "Guide to *On War*," 700–701. Brodie's translation here and elsewhere is different from that supplied by Howard and Paret in their edition of the text.

106. *On War* (book 8, chap. 2), 579. This conception is evidently opposed to the metaphor of war as a duel, reflected for Clausewitz (ibid. [book 8, chap. 1], 577) in most accounts of battle by generals.

107. "Guide to *On War*," 658.

108. *On War* (book 3, chap. 5), cited in ibid. Italics added by Brodie.

109. Peter Paret, "Clausewitz," in Paret, ed., *Makers of Modern Strategy*, 204. See also Paret, *Clausewitz and the State*, 285.

110. "Guide to *On War*," 658.

111. See chapter 7, note 10, of this book. Gerald Aronson, a psychiatrist practicing in Los Angeles, informed me that a RAND study group on this subject flourished in the early 1960s. An outline, evidently prepared for this group, entitled "Notes for Discussion—October 15, 1962—Aronson," was found among the Fawn Brodie Papers, Manuscript Collection 360, Special Collections Department, University of Utah Libraries, Salt Lake City, Box 60 (Folder 9).

112. Brodie, "Strategic Objectives and the Determination of Force Composition (see chap. 1, n. 89), 87. In *Strategy in the Missile Age*, published about the same time, he wrote that "most serious students . . . implicitly attribute to leaders of government, past and present, an abiding rationality and a dedication to logical, penetrating, farsighted thinking" (351). See also chapter 8, notes 59 and 60, of this book.

113. Brodie, "Provocation Works on People," 12 June 1959, RAND Informal Working Paper, 1

and 3–4, UCLA Collection, Box 17 (Folder 2). "Surely if statesmen were rational," he wrote in this paper, "in the sense of being regularly ruled by close and well-reasoned calculations of probabilities for gain and loss from pursuing a particular policy, we should have very little reason to fear a general war in the future" (9).

114. Ibid., 2–3 and 7.

115. Ibid., 11.

116. Ibid., 9.

117. Brodie, "The Intractability of States: A Distinctive Problem," Rand Paper P-2970, September 1964. Reproduced in *Escalation and the Nuclear Option*, 138 and 142–143.

118. Ibid., 143–145.

119. *War and Politics*, 25.

120. Ibid., 16–17.

121. Ibid., 313.

122. Ibid., 314.

123. *On War* (book 1, chap. 3), 105–106 (italics in original).

124. Clausewitz referred to psychology as an "obscure field" (ibid., cited by Paret in "Clausewitz," 204).

125. Paret, "Clausewitz," 204.

126. Ibid., 204–205.

127. *War and Politics*, 314. Compare note 124 above.

128. Parkinson, *Clausewitz* (London: Wayland Publishers, 1970).

129. Ibid., 326. Parkinson quotes Clausewitz writing at age twenty-seven, "My life is a trackless existence," and goes on to observe that "twenty years later he was to believe he had been a failure" (ibid., 19).

130. Brodie review article, "On Clausewitz: A Passion for War," *World Politics* 25 (January 1973): 289 and 300.

131. Brodie to Paret, 16 October 1973, UCLA Collection, Box 9 (P Folder).

132. "Guide to *On War*," 648.

133. Cited in Parkinson, *Clausewitz*, 19.

134. Cited from *On War* (book 1, chap. 6) in "Guide to *On War*," 649. For empirical evidence challenging Clausewitz's statement that "as a rule most men would rather believe bad news than good," see Russell Baker and Charles Peters, "The Prince and His Courtiers: At the White House, the Kremlin, and the Reichschancellery," in *Inside the System*, edited by Charles Peters and James Fallows, 3d ed. (New York: Praeger, 1977), 7–9.

135. This quotation and the next are cited by Brodie in "On Clausewitz," 300. "Clausewitz still felt not sufficiently noticed," he wrote, after mentioning Clausewitz's appointment as tutor to the crown prince and the granting to him of noble status. "And he was always sad." (Ibid., 300.)

136. "Guide to *On War*," 659. Clausewitz's observation about boldness is in *On War* (book 3, chap. 6), 190.

137. See, for example, an 1817 letter cited by Parkinson but not by Brodie: "For some time I have had the unfortunate habit of keeping everything to myself, and I should have been less reserved, less hidden away. One reason has been my fear of scorn, and the need to be sure of what I was doing. A superficial opinion which brought a rough reply would easily hurt me, and would be difficult to avoid as long as people are what they are" (*Clausewitz*, 306).

138. Brodie, "On Clausewitz," 302.

139. Ibid., 302–303. In *War and Politics*, Brodie also refers to Clausewitz's inner conflict but cites his "compassion" as an element of the conflict, linking it to Clausewitz's "real anguish at the horrors he saw at the Berezina" (445). "The inner conflict between his undoubted compassion," Brodie wrote of Clausewitz, "and something much fiercer in his nature must have contributed to the depression that seems to have deepened steadily throughout his life" (445).

140. Brodie, "On Clausewitz," 305.

141. Paret may have had Dostoyevski and Kafka in mind here. See below. A contemporary writer whose sadness produced by tragic experiences has not lessened but strengthened his creativity is Elie Weisel.

142. Brodie, "On Clausewitz," 301 and 304.

143. Ibid., 306–307.

144. For the last sentence of this paragraph, I am indebted to a personal communication from Professor Paret, 18 January 1980 (cited henceforth as "Paret's Comment"). Evidence that Brodie accepted that depression impaired creativity is contained in Paret to Brodie, 4 October 1973, UCLA Collection, Box 9 (P Folder), in which Paret ascribed this view to Brodie's erroneous understanding that Paret held such an opinion. As indicated below, Brodie was highly respectful of Paret's competence on this subject.

145. Paret, *Clausewitz and the State*, 435 and 435f. See also "Paret Comment."

146. Paret to Brodie, 4 October 1973. In *Clausewitz and the State*, Paret wrote that "depression is not an unusual condition; what matters is its comprehensiveness, depth, and frequency. Neither his letters nor his actions indicate that Clausewitz's personality was essentially depressive, just as they do not indicate that he was torn by irreconcilable conflicts" (437). In the second edition of *Clausewitz* (1985; x–xi), Paret sets forward additional evidence for his views on this question. In "Paret Comment," Paret wrote that "in my opinion, BB took too encompassing a view of depression."

147. Cited in Paret to Brodie, 4 October 1973. Writing to Brodie on 19 October 1973 (UCLA Collection, Box 9 [P Folder]), Paret refuted Parkinson's assertion that Clausewitz felt paralyzed and looked forward to an honorable death, by providing what he argued was a more accurate translation of a key Clausewitz letter that Parkinson had used as evidence for this assertion. The pertinent text of this letter, dated 16 September 1820, is in Paret, *Clausewitz and the State*, 281.

148. Paret, *Clausewitz and the State*, 282.

149. Paret to Brodie, 4 October 1973.

150. Ibid.

151. Paret, *Clausewitz and the State*, 437.

152. Ibid., 285.

153. Paret to Brodie, 4 October 1973.

154. Paret, *Clausewitz and the State*, 282–283.

155. Brodie to Paret, 16 October 1973. Paret ("Paret Comment") was not in fact psychoanalytically trained, but he had studied the history of psychoanalysis, corresponded with Freud, and had recently edited *Sisyphus, or the Limits of Education*, by his stepfather Siegfried Bernfeld (Berkeley: University of California Press, 1973), a work on psychoanalysis and education. His mother, stepfather, and wife were psychoanalysts.

156. Brodie, "In Quest of the Unknown Clausewitz," 68. Paret ("Paret Comment") later recalled pointing out to Brodie that his book had in fact quoted the very passage that Brodie claimed he had not thought worth quoting; see Paret, *Clausewitz and the State*, 222. Paret interpreted this classical "Freudian slip" as reflecting Brodie's desire to see Clausewitz as severely depressed, a condition that would have increased the similarity between him and Brodie. I discuss this subject later in this chapter.

157. "Paret Comment."

158. Brodie's evaluation of Clausewitz should be contrasted with his more characteristically careful comment in a review of a study on Woodrow Wilson by Alexander L. George and Juliette L. George (*Woodrow Wilson and Colonel House: A Personality Study* [New York: John Day, 1956]). "It is one thing," Brodie wrote in that earlier review, "to observe compulsive behavior and identify it for what it is; it is quite another to find the original causes. The former is what a sensitive and appropriately educated person can discern in his friends and acquaintances as well as in himself and, in some instances, in historical figures; the latter usually requires the expert therapist and the couch" ("A Psychoanalytic Interpretation of Woodrow Wilson," *World Politics* [April 1957]: 416. For extended discussions of problems of psychohistorical explanation, see John E. Mack,

"Psychoanalysis and Historical Biography," *Journal of the American Psychoanalytic Association* 19 (January 1971); Alexander L. George, "Assessing Presidential Character," *World Politics* 26 (January 1974); and Robert C. Tucker, "The Georges' Wilson Reexamined: An Essay on Psychobiography," *American Political Science Review* 71 (June 1977).

159. Brodie, Review of *Clausewitz and the State*, by Peter Paret, *Journal of Interdisciplinary History* 8 (Winter 1978): 574. This second review of Paret's *Clausewitz and the State* omits the criticism (found in the *International Security* review) of Paret's failure to make contact with Clausewitz's deeper emotions and is even more laudatory than the first.

160. Brodie untitled statement, evidently enclosed in Brodie to Paret, 16 October 1973.

161. According to the undated statement by Brodie referred to in note 160 above, the analyst confirming Brodie's view was Ralph Greenson and the one suggesting another view was Gerald Aronson. Aronson's view of Clausewitz's depression seems to be compatible with the Freudian definition of psychic health employed by Paret, because it was not inconsistent with Clausewitz's ability to love or to work.

162. On this aspect of Clausewitz's orientation, see Paret, *Clausewitz and the State*, 357.

163. Paret, "Clausewitz," 208.

164. This point was made to me by two people closely aware of Brodie's state of mind in his last years, including his late wife, Fawn Brodie.

165. For this point and another in the next paragraph about the subjective reception by policymakers of objective analysis, I am indebted to an unpublished 1959 paper by Charles Lindblom, "Judgment and Partisanship," one of six prepared by Professor Lindblom on the missions and influence of the RAND Corporation. I have been able to read the six papers through the courtesy of Professor Lindblom and the RAND Corporation. Brodie reacted favorably to these papers, and his indebtedness to Lindblom is suggested by the following passage in his appraisal: "My own choice for RAND policy in the future, incidentally, would be what you designate as choice three on page 6 of your fifth paper . . . : 'The third avenue is through more explicit and professional attention to subjective elements in analysis, together with some softening of hostility toward Air Force partisanship'" (Brodie to Lindblom, 27 January 1960, UCLA Collection, Box 1 [L Folder]).

166. Cited in memorandum, David Novick to F. R. Collbohm, 10 March 1964 (copy sent to Brodie), UCLA Collection, Box 2 (Folder 15).

167. Among the publicly known exceptions are Nathan Leites's work on the Soviet leadership, Herbert Goldhamer's work on North Korean and Chinese prisoners of war during the Korean War, and Alexander George's writing on the problem of American provocation of the Soviet Union.

168. Kissinger, *The Necessity for Choice* (New York: Harper & Brothers, 1961), 347.

169. Sick, *All Fall Down: America's Tragic Encounter with Iran* (New York: Penguin Books, 1986), 45. This point was likely to have been neglected at RAND insofar as, according to Brodie, "diplomacy is not RAND's essential business" ("Provocation Works on People," 9).

170. See especially *War and Politics*, 392ff. When Brodie discussed vital interests, as in chap. 8 of *War and Politics*, he had relatively little to say about the contemporary Soviet-American conflict over such interests.

171. Brodie, Review of Beaufre, 209–210.

172. "Why Were We So (Strategically) Wrong?" *Foreign Policy*, no. 5 (Winter 1971/72): 161.

173. Ibid., 156. In an undated letter to Colin Gray, in which Brodie gave a lengthy portrait of his former RAND colleague Albert Wohlstetter, he wrote that "word got around in Washington and elsewhere that Wohlstetter really was RAND, and vice-versa—that all the important and original work done there was inspired and led by him" (UCLA Collection, Box 8 [G Folder]). Such views may have played some part in limiting Brodie's interaction with RAND economists, in spite of RAND's official encouragement of interdisciplinary problem solving. See note 22 above. One person closely acquainted with Brodie at RAND stated in an interview that all of Brodie's RAND work was affected by personality concerns. I was unable to confirm or disconfirm this view but conclude that it would be worth investigating.

174. Ibid., 156 and 156f.

175. Brodie to Stephen Jones, 25 February 1955, UCLA Collection, Box 1 (J Folder); italics in original. Following publication of *Strategy in the Missile Age*, Brodie wrote to Quincy Wright on 18 November 1959: "I assure you that I wrote this book with a full consciousness at all times of the unimaginable and essentially futile horror that any general war would mean in the thermonuclear age. I rather imagine that that feeling is reflected in the book. I suppose I came as close to expressing a pacifist conviction as any writer on strategy decently can" (UCLA Collection, Box 2 [W Folder]).

176. Reference has already been made (chapter 7) to Brodie's view about the need to seek "negotiated peace based on compromise" in any war between nuclear-weapon-equipped adversaries, even though this meant rejecting Clausewitz's definition of the object of war. Some years later, by contrast, Brodie wrote that "far from being the advocate of total or absolute war, as is often charged, Clausewitz might in fact be considered the originator of the modern doctrine of limited war" ("Strategy," 284). For another analysis of war limitation that adopts a Clausewitzian outlook, see Osgood, *Limited War*.

177. Recall the statement by Herbert Goldhamer in note 18 above.

178. Brodie, "Intractability of States," 140.

Chapter 10. Conclusions

1. The distinction between "stable balancer" and "war fighting" schools of thought is made by Leon V. Sigal in "Rethinking the Unthinkable," *Foreign Policy*, no. 34 (Spring 1979): 35–51. For a reference to Brodie's belief in the stability of the strategic balance, see Jervis, *Illogic of Nuclear Strategy*, 158 and 173. Jervis cites Brodie, "On the Objectives of Arms Control," *International Security* 1 (Summer 1976): 17–36.

2. On the coercive use of nuclear force, the major work remains Schelling, *Arms and Influence*. On nuclear weapons targeting, a subject of recent rising interest, see Colin S. Gray, "Targeting Problems for Central War," *Naval War College Review* 33 (January/February 1980): 3–21; David E. Rosenberg, "The Origins of Overkill: Nuclear Weapons and American Strategy, 1945–1960," *International Security* 7 (Spring 1983): 17ff; Desmond Ball, "U.S. Strategic Forces: How Would They Be Used?" *International Security* 7 (Winter 1982/83): 31–60; Ball, *Targeting for Strategic Deterrence*, Adelphi Paper no. 185 (London: International Institute for Strategic Studies, 1983); Ball and Jeffrey Richelsen, eds., *Strategic Nuclear Targeting* (Ithaca, N.Y.: Cornell University Press, 1986); and Scott D. Sagan, *Moving Targets: Nuclear Strategy and National Security* (Princeton, N.J.: Princeton University Press, 1989).

3. "In the past," Speier writes in the same letter, "I have tried whenever an occasion arose to convey my impression to you that you delight in pejorative statements about men of power. In your condemnations I hear faint echoes of the Jewish Prophets or the Puritan preachers: like them you speak with the righteousness of your cause and you are harsh if others don't serve it" (Speier to Brodie, 30 November 1954, UCLA Collection, Box 4 [Folder 19]).

4. *War and Politics*, 482.

5. Ibid., 492. In a 1959 letter to Henry Jackson, referring to his tour of duty with Vandenberg, Brodie wrote of being "appalled above all by the busyness of the senior officers with whom I came in contact, by the apparent 'cult of activism' that seemed to prevail on all sides and that effectively crowded out any chance or propensity to reflect deeply on some very baffling strategic problems that were staring at us almost unnoticed. However, even if my observation was entirely correct, I know how futile it would have been to order these officers to be less busy, that is, to accord themselves more time for reflection. The reason is that we are talking not simply about making more time available but about altering a whole cultural pattern, one in which the officers

concerned feel very much at home being busy than reflecting" (Brodie to Jackson, 13 August 1959, UCLA Collection, Box 4 [Folder 5]).

6. Brodie to Speier, 23 November 1954, UCLA Collection, Box 4 (Folder 19).

7. *War and Politics*, 479.

8. Ibid., 438f.

9. See chapter 3 of this book.

10. Cited in Roman Kolkowicz, "The Strange Career of the Defense Intellectuals," *Orbis* 31 (Summer 1987): 191. In a letter to Pierre M. Gallois, Brodie wrote: "You must excuse and forgive me for sounding like a professor, which of course I am" (Brodie to Gallois, 10 September 1965, UCLA Collection, Box 1 [G Folder]). Morris Janowitz, referring to one strategic idea that he specifically associated with Brodie, is more blunt about its limitations in this respect. "The dominant strategic 'advice' offered from 1945 to 1960 was," Janowitz wrote in reference to the United States, "on the whole, irrelevant to the central issues of the stabilization of nuclear weapons. During this period, the central strategic conception was the distinction between tactical and strategic nuclear weapons. No doubt this notion had a variety of origins, including internal military staff work, but the writings of civilian scholars contributed to its currency. Even the most superficial examination of the literature reveals no conceptual or operational basis for the distinction, which was without rational purpose and lacked precision. At the time it was offered, it encountered determined and persistent critiques. It was one of those intellectual inventions which have little effective consequence, and it perished because of its political defects. It was essentially a notion generated by the intellectuals' fascination with violence, and designed to avoid the analysis of the limitations of military intervention in a nuclear context" ("Toward a Redefinition of Military Strategy in International Relations," *World Politics* 26 [July 1974]: 488).

Although Soviet officials, many of their counterparts in NATO, and many members of the American air staff responsible for selecting targets viewed American nuclear weapons allocated to the European theater as strategic, it was not likely that American leaders would have been persuaded to send thousands of them to Europe without believing that major war in Europe could be distinguished from all-out nuclear warfare. And it is hard to understand how the overall military balance in Europe, which Janowitz admits became relatively stabilized until the mid-1960s (ibid., 493), could have been rendered stable without the supply of American nuclear weapons to Western Europe. Janowitz, for whom the "central issue" was not the existence of nuclear weapons but the decline of constraints against American ground combat on the Asian mainland, suggested no guidelines of his own for nuclear strategy.

11. Prof. Alexander George (in an unpublished paper and later in a private communication to me) characterized Brodie's correction of the overly refined and even extreme advocacy positions of others (such as on the issue of a conventional defense for NATO) as "crude navigation." Insofar as "crude navigation" was associated with systematic questioning and the search for less extreme alternatives, it was basic to Brodie's approach to strategic analysis, as is clear in a 1964 Brodie response to Paul Kecskemeti: "What you seem to be saying is that if we fight conventionally we can achieve 'an asymmetrical, superior bargaining position,' but not if we use nuclear weapons. This statement, if true, has the most profound policy implications. How do we know it is true? I happen to feel it is not true. But, I would not try to present my contrary view without a detailed consideration of why I consider your view to be questionable. This is what I presume we mean by "analysis" (memorandum, Brodie to Kecskemeti, 27 April 1964, UCLA Collection, Box 2 [Folder 15]). However, though Brodie employed "crude navigation" as a response to newer and less-tested ideas, he did not use it in appraising older ones. See below.

12. Memorandum, Brodie to J. M. Goldsen, 13 February 1964, UCLA Collection, Box 2 (Folder 15). This view should be compared with Brodie's subsequent argument with Peter Paret on psychoanalytic interpretations of Clausewitz (see chapter 9 of this volume).

13. See chapter 5 of this volume.

14. In "Must We Shoot from the Hip?" (see chap. 1, n. 20), Brodie wrote that in addition to being adopted by the air staff, the "bonus" concept was subscribed to by most of the RAND staff.

15. The strike-spacing project, which received wide discussion in the Social Science Division at RAND, led to Brodie's informal paper "Must We Shoot from the Hip?" The force employment guidance critique, a collaboration with Andrew Marshall, was reflected in separate informal papers by Brodie and Marshall and in a collective document signed by both men and submitted to the air force. Brodie's separate contribution to this project was "Commentary on the Force Employment Study" (9 January 1953, RAND Informal Working Paper). The Tactical Air Power Committee project, chaired by Brodie (1955–1956), was evidenced in interview summaries and a committee report. I have used material from each of these projects in this book. Brodie participated in two other RAND collaborative projects during this period: the committee on the effects of the H-bomb, consisting mainly of Brodie, Ernest Plesset, and Charles J. Hitch (see chapter 5, note 1, of this volume); and the committee on strategic objectives, for which an internal working paper, "The Next Ten Years" (30 December 1954), was prepared by a subcommittee consisting of Brodie, Hitch, and Marshall.

16. This point is made in chapter 2 of this book in connection with Brodie's earliest postwar writing. "I admit," Brodie wrote much later in 1978, "that I could never fully understand the pro-ABM position" ("The Development of Nuclear Strategy," *International Security* 2 [Spring 1978]: 70).

17. See chapter 5 of this volume.

18. Brodie, *Strategy in the Missile Age*, 220–221.

19. Brodie to Quincy Wright, 18 November 1959, UCLA Collection, Box 2 (W Folder). Italics in original.

20. Brodie, *Escalation and the Nuclear Option*, 21.

21. See, for example, Fred C. Iklé, "Nuclear Strategy: Can There Be a Happy Ending?" *Foreign Affairs* 63 (Spring 1985): 822–823. Much earlier, Brodie wrote in a RAND informal working paper that "the awful vulnerability of our allies to atomic weapons is something which we tend to lose sight of. . . . [T]he fact is that in a crisis our allies would be utterly unable to face up to the threat of atomic weapons being used strategically against them" ("Political Consequences of the H-Bomb" [see chap. 1, n. 70], 29).

22. *War and Politics*, 452.

23. See chapter 3, note 4, of this book.

24. "Must We Shoot from the Hip?" 244.

25. Ibid., 255. See also below.

26. See chapter 5 of this book.

27. *Strategy in the Missile Age*, 138.

28. Ibid., 215. And see also ibid., 408, in which Brodie wrote: "Almost always in the past there was time even after hostilities began for the significance of the technological changes to be learned and appreciated. Such time will not again be available in any unrestricted war of the future."

29. "War in the Atomic Age," in Brodie, *The Absolute Weapon*, 29. The strategic thinker who presaged this idea by anticipating futile, unrestricted warfare was Ivan S. Bloch, *The Future of War* (New York: Doubleday & McClure, 1899). For Brodie's few known references to Bloch, see "Implications of Scientific Advances to Military Strategy" (see chap. 4, n. 38), 8; and *War and Politics*, 416–419.

30. "Changing Capabilities and War Objectives" (see chap. 1, n. 58), 72; "Must We Shoot from the Hip?" passim.

31. *Strategy in the Missile Age*, 352.

32. "The Issue of Strategic Superiority: A Comment," RAND Informal Working Paper, 19 July 1963. "One of the reasons I think that the simple kind of superiority still matters," Brodie wrote in this paper, "is that no amount of sophisticated argument can shake the basic feeling that in the clutch it's better to be the man with more rather than the man with less, especially when more means lots more" (1).

33. See chapter 8 of this volume.

34. A fine study that uses a focused case study method to test theory with reality is George and Smoke, *Deterrence in American Foreign Policy*. See also Alexander L. George, Philip J. Farley, and Alexander Dallin, eds., *U.S.-Soviet Security Cooperation: Achievements, Failures, Lessons* (New York: Oxford University Press, 1988).

35. See chapter 8 of this volume.

36. *Strategy in the Missile Age*, 331 and 330.

37. "Political Consequences of the H-Bomb," 25.

38. *Strategy in the Missile Age*, 313.

39. Ibid., 313–314.

40. "New Techniques of War and National Policies," in Ogburn, ed., *Technology and International Relations*, 165.

41. Ibid., 158.

42. See chapter 5 of this book.

43. See chapter 2 of this book. Brodie wrote in July 1947 that "it is now far more necessary than ever before that we maximize the force available at the start of hostilities" ("Navy Department Thinking on the Atomic Bomb," *Bulletin of the Atomic Scientists* 3 (July 1947): 199.

44. See chapter 2 of this book.

45. See chapter 2 of this book.

46. See chapter 5 of this book.

47. "New Techniques of War and National Policies," 166.

48. Brodie, "Implications for Military Policy," in *The Absolute Weapon*, 76.

49. *Strategy in the Missile Age*, 269.

50. Ibid., 277.

51. Ibid., 408–409. For a challenge to this statement of priorities, see Herman Kahn, *Thinking about the Unthinkable in the 1980s*.

52. *Strategy in the Missile Age*, 271.

53. Ibid., 292 (italics in original). See also Rowen, "Future of General War," in Berkowitz and Bock, eds., *American National Security*, 71; and Albert Wohlstetter, "Bishops, Statesmen, and Other Strategists on the Bombing of Innocents," *Commentary* 75 (June 1983): passim. See also below.

54. *Strategy in the Missile Age*, 293.

55. "Strategic Objectives and the Determination of Force Composition" (see chap. 1, n. 89), 87. In *Strategy in the Missile Age*, published at about the same time, Brodie wrote that "it is . . . impossible for us to predict with absolute assurance our own behavior in extremely tense and provocative circumstances" (274). Brodie was inclined at this time, as we have seen, to dramatize the importance of emotion-based behavior in international politics. A different endorsement of threatening massive retaliation was provided in 1960 by Robert W. Tucker, who maintained that "if men presently show less restraint in threatening their adversaries, it is largely because they are less secure than in an earlier age" (Cited in Wohlstetter, "Bishops, Statesmen, and Other Strategists," 23).

56. "Strategic Objectives and the Determination of Force Composition," 91.

57. *Strategy in the Missile Age*, 293–294.

58. "Strategic Objectives and the Determination of Force Composition," 91.

59. Ibid., 86.

60. "Political Impact of U.S. Force Postures" (see chap. 1, n. 66), 243.

61. Here Brodie sidestepped a major difference between Albert Wohlstetter and Thomas Schelling over the value of cities as hostages for nuclear attack. Unlike Wohlstetter, Brodie continued to insist that cities were useful as targets for coercion to restrain a nuclear-armed adversary, and unlike Schelling, he presumed that Soviet and American leaders would successfully control their behavior in a crisis, lessening the danger of coercive efforts.

62. See chapter 8 of this book. One of the reasons that Brodie no longer highlighted threats

of a general war was that he no longer believed that emotion-based behavior was important in statecraft. By contrast, Schelling adhered to Brodie's earlier views. He wrote in 1966 that "while it is hard for a government, particularly a responsible government, to appear irrational whenever such an appearance is expedient, it is equally hard for a government, even a responsible one, to *guarantee* its own moderation in every circumstance" (*Arms and Influence*, 41; italics in original). Schelling argued that "deterrent threats . . . do not need to depend on a willingness to commit anything like suicide in the face of a challenge" (ibid., 97).

63. *War and Politics*, 425.

64. "Strategic Objectives and the Determination of Force Composition," 86.

65. Schell, *The Fate of the Earth* (New York: Alfred A. Knopf, 1982), 202.

66. Ibid., 203.

67. Gray, "Nuclear Strategy: A Case for a Theory of Victory," *International Security* 4 (Summer 1979): 69–70. Not fully consistent is Gray's remark that "U.S. operational planning never reflected any close approximation to the assured destruction concept" (ibid., 59).

68. Ibid., 61.

69. Ibid., 82.

70. Ibid., 75f.

71. "Strategy as a Science," *World Politics* 1 (July 1949): 474–475. More recently, Edward N. Luttwak wrote of strategy as serving "to connect the diverse issues into a systematic pattern of things; then to craft plans—often long range—for dealing with the whole" (*On the Meaning of Victory: Essays on Strategy* [New York: Simon & Schuster, 1986], 243).

72. "What we get from Clausewitz," he wrote, "is a deepening of sensibility or insight rather than a body of rules, because insofar as he does offer us rules he is at once avid to show us all the qualifications and historical exceptions to them" (*War and Politics*, 452).

73. In the margin of "Notes on the Term 'Strategy,'" prepared for a Naval War College lecture, 22 August 1949, Edward Mead Earle penned the following: "Foreign policy concerned with broad principles, objectives, interests. Military strategy concerns itself with 'What will we do if . . .'" (Edward Mead Earle Papers, Box 25 [Folder: Strategy]).

74. This idea is associated by Earle with "The Navy Concept" (ibid.). See also Berend D. Bruins, "Should Naval Officers Be Strategists?" *United States Naval Institute Proceedings* 108 (January 1982): 55.

75. "It is not enough to prescribe an approach to strategic studies," Lawrence Freedman wrote, "without discussing whether it can only prosper in particular political and institutional conditions" ("The Strategist's Vocation," *Survival* 25 [July/August 1983]: 172).

76. Scott Sagan wrote that "in a democracy, the making of nuclear operational plans [is] often easier done than said: excessive rhetoric about war-fighting can frighten the public as much as a potential adversary" (*Survival* 25 [July/August 1983], 192).

77. See chapter 2, note 82, of this volume.

78. A survey of footnotes in chapters 8 ("The Anatomy of Deterrence") and 9 ("Limited War") of *Strategy in the Missile Age* reveals twenty-two names and/or publications outside of Rand and sixteen names and/or publications associated with Rand; counted as additional were repeated references to the same individual or publication. The former category includes a list of six items applying depth psychology to questions of war and peace. In an earlier draft of these chapters, entitled "Alternative Strategic Policies II" (27 March 1958, Rand Informal Working Paper), the totals are fourteen and eleven, respectively, and the latter number includes three attributions to Andrew Marshall and one to a Rand informal working paper written by Marshall and Harvey DeWeerd; these two were not mentioned in the published version.

79. The well-known ceramics designer Eva Zeisel observed: "I came to the conclusion that what was called limits—yes, industrial design is very limiting—was just the opposite; it was very unlimiting. I set my students this project. I said, 'Please sit down and do the most beautiful thing you can imagine. You must have been thinking a lot about it.' And they were sitting around totally

frustrated, without the slightest idea of how to fulfill their dream. Then I gave them limitations —
'Make something this high, with this function' — and suddenly they were all sitting there working
like beavers" (Suzannah Lessard, "The Present Moment [Profile of Eva Zeisel]," *New Yorker* 63
[13 April 1987]: 57).

80. "For enormous periods of time, even in Western Europe, crucible of the conquering impulse," John Keegan wrote, "warfare was not triumphalist but a cautious, local, piecemeal, pro-
tracted and indecisive business" (*The Mask of Command* [New York: Viking, 1987], 7).

81. The following recent evaluation of Mao Tse-tung as a strategic thinker also applies to Brodie:
"Mao was obsessed by the problem of knowledge, and his polemical attacks on heretical views,
while directed against personal and political targets, deal with failures of systematic learning and
thinking. . . .

"Mao wrote as if only he, with his enormous strength and vision, had the capacity to recognize
the problem of superficial knowledge and impulsive decision and to cope with it. . . . [H]e reiterates that every situation must be totally understood and rigorously analyzed before action is
taken. . . . [T]hese passages reveal as clearly as is possible in cold translated print, the passion of
the revolutionary evangelist trying to confront the original sin of lazy, subjective thinking. The
clichés of his now-famous strategic doctrine were, for him, no more than simple guidelines that
could set the right direction for revolutionary strategy and warn against the worst kinds of strategic blunders. But only realistic application, which required the utmost intellectual effort, could
turn these strategic formulae into actual victory" (John Shy and Thomas W. Collier, "Revolutionary War," in Paret, *Makers of Modern Strategy*, 842–843).

82. On the balance between closure and openness to incoming information, see Robert Jervis,
"Hypotheses on Misperception," *World Politics* 20 (April 1968): 454–479.

83. See chapter 5 of this book.

84. Referring in 1955 to his manuscript that was to be published in 1959 as *Strategy in the
Missile Age*, Brodie wrote of never before having had so many "false and wasteful starts" (Brodie
to Herbert S. Bailey, Jr., 8 February 1955, UCLA Collection, Box 1 [B Folder]).

85. For an essay about the limitations of grand strategy that does not focus primarily upon
nuclear weaponry, see Seyom Brown, "An End to Grand Strategy," *Foreign Policy*, no. 32 (Fall
1978): 22–46.

86. Jervis, "MAD Is the Best Possible Deterrence," *Bulletin of the Atomic Scientists* 41 (March
1985): 43.

87. See, for example, "Development of Nuclear Strategy," 65–66.

88. See chapter 5 of this volume.

89. See Jervis's discussion of what he terms the "stability-instability" paradox in chapter 2 of
The Illogic of American Nuclear Strategy. Jervis writes: "Note the odd congeries of beliefs: those
like Brodie who see the strategic balance as robust . . . also tended to downplay the significance
of the stability-instability paradox, whereas those who see the balance as more delicate focus more
on the dangers of limited Soviet adventures" (ibid., 173f). In this book, I have noted that during
the 1950s, Brodie played down the delicacy of the strategic balance yet also emphasized the dangers
of limited Soviet war-making.

Selected Bibliography

Abbreviations used:

AFHRC   Air Force Historical Research Center
USSBS   United States Stretegic Bombing Survey
ETO   European Theater of Operations
CWE   Conventional War in Europe

Unpublished Sources

Personal Papers

Depository Collections
Brodie, Bernard. Papers. Special Collections Division, University Research Library, University of California, Los Angeles.
Brodie, Fawn. Papers. University of Utah Libraries, Salt Lake City.
Earle, Edward Mead. Papers. Seeley G. Mudd Manuscript Library, Princeton University, Princeton, New Jersey.
LeMay, Curtis E. Papers. Manuscript Division, Library of Congress, Washington, D.C.
Oppenheimer, J. Robert. Papers. Manuscript Division, Library of Congress, Washington, D.C.
Vandenberg, Hoyt S. Papers. Manuscript Division, Library of Congress, Washington, D.C.
Private Collections
Brodie, Fawn. Unpublished writings by Bernard Brodie, including a projected lecture course (was to be given in Japan) on "Modern Military Strategic Doctrine," [1978].
Golden, William T. Correspondence between Golden and Bernard Brodie and between Golden and Sidney Souers; bound volume of unpublished collection of memoranda of interviews, "Government Military-Scientific Research: Review for the President of the United States, 1950–1951," [1950–1951].
Hoag, Malcolm. Excerpts from selected unpublished papers by Hoag.
Jervis, Robert. Published and unpublished papers by Bernard Brodie (supplied to the author by Roman Kolkowicz).
King, James E. Correspondence between King and Bernard Brodie; draft of unpublished manuscript, "On Clausewitz: Master Theorist of War."
Lambeth, Benjamin. Parts 3 and 4 of an unpublished manuscript by James E. King, "The New Strategy."
Lindblom, Charles E. Unpublished papers by Lindblom.

Loftus, Joseph E. Published and unpublished papers by Loftus and others relating to strategic bombing in World War II; commentary on postwar target-selection questions and on contributions by Bernard Brodie.

Public Records in Depository Collections

National Archives. Branch Depository, Suitland, Maryland. Records of the Secretary of the Air Force. Record Group 340. Correspondence Files of Secretary of the Air Force Thomas K. Finletter, 1951. "Defensive and Offensive Plans for Fighting War, 1951," File IJ(2) (partially declassified under Mandatory Freedom of Information Act Review).
———. Washington, D.C. Records of the Chief of Staff, U.S. Air Force. Record Group 341. Operational Files of the Air Force Directorate of Intelligence (entry 214). Special File on the Strategic Air Offensive, Plans and Operations Division, 1942–1954. Files and Logs of the Air Staff Correspondence Control Branch (entry 3 and entry 7).
———. Records of the Joint Chiefs of Staff. Record Group 218. Central Decimal File, 1948–1950. Records of the Joint Strategic Plans Committee (CCS 334). Evaluation of Plans for Strategic Air Offensive (CCS 373). Target Systems for the Joint Outline Emergency War Plan (CCS 373.11).
———. Records of the Office of Strategic Services (OSS). Record Group 226. War Diary, vol. 5, OSS Research and Analysis Branch, London (entry 91).
———. Records of the United States Strategic Bombing Survey (USSBS). Record Group 243. "Anti-Nazi Opposition" (File 64.b.t.[8]). "Morale Division (ETO)" (File 300.6-G). "USSBS Division Histories" (File 314.7). "Conferences, Military, Naval, and Other" (File 337).

Other Public Records

U.S. Air Force Headquarters. Directorate of Intelligence. Washington, D.C. Collection of nine documents on intelligence planning and on air force solicitation of RAND Corporation studies, 1953–1956 (released by Air Force Directorate of Estimates [now part of Air Force Intelligence Agency] and by Air Force Directorate of Intelligence Plans and Systems [now Directorate of Policy Plans and Programs] under Freedom of Information Request, 1983).
———. Intelligence Service. Fort Belvoir, Virginia. Air Staff Summary Sheet and Memorandum on "Project RAND," 12 February 1954; and letter, George J. Keegan, Jr. (major, USAF), to Edward M. Collins (lt. col., USAF), 16 April 1956, regarding release of RAND studies to the Air Ministry of the United Kingdom (declassified and released under Freedom of Information Request, 1983).

RAND Corporation Papers, Memoranda, and Reports

Informal Working Papers
Brodie, Bernard. "Afterthoughts on CWE from the Meeting (with Herr Erler) of April 16." 22 April 1963.
———. "Alternative Strategic Policies II." 27 March 1958.
———. "Commentary on the Force Employment Study." 9 January 1953.
———. "The Issue of Strategic Superiority: A Comment." 19 July 1963.
———. "Must We Shoot from the Hip?" 4 September 1951.
———. "Provocation Works on People." 12 June 1959.
———. "The Rejection of the Airborne Alert: Another Facet of the 'Provocation' Problem." 8 February 1960.
———. "Some Considerations Governing Escalation." 4 September 1964.
———. Unpublished, unclassified notes, 1955–1956.
Brodie, Bernard, Charles J. Hitch, and Andrew W. Marshall. "The Next Ten Years." 30 December 1954.

RAND Corporation. "Fourteen Informal Writings from the Unpublished Work of Bernard Brodie, 1952–1965." Unbound collection, 1980.

Formal Papers

Averch, H., and M. M. Lavin. "Dilemmas in the Politico-Military Conduct of Escalating Crises." RAND Paper P-3205, August 1965.

Brodie, Bernard. "The American Scientific Strategists." RAND Paper P-2979, October 1964.

————. "Attitudes towards the Use of Force." RAND Paper P-360, December 1952; revised December 1953.

————. "The Intractability of States: A Distinctive Problem." RAND Paper P-2970, September 1964.

Brodie, Bernard, and Nathan Leites. "A Proposal on the Projection of American Attitudes towards French Nuclear Policies." RAND Research Memorandum RM-3343-ISA, October 1962.

Cohen, Samuel T. "On the Stringency of Dosage Criteria for Battlefield Nuclear Operations." RAND Paper P-5332, January 1975.

Goldhamer, Herbert. "Communist Reaction in Korea to American Possession of the A-Bomb and Its Significance for U.S. Political and Psychological Warfare." RAND Research Memorandum RM-903, August 1952.

————. "Human Factors in Systems Analysis." RAND Research Memorandum RM-388, April 1950.

Hirshleifer, Jack. "Disaster and Recovery: A Historical Survey." RAND Research Memorandum RM-3079-PR, April 1963.

Implications of Large-Yield Nuclear Weapons. RAND Report R-237, July 1952 (released in sanitized form under Freedom of Information Request, 1983).

Kaysen, Carl. *Notes on Strategic Air Intelligence in World War II (ETO).* RAND Report R-165, October 1949.

Reinhardt, G. C. "Nuclear Weapons and Limited Warfare: A Sketchbook History." RAND Paper P-3011, November 1964.

Sallagar, F. M. *The Road to Total War: Escalation in World War II.* RAND Report R-465-PR, April 1969.

Speier, Hans. *German Rearmament and Atomic War.* RAND Report R-298, February 1957.

"The Warning of Target Populations in Air War: An Appendix of Working Papers." RAND Research Memorandum RM-275, November 1949.

Lecture Transcripts

Brodie, Bernard. "A-Bombs and Air Strategy." Air War College lecture, 24 March 1949. AFHRC, Maxwell Air Force Base, Montgomery, Alabama. Catalog no. K239.716249-13(R).

————. "Air Power in an Overall Strategy." Air War College lecture, 23 May 1951. AFHRC, Maxwell Air Force Base, Montgomery, Alabama. Catalog no. K239.716251-26.

————. "The Atomic Bomb as a Weapon." National War College lecture, 6 September 1946. Air University Library, Maxwell Air Force Base, Montgomery, Alabama. Catalog no. M-33507-C.

————. "Changing Capabilities and War Objectives." Air War College lecture, 17 April 1952. AFHRC, Maxwell Air Force Base, Montgomery, Alabama. Catalog no. K239.716252-105.

————. "The Impact of New Weapons on War." National War College lecture, 4 September 1946. Air University Library, Maxwell Air Force Base, Montgomery, Alabama. Catalog no. M-33506-C.

————. "The Problem of Integrating the Factors of National Strategy." Air War College lecture, 17 March 1950. AFHRC, Maxwell Air Force Base, Montgomery, Alabama. Catalog no. K239.716250-12(R).

————. "Sea Power in the Atomic Age." Naval War College lecture, 19 January 1949. Naval War College Library, Newport, Rhode Island. Catalog no. 6890-7770.

Dyer, Dan B. "Generation of Target Systems." Air War College lecture, 7 April 1950. AFHRC Catalog no. K239.716250-22(S). Microfilm copy consulted at the Office of Air Force History, Bolling Air Force Base, Washington, D.C.

————. "Horizontal Approach to Target Analysis." Air War College lecture, 12 December 1951. AFHRC, Maxwell Air Force Base, Montgomery, Alabama. Catalog no. K239.716251-55.

Lowe, James T. "The Intelligence Basis of Selection of Strategic Target Systems." Air War College lecture, 13 November 1947. AFHRC, Maxwell Air Force Base, Montgomery, Alabama. Catalog no. K239.716247-50.

————. "Last 5 Minutes of Discussion Period." Air War College transcript, 1 March 1951. AFHRC, Maxwell Air Force Base, Montgomery, Alabama. Catalog no. K239.716251-184.

————. "Theory of Strategic Vulnerability." Air War College lecture, 6 April 1950. AFHRC Catalog no. K239.716250-43. Microfilm copy consulted at the Office of Air Force History, Bolling Air Force Base, Washington, D.C.

Other Unpublished Documents

Cohen, Victor. "Air Intelligence," declassified U.S. Air Force Historical Study no. 106–87, n.d. Air Force Historical Research Center. Maxwell Air Force Base, Alabama. Microfilm copy, AFHRC microfilm reel K1021.

Brennan, Donald G. "Review of Clausewitz's *On War*." Hudson Institute Paper HI-2713-P, October 1977. Published in part (see under "Articles and Book Chapters").

"History of the U.S. Strategic Bombing Survey (European Theater): Appendix of Supporting Documents, 1944–1945." Center of Military History. U.S. Army. Washington, D.C. File 1-1.3/UN. Photocopy.

Isoardi, Steven L. "Bernard Brodie—Bibliography: Articles, Monographs, Speeches, Drafts, etc.," 19 March 1979. Typescript.

Liberatore, M. A. Letter to author, 8 December 1988. (Information about Bernard Brodie's naval duty assignments, 1943–1945, from his naval records at the National Personnel Records Center, St. Louis, Missouri.)

U.S. Naval Administration in World War II: Chief of Naval Operations, Office of Naval Intelligence. Vol. 3 (Part 14: Special Warfare ["W" Branch]), 1335–1390, n.d. Navy Department Library. Washington Navy Yard. Washington, D.C. Microfilm copy.

Published Works

Government Reports

King, Admiral Ernest J., Jr., *U.S. Navy at War, 1941–1945: Official Reports to the Secretary of the Navy, by Fleet Admiral Ernest J. King, U.S. Navy.* Washington, D.C.: U.S. Navy Department, 1946.

USSBS Reports

Aircraft Division Industry Report. USSBS Report no. 4 (European War), 1947. Facsimile reprint. *The United States Strategic Bombing Survey*, edited by David MacIsaac, vol. 2. New York: Garland, 1976.

Defeat of the German Air Force. USSBS Report no. 59 (European War), 1947. MacIsaac edition facsimile reprint, vol. 3. See *Aircraft Division Industry Report.*

Effects of the Atomic Bomb on Nagasaki, Japan. 3 vols. USSBS Report no. 93 (Pacific War). Washington, D.C.: Government Printing Office, 1947.

The Effects of Atomic Bombs on Hiroshima and Nagasaki. USSBS Report no. 3 (Pacific War), 1946. MacIsaac edition facsimile reprint, vol. 7. See *Aircraft Division Industry Report.*

The Effects of Strategic Bombing on German Morale. USSBS Report no. 64b (European War), 1947. MacIsaac edition facsimile reprint, vol. 4. See *Aircraft Division Industry Report.*

The Effects of Strategic Bombing on Japanese Morale. USSBS Report no. 14 (Pacific War). Washington, D.C.: Government Printing Office, 1947.

The Effects of Strategic Bombing on the German War Economy. USSBS Report no. 3 (European War), 1945. MacIsaac edition facsimile reprint, vol. 1. See *Aircraft Division Industry Report.*

The Electric Power Industry of Japan. USSBS Report no. 40 (Pacific War). Washington, D.C.: Government Printing Office, 1945.

The Electric Power Industry of Japan (Plant Reports). USSBS Report no. 41 (Pacific War). Washington, D.C.: Government Printing Office, 1947.

German Electric Utilities Industry Report. USSBS Report no. 205 (European War), 1947. MacIsaac edition facsimile reprint (without appendices), vol. 6. See *Aircraft Division Industry Report.*

Oil Division Final Report. USSBS Report no. 109 (European War), 1947. MacIsaac edition facsimile reprint, vol. 3. See *Aircraft Division Industry Report.*

Over-all Report. USSBS Report no. 2 (European War), 1945. MacIsaac edition facsimile reprint, vol. 1. See *Aircraft Division Industry Report.*

The Strategic Air Operations of Very Heavy Bombardment in the War against Japan (20th Air Force). USSBS Report no. 66 (Pacific War), 1946. MacIsaac edition facsimile reprint, vol. 9. See *Aircraft Division Industry Report.*

Summary Report. USSBS Report no. 1 (European War), 1945. MacIsaac edition facsimile reprint, vol. 1. See *Aircraft Division Industry Report.*

Books

Ball, Desmond, and Jeffrey Richelson, eds. *Strategic Nuclear Targeting.* Ithaca, N.Y.: Cornell University Press, 1986.

Batchelder, Robert C. *The Irreversible Decision: 1939–1950.* Boston: Houghton, Mifflin, 1962.

Beaufre, André. *An Introduction to Strategy.* Translated by R. H. Barry. New York: Praeger, 1965.

Bell, Coral. *Negotiation from Strength.* New York: Alfred A. Knopf, 1963.

Blackett, P. M. S. *Atomic Weapons and East-West Relations.* Cambridge: Cambridge University Press, 1956.

———. *Military and Political Consequences of Atomic Energy.* London: Turnstile Press, 1948.

———. *Studies of War: Nuclear and Conventional.* London: Oliver & Boyd, 1962.

Bloch, Ivan S. *The Future of War.* New York: Doubleday & McClure, 1899.

Borden, William L. *There Will Be No Time.* New York: Macmillan, 1946.

Bracken, Paul. *The Command and Control of Nuclear Forces.* New Haven, Conn.: Yale University Press, 1983.

Brodie, Bernard. *Escalation and the Nuclear Option.* Princeton, N.J.: Princeton University Press, 1966.

———. *A Layman's Guide to Naval Strategy.* Princeton, N.J.: Princeton University Press, 1942.

———. *Sea Power in the Machine Age.* Princeton, N.J.: Princeton University Press, 1941.

———. *Strategy in the Missile Age.* Princeton, N.J.: Princeton University Press, 1959.

———. *War and Politics.* New York: Macmillan, 1973.

Brodie, Bernard, ed. *The Absolute Weapon: Atomic Power and World Order.* New York: Harcourt, Brace, 1946.

Brodie, Bernard, and Fawn Brodie. *From Crossbow to H-Bomb.* Revised edition. Bloomington: Indiana University Press, 1973.

Canby, Steven. *The Alliance and Europe, Part IV: Military Doctrine and Technology.* Adelphi Paper no. 109. London: International Institute for Strategic Studies, 1974/75.

Clausewitz, Carl von. *On War.* Edited and translated by Michael Howard and Peter Paret. Princeton, N.J.: Princeton University Press, 1976.

Cohen, Samuel T. *The Neutron Bomb: Political, Technological, and Military Issues.* Cambridge, Mass.: Institute for Foreign Policy Analysis, n.d.

Craven, Wesley F., and James L. Cate, eds. *The Army Air Forces in World War II.* 5 vols. (1949–1953). Reprint. Chicago: University of Chicago Press, 1983.

Davis, Lynn E. *Limited Nuclear Options: Deterrence and the New American Doctrine.* Adelphi Paper no. 121. London: International Institute for Strategic Studies, 1976.

Dyson, Freeman. *Weapons and Hope.* New York: Harper & Row, 1984.

Earle, Edward M., ed. *The Makers of Modern Strategy.* Princeton, N.J.: Princeton University Press, 1943.

Etzold, Thomas H., and John Lewis Gaddis, eds. *Containment: Documents on American Policy and Strategy, 1945–1950.* New York: Columbia University Press, 1978.

Feis, Herbert. *Japan Subdued: The Atomic Bomb and the End of the War in the Pacific.* Princeton, N.J.: Princeton University Press, 1961.

Freedman, Lawrence. *The Evolution of Nuclear Strategy.* New York: St. Martin's, 1981.

George, Alexander L., and Juliette L. George. *Woodrow Wilson and Colonel House: A Personality Study.* New York: John Day, 1956.

George, Alexander L., and Richard Smoke. *Deterrence in American Foreign Policy: Theory and Practice.* New York: Columbia University Press, 1974.

Gray, Colin S. *Nuclear Strategy and National Style.* Lanham, Md.: Hamilton Press, 1986.

————. *Strategic Studies: A Critical Assessment.* Westport, Conn.: Greenwood Press, 1982.

Greenfield, Kent R. *American Strategy in World War II: A Reconsideration.* Baltimore: Johns Hopkins University Press, 1963.

Grodzins, Morton, and Eugene Rabinovitch, eds. *The Atomic Age.* New York: Basic Books, 1963.

Hansell, Haywood S., Jr. *Strategic Air War against Japan.* Washington, D.C.: Government Printing Office, 1980.

Harris, Arthur. *Bomber Offensive.* New York: Macmillan, 1947.

Heisenberg, Wolfgang. *The Alliance and Europe, Part I: Crisis Stability in Europe and Theatre Nuclear Weapons.* Adelphi Paper no. 96. London: International Institute for Strategic Studies, 1973.

Herken, Gregg. *Counsels of War.* New York: Alfred A. Knopf, 1985.

————. *The Winning Weapon: The Atomic Bomb in the Cold War, 1945–1950.* New York: Alfred A. Knopf, 1980.

Higham, Robin. *The Military Intellectuals in Britain: 1918–1939.* New Brunswick, N.J.: Rutgers University Press, 1966.

Howard, Michael. *The Causes of Wars.* Cambridge, Mass.: Harvard University Press, 1983.

————. *Studies in War and Peace.* New York: Viking, 1971.

Howard, Michael, ed. *Restraints on War: Studies in the Limitation of Armed Conflict.* Oxford: Oxford University Press, 1979.

————. *The Theory and Practice of War.* London: Cassell, 1965.

Hughes, H. Stuart. *Consciousness and Society.* New York: Alfred A. Knopf, 1958.

————. *History as Art and as Science.* New York: Harper & Row, 1964.

In the Matter of J. Robert Oppenheimer: Transcript of Hearing before Personnel Security Board and Texts of Principal Documents and Letters. 1955. Reprint. Cambridge, Mass.: MIT Press, 1971.

Irving, David. *The Destruction of Dresden.* London: William Kimber, 1963.

————. *The Mare's Nest.* London: William Kimber, 1964.

Janis, Irving. *Air War and Emotional Stress.* 1951. Reprint. Westport, Conn.: Greenwood Press, 1976.

Jervis, Robert. *The Illogic of American Nuclear Strategy.* Ithaca, N.Y.: Cornell University Press, 1984.

Kahn, Herman. *On Escalation: Metaphors and Scenarios.* New York: Praeger, 1965.

————. *On Thermonuclear War.* Princeton, N.J.: Princeton University Press, 1961.

————. *Thinking about the Unthinkable in the 1980's.* New York: Simon & Schuster, 1984.

Kaplan, Fred. *The Wizards of Armageddon.* New York: Simon & Schuster, 1983.

Kaufmann, William W. *The McNamara Strategy.* New York: Harper & Row, 1964.

Kaufmann, William W., ed. *Military Policy and National Security.* Princeton, N.J.: Princeton University Press, 1956.

Kecskemeti, Paul. *Strategic Surrender.* Stanford, Calif.: Stanford University Press, 1964.

Keegan, John. *The Mask of Command.* New York: Viking, 1987.

Kissinger, Henry A. *The Necessity for Choice.* New York: Harper & Brothers, 1961.

————. *Nuclear Weapons and Foreign Policy.* New York: Harper & Brothers, 1957.

Klein, Burton H. *Germany's Economic Preparations for War.* Cambridge, Mass.: Harvard University Press, 1959.

Knorr, Klaus. *Military Power and War Potential.* Princeton, N.J.: Princeton University Press, 1956.

Knorr, Klaus, ed. *NATO and American Security.* Princeton, N.J.: Princeton University Press, 1959.

Knorr, Klaus, and Thornton Read, eds. *Limited Strategic War.* Princeton, N.J.: Princeton University Press, 1962.

Kolkowicz, Roman, ed. *The Logic of Nuclear Terror.* Boston: Allen & Unwin, 1987.

Lapp, Ralph. *Atoms and People.* New York: Harper & Brothers, 1956.

Lasswell, Harold D. *Propaganda Technique in the World War.* New York: Alfred A. Knopf, 1927.

Lee, Asher. *Airpower.* London: Duckworth, 1955.

Leitenberg, Milton, ed. *Tactical Nuclear Weapons: European Perspectives.* New York: Crane, Russak, 1978.

Leites, Nathan. *Once More about What We Should Not Do Even in the Worst Case: The Assured Destruction Attack.* Los Angeles: California Arms Control and Foreign Policy Seminar, 1974.

―――. *The Operational Code of the Politburo.* New York: McGraw-Hill, 1951.

―――. *A Study of Bolshevism.* Glencoe, Ill.: Free Press, 1953.

Lerner, Daniel. *Psychological Warfare against Nazi Germany.* 1949. Reprint. Cambridge: MIT Press, 1971.

Licklider, Roy E. *The Private Nuclear Strategists.* Columbus: Ohio State University Press, 1971.

Liddell Hart, B. H. *The Liddell Hart Memoirs.* Vol. 1 (1895–1938). New York: G. P. Putnam's Sons, 1965.

―――. *Strategy: The Indirect Approach.* New York: Praeger, 1954.

Linebarger, Paul M. A. *Psychological Warfare.* Washington, D.C.: Combat Forces Press, 1954.

Luttwak, Edward N. *On the Meaning of Victory: Essays on Strategy.* New York: Simon & Schuster, 1986.

MacIsaac, David. *Strategic Bombing in World War Two: The Story of the United States Strategic Bombing Survey.* New York: Garland, 1976.

Mandelbaum, Michael. *The Nuclear Question: The United States and Nuclear Weapons, 1946–1976.* Cambridge: Cambridge University Press, 1979.

Middlebrook, Martin. *The Battle of Hamburg.* New York: Charles Scribner's Sons, 1981.

Morison, Elting E. *Men, Machines, and Modern Times.* Cambridge, Mass.: MIT Press, 1966.

Newman, James R., and Byron S. Miller. *The Control of Atomic Energy.* New York: McGraw-Hill, 1948.

O'Brien, T. H. *Civil Defense.* London: Longmans, Green, 1955.

Paret, Peter. *Clausewitz and the State.* New York: Oxford University Press, 1976.

Paret, Peter, ed. *Makers of Modern Strategy: From Machiavelli to the Nuclear Age.* Princeton, N.J.: Princeton University Press, 1986.

Parkinson, Roger. *Clausewitz.* London: Wayland Publishers, 1970.

Powers, Thomas. *Thinking about the Next War.* New York: Alfred A. Knopf, 1983.

Quade, Edward S., ed. *Analysis for Military Decisions.* Chicago: Rand McNally, 1966.

Ropp, Theodore. *War in the Modern World.* Revised edition. New York: Collier, 1962.

Rostow, Walt W. *Pre-Invasion Bombing Strategy.* Austin: University of Texas Press, 1981.

Schell, Jonathan. *The Fate of the Earth.* New York: Alfred A. Knopf, 1982.

Schelling, Thomas C. *Arms and Influence.* New Haven, Conn.: Yale University Press, 1966.

―――. *The Strategy of Conflict.* New York: Oxford University Press, 1960.

Slessor, John. *The Central Blue.* New York: Praeger, 1957.

Smith, Alice Kimball. *A Peril and a Hope.* Cambridge, Mass.: MIT Press, 1965.

Smith, Bruce L. R. *The RAND Corporation: Case Study of a Non-Profit Advisory Corporation.* Cambridge, Mass.: Harvard University Press, 1966.

Smoke, Richard. *War: Controlling Escalation.* Cambridge, Mass.: Harvard University Press, 1977.

Tedder, Arthur M. *Air Power in War.* London: Hodder & Stoughton, [1948?].

Titmuss, Richard M. *Problems of Social Policy.* London: Longmans, Green, 1950.

Trachtenberg, Marc, ed. *The Development of American Strategic Thought: Writings on Strategy: 1945–1951.* Vol. 2 of *The Development of American Strategic Thought: Writings on Strategy, 1945–1969.* Edited by Trachtenberg. 6 vols. New York: Garland, 1987.

―――. *The Development of American Strategic Thought: Writings on Strategy, 1952–1960* (1). Vol. 3 of *The Development of American Strategic Thought: Writings on Strategy, 1945–1969,* edited by Trachtenberg. 6 vols. New York: Garland, 1988.

————. *The Development of American Strategic Thought: Writings on Strategy, 1952–1960* (3). Vol. 5 of *The Development of American Strategic Thought: Writings on Strategy, 1945–1969*, edited by Trachtenberg. 6 vols. New York: Garland, 1987–1988.

————. *The Development of American Strategic Thought: Writings on Strategy, 1961–1969.* Vol. 6 of *The Development of American Strategic Thought: Writings on Strategy, 1945–1969*, edited by Trachtenberg. 6 vols. New York: Garland, 1988.

Treverton, Gary. *Nuclear Weapons in Europe*. Adelphi Paper no. 168. London: International Institute for Strategic Studies, 1981.

Turner, Stansfield. *Secrecy and Democracy*. Boston: Houghton, Mifflin, 1985.

Webster, Charles, and Noble Frankland. *The Strategic Air Offensive against Germany, 1939–1945*. 4 vols. London: Her Majesty's Stationery Office, 1961.

Weitz, Benjamin I., et al. *Electric Power Development in the USSR*. Moscow: INRA Publishing Society, 1936.

Woodward, Ernest L. *Some Political Consequences of the Atomic Bomb*. London: Oxford University Press, 1945.

York, Herbert. *The Advisors: Oppenheimer, Teller and the Superbomb*. San Francisco: W. H. Freeman, 1976.

Zuckerman, Solly. *From Apes to Warlords*. London: Hamish Hamilton, 1978.

————. *Nuclear Illusion and Reality*. New York: Viking, 1982.

————. *Scientists and War*. London: Hamish Hamilton, 1956.

Articles

Ball, Desmond. "U.S. Strategic Forces: How Would They Be Used?" *International Security* 7 (Winter 1982/83): 31–60.

Beaufre, André. Reply to Bernard Brodie's review of Beaufre's *Introduction to Strategy* and *Dissuasion et Stratégie*. *Survival* 7 (December 1965): 342–343.

Brennan, Donald. "Review of Clausewitz's *On War*." *Survival* 20 (January/February 1978): 38–39.

Brodie, Bernard. "The Atom Bomb as Policy Maker." *Foreign Affairs* 27 (October 1948): 17–33.

————. "A Critique of Army and Navy Thinking on the Atomic Bomb." *Bulletin of the Atomic Scientists* 3 (August 1947): 207–210.

————. "Defense Policy and the Possibility of Total War." *Daedalus* 91 (Fall 1962): 733–748.

————. "The Development of Nuclear Strategy." *International Security* 2 (Spring 1978): 65–83.

————. "The Heritage of Douhet." *Air University Quarterly Review* 6 (Summer 1953): 64–69, 121–127.

————. "The Impact of Technological Change on the International System: Reflections on Prediction." In *Change and the Future International System*, edited by David S. Sullivan and Martin J. Sattler, 1–15. New York: Columbia University Press, 1972.

————. "In Quest of the Unknown Clausewitz: A Review of *Clausewitz and the State*, by Peter Paret." *International Security* 1 (Winter 1977): 62–69.

————. "Learning to Fight a Limited War." *Los Angeles Times*, 3 December 1967, G-7.

————. "The McNamara Phenomenon." *World Politics* 17 (July 1965): 672–686.

————. "Morals and Strategy." *Worldview* (September 1964): 4–8.

————. "More about Limited War." *World Politics* 10 (October 1957): 112–122.

————. "Navy Department Thinking on the Atomic Bomb." *Bulletin of the Atomic Scientists* 3 (July 1947): 177–180, 198–199.

————. "New Techniques of War and National Policies." In *Technology and International Relations*, edited by William F. Ogburn, 144–173. Chicago: University of Chicago Press, 1949.

————. "Nuclear Weapons: Strategic or Tactical?" *Foreign Affairs* 32 (January 1954): 217–229.

————. "On Clausewitz: A Passion for War." *World Politics* 25 (Janaury 1973): 288–308.

————. "On the Objectives of Arms Control." *International Security* 1 (Summer 1976): 17–36.

————. "Paying in Full for Limited War." *Los Angeles Times*, 17 October 1968, II–7.

————. "A Psychoanalytic Interpretation of Woodrow Wilson." *World Politics* 9 (April 1957): 413–422.

————. Review of *Clausewitz and the State*, by Peter Paret. *Journal of Interdisciplinary History* 8 (Winter 1978): 572–574.

————. Review of *Introduction to Strategy* and *Dissuasion et Stratégie*, by André Beaufre. *Survival* 7 (August 1965): 208–210.

————. "Scientific Progress and Political Science." *Scientific Monthly* 85 (December 1957): 315–319.

————. "Some Notes on the Evolution of Air Doctrine." *World Politics* 7 (April 1955): 349–370.

————. "Strategic Bombing: What It Can Do." *Reporter* 3 (August 1950): 28–31.

————. "Strategic Implications of the North Atlantic Pact." *Yale Review* 39 (December 1949): 193–208.

————. "Strategy." In *The International Encyclopedia of the Social Sciences*, edited by David L. Sills, vol. 15, 281–287. New York: Macmillan & Free Press, 1968.

————. "Strategy as a Science." *World Politics* 1 (July 1949): 467–488.

————. "Strategy Hits a Dead End." *Harper's* 211 (October 1955): 33–37.

————. "Unlimited Weapons and Limited War." *Reporter* 11 (November 1954): 16–21.

————. "War Department Thinking on the Atomic Bomb." *Bulletin of the Atomic Scientists* 3 (June 1947): 150–155, 168.

————. "What Price Conventional Capabilities in Europe?" *Reporter* 28, (May 1963): 25–29, 32–33.

————. "Why Were We So (Strategically) Wrong?" *Foreign Policy*, no. 5 (Winter 1971/72): 151–161.

Brown, Seyom. "An End to Grand Strategy." *Foreign Policy*, no. 32 (Fall 1978): 22–46.

Bruins, Berend D. "Should Naval Officers Be Strategists?" *United States Naval Institute Proceedings* 108 (January 1982): 52–56.

Earle, Edward M. "The Influence of Air Power upon History." *Yale Review* 35 (June 1946): 20–31.

Fisher, Roger. "Preventing Nuclear War." *Bulletin of the Atomic Scientists* 37 (March 1981): 11–17.

Freedman, Lawrence. "The Strategist's Vocation." *Survival* 25 (July/August 1983): 170–174.

Futrell, Robert F. "Air Power in World War II." In Monro MacCloskey, *The United States Air Force,* 37–60. New York: Praeger, 1967.

————. "The Strategic Bombing Campaign." In *The United States Air Force in Korea: 1950–1953,* 183–198. Revised edition. Washington, D.C.: Government Printing Office, 1983.

Gray, Colin S. "Nuclear Strategy: A Case for a Theory of Victory." *International Security* 4 (Summer 1979): 54–87.

————. "Targeting Problems for Central War." *Naval War College Review* 33 (January/February 1980): 3–21.

————. "What RAND Hath Wrought." *Foreign Policy*, no. 4 (Fall 1971): 111–129.

Higham, Robin. "The Dangerously Neglected—The British Military Intellectuals, 1918–1939." *Military Affairs* 29 (Summer 1965): 73–85.

Howard, Michael. "War as an Instrument of Policy." In *Diplomatic Investigations: Essays in the Theory of International Politics*, edited by Herbert Butterfield and Martin Wight, 193–200. London: Allen & Unwin, 1966.

Iklé, Fred C. "Can Nuclear Deterrence Last Out the Century?" *Foreign Affairs* 51 (January 1973): 267–285.

————. "Nuclear Strategy: Can There Be a Happy Ending?" *Foreign Affairs* 63 (Spring 1985): 810–826.

————. "When the Fighting Has to Stop: The Arguments about Escalation." *World Politics* 19 (July 1967): 692–707.

Janowitz, Morris. "Toward a Redefinition of Military Strategy in International Relations." *World Politics* 26 (July 1974): 473–499.

Jervis, Robert. "Deterrence and Perception." *International Security* 7 (Winter 1982/83): 3–14.

———. "Deterrence Theory Revisited." *World Politics* 31 (January 1979): 289–324.

———. "MAD Is the Best Possible Deterrence." *Bulletin of the Atomic Scientists* 41 (March 1985): 43–45.

Kahn, Herman. "The Arms Race and Some of Its Hazards." In *Arms Control, Disarmament, and National Security*, edited by Donald G. Brennan, 89–121. New York: George Braziller, 1961.

Kaplan, Fred. "Strategic Thinkers." *Bulletin of the Atomic Scientists* 38 (December 1982): 51–56.

Kaufmann, William W. "The Crisis in Military Affairs." *World Politics* 10 (July 1958): 579–603.

King, James E. "Airpower in the Missile Gap." *World Politics* 12 (July 1960): 628–639.

———. "Nuclear Plenty and Limited War." *Foreign Affairs* 35 (January 1957): 238–256.

———. "On Clausewitz: Master Theorist of War." *Naval War College Review* 30 (Fall 1977): 3–36.

Kolkowicz, Roman. "The Strange Career of the Defense Intellectuals." *Orbis* 31 (Summer 1987): 179–192.

Lee, Asher. "Trends in Aerial Defense." *World Politics* 7 (January 1955): 233–254.

Leghorn, Richard. "No Need to Bomb Cities to Win War." *U.S. News and World Report*, 28 January 1955, 78–94.

Liddell Hart, B. H. "War, Limited." *Harper's* 192 (March 1946): 193–203.

Loftus, Joseph E. "Strategy, Economics, and the Bomb." *Scientific Monthly* 68 (May 1949): 310–320.

Michael, Donald N. "Civilian Behavior under Atomic Bombardment." *Bulletin of the Atomic Scientists* 11 (May 1955): 173–177.

Read, Thornton. "Nuclear Tactics for Defending a Border." *World Politics* 15 (April 1963): 390–402.

Rosenberg, David E. "American Atomic Strategy and the Hydrogen Bomb Decision." *Journal of American History* 66 (June 1979): 62–87.

———. "The Origins of Overkill: Nuclear Weapons and American Strategy, 1945–1960." *International Security* 7 (Spring 1983): 4–71.

———. "A Smoking, Radiating Ruin at the End of Two Hours: Documents on American War Plans for Nuclear War with the Soviet Union, 1954–55." *International Security* 6 (Winter 1981/82): 3–38.

Rowen, Henry S. "The Evolution of Strategic Nuclear Doctrine." In *Strategic Thought in the Nuclear Age*, edited by Laurence Martin, 65–79. Baltimore: Johns Hopkins University Press, 1979.

———. "The Future of General War." In *American National Security: A Reader in Theory and Policy*, edited by Morton Berkowitz and P. G. Bock. New York: Free Press, 1965.

Rowen, Henry S., and Albert Wohlstetter. "Varying Response with Circumstance." In *Beyond Nuclear Deterrence: New Aims, New Arms*, edited by Johan J. Holst and Uwe Nerlich, 225–238. New York: Crane, Russak, 1977.

Schelling, Thomas C. "Bargaining, Communication, and Limited War." *Journal of Conflict Resolution* 1 (March 1957): 19–36.

———. "Nuclear Strategy in Europe." *World Politics* 14 (April 1962): 421–432.

Sigal, Leon V. "Rethinking the Unthinkable." *Foreign Policy*, no. 34 (Spring 1979): 35–51.

Spaatz, Carl. "Strategic Air Power: Fulfillment of a Concept." *Foreign Affairs* 24 (April 1946): 6–17.

Viner, Jacob. "The Implications of the Atomic Bomb for International Relations." *Proceedings of the American Philosophical Society* 90 (January 1946): 53–58.

Walt, Stephen M. "The Search for a Science of Strategy: A Review Essay on *Makers of Modern Strategy*." *International Security* 22 (Summer 1987): 140–165.

Wohlstetter, Albert. "Bishops, Statesmen, and Other Strategists on the Bombing of Innocents." *Commentary* 75 (June 1983): 15–35.

———. "The Delicate Balance of Terror." *Foreign Affairs* 37 (January 1959): 212–234.

Wolfers, Arnold. "Could a War in Europe Be Limited?" *Yale Review* 45 (Winter 1956): 214–228.

———. "Superiority in Nuclear Weapons: Advantages and Limitations." *Annals* 290 (November 1953): 7–17.

Zuckerman, Sir Solly. "Judgment and Control in Modern Warfare." *Foreign Affairs* 40 (January 1962): 196–212.

Acknowledgments

Excerpts from *The Absolute Weapon* edited by Bernard Brodie, copyright 1946 by the Yale Institute of International Studies and renewed 1974 by The Yale Center for International and Area Studies, reprinted by permission of Harcourt Brace Jovanovich, Inc.

Quotations from *Bomber Offensive* by Sir Arthur Harris, copyright 1947 by The Macmillan Company. Reprinted by permission.

Excerpts from "Strategy Hits a Dead End" by Bernard Brodie, copyright © 1955 by *Harper's Magazine.* All rights reserved. Reprinted from the October issue by special permission.

Excerpts from "The Impact of Technological Change on the International System: Reflections on Prediction" by Bernard Brodie. Published by permission of the *Journal of International Affairs* and the Trustees of Columbia University in the City of New York.

Excerpts from "New Techniques of War and National Policies" by Bernard Brodie, in *Technology and International Relations,* edited by William F. Ogburn, copyright 1949 by University of Chicago Press. Reprinted by permission of University of Chicago Press.

Excerpts from "The Atom Bomb as Policy Maker" by Bernard Brodie. Reprinted by permission of *Foreign Affairs,* Summer 1990. Copyright 1948 by the Council on Foreign Relations, Inc.

Excerpts from "Nuclear Weapons: Strategic or Tactical?" by Bernard Brodie. Reprinted by permission of *Foreign Affairs,* Summer 1990. Copyright 1954 by the Council on Foreign Relations, Inc.

Excerpts from "The Development of Nuclear Strategy" by Bernard Brodie. Reprinted from *International Security* 2, 4, by permission of The MIT Press, Cambridge, Massachusetts, and the President and Fellows of Harvard College. Copyright © 1978 by the President and Fellows of Harvard College.

Excerpts from "In Quest of the Unknown Clausewitz" by Bernard Brodie. Reprinted from *International Security* 1, 3, by permission of The MIT Press, Cambridge, Massachusetts, and the President and Fellows of Harvard College. Copyright © 1977 by the President and Fellows of Harvard College.

Excerpts from "Navy Department Thinking on the Atomic Bomb" by Bernard Brodie. Reprinted by permission of the *Bulletin of the Atomic Scientists.* Copyright 1947 by the Educational Foundation for Nuclear Science, 6042 South Kimbark Avenue, Chicago, IL 60637.

Excerpts from "MAD Is the Best Possible Deterrence" by Robert Jervis. Reprinted by permission of the *Bulletin of the Atomic Scientists.* Copyright 1985 by the Educational Foundation for Nuclear Science, 6042 South Kimbark Avenue, Chicago IL 60637.

Excerpts from "Civilian Behavior under Atomic Bombardment" by Donald Michael. Reprinted by permission of the *Bulletin of the Atomic Scientists.* Copyright 1955 by the Educational Foundation for Nuclear Science, 6042 South Kimbark Avenue, Chicago IL 60637.

Excerpts from "Review of *Introduction to Strategy,* and *Dissuasion et Strategie,* by André Beaufre," by Bernard Brodie, *Survival* 7 (August 1965). Reprinted by permission of the International Institute for Strategic Studies.

Excerpts from "Reply to Bernard Brodie's *Review of Introduction to Strategy,* and *Dissuasion et Strategie,* by Beaufre,*" by André Beaufre, *Survival* 7 (December 1965). Reprinted by permission of the International Institute for Strategic Studies.

Excerpts from "Rejoinder to the Reply by André Beaufre" by Bernard Brodie, *Survival* 7 (December 1965). Reprinted by permission of the International Institute for Strategic Studies.

Excerpts from "Review of Clausewitz's *On War*" by Donald Brennan, *Survival* 20 (January/February 1978). Reprinted by permission of the International Institute for Strategic Studies.

Excerpts from *Nuclear Weapons in Europe* by Gary Treverton, Adelphi Paper no. 168, 1981. Reprinted by permission of the International Institute for Strategic Studies.

"Using the Absolute Weapon: Early Ideas of Bernard Brodie on Atomic Strategy," by Barry H. Steiner. Adapted with minor changes from the *Journal of Strategic Studies* 7 (December 1984), by permission of Frank Cass & Co., Ltd.

Excerpts from "More about Limited War" by Bernard Brodie. From *World Politics* 10 (October 1957). Reprinted by permission of Princeton University Press.

Excerpts from "On Clausewitz: A Passion for War" by Bernard Brodie. From *World Politics,* 25 (January 1973). Reprinted by permission of Princeton University Press.

Excerpts from "Strategy as a Science" by Bernard Brodie. From *World Politics* 1 (July 1949). Reprinted by permission of Princeton University Press.

Excerpts from "Trends in Aerial Warfare" by Asher Lee. From *World Politics* 7 (January 1955). Reprinted by permission of Princeton University Press.

Excerpts from Clausewitz's *On War,* edited by Michael Howard and Peter Paret. Copyright © 1976 by Princeton University Press. Reprinted by permission of Princeton University Press.

Excerpts from *War and Politics* by Bernard Brodie. Copyright © 1973 by Bernard Brodie. Reprinted by permission of Bruce Brodie and Macmillan Publishing Co., Inc.

Excerpts from *Escalation and the Nuclear Option* by Bernard Brodie. Copyright © 1966 by Bernard Brodie. Reprinted by permission of Bruce Brodie.

Excerpts from *Strategy in the Missile Age* by Bernard Brodie. Copyright © 1959 by the RAND Corporation. Reprinted by permission of the RAND Corporation.

Excerpts from *The Causes of Wars,* by Michael Howard. Copyright © 1983 by Michael Howard. Reprinted by permission of Michael Howard.

Quotations from the unpublished papers of Bernard Brodie, in the Special Collections Department (collection #1223) of the University Research Library at the University of California, Los Angeles; in the Air Force Historical Research Center, Maxwell Air Force Base, Montgomery, Alabama; and in the Naval Historical Collection, Naval War College, Newport, R.I. Published by permission of Bruce Brodie, the Department of Special Collections at UCLA, the Air Force Historical Research Center, and the Naval War College.

Quotations from the unpublished papers of William T. Golden, New York City, published by permission of William T. Golden.

Quotations from the unpublished papers of Edward Mead Earle, Seeley G. Mudd Manuscript Library, Princeton, N.J. Published by permission of Rosamond Earle Matthews and Princeton University Libraries.

Quotations from RAND Corporation reports, research memoranda, and papers, by Bernard Brodie and others; and from informal RAND Corporation papers by Bernard Brodie. Published by permission of the RAND Corporation.

Index